Software Engineering with Abstractions

Valdis Berzins
Luqi
NAVAL POSTGRADUATE SCHOOL

ADDISON-WESLEY PUBLISHING COMPANY

Reading, Massachusetts ■ Menlo Park, California ■ New York
Don Mills, Ontario ■ Wokingham, England ■ Amsterdam ■ Bonn
Sydney ■ Singapore ■ Tokyo ■ Madrid ■ San Juan

Library of Congress Cataloging-in-Publication Data

Bērzins, Valdis Andris.
    Software engineering with abstractions / Valdis Berzins, Luqi.
      p. cm.
    Includes index.
    ISBN 0-201-08004-4
    1. Computer software--Development. 2. Ada (Computer program
    language) I. Luqi. II. Title.
QA76.76.D47B47 1990   88–7517
005.13′3--dc19   CIP

ABCDEFGHIJ–MA–943210

Preface

This book explains how to employ formal methods in modern software engineering with emphasis on approaches amenable to computer assistance. We provide a consistent treatment of the entire software development process and strive to present a single approach with sufficient depth to let the readers carry out the process, with concern for compatibility and integration, rather than a broad survey of popular techniques. The main theoretical concepts of the field are introduced, explained, and linked to practical applications via examples.

This book is intended primarily for three groups of people: computer science students who wish to become practicing software engineers, experienced software engineers who wish to acquire skill in applying formal methods, and people interested in creating new software tools for automating parts of the software development process.

The first six chapters support an advanced one-year course sequence on software engineering and large-scale software development for computer science students, mainly for seniors and graduate students. A one-quarter or one-semester course can be based on the first four chapters if the more advanced sections are omitted. Chapters 7 and 8 can support an advanced seminar in software engineering and will be of interest to software toolsmiths.

The book can also be used as a reference and self-study guide for experienced software engineers who wish to strengthen their understanding of modern software engineering. We have included sections that summarize and review the relevant mathematical background to make the book self-contained and numerous examples to clarify the abstract concepts introduced. We present principles and methods for large-scale software development, and show (via examples) how these principles and methods can be realized in practice using Ada.

We use a combination of abstractions, formal specifications, mathematical concepts, and software tools to gain and maintain intellectual control over complicated systems. It is difficult to convince many computer science students of the importance of systematic methods and formal specifications because their experience is limited to programming on a relatively small scale, and the advantages of modern methods are least apparent for small examples. Classroom situations do not allow complete treatment of large or complex examples. The book is organized around a complete running example—a simplified airline reservation system—which starts from requirements formulation, goes all the way to code, and then includes some evolutionary changes. This example illustrates features typical of large-scale systems, such as multiple user interfaces, parallel processing, and time-sensitive processing, and shows how the principles presented in the book can be realized in realistic situations. Although the example does need not to be covered in detail in a classroom situation, it provides the basis for illustrating motivations for formal approaches and shows how specifications can be used to help make evolutionary changes, including the conversion of a single-processor design to a multiple-processor design. Parts of the example can be cited in classroom situations to illustrate particular points, and students can read the details to see how the parts fit together. The example can help experienced software engineers realize the potential benefits of the Ada language.

Spec, the formal specification language used in the book, has been explicitly designed for large-scale applications, including parallel, distributed, and real-time systems. The language uses second-order temporal logic, which has the familiar first-order logic as a subset. Spec is compatible with Ada, and can be used to write specifications in common styles for different types of software systems. The basics of the language are introduced as they are needed in the development of the extended example; reference material on the more advanced parts is provided in separate sections and in the appendixes. A simple subset of the language can be used in an initial presentation; more advanced features can be introduced as needed, or can be ignored for shorter or more elementary courses.

The specifications for the example have been run through the Spec syntax checker; the Ada code for the example has been compiled and tested using the Verdix Ada Compiler version 5.7, on a Sun 3 workstation running Sun Unix version 3.5. The code runs in accordance with the specification on all test cases we have tried, but has not been verified mathematically.

The book is organized according to the stages of software development, with additional chapters discussing computer-aided design tools for software development and future research directions. Each chapter starts with basic concepts and a set of procedures and guidelines. The basic concepts are illustrated using small examples, and the procedures are illustrated using a running example. Quality assurance and management issues are discussed after the example, followed by supporting theoretical material relevant to the chapter. The appendixes contain supplementary reference material on the notations used, sets of reusable components for requirements models, interface specifications, and Ada code. A simple preprocessor for simplifying Ada implementations of generators is also included. Online software for Spec may be obtained through the Open Software Foundation, Cambridge, MA.

We would like to thank all the computer scientists who helped to form the ideas in this book, and the co-instructors and the students in our software engineering courses whose questions, criticisms, and discussions, helped us create the framework presented in this book. We would also like to thank David Beebe, Gordon Bradley, Jerry DePasquale, Tim Fossum, David Gelperin, Helen Goldstein, Peter Gordon, Mike Gray, Yingli Hong, Mohammad Ketabchi, Robert Kopas, Yuhjeng Lee, Robert McGhee, Karen Myer, David Naumann, Peter Ng, Tim Shimeall, Alan Snyder, Wei Tek Tsai, Jill Weigand, Laurie Werth, and Raymond Yeh for their help and support.

Monterey, California   Valdis Berzins
                                                               Luqi

Contents

1

Introduction

The purpose of this book is to teach the theory and practice of software engineering. *Software engineering* is the application of science and mathematics to the problem of making computers useful to people via software. *Software* is the entire set of documentation, operating procedures, test cases, and programs associated with a computer-based system. These definitions indicate that software engineering is not just programming; its goal is to provide effective scientific methods for producing software systems that meet the needs of the customer, while conforming to the customer's schedule and budget constraints.

We want to make software development less labor intensive and to enable the development of higher quality software products by providing an integrated approach that draws on both industrial experience with software development and theoretical research in computer science. Industrial practice has relied on largely informal methods to cover the entire range of activities needed to produce software systems. Such methods are easy to understand and require less training to apply than formal methods, but they depend strongly on the artistic ability of skilled individuals; lack of a theoretical foundation makes them difficult to automate and easy to misinterpret. Computer science research has addressed some problems faced by software engineers, but many of the results are not directly applicable to software development.

This book provides a set of methods and tools for software development that integrate successful informal approaches with available theoretical results. We focus on ideas and techniques that make it possible to systematically produce software systems that meet user requirements. Our intention is to make computer-aided software engineering possible for a wide range of software development tasks. Computers have been used to aid the development of software since the construction of the first assemblers and compilers. As the

1

cost of hardware decreases, it becomes practical to accomplish more complex development tasks with software and computers.

We also want to make software simple and easy to understand. Abstractions let us use and develop more powerful software systems with simpler concepts. An *abstraction* is a simplified view of a system containing only the details important for a particular purpose. Abstractions with mathematical definitions can support automation and provide brief, simple, and precise descriptions of software systems. Abstractions are essential for large-scale projects because complex systems must be simplified before they can be understood and synthesized by individual people.

Formal languages have an important part in our approach because only the aspects of a language that have been precisely defined can be mechanically processed. A highly automated software development system depends on notations with a precisely defined syntax and semantics. We discuss such languages at three different levels: conceptual modeling, specification, and programming. Notations based on logic are used for conceptual modeling and specifications, and Ada is used for constructing programs.

Supporting large-scale software development via abstractions was one of the goals for the development of the Ada programming language. Because a fundamental change in thinking habits is needed for many experienced programmers to reap the full benefits of Ada, learning just the facilities provided by the language is not enough to help them become skilled Ada users. This book shows how to use Ada as the implementation language in a systematic software development process amenable to partial automation.

It is important to bring the state of the art in software engineering closer to the point where we will be able to produce useful and reliable software at a reasonable cost. Software development has not been very successful in this respect. The methods presented here are aimed at the production of software with specified properties, using a systematic and predictable process. The practical use of the approach developed in this book is illustrated via a complete example of sufficient size to show many common properties of large software systems. The theory supporting the approach is included to make the treatment self-contained, and to aid practitioners in adapting the approach to their needs and applications.

1.1 Why Software Engineering is Important

Software engineering is important because

1. Software has a large and increasing effect on people's lives, and
2. Software has a large and increasing cost.

Software is needed to enable computers to perform useful tasks. People's lives are being affected by software in increasingly critical ways as software is developed to automate many new tasks. Some of the areas being partially automated include financial services, communications systems, design and manufacturing operations, management information systems, control of power generation and distribution systems, medical services, air travel, space exploration, and weapons systems. Computers can perform tasks that are too complicated or too time consuming for people to do manually, and they can often do those tasks faster, at lower cost, and with greater reliability than people can. As software technology improves, the range of functions that can be usefully automated will continue to expand. However, computers are useful only if the software operates correctly and performs the functions needed by the people using the computers. Most computer system faults are due to design errors in the software rather than unpredictable behavior of the hardware. Software failures have potentially high costs in terms of human life and money, and the quality of most people's lives is increasingly being affected by the quality of the software with which they interact. Other common problems with computers are caused by software that "correctly" performs functions not intended by the people using the computer systems, either because the software developers did not understand the user's needs initially, or because the software is too inflexible to adapt to changing user needs. Developing reliable, useful, and flexible software systems is one of the great challenges facing software engineers today.

The large effect of software has been driven by the rapidly falling cost of computer hardware, which has been cut in half roughly every 2 years. This trend has been in effect for 30 years, and current technological developments support the belief that the trend will continue in the near future. As a result, it is becoming economically attractive to automate increasingly more tasks, provided that the required software can be produced. This automation is affecting more and more people. According to a software economic study, costs related to software accounted for about 2% of the U.S. gross national product in 1980 (about $40 billion), and a projection indicates that about 40% of the U.S. labor force relied on computers in 1985 [1]. According to a recent estimate, software-related expenses accounted for about 5% of the U.S. gross national product in 1986 (about $228 billion) [3]. Development effort for software systems is usually measured in person-years. For example, Brooks' famous book contains an estimate that IBM's operating system OS/360 took about 5000 person-years to develop and document, which implies a multi-million dollar cost [4]. The cost of software is thus large both in the aggregate and in terms of individual systems.

1.2 Factors Influencing Software Development

Because hardware is becoming cheaper and faster, the demand for increasingly sophisticated computer applications has increased to the point where no single person can hope to build an entire large system. This implies the need for a software development organization. As the number of people in the organization increases, the fraction of each worker's time devoted to communication increases, and the fraction of time left for software development work decreases. Consequently, larger software development teams are less efficient than small ones. Communication costs can be reduced by producing and maintaining precise documentation for the development. Although it takes some work to produce this documentation, once written, it can be read by many people during the lifetime of the software without depending on personal contact with the author, so that the communications overhead per person does not increase dramatically with project size. This is important for large projects, where the number of people is large and many people enter and leave the project. When a member of the original design team leaves the project, undocumented critical information that is lost can be very costly or impossible to recover. Communication problems are reduced if the documentation is kept in a computer system with tools for distributing changes and maintaining consistency. Such a computer system is known as a *project database*.

Sophisticated computer applications are constrained by the limits of human understanding. It is not possible for a single person to completely understand the implementation that took many person-years to produce. A well known example is the software for the SDI ("Star Wars") system, estimated at 10 million lines of code. Assuming 60 lines per page and 250 pages per inch, that implies a program listing more than 50 feet thick, which is a stack of paper higher than a five story building. This is much too large for human analysis if the entire program must be examined as a single unit. Since reliability is very important for large systems, extensive analysis and checking of the software is required. It is practically impossible for a program to work correctly unless its author clearly understands what it does and how it works. This implies that the system must be organized as a set of modules that can be understood independently of each other and are small enough to be thoroughly analyzed by a single person. The need for independent modules will remain even if advances in automation allow the analysis of a system to be carried out by a program rather than a person, because the execution times of programs involving deductive reasoning are rapidly increasing functions of the size of the problem to be analyzed.

As software systems get larger, reliability requirements get more stringent. A simple statistical method can be used to explain this fact. A conventionally designed system fails when one of its modules fails. If we define

N: the number of modules in a software system,

P: the probability a typical module is free from design faults,

and assume design faults in different modules are equally likely and independent of each other, we get

P^N: the probability the entire system is free of design faults, which gets small as N gets large unless P is very close to one. It is reasonable to assume that faults in modules with different functions are independent, although similar assumptions for redundant implementations satisfying a common specification are not realistic [2]. We can estimate the reliability for the process of producing an individual module needed to achieve a given level of confidence in the reliability of the entire system, if we assume the entire system must have a low probability of containing a fault. In such a case, P^N must be close to one, and the quantity

$1 - P$: the probability a typical module has a fault,

must be small. If we define

$$Q = 1 - P$$

we get

$$P^N = (1 - Q)^N = 1 - NQ + higher\ order\ terms,$$

using a binomial expansion. If the entire system must be reliable, NQ must be small, and we can neglect the higher-order terms to give the approximation

$$P^N \cong 1 - NQ.$$

Since we have

$1 - P^N \cong NQ$: the probability that the entire system has a fault,

the probability of a fault in a typical module must be N times smaller than the probability of a fault in the entire system, provided that the probability of a fault in the entire system must be much less than one. For example, if the probability of a fault in the entire system must be less than 1%, the probability of a fault in a typical module must be less than $1/100N$. Systems with $N > 1000$ are relatively common, so this is a very stringent requirement on the accuracy of the software development process.

The previous analysis addresses the probability that a manual process produces a software system free of defects. We have modeled human designers as random processes that produce correct designs with some probability that is strictly less than one. The mathematics leads to the conclusion that a large system that does not have a fault tolerant design and is produced by manual techniques is likely to contain at least one fault. This conclusion is consistent with practical experience: very few of the software systems currently in use are entirely free from faults. The analysis does not say anything about the frequency with which such an imperfect system will fail during operation. The failure rate of an imperfect system depends critically on the distribution of the actual input values, and can vary widely for different input distributions.

Although the previous analysis is a simplification of the actual situation, we can see that reliable large systems must be built from very reliable modules. Because routinely perfect software modules are beyond the current state of the art in software development, very large systems must have *fault tolerant* designs. This means software redundancy and error recovery facilities must be provided to enable the entire system to operate correctly despite failures in some of its modules. Several different methods for calculating the most critical functions must be implemented and executed, results must be compared, and some method for handling discrepancies must be provided; therefore fault tolerance adds considerably to development time and cost, and increases execution time and memory requirements. Recent research on software fault tolerance indicates that, due to correlations between errors in different implementations of the same module, the degree of redundancy needed to achieve reliability via fault tolerant designs can be much larger than indicated by predictions based on the independence assumption commonly used in estimating reliability of fault tolerant hardware systems [2].

To summarize, building a very large system is qualitatively different from writing a small program. You need:

1. A group of people, carefully organized

2. Precise design documents, in a computerized project database

3. A modular design, with limited interactions between modules

4. Extreme reliability, with backup systems.

A large software development effort is likely to fail if these points are not respected. The development of any software product with a large user community will benefit from these goals, although smaller products may not need software redundancy for fault tolerance. Developing a large system is very different from most individual programming assignments in computer science courses because small single-user programs can be produced in more arbitrary ways.

1.3 The Software Development Process

There are many different views of the software development process. While the names and boundaries of the stages in the process differ from author to author, everyone agrees software development consists of several qualitatively different kinds of activities. We refer to the construction activities in the software development cycle as *requirements analysis, functional specification, architectural design, implementation,* and *evolution.* Each of these activities has quality assurance tasks associated with it. One of the quality assurance tasks associated with implementation, *testing,* is sometimes treated as a separate activity. The relationships between the activities of the software development cycle are illustrated in Fig. 1.1. The arrows in the diagram indicate data flows

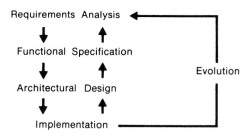

FIGURE 1.1
Relationships Between Software Development Activities

between the activities. Requirements analysis is the process of determining and documenting the customer's needs and constraints. Functional specification is the process of developing and formalizing a proposed systems interface for meeting the customer's needs. Architectural design is the process of decomposing the system into modules and defining internal interfaces. Implementation is the process of producing a program for each module. Evolution is the process of adapting the system to the changing needs of the customer. These activities are most efficiently performed in pipeline fashion, and usually overlap in time. Although the stages in the pipeline occur in the order listed above, it is incorrect to assume one stage stops when the next one starts, because insights gained in the later stages often trigger extensions or modifications to the results of earlier stages. The short upward arrows represent feedback containing insights gained at the more detailed levels.

The large loop represents evolution, which is a repetition of the same basic activities as the initial development. Large systems go through the stages of the software development cycle many times, once for each version of the system. Evolution is needed because the customer's needs change in response to changes in the environment and from experience with using the previous version of the system. The main difference between the initial development and later evolution is that a nonempty previous version of the system is available during evolution. Many parts of the previous version, which ideally consists of an entire project database, can be reused in the next version.

The word "design" is sometimes used for describing the synthesis part of software development, even though the word can mean different things in different contexts. Requirements analysis can be viewed as the design of a set of goals for the proposed system; functional specification can be viewed as the design of the external interfaces; architectural design can be viewed as the design of internal interfaces; implementation can be viewed as the design of data structures and algorithms; and evolution can be viewed as the design of new versions of the entire system.

TABLE 1.1
QUALITY ASSURANCE ACTIVITIES

Stage	Quality Assurance Activities
Requirements analysis	Customer reviews Consistency checking
Functional specification	Customer reviews Consistency checking Requirements tracing
Architectural design	Design reviews Consistency checking Dependency tracing
Implementation	Design reviews Testing Consistency checking Correctness proofs Performance analysis

Each stage of the software development cycle involves quality assurance in addition to synthesis. The quality assurance activities associated with each stage are summarized in Table 1.1. Customer reviews and design reviews are manual processes, where groups of people review the project documentation for particular properties. Consistency checking, requirements tracing, dependency tracing, testing, correctness proofs, and performance analysis are computer-aided processes, where people review the project documentation for particular properties with the help of software tools. These activities are explained in detail in the quality assurance sections of later chapters.

The trend towards a higher degree of automation is blurring the distinction between tools for consistency checking and computer-aided synthesis. For example, any program constructed using a syntax-directed editor is guaranteed to be free of syntax errors. As the state of the art in computer-aided software engineering improves, tools that guarantee other aspects of consistency by construction may eliminate explicit quality assurance activities for those aspects.

The next section briefly explains the stages in the software development cycle. Detailed explanations and examples can be found in later chapters.

1.3.1 Requirements Analysis

The goals of requirements analysis are to define the purpose of the proposed software system and to determine the constraints on its development. Requirements are typically prepared by analysts on behalf of the customer, although the analysts may be part of the development organization. Details of specific interfaces are worked out in the functional specification activity and are not specified at this stage.

The purpose of the system is described by listing the individual goals of the customer. These goals are described in the user's terms, using the vocabulary of the existing system and its environment. This vocabulary is standardized by building a formal model of the environment for the proposed system. The goals are organized into a hierarchy in which informal high-level goals are refined into more specific lower-level goals. The lowest-level goals are explicitly defined in terms of the environment model.

An important part of the requirements analysis activity is formalizing and completing the customer's initial problem statement. A formal statement is self-contained relative to a fixed definition of the syntax and meaning of the underlying notation. Since computer programs are formal statements, a problem must be formalized before it can be solved by a computer. The customer's initial problem statement is usually informal, depending on a set of concepts from the application area that are assumed to be understood. Formalizing the requirements involves identifying and developing precise definitions for the undefined concepts in the initial problem statement. A large amount of interaction with the customer and the users is needed to formalize the requirements, because the developers are usually not experts on the customer's problem and may not be familiar with the special terminology of the area, or may have informal interpretations for some of the terms that differ from the customer's intended meaning. The analyst's job is to create a formal problem statement that corresponds to the customer's real problem.

The customer's initial problem statement is usually incomplete because some of the requirements corresponding to the customer's problem are motivated by properties of computer systems unknown to the customer. Another class of unstated requirements stems from constraints on the problem so familiar that the customer is not aware of them, and has difficulty imagining situations in which they might be violated. The analyst must produce a simple formalization of the customer's problem that captures enough of its essential aspects to ensure that the system for solving the formalized problem will be useful in the customer's real application. This requires discovering unstated requirements and checking them with the customer.

The requirements record the results of a process of negotiation between the customer and the developer that identify the goals to be met in the version of the system to be developed, and those to be addressed in future versions or not at all. These negotiations are affected by the constraints on the development specified by the customer.

Constraints limit the choices available to the developers. Typical kinds of constraints are summarized in Table 1.2. The constraints affect how many of the customer's goals can be met by the system to be developed, because the resource constraints determine how much effort is available for the development project, and the other constraints affect the amount of work involved.

It is important to detect errors in the requirements as early as possible because the cost of fixing an error during implementation can be several orders of magnitude higher than fixing the error at the initial requirements analysis

TABLE 1.2
TYPES OF CONSTRAINTS

Constraint Type	Examples
Resource	Schedule, budget, manpower
Performance	Execution time, memory space, system down time
Environment	Hardware, operating system, external systems
Form	Programming language, coding standards, documentation standards
Methods	Development tools, testing procedures, performance benchmarks

stage. Confidence in the accuracy of the requirements is established via user reviews and consistency checks. A user review is a meeting in which consequences of the requirements are presented to the customer, to determine whether the implications of the requirements agree with their intentions. This process is needed because the customer is the ultimate judge of what is a requirement and what is not. Some aspects of the environment model can be checked for consistency and completeness via internal review meetings or automated tools. Consistency checking is important because inconsistent requirements cannot be met by any system. For systems that must be very reliable, the accuracy of the goals can be improved by having two versions of the requirements developed by independent teams of analysts and checking the correspondence between the two versions. Such a process is expensive, but it can detect missing or ambiguous requirements at an early stage.

The initial requirements consist of the goals, constraints, and environment model. The goals and constraints are often represented as informal outlines augmented with diagrams. The environment model is sometimes expressed in a formal conceptual modeling language. The functional specifications for the system usually become part of the requirements when they have been completed and accepted by the customer.

1.3.2 Functional Specification

The goal of the functional specification stage is to define precisely the external interfaces of the proposed system. Functional specifications are typically prepared by analysts and designers working for the developer. The system concepts that the users will be expected to know and the details of the user interfaces are determined and defined at this point. The functional specification should contain all of the information needed by the eventual users of the proposed system, and information needed by the designers of any external systems that will interact with the proposed system. Any other information should not appear in the functional specification. The internal structure of the system is determined in the architectural design activity and is not included in the functional specification.

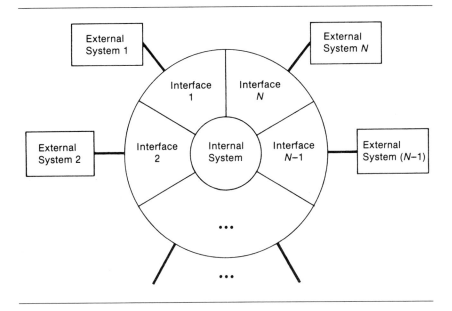

FIGURE 1.2
The Interfaces of a Proposed System

Functional specifications define the external interfaces using the vocabulary of the proposed system. An *interface* is the boundary between a system
and the other systems with which it interacts. An external interface is the boundary between the proposed system and an external system such as a user, a
piece of hardware, or a software system outside the scope of the development
project. Each external interface provides a simplified view of the proposed system, as illustrated in Fig. 1.2. Interfaces are defined by the types of the data
objects flowing across the boundary, the properties that must be satisfied by the
objects coming in and the objects going out, and the conditions under which
each output is produced. Each data object flowing across the boundary of the
system is an instance of an abstract data type.

An *abstract data type* consists of a set of instances and a set of primitive
operations that provide the only means for creating and interacting with the
instances. Abstract data types can be defined by the developer or predefined by
the programming language. Each abstract data type is itself a system whose
interface consists of the interfaces of the associated primitive operations. Each
interaction with a primitive operation involves the flow of one or more data
objects across the boundary of the abstract data type, at least one of which must
be an instance of that type.

Each system can be classified as a function, machine, or type according to
the following table.

Classification	Instances	Memory
Function	One	No
Machine	One	Yes
Type	Many	Optional

Functions and machines are individual systems. Types define and manage collections of individual instances. Machines have internal memory but functions do not. The data objects produced by a function as a result of an interaction are completely determined by the data objects flowing into the function during the same interaction. A function is a single-valued mapping in the mathematical sense. The data objects produced by a machine can depend on data objects flowing into the machine during previous interactions. A machine is an abstract state machine. An abstract state machine is a collection of operations, where each operation is characterized by a single-valued mapping that determines the current outputs and the next state in terms of the current inputs and the previous state. The state of a state machine is a data object that summarizes the effects of the sequence of inputs previously received by the machine. Types are abstract data types, as previously defined. A type can be further classified as *mutable* if it has internal memory and as *immutable* if it does not. An immutable type has a fixed set of instances, and all of its primitive operations are functions. The instances of a mutable type can be created, modified, and destroyed by its primitive operations.

Many common kinds of software systems are machines, because they have a single instance and maintain a long term memory. For example, most operating systems are machines, since the file system and the state of each process act as components of the operating system state. Software systems that can be classified as functions or types are less common, but they are by no means rare. Most compilers are functions since the machine code produced by the compiler is completely determined by the source program and options supplied when the compiler is invoked. Most software applications in a window-style system are types, because a new instance of the application is created whenever a new window is opened, and multiple windows can exist at the same time.

The quality assurance activities associated with functional specification are customer reviews, consistency checking, and requirements tracing. The customer is the final judge of the acceptability of a user interface, so that customer reviews of the functional specifications are needed. The information in the user's manual about the commands and data that the user will supply is derived from the functional specification. A first draft of such a user's manual is a good vehicle for a customer review.

Consistency checking is important because only consistent specifications can be implemented. Because the functional specification is a formal document, there is a potential for a large amount of computer aid in checking its consistency, but there is a need for further tool development in this area. At the current time, the most practical approach is a combination of automated and manual checking.

Each interaction described in the functional specification should be traceable to one or more requirements, and each requirement should be met by some combination of the interactions described. Checking these conditions is known as *requirements tracing*. Measuring the degree to which a particular functional specification meets a given requirement currently depends on human value judgements, because refinement and interpretation of incompletely stated requirements is part of the measuring process. Such human value judgements are necessary at the boundary between informal descriptions and formal descriptions. This boundary must exist for any approach to software development. In our approach, the boundary falls between the informally stated goals in the requirements and the formally defined interfaces in the functional specifications.

The result of the functional specification stage is a set of definitions for the system concepts and interfaces. It is presented to the customer in the form of diagrams and a user's manual, and to the designers as a statement in a formal specification language. The functional specification is the basis for the final acceptance testing of the completed system.

1.3.3 Architectural Design

The goal of architectural design is to decompose the system into software modules. A *module* is a conceptual unit in a software system that corresponds to a clearly identifiable region of the program text. The set of software modules that will be used to realize the system are identified at this point, and their interfaces are defined. These interfaces are internal to the system, and are not directly visible to its users. The data structures and algorithms for realizing each module are determined in the implementation activity, and are not specified in the architectural design.

The modules identified in the architectural design should be small enough to be readily understood, independent from the rest of the system, and implementable in a short period of time. Simplicity is important because complicated structures are error prone. Independence is needed to let different designers work on different parts of the system at the same time without interfering with each other. The ability to implement a module in a short period is important for project management reasons, because tasks associated with individual modules are the natural units in the work schedule. These tasks have to be relatively small for accurate estimation and scheduling flexibility.

The choice of modules depends to some extent on the programming language used in the implementation, since the specified modules must be readily implementable in terms of the primitives available. Since Ada supports many kinds of abstractions and independent tasks, an architectural design geared towards Ada can stay close to the most natural logical problem decomposition without incurring an implementation penalty.

Architectural design results in interface descriptions for all modules in the proposed implementation. This information is typically summarized and presented to all concerned in the form of a module dependency diagram (see Chapter 4). The detailed interface descriptions are presented to designers and programmers as a set of statements in a formal specification language. Precise interface descriptions are an essential part of any large-scale project because they allow the uses of a module to be designed and checked without examining the implementation of a module. For this reason, interface descriptions must include the intended meaning of each module in addition to the format for invoking each of the services the module provides.

1.3.4 Implementation

The goal of implementation is to construct a program that correctly realizes the specified interface for each module identified during architectural design, and that meets the associated performance requirements. Implementation consists of three main subtasks: choosing data structures and algorithms, working out the details of the code, and checking the correspondence between the implementation and the specified interface.

The high-level design of a module involves choosing the types of data structures and algorithms that will be used in its realization. Programming skill, experience, and familiarity with standard data structures and algorithms for solving common problems are important for this task. We assume you are already competent in these areas, and focus on systematic ways of recording the results of the designer's carefully considered decisions.

It has long been recognized that the overall design of a module should be worked out, recorded, and checked over before the programmer gets immersed in the details of the code. Flowcharts and pseudocode are two early notations for doing this. A flowchart is a directed graph whose nodes represent actions and whose edges represent sequencing relations between actions. Pseudocode uses control structures common in high-level programming languages to define the sequencing relations among a set of actions. The purpose of both notations is to record control information, either graphically or as structured text. In both cases, the primitive actions can be defined informally or in any programming language. The motivation for these notations was to provide a simpler and more abstract description of the intended algorithm than was possible in the programming languages of the time.

As programming languages have improved, it has become possible to express many of the abstractions supported by these techniques directly in the programming language. A powerful programming language such as Ada can be used for the same purpose as a flowchart, and can do better because it supports more abstractions. For example, Ada supports data abstractions for simplifying complicated data structures, but flowcharts do not. It is convenient to use the same notation for the design and the detailed coding, because the later stages of the programming effort can be recorded as refinements of the earlier stages. This avoids translation steps that would be necessary if the program design information was recorded in a notation other than the implementation language. For this reason, we use the implementation language to express the aspects of the design it is capable of describing, and use other notations embedded in comments for describing the remaining aspects.

Aspects of the design that are difficult or inconvenient to express using Ada include assumptions about the relationships between different parts of a data structure. We record such information using annotations expressed in a formal specification language. These annotations are embedded in Ada comments so that they can be part of the final program. Some of the major design decisions that are recorded in annotations are data invariants, loop invariants, and bounding functions for loops and recursive functions. Such annotations are important as aids for deriving the detailed code, checking the correctness of the implementation, and designing new versions of the module in the evolution stage.

Testing is a large part of the quality assurance activity associated with implementation in most current development projects. Testing is the process of running programs on selected input data to detect and locate faults. Much of the work involved in testing consists of test case generation and design and implementation of test scaffolding. Test scaffolding is extra code that is needed to run test cases, which includes drivers, stubs, metering operations, and output analyzers. Other aspects of quality assurance include user and design reviews, automated consistency checks, and sometimes formal proofs of correctness.

Programs are usually represented in high-level programming languages that can be compiled into executable machine language. We use Ada in our examples of detailed code, with annotations in a formal specification language.

1.3.5 Evolution and Repair

Evolution is a process of modifying or extending the functionality of a software system. This may be in response to changes in user requirements or part of a planned phased development of a system as a series of increasingly sophisticated versions. Evolution is usually guided by the customer's experience with using the previous version of the system. Repair is the process of making design changes to eliminate discrepancies between the system specification and the implementation that were discovered after the system was delivered. The combination of evolution and repair is called maintenance by some authors. These activities have great practical importance because they account for a large fraction of the cost of current software systems.

Repairs are usually necessary in practice because the development of absolutely correct large systems is beyond the current state of the art in most software development organizations. The operation of a system after delivery can be viewed as a part of the quality assurance activity associated with implementation (sometimes called field testing), which produces requests for repairs. However, repairs are more often considered to be separate from implementation because they usually occur after the contract governing the initial development work has expired.

Evolution is really a repetition of the previous steps in the software development process. In current practice these steps are not always carried out as systematically as we have previously described, due to concerns about cost. Such concerns reflect a short-term view, because long-term costs can be increased by cutting corners in designing enhancements and repairs, due to extra repetitions of the evolution/repair cycle. Cutting corners results in discrepancies between the current versions of the design documentation and the implementation. Such discrepancies make further modifications progressively more difficult to make, so that new errors are introduced more frequently. Eventually the system degrades to the point where it must be retired because no one can understand it any more. The next version of such a system is developed as a new project.

1.4 Why Software Engineering is Difficult

The current high costs, long development times, and unpredictable quality of software indicate that there are some difficult problems in software development. Some of these problems are technical and others involve human factors and economics. Many of them are linked to difficulties in dealing with uncertain information, communication problems, and the labor-intensive nature of current software development practices.

Schedule and cost overruns are a common problem in software development. The effort for constructing a software system is very hard to predict based on just the requirements or functional specifications, because many tasks in the development are unknown at that stage and apparently small changes in the requirements can lead to large differences in cost. Effort is also hard to predict because the ratio between the productivities of the best and worst programmers in a team is usually at least a factor of 10. The earliest time accurate estimates (10-20%) are possible is during architectural design, when all of the modules to be built have been identified.

Repeated reestimation and rescheduling is often needed as the project proceeds and more information becomes available. This usually requires flexibility in either schedule, cost, or functionality of the product to be delivered.

Such flexibility is not always provided by contracts for software development. Large systems should be delivered as a series of relatively small enhancements to a simple kernel system; this allows the delivery of a system that performs some useful functions in a reasonable amount of time. Small enhancements can be delivered with less risk of exceeding the schedule and budget. There is also less risk of the customer's perceptions of the problem changing so much that the system is obsolete before it is delivered.

The theory of software engineering is incomplete, in the sense that there are no universal methods that guarantee a working system will appear after a finite number of steps. In practice, there are usually places where you have to throw away your original design and start over. There is rarely enough room in the schedule for doing that unless the problem is recognized before a large effort has been invested in the faulty design decision. Current wisdom is to invest heavily in design reviews early in the project.

The quality of software products has been unstable and difficult to predict, partially because it is difficult to determine accurate requirements for a software system. Communication problems are one source for this difficulty. Most customers can explain the symptoms of their problems, but they have difficulty in understanding the underlying causes, or in explaining what a system must do to solve their problems. Reaching an agreement between two groups of people with very different backgrounds and formulating the requirements accurately is a time-consuming process that depends on feedback, and may take many iterations to converge. Customers can usually recognize what they need when they start using it, which makes prototyping an important tool in requirements analysis. However, solutions that require the users to change their thinking habits may have to be demonstrated in detail and sold gently to be accepted. Consulting and training support for such solutions can be essential.

An important part of requirements analysis is arriving at a consistent view of the problem. There are many different views of the problem because the customer is usually an organization rather than an individual person. Individual descriptions of the problem usually reflect limited viewpoints. Different people are concerned with different aspects of the problem, and in large projects, often there is no single person who understands all aspects simultaneously. Many overlapping descriptions use different concepts and terms for similar things. The analysts must recognize when different people use the same word for different concepts or different words for the same concept. Sometimes the individual views conflict in substance as well as form, and internal negotiations between customer representatives are needed to reach an agreement.

As in any engineering effort, software projects generally have conflicting goals that must be weighed against each other as the design proceeds. Everyone wants their system to be easy to use, efficient in time and space, inexpensive to build, and easy to extend and modify. It is usually impossible to satisfy all of these goals simultaneously; tradeoff decisions must be made based on the relative importance of conflicting goals. Trouble can arise when the tradeoff criteria serving the best interests of individual analysts differ from those serving the best interests of the customer or the development organization as a whole.

The requirements must be feasible to implement with available resources. Because resources are usually scarce, a cost-benefit analysis is needed to determine which aspects of the problem to include in the requirements and which to delay or ignore. This process is difficult because cost estimates at the requirements analysis stage are highly uncertain.

Many software products are so complicated that no single person can hope to understand the entire system; yet it must be designed and implemented nearly perfectly to work at all. Such perfection is not practical without automated tools for detailed correctness and consistency checking. Appropriate tools are not widely available, and considerable research and technical development efforts are needed to provide them. The state of the art in computer science and software engineering has not provided such sophisticated tools in the past. Many of the more powerful tools currently in existence are experimental systems developed to demonstrate the feasibility of new approaches, and are not user friendly, robust, or efficient.

Turning experimental tools into production-quality systems requires a large up-front investment. Companies have been reluctant to spend large amounts of money on tools rather than on the direct production of software products. The perception that investment in tools is wasteful may be partially due to the intangible nature of software. It is widely recognized that sophisticated equipment is needed for large-scale production of tangible commodities. For example, there is little enthusiasm for raising wheat using hoes instead of combines even though a hoe is much cheaper than a combine.

Another factor affecting the use of sophisticated tools is the rapid advance of the state of the art in computer science. There are many people experienced in software development and software applications without the training needed to use and understand sophisticated software tools. Such tools are largely based on formal methods whose application requires good knowledge of basic mathematics and training in computer science. To summarize, successful automation of software development depends on research and development efforts, investment policies, and training.

1.5 Why a Mathematical Approach is Needed

A mathematical approach is needed in large-scale software development to achieve precise communication and a high degree of automation. Precise communication is critical because in large projects a group of people must arrive at a consistent understanding of the proposed system to successfully build it.

Automation is important at all stages of software development to improve accuracy and productivity.

A mathematical approach also provides a framework for organizing the mental processes of design that can be taught and transferred. Systematic approaches are much easier to teach than those that rely on common sense without much explicit guidance. Mathematics provides a set of general concepts that can be used as building blocks in solving many different kinds of problems. Recognizing that a particular problem in software development is a special case of a familiar general structure can help to impose order and simplicity on an otherwise bewildering maze of details. This is important because conceptual complexity imposes the ultimate limits on the software systems we can build.

Even though a mathematical approach is needed for precision and a high degree of automation, currently few large software systems are developed using formal methods. One factor limiting the application of formal approaches has been the perception that producing precise and accurate specifications before the coding stage is wasted effort. Although it may be possible to start producing deliverable code immediately in some small programming projects, doing so in a large project requires a miracle for success. An analogy helps to illustrate this point. Starting to pour the foundation for a high-rise building before the detailed plans are available requires the same kind of miracle. If factors discovered after the foundation is poured require a change in the location, size, shape, or bearing strength of the foundation, it will take much more time and effort to modify the partially constructed structure than to build it according to the corrected plans from the beginning, because parts of the existing structure will have to be demolished before it can be rebuilt. The situation is even worse if the first few floors of the building have been erected before the need to modify the foundation is discovered. Similar effects apply to large software systems, where formal specifications play the role of detailed plans. According to [1], fixing an error in the requirements analysis stage costs one hundred times less than fixing it in the maintenance stage. Accurate specifications can help to reduce costs, and formalism and automation are needed to achieve accuracy.

The application of formal methods requires more technical background than using informal techniques. Many programmers think in terms of concepts appropriate for low-level code and systems of small to moderate size even in the development of large and complex systems. The effort needed to learn new concepts and methods is justified by the potential for automating a larger part of the routine tasks faced by software engineers.

Another factor limiting the use of formal methods is lack of investment in the automated tools needed to reduce the effort of applying these methods. Such tools are expensive, but they allow many development tasks to be done much faster and more thoroughly than is possible manually, allowing the production of more powerful and better software products with the same amount of human effort. Some of the tools needed for such an approach are discussed in

Chapter 7. In addition to the tools for carrying out the individual tasks in software development, a project database is needed to let the many people and tools involved in a large software development project work together in smooth harmony.

1.6 Role of the Project Database

The purpose of the project database is to record, manage, and distribute all information about the state of a software development project. The project database contains many documents including requirements, designs, justifications, code, test cases, manuals, schedules, estimates, work assignments, and so on. The documents in the project database generally exist in many versions, are updated by many people working concurrently, and are related by several kinds of dependencies. The project database for a large project can contain many thousands of documents, leading to a significant database management task that can profit from the application of software tools.

It is important to record all aspects of a development project because human memory is volatile, is not always available, and is not directly subject to automated aid. People enter and leave large projects regularly, so that direct communication between designers may not always be possible. Even when it is possible, direct communication can be inefficient, since most design decisions have a single author and many affected parties whose needs for information occur at unpredictable times. Keeping all of the project information in a computerized database management system enables the development of software tools for many tasks necessary in software development, such as global consistency checking and status reporting.

Inconsistencies are sometimes introduced because the author of a design decision is unaware of conflicting decisions made by other designers. Some inconsistencies of this variety can be detected by software tools for global consistency checking operating on the project database. The benefits of automating this function are a reduction in the amount of explicit communication needed between designers and earlier detection of inconsistencies.

It is important for project managers to check on the status of a development project at frequent intervals because remedies for late projects must be applied early to be effective. Progress reports can be prepared without direct participation by the designers if all project information is kept in a database with appropriate software tools for generating progress reports. This is important because manual preparation of progress reports interrupts the thought processes of the designers, which can cause important ideas to be lost and slow down progress. These factors argue for an explicit project database that is maintained online and coupled with tools for automating some aspects of design and project management.

Databases for engineering applications are different from those for classical business applications in several important ways. A database for engineering applications must maintain the historical information embodied in the alternatives and refinements developed for each document to avoid wasting effort on repeating previous steps when a designer has to go back to a previous version of the design. Engineering applications involve a wide variety of data. The documents in the project database for a software development effort contain expressions in formal languages with a flexible tree structure, diagrams containing graphical information, and informal descriptions consisting of unstructured text. Transactions involving extensions and updates to these documents are long, typically taking days or weeks, and may not block concurrent access by different members of the development team. Ordinary database management systems are designed for business applications, which have different characteristics. Such systems maintain only the current state of the data, represented as large sets of fixed format records, and are optimized for short transactions typically taking less than a second to complete.

Although ordinary database management systems can be used to maintain the project database for a software development project, the mismatches described previously often lead to cumbersome interfaces and poor performance. Consequently, specialized systems are needed for effectively implementing project databases. Specialized database management systems for engineering applications are known as *engineering database systems*. Many of the proposed engineering database systems are object oriented, while ordinary database systems are usually set oriented. Engineering database systems are a recent development and mature systems are not yet widely available. There are many currently active research and development efforts focused on engineering database systems. Software development techniques are likely to be strongly affected by progress in this area.

References

1. B. W. Boehm, *Software Engineering Economics*, Prentice Hall, Englewood Cliffs, NJ, 1981.

2. D. Eckhardt and L. Lee, "A Theoretical Basis for the Analysis of Multiversion Software Subject to Coincident Errors," *IEEE Transactions on Software Engineering SE-11*, 12 (Dec. 1985), 1511–1517.

3. J. E. Hopcroft and D. B. Kraft, "Toward Better Computer Science," *IEEE Spectrum 24*, 12 (Dec. 1987), 58–60.

4. F. P. Brooks, Jr., *The Mythical Man Month: Essays on Software Engineering*, Addison-Wesley, Reading, MA, 1975.

2

Requirements Analysis

The purpose of requirements analysis is to determine a customer's needs in sufficient detail to plan the construction of a software system meeting those needs. The customer for a software development project is usually an organization that will use or market the proposed software system. The process of requirements analysis often starts with a short informal problem statement written by a representative of the customer, in response to a request from someone with the resources to pay for the project. Analysts organize, transform, and abstract information from the customer to produce a coherent written description of the customer's problem, known as a requirements document. The process of producing a sufficiently complete set of requirements requires much additional information from the customer, and possibly also from experts on the customer's problem domain. The analysts must seek out missing aspects of the problem, detect inconsistencies, and ensure that the requirements accurately reflect the real needs of the customer.

The results of requirements analysis should include the following:

1. A simplified model of the system's environment
2. A description of the goals of the system and the functions it must perform
3. Performance constraints on the system
4. Constraints on the implementation of the system
5. Resource constraints for the development project
6. A specification of the external interfaces of the system.

The components of the requirements and their relationship to the processes of requirements analysis and functional specification are illustrated in Fig. 2.1.

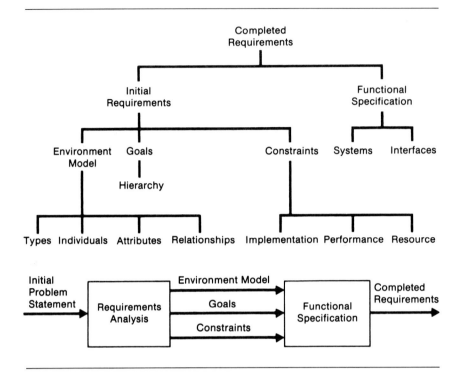

FIGURE 2.1
Structure and Derivation of the Requirements

We present a formal approach to recording the requirements, and examine guidelines for identifying missing information and checking the consistency and acceptability of the requirements. This chapter focuses on the first five components of the requirements; the next chapter focuses on specifications for interfaces. The approach is illustrated by examples, including an extended case study. Techniques for interviewing customers and negotiating agreements are beyond the scope of this book. Communicating with people is an essential skill for a requirements analyst because much of the information in a requirements document is gained by interviewing people.

2.1 Goals of Requirements Analysis

A major part of the requirements analysis task is turning the informal problem statement into a precise, testable, and feasible set of requirements. This is difficult because the initial problem statement is usually ambiguous, incomplete, contradictory, and may not reflect cost considerations. Because the customer is an organization with many members, there are usually conflicting goals and opinions. Different people are concerned with different aspects of the system, and have overlapping localized viewpoints. The analysts usually cannot have extended working sessions with customers who have a global understanding of the needs of the customer organization, because such people are usually high-level managers with little spare time. Thus it is often necessary to construct a global picture by combining many overlapping partial views at different levels of detail. The requirements analysts must work out the implications of the customer's goals, combine and unify diverse views of the system, identify and acquire missing pieces of information, abstract from concrete descriptions to identify the real problems, and detect conflicting goals. Conflicting goals must be resolved by the customer. There is not much point to developing a system unless the customers can agree on a consistent set of requirements for the system. If the customers have irreconcilable differences, it may be necessary to develop a separate system for each faction.

To refine and formalize the requirements, the analyst usually builds a model of the system's environment that captures the problem the system must solve. This model helps to identify the goals and constraints of the customer organization, which motivate the goals and constraints of the proposed software system. The model is an idealization of the environment that can be written down and analyzed. This model forms the basis for communication between the customer, the systems analyst, and the developers of the software system by establishing a standard vocabulary for the problem domain, where each term has an explicitly defined interpretation. These definitions are formulated in terms of the model. The model also introduces a logical structure that allows implications of the customer's requirements to be determined, and aids detection of contradictions and conflicts.

To carry out a requirements analysis, the informal requirements in the initial problem statement must be *formalized*, or transformed into specific measurable statements in terms of the environment model. The requirements are described as goals for controlling or interacting with the environment of the system. This process involves discovering details of customer needs that are not described in the initial problem statement, and abstracting the problem to remove unnecessary implementation details. All of these steps may cause significant changes in the initial problem statement.

The constraints on the required performance of the system, the form of its implementation, and the resources available for its development, must be determined and documented. The feasibility of the system with respect to these constraints must be examined, and adjustments made if necessary. The analysts examine possible implementation strategies to evaluate whether the requirements can be met with available resources. This evaluation should be coupled with a cost/benefit analysis to help the customer make the best use of scarce

resources, since needs almost always exceed means. A goal of the requirements analysis process is to decide which of the customer's problems will be
solved by the initial version of the proposed system, which ones will be handled
by later versions of the proposed system, and which ones will be solved outside
the proposed system. This should be done in a way that allows the system to be
built with available resources and that provides the largest possible benefit to
the customer within the resource constraints.

To complete the requirements, the analysts must define a set of external
interfaces of a system meeting the formalized requirements. This process is
called *functional specification*, and is described in detail in Chapter 3. For large
systems, each interface is defined by a separate team. As the individual interfaces are specified, interactions between them must be identified, and adjustments made as needed to integrate the individual views of the system into a
consistent whole.

The correspondence between the formalized requirements and the
customer's real needs must be checked at each level. This process is known as
requirements validation, and is very important because software development
will be based on the formalized requirements. The cost of fixing a requirements error increases sharply as a project goes into its later stages, often by
several orders of magnitude. Therefore it is important to update inappropriate
requirements to reflect the customer's needs as quickly as possible. In the
worst case, undiscovered inappropriate requirements can result in the delivery
of a system that does not meet the customer's needs.

The requirements should be kept up to date when the customer's needs
change, to keep a record of what needs to be done and to help determine which
parts of the system will be impacted by future changes. This process should be
carried out with computer aid; in real development projects the amount of
information involved is staggering, and the consequences of each change must
be completely propagated to maintain the consistency and accuracy of the
requirements. Consequently, requirements analysis and validation tasks must
continue throughout the lifetime of the software system. The requirements con-
stitute the justification for each part of the system. The link between the
requirements, the design, and the implementation contains the information
needed to explain why a given aspect of the system appears the way it does.
This is important both for educating people that come into the project, and for
making evolutionary changes to the system. If justifications for decisions are
recorded, then designers can assess whether a decision can be changed safely,
and can detect when requirements changes remove the support for earlier decisions. This can help software developers to avoid repeating mistakes that have
been explored earlier in the development. Computer aid in maintaining an
explicit representation of the relationships between the requirements and the
parts of the system they support is desirable for improving the currently
difficult and expensive evolution and repair process.

For large systems, requirements analysis is too time consuming to be carried out by a single person; teams of analysts must often work together. The need for communication among a team of analysts and eventually with a team of developers makes it imperative that the requirements be explicitly and precisely recorded, so that they can be effectively communicated. Requirements change repeatedly and often, and participate in complex relationships with the parts of the software system to be developed. Therefore, it is desirable to keep the requirements in a computer, preferably in a project database along with all of the other project information. The project database should be logically centralized and physically distributed among the work stations of the analysts and developers. Software aid for managing the evolving versions of the requirements and the dependencies between the components of the requirements and the other parts of the software is very helpful, and necessary for realizing the full benefits of a formal approach.

2.2 Basic Concepts

Requirements are a critical part of software development because of their strong effect on total software costs. It can cost one hundred times more to fix a requirements error after the system has been delivered than to fix the same error during the requirements analysis activity. Software evolution accounts for 50% to 80% of the costs associated with most software systems, and a substantial fraction of these costs stem from repairing requirements errors. Another aspect of the impact on system cost is the effect on the useful lifetime of the system. If accurate requirements are developed and kept up to date, they can guide evolutionary changes, helping the maintainers of the system to make changes using rational and systematic methods rather than guesswork. This enables changes to be made more rapidly and reliably, reducing the number of new errors that will have to be fixed in the future. At the current state of the art, all systems eventually become degraded by imperfect modifications to the point where they become unreliable and cannot be economically repaired. By lowering the error rate in system modifications, accurate and up-to-date requirements can extend the useful lifetimes of software systems.

The process of requirements analysis is dominated by the fact that the members of the customer organization cannot describe the system they need clearly, and do not understand all of the implications of the problems to be solved. This effect is amplified in large systems, where the customer organization almost always contains many individuals with different and sometimes conflicting views about the requirements. The key to detecting conflicts is maintaining an explicit record of the environment model, goals, and constraints for the proposed system, in a form that has only one place for each piece of information. The analysts gather information from the customers and enter it into the official record. This approach supports conflict detection because conflicting statements are recorded in close proximity. Consistency should be checked as each piece of information is entered.

2.2.1 Components of the Requirements

We describe the components of a requirements document in detail next.

The Environment Model. The environment model forms the basis for communication and agreement between the customer and the developer. An environment model defines the concepts needed for describing the world in which the proposed system will operate. These concepts consist of the types of objects and the distinguished individual objects in that world, the attributes of those types of objects, the relations between those types of objects, and the laws governing the objects, attributes, and relations. These primitives are illustrated in Fig. 2.2.

A type is a set of objects that has a common set of attributes, relationships, and laws. The objects in the set are known as the *instances* of the type. Types include object classes familiar from mathematics, such as numbers and sets, as well as object classes from the application domain, such as flights and airports. An attribute is a single-valued mapping from one or more types to another type. A relationship is a mathematical relation; that is, a set of n-tuples drawn from a Cartesian product of n types. A relationship is represented by a predicate that is

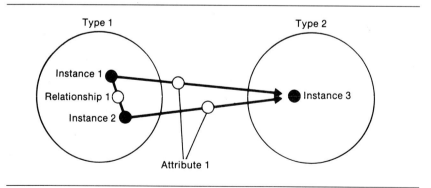

FIGURE 2.2
Components of the Environment Model

true for exactly those n-tuples contained in the relation. The number of tuples in a relation need not be finite. Laws are relationships that must be true for all possible n-tuples of objects from the given types. Examples of types, attributes, relationships, and laws can be found in Section 2.4.

An environment model is specified by giving a finite number of explicit definitions for types, attributes, relationships, and laws. Some of these definitions can be generic templates with parameters. A single generic definition can introduce a potentially unbounded set of related concepts, which is indexed by the actual values for the parameters.

The model presents a simplified view of the world containing only a fixed set of types, attributes, and relationships. The analysts arrive at such a model by including *only* those aspects of the world relevant to the customer's problem and the proposed software system for solving that problem. This includes both the aspects of the world that will have to be represented in the proposed software, and the aspects that impose external constraints on the system and motivate the customer's requirements. For example, the relationship between travel agents and airline tickets should be part of the environment model for an airline reservation system; the relationship between travel agents and their parents should not be included.

The environment model includes the laws governing the behavior of the environment. In many applications, domain experts may be needed to formulate the laws describing the behavior of the environment. The laws may describe properties inherent in the environment, assumptions about the environment that must be satisfied for the proposed system to act properly, or properties that must be maintained by the system. The environment model should include the laws that have an essential bearing on the required behavior of the proposed software system. For example, the equations of orbital mechanics describe inherent properties of the environment for the navigation system of a space shuttle. An example of a law expressing a constraint that the environment must satisfy for proper operation of the system is a limit on the maximum transaction rate for a hard real-time system. A more specific example is the assumption that a person waiting for service from an elevator system will push the elevator button if it is not already lit. Such an assumption is needed to express a requirement of guaranteed service. Properties that must be maintained by a software system are often motivated by safety considerations. For example, in an elevator system, the doors must not be open on a given floor unless the elevator is stopped at that floor. In a system for controlling a telescope at an observatory, a similar safety requirement is that the telescope must never point directly at the sun.

Formalizing the Requirements.   The requirements for the proposed system are formalized by writing a description of the goals of the system and the functions it must perform in terms of the model. This requires passing from the initial informal view, which depends on the customer's understanding of many undefined terms, to a formal view where all of the concepts are explicitly defined in terms of a model. There are intermediate levels of formality, where some of the definitions are expressed informally, using English or pictures; other definitions are expressed in mathematically defined formal languages, such as logic or differential equations. In current practice, requirements are not completely formal, but the trend is to make them more formal as more automated analysis becomes possible. It is accepted practice to require explicit but possibly informal definitions of all the concepts used in the model. We follow this practice, using a mixture of formal and informal definitions.

The process of formalizing the requirements is needed to make them explicit, well defined, and objectively testable. These properties are needed for effective communication with the developer, and for formulating a contract agreement governing the development work. Formalization is also a necessary step for computer-aided checking and analysis. The degree of computer aid available determines to a large extent the degree of formality that is most useful in practice.

For large projects, it is useful to describe the goals of the system in a hierarchical structure, where each high-level goal is refined into a set of lower-level subgoals that will realize the high-level goal. The functions the system must perform are some of the nodes in the goal hierarchy. The goals in the hierarchy should be prioritized, and should include plausible goals that are not going to be addressed in the initial version of the system due to budget and schedule limitations. If there is going to be a phased delivery plan, the phase in which each goal is to be met should be specified.

The highest-level goals are close to the customer's initial problem statement, and are often informal, qualitative, and hard to test. For example, the initial problem statement for a word processing system might contain a high-level goal stating that the system must be easy to use. When a higher-level goal is refined into subgoals, the subgoals are usually expressed at a level of abstraction closer to the system, where details are visible that the customer may not have been aware of initially. The lower-level subgoals should be more precise and easier to test that the higher-level goals they refine. In the word processing example, the ease of use requirement might be refined into subgoals stating that the system must support command menus and must maintain its text displays according to the "what-you-see-is-what-you-get" principle. At the lowest levels of refinement there might be mathematically defined interfaces with these properties. In general, the requirements get more formal at the lower levels of the hierarchy.

In practice, the model is refined as the goals are described in more detail, and the analyst discovers which aspects of the world are relevant to the proposed system. This process adds much information in the form of interpretations for concepts that were undefined or ambiguous at the higher levels. These interpretations are proposed by the analysts based on educated guesswork and general knowledge of the customer's problem area, and the potential capabilities of software systems. Consequently, goal refinements must be considered uncertain, and should be reviewed frequently by customers and users to reduce the risk of spending significant effort in inappropriate directions. If the analyst realizes that a goal refinement depends on an uncertain assumption about the customer's situation, the analyst should ask the customer a question to verify or refute the accuracy of the assumption before working out many details of the refinement.

As the requirements are refined, they are also modified to reflect the developing understanding of the customer's problem. As dependencies between the goals are recognized, they are restated in more specific terms and reorganized to make them independent. Unnecessary implementation decisions are removed as they are recognized; often, this will significantly simplify the requirements and avoid unnecessary conflicts. Such decisions should be recorded along with the reasons why they were removed, so that insights gained during analysis can be used in later stages. The process of simplifying the requirements involves generalizing the view of the customer's problem to retain only the logical essentials, while discarding arbitrary assumptions about how the system will be built, and may require a substantial intellectual effort.

Conflicts between goals must be detected and resolved. Conflicting goals may be either misunderstandings or tradeoff situations. Sometimes the customer's needs are described in an overly general way, and a narrower requirement can be found that will avoid the conflict while still solving the customer's problem. If the customer wants more than is feasible, the conflict is unavoidable, and the conflicting goals must be resolved by weakening one or both of the conflicting goals, based on the priorities of the customer. The results of conflict resolution and the rationale for resolving each conflict should be recorded for future reference, because the same issues will arise again during more detailed specification and design of the system. Resolving a conflict between goals is commonly referred to as an engineering tradeoff. Conflicts between goals may be due to logical contradictions, physical laws, hardware limitations, or development time and cost limits.

Even though the goals at the higher levels of the goal hierarchy are imprecise and often impossible to test, it is useful to record them because they serve as justifications for the lower level goals subordinate to them. This structure can serve as the basis of a systematic review process, and can be useful for identifying the impact of a proposed requirements change because requirements changes often originate at the higher levels.

Determining Constraints. Three kinds of constraints are relevant to requirements analysis: implementation constraints, performance constraints, and resource constraints, as illustrated in Fig. 2.3.

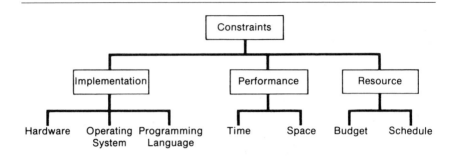

FIGURE 2.3
Constraints in Requirements Analysis

Large systems often are subject to implementation constraints. The most common kind of implementation constraint is a predefined interface to an existing external system. Such interfaces should be defined using the notations and guidelines for functional specifications presented in Chapter 3. Other kinds of implementation constraints are prespecified hardware configurations, operating systems, or implementation languages.

These implementation constraints usually come from the customer and are straightforward to specify. Some of the more challenging implementation constraints to describe are portability and maintainability requirements, which must often be refined by the analyst into objectively testable properties. Portability requirements can be defined either extensionally, by listing a set of operating environments in which the software must operate, or intensionally, by specifying a fixed virtual interface through which all interactions with the environment must occur. Maintainability requirements can be described by listing future enhancements that must be easy to make, or by listing attributes of the proposed system that must be localized in closed modules because they are likely to change.

The functions that must be performed by the proposed system are often subject to performance constraints. There may be some aggregate performance constraints that apply to the system as a whole, such as limits on memory consumption or down time. There also may be a set of performance constraints specific to each function, such as bounds on response times, transaction frequencies, and error rates. Performance constraints are sometimes derivable from the characteristics of the problem domain, especially for real-time control systems. For example, the maximum response time for an autopilot of an airplane is chosen to guarantee that the airplane will remain on course under all expected environmental conditions. In cases like this, the performance constraints are subgoals that are directly motivated by higher-level functional constraints. While the underlying laws of the problem domain may provide a means for systematically determining such performance constraints, current practice tends to rely on experience with previous systems and accepted guidelines of the application area, rather than derivations from first principles.

In other applications, performance constraints are flexible rather than absolute. Flexible performance constraints are usually based on human factors or economical considerations. The human factors aspect of performance includes the amount of delay a typical user is willing to tolerate, and the predictability of the delay. The economic aspect involves beating or matching the performance of the best competing product on the market. Unfortunately, both of these aspects usually change with time. In these situations, performance requirements are often adjusted relative to what is feasible on a given hardware configuration, as opposed to systems with hard real-time constraints, where the hardware or the functionality of the software may have to be adjusted to make absolute performance constraints feasible. It may be more accurate to refer to flexible performance constraints as design goals rather than requirements.

Reliability is another aspect of performance often specified in the requirements. Reliability requirements can be expressed as goals of immunity to specified classes of hardware failures, or in terms of acceptance tests that must be passed (such as requiring mathematical proofs of correctness for key functions and properties, or specifying a maximum acceptable error frequency with respect to a given input distribution).

It should be noted that mean time between failures, which is commonly used as a measure of hardware reliability, is not by itself a good measure of software reliability because software malfunctions are caused by fixed design faults rather than randomly occurring events such as memory errors due to hard radiation. The failure rate due to a fixed design fault is sensitive to the input distribution, and can be made to vary from 0% to 100% by choosing different input distributions.

For programs whose results do not depend on the relative execution rates of parallel processes, the occurrence of faults is completely determined by the choice of the input data. This makes the mean time between failures of the software critically dependent on the distribution of the input data as well as on the execution frequency. Any software package operates correctly on some subset of its input space and incorrectly on the complement of that subset, which we call the error input space. If the error input space is nonempty, then the software can be made to fail arbitrarily often, by an input distribution that takes samples only from the error input space. Conversely, if the error input space does not cover the whole input space, then the software can be made to appear correct by choosing an input distribution that takes samples only from the complement of the error input space. Consequently, the only meaningful reliability requirement for software that does not refer to the input distribution is a certification of correctness for all possible inputs. Such certifications are difficult, since they require either exhaustive testing or mathematical proofs of correctness. Specifying bounds on the error rates for given input distributions appears to be the most practical approach for reliability requirements of sequential programs without real-time constraints. For parallel or time sensitive programs, it may also be necessary to specify distributions for the system load and the arrival times of the data. As hardware systems get more complicated, it may become more usual to find delivered hardware products with fixed design errors. In such cases, specifying hardware reliability will also be subject to the same difficulties, and mean times between failures will have to be augmented with input distribution and load information for hardware systems also.

Analysts are expected to formulate requirements that can be met with available resources. It is necessary to find out the constraints on resources available for the software development effort, because they determine how large and powerful a system is feasible. The most visible resource constraints are budget and development schedule. In common practice, limits on cost and schedule are given by the customer with relatively little flexibility, and the analyst is called upon to specify the best system that can be achieved within those limits. This happens because most customers are themselves operating within fixed budget constraints.

Costs cannot be predicted very accurately based on an incomplete set of requirements, but it is useful for analysts to be aware of whether they are specifying requirements for a project with a tight budget, a moderate budget, or an ample budget. In cases where resources are fixed, a rough cost/benefit analysis and information about the priorities of the customer should be used to determine how much to require for each aspect of the system. In cases where there is some flexibility in the budget, the analyst should help the customer decide how much to require the proposed system to do by providing rough cost estimates for a series of increasingly ambitious options.

Validating Requirements. Validating the requirements is essential because the delivered software system will meet the users' needs only if the requirements accurately reflect those needs. The primary goal of the validation effort is to make sure the requirements are implementable and sufficiently complete; a secondary goal is to make sure they are sufficiently general. A set of requirements is implementable if a software system exists that meets the requirements and can be developed with available resources. A set of requirements is sufficiently complete if every software system that meets the requirements also meets the customer's real needs. A set of requirements is sufficiently general if it does not rule out any economically implementable systems that meet the customer's real needs.

Because the essence of requirements analysis is refining and formalizing an imprecise set of informal concepts, there is no way to mechanically guarantee the appropriateness of the result. The customers are the final judges of what they need and are willing to pay for. Review sessions, where the customers and users examine and review implications of the requirements, are an important part of ensuring that the formal requirements correspond to the customer's needs. Such reviews must be conducted in terms the customers can understand, keeping in mind that most customers are experts on their application area but not on computers or computer science. Demonstrating selected aspects of proposed system behavior via a prototype can be valuable for this purpose, if the aspects to be demonstrated are properly chosen and explained. The customers should also review the correspondence between the high-level requirements and the lower-level subgoals into which they are refined. Some aspects of the correspondence should also be reviewed by technical experts from the application domain. In large projects, independent consultants are useful for this purpose. Since decisions made at lower levels often change some of the requirements at higher levels, customer reviews should be scheduled regularly, as different aspects of the requirements are clarified.

2.2.2 The Spec Language: Requirements Subset

We use the Spec language for defining environment models to help develop precise descriptions of complex problems. Spec is a formal specification language based on logic. Logic is useful for requirements analysis as well as other phases of software development because it has the following properties.

1. Each statement in logical notation has an unambiguous and clearly defined meaning. Natural languages such as English are imprecise and can easily express ambiguous statements, which are useful in politics and diplomacy but not in software engineering. Ambiguous specifications for software components lead to systems that do not work correctly, irritating customers and possibly causing dangerous situations or financial losses. Translating informally specified requirements into statements in logic is an effective way to detect and to resolve ambiguities. This can eliminate many difficulties in communication that are caused by the need for designers and programmers to give precise interpretations to vague English documents.

2. There are known mechanical procedures for transforming and simplifying logical statements that are guaranteed to preserve their meaning. These mechanical procedures can be summarized by a set of rules expressing the laws of logic. Such procedures can significantly aid understanding by reducing complicated statements to simpler forms. One way to unscramble obscure English is to translate it into logic, simplify the sentence using the logical laws, and then translate it back into English. Aids to human understanding can be very important for solving difficult programming problems, because an engineer cannot create a correct program without understanding what it is supposed to do.

3. There are known mechanical procedures for detecting inconsistencies between statements. This is important because inconsistencies in program specifications lead to faults in computer systems. Because many practical problems have specifications that are too large to be understood by one person, mechanical aids for detecting and locating inconsistencies are very important for producing correct and reliable systems.

4. There are known mechanical procedures for checking whether one statement is a logical consequence of another. This allows an automated system to partially check the reasoning of the analysts, designers, and programmers building a software system. This is important because the mean distance between errors in text produced by people is small compared to the size of typical software products, and most software systems will not work reliably unless they are very nearly free of errors.

This section briefly introduces the aspects of Spec needed for requirements analysis. Other details of the language are introduced in Chapters 3 and 4, and syntax diagrams for the full language can be found in Appendix A.

It is useful to augment expressions in any formal language with informal comments and explanations. Informal comments in Spec as well as in Ada extend from a - - to the end of the line. Specifications in the Spec language are organized in units called *modules*. The modules used in requirements analysis are delimited by the keywords DEFINITION and END, and contain definitions for a set of *concepts*. Concept definitions start with the keyword CONCEPT, and correspond to the types, individuals, attributes, and relationships comprising an environment model. A simple example of a definition module is shown in Fig. 2.4.

The example defines a type called person. An instance of this type could be defined as shown in Fig. 2.5. Every identifier in Spec has a specified type, and the identifier denotes values only of that type. Types can overlap, and all Spec types are subsets of the universal type any. Type specifications always contain a : that is preceded by a set of identifiers and followed by the type associated with the identifiers. The definitions of types and instances have the same form since Spec types are instances of a special predefined type called type (defined in Appendix D). Definitions of attributes and relationships also have a common form, illustrated by the definition of the attribute name. Attributes and relationships have arguments and values whose types are declared in parentheses ( ). The value of a relationship has the predefined type boolean; the value of an attribute can have any other type. To make specifications easier to read, we follow the convention that the names of attributes and relationships that operate on individual objects begin with a lowercase letter, and the names of attributes and relationships that operate on types or functions begin with an upper-case letter. Spec keywords are entirely in upper-case letters.

The laws associated with a concept are listed after the keyword WHERE.

```
DEFINITION person   -- Concepts for describing people.
  INHERIT cause   -- The module "cause" defines the type "agent."
  IMPORT Subtype FROM type

  CONCEPT person: type   -- The set of human beings.
    WHERE Subtype(person, agent)   -- People are active agents.

  CONCEPT name(p: person) VALUE(s: string)
END
```

FIGURE 2.4
Example of a Type

Laws can refer to attributes and relationships using the prefix notation commonly used in mathematics. The law Subtype(person, agent) means
that the types person and agent are related by the Subtype relationship.
The Subtype relationship is a predefined concept in Spec associated with the
type module, which states that one type is a subset of another type, and
implies every instance of the first type has all of the properties of an instance of
the second type. Subtypes are used in requirements analysis to relate specific
types, which are often application specific, to general types, which are often
application independent and reusable. A small set of reusable definitions for
requirements analysis is given in Appendix C, including the modules person
and cause. The laws associated with an attribute or relationship can refer to
the arguments or values using the formal names introduced in the associated
declarations. Laws can also be expressed using the logical operators introduced
in the next section.

The keyword INHERIT includes all of the definitions from another
module, which is specified by giving its name. This provides a concise way to
share the definitions of reusable concepts without making multiple copies.
Inherited concepts can be refined by adding more constraints. If the same concept is defined locally and also inherited, then the laws associated with both
definitions are combined. This is useful for tailoring general-purpose concepts
to particular situations by inheriting the general concept and defining additional
constraints as laws.

```
CONCEPT albert_einstein: person
```

FIGURE 2.5
Example of an Instance

Concepts can be overloaded: There can be several different versions of a concept with the same identifier if they have different types of arguments. Thus, people can have an attribute called `name`, and software systems can have an attribute called `name`, where the two attributes are distinct concepts and can have different properties even though they are represented by the same symbol. Inherited concepts are merged with locally defined concepts only if they have the same identifier and the same types of arguments.

Individual concepts can be imported into a module using the keyword `IMPORT`, as shown in Fig. 2.4 for the Subtype concept. The effect of an import declaration is to include copies of the listed concept definitions from another module. The import mechanism allows selective sharing of concepts without explicitly replicating definitions, and explicitly records the logical dependencies such shared concepts introduce. In contrast to inherited concepts, imported concepts cannot be refined by adding additional constraints unless either the imported concept or the refined concept is given a new name. A concept can be imported only if it has been exported by the module in which it is defined, using the keyword `EXPORT`. This records which concepts are local to a module and which are potentially shared between modules, to make it easier to assess the impact of changing a definition. Such a facility is useful for evolving models of complex systems.

2.2.3 Logic

Logic is the basic tool for describing the requirements and assumptions related to a software system because it provides a means for recording facts and assumptions in a way that can be understood by a machine. This opens the door to mechanical assistance in understanding and checking for errors, which are important and time-consuming activities in the software development process. Learning to understand and construct statements in formal logic is the price of such mechanical assistance. It is easier to write a precise description of the behavior of a system using logic than to write a program implementing the system, because logic provides more powerful primitives. Writing descriptions in logic has many similarities to programming. It takes practice to become fluent in the notation and to acquire the new ways of thinking that it enables and encourages.

The rest of this section briefly introduces predicate logic and gives some examples of how logic can be used to describe systems.

Definitions.   The primitives of logic are few and easy to understand. A logical statement is either true or false. Logical statements in Spec are built from functions and relationships using the connectives & (and), | (or), ~ (not), => (implies), and <=> (if and only if), and the quantifiers ALL (for all) and SOME (there exists). The following grammar gives the syntax of logical statements in Spec more precisely.

```
statement =  boolean_variable
           | predicate_name ["(" expression
                                ("," expression)* ")" ]
           | "~" statement
           | statement "&" statement
           | statement "|" statement
           | statement "=>" statement
           | statement "<=>" statement
           | "(" statement ")"
           | "ALL" "(" variable ":" type "::" statement ")"
           | "SOME" "(" variable ":" type "::" statement ")"

expression =variable
           | function_name ["(" expression
                                ("," expression)* ")"]
```

In this grammar, double quotes ("") enclose terminal symbols, square brackets ([ ]) enclose optional items, a star (*) denotes zero or more repetitions of the preceding unit, and parentheses (( )) indicate groupings. For our purposes, a variable, predicate name, or a function name consists of a letter followed by any number of letters, digits, and underscores (_). We distinguish the intended interpretation of such identifiers by context. In Spec, the symbol "::" separates identifier declarations from a description of the *values* denoted by the identifiers, and the symbol ":" separates identifier declarations from a description of the *type* associated with the identifiers.

This grammar is clear but ambiguous. The ambiguities are resolved by the following two rules.

1. Sequences of repeated operations of the same type associate to the left.

2. The precedences of the operators have the following order: (tightest binding) ~, &, |, =>, <=> (weakest binding).

According to the first rule,

x & y & z	means	$(x$ & $y)$ & z
$x \mid y \mid z$	means	$(x \mid y) \mid z$
$x => y => z$	means	$(x => y) => z$
$x <=> y <=> z$	means	$(x <=> y) <=> z$

and according to the second rule,

$\tilde{x}$ & y	means	$(\tilde{x})$ & y
$x \mid y$ & z	means	$x \mid (y$ & $z)$
w & $x => y \mid z$	means	$(w$ & $x) => (y \mid z)$
$x => y <=> z$	means	$(x => y) <=> z.$

The grammar allows functions and predicates without arguments, which are interpreted as constants. There are two Boolean constants—**true** and **false**.

All logical statements have one of these two values, provided that values are given for all variables in the statement, and that the functions and predicates in the statement are well defined.

The logical connectives correspond informally to the English words "and," "or," "not," "if then," and "whenever." The meaning of the logical connectives is defined formally by the following laws.

true & $x = x$	**false** & $x =$ **false**	$x \,\&\, y = y \,\&\, x$
true $\mid x =$ **true**	**false** $\mid x = x$	$x \mid y = y \mid x$
˜**true** = **false**	˜**false** = **true**	

$$x => y = \tilde{\ }x \mid y$$

$$x <=> y = (x => y) \,\&\, (y => x)$$

The meanings of the quantifiers are described informally as follows. A universal quantifier ALL(x: t :: s) is true if and only if the enclosed statement s is true for all possible values for the bound variable x from the data type t, and is false if and only if s is false for at least one value of x from the type t. An existential quantifier SOME(x: t :: s) is true if and only if the enclosed statement s is true for at least one value of the bound variable x from the data type t, and is false if and only if s is false for all possible values of x from the type t. These primitives are defined more precisely in Chapter 3, where they are extended to treat undefined values and to include additional quantifiers.

The notation just introduced is often extended in practice to make some predicates easier to read and write. For convenience, we sometimes use infix notations for some special functions and predicates. For example,

```
x + y   is short for    plus(x, y)
x = y   is short for    equal(x, y).
```

A list of the infix operators used in the Spec language is given in Appendix B. It is also common to allow multiple bound variables in quantifiers. For example,

```
ALL(x: t1, y: t2 :: p(x, y))   is short for
                          ALL(x: t1 :: ALL(y: t2 :: p(x, y)))
ALL(x y: t :: p(x, y))         is short for
                          ALL(x: t :: ALL(y: t :: p(x, y))).
```

A further extension is the introduction of bounded quantifiers, in which the variables range over a subset of a type rather than the entire type.

```
ALL(x: t SUCH THAT p(x) :: q(x))    is short for
                          ALL(x: t :: p(x) => q(x))
SOME(x: t SUCH THAT p(x) :: q(x))   is short for
                          SOME(x: t :: p(x) & q(x)).
```

In both of these forms, the range of the variable x is restricted to the subset of the type t for which the statement $p(x)$ is true. Informally, the expansion of the bounded universal quantifier says that the statement $q(x)$ is true for all values of x in the subset if the conditional statement $p(x) => q(x)$ is true for the entire type t. The expansion of the existential quantifier says that there exists an element in the subset for which the statement $q(x)$ is true if there exists an element of the entire type for which $q(x)$ is true and the subset membership condition $p(x)$ is also true. If bounded quantifiers are new to you, it may be worthwhile to think through the reason different connectives (=> and &) are needed in the two cases. The extended notations are abbreviations that affect the appearance of predicates and make them easier to read, but do not change what can be stated in the logic.

Examples.   The most familiar application of logic is proving theorems rather than requirements analysis, so that it is worthwhile to look at some simple examples of how logic can be used to model software systems before we consider an extended example.

The elements of an environment model are types, individuals, attributes, and relationships. These correspond to the type names, constant names, function names, and predicate names of the logic. The logical connectives and quantifiers are used to express the laws of the model. These laws describe the relationships between the different concepts forming the environment model, and allow inferences of properties of the model that were not explicitly stated, as well as consistency checking.

Let us return to the examples of laws mentioned at the end of the introduction to Section 2.2.1. The first example is a space shuttle navigation system, whose environment model includes the laws of orbital mechanics. These laws are differential equations. Equations are logical statements that state that two expressions have the same value. Any equation is expressed using the predicate =, and an infix notation is provided for this predicate because equations are commonly used in many different applications. Differential equations differ from algebraic equations because they include the differentiation operator, which operates on functions rather than on individual objects such as numbers. The logic we use includes higher order types and functions, and has no difficulty in representing differential equations. We will not take the space here to write down the equations for orbital motion, since formalizations of orbital motion are well known. Interested readers are referred to any textbook on Newtonian physics for the details of these laws. In domains with well known properties such as orbital mechanics, the analyst does not have to formulate a new model. We concentrate on domains that are not well understood, for which the analyst may have to invent and formulate new laws.

The next example from the end of Section 2.2.1 is a limit on transaction rates in a hard real-time system. A simplified version of this kind of restriction

```
DEFINITION maximum_transaction_rate
  INHERIT time

  CONCEPT Minimum_period(t: type) VALUE(mp: time)
    -- The minimum time between transactions of type t.
    WHERE ALL(tr1 tr2: t
      SUCH THAT arrival_time{t}(tr1) < arrival_time{t}(tr2)
      :: arrival_time{t}(tr2) - arrival_time{t}(tr1) >= mp )

  CONCEPT arrival_time{t: type}(tr: t) VALUE(at: time)
    -- The time the request for the transaction tr arrives.
END
```

FIGURE 2.6
Example of a Timing Restriction

can be expressed as shown in Fig. 2.6. This restriction states that any two distinct transactions of the same type have a minimum separation in time. This makes the concept of a limited transaction rate more precise than the original English description, because the formal description states that the limits apply to every pair of transactions individually, rather than to an average transaction rate. The description is not completely formalized, because the interpretation of the concept of an arrival time is informally described. This degree of precision is sufficient for many purposes, and the description can be later refined by adding laws defining the properties of the `arrival_time` attribute, if this becomes necessary during the development. A standard definition module defining some of the properties of time is given in Appendix C. A goal for a particular system can be expressed by a predicate using the concepts defined in the model, such as

```
Minimum_period(receive_sensor_data) = (50 millisec).
```

The third example from the end of Section 2.2.1 involves the expected behavior of the passenger on an elevator. This law can be expressed in logic as shown in Fig. 2.7. This example illustrates the use of shared concepts typical of real applications. The definitions of the modules `elevator` and `passenger` are not shown, but the comments indicate which concepts are used from those modules. This description is a simple first version, which has not taken into consideration factors such as interactions with multiple passengers or delay times. The concept `waiting_passenger_requirement` corresponds to a leaf node in the goal hierarchy, and provides a formal definition of what it means to satisfy that requirement. Models are built by successive approximation, starting with simple initial formulations, and adding refinements as needed to capture the essential behavior of the system. The process of building up a model is illustrated in the case study.

```
DEFINITION waiting_passenger
   INHERIT elevator  -- defines elevator, floor, button_lit
   INHERIT passenger  -- defines passenger, at

   CONCEPT waiting_passenger_requirement: boolean
     WHERE waiting_passenger_requirement <=>
       ALL(p: passenger, f: floor ::
           waiting(p) & at(p, f) & ~button_lit(f)
             => pushes_button(p, f) )
       -- Assumption: the elevator detects waiting
       -- passengers via the elevator call button.

   CONCEPT waiting(p: passenger) VALUE(b: boolean)
     -- True if p is waiting for an elevator.

   CONCEPT pushes_button(p: passenger, f: floor)
     VALUE(b: boolean)
     -- True if p pushes the elevator call button at floor f.
END
```

FIGURE 2.7
Example of a Restriction on Users

The fourth example from the end of Section 2.2.1 involves a safety requirement for an elevator system, which can be expressed in logic as shown in Fig. 2.8. In this example, the elevator safety module defines a law

```
DEFINITION elevator_safety
   INHERIT elevator  -- defines elevator, floor, position,
                     -- stopped, door_open

   CONCEPT elevator_safety_requirement: boolean
     WHERE elevator_safety_requirement <=>
       ALL(e: elevator, f: floor ::
           door_open(e, f) => position(e) = f & stopped(e))
       -- Safety requirement: doors closed if elevator
       -- moving or absent.
END
```

FIGURE 2.8
Example of a Safety Requirement

expressing a safety requirement in terms of a set of inherited types and attributes. This illustrates how a goal of the system can be expressed using logic. The example is oversimplified because the inner doors of the elevator are not distinguished from the outer doors.

The last example from the end of Section 2.2.1 involves a restriction on the direction of a telescope, which can be expressed in logic as shown in Fig. 2.9. The example shows a fragment of the environment model for a telescope control system in an observatory. This example shows the definition of a safety property in terms of the temporal operator `always`, which yields a true value if and only if the predicate on which it operates is true at all points in time. Temporal operators are discussed in detail in Section 3.8.5. Reusable definitions for the mathematical concepts of vectors and angles between vectors are inherited from a standard library module. The definitions of the modules `telescope` and `vector` are not shown.

These examples do not exhaust the types of laws that can be expressed using logic. The notation is very powerful, and can be applied to many different practical situations. An important property of all of the above examples is that they are not completely formalized. Rather, primitive concepts of the application area are identified and the expected interpretations are given via informal comments. Logical laws are then used to express the dependencies

---

```
DEFINITION telescope_safety(minimum_solar_angle: real)
  INHERIT telescope
  INHERIT vector   -- defines vector, angle

  CONCEPT safe_direction_requirement(t: telescope)
    VALUE (b: boolean)
    WHERE b <=> always(angle(direction(t), solar_direction)
                       >= minimum_solar_angle )
      -- Safety requirement:
      -- the telescope must never point at the sun.

  CONCEPT direction(t: telescope)
    VALUE(v: vector)
      -- The direction in which the telescope is pointing.

  CONCEPT solar_direction: vector
    -- The current direction of the sun.
END
```

FIGURE 2.9
Another Safety Requirement

between the concepts. This lets the analyst control the degree of detail in the model and avoid belaboring the obvious in cases where the primitive concepts are standardized and well understood, so that there are no questions about choices between alternative interpretations. The model can be left partially defined, and refined by adding more laws as questions about intended interpretations of the primitive concepts arise and answers are supplied by the customer. In the extreme case, logic can be used to provide complete axiomatizations of the primitive concepts, as is commonly done in mathematics. It is important to note however, that this degree of precision is not required by the notation, and that less exhaustive approaches are possible and useful. The choice of how much detail to formalize is left up to the analyst, and can be adjusted to the needs of each particular application.

An important difference between the use of logic and earlier approaches to requirements modeling using the entity-relationship model originally introduced in database work is the ability to formally define laws expressing or partially describing the semantics of new attributes and relationships. The older approaches are equivalent to using logical notation without defining any laws, or recording the laws as informal comments only. Formally defined laws provide precision and enable automated inferences and consistency checking.

2.3 Procedures and Guidelines

There are no universally accepted procedures for software development in general, and for requirements analysis in particular. Here, we present a set of procedures that we have found to be workable and consistent with a formal and computer-aided approach to the software development process, illustrated in Fig. 2.10.

The process of requirements analysis starts with an initial problem statement, which is usually a short memo written by the customer. After receiving this document, the following tasks need to be done.

1. Build a formal model of the environment based on the concepts appearing in the initial problem statement. When doing this, relate the model to known reusable concepts.

2. Express the goals from the initial problem statement in terms of the environment model. Refine the model as needed to express the stated goals. When this step is complete, you should have a formal requirements statement that captures the initial problem statement.

3. Examine the goals and look for aspects of the problem that the customer has overlooked. Propose some additional plausible goals, and check with the customer. If the customer agrees, add the new goals to the require-

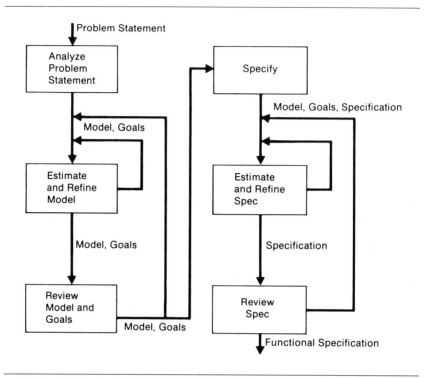

FIGURE 2.10
Procedure for Requirements Analysis

ments. If the customer does not agree, even after the consequences of not asserting the additional goals are explained, then document the rejected goals as limits on the scope of the project.

4. Refine each goal into subgoals until you identify the functions the proposed system must perform and you have testable goals each function must satisfy.

5. Develop a functional specification describing a proposed system interface. Identify missing functions that are necessary to meet the customer's needs, and reflect these in the goal hierarchy and environment model as needed.

6. Estimate costs and compare with customer resource constraints. If costs exceed means, prioritize functions and propose ways of relaxing the requirements that can be met with less expensive systems, or break the system into a set of enhancements that can be delivered in phases, and negotiate which functions will be included in the first version of the system.

7. Validate the final version of the requirements via customer reviews. If the proposed system is unfamiliar, has more ambitious requirements than previous systems, or has a strong human factors aspect in the interface, build a prototype to aid in validation.

This method for requirements analysis is illustrated via a case study in Section 2.4. This case study is an extended example, which is followed through all stages of development in later chapters.

2.3.1 Heuristics and Strategies

Requirements analysis is currently an art that has not been codified into a set of clear and mechanizable rules, but there are some informal guidelines that can be applied by human analysts. We briefly summarize some of these next.

1. Start by defining the objectives and constraints of the customer organization. Knowledge of these objectives and constraints will help identify and refine the objectives and constraints for the proposed system.

2. Identify the types of objects in the problem domain. Decide which ones are controlled by the system and which ones interact directly with the system.

3. Identify sources for each type of data affecting the proposed system.

4. Identify undefined concepts mentioned in the goals and develop definitions for them, based on information obtained from the customer. If the concept appears complicated or unclear, develop a formal definition, and identify more primitive related concepts needed in the explanation. Incorporate the new definitions into the environment model.

5. Interfaces are required for managing instances of all types controlled by a system that are maintained by users of the system. Add goals for providing such interfaces.

6. For each type controlled by the system, determine whether new instances of the type can be created and whether existing instances of the type can be updated or destroyed. Refine the environment model to incorporate this information, and add goals for providing a means to create, update, or destroy instances if these kinds of actions are possible for the type.

7. If the system has a user class that is a special case of a known user class, ask if the system should automate functions commonly handled by the known user class. For example, if a system will be used by some kind of vendor, ask if the system should handle billing and accounting functions.

The use of these heuristics is illustrated in the case study.

2.4 Case Study: Airline Reservation System

The concepts and procedures introduced in each chapter are illustrated in terms of a running case study on the development of a simplified airline reservation system. This example is developed in detail throughout the book, to ensure that all aspects of the development process are addressed. We have made every effort to follow practices in our example that scale up to much larger projects. The example is printed in **boldface** to distinguish it from explanations and discussions of the example.

We make some simplifying assumptions to keep the example from getting too large. Such assumptions must also be made in real projects to conform to budget constraints. However, due to size limitations imposed by our educational objectives, we have accepted some simplifications that would not be allowed in practice. The simplifying assumptions are summarized at the end of the section.

2.4.1 Initial Problem Statement

The initial problem statement is expressed in English, from the point of view of the customer organization; in this case, an airline. The initial problem statement for the airline reservation system is given in Fig. 2.11. This example is typical of the memo that starts most requirements analysis efforts: It is short, imprecise, and leaves out many relevant aspects of the problem. The analyst must turn this into a complete statement of the requirements.

2.4.2 Environment Model

The environment model should be developed in stages. In the first stage, the model implicit in the initial problem statement is formalized. This is done by looking at the nouns in the statement, identifying the ones representing types of

---

The purpose of the airline reservation system is to help the travel agent sell tickets to passengers on commercial airlines. The travel agent must be able to find all of the flights meeting a passenger's needs and make reservations based on the passenger's preferences.

FIGURE 2.11
Initial Problem Statement

The purpose of the **airline reservation system** is to help the **travel agent** sell **tickets** to **passengers** on commercial **airlines**. The travel agent must be able to find all of the **flights** meeting a passenger's needs and make **reservations** based on the passenger's preferences.

FIGURE 2.12
Identifying Types in the Initial Problem Statement

objects in the environment of the system, and identifying the relationships between them that are relevant for understanding the customer's problem. This is an instance of the second heuristic mentioned in Section 2.3.1, which suggests first identifying the types of objects in the problem domain, and then deciding which ones will be controlled by or interact with the proposed system. The nouns of the initial problem statement representing types are shown in boldface in Fig. 2.12.

Often, many of the types and relationships in an environment model are special cases of previously known general-purpose types and relationships common to the application area. These specializations are recorded by inheriting the applicable reusable general-purpose concepts and refining them by adding application-specific laws as needed.

The initial environment model resulting from applying the first step of our analysis procedure to the airline reservation system is shown in Fig. 2.13. The model is expressed in a formal specification language called Spec, a subset of which is explained in Section 2.3.2.

The objects explicitly mentioned in the initial problem statement are the airline reservation system, the travel agent, tickets, passengers, airlines, flights, and reservations. We start with these types of objects and identify the properties of each that are relevant to the development project. It is implicitly understood that the airline reservation system is a software product we are proposing to develop, and we make this understanding explicit. Since the initial problem statement refers to "the airline reservation system" we assume there will be only one copy of the system, and declare the airline reservation to be an individual element of the type `software_system`, rather than a subtype. Since the word "reservation" appears in "airline reservation system," the analyst decides the system is supposed to help the travel agent make reservations by managing all information about them. Similarly we record the implicitly understood relationships between the other kinds of objects mentioned so far.

The analyst uses a lot of common knowledge to model many relationships that are assumed but not explicitly described in the initial problem statement. For example, the `buy`, `sell`, `want`, and `needed_for` relationships describe the implicit relationships that motivate the need for the proposed system. The fact that the travel agent sells tickets to the passenger is explicitly mentioned in

FIGURE 2.13
Initial Environment Model

```
DEFINITION airline_environment
  INHERIT system   -- defines software_system, proposed,
                   -- controls
  INHERIT user   -- defines User_class, uses
  INHERIT business   -- defines vendor, customer, sells
  IMPORT Subtype FROM type

  CONCEPT airline_reservation_system: software_system
    WHERE proposed(airline_reservation_system),
        -- We are going to build an airline reservation
        -- system.
      Controls(airline_reservation_system, reservation)
        -- The system will help travel agents sell tickets by
        -- managing reservations.

  CONCEPT travel_agent: User_class
    WHERE ALL(ta: travel_agent
              :: uses(ta, airline_reservation_system)),
        -- Travel agents use the airline reservation system.
        -- We are only concerned with the travel agents using
        -- our system.
      Subtype(travel_agent, vendor),
        -- A travel agent is a sales person.
      ALL(t: ticket :: SOME(ta: travel_agent
                            :: sells(ta, t) )),
      ALL(r: reservation :: SOME(ta: travel_agent
                                :: supplies(ta, t) ))
        -- Travel agents are the only sources for tickets
        -- and reservations.

  CONCEPT ticket: type
    WHERE Subtype(ticket, product),
      ALL(t: trip :: Needed_for(ticket, t))
        -- A ticket is needed for every trip.

  CONCEPT trip: type
    WHERE Subtype(trip, activity),
      ALL(t: trip :: Needed_for(flight, t))
        -- A flight is needed for every trip.

  CONCEPT passenger: type
    WHERE Subtype(passenger, customer),
      ALL(p: passenger :: SOME(t: trip :: wants(p, t))),
      ALL(p: passenger :: SOME(t: ticket :: buys(p, t)))
```

FIGURE 2.13 (continued)

```
CONCEPT airline: type
  WHERE Subtype(airline, supplier),
    ALL(f: flight :: SOME(a: airline :: supplies(a, f)))
      -- Every flight is associated with an airline.
      -- We are only concerned with commercial flights.

CONCEPT flight: type
  WHERE Subtype(flight, activity)

CONCEPT reservation: type
  WHERE ALL(t: trip :: SOME(r: reservation
                            :: Needed_for(r, t) ))
END
```

the initial problem statement, and the other relationships are added by the analyst to complete the model of the commercial motivations for the system. Another example of this is the type trip. Trips are not explicitly mentioned in the initial problem statement, but they are needed to explain motivations and the connections between reservations and the system implicit in the initial problem statement. Passengers are interested in flights, tickets, and reservations because they want to take a trip, and a ticket, reservation, and flight are needed for a trip. These relationships are consequences of laws for the cause module, which is indirectly inherited via the business module, and could have been filled in by automated inference procedures once the analyst states that every passenger wants a trip. The inherited modules are defined in Appendix C.

The standard definitions given in Appendix C capture a small and simplified part of the knowledge that a requirements analyst has about the world in general, software systems, business, and human behavior. A short-term benefit of making such knowledge explicit is that it helps to standardize the vocabulary used by all of the analysts and designers in a project, reducing the confusion due to different interpretations for common words. A long-term benefit of building up a library of such knowledge is that it makes it possible for automated requirements analysis tools to derive consequences of the environment model and to detect inconsistencies.

The process of building the environment model involves educated guess-work on the part of the analyst, based on observation and common knowledge. The resulting properties are recorded, and then verified by asking the customer and the users of the system. This guess-and-check approach is needed because the customers do not fully understand and cannot describe precisely what they need. As in the classical scientific method, the verification process is very important. If discrepancies between the model and the customer's application and intentions are detected, the model must be modified to fit the true situation. The model is not accepted as representing reality until it has withstood thorough verification, and it is never treated as absolutely certain since discrepancies requiring further modifications can always be discovered in the future.

2.4.3 High-Level Goals

The high-level goals are derived from the initial problem statement. The initial high-level goals for the airline reservation system are shown in Fig. 2.14. The high-level goals are very informal. They have been factored into independent statements and organized into a two-level hierarchy. There is only one goal at the top level only because this is a very simple system. Larger systems usually have many top-level goals. Each top level goal expresses a goal of the customer organization, which in this case is to enable the travel agents to sell more tickets. This is an instance of the first heuristic in Section 2.3.1, which suggests the analysts should start with the goals of the customer organization to identify the goals for the proposed system. In other projects, especially for larger ones, the goals of the customer organization may not be apparent in the initial problem statement, and the analysts may have to interview people and ask many questions to get an accurate picture of the goals of the customer organization.

The second-level goals (G1.1 and G1.2) specify in more detail how the system is supposed to realize the top-level goal (G1). These are subgoals that should be realized by the proposed system to achieve the goals of the customer organization.

In general, the goals of a proposed system may not be sufficient to completely meet the goals of the customer organization, and there may be other subgoals identified that are needed to realize the goals of the customer organization, but will be met by means other than the proposed software system, such as hardware systems or manual procedures. Such external subgoals are not apparent at this stage of the analysis.

G1:   The purpose of the system is to help the travel agent sell tickets.

    G1.1:   The system must help the travel agent find all of the flights meeting a passenger's needs.

    G1.2:   The system must let the travel agent make reservations.

FIGURE 2.14
High-Level Goals

Implementation constraints:
C1: The airline reservation system must be implemented in Ada.

Performance constraints:
C2: The responses of the airline reservation system must be fast enough not to irritate the customers of the travel agents.

Resource constraints:
C3: The system must be developed by three people in ten weeks.

FIGURE 2.15
High-Level Constraints

2.4.4 Constraints

The constraints come from the user much like the initial problem statement, and are often part of the same document. If they are not given in the initial document, the analyst must obtain this information, either by soliciting written documents or by interviewing selected members of the customer organization. The constraints for the airline reservation system are given in Fig. 2.15. The ten-week development period was specified directly by the customer in terms of a delivery deadline. The customer specified a limit on the cost, which we have converted from dollars into person-weeks.

Interviews with travel agents and airline managers result in the more detailed characterizations of customer perceptions and expected system loads shown in Fig. 2.16.

The analyst considers these constraints to be clear, and does not formalize them further at this point.

C2.1: Response times less than a second are good.

C2.2: The average response time for travel agent requests should be less than ten seconds.

C2.3: Situations in which a travel agent request takes more than a minute should be rare.

   C2.3.1: Rare means average less than once per week per travel agent.

C2.4: The system must be able to handle 10,000 reservations per day.

C2.5: The system must be able to support 300 travel agents.

FIGURE 2.16
Refined Constraints

2.4.5 Refined Goals

The next stage in the process is to refine the goals of the system. This involves locating the undefined concepts in the high-level goals, and working out in more detail what they are supposed to mean. This is an instance of the fourth heuristic given in Section 2.3.1, which suggests clarifying the undefined concepts mentioned in the goals and incorporating the definitions in the environment model. Goal G1 says the system is supposed to find flights meeting the passenger's needs. The analyst has to find out what this is supposed to mean. This requires refining the model to reflect the aspects of the environment relevant to a passenger's needs.

A passenger can have many kinds of needs. Some of the possibly relevant factors are the starting and ending points of the trip, the departure and arrival times, the cost, the kind of airplane, the kinds of seats available, the kinds of meals served, the kinds of entertainment available, and so on. At this point, an experienced analyst would consider constraint C3, and decide that the customer is asking for an an unreasonably large system on a minuscule budget. The most reasonable response to such a situation is to pare down the goals to the barest minimum that will get the job done, in the hopes of being able to provide some useful services within budget, or to convince the customer to spend more to get a more powerful system. Flights with the wrong origin or destination are usually useless to a passenger; the other factors are generally more flexible. Most customers also will insist on knowing the arrival and departure times and the cost. Since constraints on the other factors are less frequent, the analyst tentatively decides to handle them outside the proposed system, and does not include them in the first version of the environment model. It is advisable to list aspects of the problem that have been deliberately neglected, for review with the customer. This is done in Section 2.4.9. The refinement of the environment model implied by these decisions is given in Fig. 2.17. This refinement of the initial environment model defines the attributes of a flight relevant to meeting a customer's needs from the point of view of the proposed system. The customer wants a trip from a given origin to a given destination. Such a trip can be realized by a flight from the same origin to the same destination. We have assumed that the origin and destination of a trip are airports rather than cities or other kinds of locations to simplify the processing required of the proposed system. The refinement to the goal hierarchy implied by these decisions is shown in Fig. 2.18. At this level, the goals are specific enough to link to the environment model, as shown in Fig. 2.19. The definition modules `requirement_goals` and `system_actions` are standard reusable components, which are defined in Appendix C. The relationship `goal` states that a goal of the specified system is to implement the specified concept, and is used to link concepts into the goal hierarchy. The identifiers for the goals are included as comments to provide a cross-reference between the informally described goal hierarchy and the concepts in the model.

The previous goal refinement raises a question—What is the source of the

```
DEFINITION airline_environment1
  INHERIT airline_environment  -- inherits money from
                               -- business
  INHERIT time
  INHERIT location
  IMPORT One_to_one FROM function(flight, flight_id)

  -- The passenger will choose a flight based on
  -- origin, destination, departure, arrival, and price.
  CONCEPT origin(f: flight) VALUE(a: airport)
  CONCEPT destination(f: flight) VALUE(a: airport)
  CONCEPT departure(f: flight) VALUE(t: time_of_day)
  CONCEPT arrival(f: flight) VALUE(t: time_of_day)
  CONCEPT price(f: flight) VALUE(m: money)
  CONCEPT id(f: flight) VALUE(i: flight_id)
    -- The flight id is used by the passenger to find the
    -- flight.
    WHERE One_to_one(id)   -- The id uniquely identifies
                           -- a flight.

  CONCEPT origin(t: trip) VALUE(a: airport)
  CONCEPT destination(t: trip) VALUE(a: airport)

  CONCEPT airport: type WHERE Subtype(airport, location)
  CONCEPT flight_id: type
END
```

FIGURE 2.17
Refined Environment Model

flight information to be displayed by the system? This is an instance of the third heuristic in Section 2.3.1, which says the analyst should identify the sources for each type of data affecting the proposed system. There are several possible sources for the flight information.

G1.1.1: The system must be able to find all flights with a given origin and destination.

G1.1.2: The system must display the arrival and departure times, the price, and the flight number for each flight it finds.

G1.1.3: The passenger will choose a flight based on the displayed information.

FIGURE 2.18
Refined Goals

```
DEFINITION goals
  INHERIT requirement_goals  -- defines goal
  INHERIT system_actions  -- defines displayed_to

  CONCEPT find(origin destination: airport)
  VALUE(s: set{flight})
    WHERE ALL(f: flight :: f IN s <=> origin(f) = origin
              & destination(f) = destination),
      goal(find, airline_reservation_system)  -- G1.1.1

  CONCEPT display_flight(f: flight) VALUE(b: boolean)
    WHERE b <=> (displayed_to(arrival(f), travel-agent)
              & displayed_to(departure(f), travel-agent)
              & displayed_to(price(f), travel-agent)
              & displayed_to(flight_id(f), travel-agent) ),
      goal(display_flight, airline_reservation_system)
      -- G1.1.2
END
```

FIGURE 2.19
Linking Goals to the Environment Model

1. It could be built into the system. In this case, the set of flights and their characteristics must never change.
2. It could come from an external system. In this case, the external system must be identified and its interface must be specified.
3. Flights could be controlled by the airline reservation system. In this case, an agent responsible for managing flights must be identified and a set of functions for maintaining the flight information must be provided.

The first case is unrealistic because fares change quite often. The second case is unattractive for performance reasons, because requests for flight information are frequent and interactive. Long distance communication tends to be slow, especially if information must be assembled from many different sources. This leaves the third case as the best choice. The agent responsible for flights is an airline manager. This choice implies the refinement to the model shown in Fig. 2.20. This leads to another goal for the system; to provide the means for the airline manager to manage fights. This goal is implicit in the initial problem statement, the constraints, and the relevant background knowledge, but the goal may not have been obvious to the customer. This is an instance of the fifth heuristic in Section 2.3.1, which says that interfaces should be provided for managing instances of all types controlled by a system and maintained by a user of the system. More consideration leads to the new goals shown in Fig. 2.21.

```
DEFINITION airline_environment2
  INHERIT airline_environment1
    -- inherits Maintains from user, Controls from system

  CONCEPT airline_manager: User_class
    WHERE ALL(am: airline_manager
               :: uses(am, airline_reservation_system) ),
        -- We are only concerned with the airline managers
        -- that will use the system.
      Maintains(airline_manager, flight)

  CONCEPT airline_reservation_system: software_system
    WHERE Controls(airline_reservation_system, flight)
END
```

FIGURE 2.20
Refinement of Environment Model

We link these goals to the environment model as shown in Fig. 2.22. The concepts `creates`, `destroys`, and `updates` are defined in the re-usable `system_actions` module, shown in Appendix C. This module is indirectly inherited via the `goals` module.

The sixth heuristic in Section 2.3.1 suggests that the analyst should ask whether instances of a type can be created, updated, or destroyed whenever a proposed system is going to control the type. This guideline applies to the types `ticket` and `reservation` in the example. Consulting the user, we discover that issuing or returning tickets for refunds is handled by the airline rather than the travel agent, and is not a concern of the airline reservation system. Thus, tickets are permanent as far as the proposed system is concerned. Neither tickets nor reservations can be changed. However, travel agents are often called upon to cancel reservations and issue new ones. This leads to the

G2: **The system must provide a means for the airline manager to manage flights.**

   G2.1: **The system must allow the airline manager to schedule new flights.**

   G2.2: **The system must allow the airline manager to drop flights from the schedule.**

   G2.3: **The system must allow the airline manager to change the fare for a flight.**

FIGURE 2.21
New Goals

```
DEFINITION goals1
  INHERIT goals

  CONCEPT create_flight: boolean
    WHERE create_flight <=> creates(airline_manger, flight),
      goal(create_flight, airline_reservation_system) -- G2.1

  CONCEPT destroy_flight: boolean
    WHERE destroy_flight <=> destroys(airline_manger, flight),
      goal(destroy_flight, airline_reservation_system) -- G2.2

  CONCEPT update_price: boolean
    WHERE update_price <=> updates(airline_manger, flight, price),
      goal(update_price, airline_reservation_system) -- G2.3
END
```

FIGURE 2.22
Link to Environment Model

refinement to the model shown in Fig. 2.23. We have included justifications as comments, indicating that the information recorded has come from the customer, so that it cannot be changed by the analysts without consulting with the

```
DEFINITION airline_environment3
  INHERIT airline_environment2
  IMPORT Immutable_instances Indestructible FROM type

  CONCEPT ticket: type
      -- Once issued, tickets cannot be changed or destroyed.
    WHERE Immutable_instances(ticket),
        -- Justification: customer policy.
      Indestructible(ticket)
        -- Justification: customer policy.

  CONCEPT reservation: type
      -- Once issued, reservations cannot be changed.
    WHERE Immutable_instances(reservation)
      -- Justification: customer policy.
END
```

FIGURE 2.23
Refinement of Model

G1.3:   The system must allow the travel agent to cancel reservations.

FIGURE 2.24
New Goal

customer. Such justifications are also useful because they provide a means to determine the likelihood of changes to these properties. In real projects, such comments should identify the source of the policy as specifically as possible by identifying the person or suborganization responsible for the policy. The designers of the system are going to want to know which properties are stable, because this kind of information often enables special implementations that provide performance advantages but may be expensive to change.

Since reservations can be changed, we must provide a means to do so. This is reflected in the goal shown in Fig. 2.24. This goal is linked to the environment model as shown in Fig. 2.25.

Another heuristic from Section 2.3.1 suggests asking whether the system should manage billing and accounting information whenever the user is a vendor. This heuristic applies in our case because the travel agent is a vendor. We discover that the customer (airline) would like the system to issue tickets and manage accounts, but is not willing to pay the extra development costs those functions would involve. If the proposed system controls a type, the analyst should ask whether the system should manage any common function associated with the type. The system controls flights and the analyst knows flights are assigned to gates at the airport, and that this information is displayed throughout the airport to help passengers find their flights, and therefore inquires whether these functions should be part of the airline reservation system. The customer responds that those functions are desirable but there is no budget for them at this time.

```
DEFINITION goals2
  INHERIT goals1

  CONCEPT destroy_reservation: boolean
    WHERE destroy_reservation <=> destroys(travel_agent, reservation),
      goal(destroy_reservation,
          airline_reservation_system )   -- G1.3
END
```

FIGURE 2.25
Link to Model

```
airline_reservation_system
  used_by: travel_agent, airline_manager
  controls: reservation, flight
```

FIGURE 2.26
Context Summary

2.4.6 Summary of the Model

An overview of the proposed system is provided by its context summary, shown in Fig. 2.26. The information in the context summary can also be presented graphically as shown in Fig. 2.27. The context summary lists the proposed software systems and shows the user classes of each system and the types of objects the system controls. This information can be very useful for introducing the proposal to someone unfamiliar with the analysis.

After the environment model is completed, it is often useful to reorganize the information and to factor it into smaller, logically related modules that are relatively independent. The reorganized environment model is shown in Figs. 2.28 through 2.31. The structure of the specification modules is shown in Fig. 2.32. The main view of the environment model focuses on the proposed

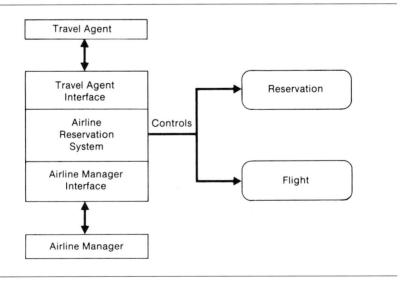

FIGURE 2.27
Context Diagram for the Airline Reservation System

```
DEFINITION flight_view
  INHERIT time
  INHERIT location
  IMPORT Subtype FROM type
  IMPORT One_to_one FROM function(flight, flight_id)

  CONCEPT flight: type
      -- The passenger will choose a flight based on origin,
      -- destination, departure, arrival, and price.
    WHERE Subtype(flight, activity)

  CONCEPT origin(f: flight) VALUE(a: airport)
  CONCEPT destination(f: flight) VALUE(a: airport)
  CONCEPT departure(f: flight) VALUE(t: time_of_day)
  CONCEPT arrival(f: flight) VALUE(t: time_of_day)
  CONCEPT price(f: flight) VALUE(m: money)
  CONCEPT id(f: flight) VALUE(i: flight_id)
    -- The flight id is used by the passenger to find
    -- the flight.
    WHERE One_to_one(id)   -- The id uniquely identifies
                           -- a flight.

  CONCEPT airport: type
    WHERE Subtype(airport, location)

  CONCEPT flight_id: type

  CONCEPT airline: type
    WHERE Subtype(airline, supplier),
      ALL(f: flight :: SOME(a: airline :: supplies(a, f)))
        -- Every flight is associated with an airline.
        -- We are only concerned with commercial flights.
END
```

FIGURE 2.28
Reorganized Environment Model: Shared Flight View

system. In larger projects, there may be several major subsystems, in which case it is natural to introduce a module for each subsystem. We have separated the concepts needed by each user class into a separate module, and the concepts needed by both user classes into another module shared by both of the modules describing the user-class views. For larger systems, we recommend factoring on a finer scale, with one module for each type or small group of related types. Such an organization makes requirements reviews easier, and helps new people entering the project to learn about the parts of the analysis that impact their work without looking through the entire description.

```
DEFINITION airline_environment
  INHERIT travel_agent_view
  INHERIT airline_manager_view
  INHERIT system
  INHERIT user

  CONCEPT airline_reservation_system: software_system
    WHERE proposed(airline_reservation_system),
        -- We are going to build an airline reservation
        -- system.
      Uses(travel_agent, airline_reservation_system),
      Controls(airline_reservation_system, reservation),
        -- The system will help travel agents sell tickets by
        -- managing reservations.
      Uses(airline_manager, airline_reservation_system),
      Controls(airline_reservation_system, flight)
        -- The system will help airline managers maintain the
        -- flight schedule.
END
```

FIGURE 2.29
Reorganized Environment Model: Context View

FIGURE 2.30
Reorganized Environment Model: Travel Agent View

```
DEFINITION travel_agent_view
  INHERIT flight_view
  INHERIT user   -- defines User_class, uses
  INHERIT business   -- defines vendor, customer, sells
  IMPORT Subtype Immutable_instances Indestructible FROM type

  CONCEPT travel_agent: User_class
    WHERE ALL(ta: travel_agent
              :: uses(ta, airline_reservation_system)),
        -- Travel agents use the airline reservation system.
        -- We are only concerned with the travel agents
        -- using our system.
      Subtype(travel_agent, vendor),
        -- A travel agent is a sales person.
      ALL(t: ticket :: SOME(ta: travel_agent
                            :: sells(ta, t) )),
      ALL(r: reservation :: SOME(ta: travel_agent
                                :: supplies(ta, t) ))
        -- Travel agents are the only sources for tickets
        -- and reservations.
```

FIGURE 2.30 (continued)

```
CONCEPT reservation: type
  WHERE ALL(t: trip :: SOME(r: reservation
                              :: Needed_for(r, t) )),
  -- Once issued, reservations cannot be changed.
  Immutable_instances(reservation)   -- Justification:
                                      -- customer policy.
CONCEPT ticket: type
  WHERE Subtype(ticket, product),
    ALL(t: trip :: Needed_for(ticket, t)),
    -- A ticket is needed for every trip.
    -- Once issued, tickets cannot be changed or destroyed.
    Immutable_instances(ticket),   -- Justification:
                                   -- customer policy.
    Indestructible(ticket)   -- Justification:
                             -- customer policy.
CONCEPT trip: type
  WHERE Subtype(trip, activity)

CONCEPT origin(t: trip) VALUE(a: airport)
CONCEPT destination(t: trip) VALUE(a: airport)

CONCEPT passenger: type
  WHERE Subtype(passenger, customer),
    ALL(p: passenger :: SOME(t: trip :: wants(p, t))),
    ALL(p: passenger :: SOME(t: ticket :: buys(p, t))),
    ALL(t: trip :: Needed_for(flight, t))
      -- The system is only concerned with trips on
      -- airplanes.
END
```

```
DEFINITION airline_manager_view
  INHERIT flight_view
  INHERIT user   -- defines User_class, uses

  CONCEPT airline_manager: User_class
    WHERE ALL(am: airline_manager
              :: uses(am, airline_reservation_system) ),
      -- We are only concerned with the airline managers
      -- that will use the system.
    Maintains(airline_manager, flight)
END
```

FIGURE 2.31
Reorganized Environment Model: Airline Manager View

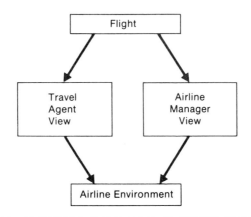

FIGURE 2.32
Inheritance Structure of the Environment Model

2.4.7 Summary of the Goals

The completed goal hierarchy is shown in Fig. 2.33. The formal definitions of
the leaf goals are gathered together in Fig. 2.34. The goals have been reordered

---

G1: **The purpose of the system is to help the travel agent sell tickets.**

    G1.1: **The system must help the travel agent find all of the flights meeting a
passenger's needs.**

        G1.1.1: **The system must be able to find all flights with a given origin
and destination.**

        G1.1.2: **The system must display the arrival and departure times, the
price, and the flight number for each flight it finds.**

        G1.1.3: **The passenger will choose a flight based on the displayed
information.**

    G1.2: **The system must let the travel agent make reservations.**

    G1.3: **The system must allow the travel agent to cancel reservations.**

G2: **The system must provide a means for the airline manager to manage flights.**

    G2.1: **The system must allow the airline manager to schedule new flights.**

    G2.2: **The system must allow the airline manager to drop flights from the
schedule.**

    G2.3: **The system must allow the airline manager to change the fare for a
flight.**

FIGURE 2.33
Completed Goal Hierarchy

```
DEFINITION airline_reservation_system_goals
  INHERIT requirement_goals
  INHERIT system_actions

  CONCEPT find(origin destination: airport)
         VALUE(s: set{flight})
    WHERE ALL(f: flight :: f IN s <=> origin(f) = origin
              & destination(f) = destination),
      goal(find, airline_reservation_system) -- G1.1.1

  CONCEPT display_flight(f: flight) VALUE(b: boolean)
    WHERE b <=> (displayed_to(arrival(f), travel-agent)
               & displayed_to(departure(f), travel-agent)
               & displayed_to(price(f), travel-agent)
               & displayed_to(flight_id(f), travel-agent) ),
      goal(display_flight,
           airline_reservation_system) -- G1.1.2

  CONCEPT destroy_reservation: boolean
    WHERE destroy_reservation <=> destroys(travel_agent, reservation),
      goal(destroy_reservation,
           airline_reservation_system) -- G1.3

  CONCEPT create_flight: boolean
    WHERE create_flight <=> creates(airline_manger, flight),
      goal(create_flight, airline_reservation_system) -- G2.1

  CONCEPT destroy_flight: boolean
    WHERE destroy_flight <=> destroys(airline_manger, flight),
      goal(destroy_flight, airline_reservation_system) -- G2.2

  CONCEPT update_price: boolean
    WHERE update_price <=> updates(airline_manger, flight, price),
      goal(update_price, airline_reservation_system) -- G2.3
END
```

FIGURE 2.34
Definitions of Leaf Goals

to correspond to the hierarchy. For larger systems, the concepts related to the
goals would be factored into smaller modules according to the structure of the
goal hierarchy, where each definition module would correspond to a subtree of
the goal hierarchy. Such an organization allows the goals to be reviewed in
small, coherent, and independently understandable units. A summary of the
constraints can be found in Section 2.4.4.

2.4.8 Summary of the Assumptions

Most real projects will have tight budgets requiring some simplifying assumptions. In practice, those assumptions will be approved by the customer in the process of budget negotiations. The simplifying assumptions for our example follow. Several of these assumptions would be considered unacceptable by a real airline or travel agent, but they have been necessary to meet our tight budget constraints, and to keep the example small enough to allow a complete treatment.

1. The type of airplane on a flight is not important to the travel agent.
2. The kinds of seats available on a flight are not important to the travel agent.
3. The kinds of meals served on a flight are not important to the travel agent.
4. The type of entertainment offered on a flight is not important to the travel agent.
5. Each flight has a single origin and a single destination.
6. Flights occur at the same time every day.
7. All seats on a flight have the same price.
8. The origin and destination of a passenger's trip are specified as airports rather than cities.
9. The ticket clerk and gate agent at the airport are travel agents as far as the system is concerned.
10. The system is not responsible for individual seat assignments.
11. The system is not responsible for issuing tickets.
12. The system is not responsible for billing or accounting functions.
13. The system is not responsible for maintaining arrival and departure displays at the airport or gate assignments for flights.

These assumptions were all made in the process of formulating the environment model, although they have not all been noted in the explanatory text. A suggested exercise is locating the aspects of the environment model corresponding to each of the above simplifying assumptions.

2.5 Quality Assurance

Currently, review meetings in which groups of people examine the requirements are the most popular ways to find faults in the requirements. Review meetings are particularly cost effective at finding faults in initial proposals or newly proposed modifications. There are three different kinds of review meetings: customer reviews, internal reviews, and reviews by domain experts. These meetings are conducted by the analysts who developed the requirements, together with representatives of the customer organization for customer reviews; analysts who were not involved in formulating the requirements for internal reviews; or experts in the application domain for reviews by domain experts. The purpose of a customer review is to find places where the formalized requirements do not correspond to the real problem. The purpose of an internal review is to find incomplete aspects of the requirements; internal inconsistencies; unwanted implementation details; and potential feasibility, performance, or cost problems. The purpose of a domain expert review is to find inaccuracies in the formalized laws of the environment, and to locate common problems in the application domain that have not been addressed by the requirements.

There are some general guidelines for conducting review meetings. The most effective meetings consist of three to six people and last one to two hours. Each meeting must have a chairman and a secretary, both of whom should be different from the people presenting the requirements. The requirements should be presented by the analysts who formulated them. The role of the chairman is to make sure that meeting time is spent effectively. The chairman should break up arguments and avoid spending meeting time trying to solve problems with the requirements. The purpose of a review meeting is to locate and diagnose as many problems as possible and to assign responsibilities for resolving the detected problems, not to work out solutions. The secretary's job is to write down the list of problems detected at the meeting, along with explanations of each problem and lists of people responsible for the solution of each problem. Because the secretary must understand the discussions to do a proper job, this function is usually performed by an analyst or a member of the technical staff. The person responsible for the part of the requirements containing a fault should contact the people assigned to help with the solution after the meeting is over. Each participant should be given a hard copy of the material to be presented, preferably in advance of the meeting. The presentation material should contain diagrams, pictures, and summaries in addition to the formal texts of the requirements. The summary material should be used to guide an oral presentation. The details of the requirements should be displayed only as needed to answer questions or locate suspected errors. The information can be displayed using chalkboards, overhead projectors, or large-screen computer terminals, depending on available resources.

Prototypes are useful for demonstrating implications of the requirements to the customer, validating interfaces, and establishing feasibility. A prototype is a mockup of the proposed system that faithfully models some selected aspects of its operation. A demonstration of some sample sessions with a prototype of the proposed system can spark customers into recognizing inappropriate or missing functions and can provide a clear picture of what it will be like to use the finished system, unobtainable in any other way. This is very important because typical customers are not very good at recognizing the implications of a set of requirements statements, especially if they are expressed in unfamiliar notations and words. Customers are much better at recognizing that something is wrong than they are at describing what they need. A demonstration to a group of potential users of the system familiar with the old approaches to solving the problem can quickly pinpoint human-factors problems in the interfaces and assumptions about system operation implicit in the requirements that may not be practical in realistic situations.

To properly prepare a demonstration of a prototype, it is necessary to develop a script for the demonstration consisting of several test cases. The process of developing the script can act as a completeness check on the model of the environment of the proposed system, and of the system's intended use. Every incentive should be given to the developers of the test cases to locate missing or inconsistent aspects of the requirements.

Some aspects of the completeness and consistency of the requirements can be checked mechanically. Examples of constraints that can be automatically checked are definition completeness and type consistency. Definition completeness means that every concept mentioned in the requirements has an explicit definition and that every defined concept has been used at least once. Type consistency means that the types of the objects involved in each concept agree for the definition and each use of the concept. Other kinds of automated checks are also possible, many of which are more difficult to implement. Broadening the class of requirements checks that can be effectively automated is an active research area.

Requirements tracing refers to the process of establishing the justification relationships between the high-level requirements and their lower-level refinements. Requirements tracing is a process that should be performed by the authors of the requirements prior to any external review of the part of the requirements. The goal of this process is to make sure that all high-level requirements correspond to at least one precise low-level requirement; every low-level requirement corresponds to at least one high-level requirement; and the low-level requirements supporting each high-level requirement are sufficient for realizing the high-level requirement. The first two checks can be readily automated, provided that the structure of the hierarchy has been recorded and the precise requirements have been marked. The third check is more difficult and is usually done manually. A set of requirements cannot be considered well formed unless it meets these criteria.

An explicit representation of the requirements hierarchy is also useful for estimating the impact of a proposed requirements change and identifying features that should be dropped from the system due to the requirements change. Getting rid of obsolete components of the requirements, the design, and the code is essential if large evolving systems are to remain tractable.

Another kind of consistency checking that should be performed by the authors of the requirements is view integration. This refers to the process of putting together the views of the proposed system as seen by different external interfaces. These may correspond to user classes with different privileges, or interfaces to existing software systems. A formal review to certify the global consistency of the completed requirements is recommended whenever the proposed system is large enough to have more than one interface.

The main goals of the view integration task are to remove redundancies and to reconcile inconsistent definitions. To effectively achieve view integration, project management must establish a policy of maintaining a *definition dictionary* containing the official definitions of all the technical terms or concepts used in the project, and must provide a means for carrying out the policy. Usually, this requires assigning the responsibility for maintaining the consistency and independence of the definitions in the definition dictionary to some particular person, providing the tools, and scheduling the review meetings necessary to fulfill this responsibility. This task is difficult because different analysts may have called the same concept by different names, with slightly different definitions for each version. Recognizing when two syntactically different definitions have the same intent and ought to be reconciled depends on a fairly large amount of knowledge about the problem area, and is relatively difficult to automate. In current practice, the analysts from the various components of the project must review each other's work, and identify areas of overlap. When an overlap is found, a common name, interface, and definition for the affected parts of the model must be chosen, and the requirements must be reformulated in terms of the new standard. Any disagreements about how to standardize concepts and their names are settled by the person responsible for the definition dictionary, or ultimately by the project manager. Ensuring that common concepts have consistent names is easier if the analysts communicate their results as the environment model is developed. Relating the particular concepts used in the model to a standard library of general-purpose concepts can help locate correspondences between similar concepts defined by different analysts. Communication between analysts can be enhanced by keeping the environment model in a central database, especially if the database keeps track of links to library components and the database provides tools for identifying concepts that are direct specializations of the same library component (related to it by the Subtype relationship).

2.6 Management Aspects

From the customer's point of view, the management of a requirements analysis effort centers on the contract monitor. The responsibilities of the contract monitor are to make sure that the requirements reflect the real needs of the customer organization, to determine limits on budget and delivery schedule, and to determine the value of each aspect of the requirements to the customer, so that cost/benefit tradeoffs can be made on a reasonable basis. Getting this information will often require consulting many people in the customer organization and securing the necessary approvals for committing resources. The contract monitor is usually a member of the customer organization.

From the developer's point of view, the management of a requirements analysis effort centers on coordinating the activities of the individual analysts. In case the developer organization is responsible for both the requirements and the rest of the project, the higher levels of management may also be concerned with planning the whole development process as requirements analysis proceeds.

2.6.1 Organization and Control

Managing a team of analysts is a difficult job, because the manager must be skilled in both classical management tasks and requirements analysis. Finding people with such a combination of skills may be difficult, so that it is reasonable to split the job into two roles: manager and technical advisor. The manager should be an expert in management familiar with software development projects, while the technical advisor should be an expert in requirements analysis with some management skills. For this arrangement to be successful, it is essential that the manager and the technical advisor be able to work well together, and that the manager consult the technical advisor whenever technical issues influence management decisions, which occurs often in a software development project.

The responsibilities of the technical advisor are to monitor the progress of the effort and and to assess the difficulty of each task. The technical advisor should review the results produced by each analyst, to make sure that everyone concentrates on the logical structure of the problem and does not get bogged down in specifying unimportant details. A common reason for failures in requirements analysis is spending too much time documenting irrelevant details of existing systems or in working out irrelevant details of a proposed system, such as detailed internal data layouts. People are naturally attracted to this direction because specifying details is relatively easy, and gives the illusion of accomplishing something because a large amount of visible documentation is produced. It is also an important danger sign, because it often indicates that the people working on the project are trying to avoid some conceptual difficulty that they do not know how to solve. The technical advisor must recognize such signs and bring them to the attention of the manager.

Keeping the analysis on track is difficult because recognizing which aspects are important requires a great deal of experience and judgement. The technical advisor must be able to judge the difficulty of each subtask accurately. Classifying the tasks to be performed according to difficulty and identifying the prerequisite knowledge needed for the task require good technical insight. The results of the technical advisor's assessments are used by the manager to assign tasks to particular analysts by matching them to the individual talents and abilities of the people available to do the work. Doing a good job of task assignment is important because the capabilities of the people on a team vary widely, and people often have relatively narrow areas of expertise in which they are much more productive than when doing different tasks.

The responsibilities of the manager are to keep the effort on track, establish policies necessary to ensure progress, assign tasks to people, coordinate contact with the customer, make sure the analysts have the resources they need to do their jobs, and recruit people. Most of these tasks require support from the technical advisor.

Successful recruiting depends on planning ahead. Capable analysts are scarce because many talents and abilities are required. A good analyst must know a great deal about software, must be able to communicate well with both customers and engineers, must have the ability to move between different levels of abstraction, and must be able to construct precise formal definitions. An analyst must also be able to learn about the customer's application quickly, so that previous familiarity with the general application area is a significant advantage. Requirements analysis requires a combination of natural talent, training, and experience. A good manager will always be on the lookout for qualified people, and either create a position when a good candidate comes along, or maintain a list of qualified prospects against the day when an unfilled position becomes available. All potential new analysts should be evaluated by the technical advisor, to make sure they are really qualified.

Resources for supporting the analysts include people and systems. The analysts should have assistants available for doing some of the less demanding tasks involved in requirements analysis. These tasks include keeping a record of questions sent to the customer, making sure that answers are received and recorded, preparing displays for reviews, maintaining a record of the different versions of the requirements, recording justifications and alternative choices, and doing the aspects of completeness and consistency checking that have not yet been automated. As the state of the art improves, some of these functions will be performed by software rather than by people. Progressive automation of the more routine tasks is desirable because once the software tools are working correctly, they will make fewer mistakes than people performing the same functions manually.

There should be adequate hardware and software for supporting the analysts' work. The hardware should include an integrated system that provides adequate processing power, convenient access for all project members, and has enough secondary storage to keep all project information online. A network of computers can be attractive because the failure of a single computer need not block the progress of the entire project, but the benefits of such an approach depend on the availability of software providing a logically centralized project database with a robust distributed implementation. Portable computers that can communicate with the main network can be useful for supporting analysts in on-site visits. A possible hardware configuration is shown in Fig. 2.35. The software should include a project database, data entry and graphics facilities, facilities for supporting communication between analysts, summary and paraphrasing facilities, as much automated completeness and consistency checking as possible, a library of reusable model components, synthesis tools, prototyping tools, archival version control facilities, and planning and estimation tools. A possible software configuration is illustrated in Fig. 2.36. The computer system should support a large part of the necessary communication within the team of analysts, and should provide a large part of the information needed to assess the current status of the project. Currently, available software support leaves much to be desired, so that the technical advisor should help the manager to follow new developments. The adequacy of the hardware should be reevaluated as the software for automating more of the requirements analysis functions becomes available, since processing loads will increase as the machines start doing more of the work.

Contact with the customer must be managed to ensure that the necessary information is obtained without straining relations. The manager should establish a forum for communication with the customer, such as a software control and evaluation board with regular meetings and the authority to make decisions about the characteristics of the system to be developed. The manager should also arrange for the customer organization to designate a contact person in the customer organization formally responsible for getting questions answered, and establish an agreement on expected time delays for responses. As continual interruptions may be a source of irritation, question deliveries should be

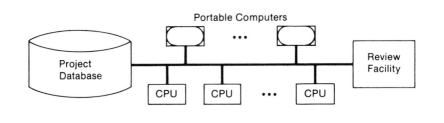

FIGURE 2.35
A Hardware Configuration for Requirements Analysis

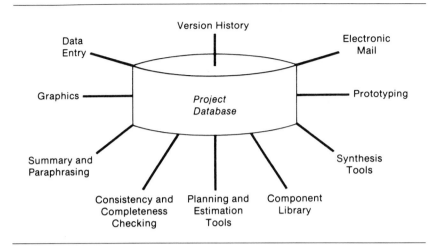

FIGURE 2.36
Software Support for Requirements Analysis

scheduled at fixed periodic intervals, to make them predictable. There should also be a designated person in the development organization responsible for gathering questions and delivering them to the customer at the scheduled times, and making sure that the answers get back to the analysts who need them, preferably via the project database. At the peak of the analysis effort there will be a lot of questions, so that a daily question cycle is reasonable. The purpose of this second channel of communication is to gather information about the customer's problem, while the purpose of the software control and evaluation board is to make decisions about the scope of the proposed project.

Contract negotiation depends on how the customer does business. If there are going to be competitive bids, then direct meetings may be inappropriate. Bids can be formulated based on the customer's answers to questions about priorities of different functions and cost/benefit tradeoffs, and opinions expressed in requirement review meetings and prototype demonstrations. In other cases, a direct discussion between the manager and someone in the customer organization responsible for the procurement may be the most effective way to make sure that the emphasis of the proposed contract is in the right place. The cost and schedule proposed in the contract critically depend on the developer's best estimate of the amount of work that will be involved.

2.6.2 Planning and Estimation

One of the important goals of requirements analysis is to support the planning of the rest of the software development effort. The planning effort is often performed by the manager of the requirements analysis effort, as the prerequisite information becomes available. The basis for the planning task is an estimate of the amount of work that will be involved. Such estimates are highly uncertain as long as the requirements are in flux, because a requirements change can easy add large subsystems to the product, with correspondingly large costs. A useful approach is to maintain a task breakdown and cost estimate from the beginning, and to constantly refine it as more detailed requirements information becomes available.

The cost estimates will be used in contract negotiation, establishing delivery schedules, and in choosing subcontractors. The contract usually will have to specify costs and timetables, and sometimes will have penalties for late delivery. It is important to be able to estimate the real costs, because bids that are too low will lose money and bids that are too high will lose the contract to a competitor.

Even imprecise estimates can be useful for establishing the overall structure of the development effort. A phased implementation and delivery plan is recommended for large systems. Most customers will get uncomfortable with funding a development project that does not deliver some working software every one to two years. If the initial estimate says it will take five years to build the system, then the requirements should identify capabilities that can be delivered at yearly intervals, in a phased delivery schedule. The subsystems delivered at intermediate points should be chosen so that some useful work can be accomplished with each version. The intermediate systems may leave out some functions entirely, and may have primitive temporary facilities for accomplishing some of the essential but rarely executed functions.

If the customer wants the entire system to be completed in less time than the developer can accomplish, it may be necessary to find subcontractors who can build some of the subsystems, especially if the long estimated development time is due to insufficient skilled staff. If subcontractors are going to be used, then the subsystems to be contracted out must be identified early in the process, and their interfaces must be pinned down. Subsystems built by separate subcontractors should have clearly specified functions that are independent of the rest of the system, to avoid integration problems, and to reduce the need for communication between different groups. The choice of which subsystems to contract out should also be based on the availability of contractors who can do a creditable job, and the lack of inhouse expertise in given areas.

Estimation is very difficult at the early stages, and there are no proven techniques that guarantee good results. A useful general principle is to decompose the project into subtasks to as fine a level of detail as possible, and to add up the estimates for the subtasks. This is motivated by the law of large numbers in statistics, which roughly states that the relative error in a sum of independent estimates decreases roughly in proportion to the square root of the number of terms. Consequently, breaking the project into a hundred subtasks and summing the individual estimates will result in an estimate roughly ten times more accurate than simply estimating the entire project as a single task by the same method.

The above analysis assumes that the accuracy of the individual estimates is uniform and that no subtasks are left out entirely. The reason for the inaccuracy inherent in estimates at the initial requirements stage is the difficulty of anticipating all of the tasks when the architecture of the system to be built is still unknown. Large errors in estimation are often caused by entirely neglecting some large subsystems that will eventually have to be implemented.

Since accurate estimates of project costs are not possible in the requirements analysis stage, it is reasonable to arrange the work under several smaller contract agreements rather than under one large contract. Each agreement should cover a small amount of work with a clear deliverable at the end of a short period of time. For example, requirements analysis can be broken up into a number of subtasks, such as developing an environment model, specifying goals and constraints for each subsystem, developing functional specifications for each subsystem, view integration, and constructing a prototype. Since each task is relatively simple and well defined, it can be accomplished with a reasonable chance of meeting schedule and budget constraints. The developer is paid for the work as it is completed, and based on the results, the customer can decide if it is worth going on to the next stage. The budget and schedule for each step can be reasonably estimated based on the results of the previous steps, leading to a more predictable process than negotiating a single large contract at a stage where the developer can only guess at the actual effort and costs involved in the project.

2.7 Summary of Requirements Analysis

In the initial stages of requirements analysis, the goals and constraints for the proposed system are elicited from the user. An explicit model of the user's problem domain is constructed in order to precisely define and analyze the goals and constraints. This model documents the conceptual environment of the proposed system. The goals and constraints are expressed in terms of the environment model, adjusted to make them implementable and sufficiently complete, and carefully validated to ensure that they correspond to the real needs of the user. In the final stages of requirements analysis, the external interfaces of the system are proposed, precisely specified, and validated. This process, known as *functional specification*, is the subject of the next chapter.

2.8 Related Research

Requirements analysis is still poorly understood, and there is a great deal of ongoing research in the area. Surveys of research in the area can be found in [1, 12] and surveys of requirements languages can be found in [10, 14]. A well known practical experiment on systematic ways to describe requirements for embedded systems is described in [9]. Application-specific requirements languages are explored in [7]. Knowledge-based representations are also being applied to requirements analysis, discussed in [3]. Issues involving concurrency are examined in [13, 14]. The use of requirements in testing real-time systems is discussed in [5]. Some informal approaches to requirements validation are discussed in [2], and the use of computer-aided prototyping for firming up requirements is described in [11]. Advanced tool support for requirements analysis includes truth maintenance and contradiction detection facilities, described in [6]. Transformations elaborating the requirements model have been proposed for representing justifications for decisions made by the analysts, discussed in [8]. A framework for computer-aided project management is described in [4].

Exercises

1. Express the following requirement using logic: "A student can register for no more than five courses." Define any concepts you need to use.

2. Express the following requirement using logic: "The microwave must automatically turn off the power when the door is opened." Define any concepts you need to use.

3. Express the following requirement using logic: "Employees are uniquely identified by their social security numbers." Define any concepts you need to use.

4. Redefine the concept "price" to allow different fares for different types of seats on a flight. How does this change affect the goals of the airline reservation system and the other concepts in the environment model? Show the revised goals and concepts.

5. Redefine the concept "flight" to allow multiple stops on the same flight. How does such a change affect the goals of the airline reservation system? How would you assess the effect of such a change on the cost of developing the proposed system?

6. Redefine the concept of a trip so that the origin and destination of a trip demanded by the passenger is a city rather than an airport. How does this change affect the goals of the airline reservation system? Identify the additional concepts needed to express the new goals, and write down formal definitions for them, including any new laws that become relevant.

7. Suppose that maintaining the displays of arrival times and departure times at the airport is added as a new goal for the airline reservation system. Does this change introduce new user classes? Work out the next level of subgoals refining this new goal, and the extensions to the environment model necessary to support the new goal and its subgoals.

Projects

The following problems are suitable subjects for team projects, although simplifying assumptions will be necessary to complete most of them in a reasonable amount of time.

1. Work out a set of requirements for the control system of an elevator.

2. Work out a set of requirements for an automated teller machine at a bank.

3. Work out a set of requirements for a spreadsheet program.

4. Work out the requirements for an electronic mail system.

5. Work out the requirements for a payroll system.

6. Work out the requirements for a text editor.

7. Work out a set of requirements for a software system that helps an architect draw plans for buildings.

8. Work out a set of requirements for a system that schedules classes and rooms at a university.

9. Work out a set of requirements for the software support system for a requirements analyst.

References

1. T. Anderson, *Software Requirements: Specification and Testing*, Blackwell Scientific Publishing, Oxford, England, 1985.

2. B. Boehm, "Verifying and Validating Software Requirements and Design Specifications," *IEEE Software 1*, 1 (Jan. 1984), 75–88.

3. A. Borgida, S. Greenspan and J. Mylopoulos, "Knowledge-Based Representation as the Basis for Requirements Specifications," *IEEE Computer 18*, 4 (Apr. 1985), 82–91.

4. R. Campbell and R. Terwilliger, "The SAGA Approach to Automated Project Management," *Advanced Programming Environments*, R. Conradi, T. Didriksen and D. Wanvik (editors), Springer-Verlag, 1986, 142–155.

5. M. Chandrasekharan, B. Dasarathy and Z. Kishimoto, "Requirements-Based Testing of Real-Time Systems: Modeling for Testability," *IEEE Computer 18*, 4 (Apr. 1985), 71–80.

6. A. Czuchry, "Where's the Intelligence in the Intelligent Assistant for Requirements Analysis?" *Proceedings Second Annual RADC Knowledge-based Assistant Conference*, RADC(COES), Grifiss AFB, NY, 1987.

7. A. M. Davis, "The Design of a Family of Application-Oriented Requirements Languages," *IEEE Computer 15*, 5 (May 1982), 21–28.

8. M. Feather, "Constructing Specifications by Combining Parallel Elaborations," *IEEE Transactions on Software Engineering 15*, 2 (Feb. 1989), 198–208.

9. K. L. Heninger, "Specifying Software Requirements for Complex Systems: New Techniques and Their Applications," *IEEE Transactions on Software Engineering SE-6*, 1 (Jan. 1980), 2–12.

10. A. A. Levene and G. P. Mullery, "An Investigation of Requirements Specification Languages: Theory and Practice," *IEEE Computer 15*, 5 (May 1982), 50–59.

11. Luqi and V. Berzins, "Rapidly Prototyping Real-Time Systems," *IEEE Software*, Sep. 1988, 25–36.

12. Roman and Gruia-Catalin, "A Taxonomy of Current Issues in Requirements Engineering," *IEEE Computer 18*, 4 (Apr. 1985).

13. R. Sidwell, "Modeling and Analysis of Concurrent Systems," *Technical Report 87–03* (1987), University of California, Irvine.

14. S. White, "A Pragmatic Formal Method for Computer System Definition," Ph. D. thesis, Computer Science Department, Polytechnic University, Brooklyn, NY, June 1987.

3

Functional Specification

A functional specification is a precise black-box model of the proposed software system capturing just the aspects of its behavior relevant to the users of the system. The behavior of a system consists of its interactions with other systems. The systems with which a software system can interact may consist of people, software, or hardware in any combination. A black-box model views a system as a single entity; a glass-box model views a system as a set of interconnected parts. Because it is a black-box model, a functional specification does not describe the set of parts that will be used to realize the system or their interconnections. System decompositions and glass-box models are developed in the architectural design activity, which is discussed in Chapter 4.

Black-box models of systems are important in engineering applications because they can be understood and analyzed without reference to the parts of the system. The process of building black-box models is called *abstraction*, and the models themselves are sometimes called abstractions. Abstraction is used to simplify the design of a complex system by reducing the number of details that must be considered at the same time. Conceptual complexity is the main limiting factor in the development of software systems; therefore, reducing the amount of detail a designer must consider at the same time is very important in software engineering. We emphasize abstraction and consider only black-box functional specifications because we are primarily concerned with the development of large and complex systems. As systems being developed get larger, jumping directly to code and jumping directly to decomposing the system into software modules become counterproductive approaches. The programmer interested in constructing large systems should get into the habit of black-box thinking, even though it may seem strange and difficult at first. The concepts and notations introduced in this chapter are intended to help develop that habit.

The functional specifications are produced by the analysts in the final stages of the requirements analysis effort and are usually incorporated into the requirements document when they are completed. A major difference between the initial requirements and functional specifications is how they are produced and used. The initial requirements are produced by, or on behalf of, the organization sponsoring the development effort, to describe the customer's needs. Functional specifications are developed by the organization seeking to build the software system, to describe a proposed solution to the customer's problem. These two documents have different roles in the contract negotiation process: requirements are requests for proposals, and functional specifications are the responding proposals. When agreement is reached, both documents are usually included in the contract governing the development work. At this point, the functional specification becomes part of the customer's requirements. We believe this transition is one of the causes of the widespread disagreement in the field about the differences between requirements and specifications. To avoid confusion, we refer to the combination of the initial requirements and the functional specification as the final requirements. The initial requirements consist of the environment model, the goals, and the constraints, as described in the previous chapter. The functional specification is a model of the external interfaces of the proposed system.

Another difference is the point of view of the two documents. The initial requirements are cast in terms of the customer's problem, and should be independent of particular solutions to the problem. A functional specification is cast in terms of a particular proposed system. This difference is reflected in the language and concepts used: the initial requirements use the terminology of the customer's application, and the functional specification uses the terminology of the proposed software system, which ideally should be a compatible extension of the application terminology.

The initial requirements and the functional specification should contain qualitatively different kinds of information. The initial requirements contain goals and constraints; a specification defines a set of behaviors. We note that this distinction is not always respected in practice. If we take a formal view, each goal can be associated with an objective function that gives a quantitative measure of how well a specified behavior meets the goal. A constraint is a limit on the resources required to realize a behavior. A specification is a predicate that determines which classes of system behavior are acceptable and which are not. From the formal point of view, requirements define the objective function and the constraints of an optimization problem, and a specification defines a solution to the optimization problem—a system that maximizes the goal functions subject to the resource constraints. In practice, things are not quite so simple, because the goals are incompletely known and the values of both the goal functions and the constraints (cost of implementing a proposed specification) are not precisely determined or mechanically computable. Instead of solving the optimization via a computer program, analysts typically use an informal manual process based on experience and guesswork.

3.1 Goals

The goal of the functional specification activity is to construct a black-box model of the proposed system. This contrasts with the goals of the initial requirements analysis and those of architectural design. The goals of the initial requirements analysis are to discover the customer's goals and constraints, and to capture a formal model of the customer's problem domain. The goal of the architectural design activity is to construct a hierarchy of glass-box models of the proposed system, which shows the decomposition of the system into the individual software components that will be used to realize the proposed system.

Functional specification is separated from architectural design because it is useful to decide what is to be built before investing much effort in deciding how to build it. This should always be done for large systems because it is more efficient and it leads to a better product. The claim of efficiency is based on avoiding the design and specification of functions that are not going to be implemented. The claim of improved quality is based on separation of concerns: if the designer focuses on just one issue there are fewer details to consider, enabling a better understanding of the problem and therefore a better and more coherent solution.

The black-box model constructed during the functional specification activity must meet the goals specified in the initial requirements and must also provide a solution to the customer's real problem. Because changes have significantly higher costs at each later stage of the project, it is a good idea to thoroughly check the correspondence of each part of the functional specifications to the customer's needs before committing much design effort to that part.

The functional specification should be consistent with the initial requirements document, but the ultimate test of its correctness is acceptance by the customer. In cases where the customer claims the functional specification is incorrect even though it conforms to the initial requirements document, both documents must be changed to reflect the customer's needs. It is important to maintain the consistency of the two documents to propagate requirements changes correctly during the evolution of the system [10]. A change to the functional specification dictated by the user may signal an implied change in the initial requirements, which can impact other features of the functional specification in ways that may not be obvious without explicit requirements tracing.

Often, there is a need for additions or changes to the initial requirements during functional specification because a detailed analysis of the proposed interface exposes new aspects of the problem, usually concerning required responses to infrequent situations. The functional specifications are generally more precise and more complete than the initial requirements. It is a mistake to think that the requirements analysis activity can stop as soon as the functional specification activity starts. The two activities are concurrent and pipelined, in the sense that a draft of the initial requirements is needed before functional specification can start. The requirements analysis effort is guided by feedback from the functional specification activity, and vice versa. The environment model, goals, and constraints continue to evolve as the functional specification is developed.

Requirements analysis is an empirical process that involves extracting information from the customer about the problem to be solved. The resulting document is a record of the results, together with some of the implications of the customer's statements. As with any experimental data gathering process, the information in the initial requirements document is to some degree uncertain and inherently incomplete. The functional specification is a theoretical object rather than an experimental one, and has a completely determined set of properties. The set of properties is usually infinite, and cannot be completely exhibited by any experimental process such as testing or simulation; but some regularities of the entire infinite set can be established by mathematical proofs. For this reason, the functional specification should be sufficiently formal to allow mathematical analysis supporting automated checking and synthesis. The functional specification is the starting point for the design of the system, so it is important to ensure its internal consistency and accuracy, and to obtain the approval of the customer before investing much design effort.

3.2 Basic Concepts

In our approach, the result of the functional specification phase is an event model of the system to be built, expressed using the Spec language. The subset of Spec dealing with concepts, definitions, inheritance, and the import/export relations is described in Section 2.2.2, and the subset dealing with primitives for modeling the behavior of software systems is described in Section 3.2.1. The formal specification in the Spec language is usually augmented by a set of mechanically derivable diagrams for review purposes.

The functional specification is developed in two stages: the first defines the behavior of the system in terms of abstract inputs and outputs, and the second defines the concrete formats and editing facilities for the inputs and outputs. The result of the first stage is called the abstract functional specification and the result of the second stage is called the concrete functional specification. The abstract functional specification is a black-box description of each major sub-system to be built that describes the information content rather than the format of the data crossing the boundaries of the system. The concrete functional specification is a black-box specification of an encapsulation of each external system, that describes the formats of the data crossing the boundaries of the system via transformations from concrete external inputs into abstract inputs, and abstract outputs into concrete external outputs.

The split between these two phases is motivated by separation of concerns and concurrency of development tasks. The analyst is likely to design a better interface by concentrating first on the abstract behavior, and worrying about the formats only when the meaning and contents of the messages are stable. This implies the need for a verification and validation step between the two phases, to make sure that the intended behavior of the system is correctly modeled before continuing. Once the abstract functional specification is complete and certified, several other activities can proceed in parallel with concrete functional specification. These include architectural design for the central functions, the development of a draft user's manual, and the development of test cases for the systems integration tests and the customer's acceptance tests. The encapsulation of the external systems also makes it easier to move a specified system to a different environment, since the central functions are less likely to change than is the packaging for the external interfaces. This can be important in the concurrent development of several major software and hardware systems that have to interact with each other, because the detailed characteristics of the external systems may not be completely known at the beginning of the functional specification stage.

Our approach differs from many popular informal approaches because we do not decompose the central modules into lower-level modules in the functional specification. We defer such glass-box decompositions until the architectural design stage, where the internal structure and interfaces of the system are defined. Our black-box approach does not treat large functional specifications as monolithic entities, however. We divide complex black-box specifications into simpler pieces in several qualitatively different ways.

1. Very large systems often contain several nearly independent major subsystems with different purposes. For example, a spacecraft may have a navigation subsystem, a communication subsystem, and a subsystem for controlling an exploration robot. Such major subsystems should be modeled as distinct central modules, especially if they are going to be assigned to different subcontractors.

2. Each major subsystem typically has more than one interface. For example, the navigation subsystem may have interfaces with the pilot and with several different sensors. We specify each interface of a central module as a separate view.

3. The description of each interface is partitioned based on the messages it accepts, and the normal and exceptional responses to each message.

4. The concepts needed to describe the behavior of each message are described by a set of definitions. In complex systems, the definitions of these concepts can have a hierarchical structure, in which the more abstract concepts are defined in terms of more primitive ones at several levels of detail. The concept hierarchy replaces the data dictionaries used in earlier approaches, and is more general because it includes predicates and functions in addition to data types and constants.

5. The individual events of a system can be organized into atomic transactions to describe the degree of interleaving allowed between concurrent interactions. The transactions in a complex protocol can also be defined hierarchically.

Black-box specifications of large systems are partitioned by subsystems, interfaces, messages, and responses to show the structure of the system's functionality. The concept hierarchy and the transaction hierarchy impose structure on other aspects of the specification.

The Spec language uses the event model to define the black-box behavior of proposed and external systems. The event model and the Spec language are described next. Syntax diagrams for the Spec language can be found in Appendix A. Some small examples of Spec can be found in Section 3.2.1, and an extended example (the airline reservation system) can be found in Section 3.4.

3.2.1 The Spec Language: Constructs for Specifying Software Systems

The Spec language is a formal specification language intended to span the entire process of software development. The subset of the language needed for requirements analysis has been introduced in Chapter 2. This section provides an introduction to the aspects of the language needed for functional specification at a level sufficient to handle many conventional applications. Some of the subtler and more technical issues associated with the language are discussed in Section 3.9. These issues are of interest to analysts working on advanced applications such as concurrent, distributed, and real-time systems; and to tool builders working on computer-aided software engineering environments.

Spec has been designed to encourage designs that separate different concerns into different modules, to make review and evolution easier. The language is intended to support top-down conceptual modeling, and is not intended to describe systems that do not have a factored structure. The language can be used in *reverse engineering*, the process of reconstructing the specifications for existing systems for which the documentation has been lost or allowed to become obsolete. Such a process is sometimes applied to the previous version of a system to aid in the specification of a proposed replacement system. The Spec language does not make it easy to record information haphazardly, but does help analysts impose structure on apparent chaos by factoring out coherent pieces in an active process that combines discovery with reformulation, concept formation, generalization, and reorganization. The Spec language provides several kinds of building blocks to help analysts and designers organize their thoughts. These building blocks are described in the rest of this section.

Spec can specify the behavior of three different types of software modules: functions, machines, and types. These modules can interact via three different types of messages: normal messages, exceptions, and generators. These types of modules and messages form a simple set of primitives sufficient to describe all common varieties of software components. The properties of these kinds of modules and messages are described next, with examples of each.

It is useful to classify modules as mutable or immutable because immutable modules are easier to analyze and are subject to fewer restrictions when used in an implementation. A module is *mutable* if the response of the module to at least one message can be affected by previous messages it has received; otherwise, it is *immutable*. Mutable modules behave as if they had internal states or memory; the behavior of immutable modules is independent of the past. Immutable modules can be shared by the implementations of two separate processes without risk of interference, and can be replicated without changing their semantics, but mutable modules cannot. Formal definitions of these concepts can be found in Appendix D, in the specification of the type "type." The distinction between mutable and immutable modules is a property of the behavior of a module rather than a property of its internal structure. It is possible to implement immutable modules using mutable components if the components are properly protected against unintended interactions.

In Spec, all functions are immutable modules. Machines are intended to be mutable, although Spec does not prevent the specification of trivial machines that are immutable because they have only a single state. Types can be either mutable or immutable.

Functions. The response of a function module is influenced only by the most recent stimulus, so that function modules do not exhibit internal memory. Completely specified function modules calculate single-valued functions in the mathematical sense; incompletely specified function modules can exhibit

nondeterministic behavior. An example of a specification for a `square_`
`root` function is shown in Fig. 3.1. The basic unit of a black-box specification
written in Spec describes the required responses to a stimulus. The keyword
`MESSAGE` introduces the description of a stimulus recognized by a module,
which consists of an incoming message. A message can have a name and zero
or more formal arguments representing input values. Message names are used
to distinguish different types of stimuli, corresponding to requests for different
services. Most function modules provide a single service, and are usually
designed to accept anonymous messages; that is, messages whose name is the
null string. The `square_root` function accepts anonymous messages containing a single real number denoted by the formal argument x. The Spec
language requires the types of all data values to be declared to allow type consistency checks. This does not impose any restrictions on the designer because
Spec has union types, and types can have subtypes. There is a universal type
called *any* that is the union of all other types and can be used to describe operations applicable to all types of objects and to express general laws. A mature
specification environment for supporting the use of the Spec language is
expected to have type-inferencing capabilities for automatically filling in and
maintaining type declarations in the cases where they can be determined from
the context.

The response of a module to a message can be defined with several cases
introduced by `WHEN` clauses. The example illustrates such a case analysis with
two cases, one corresponding to a normal response and the other to an excep-

---

```
FUNCTION square_root (precision: real SUCH THAT precision > 0.0)

   MESSAGE(x: real)
     WHEN x >= 0.0
       REPLY(y: real)
       WHERE y >= 0.0 & approximates(y * y, x)
     OTHERWISE REPLY EXCEPTION imaginary_square_root

   CONCEPT approximates(r1 r2: real)
     -- True if r1 is a sufficiently accurate approximation of r2.
     -- The precision is relative rather than absolute.
     VALUE(b: boolean)
       WHERE b <=> abs(r1 - r2) <= abs(r2 * precision)
END
```

FIGURE 3.1
Specification for Square Root

tion. The predicate after each WHEN is a precondition, describing the conditions under which the associated response must be triggered by an incoming message with a given name and condition. The preconditions in each WHEN statement are stated independently, so that the order of the WHEN statements does not matter. If the preconditions of several WHEN clauses are satisfied by the same stimulus, all of the associated responses must be produced and all of the associated postconditions must be satisfied simultaneously. Overlapping preconditions are not recommended because they can lead to inconsistencies: specifications that cannot be satisfied due to conflicting constraints from different descriptions of the same response.

OTHERWISE represents the case where the other preconditions are false. In the example, the OTHERWISE means the same thing as WHEN x < 0.0. In Spec, each series of WHEN statements must be terminated by an OTHERWISE to make sure all cases are covered. If a case is to be left undefined, the designer must say so explicitly, by including a WHEN or OTHERWISE clause with the undefined postcondition, represented as a ! in Spec.

A REPLY describes the message sent back in response to a stimulus. The reply is sent to the module that sent the stimulus, which is determined from the implicit origin attribute of the message (see Section 3.2.3). A REPLY corresponds to the call/return interface convention followed by most subprograms. A REPLY can have any number of data components, representing output data values that are all delivered at the same time. In the example, the REPLY for the normal case has no name and a single data component, while the REPLY for the exceptional case has a name but no data components. If REPLY is followed by EXCEPTION then the message represents an exceptional response (with a condition tag **exception**); otherwise the message represents a normal response (with a condition tag **normal**). EXCEPTION can also appear after MESSAGE in the specification of an exception handler, indicating that the stimulus must represent an exception condition.

An outgoing message can have a WHERE clause containing a postcondition that must be satisfied by the outgoing message. The WHERE keyword is followed by a statement in predicate logic describing the required relation between the contents of the message that was received and the contents of the reply message. This predicate states how to recognize a correct result, but it does not specify how to compute the required output. In the example, the normal reply must contain a nonnegative value whose square is approximately equal to the input. This provides sufficient information to distinguish correct outputs from incorrect ones, but does not give any hint about how to implement the required function. This is desired when specifying black-box behavior. In later stages of design, the black-box specification can be augmented with annotations containing implementation advice, such as the name of an algorithm for realizing the module.

The behavior of a module can be summarized in a stimulus-response diagram for review purposes. Such a diagram for the `square_root` module is shown in Fig. 3.2. The diagram shows the incoming and outgoing messages for each case of the response. The responses have been labeled with mnemonic names derived from the comments. Normal messages are shown using solid arrows and exception messages are shown using dotted arrows. Responses involving state changes are shown as squares and responses without state changes are shown as circles. In the `square_root` example, there are no state changes, so all nodes are round.

A CONCEPT in Spec introduces a new predicate symbol, a new function symbol, a new constant symbol, or a new type symbol, and defines the intended properties of the new symbol. Concepts were used in Chapter 2 to describe the environment model. In this chapter, concepts are used to simplify descriptions of the behavior of the proposed system. Concepts represent abstractions that are needed to explain the behavior of a system but do not represent parts of the system being specified. In the example, the concept *approximates* defines the intended meaning of "sufficiently accurate approximation" in terms of the generic parameter *precision*. Some notion of approximation is needed to specify a practical square root function because it is not possible to implement exact square roots using machine arithmetic. In this case, the size of the acceptable interval is defined relative to the size of the input value rather than as an absolute constant. The generic parameter allows a single definition for a square root module to be adapted to many applications with different precision requirements. Introducing explicitly defined concepts modularizes the specification. This helps simplify the postcondition and supports stepwise refinement and localization of information. The definition of a concept can be delayed or left

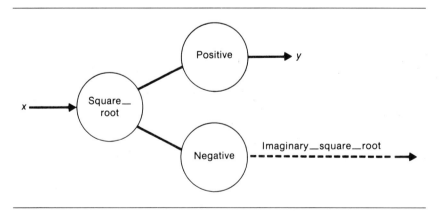

FIGURE 3.2
Stimulus-Response Diagram for Square_Root

as an informal comment when the concept is identified and the postcondition is developed.

A facility for introducing names for concepts with explicit definitions and interfaces is important for organizing and simplifying descriptions of complex software systems. Even in an example as small and simple as square_root, the concept *approximates* makes the specification easier to read and understand. The specification would mean exactly the same thing formally if the use of *approximates* in the postcondition were eliminated by substituting the definition of the concept, but the resulting predicate would be longer and harder to read, and some important information would be lost from the perspective of a human reader.

The structure of a specification is very important, because people cannot remember or understand many details simultaneously. For example, the postcondition for the normal case of square_root says the square of the output must approximate the input. This description is adequate for an initial understanding, and a human reader can get this much information from the postcondition without looking at the definition of approximates. The definition must be consulted only when the software engineer is interested in the accuracy of the approximation, or whether the accuracy is relative or absolute. The summary provided by the simple high-level description is lost if the definition is expanded in line and the concept is eliminated. Because communication is a major motivation for producing specifications, it is important to structure specifications so that they can be understood a little piece at a time. Concepts should be used to factor out the aspects of a specification that do not have to be considered on a first reading. This implies using concepts with illuminating names, and augmenting the formal definitions with informal comments capturing the intent of the concepts that have been used in a definition. If you find yourself writing a predicate that is filling up a page, you are doing something wrong, and you should look for some higher-level concepts that simplify what you are doing.

Every concept is local to the module in which it is defined unless it is exported (see Section 3.9.1) or inherited (see Section 3.9.5). Concepts without formal arguments are interpreted as constants. A constant can represent either a data type or a data value. Concepts with formal arguments are interpreted as functions. A function can represent a predicate or relationship if its value is boolean, and can represent an attribute if its value belongs to some other type.

Concepts represent objects and properties that are needed to describe the intended behavior of a proposed software system, and to test implementations of the system. Concepts are delivered to the customer in the manuals explaining how the system is supposed to operate, where they may be presented less formally than in the functional specifications and architectural design. Concepts do not necessarily represent components of the code to be delivered, although it may be useful to implement them for testing purposes.

A function should be defined as a module of type `FUNCTION` if it is part of the model of the software system, and it should be defined as a concept that is part of a module if the function is needed to specify the behavior of the module, but it is not directly involved in representing the behavior of the software system at a given level.

The `square_root` function in the example is a *generic module*. A generic module represents an entire class of individual modules (called the instances of the generic module) rather than a single module. The example defines an instance of the `square_root` function for every possible value of the generic parameter *precision*, which must be a positive real number. A module definition in the Spec language is generic if there is a generic parameter declaration after the name of the module. Generic parameters are enclosed in braces ({ }). A parameter or argument declaration can be followed by an optional `SUCH THAT` clause restricting the legal values of the actual parameters or arguments. There is exactly one instance of a generic module for every set of legal values for the generic parameters. The `square_root` module has one generic parameter, `precision`, which can have any positive real number as a value. As the example shows, the number of potential instances of a generic module need not be finite.

We have made the precision of the approximation a parameter because there is no good reason for picking any particular value for this quantity. This is an instance of a general software design principle that urges avoiding magic numbers: every constant in a module should have a clear and explicitly documented justification. The precision needed in any particular case depends on the application, and the running times of most square root algorithms depend on the required precision. Therefore, freezing the precision prematurely could severely limit the range of applications in which the module can be used. Generic modules are an important means for increasing the chances that a previously specified module can be reused in a different context.

Machines.   A machine is a module with an internal state (machines are mutable modules). An example of a machine representing a simplified inventory control system for a warehouse is shown in Fig. 3.3. This example is a partial description of an inventory control system for a warehouse. Shipment of backordered items (when they come in) is not included here. Adding such a function would affect the state and the `receive` message, as illustrated in Section 3.9.6. The example has also been unrealistically simplified by leaving out the customer's address. A data flow diagram showing the context for this system is shown in Fig. 3.4.

The behavior of a machine is described in terms of a conceptual model of its state, which serves to summarize the aspects of previous messages received by the machine that can influence its future behavior. States are localized: the state of a machine can change only at an event in which the machine receives a

```
MACHINE inventory
   -- Assumes that shipping and supplier are other modules.
   STATE(stock: map{from:: item, to:: integer})
   INVARIANT ALL(i: item :: stock[i] >= 0)
   INITIALLY ALL(i: item :: stock[i] = 0)

   MESSAGE receive(i: item, q: integer)
      -- Process a shipment from a supplier.
   WHEN q > 0
      TRANSITION stock[i] = *stock[i] + q
      -- Delayed responses to backorders are not shown here.
   OTHERWISE REPLY EXCEPTION empty_shipment

   MESSAGE order(io: item, qo: integer)
      -- Process an order from a customer.
   WHEN 0 < qo <= stock[io]
      SEND ship(is: item, qs: integer) TO shipping
        WHERE is = io, qs = qo
      TRANSITION stock[io] + qo = *stock[io]
   WHEN 0 < qo > stock[io]
      SEND ship(is: item, qs: integer) TO shipping
        WHERE is = io, qs = stock[io]
      SEND back_order(ib: item, qb: integer) TO supplier
        WHERE ib = io, qb + qs = qo
      TRANSITION stock[io] = 0
   OTHERWISE REPLY EXCEPTION empty_order
END
```

FIGURE 3.3
A Simplified Warehouse

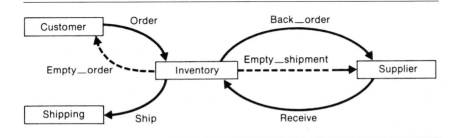

FIGURE 3.4
Message Flow Diagram for Inventory

message, and is directly visible only inside the definition of the machine. Conceptual models are described in terms of a finite set of state variables, whose types are declared after the keyword STATE. In the example, there is just one state variable, *stock*, whose value is a map from items to integers. Map is a generic type defined in the Spec type library (Appendix D). Brief informal descriptions of the types in the Spec type library can be found in Section 3.9.9. A map is a function with a finite range. The domain of a map can have an unlimited number of elements. The generic formal parameters *from* and *to* represent the types of the elements in the domain and range of the map, respectively. The actual values for these parameters have been specified using named associations, indicated by the : :, rather than by position. Named associations can be useful for reminding the reader of the intended interpretation for each parameter. The notation stock[*i*] is a special shorthand for the map operation "["(stock, *i*), which denotes the value of the map *stock* at the domain element *i*. This operation is analogous to the indexing operation for an array. In the example, stock[*i*] represents the quantity of the item *i* on hand in the current state of the inventory.

The description of a conceptual model for the state of a machine includes invariants and initialization constraints. Invariants must be satisfied in all reachable states; initialization restrictions must be satisfied only in the first state. In the example, the invariant says that the quantity on hand must be non-negative for every item at all times, and the initialization constraint says there are no items in stock at the beginning. Invariants are used to rule out meaningless or undesirable states.

As illustrated by the invariant in the example, predicates in the Spec language can include quantifiers. A quantified predicate of the form

```
ALL(x: t :: p(x))
```

is true if the condition p(x) is satisfied by all values x of type t. A quantified predicate of the form

```
SOME(x: t :: p(x))
```

is true if the condition p(x) is satisfied by at least one value x of type t. The : : is a delimiter that separates the variable declarations from the body of the expression, and corresponds to the English phrase "it is the case that" for the quantifiers shown above. The variables declared before the "::" of a quantifier are called its *bound variables*. Bound variables of a quantifier are local to the region in the matching parentheses following the quantifier name; for example, ALL. Variables that are not bound by a quantifier must be declared as generic parameters, state or model components, message components for incoming or outgoing messages, local variables of a WHEN clause (see CHOOSE), or concept parameters. All variables in Spec have type declarations. Quantifiers are introduced in Section 2.2.3 and are described more fully in Sections 3.8.1, 3.8.2, and 3.8.4. Scope rules for variables are defined in Section 3.9.1.

State changes are described in TRANSITION clauses, with the conventions that state variables of a machine or instance variables of an abstract data type do not change unless explicitly mentioned in a TRANSITION clause. State changes occur at events. There are two states associated with each event: the old state (just before the event) and the new state (just after the event). State variables in preconditions refer to the old state, and state variables in postconditions and TRANSITION clauses refer to the new state unless they are prefixed by an *, which can be read as the English word "previous." The transitions in the example are equations rather than assignment statements. Equations can describe the transition either forwards or backwards in time, whichever is simpler (compare the first two transitions in the example). The first transition in the example increases the amount of the item i on hand to reflect the arrival of an incoming shipment, and the second transition decreases the amount of the item i on hand to reflect the departure of an outgoing shipment.

Usually, the behavior of a machine is easier to describe in terms of state variables rather than directly in terms of the sequence of messages received by the machine up to the most recent event. The conceptual model of the state serves as a summary of the aspects of this message sequence relevant for determining the machine's future behavior. In the example, the interactions shown require only information about the number of items currently on hand, which is represented by the state variable stock. To add a capability for shipping backordered items when a new shipment is received, the conceptual model would be expanded to include a record of outstanding backorders by adding another state variable.

Messages sent to destinations other than the origin of the incoming message are described using SEND instead of REPLY. A SEND statement means that a message satisfying the description must be sent to the specified module. SEND statements are useful for describing distributed systems with a pipeline structure. A response can have more than one SEND statement to describe messages sent to different destinations. In such cases, the outgoing messages can be sent out concurrently or one at a time in any order, without waiting for any responses. The inventory example shows such a multiple response for the *order* message, in the case where there are not enough items on hand to fill the order completely. In this case, there are two messages in the response, one of which goes to the module *shipping*, representing the shipping department, and the other of which goes to the module *supplier*, representing the supplier for the items in the warehouse. The first message represents a request to send out a partial shipment; the second message represents a backorder for the items in the unfilled part of the order.

The postcondition of a machine is factored into several parts. Internal state changes are described in the TRANSITION clause, while outgoing messages are described in REPLY or SEND clauses. The postcondition is separated in this way to make it easier for designers and analysts to find the relevant parts of a specification, and for automated tools to determine which messages can cause state changes. This latter distinction is useful in summary diagrams.

Types. A type module defines an abstract data type. An abstract data type consists of a value set and a set of primitive operations involving the value set. The elements of the value set are called the instances of the type. In the event model, a type module manages the value set of an abstract data type, creating all of the values of the type and performing all of the primitive operations on those values. Each message accepted by the type module corresponds to one of the operations of the abstract data type. The messages of a type module usually have names, because abstract data types usually provide more than one operation.

Recall that modules are mutable if and only if they have internal states. Both immutable and mutable types are useful in practice, and both can be specified using Spec. The value set of an immutable type is fixed, and the properties of the individual instances of the type cannot be changed. A mutable type can have operations that modify the value set or change the properties of existing instances. In particular, mutable types can have operations that create new instances or modify existing instances.

The difference between mutable and immutable types is subtle and deserves some discussion. The distinction becomes most apparent when an instance of a type is shared by several program variables. If the properties of the instance can be changed by a mutating operation, the change affects all of the variables denoting the instance, whether or not those variables were explicitly mentioned in the operation. Mutable types are often implemented as pointers to pieces of storage whose contents can be modified. Mutable types must be used with care because shared instances of mutable types can introduce hidden interactions between modules. All of the components of the conceptual representation in the specification of a machine or type should be instances of immutable types to ensure that only independent abstractions are specified.

Each instance of a mutable type has a permanent identity that remains fixed despite arbitrary changes to the properties of the instance. A mutating operation without a REPLY changes the properties of an instance and does not affect the identity of the instance bound to any program variable. In contrast, an assignment to a program variable affects the identity of the instance bound to the variable without affecting the properties of either the instance bound to the variable in the old state or the instance bound to the variable in the new state. The choice between a function with a returned value and a procedure with an output variable for realizing an operation with an output value is a matter of packaging, which is completely independent of whether or not the operation can mutate instances of a data type. Subprograms with output or input/output parameters can be used to implement operations of both mutable and immutable types. An example of a specification for an immutable abstract data type is shown in Fig. 3.5.

Data types have conceptual models that are used to visualize and describe the instances of the type. The conceptual model is used to specify the behavior of a type, and forms the mental picture of the type for the programmers who use the operations of the type. The conceptual model is chosen for clarity, and is often different than the data structure used in the implementation. In case the data type must be reimplemented to improve performance, the data structure used in the implementation will change, but the conceptual model will not. The conceptual model consists of a finite set of components called instance variables. The instance variables of a type correspond to the state variables of a machine. The types of the instance variables are declared after the keyword MODEL. In the example, there are two instance variables, *num* and *den*, corresponding to the numerator and denominator of a fraction representing a rational number.

Each instance of the type can be represented as a tuple containing a unique identifier and values of the instance variables. Restrictions on the components of the model are described in the INVARIANT. The INVARIANT is a predi-

```
TYPE rational
  INHERIT equality(rational)
  MODEL(num den: integer)
  INVARIANT ALL(r: rational :: r.den ~= 0)

  MESSAGE ratio(num den: integer)
    WHEN den ~= 0 REPLY(r: rational)
      WHERE r.num = num, r.den = den
    OTHERWISE REPLY EXCEPTION zero_denominator

  MESSAGE "+"(x y: rational) REPLY(r: rational)
    WHERE r.num = x.num * y.den + y.num * x.den,
      r.den = x.den * y.den

  MESSAGE "*"(x y: rational) REPLY(r: rational)
    WHERE r.num = x.num * y.num, r.den = x.den * y.den

  MESSAGE equal(x y: rational) REPLY(b: boolean)
    WHERE b <=> (x.num * y.den = y.num * x.den)
END
```

FIGURE 3.5
Simplified Rational Numbers

cate that must be true for all meaningful conceptual representations.

In the example, we are using the standard mathematical model for rational numbers. The invariant must exclude pairs with zero denominators, because the interpretation of the pairs as ratios does not make sense in that case. The infix operator ˜= represents the inequality concept associated with the integer type, specified in the predefined type library associated with the Spec language (Appendix D). It is not necessary for there to be a 1 : 1 correspondence between conceptual representations and values of the abstract data type, although in cases without such a correspondence the model is not fully abstract and some extra care must be taken in defining the operations to avoid unintended nondeterminism. Our example does not define a unique conceptual representation. For example, the pairs [num:: 1, den:: 2], [num:: 2, den:: 4], and [num:: -1, den:: -2] are all conceptual representations for the same rational number. This lack of uniqueness is reflected in the equal operation, where equality on rationals is defined in terms of equality on integers. It is incorrect to say that two rationals are equal if and only if corresponding instance variables are equal unless the invariant is strong enough to give unique conceptual representations. Since the predefined interpretation of equality is a single-valued predicate, and hence deterministic, we must ensure the operation is defined to give the same result for all valid conceptual representations of any fixed pair of rational numbers. Some additional restrictions that would make the conceptual representation unique in the example are that the denominator must be strictly positive and that the fractions must be reduced to lowest terms.

The invariant on the conceptual representation can be chosen to make the descriptions of the operations as simple as possible, since it does not involve the implementation data structure and does not restrict the designer's choice of implementations. The invariants on the implementation data structures are often much more complicated than the conceptual invariants, because implementation invariants are often designed to provide efficiency. Most knowledge about data structures is really about the art of choosing implementation invariants that enable efficient algorithms.

Inside the module defining an abstract data type, predicates describing the effects of the operations can be written in terms of the conceptual representation, and instances of the type can be described as if they were tuples containing the components specified in the MODEL. The notation x.y can be used to refer to the y component of the conceptual representation for the abstract data value x. The specifications of other modules may describe the instances of abstract types only in terms of the MESSAGEs it provides and the CONCEPTs it EXPORTs.

It is sometimes convenient to express complicated conditions as lists of independent constraints. The predicates after INVARIANT, WHEN, and WHERE can be lists of expressions separated by commas. A list of statements is true if and only if all of the statements in the list are true individually, so that in this context a comma means the same thing as &. The comma has a lower precedence than all other operators, so that it can be used to separate statements at the top level without need for parentheses.

In the example, the standard properties of the *equal* operator, such as reflexivity, transitivity, and symmetry, are INHERITed from the predefined Spec type *equality{t}*, along with a *not_equal* operation with the standard relationship to the *equal* operation. The inherited definitions are combined with the explicitly given ones. If an operation with a given name is both inherited and explicitly defined, then the constraints introduced by both definitions must be satisfied simultaneously. The semantics of inheritance in Spec is described in detail in Section 3.9.5, which gives an example of the expansion of an inherited equality structure. Inheritance is used to avoid repeating standard definitions, and is useful for ensuring consistent treatment of standard concepts such as equality across a large number of components and for specifying uniformity constraints on interfaces in different subsystems of very large software systems.

Equality{t} is a virtual type, whose definition is given in Appendix D. A virtual type is a module defining the general properties of a class of types, which inherit those properties via an INHERIT declaration. A type *t1* is a *subtype* of a type *t2* if *t1* satisfies the specification of *t2*. The types that inherit a virtual type without hiding or renaming are subtypes of the virtual type. The set of instances of a virtual type is the union of the instances of all of its subtypes. This is what makes a virtual type "virtual:" it does not have any instances other than those of its subtypes. Any type with subtypes is a generalization of those subtypes that captures some of their common properties and ignores their differences. Generalization and inheritance are a means of recording some required regularities in a class of related modules, as well as a means of reusing a set of definitions for the required common properties. This kind of structure can become increasingly important for very large systems, because it is a means for specifying required regularities across large interface classes. Many existing systems have incompatible meanings for the same commands in different subsystems because no explicit effort was made to keep the interfaces consistent. This can have a very detrimental effect on the effort required to learn how to use a system.

Spec provides special infix notations for user-defined operations as a convenience to the designer. These infix operators must be chosen from a fixed set of operator symbols with predefined operator precedences. In the example, the standard symbols for addition (+) and multiplication (*) are introduced in this fashion. These symbols can be given any definitions, but to avoid confusion they should be used only for operations that conform to the standard interpretations for these symbols. These symbols should be defined as binary operations to be compatible with the usual infix format. The special symbols can also be used in standard functional notation when they are quoted, so that if a data

type defines + to take a variable number of arguments it is legal to write
`"+"`(a, b, c) as well as a + b for values of that type.

The - and * symbols can appear either as binary infix operators or as
unary prefix operators. The unary version of * has a special meaning that may
not be redefined by the user. This symbol denotes values in the previous state,
and is used primarily in Spec `TRANSITION` clauses. A complete list of the
special operator symbols provided by Spec is given in Appendix B.

Spec provides facilities for specifying mutable types because they are used
for efficiency reasons in internal interfaces of many systems. We recommend
avoiding instances of mutable types as components of messages appearing in a
functional specification. Mutable types can be useful in a functional
specification for modeling proposed or external systems with a variable number
of instances that can be created or destroyed as the system operates, such as
display windows or nodes in a dynamic network. An example of a definition
for a mutable type commonly found in programs is shown in Fig. 3.6. In mutable types, the instances of the type have internal states, and operations are
provided for changing the internal states of the instances. `TRANSITION`
clauses are allowed in types as well as machines. A type is mutable if and only
if it has a nontrivial `TRANSITION` clause (a `TRANSITION` that implies `*x ~=`
x for some value of x). Mutating operations, such as *enqueue* in the example
above, are described using `TRANSITION` clauses.

Object identity is an important issue for mutable types because all of the
program variables bound to the same mutable object will be affected if a state
changing operation is applied to the object. In the example, the `create` operation is specified to return a newly created instance of the type `queue{t}` via
the predicate `new`. A newly created object is guaranteed to be distinct from all
objects defined in the previous state. The concept `new` is not part of the Spec
language, but it is provided by the predefined generic definition module
`mutable{t}`. The specification of any mutable type should inherit an
instance of this module. This is illustrated in the mutable queue example,
which inherits the instance `mutable{queue{t}}`. The definition of
`mutable{t}` is given in Appendix C and repeated in Fig. 3.7. `New(x)` is
true in a state for all objects x that are newly created in that state. `Id(x)` is the
permanent unique identifier of the object x. The properties of a mutable object
can change, but its id cannot change.

The concepts defined in the previous module are used to specify which
objects exist in the current state, and which objects were newly created in the
most recent state transition. This is an example of a definition module, such as
those used in Chapter 2 to represent environment models. Definition modules
can contain only concept definitions, and are used in functional specifications
for providing convenient access to widely shared concepts. The effect of inheriting a definition module is the same as importing all of the concepts defined in
that module, except that inherited concepts can be further constrained.

```
TYPE queue(t: type)
  INHERIT Mutable(queue(t))
    -- Inherit definition of the concept "new."
  MODEL(e: sequence(t))
    -- The front of the queue is at the right end.
  INVARIANT true -- Any sequence is a valid model for a queue.

  MESSAGE create -- A newly created empty queue.
    REPLY(q: queue(t)) WHERE q.e = [ ]
    TRANSITION new(q)

  MESSAGE enqueue(x: t, q: queue(t))
      -- Add x to the back of the queue.
    TRANSITION q.e = append([x], *q.e)

  MESSAGE dequeue(q: queue(t))
      -- Remove and return the front element of the queue.
    WHEN not_empty(q)
      REPLY(x: t)
      TRANSITION *q.e = append(q.e, [x])
    OTHERWISE REPLY EXCEPTION queue_underflow

  MESSAGE not_empty(q: queue(t))   -- True if q is not empty.
    REPLY(b: boolean) WHERE b <=> (q.e ~= [ ])
END
```

FIGURE 3.6
A Mutable Queue Type

An instance of a mutable data type is very similar to a state machine, except that the state machine is implicitly created and initialized at the start of the computation, and the instances of a mutable data type are explicitly created as a computation proceeds. A state machine has exactly one instance; a mutable data type can have any number of instances.

Correctly programming with mutable data types is difficult, because mutating operations can indirectly affect the properties of variables that were not explicitly mentioned in the code. Mutable data types should be used only if required to faithfully model the behavior of a system containing objects whose properties change with time or to meet tight performance constraints.

Machines and data types are related but different. There is a single instance of a machine that is created implicitly at the beginning of the computation, with an initial state set up according to the INITIALLY clause. A type can have any number of instances that are explicitly created via the operations

```
DEFINITION mutable(t: type)
  CONCEPT new(x: t) VALUE(b: boolean)
    WHERE b <=> x IN t & ~(x IN *t),
          -- An object is new if it belongs to the type
          -- in the current state and it did not belong
          -- to the type in the previous state.
      ALL(a c: t :: new(a) & c IN *t => id(a) ~= id(c))
          -- A new object is distinct from any object existing
          -- in the previous state.

  CONCEPT id(x: t) VALUE(n: nat)
    WHERE ALL(y z: t :: id(y) = id(z) => y = z),
      ALL(y: t :: *y IN *t => id(y) = id(*y))
          -- Every object has a permanent unique identifier.
END
```

FIGURE 3.7
Reusable Concepts for Mutable Types

of the type as the computation proceeds. Another difference is that all machines are mutable modules, but data types can be either mutable or immutable. These differences are illustrated by the following examples, which define a stack machine and mutable and immutable versions of a stack data type. The definition of the machine is shown in Fig. 3.8. In a machine, the internal state is hidden inside the module, and does not appear in the message interfaces.

This example also illustrates the use of the $ notation. When an expression inside a sequence literal is preceded by a $, the expression refers to a contiguous subsequence containing zero or more elements, rather than a single element. The notation has the following properties.

$[\$s1, \$s2] = s1 \parallel s2$
$[x, \$s] = [x] \parallel s$
$[\$s, x] = s \parallel [x]$

The infix operator $\parallel$ denotes sequence concatenation. The $ can also be used in declarations of formal arguments and formal parameters. For example, the message

```
MESSAGE max(x: integer, $y: integer)
```

can accept one or more arguments of type integer, where x is bound to the first argument, and y is bound to the sequence containing the rest of the arguments, in the order in which they are given. This notation is useful for defining operations with variable numbers of arguments or parameters. The $ can also appear

```
MACHINE stack(t: type)
  STATE(e: sequence(t))
    -- The top of the stack is at the right end.
  INVARIANT true -- Any sequence is a valid model for a stack.
  INITIALLY e = [ ]

  MESSAGE push(x: t) TRANSITION e = [$ *e, x]

  MESSAGE pop
    WHEN ~is_empty TRANSITION SOME(x: t :: *e = [$ e, x])
    OTHERWISE REPLY EXCEPTION stack_underflow

  MESSAGE top
    WHEN ~is_empty
      REPLY(x: t)
        WHERE SOME(prefix: sequence(t) :: e = [$ prefix, x])
    OTHERWISE REPLY EXCEPTION no_top

  MESSAGE is_empty
    REPLY(b: boolean) WHERE b <=> (s.e = [ ])
END
```

FIGURE 3.8
A Stack Machine

inside of set literals, in which context it refers to a subset rather than a subsequence, as illustrated next.

{$s1, $s2} = s1 U s2
{x, $s} = {x} U s
{$s, x} = s U {x}

The infix operator U denotes the set union operation.

A definition of a mutable stack data type is shown in Fig. 3.9, to illustrate the distinction between a machine and a mutable type. In a data type, there can be zero or more values of the type, which are explicitly created via the operations (messages) accepted by the type. Note that the operations must now have an extra argument, to specify which stack they are to act on. The initialization is replaced by a create operation.

An immutable version of the stack data type is shown in Fig. 3.10. This version is immutable because it does not have any TRANSITIONs. New instances of the type stack are created whenever some change is needed. This usually implies copying objects to modify their components. Some

```
TYPE stack{t: type}   -- Mutable version.
  INHERIT Mutable{stack{t}}

  MODEL(e: sequence{t})
    -- The top of the stack is at the right end.
  INVARIANT true -- Any sequence is a valid model for a stack.

  MESSAGE create  -- A newly created empty stack.
    REPLY(s: stack{t}) WHERE s = [ ]
    TRANSITION new(s)

  MESSAGE push(x: t, s: stack{t}) TRANSITION s.e = [$ *s.e, x]

  MESSAGE pop(s: stack{t})
    WHEN ~is_empty(s) TRANSITION SOME(x: t :: *s.e = [$ s.e, x])
    OTHERWISE REPLY EXCEPTION stack_underflow

  MESSAGE top(s: stack{t})
    WHEN ~is_empty(s)
      REPLY(x: t)
        WHERE SOME(prefix: sequence{t} :: s = [$ prefix, x])
    OTHERWISE REPLY EXCEPTION no_top

  MESSAGE is_empty(s: stack{t})
    REPLY(b: boolean) WHERE b <=> (s.e = [ ])
END
```

FIGURE 3.9
A Mutable Stack Type

optimizations that eliminate this overhead and the conditions under which they can be applied are discussed in Section 4.4.2. Immutable types are less error prone because operations on such types cannot affect program variables that are not explicitly mentioned, provided that several program variables are not stored in the same location (aliased). Immutable types may have slower operations in unoptimized single-processor implementations, but they allow more parallelism in multiprocessor machines, and do not require synchronization overhead to guarantee noninterference between concurrent operations. Immutable types can also save space in case there are many objects that can share subcomponents.

Generators.   A generator is a message that generates a sequence of values one at a time. An example of a specification for a generator is shown in Fig. 3.11.

```
TYPE stack{t: type}  -- Immutable version.
  MODEL(e: sequence{t})
    -- The top of the stack is at the right end.
  INVARIANT true -- Any sequence is a valid model for a stack.

  MESSAGE create REPLY(s: stack{t})  -- The empty stack.
    WHERE s = [ ]

  MESSAGE push(x: t, s: stack{t})
    REPLY(s1: stack{t}) WHERE s1.e = [$ s.e, x]

  MESSAGE pop(s: stack{t})
    WHEN ~is_empty(s)
      REPLY(s1: stack{t}) WHERE SOME(x: t :: s = [$ s1.e, x])
    OTHERWISE REPLY EXCEPTION stack_underflow

  MESSAGE top(s: stack{t})
    WHEN ~is_empty(s)
      REPLY(x: t)
        WHERE SOME(prefix: sequence{t} :: s = [$ prefix, x])
    OTHERWISE REPLY EXCEPTION no_top

  MESSAGE is_empty(s: stack{t})
    REPLY(b: boolean) WHERE b <=> (s.e = [ ])
END
```

FIGURE 3.10
An Immutable Stack Type

```
FUNCTION primes
  IMPORT prime FROM nat
  IMPORT sorted FROM sequence{nat}

  MESSAGE(limit: nat) GENERATE(s: sequence{nat})
    WHERE increasing_order(s),
      ALL(i: nat :: i IN s <=> 1 <= i <= limit & prime(i))

  CONCEPT increasing_order(s: sequence{nat}) VALUE(b: boolean)
    WHERE b <=> sorted{"<="@nat}(s)
END
```

FIGURE 3.11
A Prime Number Generator

The definitions of the concepts `prime` and `sorted` are part of the predefined Spec types `nat` and `sequence`, respectively (see Appendix D). The @ is used in Spec to determine the type of an overloaded operator or constant in places where it is not clear from the context. In this example, this construct is used to distinguish between the $<=$ operation on the natural numbers and the $<=$ operation on other types. The GENERATE keyword means the same thing as a REPLY except that the result is a sequence whose elements are delivered one at a time rather than all at once. The distinction between GENERATE and REPLY records the choice between representing a sequence as a time series or as a data structure. GENERATE means that the elements will be generated one at a time, and processed incrementally, rather than being generated all at once and returned in a single data structure containing all of the elements, as would be the case for a REPLY of type sequence. In a program, a generator is usually used to control a data driven loop. The implementation of generators in Ada is discussed in Section 5.7.5. Generators also can be used in specifications of other modules, for example to define the range of a quantified variable. Generators are interpreted as sequence-valued functions when they appear in specifications, as in the example shown in Fig. 3.12.

Any message with a GENERATE is a generator, so that generators can be defined as operations of an abstract data type or a machine. Generators can be used to provide an efficient way to scan all of the elements of an abstract collection without exposing the data structure used to implement the collection. Generators usually appear in the internal interfaces of software systems. An example of a generator in a user interface is the *more* function in the UNIX operating system, which generates a sequence of screen images for displaying the contents of a file or data stream.

Set Constructors and Additional Quantifiers.   A quantifier is an operation on a set of values defined by a range declaration for a set of bound variables, an optional restriction predicate, and a generating expression. Quantifiers are related to set constructors, which are explained first. The Spec set constructor is illustrated in the following example.

```
{x: boolean SUCH THAT 2 <= x <= 4 :: x MOD 2 = 0}
  = {2 MOD 2 = 0, 3 MOD 2 = 0, 4 MOD 2 = 0}
  = {true, false, true}
  = {false, true}
```

```
CONCEPT big_prime_candidate(n: integer) VALUE(x: integer)
  WHERE ALL(k: integer SUCH THAT k IN primes(n) :: x MOD k = k - 1)
```

FIGURE 3.12
Using a Generator in Another Specification

In this example, the range declaration is x: `boolean`, the restriction predicate is $2 <= x <= 4$, and the generating expression is x `MOD 2 = 0`. The generating expression in this case produces a boolean value. The three lines below the set constructor are Spec set literals that represent steps in the simplification of the constructed set, where the generating expression is instantiated for each instance in the range of the bound variable, the expressions are evaluated, and repeated elements are removed. The last step reflects the fact that the order of the elements and the number of occurrences of each element in a set do not matter.

The familiar quantifiers ALL and SOME can be thought of as forming sets of boolean values similar to the one shown above, and then performing a simple check on the result. The universal quantifier checks if this set contains any values other than **true**, and the existential quantifier checks if this set contains the value **true**. Since the set {**false, true**} contains the value **false** but also contains the element **true**, we conclude that

```
ALL(x: nat SUCH THAT 2 <= x <= 4 :: x MOD 2 = 0)  = false &
SOME(x: nat SUCH THAT 2 <= x <= 4 :: x MOD 2 = 0) = true.
```

There are other types of useful operations on sets, such as counting the number of elements in a set, finding the sum or the product of the elements, finding the largest or smallest value in the set, or taking the union or intersection of the elements of the set. These operations are also treated as quantifiers in Spec, with the names NUMBER, SUM, PRODUCT, MAXIMUM, MINIMUM, UNION, and INTERSECTION. For example,

```
SUM(i: nat :: (x ^ i)/factorial(i))
```

represents the Taylor series expansion for exp(x);

```
MAXIMUM(x: real SUCH THAT 0.0<x<1.0::x^2*(x-1)^2)
```

represents the maximum value of the polynomial $x^2(x-1)^2$ in the open interval $(0, 1)$, and

```
NUMBER(x: nat :: 12 MOD x = 0 & x > 0 :: x)
```

represents the number of positive factors for the integer 12. These quantifiers are useful for providing concise descriptions of many properties of software systems. These quantifiers are defined in Appendix C, in the module `quantifiers`, which also defines a derived quantifier called AVERAGE. The properties of these additional quantifiers are discussed in detail in Section 3.8.4.

Spec lets the designer define additional quantifiers. All quantifiers have names that contain only uppercase letters, and are linked to functions on sets whose names contain the same letters, but where all but the first letter is in lowercase. This relationship is illustrated by the following equivalence.

```
QUANTIFIER(x: t SUCH THAT q(x) :: p(x)) =
   Quantifier({x: t SUCH THAT q(x) :: p(x)})
```

Thus the quantifier notation is really a shorthand for applying a set function to a set constructor.

3.2.2 The Event Model

The primitives of the event model, which is the semantic basis for Spec, are modules, messages, events, and alarms. These four kinds of primitives are described next. Modules can be used to model external systems such as users and peripheral hardware devices, as well as software components. Modules have no visible internal structure. The behavior of a module is specified by describing its interface, which consists of the set of stimuli recognized by the module and the associated responses. A stimulus is an event, and the response is the set of events directly triggered by the stimulus. The events in the response consist of the arrivals of the messages sent out by the module because of the stimulus. State changes triggered by a stimulus are manifested in responses to future stimuli. The response of a module to a message is influenced only by the sequence and arrival times of the messages received by the module since it was created. This means there is no action at a distance: all interactions must involve explicit message transmissions. This restriction formalizes the requirement that each module must correspond to an independent abstraction, since it implies the behavior of a module can be influenced only via the operations provided by its interface.

Messages can be used to model user commands, system responses, and interactions between internal subsystems. Messages represent abstract interactions that can be realized in a wide variety of ways, including procedure call, return from a procedure, Ada rendezvous, coroutine invocation, external I/O, assignments to nonlocal variables, hardware interrupts, and exceptions. Each message has a condition, a name, a sequence of zero or more data values, and an origin. The condition has the value *normal* for messages representing normal interactions, and the value *exception* for messages representing abnormal interactions such as exceptions. The name of a message identifies the service requested by a normal message or the exception condition announced by an exception message. The data values represent either inputs or results, and may be present for any kind of message. The origin of a message is the event or alarm that caused the message to be sent. The origin records causal relationships in a computation history, and is used to identify destinations of reply messages in the Spec language.

Events are used to record and describe the behavior of a system. Each event is associated with a module, a message, and a time, and is uniquely identified by these three properties. The time records the instant at which the module accepted the message. Events at the same module happen at distinct times, and occur in a well defined sequence. Events can be classified as *reactive* or *temporal*, depending on whether the origin of the message that arrived in the event is an event or an alarm. Reactive events represent responses to external stimuli; temporal events represent actions initiated by the module based on the absolute time. Temporal events can be used to represent both regularly scheduled actions and actions initiated at unpredictable intervals by independent agents such as human users.

A reactive event in an airline reservation system is illustrated in Fig. 3.13. The event E1 is the stimulus causing the response event E2. E1 represents the arrival of a find_flights command from the travel agent at the airline reservation system. E2 represents the arrival of the message flights_3 at the travel agent module. This message contains the set of found flights, and is identified as a response to the command arriving in the event E1 via the origin attribute of the message. The set of events {E1, E2} represents a fragment of a computation history for the airline reservation system.

A temporal event is illustrated in Fig. 3.14. The alarm A1 defines the time at which the weekly run for generating paychecks is enabled at a payroll system. The temporal event E3 occurs when the generate_paychecks message is received by the payroll system, representing the instant when the process of generating paychecks actually starts. The scheduling delay between the alarm A1 and the event E3 can be constrained by the specification, and in the extreme case could be required to have zero length. The reactive event E4 occurs when the paychecks actually arrive at the printer. At this level of modeling, the set of paychecks is treated as a single unit that arrives at an

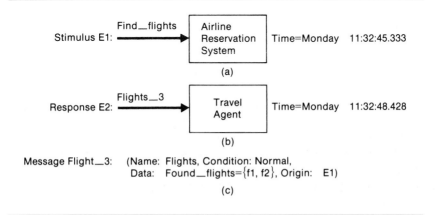

FIGURE 3.13
A Reactive Event

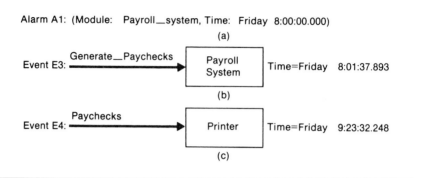

FIGURE 3.14
A Temporal Event

instant of time. In actuality, printing is an extended process. The time required to print the checks is not distinguished from message transmission delay at this level of modeling, so that the arrival of the set of paychecks corresponds to the instant when the printing job is completed.

Alarms represent discrete points in time when temporal events are triggered. Each alarm consists of a module, a message, and a time. An alarm causes the module to send the message to itself at the given time. A temporal event happens when the message arrives at the module, which can happen at or after the time the message was sent. Alarms serve as reference points for specifying constraints on scheduling delays for temporal events. Each module has a clock that measures local physical time at the current location of the module. The event model uses local physical time to support specifications of events that must happen at given absolute times (for example, at 3 A.M. every Sunday). The time of an event or alarm is determined using the clock of the module at which the event occurs.

Some care is required in comparing times at different locations because the local clocks of different modules cannot be perfectly synchronized with each other. This is most clearly apparent for distributed systems that span multiple time zones. Another consideration is that practical schemes for reading remote clocks or synchronizing clocks at different locations are inherently approximate due to imperfectly predictable communication delays.

Some consequences of imperfect synchronization of clocks at different modules are that the order of occurrence of two events cannot be determined by simply comparing the local times of the events, and that message delays cannot be calculated by taking the difference between their times of occurrence. These problems can be solved in principle by applying a transformation to each of the local clocks to convert them to readings from a clock in a standard location (for example, Greenwich Mean Time). The orderings on events derived from such transformed times are consistent with the orderings observed by physical means outside the software system, and can be determined in practice to within the accuracy of the clock synchronization. The only kind of time interval meaningful in the event model is the duration between two events. There is no distinction between computation delay and communication delay in the event model.

The response of a module to a message can be affected only by the sequence of messages received by the module since it was created. The event model and the Spec language permit nondeterminism due to partially specified communication delays or partially specified responses. Complete specifications permit only deterministic behavior for a single module. In Spec it is possible to specify that a response must be deterministic (repeatable) without completely specifying the other properties of the response.

Each module has the potential to act independently, so that there is natural concurrency in a system consisting of many modules. Modules can be used to model concurrent and distributed systems, as well as systems consisting of a single sequential process. The event model helps to expose the parallelism inherent in a problem, since a stimulus can have a set of unordered responses occurring at different locations. Because events happen instantaneously and the response of a module is not sensitive to anything but the sequence of events at the module, the event model implies concurrent interactions cannot interfere with each other at the level of individual events. Atomic transactions can be used to specify constraints on the order in which a module can accept events. This capability is useful for defining systems with modes in which only subsets of the system commands are available, and for specifying synchronization constraints involving chains of events in distributed systems.

Atomic transactions must be used with care, because they can interact with each other or with timing constraints to produce unsatisfiable specifications. Atomic transactions can lead to deadlocks if the protocols of the modules involved in a transaction are not compatible with each other, and can lead to starvation if a transaction goes on forever. Starvation and deadlock are situations in which a message that was sent cannot be accepted at its destination. Messages always arrive at their destinations, and are guaranteed to be accepted once they arrive if and only if all atomic transactions at the destination terminate and are free of deadlocks. The order in which messages arrive at a module is not usually under the control of the designer. The designer can influence the order in which a module accepts messages by specifying atomic transactions.

3.2.3 Diagrams

Diagrams are useful for summary and review of specifications and designs. Such diagrams are most effective if they follow uniform conventions, and use a relatively small and simple set of symbols. Uniformity and simplicity are more important than the particular conventions used. In this section we describe the set of conventions and diagram types used in this book.

Symbols and Conventions.   Our diagrams use the following symbols and general conventions.

1. Rectangles represent objects or actions associated with potential state changes, and circles represent objects or actions that are not associated with state changes.

2. Solid lines represent the primary relationships in a diagram, and dotted lines represent secondary relationships.

3. Arrows represent relationships involving flows, with arrowheads on both ends to indicate bi-directional links. Lines without arrows represent relationships unrelated to flows.

4. Objects with multiple instances, such as types or generator messages, are marked with a double line at the top.

5. Generic object templates or object families are shown with thick lines. Individual objects are shown with thin lines.

Flow Diagrams.   Flow diagrams are directed graphs whose nodes represent locations and whose edges represent something moving from one location to another. Common types of flow diagrams used in computer science include control flow diagrams (flowcharts), state transition diagrams, and data flow diagrams. Other kinds of flow diagrams used in this book include message flow diagrams and type flow diagrams. A message flow diagram is a kind of data flow diagram in which nodes represent Spec modules and arrows represent Spec messages. The symbols used in message flow diagrams are summarized in Fig. 3.15. Names of messages appear above horizontal arrows and to the right of vertical arrows. Names of message components, if they are shown, appear below horizontal arrows and to the left of vertical arrows. Generic modules or messages are shown with thick lines, and individual messages or modules are shown with thin lines. An example of a message flow diagram is shown in Fig. 3.4.

A type flow diagram summarizes the types of data that are carried by the messages in a system. The arrows of a type flow diagram are labeled with data type names. The nodes of a type flow diagram represent Spec modules. An example of a type flow diagram is shown in Fig. 3.36.

Decomposition Diagrams.   Decomposition diagrams are used to describe part-of relationships. In this chapter, type decomposition diagrams are used to illustrate the components of composite types such as tuples. An example of a

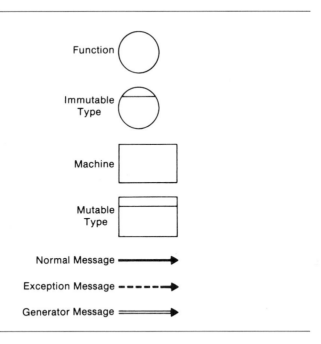

FIGURE 3.15
Symbols in Message Flow Diagrams

type decomposition diagram is shown in Fig. 3.37. In the next chapter, module decomposition diagrams are used to show the lower-level modules used in the construction of a higher-level module.

Decomposition relationships are acyclic graphs with nodes representing objects and arcs representing the part-of relationship. Each node representing an assembly is shown above the node representing its component parts. Arcs are shown without arrowheads, and have a vertical or slanted direction. Nodes representing modules are shown using the symbols of Fig. 3.15. If several parts belong to the same set of assemblies, they are shown in adjacent vertical stacks, with a single arc for the whole stack, instead of a separate arc for each node in the stack.

Event Diagrams.   Event diagrams illustrate the order in which things happen. Timing relationships are shown with earlier times at the left and later times at the right. The stimulus-response diagrams and the transaction diagrams used in this chapter are kinds of event diagrams.

A stimulus-response diagram summarizes the possible responses of a module to an event at the module. A stimulus-response diagram is a tree with two levels, in which the nodes represent events. The root node represents a stimulus event, and is labeled with the name of the module at which the event occurs. The root node has an incoming arrow labeled with the name of the message or temporal that triggers the event. The nodes at the second level represent alternative responses, and are labeled with names of the cases in which each alternative occurs. Responses are shown as rectangles if they cause state changes at the module, and are shown as circles otherwise. The arrows coming out of the response nodes represent the messages that are sent out in each case. An example of a stimulus-response diagram is shown in Fig. 3.2.

A transaction diagram is a directed graph whose nodes represent events or transactions, and whose edges represent sequencing in time. Transaction diagrams represent the constraints on the order in which events can occur at a module. Each event is connected to the events or transactions that can happen next. Individual events are shown as circles, and transactions are shown as boxes, since transactions have control states and events do not. Edges are shown as arrows with optional labels describing guard conditions. The form of a transaction diagram is similar to the syntax diagrams used to describe the syntax of Pascal. An example of a transaction diagram is shown in Fig. 3.67.

3.3 Procedures and Guidelines

The process of functional specification starts from the initial requirements document, which should contain an environment model, a goals hierarchy for the proposed system, and a constraint hierarchy for the proposed system. After this document has been accepted by the customer, the following tasks are carried out to produce the abstract functional specification.

1. Identify the major subsystems of the proposed software, and the user classes and external systems with which the proposed software will interact. Create a Spec module for each external system and subsystem.

2. Identify all external interfaces of the proposed subsystems, and make a list of the messages and temporals in each interface. Make sure the identified messages correspond to the goal hierarchy, and go over the lists with the customer. Create a Spec module for each interface. Set up the inheritance links between the interfaces and the proposed subsystems.

3. For each interface, write a skeleton specification for all of the messages. Choose names for all messages, exceptions, and message components, and identify the data type of each message component. Identify any new abstract data types needed, and create Spec modules for them. When all of the components have been identified, make an initial estimate of how much effort it will take to build the system.

4. Invent conceptual models for each machine and type. Develop the invariants and initial conditions, and define the concepts needed to specify them. Check the consistency of the interfaces, and make any adjustments needed.

5. Develop the WHEN, WHERE, and TRANSITION clauses for each message and identify the concepts needed to specify them. Refine the invariants as needed. Determine IMPORT / EXPORT relations for shared concepts, and create definition skeletons for each concept. The definition skeletons should define the types of inputs and outputs for each concept, and should have an informal description of the concept.

6. Write formal definitions for concepts, identify any necessary lower-level concepts, and write definition skeletons for them. Continue until all concepts have been defined in terms of predefined or available components. Check the internal consistency of the entire specification, and resolve any conflicts.

7. Conduct a customer review, and adjust the specifications and initial requirements until they are acceptable to the customer.

When these tasks are finished, the abstract functional specification is complete. Contractual agreements covering the remainder of the development work usually incorporate the initial requirements and the abstract functional specification. In some cases, parts of the concrete functional specification may also be needed for the contract. After the abstract functional specification is complete, the activity of concrete functional specification can proceed in parallel with architectural design for the central modules, the development of test cases, and the development of a draft user manual. The steps for developing concrete functional specifications follow.

1. Determine the capabilities of the input/output devices to be used with the proposed software, and determine the general kind of packaging for each interface (menu driven, keyboard command, light pen, voice, etc.). This step can begin before the abstract functional specifications are fully stabilized.

2. Work out the format for each command, and record the formats in the Spec modules describing the external systems. Review these formats with the customer, adjusting as needed.

3. Determine the editing facilities to be provided, and the concrete error messages associated with each top-level exception condition. Record and review these with the customer, adjusting as needed.

The task structure just described is appropriate for many software development projects. In practice, these procedures can be adapted to special circumstances or constraints due to a particular customer or development environment.

3.3.1 General Guidelines for Analysis and Design

At the current state of the art, there are no completely automatic procedures for creating functional specifications. Developing functional specifications is an art that most analysts learn by experience. The guidelines in this section are informal rules of thumb that help analysts avoid getting lost in the maze of details in any real problem. You should create a personal version of this list as you discover which approaches work for you and which ones give you trouble. We have included justifications for each guideline, to help you tailor the general rules to each particular situation.

1. Identify *all* of the cases at each level before refining any one case. This is important for estimation and planning. You cannot estimate the cost of a task or assign people to work on it until you have identified the task.

2. Try to make all of the decisions that are determined by available information before refining further. A breadth-first rather than a depth-first working style is recommended to help prevent mistakes caused by irrelevant details obscuring important information. This kind of error is commonly described as "not seeing the forest for the trees."

3. Either make a decision accurately or record questions and postpone the decision until more information is available. Avoid arbitrary decisions. Carefully calculating the proper answers at the beginning is more efficient than jumping to imperfect conclusions because faulty decisions lead to bugs that must be fixed before you get a working system. Fixing bugs late in the development cycle is wasteful because time must be spent searching for the cause of a failure. Once the cause is found, the code that was developed based on the faulty design decision must be reviewed and sometimes redeveloped. If you must make some guesses to make progress, mark them in some mechanically detectable way to make it easier to find the decisions that have to be reviewed and refined later.

4. Keep your design documents consistent: Propagate the consequences of incompatible changes completely before going on. Impatience and the desire to avoid interrupting a train of thought often lead to inconsistencies because some of the consequences of a retracted assumption were not reviewed and updated. Whenever you finish a step, go back and check for incorrect or missing parts. Your ideas change as you work, and you will not always notice when something gets obsolete. You must actively look for such errors periodically. You want to find incorrect decisions before you base other decisions on them, because otherwise you will waste your effort.

5. If some aspect of the design looks ugly, throw it away and start over. Expect to throw away a lot of paper. Replacing a bad conceptual model can save a great deal of effort in the long run because a bad model can

complicate many future decisions to the point where the system becomes impossible to understand and debug.

6. Save a version of your design before making an incompatible change, because you may need to backtrack later. Sometimes an attractive idea turns sour after you discover some new aspects of the problem, and you may want to go back to a previously discarded line of attack.

7. Record justifications for major decisions as comments. This makes repairs and evolution in response to requirements changes easier, because it is easier to determine which parts of the design are still valid under the new rules. Justifications for previously discarded decisions can be especially valuable in case you have to backtrack, because you can avoid making the same mistake twice. In a large project, people come and go, and the project may take so long that even the original designers may forget why they did what they did before the end is in sight. It is very difficult to reconstruct justifications from an uncommented design, especially after many aspects of the system have been mixed together.

3.4 Case Study: Airline Reservation System

The Spec language and the procedures and guidelines for producing functional specifications introduced in this chapter are illustrated here in terms of the running airline reservation example. We use the initial requirements developed in Chapter 2 as a starting point.

3.4.1 Abstract Functional Specification

The first step is to work out the abstract functional specification, in which we consider only the information content of the messages crossing the boundaries of the proposed system, and not the data formats of those messages.

Systems. The first step is to identify external systems and major internal subsystems. This was done in the last chapter as part of the context summary of the environment model. There is one proposed system, the `airline_reservation_system`, and two external systems, the `travel_agent` and the `airline_manager`, both of which represent classes of human users rather than external software or hardware systems. The example is not large enough to separate the proposed system into multiple major internal subsystems.

Interfaces. There is one external interface for each external system: the
`travel_agent_interface` and the `airline_manager_interface`.
Both of these interfaces are views of the proposed `airline_
reservation_system`.

  We create a Spec module for each external system and proposed subsystem, with inheritance relations between each subsystem and each external interface. Because each of these systems are potentially sensitive to past events,
they are modeled in Spec as machines. The initial specifications resulting from
these considerations are shown in Fig. 3.16. Although these specifications do
not appear to have much content, we have accomplished the important functions of identifying all of the pieces and defining their interconnections. We
note that there will be one instance each of the airline reservation system and
the airline manager, but that there will be 300 travel agents. We use a Spec
instance declaration to specify the set of instances of the generic travel agent
module interfacing to the proposed system. Given our tight budget, we propose
a system where the number of travel agents is determined statically, rather than
a dynamic one with provisions for adding new travel agents as the system runs.
Therefore we define the travel agent as a generic machine and declare all of the
required instances. The number of instances is determined from requirement
C2.5.

  We use the Spec language to record partial decisions as they are made.

```
MACHINE airline_reservation_system
  INHERIT travel_agent_interface
  INHERIT airline_manager_interface
END

MACHINE travel_agent(id: nat)
END

INSTANCE travel_agent_instance(i: nat)
    -- Declares 300 instances of the travel agent machine.
  WHERE travel_agent_instance(i) = travel_agent(i)
  FOREACH(i: nat SUCH THAT 1 <= i <= 300)
END

MACHINE airline_manager
END
```

FIGURE 3.16
Skeleton Specifications for Proposed and External Systems

Each of the modules shown in Fig. 3.16 is a syntactically correct skeleton of a specification, with places for each of the required missing pieces. The specification of the `airline_reservation_system` module is actually finished at this point, although much work remains to elaborate the two interface modules it inherits. Skeletons for the two interfaces are shown in Fig. 3.17.

The interfaces have empty state descriptions to indicate these machines have nontrivial states whose descriptions must be filled in later. The state descriptions of the airline reservation system, the travel agent, and the airline manager do not contain any state descriptions because they have been completely specified. A missing state declaration implies the airline reservation system does not have any state components or restrictions other than those inherited from its two interfaces. The missing state descriptions for the travel agent and the airline manager imply the airline reservation system does not make any assumptions about the internal states of the users. More sophisticated software systems might keep track of what each user knows, and adjust their behavior accordingly. The functional specification of such a system would model the user as a machine with a nontrivial state model.

The abstract functional specification stage will be complete when the two interface modules are done. The concrete functional specification stage involves the elaboration of the travel agent and airline manager modules, which describe the encapsulation of the external systems. If we have sufficient staff available, we could assign a separate analyst to work on each of the two interface modules at this point, although they would have to communicate each time they extend or modify the state model. The state of a machine is the means for potential interactions between the interfaces, and the state model, the invariants, and initial conditions represent the common agreements between the analysts that form the basis for describing the interactions between the interfaces of the machine.

```
MACHINE travel_agent_interface
  STATE  INVARIANT ? INITIALLY ?
END

MACHINE airline_manager_interface
  STATE  INVARIANT ? INITIALLY ?
END
```

FIGURE 3.17
Skeleton Specifications for Interfaces

Messages. The next step is to make a list of the messages in each interface. By consulting the initial requirements, we produce the lists shown in Fig. 3.18. These two interfaces have covered all of the leaf nodes in the goal tree, with the exception of G1.1.3. That goal is an assumption about the influence of the proposed software system on the behavior of the passenger, which is not directly reflected by the interface of the system. This lack of a system structure corresponding to the requirement is not a fault in this case, due to the decision that the initial version of the airline reservation system will not be responsible for issuing tickets. This decision is documented by assumption 11 in Section 2.4.9.

The customer reviews this list of messages, and agrees that a system providing such an interface should provide enough functionality to let the travel agents get their jobs done. The customer also mentions the possibility of a follow-on contract to add capabilities for the travel agent to make seat assignments and to support several different fare classes for the same flight. When asked if these features should be provided in the first version, the customer says some experience with the first version is required before additional funding can be justified.

We add message descriptions to the skeleton specifications for each interface, based on the lists above. The result for the travel agent interface is shown in Fig. 3.19.

The initial specification of the travel agent interface inherits the travel agent's view of the environment model, as defined in Section 2.4.6. We have identified the data that is needed for each of the messages, and the exceptional cases associated with each message. The behavior of the find_flights message was essentially determined during requirements analysis, in the process of refining goal G1.1. The decision was made at that point to display all of the flights from the origin to the destination of the customer's trip. According to

---

```
travel_agent_interface
    find_flights              G1.1.1, G1.1.2
    reserve                   G1.2
    cancel                    G1.3


airline_manager_interface
    add_flight                G2.1
    drop_flight               G2.2
    new_fare                  G2.3
```

FIGURE 3.18
Messages in Each Interface

the environment model, the origin and destination are airports. Since we are concerned with the abstract content of the information carried by the messages at this stage rather than formats, we can model the result of find_flights as a sequence of flights. We use a sequence rather than a set because the flights must be displayed in some order. Such a response can always be produced, because even in the extreme case where there are no flights from the origin to the destination, the system can return the empty sequence. We identify each missing part and mark it with a ?. The symbol ? represents an undefined value that must be filled in later, and can be rendered in English as the phrase "to be determined." In a specification support environment these placeholders should be produced automatically by a syntax-directed editor, along with the keywords defining the structure of a MESSAGE declaration.

The messages reserve and cancel involve the properties of flights and reservations. In the last chapter, we made the simplifying assumption that flights occur at the same time every day, which implies flights are periodic occurrences. Flights also have finite capacities that impose limits on the number of reservations that can be issued for a flight on any given day. A reservation entitles a passenger to a seat on a specified flight and day. We

```
MACHINE travel_agent_interface
  INHERIT travel_agent_view

  MESSAGE find_flights(origin destination: airport)
    -- G1.1.1, G1.1.2
  REPLY flights(s: sequence(flight_description))
    WHERE ? -- flights from the origin to the destination

  MESSAGE reserve(i: flight_id, d: date, p: passenger)   -- G1.2
    WHEN ? -- Seat available.
      REPLY done
      TRANSITION ? -- Add reservation.
    OTHERWISE REPLY EXCEPTION no_seat

  MESSAGE cancel(i: flight_id, d: date, p: passenger)   -- G1.3
    WHEN ? -- Reservation found.
      REPLY done
      TRANSITION ? -- Remove reservation.
    OTHERWISE REPLY EXCEPTION no_reservation
END
```

FIGURE 3.19
Message Skeletons for the Travel Agent Interface

refine the environment model to reflect these considerations, as shown in Fig. 3.20. We have added a law and an attribute to the type flight and a set of attributes to the type reservation in the environment model. The type nat is the set of natural numbers (non-negative integers), and is part of the Spec type library (Appendix D).

The exception condition for the reserve message is needed because of the finite capacity of a flight: if a flight is full, no more reservations can be made. The conditions under which the exception occurs are described informally in a comment, and a ? is used as a placeholder for the formal assertion to be developed later. The motivation for the exception associated with the cancel message has a less compelling justification. Travel agents usually issue a cancel command only if they expect it to have some effect. An attempt to cancel a reservation that is not there indicates the command that was issued

---

```
DEFINITION flight_view1
  INHERIT flight_view
  INHERIT period

  CONCEPT flight: type
    WHERE ALL(f: flight :: periodic(f) & period(f) = (1 day))

  CONCEPT capacity(f: flight) VALUE(n: nat)
    -- The maximum number of reservations for the flight
    -- on any day.
END

DEFINITION travel_agent_view1
  INHERIT travel_agent_view
  INHERIT flight_view1

  CONCEPT id(r: reservation) VALUE(id: flight_id)
  CONCEPT date(r: reservation) VALUE(d: date)
  CONCEPT passenger(r: reservation) VALUE(p: passenger)
END

DEFINITION airline_manager_view1
  INHERIT airline_manager_view
  INHERIT flight_view1
END
```

FIGURE 3.20
Refinement of the Environment Model

does not correspond to the travel agent's intentions, possibly due to an error such as a misspelled passenger name. The analyst decides to report an exception in this case to help the travel agent detect potential errors. The responses in the normal cases of these two commands are messages with a name but no data components. These responses are provided to let the travel agent know when a command has taken effect, which can be useful if the system goes down in the middle of a session.

A similar process leads to the skeleton specification of the airline manager interface shown in Fig. 3.21. The airline manager interface inherits the airline manager's view of the environment model, as defined in Section 2.4.6. The arguments to the add_flight message are determined from the attributes of the type flight in the environment model. The analyst considers whether the range of the capacity for a flight should be restricted, and decides it should not be because it is difficult to put useful bounds on the range that are not likely to be invalidated by a new kind of very large or very small commercial

```
MACHINE airline_manager_interface
  INHERIT airline_manager_view

  MESSAGE add_flight(i: flight_id, price: money,
                     origin destination: airport,
                     departure arrival: time, capacity: nat)
    WHEN ? -- New flight.
      REPLY done
      TRANSITION ? -- Add flight.
    OTHERWISE REPLY EXCEPTION flight_exists

  MESSAGE drop_flight(i: flight_id)
    WHEN ? -- Flight exists.
      REPLY done
      TRANSITION ? -- Remove flight.
    OTHERWISE REPLY EXCEPTION no_such_flight

  MESSAGE new_fare(i: flight_id, price: money)
    WHEN ? -- Flight exists.
      REPLY done
      TRANSITION ? -- Change fare.
    OTHERWISE REPLY EXCEPTION no_such_flight
END
```

FIGURE 3.21
Message Skeletons for the Airline Manager Interface

airplane. This decision is reflected by the lack of an exception reporting an illegal capacity for the new flight. This completes our skeleton specifications.

We consider whether any new abstract data types should be identified at this point. The data types visible in the interfaces are `set{flight}`, `flight`, `flight_id`, `money`, `airport`, `time`, `date`, and `passenger`. The type `set` is a predefined generic type that does not have to be specified anew for this problem (see Appendix D). At the moment, no operations on the rest of the types are apparent other than input and output. Because the detailed properties of those types do not impact the analysis at this stage, it is advisable to delay refining these types until more information becomes available. Thus no new abstract data type modules are introduced at this point.

The processing described so far does not involve anything very complicated, therefore the initial estimate of the effort required is less than the 30 person-weeks available. Potential complications may be introduced by the performance constraints, especially if the database must be partitioned to adequately support a large amount of concurrency. We note these issues as things to watch and continue.

Models and Invariants.   Next we invent conceptual models for the states of the machines. This is done by considering the part of the history of the machine needed to support the operations. The environment model says the airline reservation system is going to control the types `reservation` and `flight`. The airline manager interface is responsible for controlling flights. The travel agent interface is responsible for controlling reservations, and it needs information about flights to do so. This corresponds to the dependency between the two interfaces identified in the process of factoring the environment model shown in Section 2.4.6. Because the travel agent interface is the primary motivation for the system, we elaborate its conceptual model first, as shown in Fig. 3.22.

In working out the conceptual model for the state as seen by the travel agent interface, we concentrate on the aspect associated with reservations, and bring in details about the flight schedule only as needed. Our first guess is that the state consists of a set of reservations and a set of flights. When looking for invariant restrictions on the flight schedule, we notice flights are identified by `flight_id` when making and canceling reservations, so the flight schedule should not contain more than one flight with the same `flight_id`. There must be a single-valued mapping from `flight_id`'s to flights, so we change the conceptual model to make this structure more explicit, as shown in Fig. 3.22. The parameters of the generic type `map` in the conceptual model for the flight schedule represent the domain and range types of the map, in that order. In Spec, the correspondence between actual parameters or arguments and the corresponding formals is always based on the order of appearance, although named associations can be used to add redundancy. Such redundancy can be useful for error checking or for ensuring that modules with variable numbers of

```
MACHINE travel_agent_interface1
  INHERIT travel_agent_interface HIDE reserve cancel
  INHERIT travel_agent_view1

  STATE(reservations: set{reservation},
        schedule: map{flight_id, flight})
  INVARIANT existing_flights(reservations),
            no_overbooking(reservations)
  INITIALLY reservations = { }, domain(schedule) = { }
    -- Initially the reservation set and the schedule
    -- are both empty.

  MESSAGE reserve(i: flight_id, d: date, p: passenger)   -- G1.2
    WHEN ? -- Seat available.
      REPLY done
      TRANSITION ? -- Add reservation.
    WHEN ? -- Unknown flight.
      REPLY EXCEPTION no_such_flight
    OTHERWISE REPLY EXCEPTION no_seat

  MESSAGE cancel(i: flight_id, d: date, p: passenger) -- G1.3
    WHEN ? -- Reservation found.
      REPLY done
      TRANSITION ? -- Remove reservation.
    WHEN ? -- Unknown flight.
      REPLY EXCEPTION no_such_flight
    OTHERWISE REPLY EXCEPTION no_reservation

  CONCEPT existing_flights(s: set{reservation}) VALUE(b: boolean)
    WHERE ALL(r: reservation SUCH THAT r IN s ::
              id(r) IN schedule)

  CONCEPT no_overbooking(s: set{reservation}) VALUE(b: boolean)
    WHERE ALL(i: flight_id, d: date SUCH THAT i IN schedule
              :: bookings(i, d, reservations) <=
                 capacity(schedule[i]) )

  CONCEPT bookings(i: flight_id, d: date, rs: set{reservation})
    VALUE(n: nat)
    WHERE n = NUMBER(r: reservation SUCH THAT
                     r IN rs & id(r) = i & date(r) = d :: r)

  CONCEPT flight_description: type
END
```

FIGURE 3.22
Conceptual Model for the Travel Agent Interface

parameters have unambiguous parameter associations. The type specification for the flight schedule with named parameter associations would look like `map{from:: flight_id, to:: flight}`.

When looking for invariant restrictions on reservations, we note there should not be any reservations for flights that do not appear on the flight schedule, and that we should not issue more reservations than the capacity of each flight. Airlines commonly have a policy of overbooking, but we assume this is handled by making the recorded capacity of a flight larger than the actual number of seats. This simplifies the world from the point of view of the software, since the program need not be concerned with the distinction between the capacity of a flight and the actual number of seats on the flight. Such simplifications are important because the project has limited resources.

The concepts needed to define these invariants are identified and defined as part of this refinement. We adopt the convention that a flight exists if and only if it is contained in the flight schedule mapping. The restriction on reservations due to finite capacities of the flights is defined in terms of an auxiliary concept: the number of bookings for a flight on a given day. This concept was introduced because the definition of `no_overbooking` was getting too complicated without it, and it corresponds to a concept that arises naturally when the concept is explained informally. A heuristic that may be useful for learning how to structure formal specifications is to consider introducing an intermediate concept whenever a definition would otherwise involve nested quantifiers. While this heuristic has no absolute justification, it leads to good concept structures most of the time. The `NUMBER` quantifier used in the definition of the `bookings` concept is used to count the number of reservations satisfying the specified conditions. Extended quantifiers such as `NUMBER` are explained in Section 3.8.4.

When reviewing the messages with respect to the invariants, we find that an exception condition associated with making or canceling a reservation for a flight not in the schedule was neglected in the initial message skeletons, and the messages are refined accordingly.

The previous definitions of `reserve` and `cancel` are not inherited, as indicated by the keyword `HIDE`, because we have made an incompatible change to the interface of those messages by adding an additional case to the response. The effect of the `HIDE` is to replace the previous definitions with those shown, rather than attempting to combine the constraints given in both versions. Since the interfaces of the two versions do not match, trying to combine them would lead to a conflict (i.e., the undefined element !).

The types `reservation` and `flight` are not made into abstract data types at this point because they do not have any significant primitive operations. Since reservations and flights are created by the system, the initial state is defined to have an empty set of reservations and an empty flight schedule.

This level of refinement is now complete, and we turn to the conceptual model of the airline manager interface. The airline manager is concerned with the flight schedule, but not with the details of the reservations. We start with the conceptual model of the flight schedule developed for the travel agent interface, to help maintain consistency. We do not find any additional invariant restrictions for the flight schedule, and define an initial state in which no flights are scheduled. The result is shown in Fig. 3.23. We incorporate the refinement of the component of the environment model dealing with flights by inheriting the refined module `airline_manager_view1`, because the capacity of a flight is involved in scheduling a new flight. The definitions of the messages are not shown because we have discovered no new restrictions, and the interfaces of the messages have not changed. We compare the state models of the two interfaces, and note that they are consistent with each other. This completes step four of the analysis procedure.

Preconditions, Transitions, and Postconditions. The next step involves writing the assertions needed to specify the effects of the messages. Because the interactions between the two interfaces are limited to the invariants, and those have been developed and checked, we can assume the remaining parts of the development are relatively independent for the two interfaces, and can be pursued concurrently without much concern about interactions. The results of the next step for the travel agent interface are shown in Fig. 3.24. We find that the `bookings` concept developed for the invariant is also useful in describing the `reserve` message. Reconsidering the behavior of `reserve` in the light of the state model exposes a new issue—can a passenger have more than one reservation on the same flight and date? We assume the answer is no, to simplify the design of the system, and add this to our list of simplifying assumptions for review by the customer. If we were to allow multiple reservations, we would reconsider the state model and the `cancel` message. The state model for reservations would change from a set to a multiset, and the `cancel` message would specify how many of the customer's reservations are to be canceled. The type `multiset` is part of the Spec type library (Appendix D).

```
MACHINE airline_manager_interface1
  INHERIT airline_manager_interface
  INHERIT airline_manager_view1

  STATE(schedule: map(flight_id, flight)) INVARIANT true
  INITIALLY domain(schedule) = { }
    -- Initially the schedule is empty.
END
```

FIGURE 3.23
Conceptual Model for the Airline Manager Interface

FIGURE 3.24
Assertions for the Travel Agent Interface

```
MACHINE travel_agent_interface2
  INHERIT travel_agent_interface1 HIDE reserve

  STATE(reservations: set{reservation},
        schedule: map{flight_id, flight})
  INVARIANT existing_flights(reservations),
            no_overbooking(reservations),
            single_reservation(reservations)
  INITIALLY reservations = { }, domain(schedule) = { }
    -- Initially the reservation set and the schedule
    -- are both empty.

  MESSAGE find_flights(origin destination: airport)
    -- G1.1.1, G1.1.2
  REPLY flights(s: sequence{flight_description})
    WHERE ALL(f: flight :: description(f) IN s <=>
              f IN range(schedule) & origin(f) = origin &
              destination(f) = destination )
    -- Flights from the origin to the destination.

  MESSAGE reserve(i: flight_id, d: date, p: passenger) -- G1.2
    WHEN i IN schedule &
        bookings(i, d, reservations) < capacity(schedule[i])
        & ~holds(p, i, d, *reservations)  -- Seat available.
      CHOOSE (r: reservation SUCH THAT
              passenger(r) = p & id(r) = i & date(r) = d)
      REPLY done
      TRANSITION reservations = *reservations U {r}
        -- Add reservation.
    WHEN holds(p, i, d, *reservations)
      REPLY EXCEPTION reservation_exists
    WHEN ~(i IN schedule)   -- Unknown flight.
      REPLY EXCEPTION no_such_flight
    OTHERWISE REPLY EXCEPTION no_seat

  MESSAGE cancel(i: flight_id, d: date, p: passenger)  -- G1.3
    WHEN i IN schedule & holds(p, i, d, *reservations)
      -- Reservation found.
      CHOOSE (r: reservation SUCH THAT
              r IN *reservations & passenger(r) = p & id(r) = i &
              date(r) = d )
      REPLY done
      TRANSITION reservations = *reservations - {r}
        -- Remove reservation.
```

```
WHEN ~(i IN schedule)   -- Unknown flight.
   REPLY EXCEPTION no_such_flight
OTHERWISE REPLY EXCEPTION no_reservation

CONCEPT description(f: flight) VALUE(fd: flight_description)

CONCEPT flight_description: type

CONCEPT holds(p: passenger, i: flight_id, d: date,
              rs: set(reservation))
   VALUE(b: boolean)
      -- True if the passenger has a reservation for the flight
      -- on the date in the reservation set.

CONCEPT single_reservation(s: set(reservation))
   VALUE(b: boolean)
   WHERE ALL(r1 r2: reservation SUCH THAT r1 IN s & r2 IN s
             :: id(r1) = id(r2) & date(r1) = date(r2) &
                passenger(r1) = passenger(r2) => r1 = r2 )
END
```

The state model is augmented with a new invariant expressing the new restriction on reservations, expressed in terms of the new concept single_reservation. The concept holds is introduced to express whether a passenger already holds a reservation. The new restriction also introduces a new exception condition reservation_exists, and an incompatible change to the interface of the reserve message, as indicated by the HIDE.

The result of refining the airline manager interface is shown in Fig. 3.25. The state model is not shown since it did not change. No new concepts are needed to write the assertions. The operations bind and remove are part of the predefined map type (Appendix D).

Concepts. The next step is to define any new concepts introduced in the assertions defining the behavior of the messages. The new concepts used to define the messages in the travel agent interface are shown in Fig. 3.26. The attributes of a flight that must be displayed are given by goal G1.1.2, and are reflected in the definition of a flight description. The definition of the holds attribute is straightforward.

In the airline manager interface, the concepts introduced for the invariants and the operations of the predefined types set and map were sufficient for defining the messages, so there are no new concepts.

An internal review of the internal consistency of the specifications focuses on possible interactions between the two views. When the messages of each interface are reviewed with respect to the invariants of the other interface, we

```
MACHINE airline_manager_interface2
  INHERIT airline_manager_interface1

  MESSAGE add_flight(i: flight_id, price: money,
                     origin destination: airport,
                     departure arrival: time, capacity: nat)
    WHEN ~(i IN schedule) -- New flight.
      CHOOSE(f: flight SUCH THAT id(f) = i & price(f) = price &
             origin(f) = origin & destination(f) = destination &
             departure(f) = departure & arrival(f) = arrival &
             capacity(f) = capacity )
      REPLY done
      TRANSITION schedule = bind(i, f, *schedule) -- Add flight.
    OTHERWISE REPLY EXCEPTION flight_exists

  MESSAGE drop_flight(i: flight_id)
    WHEN i IN schedule -- Flight exists.
      REPLY done
      TRANSITION schedule = remove(i, *schedule)
        -- Remove flight.
    OTHERWISE REPLY EXCEPTION no_such_flight

  MESSAGE new_fare(i: flight_id, price: money)
    WHEN i IN schedule -- Flight exists.
      CHOOSE(f: flight SUCH THAT id(f) = i & price(f) = price &
             origin(f) = origin(*schedule[i]) &
             destination(f) = destination(*schedule[i]) &
             departure(f) = departure(*schedule[i]) &
             arrival(f) = arrival(*schedule[i]) &
             capacity(f) = capacity(*schedule[i]) )
      REPLY done
      TRANSITION schedule = bind(i, f, *schedule)
        -- Change fare.
    OTHERWISE REPLY EXCEPTION no_such_flight
END
```

FIGURE 3.25
Assertions for the Airline Manager Interface

discover a problem—when a flight is canceled, what happens to the reservations on that flight? If the reservation set does not change, then the
existing_flights invariant will be violated.

The internal review also considers whether there is need for any atomic
transactions. In this case, the messages are not involved in any multistep protocols, so that there is no need for atomic transactions to prevent interference

```
MACHINE travel_agent_interface3
  INHERIT travel_agent_interface2

  CONCEPT description(f: flight)
    VALUE(fd: flight_description)
    WHERE fd = [id:: id(f), dep:: departure(f),
                arr:: arrival(f), price:: price(f) ]

  CONCEPT flight_description: type
    WHERE flight_description =
      tuple{id:: flight_id, dep arr:: time, price:: money}

  CONCEPT holds(p: passenger, i: flight_id, d: date,
               rs: set{reservation} )
    VALUE(b: boolean)
    WHERE SOME(r: reservation SUCH THAT r IN rs ::
               passenger(r) = p & id(r) = i & date(r) = d )
END
```

FIGURE 3.26
Concepts for the Travel Agent Interface

between concurrent requests. If the system was designed so that travel agents first check whether a seat is available, and then make a reservation, it would be desirable to introduce an atomic transaction to ensure that some other travel agent could not assign the seat between the time it was reported available and the time a reservation was requested. In our design, everything happens in a single step, and the potential unavailability of a seat is reported via an exception, so that there is no need to consider the granularity of transactions. This simplifies the implementation considerably (important for projects on tight budgets) and helps keep the system easy to maintain and modify. The use of atomic transactions to specify the granularity of multistep activities is illustrated in Section 3.9.6. The internal review does not reveal any other problems.

The simplest solution to the problem we have discovered is to remove the reservations on the canceled flight. However, the airlines may not be satisfied if there is no way to warn the passengers holding reservations on a canceled flight. Because the system does not interact directly with the passengers, warnings must be transmitted via the travel agent. Because we are on a tight budget, we propose a solution with a minimal implementation cost, especially since we are considering a response to a rare event.

We propose to solve this problem via a combination of policies, human activities, and software support. The proposed policy is that the airline will notify travel agents of an impending flight cancellation in advance by some

---

G1.4: The system must be able to find all reservations on a given flight after a given date. -- Derived from G2.2.

FIGURE 3.27
Additional Goal

means outside the proposed software system, such as a form letter. Each travel agent is responsible for contacting the passengers who made reservations on the affected flight through the travel agent. The travel agent is responsible for the means to contact the passengers. Any passengers who hold reservations on the canceled flight and do not reschedule their trips on other flights lose their reservations when the flight is actually canceled. Reservations are highly volatile and controlled by the proposed system; therefore, this solution requires the proposed system to provide a means for the travel agent to find the reservations that would be affected by a flight cancellation. We propose the following policy to the customer, and they accept it as a reasonable cost-cutting compromise.

We have just discovered a new requirement, recorded in Fig. 3.27. Travel agents must be able to find the reservations they have made, so the environment model of a reservation must be expanded to include the travel agent that made the reservation, as shown in Fig. 3.28. We make the minimal changes required by this interface. In particular, we avoid the temptation to have the system remember the identity of each travel agent because this complicates the model of the system and introduces additional implementation costs. We ask the customer if they are willing to pay for this capability, and they say they would rather not. When asked if it is acceptable to assign short unique identifiers to the travel agents by a manual procedure outside the proposed software

---

```
DEFINITION travel_agent_view2
  INHERIT travel_agent_view1

  CONCEPT agent(r: reservation) VALUE(a: agent_id)
    -- Needed if flights are canceled.
    -- Justification: G1.3

  CONCEPT agent_id: type
    -- Each travel agent has a unique agent_id.
END
```

FIGURE 3.28
Refinement of Environment Model

```
MACHINE travel_agent_interface4
  INHERIT travel_agent_interface3 HIDE reserve
  INHERIT travel_agent_view2

  MESSAGE notify(a: agent_id, i: flight_id, d: date)
    -- Respond to an impending flight cancellation
    -- at a specified date.
    WHEN i IN schedule
      REPLY reservations(s: sequence(reservation))
        WHERE ALL(r: reservation :: r IN s <=>
                  r IN reservations & id(r) = i &
                  agent(r) = a & date(r) >= d )
    OTHERWISE REPLY EXCEPTION no_such_flight

  MESSAGE reserve(a: agent_id, i: flight_id, d: date,
                  p: passenger)   -- G1.2
    WHEN i IN schedule &
        bookings(i, d, reservations) < capacity(schedule[i]) &
        ~holds(p, i, d, *reservations)   -- Seat available.
      CHOOSE (r: reservation SUCH THAT
              passenger(r) = p & id(r) = i & date(r) = d &
              agent(r) = a )
      REPLY done
      TRANSITION reservations = *reservations U {r}
        -- Add reservation.
    WHEN holds(p, i, d, *reservations)
      REPLY EXCEPTION reservation_exists
    WHEN ~(i IN schedule)   -- Unknown flight.
      REPLY EXCEPTION no_such_flight
    OTHERWISE REPLY EXCEPTION no_seat
END
```

FIGURE 3.29
Refined Travel Agent Interface

system, the customer agrees. The updated version of the travel agent interface is shown in Fig. 3.29. The new function is provided by the notify message. This extension to the functionality of the system also requires several other refinements and modifications. The new function requires the interface of the reserve message to be changed to reflect the identity of the travel agent that made the reservation.

The type date was previously uninterpreted because it did not have any properties affecting the specification. The notify message introduces a nontrivial operation on the type date, since the behavior of the system now depends on the ordering relation on dates. This leads us to define date as an abstract data type, as shown in Fig. 3.30. The date was defined with a two-digit range for the year to reduce the amount of information that has to be input when making a reservation, because that is a frequent operation for the travel agent. This leads to the problem of defining the ordering on dates across the turn of the century. It is quite likely the software system will be in operation for a few decades, so it is not advisable to make a model that will fail on January 1, 2000. We could delay the problem as far as 2090 by making a different fixed interpretation for two-digit years, but deliberately designing a system with a "time bomb" bug is not good engineering. We are reluctant to go to

```
TYPE date
  INHERIT equality(date)

  MODEL(day month year: nat)
  INVARIANT ALL(d: date :: 1 <= d.day <= 31 &
                1 <= d.month <= 12 & 0 <= d.year <= 99 )

  MESSAGE create(d m y: nat)
    WHEN 1 <= d <= 31 & 1 <= m <= 12 & 0 <= d.year <= 99
      REPLY(d: date) WHERE d1.day = d, d1.month = m, d1.year = y
    OTHERWISE REPLY EXCEPTION illegal_date

  MESSAGE equal(d1 d2: date) REPLY(b: boolean)
    WHERE b <=> d1.day = d2.day & d1.month = d2.month &
              d1.year = d2.year

  MESSAGE "<"(d1 d2: date) REPLY(b: boolean)
    WHERE b <=> 0 < (d2.year - d1.year) MOD 100 < 50
            | d1.year = d2.year & d1.month < d2.month
            | d1.year = d2.year & d1.month = d2.month &
              d1.day < d2.day
    -- Note 12/31/99 < 01/01/00
    -- < is a total ordering on any time interval less than 50
    -- years long but it is not transitive on longer intervals.

  MESSAGE "<="(d1 d2: date) REPLY(b: boolean)
    WHERE b <=> d1 < d2 | d1 = d2
END
```

FIGURE 3.30
Specification for an Interface Data Type

four-digit dates, because that would increase the amount of input data for the system and we note that people can handle two-digit dates without any confusion. The reason for this provides the solution. Airline reservations are never made many years in advance, so that the current date provides a reliable estimate for the high-order digits of the date. The solution to the problem is thus to use modulo arithmetic to make the origin of the time interval relative to the current time. We interpret interval lengths reduced modulo 100 that are near zero to be positive and those near 99 to be negative.

We cannot inherit the messages from the virtual type `total_order(date)` because the ordering we have defined is not a total ordering on the entire type, since it is not transitive. However, the < message does give us a total ordering on any contiguous time interval less than 50 years long. We have defined a set of local orderings that cannot be combined into a global ordering because that would lead to a cycle (01/01/00 < 01/02/01 < ... < 12/31/99 < 01/01/00). Since the application never deals with very long time intervals, this is not a problem.

The updated version of the airline manager interface is shown in Fig. 3.31. This reflects the change to the operation `drop_flight` needed to maintain the

```
MACHINE airline_manager_interface3
  INHERIT airline_manager_interface2

  STATE(reservations: set(reservation),
        schedule: map(flight_id, flight) )
  INVARIANT existing_flights(reservations),
            no_overbooking(reservations),
            single_reservation(reservations)
  INITIALLY reservations = ( ), domain(schedule) = ( )
    -- Initially the reservation set and the schedule
    -- are both empty.

  MESSAGE drop_flight(i: flight_id)
    WHEN i IN schedule -- Flight exists.
      REPLY done
      TRANSITION schedule = remove(i, *schedule),
        ALL(r: reservation :: r IN reservations <=>
            r IN *reservations & id(r) ~= i)
          -- Remove flight and all reservations on the flight.
    OTHERWISE REPLY EXCEPTION no_such_flight
END
```

FIGURE 3.31
Refined Airline Manager Interface

invariant. The model of the state has been extended, because it is now apparent that both components of the state are affected by the actions of the airline manager. In hindsight, it would have been a good idea to include all the invariants that mention the schedule in the airline manager's view of the system state, and thus make the reservation set visible because it is linked to the schedule by those invariants.

This example suggests a general guideline for which state components to include in the view of a machine corresponding to an interface. Each view should include all state components explicitly mentioned in the view, and all of the invariants mentioning the visible state components. This guideline should be applied recursively, because a view includes the invariants, and should therefore also include all of the state components mentioned in the invariants. This criterion effectively partitions the state components into independent blocks. All of the components of a state model are often linked directly or indirectly by these invariants; thus this guideline often puts all of the state components in the same block. In such cases, all the state components and all the invariants should be visible in each view. Changes or extensions to the state model or the invariants should be propagated to all views of the system in which the affected blocks of state components are visible as quickly as possible, to avoid errors caused by one analyst not knowing what the others are doing.

Customer Review.   The customer review is based on the message flow diagram shown in Fig. 3.32, the stimulus-response diagrams shown in Figs. 3.33 through 3.35, the type flow diagram shown in Fig. 3.36, and the type

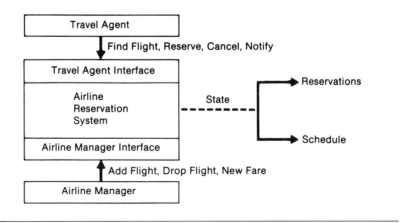

FIGURE 3.32
Message Flow Diagram for the Airline Reservation System

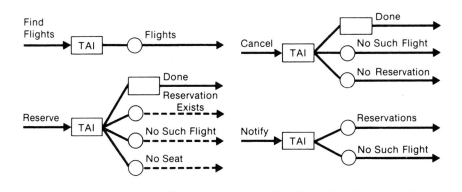

FIGURE 3.33
Stimulus-Response Diagram for the Travel Agent Interface

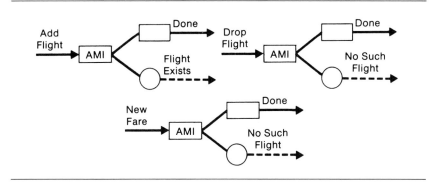

FIGURE 3.34
Stimulus-Response Diagram for the Airline Manager Interface

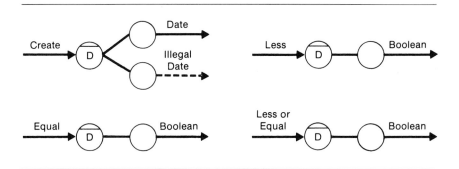

FIGURE 3.35
Stimulus-Response Diagram for the Type Date

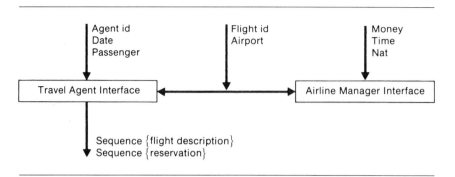

FIGURE 3.36
Type Flow Diagram for the Airline Reservation System

definition dependency diagram shown in Fig. 3.37. These diagrams form the basis for an oral explanation of the system. The message flow diagrams define the context of the system, and serve as a reference point for the more detailed explanations. The stimulus-response diagrams support the explanation of the available commands, their effects, and the possible error conditions. The type flow diagram summarizes the types of information flowing into and out of the system. The type decomposition diagrams show the components of any concrete compound types, and the stimulus-response diagrams provide a summary of the interfaces of any abstract data types.

The customer representatives review this information augmented by oral explanations, ask some questions, and find the proposed first version of the system acceptable, given the schedule and budget constraints. This completes the abstract functional specification.

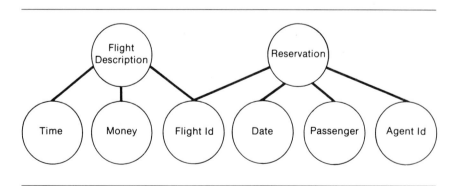

FIGURE 3.37
Type Decomposition Diagram for the Airline Reservation System

Summary of the Abstract Functional Specification. The completed travel agent interface is summarized in Fig. 3.38. The final travel agent view refers to the final environment model given in Section 3.4.3, and the definitions supporting the state model shown in Fig. 3.39. These definitions have been factored out because they are common to both views of the airline reservation system.

The completed airline manager interface is summarized in Fig. 3.40. The final airline manager view refers to the final environment model given in Section 3.4.3.

FIGURE 3.38
Completed Travel Agent Interface

```
MACHINE final_travel_agent_interface
  INHERIT final_travel_agent_view
  INHERIT airline_reservation_state_model

  STATE(reservations: set(reservation),
        schedule: map(flight_id, flight) )
  INVARIANT existing_flights(reservations),
            no_overbooking(reservations),
            single_reservation(reservations)
  INITIALLY reservations = { }, domain(schedule) = { }
    -- Initially the reservation set and the schedule
    -- are both empty.

  MESSAGE find_flights(origin destination: airport)
    -- G1.1.1, G1.1.2
  REPLY flights(s: sequence(flight_description))
    -- Flights from the origin to the destination.
    WHERE ALL(f: flight :: description(f) IN s <=>
              f IN range(schedule) & origin(f) = origin &
              destination(f) = destination )

  MESSAGE reserve(a: agent_id, i: flight_id, d: date,
                  p: passenger)   -- G1.2
    WHEN i IN schedule &
         bookings(i, d, reservations) < capacity(schedule[i]) &
         ~holds(p, i, d, *reservations) -- Seat available.
      CHOOSE (r: reservation SUCH THAT
              passenger(r) = p & id(r) = i & date(r) = d &
              agent(r) = a )
      REPLY done TRANSITION reservations = *reservations U {r}
        -- Add reservation.
    WHEN holds(p, i, d, *reservations)
      REPLY EXCEPTION reservation_exists
```

FIGURE 3.38 (continued)

```
    WHEN ~(i IN schedule) -- Unknown flight.
      REPLY EXCEPTION no_such_flight
    OTHERWISE REPLY EXCEPTION no_seat
  MESSAGE cancel(i: flight_id, d: date, p: passenger)   -- G1.3
    WHEN i IN schedule & holds(p, i, d, *reservations)
      -- Reservation found.
      CHOOSE (r: reservation SUCH THAT
              r IN *reservations & passenger(r) = p &
              id(r) = i & date(r) = d)
      REPLY done TRANSITION reservations = *reservations - {r}
        -- Remove reservation.
    WHEN ~(i IN schedule) REPLY EXCEPTION no_such_flight
      -- Unknown flight.
    OTHERWISE REPLY EXCEPTION no_reservation

  MESSAGE notify(a: agent_id, i: flight_id, d: date)   -- G1.4
    WHEN i IN schedule
      -- Respond to an impending flight cancellation.
      REPLY reservations(s: sequence{reservation})
        WHERE ALL(r: reservation :: r IN s <=>
                  r IN reservations & id(r) = i & agent(r) = a &
                  date(r) >= d )
    OTHERWISE REPLY EXCEPTION no_such_flight

  CONCEPT holds(p: passenger, i: flight_id, d: date,
                rs: set{reservation} )
    VALUE(b: boolean)
    WHERE SOME(r: reservation SUCH THAT r IN rs ::
                passenger(r) = p & id(r) = i & date(r) = d )

  CONCEPT description(f: flight) VALUE(fd: flight_description)
    WHERE fd = [id:: id(f), dep:: departure(f),
                arr:: arrival(f), price:: price(f) ]

  CONCEPT flight_description: type
    WHERE flight_description =
      tuple{id:: flight_id, dep arr:: time, price:: money}
END
```

3.4.2 Concrete Functional Specification

The next step is to determine the message formats and to develop the concrete
functional specification.

```
DEFINITION airline_reservation_state_model

  CONCEPT existing_flights(s: set(reservation))
    VALUE(b: boolean)
    WHERE ALL(r: reservation SUCH THAT r IN s ::
              id(r) IN schedule)

  CONCEPT no_overbooking(s: set(reservation))
    VALUE(b: boolean)
    WHERE ALL(i: flight_id, d: date SUCH THAT i IN schedule ::
              bookings(i, d, reservations) <=
              capacity(schedule[i]) )

  CONCEPT bookings(i: flight_id, d: date, rs: set(reservation))
    VALUE(n: nat)
    WHERE n = NUMBER(r: reservation SUCH THAT
                     r IN rs & id(r) = i & date(r) = d :: r)

  CONCEPT single_reservation(s: set(reservation))
    VALUE(b: boolean)
    WHERE ALL(r1 r2: reservation SUCH THAT r1 IN s & r2 IN s
              :: id(r1) = id(r2) & date(r1) = date(r2) &
              passenger(r1) = passenger(r2) => r1 = r2 )
END
```

FIGURE 3.39
Completed State Model Concepts

Input/Output Devices.   The customer says the travel agents will be supplied with display terminals that communicate with the central computer by a 1200 baud telephone connection. The terminals have no special graphics or input capabilities. When asked about user-friendly interfaces, the customer responds with "do the best you can, as long as you do not increase the cost." When asked about security, the customer says unauthorized access is not a major concern, because dedicated telephone lines will be used for communication.

Message Formats.   The next step is to define the concrete message formats the users of the system see. We do this in two stages: first, developing the formats for the commands and the normal responses, and then defining the editing facilities and the error messages. This gives the customer a chance to review the parts of the interface used most often and to ask for any adjustments needed before we spend effort on details of the exceptional cases.

Because we are on a tight budget, we choose a conventional command interface that is simple to implement. This decision is affected by the limited

```
MACHINE final_airline_manager_interface
  INHERIT final_airline_manager_view
  INHERIT airline_reservation_state_model

  STATE(reservations: set{reservation},
        schedule: map{flight_id, flight})
  INVARIANT existing_flights(reservations),
            no_overbooking(reservations),
            single_reservation(reservations)
  INITIALLY reservations = { }, domain(schedule) = { }
    -- Initially the reservation set and the schedule
    -- are both empty.

  MESSAGE add_flight(i: flight_id, price: money,
                     origin destination: airport,
                     departure arrival: time, capacity: nat)
    WHEN ~(i IN schedule) -- New flight.
      CHOOSE(f: flight SUCH THAT id(f) = i & price(f) = price &
             origin(f) = origin & destination(f) = destination &
             departure(f) = departure & arrival(f) = arrival &
             capacity(f) = capacity )
      REPLY done TRANSITION schedule = bind(i, f, *schedule)
        -- Add flight.
    OTHERWISE REPLY EXCEPTION flight_exists

  MESSAGE drop_flight(i: flight_id)
    WHEN i IN schedule -- Flight exists.
      REPLY done
        -- Remove flight and all reservations on the flight.
      TRANSITION schedule = remove(i, *schedule),
        ALL(r: reservation :: r IN reservations <=>
            r IN *reservations & id(r) ~= i )
    OTHERWISE REPLY EXCEPTION no_such_flight

  MESSAGE new_fare(i: flight_id, price: money)
    WHEN i IN schedule -- Flight exists.
      CHOOSE(f: flight SUCH THAT id(f) = i & price(f) = price &
             origin(f) = origin(*schedule[i]) &
             destination(f) = destination(*schedule[i]) &
             departure(f) = departure(*schedule[i]) &
             arrival(f) = arrival(*schedule[i]) &
             capacity(f) = capacity(*schedule[i]) )
      REPLY done TRANSITION schedule = bind(i, f, *schedule)
        -- Change fare.
    OTHERWISE REPLY EXCEPTION no_such_flight
END
```

FIGURE 3.40
Completed Airline Manager Interface

capabilities of the hardware to be used and the current state of our software library, which does not have an existing generic menu or display package that can be easily adapted to our needs. A specification for the initial version of the concrete command interface visible to the travel agent is shown in Fig. 3.41.

FIGURE 3.41
Concrete Command Interface for the Travel Agent

```
MACHINE travel_agent(id: nat)
  INHERIT final_travel_agent_view HIDE time money
  INHERIT travel_agent_command_formats
  INHERIT travel_agent_output_formats
  IMPORT flight_description FROM travel_agent_interface

  MESSAGE interpret_command(command: string)
    -- Command from travel agent's keyboard.
    WHEN is_find_flights(edit(command), origin, destination)
      SEND find_flights(origin destination: airport)
        TO airline_reservation_system
    WHEN is_reserve(edit(command), a, i, d, p)
      SEND reserve(a: agent_id, i: flight_id, d: date,
                   p: passenger)
        TO airline_reservation_system
    WHEN is_cancel(edit(command), i, d, p)
      SEND cancel(i: flight_id, d: date, p: passenger)
        TO airline_reservation_system
    WHEN is_notify(edit(command), a, i, d)
      SEND notify(a: agent_id, i: flight_id, d: date)
        TO airline_reservation_system
    OTHERWISE REPLY(s: string) WHERE s = "command not recognized"

  -- Normal responses.

  MESSAGE flights(sf: sequence(flight_description))
    WHEN sf ~= [ ]
      CHOOSE(rows: sequence(row) SUCH THAT
             length(rows) = length(sf) &
             ALL(i: nat SUCH THAT i IN domain(sf) ::
                 rows[i] = flight_row(sf[i]) ))
      SEND(lines: sequence(string)) TO display
        WHERE lines = table(rows, [6, 8, 8, 10])
    OTHERWISE SEND(s: string) TO display
      WHERE s = "no flights found"

  MESSAGE done
    SEND(s: string) TO display WHERE s = "done"
```

FIGURE 3.41 (continued)

```
  MESSAGE reservations(sr: sequence(reservation))
    WHEN sr ~= [ ]
      CHOOSE(rows: sequence(row) SUCH THAT
             length(rows) = length(sr) &
             ALL(i: nat SUCH THAT i IN domain(sr) ::
                 rows[i] = reservation_row(sr[i]) ))
    SEND(lines: sequence(string)) TO display
      WHERE lines = table(rows, [8, 20])
    OTHERWISE SEND(s: string) TO display
      WHERE s = "no reservations found"

  CONCEPT edit(s: string)
    VALUE(es: string)
END
```

This specification describes how concrete commands are transformed into the abstract commands defined in the abstract functional specification, and how the abstract responses are displayed to the travel agent. The first letters of the commands in each interface are unique, so we use single characters as identifiers to minimize typing and to simplify the implementation. The machine has an empty state model because the proposed interface does not keep track of past interactions with the travel agent. For example, an interface with a facility to repeat the last command would have a nontrivial state model that includes a record of the last command issued by the user. The output formats have been defined in terms of the predefined formatting concept table, which describes a two dimensional table whose columns fit in fields of specified widths. The contents of the rows in the tables are specified in the concepts flight_row and reservation_row.

We have broken up the descriptions into small groups with similar purposes to make it easier to read and review them. Each group gives a complete view of a limited aspect of the whole, thus making it easier for a reviewer to understand the proposed concrete interface. We have followed the informal guideline of looking for coherent subgroups in any specification that does not fit on a page, giving the coherence of the grouping a higher priority than the length limitation. Because supporting reviews and helping new people learn about the proposed systems are important goals of a functional specification, we recommend this practice for practical projects as well as for educational exercises.

The detailed definitions of the concrete command formats are factored out in the definition module shown in Fig. 3.42. These definitions are predicates describing the order and the components of each command, using the

```
DEFINITION travel_agent_command_formats
  INHERIT airline_reservation_type_formats
  IMPORT is_list FROM format -- Standard formatting concepts.

  CONCEPT is_find_flights(command: string,
                          origin destination: airport)
    VALUE(b: boolean)
    WHERE b <=> is_list(command, "f", origin, destination)

  CONCEPT is_reserve(command: string, a: agent_id, i: flight_id,
                     d: date, p: passenger)
    VALUE(b: boolean)
    WHERE b <=> SOME(ds: string ::
                     is_list(command, "r", a, i, ds, p) &
                     date(ds) = d )

  CONCEPT is_cancel(command: string, i: flight_id, d: date,
                    p: passenger)
    VALUE(b: boolean)
    WHERE b <=> SOME(ds: string ::
                     is_list(command, "c", i, ds, p) &
                     date(ds) = d )

  CONCEPT is_notify(command: string, a: agent_id, i: flight_id,
                    d: date)
    VALUE(b: boolean)
    WHERE b <=> SOME(ds: string ::
                     is_list(command, "n", a, i, ds) &
                     date(ds) = d )
END
```

FIGURE 3.42
Travel Agent Command Formats

predefined formatting concept is_list, which defines the format of a list of strings separated by spaces.

The detailed definitions of the concrete output formats are factored out in the definition module shown in Fig. 3.43. These definitions show the content of each line in the displays generated by the find_flights and notify commands.

The detailed definitions of the formats for the uninterpreted types of the abstract functional specification are shown in Fig. 3.44.

This specification documents the concrete message format decisions that were made. We have taken advantage of the fact that the data types

```
DEFINITION travel_agent_output_formats
  INHERIT final_travel_agent_view
  INHERIT airline_reservation_type_formats
  IMPORT flight_description FROM travel_agent_interface
  IMPORT row FROM format  -- Standard formatting concepts.

  CONCEPT flight_row(f: flight_description)
    VALUE(r: row)
    WHERE r = [f.id, f.dep, f.arr, f.price]

  CONCEPT reservation_row(r: reservation)
    VALUE(r1: row)
    WHERE SOME(ds: string ::
               r1 = [ds, passenger(r)] & date(r) = date(ds) )
END
```

FIGURE 3.43
Travel Agent Output Formats

FIGURE 3.44
Concrete Type Definitions

```
DEFINITION airline_reservation_type_formats
  INHERIT character_properties
  IMPORT Subtype FROM type

  CONCEPT date(s: string)
    VALUE(d1: date)
    WHERE SOME(m d y: string :: s = [$m, '/', $d, '/', $y] &
               digits(m) & digits(d1) & digits(y) &
               1 <= nat(m) <= 12 & 1 <= nat(d1) <= 31 &
               length(y) = 2 &
               d1 = create@date(nat(d), nat(m), nat(y)) )

  -- Format definitions for the types in the
  -- travel agent interface.

  CONCEPT flight_id: type
    WHERE Subtype(flight_id, string),
      ALL(f: flight_id :: SOME(a n: string :: f = a || n &
          letters(a) & length(a) = 2 & digits(n) &
          length(n) <= 4 ))
```

```
CONCEPT agent_id: type
  WHERE Subtype(agent_id, string),
    ALL(a: agent_id :: letters(a) & length(a) = 3)
    -- The id is a short code to minimize typing.

CONCEPT airport: type
  WHERE Subtype(airport, string),
    ALL(a: airport :: letters(a) & length(a) = 3)

CONCEPT money: type
  WHERE Subtype(money, string),
    ALL(m: money :: SOME(d c: string :: m = ['$', $d, '.', $c]
        & digits(d) & digits(c) & length(c) = 2 ))

CONCEPT time: type
  -- 24 hour time.
  WHERE Subtype(time, string),
    ALL(t: time :: SOME(h m: string :: t = [$h, ':', $m] &
        digits(h) & digits(m) & 0 <= nat(h) <= 23 &
        0 <= nat(m) <= 59 & length(h) >= 1 & length(m) = 2 ))

CONCEPT passenger: type
  WHERE Subtype(passenger, string),
    ALL(p: passenger, c: char SUCH THAT c IN p ::
        letter(c) | c = space ),
    ALL(p: passenger :: length(p) > 1 & p[1] ~= space &
                        p[length(p)] ~= space )
  -- This format implies the passenger must be the last
  -- argument, because passenger names can contain spaces.
END
```

---

flight_id, money, airport, time, date, and passenger are unconstrained by the abstract functional specification. These types are used only for
input and output, so we can reduce our work by representing them as strings.
Because these are incompatible changes from the concepts time and money in
the environment model, we hide these concepts in the views of the environment
model inherited by the concrete interface specifications of the travel agent and
the airline manager. We have used predefined formatting concepts from the
modules format and character_properties, defined in the Spec concepts library (Appendix C).

The length of the agent_id is determined from constraint C2.4 from the
initial requirements, which says the system handles 10,000 transactions per day.
We take this to imply that there are no more than 10,000 travel agents, since a

```
MACHINE airline_manager
  INHERIT final_airline_manager_view HIDE time money
  INHERIT airline_manager_command_formats

  MESSAGE interpret_command(command: string)
    -- Command from airline manager's keyboard.
    WHEN is_add_flight(edit(command), i, price, origin,
                       destination, departure, arrival, capacity)
      SEND add_flight(i: flight_id, price: money,
                      origin destination: airport,
                      departure arrival: time, capacity: nat)
        TO airline_reservation_system
    WHEN is_drop_flight(edit(command), i)
      SEND drop_flight(i: flight_id)
        TO airline_reservation_system
    WHEN is_new_fare(edit(command), i, price)
      SEND new_fare(i: flight_id, price: money)
        TO airline_reservation_system
    OTHERWISE REPLY(s: string) WHERE s = "command not
                                          recognized"
  -- Normal responses.

  MESSAGE done
    SEND(s: string) TO display WHERE s = "Done."

  CONCEPT edit(s: string)
    VALUE(es: string)
END
```

FIGURE 3.45
Concrete Command Interface for the Airline Manager

typical travel agent makes at least one transaction per day. We make a note to review this assumption with the airline managers.

A specification for the concrete commands visible to the airline manager is shown in Fig. 3.45. A specification for the command formats for the airline manager is shown in Fig. 3.46. The facilities for the airline manager are similar to those for the travel agent. In particular, we propose to use the same editing function in both interfaces to reduce implementation effort, as indicated by the IMPORT. The details of this editing function are as yet undetermined.

When the formats are reviewed by the customers, they are found Spartan but usable. The airline managers request that command names be spelled out in full. The travel agents are happy with short commands, and do not request any changes.

```
DEFINITION airline_manager_command_formats
  INHERIT format

  CONCEPT is_add_flight(command: string, i: flight_id, p: money,
                        o d: airport, dep arr: time, cn: nat)
    VALUE(b: boolean)
    WHERE b <=> SOME(ds cap: string SUCH THAT
                     d = date(ds) & cn = nat(cap) ::
                     is_list(command, "a", i, p, o, ds,
                             dep, arr, cap ))

  CONCEPT is_drop_flight(command: string, i: flight_id)
    VALUE(b: boolean)
    WHERE b <=> is_list(command, "d", i)

  CONCEPT is_new_fare(command: string, i: flight_id, p: money)
    VALUE(b: boolean)
    WHERE b <=> is_list(command, "n", i, p)
END
```

FIGURE 3.46
Airline Manager Command Formats

Editing and Error Messages.   Again, motivated by budget pressure, we
decide to propose only minimal editing facilities, which are limited to character
and line erase. Such a facility is provided by the reusable concept
basic_edit (Appendix C), which is inherited to refine the previously uninterpreted concept edit.

Simple error messages are added to complete the concrete functional
specification for the travel agent as shown in Fig. 3.47. Error messages are
added to complete the concrete functional specification for the airline manager
as shown in Fig. 3.48. The incompatible change to the airline manager interface, making the commands complete English words rather than single characters, is reflected by the HIDE keyword in the INHERIT. The revised definition
of the command formats is shown in Fig. 3.49.

The error messages for the airline manager interface are longer than the
error messages in the travel agent interface, and give more detailed explanations of the causes of potential problems and suggest ways to correct them.
This design is based on the assumption that airline managers interact with the
system less frequently than do travel agents, and hence are less familiar with
the system and need more guidance. We have also extrapolated from the previous request for full English command names to conclude that airline managers
probably do not like cryptic error messages.

```
MACHINE final_travel_agent(id: nat)
  INHERIT travel_agent(id)
  INHERIT basic_edit

  -- Error messages.

  MESSAGE EXCEPTION no_seat
    SEND(s: string) TO display WHERE s = "No seat available."

  MESSAGE EXCEPTION reservation_exists
    SEND(s: string) TO display
    WHERE s = "The passenger already has a reservation."

  MESSAGE EXCEPTION no_reservation
    SEND(s: string) TO display
    WHERE s = "The passenger does not hold a reservation."

  MESSAGE EXCEPTION no_such_flight
    SEND(s: string) TO display WHERE s = "Unknown flight id."
END
```

FIGURE 3.47
Completed Concrete Interface for the Travel Agent

```
MACHINE final_airline_manager
  INHERIT airline_manager
    HIDE is_add_flight is_drop_flight is_new_fare
  INHERIT final_airline_manager_command_formats
  INHERIT basic_edit

  MESSAGE EXCEPTION flight_exists
    SEND(s: string) TO display WHERE s =
      "The flight is already scheduled." || [newline] ||
      "To change it, use drop_flight and then add_flight."

  MESSAGE EXCEPTION no_such_flight
    SEND(s: string) TO display WHERE s =
      "No such flight was scheduled, check the flight id."
END
```

FIGURE 3.48
Completed Concrete Interface for the Airline Manager

```
DEFINITION final_airline_manager_command_formats
  INHERIT format

  CONCEPT is_add_flight(command: string, i: flight_id, p: money,
                        o d: airport, dep arr: time, cn: nat)
    VALUE(b: boolean)
    WHERE b <=> SOME(ds cap: string SUCH THAT
                     d = date(ds) & cn = nat(cap) ::
                     is_list(command, "add_flight", i, p, o, ds,
                             dep, arr, cap) )

  CONCEPT is_drop_flight(command: string, i: flight_id)
    VALUE(b: boolean)
    WHERE b <=> is_list(command, "drop_flight", i)

  CONCEPT is_new_fare(command: string, i: flight_id, p: money)
    VALUE(b: boolean)
    WHERE b <=> is_list(command, "new_fare", i, p)
END
```

FIGURE 3.49
Completed Airline Manager Command Formats

Customer Review. The proposed concrete interface is now reviewed by a group of potential users, based on the diagrams of Section 3.4.1 and the examples of type formats shown in Fig. 3.50, the examples of command formats shown in Fig. 3.51, and the examples of error message formats shown in Fig. 3.52. The users like the consistency of the order of the arguments across

Type Formats

airport:	LAX
flight_id:	aa101
date:	1/17/89
passenger:	Seymour Cray
agent_id:	rvb
time:	14:57
money:	$245.00
nat:	220

FIGURE 3.50
Examples of Interface Type Formats

Travel Agent Commands

find_flights: f SFO LAX
reserve: r rvb aa101 1/17/89 Seymour Cray
cancel: c aa101 1/17/89 Seymour Cray
notify: n rvb aa101 11/2/89

Airline Manager Commands

add_flight: add_flight aa101 $245.00 SFO LAX 9:45 12:05 220
drop_flight: drop_flight aa101
new_fare: new_fare aa101 $278.45

FIGURE 3.51
Examples of Command Formats

different commands, and accept the concrete formats. The airline managers say they would like to have a command menu and prompts for the arguments associated with each command in future versions of the system, but are not interested in paying extra for incorporating this feature in the initial development.

3.4.3 Summary of the Final Requirements

The extensions to the environment model made during functional specification were limited to the types flight and reservation. The complete descrip-

Travel Agent Error Messages

no_seat: No seat available.
reservation_exists: The passenger already has a reservation.
no_reservation: The passenger does not hold a reservation.
no_such_flight: Unknown flight id.

Airline Manager Error Messages

flight_exists: The flight is already scheduled.
                    To change it, use drop_flight and the add_flight.

no_such_flight: No such flight was scheduled, check the flight id.

FIGURE 3.52
Examples of Error Messages

tions of the final environment model are collected in Figs. 3.53 through 3.56.

The derived goal G1.4 was discovered during functional specification. The completed goal hierarchy is shown in Fig. 3.57.

The completed abstract functional specification is shown in Section 3.4.1. The concrete functional specification is given in Section 3.4.2.

3.4.4 Summary of Simplifying Assumptions

The following additional simplifying assumptions have been made during functional specification.

1. The capacity of a flight is the same every day.

2. A passenger can have only one reservation on any given flight and day.

3. Travel agents will be notified in advance of flights that are going to be removed from the schedule. This is done outside the proposed software system.

4. Short unique identifiers are assigned to the travel agents by some means outside the software system.

5. There are no more than 10,000 travel agents.

```
DEFINITION final_airline_environment
  INHERIT final_travel_agent_view
  INHERIT final_airline_manager_view
  INHERIT system
  INHERIT user

  CONCEPT airline_reservation_system: software_system
    WHERE proposed(airline_reservation_system),
        -- We are going to build an airline reservation system.
      Uses(travel_agent, airline_reservation_system),
      Controls(airline_reservation_system, reservation),
        -- The system will help travel agents sell tickets
        -- by managing reservations.
      Uses(airline_manager, airline_reservation_system),
      Controls(airline_reservation_system, flight)
        -- The system will help airline managers maintain
        -- the flight schedule.
END
```

FIGURE 3.53
Final Environment Model: Proposed System

FIGURE 3.54
Final Environment Model: Travel Agent View

```
DEFINITION final_travel_agent_view
  INHERIT final_flight_view
  INHERIT user  -- Defines User_class, uses.
  INHERIT business  -- Defines vendor, customer, sells.
  IMPORT Subtype Immutable_instances Indestructible FROM type

  CONCEPT travel_agent: User_class
    WHERE ALL(ta: travel_agent ::
              uses(ta, airline_reservation_system)),
        -- Travel agents use the airline reservation system.
        -- We are only concerned with the travel agents
        -- using our system.
      Subtype(travel_agent, vendor),
        -- A travel agent is a sales person.
      ALL(t: ticket :: SOME(ta: travel_agent :: sells(ta, t))),
      ALL(r: reservation ::
          SOME(ta: travel_agent :: supplies(ta, t)) )
        -- Travel agents are the only sources for
        -- tickets and reservations.

  CONCEPT reservation: type
    WHERE ALL(t: trip ::
              SOME(r: reservation :: Needed_for(r, t)) ),
      -- Once issued, reservations cannot be changed.
    Immutable_instances(reservation)
      -- Justification: customer policy.

  CONCEPT id(r: reservation) VALUE(id: flight_id)
  CONCEPT date(r: reservation) VALUE(d: date)
  CONCEPT passenger(r: reservation) VALUE(p: passenger)
  CONCEPT agent(r: reservation) VALUE(a: agent_id)
    -- Needed if flights are canceled.
    -- Justification: G1.3

  CONCEPT agent_id: type
    -- Each travel agent has a unique agent_id.

  CONCEPT ticket: type
    WHERE Subtype(ticket, product),
      ALL(t: trip :: Needed_for(ticket, t)),
        -- A ticket is needed for every trip.
        -- Once issued, tickets cannot be changed or destroyed.
      Immutable_instances(ticket),
        -- Justification: customer policy.
      Indestructible(ticket)  -- Justification: customer policy.

  CONCEPT trip: type
    WHERE Subtype(trip, activity)
```

```
CONCEPT origin(t: trip) VALUE(a: airport)
CONCEPT destination(t: trip) VALUE(a: airport)

CONCEPT passenger: type
  WHERE Subtype(passenger, customer),
    ALL(p: passenger :: SOME(t: trip :: wants(p, t))),
    ALL(p: passenger :: SOME(t: ticket :: buys(p, t))),
    ALL(t: trip :: Needed_for(flight, t))
      -- The system is only concerned with trips on
      -- airplanes.
END
```

```
DEFINITION final_airline_manager_view
  INHERIT final_flight_view
  INHERIT user   -- defines User_class, uses

  CONCEPT airline_manager: User_class
    WHERE ALL(am: airline_manager ::
              uses(am, airline_reservation_system) ),
      -- We are only concerned with the airline managers
      -- that will use the system.
    Maintains(airline_manager, flight)
END
```

FIGURE 3.55
Final Environment Model: Airline Manager View

FIGURE 3.56
Final Environment Model: Flight Properties

```
DEFINITION final_flight_view
  INHERIT time
  INHERIT location
  INHERIT period
  IMPORT Subtype FROM type
  IMPORT One_to_one FROM function{flight, flight_id}

  CONCEPT flight: type
      -- The passenger will choose a flight based on origin,
      -- destination, departure, arrival, and price.
    WHERE Subtype(flight, activity),
      ALL(f: flight :: periodic(f) & period(f) = (1 day))
  CONCEPT origin(f: flight) VALUE(a: airport)
  CONCEPT destination(f: flight) VALUE(a: airport)
  CONCEPT departure(f: flight) VALUE(t: time_of_day)
```

FIGURE 3.56 (continued)

```
CONCEPT arrival(f: flight) VALUE(t: time_of_day)
CONCEPT price(f: flight) VALUE(m: money)
CONCEPT id(f: flight) VALUE(i: flight_id)
  -- The flight id is used by the passenger to find the flight.
  WHERE One_to_one(id) -- The id uniquely identifies a flight.
CONCEPT capacity(f: flight) VALUE(n: nat)
  -- The maximum number of reservations for the flight
  -- on any day.

CONCEPT airport: type WHERE Subtype(airport, location)
CONCEPT flight_id: type

CONCEPT airline: type
  WHERE Subtype(airline, supplier),
    ALL(f: flight :: SOME(a: airline :: supplies(a, f)))
      -- Every flight is associated with an airline.
      -- We are only concerned with commercial flights.
END
```

G1: The purpose of the system is to help the travel agent sell tickets.

> **G1.1: The system must help the travel agent find all of the flights meeting a passenger's needs.**

>> **G1.1.1: The system must be able to find all flights with a given origin and destination.**

>> **G1.1.2: The system must display the arrival and departure times, the price, and the flight number for each flight it finds.**

>> **G1.1.3: The passenger will choose a flight based on the displayed information.**

> **G1.2: The system must let the travel agent make reservations.**

> **G1.3: The system must allow the travel agent to cancel reservations.**

> **G1.4: The system must be able to find all reservations on a given flight after a given date. -- Derived from G2.2.**

G2: The system must provide a means for the airline manager to manage flights.

> **G2.1: The system must allow the airline manager to schedule new flights.**

> **G2.2: The system must allow the airline manager to drop flights from the schedule.**

> **G2.3: The system must allow the airline manager to change the fare for a flight.**

FIGURE 3.57
Completed Goal Hierarchy

3.5 Quality Assurance

Quality assurance activities can be classified into two categories known as validation and verification. Validation refers to activities aimed at checking the correspondence between a formal model and the real world, such as checking that a functional specification corresponds to the real needs of the customer and that the environment model corresponds to the real behavior of the external systems that interact with the proposed software system. Verification refers to activities aimed at checking the correspondence between a formal model and another more detailed formal model, such as checking that the functional specification is consistent with the formal environment model or checking that an implementation corresponds to the functional specification.

Validation has great practical importance, because developing a system that does not meet the customer's needs can be a very expensive mistake. Validation is an experimental and inherently uncertain process. In any scientific or engineering enterprise the validation of a formal model with respect to a real physical system is decidable only in the negative sense: Theories can be refuted by individual experiments, but cannot be proved conclusively. Validation is a process that seeks to refute the accuracy of a formal model. Repeated failures to refute the formal model increase the level of confidence, in a statistical sense, that a formal model is an adequate representation of reality, but there is no point at which we can say that a specification has been absolutely and conclusively validated. Since validation efforts are expensive, there is a tradeoff between the cost of validation and the risk of a serious fault in the formal model remaining undetected.

The main methods for validating functional specifications are customer reviews and demonstrations of prototypes. These methods have been discussed in the previous chapter. Diagrams and draft user's manuals are also important means for supporting customer reviews.

Verification is a process that is theoretically subject to a precise mathematical analysis. At the functional specification stage, verification refers to checking the correspondence between the formal requirements model and the functional specification. Currently, most requirements models are not sufficiently formal to support much mathematical verification. The development of the models, underlying mathematics, and automated procedures needed to support such verification is a current research area. In practice, the correspondence is usually checked by a manual process of tracing each part of the requirements to some part of the formal specification, and vice versa. The adequacy of each aspect of the correspondence is checked by the analysts. They also check whether every requirement has been met by some part of the functional specification, and whether every part of the functional specification corresponds to some requirement.

Another aspect of verification is checking the internal consistency of the functional specification. An inconsistent functional specification is not acceptable because it cannot be implemented. Some of the consistency constraints that should be checked for a functional specification expressed in the Spec language are described in Section 3.9.4. Some of these constraints are well understood and could be checked by mechanical procedures.

3.6 Management Aspects

As during requirements analysis, customer reviews and estimation are important during functional specification. These aspects are discussed in Chapter 2. Another problem that gains more importance in this stage is making rational task assignments.

Most projects have tight schedules, so that it is important to schedule activities in parallel as much as possible. However, assigning too many people to a project slows it down if the people need to interact so much that they spend all of their time talking to each other, or introduce many mistakes by making decisions in ignorance of what was done in related parts of the system by other people. Because the mistakes all have to be fixed later, delays late in the project can be caused by excessive haste at the start.

Because there are many potentially parallel tasks that can start after the abstract functional specification is complete and stable, but the functional specifications have relatively few tasks that can be pursued independently, the manager may be faced with a large staff sitting idle at the beginning of the functional specification stage. There is a simple solution to this problem, motivated by the high cost of specification errors: assign the extra people to the tasks of reviewing and checking the work of the team of analysts. This also has the benefit of familiarizing the people not directly involved in writing the specifications with its goals and properties, so that they will be able to design, implement, test, and document the system with less overhead when the time comes. The people who are going to work on each part of a system should be assigned to review the corresponding specifications whenever this is possible. However, it may not be clear in the early stages how many people will be needed for each part of the project.

A clear division of teams along the boundaries of subsystems and interfaces is desirable, because that usually reduces the need for communication between teams, increasing the overall efficiency of the development process. Since it is impractical to produce systems whose structure differs significantly from the structure of the development organization, some restraint is needed to keep organizational boundaries flexible until the structure of the proposed system stabilizes. In some projects, an arbitrary organizational structure is imposed by a management decree at the start of the project. This often leads to specifications and systems architectures whose structure reflects the arbitrary organizational structures used rather than the structure of the problem. Such architectures suffer from expensive system integration and maintenance problems in the long run, because of the lack of independent units in the code. For this reason the subsystems and interfaces should be identified as early as possible, and the organizational structure should be adjusted to match the structure of the proposed system, rather than vice versa.

When several different analysts are working concurrently on interacting interfaces of the same system, or on different messages in the same interface, it is important to communicate information about conceptual models and invariants as quickly as possible. This can be done with computer aid if a good design database is available. There should also be a clearly defined mechanism for resolving conflicting requirements on the conceptual models of the developing system, and a clear assignment of responsibility for the consistency of these models. In very large projects, it may be necessary to have a group of people dedicated to maintaining the consistency of the design. In future development environments for specifications, eventually this function may be largely automated.

3.7 User Manuals

Manuals include both printed information and online help facilities. Manuals are important because they provide the means for the users to learn how to use the system. It does not matter how efficient a system is or how powerful it is if it is not coherently documented, because the users will not be able to use the system to solve their problems.

The manuals should be derived from the functional specifications. The functional specifications define the commands available to the users, the expected responses, and the concepts needed to explain what the commands do. This is the information that should be contained in the reference manual for the system.

In addition to a reference manual, most systems should have a tutorial document for each class of users that explains how the available commands can be used to solve the user's problems. The main tasks of the tutorial writers are to determine how much a typical user is expected to know, and to organize the description of the system so that users can easily learn how to get the system to solve their problems.

The first task requires determining the most common problems the users have, and finding the sequences of commands that address those problems. The requirements document should contain some of this information in the environment model and the goal hierarchy, but additional interviews with users may be necessary to get all of the information needed. This process may result in a clearer understanding of the users' needs, in the form of scenarios for expected usage patterns for the system. The tutorial writers should cooperate with the group developing the test cases from the functional specifications in working out these scenarios. The scenarios should be fed back to the requirements analysis and functional specification activities for consistency checking. A common kind of fault that can be discovered at this stage is that some common user problems are not addressed by the set of commands described in the functional specification. Such a discovery should be brought to the attention of the user, and may lead to renegotiation of the scope of the development project. Draft copies of the manuals and tutorials should be reviewed by the customer as an additional validation step for the system.

The second task can be approached by organizing the manuals according to the principle of locality of information. It should be possible for a beginning user to start to use the system to solve the simpler and most common problems by reading only a short and clearly identifiable section of the tutorial, covering the most commonly used parts of the system. This may require working out some simplified models of the system that leave out the concepts and attributes needed to understand the more advanced features of the system. The more advanced capabilities of the system should be described later in the document, and each capability or closely related set of capabilities should be described in a short, self-contained section of the manual. Each section should consist of a brief introduction, a description of a related set of commands, and a set of examples showing how the commands can be used to realize the most common operations the users perform. Such manuals should have a thorough index that includes many of the common synonyms for the operations addressed by the commands of the system.

3.8 Logic

This section provides some of the mathematical background supporting the logical notation used in the rest of the chapter. The basic concepts of standard logic were reviewed in Section 2.2.3. In this section, we extend standard logic to include undefined values, introduce some simplification and transformation laws, define an extended set of quantifiers, and introduce some temporal operators. All of these extensions are useful for defining software systems.

3.8.1 Partial Operators and Three-Valued Logic

In software design, we have to be able to record the results of a design decision, even if some aspects of the design are only partially defined. We do this by introducing the value ! (undefined). There are two symbols in Spec for representing the logical value !: ? and ! . Spec has two different symbols for this value to reflect a difference in the way undefined quantities are treated in the software development process. When a ? appears as a part of a software specification, it represents an obligation to fill in a well defined value at some future time. Thus a completed design should not contain any instances of ? . When an ! appears as a part of a software specification, it represents a value that has been deliberately left undefined in a completed design. Either kind of undefined value should never appear during the operation of the system if there are no design errors. Operationally there is no distinction between the two kinds of undefined, so that ? = ! = !.

The logical undefined element ! can represent the result of an unknown choice between **true** or **false**, the result of a computation that does not terminate, or the truth value of a statement that is neither true nor false because the statement does not have a well defined meaning. For example, ! can represent the results of a partial operation that is undefined for a given assignment of values to variables, such as the expression $x > y / z$ when $z = 0$. The logic does not distinguish between different kinds of undefined values, and represents them all by the symbol !.

Most programming languages are based on a model of computation in which all of the actual arguments to an operation are evaluated before the calculation of the operation is started. This corresponds to the popular "call by value," "call by value-result," and "call by reference" mechanisms used by subprograms and task entries in Ada. Functions computed by such mechanisms are *strict*. A function is strict if its value is ! (undefined) whenever any of its arguments take the value !. An example of an operator that is not strict is the conditional if-then-else, which satisfies the following laws.

(if **true** then x else !) = x
(if **false** then ! else x) = x

These laws reflect the fact that the conditional evaluates only one of its arms, so that the expression in the other arm can be undefined without affecting the result. Our three-valued logic includes primitives that are not strict because they are designed to make it easy to describe software systems, rather than for efficient execution. The connectives of three-valued logic agree with the boolean operators of most programming languages if all operands are well defined, but take proper values in some cases in which the boolean operators of a programming language are undefined.

If we use the above interpretation of ! and the laws of Section 2.2.3 to extend the conventional logical operators, we get a three-valued logic, in which statements can take on the values **true**, **false**, and **!**. In cases where the result of an expression is the same whether a variable x takes on the value **true** or the value **false**, we say that the value of the expression is also the same when the variable x takes on the value **!**. In all other cases, the value of an expression containing a **!** is **!**. If we apply this policy to all of the logical connectives, we get the following truth tables.

~	
false	true
true	false
!	!

&	false	true	!
false	false	false	false
true	false	true	!
!	false	!	!

|	false	true	!
false	false	true	!
true	true	true	true
!	!	true	!

=>	false	true	!
false	true	true	true
true	false	true	!
!	!	true	!

<=>	false	true	!
false	true	false	!
true	false	true	!
!	!	!	!

These tables define the meaning of the connectives and let us calculate the truth values of compound logical statements if we know the truth values of the individual predicates in the statement.

Some programming languages have conditional boolean connectives that are halfway between the strict boolean connectives and the connectives of three-valued logic. In Ada, the strict boolean connectives are called "and" and "or," and the conditional connectives are called "and then" and "or else." These connectives satisfy the following laws, which show the differences between the strict and conditional connectives.

> **false** and **!** = **!**
> **true** or **!** = **!**

> **false** and then **!** = **false**
> **true** or else **!** = **true**

Thus the conditional connectives do not evaluate the second argument if the value of the first argument determines the value of the result, and can have a well defined value even if the evaluation of the second argument would diverge or abort the computation. For example, this can be useful for checking whether the index of an array is within range before looking up the corresponding value in the array, as in the Ada expression

```
i in a'range and then a(i) > 0.
```

The difference between the conditional connectives and the connectives of three-valued logic is shown by the following laws.

! and then **false** = !
! or else **true** = !

! & **false** = **false**
! | **true** = **true**

The logical connectives "&" and "|" are commutative, but the conditional Ada connectives "and then" and "or else" are not. In particular, the connectives of three-valued logic give proper values whenever one argument has a proper value sufficient to determine the results, without regard to the order of the arguments. This allows constraints that ensure a statement is well defined to be given in any order, and makes the properties of the connectives of standard two-valued logic more similar to the connectives of three-valued logic than to the conditional boolean connectives of Ada. For example, the Ada expression

```
a(i) > 0 & i in a'range
```

is well defined for all values of i, while the corresponding statement with an and then is not. The Ada primitives differ from those of three-valued logic because conditional connectives are more efficient to implement: An implementation of & and | would have to evaluate both arguments in parallel to be able to produce a proper value in the case where the evaluation of the first argument does not terminate but the second one does. Three-valued logic simplifies the process of specifying software because it relieves the analyst from the need to be careful about the order in which constraints involving partially defined operations are written. Many familiar programming primitives are partial operations: for example, divide, square root, read (from a file), index (of a pattern in a string), car and cdr (of a LISP list), top (of a stack), and so on.

Quantifiers are extended to the three-valued logic using the same policy we applied to the boolean connectives, with the assumption that data types contain only proper values; the undefined value ! does not belong to any data type. A universal quantifier is true if the enclosed logical statement is true for all possible proper values of the bound variables, is false if the enclosed statement is false for at least one assignment of proper values to the bound variables, and is undefined otherwise. Thus ALL(x: t :: p(x)) can be false even if $p(x) =$! for some value of x in the type t, provided that $p(x) = $ **false** for some other value of x in t. However, ALL(x: t :: p(x)) can be true only if $p(x)$ has a proper value ($p(x) \neq$!) for all the proper values in the type t. Similarly, an existential quantifier is true if the enclosed statement is true for at least one assignment of proper values to the bound variables, is false if the enclosed statement is false for all possible assignments of proper values to the bound variables, and is undefined otherwise. Thus `SOME(x: t :: p(x))` can be true even if $p(x)$ is undefined for some values of x in t, but can only be false if $p(x)$ is well defined (and false) for all values if x in t.

The universal and existential quantifiers are duals of each other both in two-valued logic and in three-valued logic. This means the following laws hold for all logical statements s:

```
~ALL(x: t :: s) = SOME(x: t :: ~s)
~SOME(x: t :: s) = ALL(x: t :: ~s)
```

3.8.2 Laws and Transformations

In software engineering we are interested in laws that let us simplify logical statements while preserving their meaning in all possible states. Such laws state that two logical statements with different forms are equal, written $p1 = p2$. Such a law means that logical statements $p1$ and $p2$ have the same value in all possible states, where a state is a mapping from variables to data values from the types associated with the variables. The equality used in such laws has the following properties.

> $p = p$
> if $p1 = p2$ then $p2 = p1$
> if $p1 = p2$ and $p2 = p3$ then $p1 = p3$
> if $p1 = p2$ then $E(p1) = E(p2)$

The first of these laws says any logical statement is equal to itself, and distinguishes equality from <=> because (! = !) = **true** but (! <=> !) = ! $\neq$ **true**. Equality is the same as <=> for completely defined logical statements. The second (symmetry) and third (transitivity) laws say simplifications can be performed by stringing together chains of equalities, without regard for the order in which the terms appear in each equality. The fourth (substitution) law says you can replace a part of a logical statement with another logical statement equal to the original part without affecting the meaning of the whole logical statement. This justifies the use of substitutions for subexpressions of a statement in the simplification process. A conditional law of the form

> if h_1 and ... and h_n then $p1 = p2$

means that $p1$ and $p2$ have the same value in all states where each of the hypotheses (the expressions h_i) has the value **true**.

There is nothing mysterious about three-valued logic. Many of the laws of ordinary two-valued logic are true for this three-valued logic. Some of the most useful laws that hold for both two-valued and three-valued logic are given below, with brief explanations.

$$(x \ \& \ y) \ \& \ z = x \ \& \ (y \ \& \ z) \quad (x \mid y) \mid z = x \mid (y \mid z)$$

These are the associative laws, that say that parentheses are not needed for conjunctions (&) or disjunctions (|), because such statements mean the same thing no matter how the parentheses are inserted.

$$(x \ \& \ y) \mid (x \ \& \ z) = x \ \& \ (y \mid z) \quad (x \mid y) \ \& \ (x \mid z) = x \mid (y \ \& \ z)$$

These are the distributive laws, that show that the placement of parentheses can affect the meaning of a statement if both kinds of connectives are mixed. In logic there are two distributive laws, unlike arithmetic, where there is only one. This reflects a fundamental symmetry between & and |. These laws can be used to simplify complicated statements by factoring out common subexpressions. The laws can also be used to simplify expressions by expanding them, provided that some of the terms generated in the expansion cancel out.

$$\tilde{}(x \ \& \ y) = (\tilde{}x) \mid (\tilde{}y) \quad \tilde{}(x \mid y) = (\tilde{}x) \ \& \ (\tilde{}y)$$

These are DeMorgan's laws. These laws state the fundamental symmetry between & and | more clearly: If you interchange **true** and **false**, and also & and |, any true statement remains true, any false statement remains false, and any undefined statement remains undefined. The duality laws for quantifiers given at the end of the previous section are related to DeMorgan's laws, because the universal quantifier is a repeated conjunction (&) with one term for each possible value for the bound variable, and an existential quantifier is a repeated disjunction (|). These laws can be used to move negations from large expressions to smaller ones, where they can sometimes be eliminated by the following law.

$$\tilde{\tilde{}}x = x$$

This is the law of double negation. Note that this law is oriented left to right: Replacing the left-hand side by the right-hand side produces an equivalent but shorter statement. This kind of law is called a simplification rule. Simplification rules are very useful in mechanical simplification, because they are always applied in one direction (from left to right), and always produce transformation sequences of finite length. Transformations using simplification rules are guaranteed to stop after a finite number of steps because of the length reduction at each step. The next several laws are also simplification rules.

$$x \ \& \ x = x \quad x \mid x = x$$

These are the idempotence laws, which allow you to drop multiple copies of the same statement in a conjunction or a disjunction.

$$(\textbf{false} => x) = \textbf{true} \quad (x => \textbf{true}) = \textbf{true}$$
$$(\textbf{true} => x) = x \quad (x => \textbf{false}) = {\tilde{}}x$$

These laws for simplifying implications are all consequences of the definition of $=>$ in terms of $|$ and $\tilde{}$.

$$x \,\&\, (x \,|\, y) = x \quad x \,|\, (x \,\&\, y) = x$$

These are the basic absorption laws. These laws may be easier to understand in terms of set theory and the stronger conditional absorption laws given next.

$$\text{if } x => y \text{ then } x \,\&\, y = x \quad \text{if } y => x \text{ then } x \,|\, y = x$$

The relationships between the logical connectives and set theory can be illustrated as follows. Suppose the sets S1 and S2 are defined by the relations below, where $p(x)$ and $q(x)$ are boolean-valued functions (predicates).

$$S1 = \{x\text{: any SUCH THAT } p(x) :: x\} \quad S2 = \{x\text{: any SUCH THAT } q(x) :: x\}$$

S1 is the set of all objects x in the universe for which the predicate $p(x)$ has the value **true**, and similarly for S2. In such a case the following relationships hold.

$$S1 \cap S2 = \{x\text{: any SUCH THAT } p(x) \,\&\, q(x) :: x\}$$
$$S1 \cup S2 = \{x\text{: any SUCH THAT } p(x) \,|\, q(x) :: x\}$$
$$S1 \subseteq S2 <=> \text{ALL}(x\text{: any} :: p(x) => q(x))$$

In terms of these relationships, the conditional absorption laws say the following.

$$\text{if } S1 \subseteq S2 \text{ then } S1 \cap S2 = S1$$
$$\text{if } S1 \subseteq S2 \text{ then } S1 \cup S2 = S2$$

These laws have simple intuitive interpretations: intersecting a set with one of its supersets does not change the set, and neither does taking the union of a set with one of its subsets.

An example of how these laws can be combined to generate new laws is shown below.

$x => (y => z) = {\tilde{}}x \,|\, (y => z)$	Definition of $=>$
${\tilde{}}x \,|\, (y => z) = {\tilde{}}x \,|\, ({\tilde{}}y \,|\, z)$	Definition of $=>$
${\tilde{}}x \,|\, ({\tilde{}}y \,|\, z) = ({\tilde{}}x \,|\, {\tilde{}}y) \,|\, z$	Associativity law for $|$
$({\tilde{}}x \,|\, {\tilde{}}y) \,|\, z = {\tilde{}}(x \,\&\, y) \,|\, z$	DeMorgan's law
${\tilde{}}(x \,\&\, y) \,|\, z = (x \,\&\, y) => z$	Definition of $=>$

$$x => (y => z) = (x \,\&\, y) => z \quad \text{Transitivity law for } =$$

The last line is the new law. A sequence of steps like this is called a derivation.

Each line in a derivation must follow from a known law and the previous steps in the derivation. Each step in the derivation uses a law that is valid in the three-valued logic; therefore, the new law holds for the three-valued logic as well. Because

$$(x => y) => z = (\tilde{}x \mid y) => z$$

by the definition of =>, we can see => is not associative. However, both => and <=> are transitive:

    if $x => y$ and $y => z$ then $x => z$
    if $x <=> y$ and $y <=> z$ then $x <=> z$

Another well known and useful law for implications is shown next.

    if x and $x => y$ then y

This law allows us to draw definite conclusions from conditional statements.

The following laws hold for two-valued logic, but they do not hold in the three-valued logic. These laws can be used to simplify expressions that are known to be completely defined. The laws can be used in predicate logic if **!** does not appear explicitly, and if all of the predicates and functions used are total (have well defined values for all possible inputs).

    $x \ \& \ \tilde{}x = $ **false** $x \mid \tilde{}x = $ **true**

These are known as the law of contradiction and the law of the excluded middle. These laws are sometimes used after an expansion via the distributive laws to cancel out pairs of terms, by first reducing them to the boolean constants **true** and **false**, and then eliminating the constants using the defining laws for & and |. These laws agree with common sense and have been used by logicians for many years, but it is worthwhile to notice that they do not hold for $x = $ **!**. This may be less surprising if we note a careless designer could replace **!** by a predicate such as "$a > b \ / \ 0$," which is always undefined, or a predicate such as "$a > b \ / \ c$," which is sometimes undefined.

    $x => x = $ **true** $x <=> x = $ **true**

The self-implication and self-equivalence laws show how to evaluate implications and equivalences between identical terms. These laws also do not hold for $x = $ **!**.

Before discussing some of the laws for quantifiers, we introduce an example that is used next to illustrate the use of the laws. The example also illustrates the use of logic for describing properties of software modules such as the desired outputs. Logical statements are usually built using the primitive attributes or operations of the data types involved. The meaning of these primitive operations can be defined by giving some laws the operations must satisfy, expressed as logical statements. For example, the length attribute of a sequence of elements of type *t* can be defined by the following predicates.

L1 `length([ ]) = 0`

L2 `ALL(x: t :: length([x]) = 1)`

L3 `ALL(s1 s2: sequence(t) ::`
  `    length(s1 || s2) = length(s1) + length(s2) )`

In the preceding example, [ ] is a constant representing the empty sequence, [*x*] represents the sequence containing the single element *x*, and || represents the sequence concatenation operation. These laws define the length attribute because all sequences can be generated by the empty sequence or finite concatenations of sequences of length one. Laws of this type are known as inductive or recursive definitions.

The most useful law for quantifiers is the substitution law for universal quantifiers, shown below.

if ALL(*x*: *t* :: *p*(*x*)) then *e* IN *t* => *p*(*e*)

This law holds for any expression *e*. Since the membership operation for types has the extended interpretation (**!** IN *t*) = **false**, the preceding law lets us conclude *p*(*e*) is true in any state that yields a proper data value of type *t*. The substitution law is useful for simplifying predicates and expressions. For example, the expression length(*s* || [*y*]) can be simplified as follows. We can substitute the expression *s* for the variable *s*1 and the expression [*y*] for the variable *s*2 in the predicate L3 to get

length(*s* || [*y*]) = length(*s*) + length([*y*])

Substituting *y* for *x* in L2 gives

length([*y*]) = 1

and applying the substitution law gives us the following simplification.

length(*s* || [*y*]) = length(*s*) + 1

Another set of laws that is sometimes useful is the following.

if ALL(*x*: *t* :: *p*(*x*)) then ALL(*y*: *t* :: *p*(*y*))
if SOME(*x*: *t* :: *p*(*x*)) then SOME(*y*: *t* :: *p*(*y*))

This set of laws is valid only if the variable *y* does not occur free in the predicate *p*(*x*). A free occurrence of a variable in an expression is an occurrence that is not bound by a quantifier contained in the expression. The bound variables of a quantifier are listed before the : : . These laws say that the bound variables of a quantifier can be renamed without affecting the meaning, provided that there are no name collisions. For example, the inner bound variable *x* cannot be renamed to *y* in the following predicate because of the free occurrence of *y* in $q(x, y)$.

```
ALL(y: t1 :: SOME(x: t2 :: q(x, y)))
```

The renaming can be done if the outer bound variable y is first renamed to z as shown next.

```
ALL(z: t1 :: SOME(y: t2 :: q(y, z)))
```

Similar laws for renaming bound variables also apply to the additional quantifiers introduced later.

3.8.3 Formal Definition of the Semantics of Logical Statements

This section contains a formal definition of the meaning of logical statements; you can skip it if you understood the informal explanations in the previous section, and if you are more interested in applications than in precise formulations of the logic.

The meaning of a predicate is specified with respect to a state. A state associates a value of some data type with each variable, and a mapping from an n-tuple of data types to another data type with each function name and predicate name. These values and mappings are known as *interpretations* for the variables, function names, and predicate names. The range of the interpretation of each predicate name must be the boolean data type consisting of the values **true** and **false** introduced in the previous section. The interpretation of a variable v, a function name f, and a predicate p in a state s is denoted by $s(v)$, $s(f)$, and $s(p)$ respectively.

The meaning $m(p, s)$ of a predicate p in the state s is defined as follows.

$m(v, s) = s(v)$
$m(\~p1, s) = \~m(p1, s)$
$m(p1 \,\&\, p2, s) = m(p1, s) \,\&\, m(p2, s)$
$m(p1 \mid p2, s) = m(p1, s) \mid m(p2, s)$
$m(p1 => p2, s) = m(p1, s) => m(p2, s)$
$m(p1 <=> p2, s) = m(p1, s) <=> m(p2, s)$
$m(p(e_1, \dots, e_n), s) = s(p)(m(e_1, s), \dots, m(e_n, s))$
$m(\text{ALL}(v: t :: p), s) = $ **true** if and only if $m(p, s1) = $ **true** for all states $s1$
  such that $s1(v)$ IN t and $s1(x) = s(x)$ if $x \neq v$
$m(\text{ALL}(v: t :: p), s) = $ **false** if and only if $m(p, s1) = $ **false** for at least one state $s1$
  such that $s1(v)$ IN t and $s1(x) = s(x)$ if $x \neq v$
$m(\text{SOME}(v: t :: p), s) = $ **true** if and only if $m(p, s1) = $ **true** for at least one state $s1$
  such that $s1(v)$ IN t and $s1(x) = s(x)$ if $x \neq v$
$m(\text{SOME}(v: t :: p), s) = $ **false** if and only if $m(p, s1) = $ **false** for all states $s1$
  such that $s1(v)$ IN t and $s1(x) = s(x)$ if $x \neq v$
$m(f(e_1, \dots, e_n), s) = s(f)(m(e_1, s), \dots, m(e_n, s))$

The meaning of a variable, whether it is boolean or of some other type, is given by the interpretation of the variable in the state. The meanings of the propositional connectives ˜, &, |, =>, and <=> are determined by finding the meanings of the subpropositions $p1$ and $p2$, which should be truth values, and combining them according to the rules given in the previous section. The meaning of a predicate or function call is determined by finding the meanings of the arguments and applying the mapping given by the interpretation of the predicate or function name in the state. The meaning of the universal quantifier ALL is true if and only if the enclosed predicate is true for all possible interpretations of the bound variable v in the specified data type t and is false if the enclosed predicate is false for at least one interpretation of the bound variable v. The meaning of the existential quantifier SOME is true if and only if the enclosed predicate is true for at least one interpretation of the bound variable v in the specified data type t and is false if the enclosed predicate is false for all possible interpretations of the bound variable v. The meaning of the quantifiers is ! (undefined) in all other cases.

3.8.4 Extended Quantifiers

The Spec language supports the universal and existential quantifiers familiar from logic as well as several less familiar ones, which were introduced in Section 3.2.1. In this section, we define the meaning of these quantifiers more carefully and give some of the laws they satisfy.

We discuss the set constructor first because all of the other quantifiers can be defined in terms of it. In general, quantifiers are used to describe properties of sets. The set constructor is explained informally in Section 3.2.1. Set constructors have the form

```
{x: t SUCH THAT p(x) :: f(x)},
```

and satisfy the following law.

```
ALL(y: any :: y IN {x: t SUCH THAT p(x) :: f(x)}
              <=> SOME(x: t :: p(x) & y = f(x)) )
```

A set constructor forms the set containing the value of $f(x)$ for all proper elements x of the data type t that satisfy the predicate $p(x)$. The range of values for the variable x includes only the defined objects of the type, excluding !, ?, and objects that have not yet been created. The resulting set is always a subset of the range of the function f augmented by the improper value !, and contains ! if f is undefined for at least one proper element x of t such that $p(x) = $ true. The predicate $p(x)$ can be replaced by any logical statement involving x, and the function $f(x)$ can be replaced by any expression involving x. The predicate can be left out if the variable ranges over all elements of the type, as illustrated:

```
{x: t SUCH THAT true :: f(x)} = {x: t :: f(x)}.
```

For example, the set of all even integers can be described by either of the following set constructors.

```
{x: integer :: 2 * x}
```

```
{x: integer SUCH THAT x MOD 2 = 0 :: x}
```

The following laws apply to the set constructor.

```
{x: t :: x} = t
```

```
{x: t SUCH THAT p1(x) :: x} U {y: t SUCH THAT p2(y) :: y}
   = {z: t SUCH THAT p1(z) | p2(z) :: z}
```

```
intersection({x: t SUCH THAT p1(x) :: x},
             {y: t SUCH THAT p2(y) :: y})
           = {z: t SUCH THAT p1(z) & p2(z) :: z}
```

The first law says the set of all elements of a type is the same as the type. The last two laws show how to form unions and intersections of constructed sets.

The most familiar quantifiers are ALL and SOME. These can be defined in terms of the set constructor as follows.

```
ALL(x: t SUCH THAT p1(x) :: p2(x))
   =   ({p2(x) :: x IN t & p1(x)} ⊆ {true})
```

```
SOME(x: t SUCH THAT p1(x) :: p2(x))
   =   (true IN {p2(x) :: x IN t & p1(x)})
```

In the above expressions, the range of $p2$ must be boolean, and $p2(x)$ can be replaced by any logical statement. This definition agrees with the standard interpretation for the universal and existential quantifiers. The universal quantifier ALL says $p2(x)$ must be **true** for all values of x for which $p1(x)$ is true. The existential quantifier SOME says $p2(x)$ must be **true** for at least one value of x for which $p1(x)$ is true. The set constructor in the definitions produces a set containing boolean values. Note that all of the sets in the definitions of the quantifiers ALL and SOME are finite, because there can be at most three distinct values produced by the predicate $p(x)$: **true**, **false**, and **!**. The AND combination of such a set is **true** if all of the values in the set are **true**; the OR combination of such a set is **true** if at least one of the values in the set is **true**. An ALL quantifier over an empty set is **true**, and a SOME quantifier over an empty set is false. An ALL quantifier over a set containing **!** is false if the set contains false and is **!** otherwise. A SOME quantifier over a set containing **!** is **true** if the set contains **true** and is **!** otherwise.

The ALL and SOME quantifiers obey these laws:

ALL(x: t SUCH THAT $p\,1(x)$ :: $p\,2(x)$) = ALL(x: t :: $p\,1(x)$ => $p\,2(x)$)

SOME(x: t SUCH THAT $p\,1(x)$ :: $p\,2(x)$) = SOME(x: t :: $p\,1(x)$ & $p\,2(x)$)

~ALL(x: t SUCH THAT $p\,1(x)$ :: $p\,2(x)$)
    = SOME(x: t SUCH THAT $p\,1(x)$ :: ~$p\,2(x)$)

~SOME(x: t SUCH THAT $p\,1(x)$ :: $p\,2(x)$)
    = ALL(x: t SUCH THAT $p\,1(x)$ :: ~$p\,2(x)$)

ALL(x: t SUCH THAT $p\,1(x)$ :: $p\,2(x)$ & $p\,3(x)$)
    = ALL(y: t SUCH THAT $p\,1(y)$ :: $p\,2(y)$)
      & ALL(z: t SUCH THAT $p\,1(z)$ :: $p\,3(z)$)

SOME(x: t SUCH THAT $p\,1(x)$ :: $p\,2(x)$ | $p\,3(x)$)
    = SOME(y: t SUCH THAT $p\,1(y)$ :: $p\,2(y)$)
      | SOME(z: t SUCH THAT $p\,1(z)$ :: $p\,3(z)$)

The first two laws explain the relation between restricted quantifiers and unrestricted quantifiers. Note the difference between the two cases. The next two laws are the generalized version of DeMorgan's Laws, which govern the interaction between the quantifiers and logical negation. The last two laws show the cases in which a complex quantifier can be split into two simpler ones. These two laws are valid only if the variable names y and z do not occur as free variables in the predicates $p1(x)$, $p2(x)$, and $p3(x)$. The analogous laws for ALL and | or SOME and & do not hold.

The NUMBER quantifier can be defined as follows.

NUMBER(x: t SUCH THAT $p(x)$ :: $f(x)$)
    = size(\{x: t SUCH THAT $p(x)$ :: $f(x)$\})

This quantifier counts the number of distinct values in the constructed set. The range of the function f can be any data type with an equality operation. The result of the NUMBER quantifier is a natural number. The NUMBER of an empty set is zero. The NUMBER of a finite set containing ! is one more than the number of proper elements in the set. The NUMBER of an infinite set is ! (undefined). Some examples are shown next.

NUMBER(x: integer SUCH THAT -5 <= x <= 5 :: x) = 11

NUMBER(x: integer SUCH THAT -5 <= x <= 5 :: $x\,\hat{}\,2$) = 6

The SUM and PRODUCT quantifiers require that the value of $f(x)$ be of some data type with + and * operations that are both associative and commutative. Some of the data types with these properties are integer, rational, real, and complex. These two quantifiers can be defined as follows.

SUM(x: t SUCH THAT p(x) :: f(x))= $\displaystyle\sum_{x\epsilon t \& p(x)} f(x)$

PRODUCT(x: t SUCH THAT p(x) :: f(x))= $\displaystyle\prod_{x\epsilon t \& p(x)} f(x)$

These quantifiers correspond to the familiar summation and product notations used in most mathematics books. The SUM of the empty set is zero, and the PRODUCT of the empty set is one. The value of a divergent SUM or PRODUCT is !. The value of a SUM or PRODUCT with an undefined term is !. Some examples of these quantifiers are:

SUM(x: nat :: 0.5 ^ x) = 2.0

PRODUCT(x: integer SUCH THAT 1 <= x <= 4 :: x) = 24.

The first example is the sum of an infinite geometric series, and the second example is an instance of the factorial function.

The UNION and INTERSECTION quantifiers require that the range of f have pairwise union and intersection operations that are associative and commutative. For example, these quantifiers apply to any instantiation of the generic types set and relation. These quantifiers can be defined as follows.

UNION(x: t SUCH THAT p(x) :: f(x))= $\displaystyle\bigcup_{x\epsilon t \& p(x)} f(x)$

INTERSECTION(x: t SUCH THAT p(x) :: f(x))= $\displaystyle\bigcap_{x\epsilon t \& p(x)} f(x)$

The UNION of the empty set is the empty set. The INTERSECTION of the empty set is the entire type t. The UNION or INTERSECTION of a set with an undefined element is !. Some examples of these quantifiers are:

UNION(x: nat :: {y: nat SUCH THAT y < x :: y}) = nat

INTERSECTION(p: person SUCH THAT invited(p)
                :: free_hours(p)).

The first example states that the set of all finite initial subranges of the natural numbers covers the entire set of natural numbers. The second example describes the set of times at which all of the invited people do not have existing commitments. Such a set is useful for describing systems for scheduling meetings. The function free_hours(p) is assumed to return the set of hour-long time slots during which the person p has no activities scheduled.

The MAXIMUM and MINIMUM quantifiers require that $f(x)$ be of some data type t with a <= operation that is a partial order. These quantifiers can be defined as follows.

```
MAXIMUM(x: t SUCH THAT p(x) :: f(x))
    = lub {f(x) :: x IN t & p(x)}
MINIMUM(x: t SUCH THAT p(x) :: f(x))
    = glb {f(x) :: x IN t & p(x)}
```

The symbol `lub` stands for the least upper bound or supremum of standard mathematics; `glb` stands for the greatest lower bound, or infimum. These quantifiers are well defined in all situations if the data type `t` is a complete lattice with respect to the `<=` operation, which means that every subset of the data type must have a least upper bound and a greatest lower bound. An example of a complete lattice is a closed interval of numbers, such as `{r: real SUCH THAT 0.0 <= r <= 1.0 :: r}`. If the least upper bound of the constructed set does not exist, then the value of the `MAXIMUM` quantifier is `!`. If the greatest lower bound of the constructed set does not exist, then the value of the `MINIMUM` quantifier is `!`. The `MAXIMUM` of the empty set is the `MINIMUM` of the entire data type. The `MINIMUM` of the empty set is the `MAXIMUM` of the entire data type. The `MAXIMUM` or `MINIMUM` of a set with an undefined element is `!`. Some examples of these quantifiers are shown next.

```
MAXIMUM(e: employee SUCH THAT e.dept = "sales"
        :: e.salary)
MINIMUM(r: route SUCH THAT
        origin(r) = a & destination(r) = b :: cost(r))
```

The first example represents the highest salary earned by anyone in the sales department. The second example is the cost of the cheapest route from *a* to *b*.

To summarize, a quantifier specifies a set of values, and combines those values via some operation. Quantifiers are related to the reduction operator of APL: `ALL` is an and-reduction, `SOME` is an or-reduction, `SUM` is a plus-reduction, and so on. The Spec types `set` and `sequence` have a `reduce` operation similar to the reduction operation of APL (Appendix D). The difference between the logical quantifiers and the corresponding reduction operators in a programming language is that the quantifiers can have well defined values even if the ranges of the bound variables are not finite, and programming language operators are usually defined only for finite ranges. Spec definitions of the predefined quantifiers discussed in this section are given in the definition module `quantifiers` at the end of Appendix C. Additional quantifiers can be defined by the designer as needed (see the last exercise at the end of this chapter).

3.8.5 Temporal Operators

Sometimes it is necessary to talk about properties of the system that involve more than one point in time, or more than one state. If we are willing to make the time an explicit argument to all functions and predicates, this can be done using ordinary logic. However, a kind of modal logic called temporal logic has been developed that supports statements about properties of different states without requiring explicit arguments representing the time at which each statement is true. We adopt this approach because introducing arguments representing time into all predicates, including those that are not sensitive to the time, is artificial and adds unnecessary complexity.

There is more than one kind of temporal logic. Because software modules can be potentially nondeterministic, we use a branching-time logic rather than a linear-time logic. The model underlying such a logic allows nondeterministic state transitions, so that there can be several possible next states for a given starting state. The past is determined, so that in such a model there is a single chain of past states. In Spec, logical predicates are used to describe the behavior of a module in terms of events at that module only, and the events occurring at a single module are totally ordered: They occur in a well defined sequence, without any observable concurrency. Events at different modules can be concurrent, but such events cannot be compared directly in the specification of a single module. Thus it is appropriate to use a logic in which past states are totally ordered. Approaches to specifications that are based on global states rather than localized states need temporal logics in which events are partially ordered, to describe pairs of events whose relative order in time is not determined.

Temporal logic extends predicate logic by adding a set of temporal operators. There are two basic operators that apply to expressions, `previous` and `next`. Syntactically these operators look like functions. The expression `previous(e)` represents the value of the expression *e* in the previous state. In Spec `previous(e)` can also be written as `*e`. This operator is used extensively to specify state machines and mutable types. Since the previous state is unique if it exists, the `previous` operator can be treated as a partial function. The initial state of a machine or type has no previous state, and satisfies the following law:

```
ALL(x: any :: *x = !)
```

that says that the value of every object in the previous state is undefined. This implies that * can be used in invariants only if it is guarded by a constraint that ensures that the * is well defined, as illustrated in the following example.

```
INVARIANT ALL(e: employee SUCH THAT *e ~= !
              :: e.salary >= *e.salary)
```

The * operator is used much more frequently than the other operators defined next, and is sufficient for specifying many systems. The rest of this section discusses operators needed by more advanced applications, and can be skipped on a first reading.

The operator `next(e)` represents the value of the expression *e* in the next state. There can be several different next states for nondeterministic operations. A predicate containing instances of `next(e)` is true only if the predicate is satisfied by the value of the expression *e* in all states that can occur immediately following the current state. A nondeterministic operation can have more than one possible next state, but the next state of a deterministic operation is unique. A module has a final state if it has a finite computation history. The final state of a module has no next state, and satisfies the following law,

```
ALL(x: any :: next(x) = !)
```

which says that the value of every object in the next state is undefined. This operator is used relatively rarely in module specifications because the response of a module usually depends only on the current and past states, rather than on future states.

The operators `next` and `previous` can also be applied to entire logical statements, with the interpretation that the statement must be true in the next state or the previous state, respectively.

For some applications, it is necessary to refer to more remote states than just the current state, the immediately preceding state, and the immediately following state. The `next` and `previous` operators can also have parameters that restrict attention only to events of a particular kind or refer to events farther in the past or future via an index. The operator `previous{name: identifier}` refers to the state just before the arrival of the most recently received message with the given name, and the operator `next{name: identifier}` refers to the state just after the arrival of the next future message with the given name. The indexed versions of the operators `previous{index: nat}`, `previous{name: identifier, index: nat}`, `next{index: nat}`, and `next{name: identifier, index: nat}` can refer to events that are more remote in time that are defined by fixed offsets relative to the current state. These operators satisfy the following laws.

```
previous{0}(e) = e
previous{n+1}(e) = previous(previous{n}(e))

previous{id, 0}(e) = e
previous{id, n+1}(e) = previous{id}(previous{id, n}(e))

next{0}(e) = e
next{n+1}(e) = next(next{n}(e))

next{id, 0}(e) = e
next{id, n+1}(e) = next{id}(next{id, n}(e))
```

Previous and next are the local temporal operators in our logic.

Our logic also contains the following global temporal operators:

henceforth, eventually, so_far, has_been, always, and sometime. The statement henceforth(s) means *s* is true in the current state
and will continue to be true in all possible future states. The statement
eventually(s) means *s* is true now or will be true in some future state, for
all possible choices of future computation paths. These two operators satisfy
the following laws.

```
henceforth(s) => s & (next(true) => next(henceforth(s)))
eventually(s) => s | (next(true) & next(eventually(s)))
```

The guard next(true) ensures that the laws have the proper meaning in the
final state, in which next is undefined. These two operators are not (in general) duals of each other, due to the possibility of nondeterminism:
eventually(s) means *s* is guaranteed to become true no matter what
choices are made by all nondeterministic operations; ˜henceforth(˜s)
means that it is possible for *s* to become true for some possible choices by the
nondeterministic operators, but there is no guarantee that these choices will
actually be taken. In systems with only deterministic operations, the above distinction disappears, so that henceforth and eventually become duals in
such contexts. We have defined these operators to correspond to the most
likely needs of analysts and software engineers, rather than to give the simplest
mathematical formulation.

The statement so_far(s) means *s* is true now and was true in all past
states. The statement has_been(s) means *s* is true now or was true in some
past state. These two operators are duals, since they satisfy the following laws:

```
˜so_far(s) = has_been(˜s)
˜has_been(s) = so_far(˜s)
```

The statements always(s) and sometime(s) are defined by the following
laws:

```
always(s) = so_far(s) & henceforth(s)
sometime(s) = has_been(s) | eventually(s)
```

Some other authors use always and sometime to mean henceforth and
eventually, as defined previously.

The always operator is useful in expressing global invariance properties,
and is implicit in the Spec keyword INVARIANT. It is also useful in defining
concepts such as Immutable for the type type (Appendix D). Future operators such as next and henceforth can be useful to express the effect of an
operation on future state changes. For example, in a version control system, the
operation that freezes a version should have the effect of preventing any future
changes to the version. This can be expressed as henceforth(x =
next(x)). Eventually is useful for describing guarantees of service, such
as expressing that a scheduling policy must avoid starvation.

3.9 Spec Language Issues

This section contains a more detailed description of the properties of the Spec language, and is intended as reference material for answering detailed technical questions about the language. This section can be skipped on a first reading.

3.9.1 Name-Scoping Rules

Names in the Spec language can have carefully controlled scopes. The scoping rules define the region of text in which a name is visible. These rules are given next, going from least restrictive to most restrictive.

1. The names of modules, messages and exceptions are global. Message names in expressions may need an @module_name qualifier to uniquely identify the intended operation.

2. The names of concepts are visible only in the module in which they are defined and its descendents, unless they are explicitly exported in an EXPORT clause. The *descendents* of a module *m* are the modules that inherit *m*, either directly or indirectly. The names of concepts that are explicitly exported are also visible inside other modules that explicitly import those names using an IMPORT clause. The scope of a concept is the entire specification of each module in which the concept is visible according to the above rules. Only the names of concepts can be exported and imported.

3. The component names of the MODEL of a type and the component names of the STATE of a machine are visible in the entire specification of the module in which these names are defined, and the specifications of any of its descendents.

4. The scope of the formal parameters of a generic module is the entire specification of the module. The formal parameters are not visible in the descendents of the module, since only instances of generic modules can be inherited. The formal parameters of the generic module are replaced by the actual parameters used to specify the inherited instance.

5. The scope of the formal arguments and formal parameters of a message is the entire specification of that message.

6. The scope of the formal arguments of a REPLY, SEND, or GENERATE and any local variables declared in a CHOOSE extends from the point where the variables are declared to the end of the WHEN or OTHERWISE clause in which they are declared. If there is no WHEN or OTHERWISE, the scope of

the variables extends from the point where they are declared to the end of the message specification.

7. The scope of the variables bound to a quantifier extends from the "(" following the name of the quantifier to the matching ")".

All identifiers in Spec must fall into one of the preceding categories. In particular, specifications may not contain any free variables.

3.9.2 Overloading and Type Conversions

Spec allows names to be overloaded. This means that several different modules or operations visible in the same scope can have the same name, provided they have different *signatures*. The signature of an individual module consists of its name. The signature of a message or concept consists of its name and the sequence of types of its arguments. The signature of a generic module, concept, or message also includes the sequence of types of its generic parameters, which is distinct from the sequence of argument types. Modules and concepts are uniquely identified by their signatures. Messages are uniquely identified by their signature and the signature of the module in which they are defined. Exception names can be overloaded in the same way as message names. Exceptions in Spec can have generic parameters and arguments, just like other kinds of messages.

Messages defined in different modules can have the same names without any restrictions. A message can be used in an expression with the explicit form `message@module(argument, ... , argument)`, which specifies both the message and the module to which the message is to be sent. For generic modules, the explicit form must include the generic parameters, as in `message@module{parameter, ... , parameter}(argument, ... , argument)`. The explicit form applies to messages but not to concepts.

Because the explicit form can get long, expressions in Spec can also have an abbreviated implicit form `operator(argument, ... , argument)`. The implicit form can refer to either concepts or messages, and can be used only if there is a unique candidate operation with the given signature. The candidate operations consist of global function modules, the concepts visible in the module containing the implicit form, all of the messages defined in or inherited by that module, and all of the messages defined in or inherited by the types of the arguments to the implicit form. If there are no candidates, then there is either a missing definition or a missing `IMPORT` or `EXPORT`. If there is more than one candidate, then the implicit form is illegal due to ambiguity, and an explicit form must be used to specify which of the candidate operations is intended. To summarize, the implicit short form can be used only if it would be unambiguous.

Variants of the operations defined, inherited, or imported in a module are implicitly generated by the type conversions defined in the module. These variants are included in the candidate operations for the implicit expression form discussed above. Implicit variants are generated for both messages and concepts. Only locally defined and inherited type conversions can generate implicit variants of operations. A *type conversion* is a message of the form

```
MESSAGE type1_to_type2(x: type1)
REPLY (y: type2)
```

where the name of the message contains the names of the two types being converted. A type conversion such as the one just shown induces a variant for each message with an argument of type `type2`, and the corresponding argument of the generated variant has type `type1`. The meaning of the generated variant is defined by first applying the conversion to the argument to convert it to `type2`, and then applying the explicitly defined operation. Conversions apply also to generated variants, so that multiple conversions can be applied to either the same or different arguments of an operation. Conversions are intended primarily for mixed-mode arithmetic, but they can also be applied to any pair of user-defined data types where one type can be viewed as a subset of the other. Type conversions must be designed with care to avoid generating multiple definitions for the same signature.

3.9.3 Import and Export

Only concepts can be imported and exported by modules. A concept can only be imported from an individual module. To import a concept from a generic module, you have to specify actual values for the generic parameters to identify one of its instances. The actual parameters can be expressions involving formal parameters of the module importing the concept.

A concept can only be exported by the module in which it was defined. Imported concepts cannot be exported. Inherited concepts can be exported only if they are refined by a locally defined concept or renamed.

A concept can be imported only if another concept with the same signature has not been defined locally or inherited. The meaning of an imported concept is given by the imported definition. Unlike an inherited concept, an imported concept cannot be refined by a local definition with the same signature. Refinements of imported concepts must have different names.

Concepts are imported and exported by name, so that all versions of overloaded concepts are imported and exported as a block.

3.9.4 Consistency and Completeness Constraints

The *unique definition* constraint allows only one definition of a concept or message with the same signature to be visible in any of the modules in a well formed specification. The signature of an operation is defined in Section 3.9.2, and is determined by the name of the operation and the sequence of argument types. The number of arguments and the order of the argument types is significant in determining the signature. The names of the formal parameters, the names and conditions of the responses, and the names and types of the result parameters are not part of the signature. Because two distinct operations with the same signature cannot be visible at the same place, the type and condition of the reply are determined by the operation's signature and the input data. Constants are treated as operations with empty sequences of arguments. It is legal for a module and a constant to have the same signature. Two different constants with the same name cannot be defined, inherited, or imported into the same module, even if the constants have different types.

The definition consistency constraint implies some concepts may have to be renamed before they can be imported or inherited. Suppose you want to import the concept c from the module m, but you have already defined a local concept with the same name and argument types, but with a different meaning. You can either change the name of the local concept, or rename the imported one. If you have chosen a good name for your local definition, it is better to rename the imported definition. This can be done by creating a new module that inherits m, as shown next for the case where m is a function:

```
FUNCTION new_m
  INHERIT m RENAME c AS new_c
END
```

The renamed concept can be imported as follows.

```
IMPORT new_c FROM new_m
```

The *import consistency* constraint says that a concept can be imported from another module only if the other module defines and EXPORTs the concept.

The *type consistency* constraints of the Spec language are the following.

1. For each expression using prefix functional form with an @module qualifier, the specified module must define or inherit a message matching the types of the actual parameters and actual arguments.

2. For each expression using infix operators or prefix functional form without an @module qualifier, there must be exactly one candidate operation matching the types of the actual parameters and actual arguments (see Section 3.9.2).

3. Arguments and parameters in Spec are always specified by position. When names are given for the actual arguments or parameters, the names must match the names of the corresponding formal arguments or parameters. For example, the form map{from:: t1, to:: t2} is legal, but the form map{to:: t2, from:: t1} is not.

4. The types of the expressions following a WHERE, WHEN, SUCH THAT, or IF must be *boolean*.

5. All of the cases of a conditional expression must produce the same type of value.

6. The types of the generating expression following the :: of a quantifier must match the type requirements of the quantifier. These type requirements are summarized in Fig. 3.58. Additional semantic constraints on the types of generating expressions are given in Section 3.8.4.

7. For each operation with a variable number of parameters, there must be a unique correspondence between the actual parameters and the formal parameters. For example, the expressions f(x:: 1, y:: 2, b:: 3) and f(x:: 1, b:: 2, y:: 3) are legal for the message MESSAGE f($a: nat, b: nat, $c: nat), but the expression f(1, 2, 3) is not, because the formal parameter *a* could be bound to any of the sequences [ ], [1], or [1, 2].

8. All of the normal REPLY clauses of the same message must be of the same type.

9. All of the REPLY clauses of the same message with the same exception condition must be of the same type.

Quantifier	Type of Generating Expression
ALL	boolean
SOME	boolean
NUMBER	any type
SUM	any type with +
PRODUCT	any type with *
MAXIMUM	any type with <=
MINIMUM	any type with <=
UNION	any type with union
INTERSECTION	any type with intersection

FIGURE 3.58
Quantifier Type Requirements

10. The definition of each message used in an expression must not contain any TRANSITION clauses.

The *instance consistency* constraints require the actual parameters of an instance of a generic module to satisfy any conditions mentioned in a SUCH THAT clause in the generic parameter declaration. Some of these constraints can be difficult to check. Checking instance consistency can involve proving some difficult theorems and is an undecidable problem in the general case. An instance consistency checking tool can perform the easier checks, and print out a list of the constraints that must be checked but could not be decided by the tool.

The *input coverage* constraints require every concept to have proper values for all possible inputs satisfying the precondition and require the WHERE and TRANSITION clauses of each message to have proper values for all states and input values satisfying the associated preconditions. The extended interpretation of & and | is important for input coverage (Section 3.8.1). For example, both of the predicates $x > 0 \ \& \ y = z \ / \ x$ and $y = z \ / \ x \ \& \ x > 0$ are well defined in all states because of the law (**false** & **!**) = **false** = (**!** & **false**). The precondition of a concept is true unless explicitly stated otherwise. An example of a concept with a precondition is type_of in the predefined type union{$ts} (Appendix D).

Each message and concept definition should be *satisfiable*. A concept is satisfiable if, for all values of the input parameters, there exist values of the output parameters for which the predicates in the WHERE clauses are true. A message is satisfiable if, for all values of the input parameters satisfying the precondition of each WHEN clause and the invariants of the module, there exist values for the output parameters satisfying the postconditions and the invariants; there exist values for the local CHOOSE variables satisfying the associated restrictions; and there exist values for the state variables satisfying the TRANSITION predicates and the invariants. Checking satisfiability can involve proving some difficult theorems and is an undecidable problem in the general case.

The deterministic messages and concepts of a type are subject to *congruence consistency* constraints. Concepts and messages have *congruence consistency* if they mean the same thing for all equivalent conceptual representations. Two conceptual representations are equivalent if they represent the same instance of the type, as determined by its equal operation. Congruence consistency is trivial for types with unique conceptual representations or without an equal operation. For example, consider a representation of the rational numbers as ratios of pairs of integers that are not necessarily reduced to lowest terms. The congruence consistency constraint would fail for an operation num that returned the numerator component of the model: if the model of x is the pair [1, 2] and the model of y is the pair [2, 4] then $x = y$ but num(x) = 1 $\neq$ 2 = num(y). This example shows that an operation on an abstract type that lacks congruence consistency can appear to be nondeterministic even if the operations on the concrete representations are deterministic. Congruence consistency is a useful thing to check because the operations of most abstract data types are intended to be deterministic. Operations that are intended to be nondeterministic, such as "choose an arbitrary element of a set," should be explicitly marked as nondeterministic to enable a congruence consistency checking tool to avoid spurious error messages.

Modules with atomic transactions should be free of *deadlock* and *starvation*. Deadlock is a situation in which several modules are in a control state where each is waiting for a response from one of the others, and there are no messages in transit. A set of modules in this state can accept no further messages, which is clearly undesirable. A set of modules is free from deadlock if there is no reachable state in which the modules are deadlocked. Starvation is a situation in which messages have been sent that cannot be accepted by the destination module because it is in the middle of a nonterminating atomic transaction. A system is free from starvation if there can be no nonterminating atomic transactions. An atomic transaction can fail to terminate because it contains an infinite number of events, because of a deadlock, or because the response to some event has an infinite delay. The first two cases are properties of the specification whose absence can be checked; the last case can arise only for implementations that do not conform to the specification, because every specified response must be produced in a finite time by a correct implementation.

A completed specification should contain no instances of ? .

3.9.5 Inheritance

The Spec language has an inheritance mechanism that can be used for view integration and for specifying constraints common to the interfaces of many modules. View integration is useful because the interface of a module to each user class can be usefully defined as a separate view of the module, perhaps by different designers. A total picture of the module is then formed by inheriting all of the individual views. Specifying constraints common to many interfaces is essential for achieving interface consistency in very large systems.

A module can inherit the messages, concepts, and model or states of another module. Inheritance is illustrated by the following example. Consider the simple data type shown in Fig. 3.59. This data type inherits properties of the `equal` operation from the generic virtual type `equality` shown in Fig. 3.60. The definition of `name` shown in Fig. 3.59, which inherits `equality`, is equivalent to the expanded definition shown in Fig. 3.61, which does not contain any explicit inheritance. We have expanded the previous definition of `name` by inserting the implicitly inherited parts of the definition from `equality`. The models and the invariants of the original module and those of its ancestors are combined. The properties of the `equal` operation from the `name`

```
TYPE name
  INHERIT equality(name)
  MODEL(s: string)
  INVARIANT ALL(n: name :: length(n.s) > 0)

  MESSAGE create(text: string)
    WHEN length(text) > 0
      REPLY(n: name) WHERE n.s = text
    OTHERWISE REPLY EXCEPTION empty_name

  MESSAGE equal(n1 n2: name)
    REPLY(b: boolean)
      WHERE b <=> n1.s = n2.s
END
```

FIGURE 3.59
Simple Data Type

type have been combined with the properties of the `equal` operation from
`equality`. Note the actual type `name` has been substituted for the formal
parameter `t` of the generic module `equality`. Such actual parameters must
be provided whenever a generic module is inherited. In this example, the
definition of `equal` in the `equality` module does not mention the message
parameters `x` and `y` or the reply parameter `b`. If there had been references to
these parameters, they would have been renamed as needed to match the
corresponding message parameters `n1` and `n2` and the reply parameter `b` of the
`equal` operation of the `name` module. The definition of the `not_equal`
operation and the concepts `Reflexive`, `Strongly_reflexive`, `Sym-`
`metric`, `Transitive`, `Identity_relation`, and `Eternal` have been
inherited from the `equality` module without any changes, because these
definitions do not involve the generic parameter `t` and their names and interfaces do not match any of those in the `name` module. The aspects of a module
that can *not* be inherited are its name, its generic formal parameters, and its
`EXPORT` list.

In the general case, the expanded module definition contains the union of
the features of the original module definition and its ancestors. In this context,
`feature` refers to either messages, concepts, model components, or state components. Any module can inherit a function, but only types can inherit other
types and only machines can inherit other machines. These restrictions are
needed because the same module cannot simultaneously act both as a type and
as a machine. Formal parameters, and formal arguments in `MESSAGE`, `REPLY`,
`GENERATE`, and `SEND` statements are renamed as necessary to make the names
in the ancestors consistent with the names in the definition to be expanded. The

FIGURE 3.60
Inherited Virtual Type

```
VIRTUAL TYPE equality (t: type)
  EXPORT Reflexive Symmetric Transitive Identity_relation Eternal

  MESSAGE equal(x y: t)   -- Weak equality, can be computed.
    REPLY(b: boolean)
    WHERE Reflexive(equal), Symmetric(equal), Transitive(equal),
      Identity_relation(equal),
        -- Equals can be substituted for equals.
      Eternal(equal)
        -- If two objects are equal,
        -- they are equal in all states.

  MESSAGE not_equal(x y: t)
    REPLY(b: boolean) WHERE b <=> ~equal(x, y)

  CONCEPT "="(x y: t) VALUE(b: boolean)
      -- Strong logical equality, not computable.
    WHERE Strongly_reflexive("="),
        -- (! = !) = true but equal(!, !) = !
      ALL(x y: t :: (x = y) <=> equal(x, y))
        -- "=" is the same as "equal" for all well defined
        -- data values.

  CONCEPT "~="(x y: t) VALUE(b: boolean)
      -- Strong logical inequality, not computable.
    WHERE b <=> ~(x = y)

  CONCEPT Reflexive(f: function(t, t, boolean)) VALUE(b: boolean)
    WHERE b <=> ALL(x: t :: f(x, x))
      -- x ranges over well defined values of type t.

  CONCEPT Strongly_reflexive(f: function(t, t, boolean))
    VALUE(b: boolean)
    WHERE b <=> Reflexive(f) & f(!, !)
      -- Reflexive also for the undefined element "!".

  CONCEPT Symmetric(f: function(t, t, boolean)) VALUE(b: boolean)
    WHERE b <=> ALL(x y: t :: f(x, y) => f(y, x))

  CONCEPT Transitive(f: function(t, t, boolean))
    VALUE(b: boolean)
    WHERE b <=> ALL(x y z: t :: f(x, y) & f(y, z) => f(x, z))

  CONCEPT Identity_relation(f: function(t, t, boolean))
    VALUE(b: boolean)
```

```
WHERE b <=>
    ALL(a b: t, ts1 ts2: sequence(type), s1: ts1, s2: ts2,
        range: type, g: function($ts1, t, $ts2, range) ::
        f(a, b) => g($s1, a, $s2) = g($s1, b, $s2) )
            -- If f(x, y) there is no way
            -- to distinguish x from y.
            -- This means x and y are identical,
            -- so you can substitute x for y.

CONCEPT Eternal(f: function(t, t, boolean)) VALUE(b: boolean)
    WHERE b <=> ALL(a b: t :: f(a, b) => always(f(a, b)))
        -- This means the relation f cannot be affected by
        -- state changes.
END
```

---

correspondence is established via the order in which the parameters or arguments appear. If there is more than one feature with the same name in the primary module and its ancestors, all of the definitions of each feature that share the same name are merged, according to the following rules.

1. Components with parts are merged by merging corresponding parts. Components of a STATE or MODEL are matched up by name. Messages and concepts are matched up by signature (name and sequence of argument types). Parameters and arguments are matched by position.

2. Type specifications are merged according to the following laws.

> if Subtype(x, y) then merge(x, y) = x
> if ~(Subtype(x, y) or Subtype(y, x)) then merge(x, y) = !

The result of merging a type with one of its subtypes is the subtype. Recall that ! is an error value. Two different type specifications are considered to be inconsistent unless one of them is is a subtype of the other. As a special case, merge(x, x) = x since each type is a subtype of itself. Because messages and concepts are matched up by signature, and predicates are merged by conjunction (see the following cases), type specifications are merged only for declarations of output variables, STATE components, and MODEL components. This allows a constraining interpretation for type merging without introducing antimonotonicity problems for input variables.

3. Predicates are merged according to the following rule.

> merge(p, q) = p & q

The simplifications p & p = p, p & true = p, and p & false = false are sometimes helpful.

FIGURE 3.61
Expansion of Simple Data Type

```
TYPE name
  MODEL(s: string)
  INVARIANT ALL(n: name :: length(n.s) > 0), true

  MESSAGE create(text: string)
    WHEN length(text) > 0
      REPLY(n: name) WHERE n.s = text
    OTHERWISE REPLY EXCEPTION empty_name

  MESSAGE equal(n1 n2: name)
    REPLY(b: boolean)
      WHERE b <=> n1.s = n2.s,
        Reflexive(equal), Symmetric(equal), Transitive(equal),
        Identity_relation(equal),
          -- Equals can be substituted for equals.
        Eternal(equal)
          -- If two objects are equal,
          -- they are equal in all states.

  MESSAGE not_equal(x y: t)
    REPLY(b: boolean) WHERE b <=> ~equal(x, y)

  CONCEPT "="(x y: t) VALUE(b: boolean)
    -- Strong logical equality, not computable.
    WHERE Strongly_reflexive("="),
        -- (! = !) = true but equal(!, !) = !
      ALL(x y: t :: (x = y) <=> equal(x, y))
        -- "=" is the same as "equal" for all well defined
        -- data values.

  CONCEPT "~="(x y: t) VALUE(b: boolean)
    -- Strong logical inequality, not computable.
    WHERE b <=> ~(x = y)

  CONCEPT Reflexive(f: function{t, t, boolean}) VALUE(b: boolean)
    WHERE b <=> ALL(x: t :: f(x, x))
      -- x ranges over well defined values of type t.

  CONCEPT Strongly_reflexive(f: function{t, t, boolean})
    VALUE(b: boolean)
    WHERE b <=> Reflexive(f) & f(!, !)
      -- Reflexive also for the undefined element "!".

  CONCEPT Symmetric(f: function{t, t, boolean}) VALUE(b: boolean)
    WHERE b <=> ALL(x y: t :: f(x, y) => f(y, x))
```

```
CONCEPT Transitive(f: function(t, t, boolean))
  VALUE(b: boolean)
  WHERE b <=> ALL(x y z: t :: f(x, y) & f(y, z) => f(x, z))

CONCEPT Identity_relation(f: function(t, t, boolean))
  VALUE(b: boolean)
  WHERE b <=>
    ALL(a b: t, ts1 ts2: sequence(type), s1: ts1, s2: ts2,
        range: type, g: function($ts1, t, $ts2, range) ::
        f(a, b) => g($s1, a, $s2) = g($s1, b, $s2) )
        -- If f(x, y) there is no way to distinguish x
        -- from y.  This means x and y are identical,
        -- so you can substitute x for y.

CONCEPT Eternal(f: function(t, t, boolean)) VALUE(b: boolean)
  WHERE b <=> ALL(a b: t :: f(a, b) => always(f(a, b)))
    -- This means the relation f cannot be affected
    -- by state changes.
END
```

4. Sets of WHEN clauses are merged by forming the cross product set and merging the components of each tuple in the cross product. Formal parameters of the inherited clause are renamed as necessary to match the interface of the inheriting clause. Bound variables of quantifiers are renamed as needed to avoid name conflicts. For example, the merge of the set of clauses attached to a message in the primary module

```
WHEN p1 REPLY (x: t) WHERE q1(x)
OTHERWISE REPLY (x: t) WHERE r1(x)
```

and the set of clauses attached to the same message in a parent module

```
WHEN p2 REPLY (y: t) WHERE q2(y)
OTHERWISE REPLY (y: t) WHERE r2(y)
```

is the following set of clauses.

```
WHEN p1 & p2 REPLY (x: t) WHERE q1(x) & q2(x)
WHEN ~p1 & p2 REPLY (x: t) WHERE r1(x) & q2(x)
WHEN p1 & ~p2 REPLY (x: t) WHERE q1(x) & r2(x)
OTHERWISE REPLY (x: t) WHERE r1(x) & r2(x)
```

Recall that OTHERWISE is the same as a WHEN clause with a guard predicate that is true if none of the guard predicates of the preceding WHEN clauses are true. Note the renaming of variables. Simplifications that eliminate clauses are sometimes possible. Cases where the guard predicate is always false can be dropped, because they can never apply. This happens if $p1 = p2$, since $p1$ & $~p1$ = false.

5. Responses are matched up by response type (REPLY, SEND, or GEN-ERATE), name of the outgoing message, and destination of the outgoing message (for multiple SENDs). The combination of two different responses means that both are done in parallel. If a normal response must be merged with an exceptional response, the result is the error value !.

These rules can be applied mechanically. Such a program should locate inconsistencies (! values) and apply at least the elementary simplification transformations mentioned in step 4. Expansion of inheritance structures is useful for producing summary views of a development.

The previous discussion ignores the effects of HIDE and RENAME. The effect of INHERIT m HIDE n is to remove all components from the module *m* with the name *n* and then to inherit the result. This applies to messages, concepts, and state or model components. An ordinary INHERIT describes a specialization step, which adds additional properties and constraints to the inherited module. An inherit with a HIDE is a two-step process, where a generalization step first removes the named properties, and then a specialization step constrains the result. HIDE is used to describe incompatible changes, as illustrated in Section 3.4.1.

The effect of INHERIT m RENAME n1 AS n2 is to substitute the name n2 for the name n1 in the module *m* before inheriting it. This mechanism is used to avoid name conflicts, especially when inheriting reusable specification components from a library.

3.9.6 Timing and Response Sets

The Spec language has facilities for specifying real-time constraints. An example of a specification with timing constraints is shown in Fig. 3.62. The example shows a simple traffic ticket system that keeps track of unpaid tickets and sends dunning letters to the violators with overdue payments every 30 days until they pay up. The delay is determined with respect to the local clock of the module containing the assertion involving the keyword DELAY. When attached to a response message, DELAY refers to the time interval between the event where the stimulus message arrives at the module and the event where the associated response message is accepted by its destination module. When attached to an atomic transaction, the DELAY keyword refers to the time interval between the earliest event in the transaction and the latest event in the transaction. In the first case, checking the constraint can involve measurement errors due to imperfect clock synchronization. In the second case, the two events defining the time interval occur at the same module, so that the time interval between the two events can be determined without any approximations to account for communication delays in reading remote clocks. Upper and lower bounds on the delay associated with a response can be specified by using

```
MACHINE ticket_system
  INHERIT time_unit
  STATE(outstanding: set{ticket_id})
  INVARIANT true
  INITIALLY outstanding = { }

  MESSAGE ticket(violator: person, ticket_id: integer)
    SEND check_on_payment(violator: person, ticket_id:
                                                 integer)
      TO ticket_system
      WHERE (30 days) <= DELAY < (31 days)
    TRANSITION outstanding = *outstanding U {ticket_id}

  MESSAGE payment(violator: person, ticket_id: integer)
    TRANSITION outstanding = *outstanding - {ticket_id}

  MESSAGE check_on_payment(violator: person, ticket_id:
                                                 integer)
    WHEN ticket_id IN outstanding
      SEND letter(s: string) TO violator WHERE warning(s)
      SEND check_on_payment(violator: person, ticket_id:
                                                 integer)
        TO ticket_system
        WHERE (30 days) <= DELAY < (31 days)
    OTHERWISE -- Do nothing.

  CONCEPT warning(s: string) VALUE(b: boolean)
    -- True if s is a letter requesting immediate payment
    -- of the fine.
END
```

FIGURE 3.62
A Specification with Delay Constraints

inequalities, such as (30 days) <= DELAY < (31 days).

In Spec, a dimensioned literal consists of a numeric expression and a unit name enclosed in parentheses. The time unit names for describing time intervals are defined in the definition module time_unit (Appendix C), and include picosec, nanosec, microsec, millisec, seconds, minutes, hours, days, and weeks. Similar definitions can be given for other physical quantities such as distance, weight, voltage, and so on.

Events triggered at absolute times are specified as temporal events; events triggered at times defined relative to other events are specified as ordinary messages with a specified DELAY. Specified delays are illustrated by the ticket

```
MACHINE payroll_system
  INHERIT time   -- Defines weekday.
  INHERIT time_unit   -- Defines days.

  STATE(salary: map{person, money})
  INVARIANT true
  INITIALLY domain(salary) = { }

  MESSAGE hire(p: person, s: money)
    TRANSITION salary = add(p, s, *salary)

  MESSAGE fire(p: person)
    TRANSITION salary = remove(p, *salary)

  TEMPORAL pay
    WHERE weekday(TIME) = #friday & PERIOD = (14 days)
      SEND paycheck(amount: money) TO p
        WHERE amount = salary[p]
      FOREACH(p: person SUCH THAT p IN domain(salary))
END
```

FIGURE 3.63
A Specification with Temporal Events

example. An example of a specification with temporal events is shown in Fig.
3.63. The example shows an oversimplified bi-weekly payroll. The specified
system is unrealistic in the sense that workers get paid every two weeks
whether or not they spent any time working, but it is sufficient for illustrating
the use of temporal events. The temporal event pay is triggered every other
Friday. When attached to the definition of a message or temporal event,
PERIOD refers to the duration between every pair of consecutive events matching the definition. The implicit universal quantifier over consecutive pairs of
events makes constraints on the period vacuously true in histories that do not
contain at least two events of the required type, thus preventing complications
with initial conditions. When attached to an atomic transaction, PERIOD refers
to the duration between the first events of any two consecutive transactions of
the specified type.

The PERIOD is used to specify the frequency of an event, and predicates
involving the TIME can be used to specify the phase. The phase of the payroll
has not been specified exactly, since any time on Friday is acceptable. Such
imprecision makes the constraint on the period needed in addition to the constraint on the triggering time. A period would be specified even if paydays
came every week instead of every other week to avoid triggering the temporal

event more than once each Friday, because in this example the phase is restricted to an interval rather than being specified exactly. An exact time constraint, such as "noon on Fridays," would make the period unnecessary.

The precondition of a temporal defines an alarm in the event model (see Section 3.2.2), which is the point in time when the response is enabled via a message the module sends to itself. The actual temporal event occurs when this implicit message arrives at the module and can occur with any finite delay unless the DELAY is restricted in the precondition of the temporal, represented in the first WHERE clause. This corresponds to a scheduling delay in the implementation. The arrival of the message implicitly generated by the temporal event corresponds to the time the operation is actually started. Restrictions on the time at which the response must be delivered can be specified by including a restriction on the DELAY in the postcondition attached to the response, represented in the second WHERE clause. The payroll example specifies only when the temporal event is enabled, but does not impose any constraints on when the operation must actually be started or when it must be completed. You are invited to extend the example by adding such hard timing constraints.

The temporal event in the example also illustrates the use of FOREACH to specify sets of responses containing variable numbers of events. FOREACH can be used to describe a response in which a similar message is to be sent to every element of a specified set of destinations; in this case, the set of workers to be paid. It can also be used to describe a set of similar messages to be sent to the same destination, as in the elaboration of the warehouse example shown in Fig. 3.64, which supports the processing of backorders. The FOREACH is used to define a situation where a single message can trigger a variable number of responses. In this case, the arrival of a shipment from the supplier triggers sending out delayed responses to zero or more backorders.

The extended inventory example also illustrates how variables local to a WHEN clause can be introduced via CHOOSE. This is useful when the same value is needed in more than one predicate. In this case, the set of backorders s is used in both a SEND and a TRANSITION. This cannot be done using a quantifier without repeating the definition of s, since the scope of a variable bound to a quantifier is limited to a single predicate. This example also illustrates the use of the SUM quantifier for adding up the quantities shipped out to meet outstanding backorders.

3.9.7 Atomic Transactions

Atomic transactions are used to specify the noninterference requirements for a set of potentially concurrent transactions in a distributed environment. An example of a specification with atomic transactions is shown in Fig. 3.65. This example shows the specification for the sender half of a simplified protocol for transferring files over a noisy channel (such as a telephone line). A practical

```
MACHINE inventory
    -- Assumes shipping and supplier are other modules.
  STATE(stock: map{item, nat},
        backorders: map{item, sequence{nat}} )
  INVARIANT ALL(i: item, q: nat SUCH THAT q IN backorders[i] ::
                stock[i] <= q )
  INITIALLY ALL(i: item :: stock[i] = 0 & backorders[i] = [ ])

  MESSAGE receive(i: item, qr: nat)
    WHEN qr > 0
      CHOOSE(s: set{nat} SUCH THAT
             s = fillable(backorders[i], stock[i] + qr) )
        SEND shipping_order(is: item, qs: nat) TO shipping
          WHERE is = i, qs = q
        FOREACH(q: nat SUCH THAT q IN s)
      TRANSITION
        SOME(tb: nat SUCH THAT
             tb = SUM(q: nat SUCH THAT q IN s :: q) ::
             stock[i] = *stock[i] + qr - tb )
    OTHERWISE REPLY EXCEPTION empty_shipment

  MESSAGE order(io: item, qo: nat)
    WHEN 0 < qo <= stock[io]
      SEND shipping_order(is: item, qs: nat) TO shipping
        WHERE is = io, qs = qo
      TRANSITION stock[io] + qo = *stock[io]
    WHEN 0 < qo > stock[io]
      SEND shipping_order(is: item, qs: nat) TO shipping
        WHERE is = io, qs = stock[io]
      SEND back_order(ib: item, qb: nat) TO supplier
        WHERE ib = io, qb + qs = qo
      TRANSITION stock[io] = 0
    OTHERWISE REPLY EXCEPTION empty_order

  CONCEPT fillable(bs: sequence{nat}, on_hand: nat)
    VALUE(s: set{nat})
      -- The subset of the backorders in bs that can be filled
      -- with the given number of items on hand.
END
```

FIGURE 3.64
Extended Inventory Example

```
MACHINE sender
  STATE(data: sequence[block])
  INVARIANT true
  INITIALLY data = [ ]

  MESSAGE send(file: sequence[block])
    WHEN length(file) > 0
      SEND first(b: block) TO receiver WHERE b = file[1]
      TRANSITION data = file
    OTHERWISE REPLY EXCEPTION empty_file

  MESSAGE echo(b: block)
    WHEN b = data[1] & length(data) > 1
      SEND next(b1: block) TO receiver WHERE b1 = data[1]
      TRANSITION *data = b || data
    WHEN b = data[1] & length(data) = 1
      SEND done TO receiver
      SEND done TO sender
      TRANSITION data = [ ]
    OTHERWISE SEND retransmit(b2: block)
      TO receiver WHERE b2 = data[1]

  MESSAGE done

  TRANSACTION transfer = send ; DO echo OD ; done
END
```

FIGURE 3.65
Specification of a Sender Protocol

system would transfer the name as well as the contents of a file. The example represents a preliminary design, in which the type block is unspecified. The system in the example contains three interfaces.

1. The user interface consisting of the send message

2. The channel interface consisting of the first, next, and retransmit messages

3. The file system interface consisting of the save message.

We assume that messages always arrive, but their contents may be corrupted on the way. The protocol shown in the example depends on the assumption that a transmission error in the echo message does not undo the effects of a previous transmission error.

The atomic transactions of a module are specified between the messages and the concepts defined in the module. The transaction `transfer` says the sender accepts only `echo` messages between a `send` and the next `done` message, which implies that the next `send` must wait until all of the activity associated with the previous `send` has been completed. This prevents another user from interrupting a transmission already in progress.

The receiver half of the protocol is specified in Fig. 3.66. The atomic transaction allows only `next` or `retransmit` events between the `first` and `done` events. This constraint keeps different transmissions from interrupting the work of the receiver even if there is more than one sender operating concurrently, provided they all follow the specified sender protocol. The deadlock and starvation properties of this protocol are discussed in Chapter 7.

Atomic transactions are defined in terms of sequencing (action ; action), parallel combination (action action ... action), choice (`IF` action | ... | action

---

```
MACHINE receiver
  STATE(data: sequence{block})
  INVARIANT true
  INITIALLY data = [ ]

  MESSAGE first(b: block)
    SEND echo(b: block) TO sender
    TRANSITION data = [b]

  MESSAGE next(b: block)
    SEND echo(b: block) TO sender
    TRANSITION data = *data || b

  MESSAGE retransmit(b: block)
    SEND echo(b: block) TO sender
    TRANSITION data[length(*data)] = b
      -- Replace the last element of data.

  MESSAGE done
    SEND save(file: sequence{block})
      TO file_system WHERE file = data
    TRANSITION data = [ ]

  TRANSACTION receive = first ; DO next | retransmit OD ; done
END
```

FIGURE 3.66
Specification of a Receiver Protocol

FI), and repetition (DO action | ... | action OD). Sequencing implies one instance of the action on the left must occur before one instance of the action on the right. Parallel combination implies one instance of each action listed must occur in some unspecified order. A choice implies exactly one instance of the actions listed must occur. A repetition implies a sequence of zero or more instances of the actions listed may occur. The actions can be either message names or transaction names. Message names preceded by EXCEPTION match only events with the given name and the condition *exception*, and message names without EXCEPTION match only events with the given name and the condition *normal*. Actions can be preceded by guard predicates that specify conditions under which the action can be accepted. The transaction names used in actions can be mutually recursive. The definition of a set of atomic transactions can be presented as transaction diagrams such as the ones shown in Fig. 3.67. Transaction diagrams represent the constraints on the order of events associated with atomic transactions, and are discussed in more detail in Section 3.2.3.

The use of guarded actions in a transaction preventing overflow and underflow of a bounded buffer is shown in Fig. 3.68. As illustrated in the example, the guard predicates can refer to the state variables of a state machine.

If an atomic transaction is associated with a type, the constraints it defines apply independently to each instance of the type. An event in such an atomic transaction consists of a message arriving at the type module. Such an event affects the copies of the atomic transactions associated with each instance of

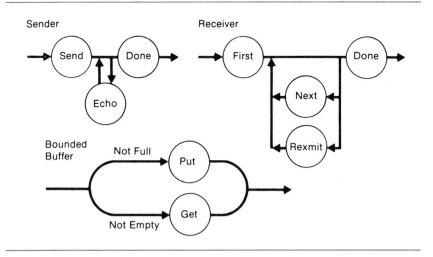

FIGURE 3.67
Transaction Diagrams

```
MACHINE bounded_buffer(t: type, size: nat SUCH THAT size > 0)

  STATE (contents: sequence(t))
  INVARIANT length(contents) <= size
  INITIALLY contents = [ ]

  MESSAGE put(x: t)
    TRANSITION contents = *contents || [x]

  MESSAGE get
    REPLY(x: t)
    TRANSITION [x] || contents = *contents

  TRANSACTION input_output =
    IF WHEN length(contents) < size -> put  -- Not full.
    | WHEN length(contents) > 0 -> get  -- Not empty.
    FI
END
```

FIGURE 3.68
Specification of a Bounded Buffer

the type that appears as an actual argument in the arriving message. If the message has no arguments of the type, then the event affects the atomic transactions at all of the instances of the type.

The guard predicate for an event in an atomic transaction associated with a type can refer to the components of the model for the associated instance, if there is one. The associated instance is the first actual argument of the message arriving at the event, if the first actual argument belongs to the type. If the first actual argument does not belong to the type, then the instance associated with the event is undefined, and it is illegal to refer to model components in guard predicates for the event.

3.9.8 Sending Messages to Types and Instances

In Spec, a type module is viewed as an object manager that performs operations on behalf of its instances. Thus formally all primitive operations on the type correspond to messages sent to the type module. Spec was designed in this way to allow all messages to be treated uniformly. It is not possible to make all the primitive operations of a mutable type correspond to messages sent to the instances of the type, because in that case there would be no way to create the first instance of a mutable type, which has an empty set of instances in the initial state. Object-oriented programming languages that have tried to associate messages with the individual instances of a type have been forced to include some messages sent to the type (class) itself, which must then be treated as an instance of a higher-order type (meta-class). We have found that the distinction between messages that must be sent to instances of a class and those that must be sent to instances of the meta-class confuses people. Spec has been designed to avoid this distinction, as well as the asymmetry that has to be introduced into messages that operate on more than one instance of a type if all messages must be sent to instances.

Sometimes it is convenient to be able to send messages to instances of a type, such as in the payroll example of Fig. 3.63. This point of view is particularly appropriate for dynamic systems that interact with types of external systems that have a variable number of instances. It is natural to model such system classes as types, whose instances are treated as modules rather than as passive data objects. Typically such systems have internal states, so that in the context of a functional specification we would like to model such a system class as a mutable type, with operations for creating and destroying instances, and we would like to treat the instances as machines. Motivated by this class of applications, we define the effect of a SEND of the form

```
SEND m(x₁: t₁, ... , xₙ: tₙ) TO e,
```

where e is an expression of type t, to be equivalent to the operation

```
SEND m(e, x₁, ... , xₙ) TO t.
```

The discussion of atomic transactions for types at the end of the previous section is also motivated by this view of types.

3.9.9 Predefined Types and Expressions

The Spec language has a predefined library of type specifications that can be used in building conceptual models for new types defined by the analyst or designer. Spec definitions of the predefined types can be found in Appendix D, and a summary of the standard interpretations of the predefined prefix and infix operators can be found in Appendix B. This section describes the predefined types informally.

All of the types in the Spec library are immutable, which means the instances of the predefined types do not have any internal states that are subject to change. All operations that change components of composite data objects do so by creating new instances, without affecting the properties of the original objects. This property avoids unintended interactions. We recommend using only immutable types for components of messages in functional specifications. It is appropriate to use instances of mutable types as destinations of messages if the proposed software system must interact with variable numbers of similar external systems, such as airplanes entering and leaving the airspace controlled by an air traffic control system.

Improper Values.   There are two improper values in Spec: ? (to be determined) and ! (error). The value ? represents a decision that has not yet been made, and implies an obligation to fill in a proper value at a later date. A complete design does not contain any ? s. The value ! represents a deliberately undefined value, which should never be generated at runtime. It is used to represent deliberately uninitialized objects and states components whose values do not matter. Formally both of these symbols represent the same undefined value.

Any.   The type any is the union of all of the other types in the system. It does not have any operations.

Equality{t: type}.   The standard definition of equality is inherited by all of the types in the Spec library. For this reason, the equality operations are not mentioned when the types are discussed individually in the rest of this section. The weak equality operations equal and not_equal are strict functions and are computable. These operations are inherited by user-defined data types, and are expected to appear as part of the implementation of any type *t* which inherits the type equality{t}. Equality is reflexive, symmetric, transitive, and obeys the substitution law. For mutable types, two objects are equal only if they have the same identity and the same properties.

The type equality{t} also defines the concepts = and ~=, which represent the strong logical equality and inequality relations for the type, which are not strict. These relations are the same as equal and not_equal for well defined data values, and are extended to the undefined value ! by the conventions ! = ! and ALL(x: t :: x ~= !). Because logical equality can be used to check whether a value is undefined, it is not computable. Logical equality is useful in specifications but should not appear in implementations. Consequently these operations are defined as concepts rather than as messages.

Boolean.   The type boolean is the usual truth value domain. The boolean literals are true and false. The operations on booleans are and, or, implies, &, |, ~, =>, <=>, =, and ~=. The weak boolean operations and, or, and implies are strict, and are defined as messages to indicate they appear in implementations of the type boolean. The concepts &, |, and => correspond to the strong boolean connectives of the three-valued logic discussed in Section 3.8. The strong connectives are useful in specifications because they can give well defined results even if some of the arguments are undefined. The strong connectives agree with the weak versions for all well defined values, and are similar to the conditional boolean connectives provided by some programming languages, except that the order of the arguments does not matter. The strong connectives are defined as concepts rather than messages because they are not easy to implement efficiently and are not provided by most implementations, even though they are computable in principle.

Total_order{t: type}.   Many of the predefined types inherit the standard definitions of the total ordering operations $<$, $<=$, $>$, and $>=$. The $<=$ operation is reflexive, antisymmetric, transitive, and exhaustive ($x <= y$ or $y <= x$ for all x and y).

Char.   The type char consists of individual characters. The predefined char type is seven-bit ASCII. Character literals are written using single quotes (for example, 'a'). The operations on characters are create, ordinal, the letter and digit predicates, and the total ordering operations.

String.   The type string is the same as sequence{char}, and has the same operations. An additional feature of the string type is a predefined literal syntax for string-valued constants. String literals are surrounded by double quotes (e.g. "sample string"), where embedded double quotes and backslashes (\) are quoted by preceding them with a backslash. For example, the string literal "a\" and a\\" would appear as

   a " and a \

when printed.

Enumeration{i1:: identifier, ... , in:: identifier}.   Enumeration types are finite ordered sets, similar to the enumeration types in Ada. Enumeration literals are identifiers prefixed with a #, for example, #red is a literal of type enumeration{red, yellow, green}. The only identifiers that can appear in an enumeration literal are the parameters of the type. The order of the values is the order in which they appear in the parameter list. An enumeration literal can belong to several different enumeration types. When it is necessary to be precise, a type qualification can be added to a literal, (e.g. #red@enumeration{red, white, blue}). The operations on enumerations are create, ordinal, and the total ordering operations.

Null.   The only value of the type null is represented by the literal nil. This type is used for representing variants of union types that do not contain any meaningful data values. Such constructions are used in list, tree, and graph data structures.

Tuple{t1:: type, ... , tn:: type}.   Tuples are finite, labeled Cartesian products. Tuple literals are enclosed in square brackets, and contain name-value pairs separated by commas; for example, [name:: "Fred", age:: 7] is an element of the type tuple{name:: string, age:: integer}. The components can be retrieved by name (t.age or "."{age}(t) or

get(t, "age")) or by position (t[2]). The operations on tuples are
create, "." (component selection, t.c), get, "[" (indexing, t[n]),
remove, "||" (append, t1 || t2), and contains. Tuples are used to
represent data objects with a fixed number of components of different types.
They are similar to Ada records, except they are not mutable.

Union{t1:: type, ... , tn:: type}. Union types are labeled finite disjoint
unions. A union literal looks like a singleton set with a component name; for
example, {leaf:: 17} and {node:: [left :: t1, right ::
t2]} are elements of the type union{leaf:: integer, node::
tuple{left right:: tree}}. The selectors for the type parameters act
as the tags identifying the components of the disjoint union. The components
can be retrieved by name (u.leaf or "."{leaf}(u)) if the tag matches
(is{leaf}(u)). The union operations are create, ".", and is. Unions
are similar to variant records in Ada, except that they are not mutable and each
variant has exactly one component.

Sequence{t:: type}. The type sequence{t} consists of finite ordered
sequences of elements. Sequences can have any length, but the elements must
all belong to the type t. This last condition is not restrictive because t can be
the universal type any. A sequence literal is a list of expressions in square
brackets (for example, [1, 4, -5] is an element of sequence
{integer}). The sequence operations are empty, add, remove, "||"
(append, s1 || s2), "[" (indexing, s[n]), length, domain, "IN" (infix
membership test), the predicate subsequence, ".." (interval, [a .. b]),
apply (pointwise function application, like mapcar in LISP), reduce (as in
APL), and the total ordering operations. The ordering is the lexicographic ordering on the element type, and exists if and only if "<"@t does. This gives
the usual alphabetic ordering on strings, as defined by the ASCII collating
sequence. The interval operation is defined only if "<"@t exists and defines a
total ordering. The result is an ordered closed interval with a given pair of endpoints. An interval can be written as a sequence literal of the form [a .. b].
Sequence literals can also contain the $ notation (for example, [$a, x, $b]
is the same as (a || [x] || b)). Components can be extracted by posi-
tion (s[3]) and by subrange (s[1 .. 10]), corresponding to the two variants of the overloaded "[" operation.

Partial_ordering{t: type}. Some of the predefined types inherit partial ordering relations. The partial ordering operations are <, <=, ~<, >, >=, and ~>=.
The operation <= is reflexive, antisymmetric, and transitive, but not necessarily
exhaustive (there can be values x and y such that neither $x <= y$ nor $y <= x$ is
true). In a partial ordering the operations <= and ~> can be different. Examples of partial orderings are the => relation on predicates and the subset relation on sets. Every total ordering is also a partial ordering.

Set{t:: type}. The type set{t} consists of finite mathematical sets with elements from the type t. A set literal is a sequence of expressions enclosed in braces, (for example, {"John", "Mary"} is an element of type set{string}). The set operations are empty, add, remove, "IN" (infix membership test), "U" (union, s1 U s2), "-" (infix set difference, s1 - s2), intersection, Cartesian product (infix *), size (cardinality), ".." (interval, {a .. b}), apply (pointwise function application, like mapcar in LISP), reduce (as in APL), and the partial ordering operations. Sets are partially ordered by the subset relationship. The interval operation is defined only if t$"<" exists and defines a partial ordering. The result is an unordered closed interval with a given pair of endpoints. An interval can be written as a set literal of the form {a .. b}. The $ notation can also be used in set literals (for example, {$a, x, $b} is the same as (a U {x} U b)).

Unbounded_set{t:: type}. The type set{t} is a subtype of unbounded_set{t}. Unbounded_set{t} has all of the operations of the type set{t}, together with a set constructor operation capable of creating infinite sets. This constructor operation is usually used via the literal syntax; for example, {x: nat SUCH THAT prime(x) :: x ^ 2} represents the set of all squares of prime numbers.

Multiset{t: type}. Multisets are like sets except they can contain repeated elements. A multiset literal looks like a set literal with a type qualifier (for example, {1, 2, 2, 5}@multiset{nat}). The operations on multisets are empty, add, remove, U (union, s1 U s2), IN (infix membership test), frequency, size, domain, and scan. Multisets are like sequences in that they can contain multiple copies of the same element. Multisets are like sets in that the elements of a multiset are not ordered. Multisets are useful for keeping track of frequencies. You should think of multisets whenever it would be useful to have a histogram for some collection of data elements.

Map{from:: type, to:: type}. Maps are single-valued functions from an arbitrary data type to another that have the same value (the default) at all but a finite number of points. A map literal contains a list of pairs, a semicolon, and the default value, all enclosed in curly brackets; for example, {["red shoes", 3], ["black shoes", 28] ;0} is an element of the type map{from:: string, to:: integer}. The operations on maps are create, bind, remove, "[" (indexing, m[x]), "IN" (infix membership test), domain, range, and default. The domain of a map is the set of elements for which the value of the map differs from its default value. The domain of any instance of the type map{t1, t2} is a subset of t1, and the range is a subset of t2. Maps are partially ordered by the function extension relationship (m1 <= m2 iff m1 agrees with m2 on all elements of domain(m1)). Maps are generalized lookup tables, and can be used much like arrays in programming languages, except that maps are more flexible and powerful. The from type of a map can be any data type with an equal operation, and need not be finite. Multiple valued associations can be represented as maps with a range type of the form set{t}.

Relation{t1: type, ... , tn: type}. Relations are finite mathematical relations. A relation literal looks like a set of tuples. Type ambiguities can be resolved with an explicit type qualification if the type of the literal is not clear from the context. For example, {[parent:: "Joe", child:: "Sally"], [parent:: "Joe", child:: "John"]}@relation {parent child:: string} is a relation literal with an explicit type qualification. The operations on relations are create, add, "IN" (infix membership test), domain, select, project, join, "U" (union, r1 U r2), intersection, and the partial ordering operations. Relations are partially ordered by the subset relationship. Relations are useful for describing associations that are multiple valued and are accessed based on more than one different attribute.

Number. The standard properties of numbers are inherited from the number type. All of the number types have "+" and "*" operations with identity elements zero and one. Both operations are associative and commutative, and "+" distributes over "*". Mixed-mode arithmetic is allowed, and behaves according to the standard embedding that lets us view nat as a subset of integer, integer as a subset of rational, rational as a subset of real, and real as a subset of complex. The predefined numeric types in Spec correspond to standard mathematics, and hence have unbounded range and precision.

Nat. The type nat consists of the natural numbers (non-negative integers). A natural number literal is a sequence of digits in standard decimal notation (for example, 128 is a natural number). The operations on natural numbers are the constants zero (0) and one (1), succ (add one), pred (subtract one), "+" (addition, a + b), "-" (the partial subtraction operation, a - b), "*" (multiplication, a * b), "/" (division, a / b), "MOD" (remainder, a MOD b or a \ b), "^" (exponentiation, a ^ b), "|" (the divides relation, a | b), and the total ordering operations. The divides relation is a partial order, and n1 | n2 means n1 is a factor of n2. Subtraction is undefined if the result is less than zero, and division and remainder are undefined if the second argument is zero.

Integer. Integers are the signed whole numbers of standard mathematics, with an unbounded range. Integer literals have the standard form in decimal notation (for example, -5 and 17@integer are integers). Usually nat literals can be used instead of positive integer literals because of the type conversion operation `nat_to_integer` (see Section 3.9.2). The `integer` operations are the predicate `is_nat`; the constants `zero` (0) and `one` (1); and the functions `succ` (add one), `pred` (subtract one), `abs` (absolute value), `"+"` (addition, `a + b`), `"-"` (negation - `a`, or subtraction `a - b`), `"*"` (multiplication, `a * b`), `"/"` (division, `a / b`), `"MOD"` (remainder, `a MOD b` or `a \ b`), `"^"` (exponentiation, `a ^ b`), and the total ordering operations. Remainder always gives a positive result, as in standard mathematics. (Warning: most computer languages, including Ada, do not respect this interpretation for negative numbers.)

Rational.   Rational numbers are ratios of pairs of integers, with unbounded precision. A rational literal looks like a fraction with a type qualifier (for example, `1/3@rational` is a rational number). The `rational` operations are the constructor `ratio`; the predicates `is_nat` and `is_integer`; the constants `zero` and `one`; and the functions `abs` (absolute value), `"+"` (addition, `a + b`), `"-"` (negation, - `a`, or subtraction, `a - b`), `"*"` (multiplication, `a * b`), `"/"` (division, `a / b`), `"MOD"` (remainder, `a MOD b` or `a \ b`), `"^"` (exponentiation, `a ^ b`), and the total ordering operations. The type conversion operations `nat_to_rational` and `integer_to_rational` are usually left implicit.

Real.   The type `real` is the standard mathematical domain of real numbers. The precision of reals is unbounded. Real literals are decimals, with at least one digit on each side of the decimal point (for example, `0.0` is a real number). The `real` operations are the predicates `is_nat`, `is_integer`, and `is_rational`; the constants `zero` and `one`; and the functions `abs` (absolute value), `"+"` (addition, `a + b`), `"-"` (negation, - `a`, or subtraction `a - b`), `"*"` (multiplication, `a * b`), `"/"` (division, `a / b`), `"MOD"` (remainder, `a MOD b` or `a \ b`), `"^"` (exponentiation, `a ^ b`), and the total ordering operations. The type conversion operations `nat_to_real`, `integer_to_real`, and `rational_to_real` are usually left implicit.

Complex.   The type `complex` is the standard mathematical domain of complex numbers. The precision of complex numbers is unbounded. Complex literals are combinations of real literals and the complex constant i (for example, `(1.0 + 2.5 * i)@complex` is a complex number). The complex operations are the predicates `is_nat`, `is_integer`, `is_rational`, `is_real`, and `is_imaginary`; the constant `zero`, `one`, and `i`; and the functions `conjugate`, `magnitude`, `"+"` (addition, `a + b`), `"-"` (negation, - `a` or subtraction, `a - b`), `"*"` (multiplication, `a * b`), `"/"` (division, `a / b`), `"MOD"` (remainder, `a MOD b` or `a \ b`), and `"^"` (exponentiation, `a ^ b`). The type conversion operations `nat_to_complex`, `integer_ to_ complex`, `rational_to_complex`, and `real_to_complex` are usually left implicit.

Type. The instances of the type `type` are all of the data types. The type `type` is an instance of itself. The only operation of `type` other than the equality operations is `"IN"` (infix membership test), which checks whether a given object is an instance of a given type. The concept `Has_operation` can be used to check whether a function is a primitive operation of a type. The improper values ? and ! are not instances of any type. If $t1$ is a `Subtype` of $t2$, then every instance of $t1$ is also an instance of $t2$, and every primitive operation of $t2$ is also a primitive operation of $t1$. There is also a set of concepts for classifying types according to whether instances can be created, modified, and destroyed. The type `type` is used most often as a parameter for generic modules that can provide the same service for many different data types, such as `set{t}` and `sequence{t}`. Quantifiers can range over types to describe general properties, such as the concept `Transitive` defined in `equality{t}`.

Function{t1: type, ... , tn: type}. `Function` is a generic type without any operations other than equality. The last generic parameter describes the range of the functions in the type; the rest of the generic parameters describe the domain of the functions in the type. This type defines the concepts `Domain`, `Range`, `Total`, `One_to_one`, `Onto`, and `Strict`, which are used in defining general properties of other types. The type `function` is used most often as a parameter for generic modules or concepts, such as the concept `sorted{f}` in the type `sequence{t}`, in which the parameter f specifies the ordering to be used by the sorting process. Quantifiers can range over functions to describe general properties, such as the substitution property of $=$ in the type `equality{t}`. Quantifiers ranging over types and functions are not needed very often in developing functional specifications, but they may be needed to extend the Spec type library to support particular application areas. All of the laws given for quantifiers apply also if they range over types and functions. Second-order logic, which allows quantifiers over sets and functions, is often avoided in logic books because there is no complete inference procedure, but this does not introduce any new problems in our application because first-order logic with integers has an undecidable theory already. Most of the inferences needed in practical situations can be handled with the available inference techniques for first-order logic. These techniques also apply to second-order logic, although they are not complete for second-order logic.

Equivalence{t: type}. The virtual type `equivalence` defines the operations `equivalent`, `not_equivalent`, and `copy`, and the concepts `"=="` and `"~=="`, which are the strong logical versions of equivalent and not_equivalent. The distinction between strong and weak operations is described in the section describing the type `equality{t}`. These operations make sense only for mutable types, and should be inherited by all such types with the need to compare the states of distinct instances or make copies. If x ˜= y and x == y, *x* and *y* are distinct copies of an object that have the same properties in the current state, except for their identity. A `copy(x)` operation should produce a new object *y* with the preceding properties. Such a copy *y* should provide a snapshot of the state of *x* at the time the copy was made, in the sense that *y* should not be affected by any state changing operations that may be applied to *x* in the future.

3.10 Related Research

The initial integration of logic and the event model for functional specifications is described in [3]. A system using logic to specify modules and then using meaning-preserving transformations to turn the specification into an efficient implementation is described in [2], and in other work cited there. Some other specification techniques are surveyed in [6]. The use of test cases for evaluating the completeness of the specification of a data type is discussed in [9]. Theory and tools related to atomic transactions are discussed in [7], and in other work cited there. Some work on human factors relevant to concrete interface design can be found in [1, 5]. Some recent work on estimating software development effort for business applications based on functional specifications is described in [11]. Useful information on technical writing and designing and testing user manuals can be found in [4, 8].

Exercises

1. Extend the specification of the warehouse system to include the address of the customer to which the ordered items are to be shipped.

2. Extend the specification of the airline reservation system to support different fare classes for each flight. How does this change impact the environment model?

3. Extend the specification of the airline reservation system to let the travel agent make seat assignments. How does this change impact the environment model?

4. Extend the functional specification of the airline reservation system to include the function of issuing tickets. Modify the environment model accordingly.

5. Redefine the concrete functional specification for the airline manager interface to provide a command menu and prompting for the command arguments.

6. Define a new quantifier MEDIAN that yields the middle value in the rank ordering of a set. Examples: Median({1, 3, 6}) = 3 = Median({1, 3, 6, 7}).

Projects

1. Develop an environment model and write a functional specification for a text editor.

2. Work out the functional specifications for any of the projects at the end of Chapter 2.

3. (Research project.) Work out a scheme for defining quantifiers that operate on sequences rather than sets. Such a facility is useful for defining quantifiers based on binary operations that are associative but not commutative. Illustrate your method by defining an APPEND quantifier that operates on sequences of strings, and a CARTESIAN_PRODUCT quantifier that operates on sequences of sets.

References

1. R. Baecker and W. Buxton, eds., *Readings in Human-Computer Interaction: A Multidisciplinary Approach*, Morgan Kaufman, Los Altos, CA, 1987.

2. F. Bauer, B. Moller, H. Partsch and P. Pepper, "Formal Program Construction by Transformations—Computer-Aided, Intuition-Guided Programming," *IEEE Transactions on Software Engineering 15*, 2 (Feb. 1989), 165–180.

3. V. Berzins and M. Gray, "Analysis and Design in MSG.84: Formalizing Functional Specifications," *IEEE Transactions on Software Engineering SE-11*, 8 (Aug. 1985), 657–670.

4. M. Bolsky, *Better Technical Writing*, Prentice Hall, Englewood Cliffs, NJ, 1988.

5. J. Carol, ed., *Interfacing Thought*, MIT Press, Cambridge, MA, 1987.

6. B. Cohen, W. T. Harwood and M. I. Jackson, *The Specification of Complex Systems*, Addison-Wesley, Reading, MA, 1986.

7. L. Dillon, G. Avrunin and J. Wiledon, "Constrained Expressions: Towards Broad Applicability of Analysis Methods for Distributed Software Systems," *Transactions on Programming Languages and Systems 10*, 3 (July 1988), 374–402.

8. S. Grimm, *How to Write Computer Manuals for Users*, Lifetime Learning Publications, Belmont, CA, 1982.

9. P. Jalote, "Testing the Completeness of Specifications," *IEEE Transactions on Software Engineering 15*, 5 (May 1989), 526–531.

10. D. L. Parnas and P. C. Clements, "A Rational Design Process: How and Why to Fake It," *IEEE Transactions on Software Engineering SE-12*, 2 (Feb. 1986), 251–257.

11. C. Symons, "Function Point Analysis: Difficulties and Improvements," *IEEE Transactions on Software Engineering 14*, 1 (Jan. 1988), 2–11.

4

Architectural Design

An architectural design is a model of the proposed system that captures the aspects of its behavior and structure relevant to the development team. The behavior of a system consists of its interactions with other systems; the structure of a system consists of its component parts and their interconnections. An architectural design describes the system at several levels of abstraction, and can be viewed as a set of models that give increasingly detailed views of internal events as more modules are treated as glass boxes.

The functional specification and architectural design have different purposes. A functional specification describes the external interfaces along with the concepts needed to *use* the proposed system. An architectural design describes the internal and external interfaces along with the concepts needed to *build* the proposed system.

The functional specification is a subset of the architectural design. A functional specification defines the external interfaces of the proposed system— which capture its observable behavior—and enough of its structure to capture the distinction between the inside and the outside of the proposed system. This information is included in the architectural design because it is relevant to the development team as well as to the users. The functional specification is the least detailed view of the system; the only internal events shown correspond to transformations between abstract and concrete message formats for externally visible messages. The architectural design contains information needed by the development team but not by the users, such as the decomposition of the system into implementation modules and the behavior of the internal interfaces of the proposed system visible in more detailed views of the system.

4.1 Goals

The goal of the architectural design activity is to break up the proposed system into a set of small independent modules. A *module* is a self-contained unit of code. Large systems must be decomposed into modules to enable a team of people to work on different parts of the system concurrently, to enable independent analysis and design of individual modules, and to enable accurate estimation of costs and schedules. Parallel design, implementation, or testing activity is effective only if different people can perform their tasks without interfering with each other. This suggests implementation modules should be as independent as possible, and that interactions between them should be limited and explicitly defined. Because software systems are often too large to be understood completely by a single person, it is important to be able to understand and design individual modules in isolation from the rest of the system. This suggests that each module should correspond to a single coherent abstraction: Modules should have self-contained descriptions simple enough to be humanly tractable. The boundaries of most individual work assignments in a software development project usually correspond to modules. The need for accurate effort estimation also suggests modules should be small and simple, because the effort required to build a module cannot be accurately estimated unless the structure of the module can be readily predicted and understood.

Modules are decomposed at many levels of abstraction, until the specified submodules either match existing reusable software components, or are simple enough to be implemented directly in terms of the primitives of the implementation language. Important goals for this decomposition are feasibility and ease of implementation: The proposed set of parts in the decomposition of a module must be sufficient to realize the behavior specified in the black-box description of the module with a small and simple implementation.

At this stage, the goal for quality assurance is feasibility rather than correctness, because correctness depends on details of the interconnection that are not available until the module design stage. Because the choice of lower-level abstractions in the decomposition limits the choice of data structures and algorithms to be made in the module design stage, the proposed structure must be feasible with respect to the performance constraints. Checking the feasibility of a decomposition involves sketching algorithms for the performance-critical parts of the system in sufficient detail to support rough time and space complexity analysis. Such a sketch also aids estimating the required implementation effort.

Other goals for the proposed system structure are insensitivity to expected changes and support for testing and repairs. A system structure is insensitive to an expected change if the modifications required to implement the change are limited to a small number of modules, and extensions can be made by adding new modules without rearranging the existing modules. Insensitivity to change is increased if restrictive global assumptions are avoided, because such assumptions may lead to implementation restrictions that are expensive to remove in later versions of the system. A system structure supports testing if it is easy to put the system into all possible states and to observe all system properties relevant to correct operation. A system structure supports repairs if it is easy to trace each element of the behavior in the functional specification to a small localized segment of code. These goals are important because evolution, testing, and repair account for a large fraction of the cost of system development.

To summarize, the desirable properties of an architectural design include the following.

1. Modules should be understandable in isolation
2. All interaction between modules should be explicit
3. Each module should be small and simple
4. Each module should correspond to a single coherent abstraction
5. Decisions subject to change should be confined to a single module
6. Each module should be readily implementable with the specified parts
7. The decomposition should be consistent with the performance constraints
8. Each module should have a clear relation to the functional specification
9. Each module should be easy to test
10. Restrictive global assumptions should be avoided.

4.2 Basic Concepts

The process of transforming a functional specification into an architectural design is a significant design activity in which many important and difficult decisions are made. The main tasks in the architectural design activity are decomposition and concrete interface generation. The decomposition task consists of the following kinds of activities:

1. Deciding whether a module should be decomposed or implemented by a single module
2. Decomposing a module or subsystem into a network of more primitive modules
3. Evaluating relative merits of alternative decompositions
4. Specifying lower-level modules.

Guidelines for performing these activities are given in Section 4.3. Concrete interface generation is the process of mapping the abstract definitions of the interfaces of a black box into the constructs of the implementation language. In terms of Ada, the result of this task is a set of specification parts for a set of subprograms and packages. Once the conventions for representing interfaces in a particular language have been fixed, the process of generating concrete interface specifications is straightforward and largely automatable. A typical set of conventions for mapping abstract interfaces expressed in the Spec language into concrete interfaces expressed in Ada is presented in Section 4.4.2.

A *module* is both a self-contained abstraction and a unit of work. Modules have several different views: black-box specifications, parts lists, glass-box specifications, and programs. A parts list identifies the lower-level modules to be used in the implementation of a composite module. A glass-box specification defines the interconnection of the parts identified in the parts list for realizing the composite module. We use Spec to represent black-box specifications, module dependency diagrams to represent parts lists, an extended form of Ada augmented with Spec annotations to represent glass-box specifications, and standard Ada to represent programs. Module dependency diagrams are used mostly for planning and review purposes. Glass-box specifications are sketched during architectural design and details are worked out during module design. Programs are produced in the implementation stage, and are not discussed further in this chapter.

Black-box specifications are expressed in terms of the event model at the architectural design stage as well as at the functional specification stage. Modules are classified as functions, machines, or types. Interactions between modules are modeled as messages, which are classified as normal or exceptional. Responses are classified as complete or incremental, depending on whether the message is delivered in one piece (REPLY or SEND) or a little bit at a time (GENERATE).

The *parts list* of a module contains the set of lower-level modules used directly in its implementation if the module is implemented using new or modified code. Existing components that can be used without modification are treated as atomic units, and have empty parts lists. A module is *primitive* if its parts list is empty and *composite* otherwise.

The *module dependency diagram* is a graph representing the *part_of* relationship defined by the parts lists. A module dependency diagram has the same format as the decomposition diagrams discussed in Section 3.2.3. The graph contains one node for each module in the proposed implementation, and an arc from the node representing a module to each node in its parts list. Primitive modules appear as leaf nodes. The modules in the functional specification appear as source (root) nodes. The module dependency diagram is a general directed graph. The diagram is usually not a tree or forest because general-purpose low-level modules are used as components of more than one module.

The diagram can contain cycles, indicating designs involving direct or mutual recursion. In systems with recursive implementations, the nodes on each cycle should form an independent subsystem corresponding to a single coherent abstraction.

We describe algorithms and module interconnections in an extended form of Ada that includes the primitives described below. Invariants and preconditions can be included as Spec annotations in Ada comments. Boolean expressions used in conditionals and loops are extended to allow Spec quantifiers. FOR loops are extended to range over the elements of sets specified by predicates or the elements of sequences generated in response to a message. We also allow data objects to be described using the CHOOSE syntax of Spec, and state transitions to be described using the TRANSITION syntax of Spec, both embedded in Ada comments. Such statements represent deferred decisions, where some steps of an algorithm have been specified by describing the intended effects of the step rather than describing the details of how to implement the step. Such deferred decisions are useful for delaying routine details until after the more critical design decisions have been reviewed and stabilized.

The architectural design of a system contains an interface specification for each of the modules appearing in the module dependency diagram. The module design specifies the interconnections of the parts realizing each composite module, where interconnections are algorithms and data structures. Module design is often described as occurring after architectural design. However, the early stages of module design must often be interleaved with architectural design in practice, because a tentative picture of the interconnections is needed to develop a realistic parts list and assess the quality of the decomposition.

The degree to which the module design must be worked out during the architectural design activity depends on the experience and ability of the designer. More experienced designers typically need less detailed module designs for visualizing and evaluating the interconnection patterns. Regardless of the experience level of the designer it is important to record the partial module designs on which the decomposition is based, because working out detailed module designs is often the responsibility of less skillful people. Reconstructing the original intent at a later time rather than recording it as it is determined is wasteful, and the quality of the design may suffer because the reconstruction is likely to be imperfect. If the detailed module design requires a modification rather than a refinement of the initial sketch, the part of the architectural design rooted at the troublesome module must be re-evaluated to see if the lower-level interfaces are still valid. For this reason it is useful to pursue the architectural design and module design activities concurrently, in a pipelined fashion, so that errors at the higher levels of the decomposition can be detected before too much effort has been expended on decomposing the affected lower-level modules.

4.2.1 Decompositions as Refinements

A decomposition identifies the set of parts to be used in building a composite module. Such a decomposition induces a *refinement* of the behavior determined by its black-box specification. A refinement is a more detailed description that is consistent with the original. To be more precise, let us consider the two views of the module's behavior in terms of the event model.

Consider a composite module m whose parts list contains the modules m_1 ... m_n. A black-box view of the behavior of this module contains all of the events at m and none of the events at m_1, ... , m_n. A glass-box view of the behavior of this module contains all of the events at m_1, ... , m_n in addition to all of the events at m. Thus the black-box view of a computation history can be recovered from a glass-box view by deleting the events occurring at the component modules. A refinement proposes a more detailed view of a computation by including the intermediate events necessary to construct a high-level response in terms of the primitives at the next lower level of abstraction. A refinement takes the top off a black box, and exposes the events occurring at the components contained in the box.

4.2.2 Spec Pragmas

A *pragma* is an annotation expressing some implementation advice for a software component. In Ada, pragmas provide a means for the programmer to give advice to the compiler about the preferred form of implementation for a language construct in a particular situation, such as requesting that the state variable of a tight loop be kept in a register rather than in main memory. Pragmas in Spec provide a means for the designer to give advice about the preferred concrete interface design or module design for a given module. This advice may be addressed either to other designers on the development team or to automated tools for concrete interface generation or computer-aided module design. Spec pragmas appear in comments, and have the form of the keyword PRAGMA followed by a predicate. The pragmas associated with Spec are listed in Appendix E, and their effect on Ada implementations is discussed in Section 4.4.2.

4.3 Procedures and Guidelines

The process of architectural design starts by considering an entire major subsystem as a single black box, and proceeds to decompose each black box into more primitive ones, until all of the primitive black boxes are simple enough to be implemented by a single module of code.

Accepted engineering practice dictates that decomposition should be done systematically, and that at each stage several alternatives should be considered and the best one chosen based on objective criteria. As is usual for engineering problems, there are more constraints than degrees of freedom. At the current state of the art, human judgement must be used in making tradeoffs between conflicting goals. Because the long-term costs of software systems are dominated by evolution and repair efforts, a useful general rule is to emphasize simplicity and localization of information unless there is a performance constraint that cannot be met without compromising these goals.

For large systems, the best way to achieve good performance is by identifying the parts of the system limiting the performance, and by making careful choices of algorithms and data structures in those parts. A clever algorithm can speed up a system by a large factor, but only if it is applied to a module that the system spends a majority of its time executing. Improving the speed of a rarely invoked module is wasteful of effort and has a negligible effect on performance. It can also be counterproductive due to increased maintenance costs, because clever algorithms and data structures are often inflexible and difficult to understand. Since it is notoriously difficult to predict which modules are the bottlenecks in a proposed system, it is a good idea to design the system with a highly modular structure, do a quick and simple implementation, and then run benchmarks and measure execution times to determine the critical modules of the system, which are usually a small fraction of the whole. If a prototype has already been built it can be very useful for this purpose. After the bottlenecks have been identified, the offending modules can be redesigned for efficiency. This is much easier if the original design minimizes the scopes in which data structures are visible by means of abstract machines and abstract data types.

Currently there is no procedure for doing architectural design that is precise enough to be carried out by a computer, but there are some informal guidelines useful for human designers.

4.3.1 Decomposition Procedure

For modules that have to be decomposed, the designer should imagine an idealized machine on which it would be very easy to implement the module. The decomposition step consists of identifying and specifying the primitive types and operations of this idealized machine. Each decomposition step should be followed by a verification step in which an outline of an algorithm implementing the module in terms of the proposed primitives is sketched to establish feasibility. In practice it is often easier to do the feasibility check first, and then to identify the types and operations that were introduced. The steps of this process are sketched in more detail next.

There are two different cases, depending on whether or not the module being decomposed is a function. The procedure for decomposing functions is the following:

1. Sketch an informal algorithm for the module, limited to about 10 lines. The limit of 10 lines for the informal algorithm can be relaxed for regular structures such as case statements with many independent cases at the same level of abstraction, provided that the actions to be performed in each case are encapsulated in lower-level modules.

2. Identify the primitives used that are not already available, and specify them as modules using the techniques for functional specification.

3. Repeat the process for the new primitives introduced in the previous step, if there are any.

The procedure for decomposing types and machines is the following:

1. Consider all of the messages, and choose a suitable data structure for providing all of these operations, using your knowledge of data structures and algorithms. Consult reference books as needed for special-purpose data structures and algorithms.

2. Specify any new abstract data types or machines used in the representation as lower-level modules.

3. Apply the procedure for decomposing functions to each message of the type or machine.

4.3.2 Heuristics for Decomposition

Each level of a decomposition should have a single clear and coherent purpose. The information-hiding principle suggests introducing a module to hide each major design decision that is likely to change. Other useful heuristics for generating plausible building blocks are to encapsulate input and output functions, to encapsulate each level of nested loops, to encapsulate each level of nested data structures, and to encapsulate the individual actions on the arms of a case statement. When these heuristics produce too many small modules, the smaller modules can be eliminated by expanding them in-line at the level above. The concepts defined in the module to be decomposed often suggest lower-level components of the decomposition, especially the ones used in preconditions of messages.

This raises a fine point about the distinction between concepts and messages in a black-box specification. If a function is needed to specify the behavior of a module at some level of an architectural design, and is also one of the components used to realize that module at a lower level of the architectural design, then the function should be defined as a concept attached to the module at the higher level and exported. At the lower level, the function should be specified as a FUNCTION module, which imports the concept from the higher-level module and is defined in terms of it. The transformation creating the specification for such a lower-level module can be largely automated, and should be provided as a high-level editing operation in the computer-aided specification tool of the software development environment.

4.3.3 When to Stop

An important decision to be made in this stage of architectural design is whether or not a given module should be decomposed further. Our experience suggests that each module should be small enough to code and compile with about one person-day of effort, not including the associated design and testing activities. If such a module can be built using just the primitives of the programming language, there is no need to decompose.

The best size for software modules is a controversial subject. Project management considerations indicate that a single module should be implementable by one person in about a day, which is consistent with the popular guideline that a module usually should fit on a single page of code. This effort limit is motivated by the need to allow some flexibility in task assignments when compensating for unexpected developments, and by the desire for reasonably accurate estimates of the effort required for each task. In our experience, tasks of about a person-day are almost always accurately estimated, and tasks of more than two person-days are subject to occasional severe underestimates (off by a factor of five or more). Individual modules and tasks are of direct concern mostly for the lowest-level managers leading development teams. Higher-level managers in larger projects need aggregated status descriptions expressed in terms of larger scale subsystems to avoid being overwhelmed with excessive detail.

The guideline of about 10 lines of informal algorithm description mentioned previously was chosen to correspond to the one person-day size guideline. The exception for case statements is motivated by the simplicity of the control structure and a relatively low implementation effort per line. You should keep track of the implementation effort requirements for your own designs, and adjust the length guideline for algorithm sketches to match the one person-day unit of implementation effort in the context of your own development environment. The ten-line length for the algorithm sketch was based on an average expansion factor of five to one from implementation sketch to Ada code. If your expansion factor is significantly smaller you are probably making your algorithm sketches too detailed, a common problem for beginners.

4.3.4 Efficiency Considerations

It is not a good idea to complicate a design because of a marginal efficiency gain, unless that efficiency gain contributes directly to meeting a tight performance requirement. Clarity should normally be the primary design consideration. Efficiency considerations are best reflected in the architectural design stage by making rough estimates of expected sizes for data sets, and by identifying the processes that require the most computation and the data structures that require the most memory space. In the case of such critical parts, it is worthwhile to choose representations and algorithms carefully, especially if standard reusable components embodying particularly efficient algorithms and data structures for the expected range of loads can be found. Experienced engineers are aware of which aspects of the system will have the most pronounced effects on its overall performance, and spend their effort optimizing the aspects of the system that will have a large impact on the performance, emphasizing the functions that have stringent performance requirements.

4.3.5 Partitioning for Concurrency

Sometimes the performance constraints are so stringent that the specified functions cannot be implemented on a single processor with sufficient speed. Such problems can sometimes be solved by software systems structured as sets of concurrent processes, each of which can be run on a separate processor. Because hardware is relatively inexpensive and getting more so, distributed implementations are gaining popularity.

The most effective places to introduce concurrency are usually at the highest levels of decomposition, since starting a new process and interprocess communication often carry significant overhead costs. Thus the designer should check the performance constraints at the time each module of the functional specification is decomposed, and introduce partitions for concurrency if the constraints are too tight.

4.4 Case Study: Airline Reservation System

The procedures and guidelines for architectural design are illustrated in this section in terms of our running airline reservation system example. We start by listing the modules appearing in the functional specification:

1. Airline_reservation_system
2. Travel_agent

3. Airline_manager

4. Date.

The airline reservation system is the single central subsystem, and the travel agent and airline manager modules encapsulate the concrete data formats provided by the two external interfaces of the system. The date is an abstract data type whose instances flow across the interface between the travel agent and the airline reservation system. The travel agent interface and the airline manager interface modules are not included in this list because they are just restricted views of the airline reservation system that do not require independent implementations.

4.4.1 Decomposition

If we had enough designers, we would assign the decomposition of each module to a separate person, to be done concurrently. If there are not enough designers to do all of the modules, the most difficult and the largest ones should be decomposed first. It is good practice to decompose the biggest pieces first, because those pieces have the largest effect on the uncertainty about how much work is required to complete the proposed system. Reducing this uncertainty reduces the risk of missing the scheduled completion date due to a last minute surprise. We start with the central subsystem because we judge this to be the most complicated module.

Airline Reservation System. In the functional specification activity we were concerned only with logical clarity, but in architectural design we must also consider time and space efficiency. The first question we consider is whether the airline reservation system must be broken into concurrent tasks at the top level. Such concurrency may be needed to meet otherwise infeasible performance constraints by using multiple processors. We would like to avoid partitioning for concurrency if we can because partitioning increases the development effort. Requirement C2.4 says the expected load is 10K reservations per day. We make the conservative assumption that all of these requests occur during the normal working day, which is eight hours long. This gives an average time between requests of 2.88 seconds. Because each of the travel agent's frequent requests is relatively simple computationally, we expect 2.88 seconds to be ample for responding to a request if the machine is not doing anything else at the time. Because the airline reservation system does not contain any atomic transactions, there cannot be any long uninterruptible sequences of actions that can lock out other users for extended periods of time. We conclude the airline reservation system can be implemented as a single task. This implies the airline reservation system corresponds to a single unit of code at the top level, which implements an individual state machine.

The constraints on time efficiency appear to be feasible, but we notice a potential space problem because the reservations component of the state model grows without bound unless the travel agent explicitly cancels each reservation after the date of the flight. This is not practical since the travel agent would have to keep track of which passengers hold reservations, defeating the original purpose of the system. The natural expiration of a reservation is based on the date rather than on any of the other operations of the system; therefore, we decide to add a periodic temporal event for retiring stale reservations. We specify the temporal event to occur at 4 a.m. because we expect a low transaction rate at that time. This decision is recorded in Fig. 4.1. The retire temporal was not identified during functional specification because it does not affect the behavior of the system as observed by the users. In general, temporal events directly interacting with the users are included in the functional specification, although our case study does not provide any examples of this. The purpose of the temporal introduced in our design is to improve the resource consumption characteristics of the system, particularly with respect to secondary storage.

A new module for the airline reservation system design has been created to allow implementation concepts to be added without cluttering the user view of the system contained in the functional specification. Everything in the functional specification for the airline reservation system has been inherited by this module. It is important to maintain this distinction to support the creation of clear user manuals, which should contain user concepts but not implementation concepts. We have decided to implement the airline reservation system as a task because of the need to provide mutual exclusion between the temporal

```
MACHINE airline_reservation_system_design
    -- PRAGMA task(airline_reservation_system_design)
  INHERIT airline_reservation_system
  INHERIT time
  INHERIT time_unit

  TEMPORAL retire
    WHERE hour(TIME) = 4 & PERIOD = (1 days)
    TRANSITION ALL(r: reservation ::
                   r IN reservations <=>
                   r IN *reservations & date(r) >= date(TIME) )
END
```

FIGURE 4.1
Top Level of the Architectural Design

event and the requests from the travel agents and airline managers. This decision is recorded via a pragma on the second line of the specification. Pragmas are discussed in Section 4.4.2, and in Appendix E.

Because the module to be decomposed is a machine, we must consider all of the operations and choose a suitable data structure for providing a good implementation. At this point we do not have to work out the details of the representation, but we do have to commit ourselves to an overall representation approach, because the components of the implementation data structure influence the choice of modules at the next lower level.

The abstract components of the state are a set of reservations and a mapping from `flight_ids` to `flights`. We estimate the sizes of these data structures as follows. Requirement C2.4 says there are 10K reservations per day, and our experience with air travel indicates booking a reservation several months in advance is not unusual, so we estimate an average lifetime for a reservation to be 100 days, leading to a 1M set size for reservations. Because there are less than 100 major airline companies (our phone book lists about 30) and most flight numbers are three digits long, we expect no more than 100K flights. We make a note to check our assumptions about the lifetime of a reservation and the number of flights with the customer.

The volume of the data and our desire for the state of the airline reservation system to survive possible machine crashes suggest both state components should reside on a secondary storage device. Examining the operations of the airline reservation system, we note `reservations` are accessed by `flight_id` and `date` or range of `dates`, and `flights` are accessed by `flight_id` or by `origin` and `destination`. In all cases the number of data elements to be retrieved is small compared to the size of the entire data structure. The performance constraints do not allow us to scan the entire data structure on each access, since the data structures are very large and require potentially slow accesses to secondary storage. This makes it important to provide indexes that allow the speedy retrieval of relatively small amounts of information that can be used to satisfy these kinds of requests. Because both components of the state need nontrivial operations that do not match those of the standard types, we introduce some new abstract data types.

The next decision is whether each state component should be a separate type, or whether the two should be combined in some fashion. Because there is little interaction between the two components and the access patterns for each component are different, there is little to be gained by combining them. If we keep the components separate, we gain some locality of information. Consequently, we introduce one abstract data type for each component of the state.

We use types rather than machines for representing the components of the state because it introduces extra flexibility at little cost. Flexibility is desirable in general, and it is especially important for our example because we probably have to partition the system for concurrency in future versions. A natural way to do this is by cutting the data space into disjoint subsets (buckets) via a hashing function, and introducing an independent task for managing the items in each bucket. This is attractive because the tasks managing the buckets can all be instances of the same task type, and hence can be implemented by the same code. Such a partition has many distinct fragments of the flight_schedule and the reservation_set, one for each bucket. Each of these fragments is an instance of the abstract data types we define below. We do not expect the initial version of the system to need more than one instance for these types.

The specification for the type flight_schedule is given in Fig. 4.2. The purpose of this mutable type is to represent all aspects of the flight

FIGURE 4.2
Specification for Flight_Schedule

```
TYPE flight_schedule
  INHERIT final_flight_view
    -- Flight concepts from the environment model.
  IMPORT flight_description description
    FROM final_travel_agent_interface

  MODEL(m: map{flight_id, flight}, name: string)
  INVARIANT ALL(fs: flight_schedule :: same_id(fs)),
    ALL(fs1 fs2: flight_schedule ::
        fs1.name = fs1.name => fs1 = fs2 )
    -- PRAGMA persistent(flight_schedule)
    -- PRAGMA direct_allocation(flight_schedule)

  MESSAGE open(name: string, fs: flight_schedule)
    -- PRAGMA update(fs, fs1)
    -- PRAGMA representation(string, text)
    WHEN SOME(fs1: flight_schedule :: fs1.name = name)
      REPLY (fs1: flight_schedule) WHERE fs1.name = name
    OTHERWISE REPLY (fs1: flight_schedule)
      TRANSITION new(fs1), domain(fs1.m) = { }, fs1.name = name

  MESSAGE add(i: flight_id, price: money,
              origin destination: airport,
              departure arrival: time, capacity: nat,
              fs: flight_schedule)
    CHOOSE(f: flight SUCH THAT id(f) = i & price(f) = price &
           origin(f) = origin & destination(f) = destination &
           departure(f) = departure & arrival(f) = arrival &
           capacity(f) = capacity )
    TRANSITION fs.m = bind(i, f, *fs.m) -- Add flight.
    -- Replaces the previous flight if there was one.
```

```
MESSAGE remove(i: flight_id, fs: flight_schedule)
  TRANSITION fs.m = remove(i, *fs.m)

MESSAGE member(i: flight_id, fs: flight_schedule)
  REPLY(b: boolean) WHERE b <=> i IN fs.m

MESSAGE capacity(i: flight_id, fs: flight_schedule)
  WHEN i IN domain(fs.m)
    REPLY (n: nat) WHERE n = capacity(fs.m[i])
  OTHERWISE REPLY EXCEPTION no_such_flight

MESSAGE find_flights(fs: flight_schedule, o d: airport)
  GENERATE(s: sequence[flight_description])
  WHERE ALL(f: flight :: description(f) IN s <=>
            f IN range(fs.m) & origin(f) = o &
            destination(f) = d )

CONCEPT same_id(fs: flight_schedule)
  VALUE(b: boolean)
  WHERE b <=> ALL(i: flight_id SUCH THAT i IN fs.m ::
                  id(fs.m[i]) = i )
END
```

schedule relevant to the airline reservation system. The first step in defining a new abstract data type such as flight_schedule is to identify the operations of the type. The operations of the type are chosen to handle the aspects of each operation of the airline reservation system affecting the flight schedule. The intended relationship between the operations of the airline reservation system and those of the flight_schedule type is summarized in Table 4.1. The table shows which operations of the flight_schedule are used in the implementation of each operation of the airline reservation system. The operations of the type were invented by constructing this correspondence, and it is included in the design documentation for future reference. To serve our educational objective, we record the dependency information in this chapter. In a real project these relationships would be recorded in the project database. The operation dependency table is used to review the design. Inspection of the table shows all the specified flight_schedule operations are needed for the implementation of the airline reservation system.

The designer has to consider the implementation strategy for each operation of a high-level module to define the operations needed at the next lower level, and to check that a simple implementation with adequate performance and reliability is feasible. During architectural design the designer is not

TABLE 4.1
INTENDED USE OF THE FLIGHT SCHEDULE OPERATIONS

A_r_s_d	Flight_schedule
INITIALLY	Open
Find_flights	Find_flights
Reserve	Capacity
Cancel	Member
Notify	Member
Add_flight	Member, add
Drop_flight	Member, remove
New_fare	Member, add
Retire	

concerned about the details of the implementation except as needed to achieve these goals. In this case the implementation of each operation is very simple, and corresponds directly to the descriptions in the functional specification. The designer relies on insight and past experience to evaluate the design. Because no implementation difficulties are apparent, the implementation structure is not refined any further, and the dependency relationships are the only explicit descriptions of the implementation structure that are produced at this point.

The next step in the design of a new abstract type is to invent a conceptual model for the instances of the type. The first approximation to the model for the flight_schedule is taken from the schedule component of the state model for the airline reservation system in the functional specification, which is a mapping from flight_ids to flights. The conceptual model is reviewed and refined by analyzing the information needed to support the operations of the type. We extend the model by associating names with the schedule objects because we want the state of the system to survive system crashes. The open operation is used to initialize the state of the airline reservation system when it is started. Rather than creating a new flight_schedule every time the system comes up, the open operation checks whether a flight_schedule with the given name already exists, and if it does (when the system is brought up after a crash rather than for the first time) it returns the existing flight_schedule rather than creating a new one. The design reflects a decision to implement the flight_schedule using secondary storage. This decision is recorded using the pragma persistent(flight_schedule).

Our design is based on the assumption that files survive system crashes, which is not always true in practice. The contents of a file can get corrupted if the system crashes while it is halfway through a file update. Such events are relatively rare but possible. If the system is corrupted in such a way, the corrupted files can be restored to a previous consistent state from a backup tape, at the cost of losing the effects of the transactions between the time of the most recent backup copy and the crash. We assume backup copies of the file system are made regularly by the computer center by some means outside the system we are developing, and we rely on backup tapes to restore a relatively recent consistent state in the event of a crash. This decision is based on the sparseness of the budget for the development of the initial version of the system.

One way to achieve a reliable implementation of stable storage requires two copies of each file to guarantee that at least one copy is always in a consistent state, and a checksum for detecting whether each file is in a consistent state. Such implementations have more complicated code and impose a penalty of roughly a factor of two in both time and space for better reliability. An implementation based on this strategy would always be able to recover from a software crash without relying on backup tapes, and would not lose the effects of any transactions except in the event of irreversible hardware damage such as a disk head crash. We do not provide stable storage in our first implementation, but we acquaint the customer with the possibility of adding this feature in a future enhancement, for a suitable price.

We would like to avoid dynamic storage allocation for instances of the type flight_schedule, because this makes implementation easier. Since implementations of Ada are not required to provide a garbage collector, portable robust use of dynamically allocated storage would require the implementation of the flight_schedule to reclaim unused storage, which would add to the difficulty of the implementation. The decision to avoid dynamic storage allocation is recorded explicitly using the pragma direct_allocation (flight_schedule), which signifies that the main memory associated with each instance of the type is directly associated with a program variable, rather than being dynamically allocated from the heap and referenced via pointers (Ada access types). This decision is also reflected in the abstract interface of the open operation, which takes a flight_schedule as an input in addition to producing one as an output. The input fs is interpreted as an object that is not needed in the next state, so that its primary storage can be recycled to represent the new flight_schedule. Since the output does not depend on the properties of the incoming flight_schedule, fs can have an arbitrary value, including undefined (uninitialized) values. This pattern is characteristic of implementations using the direct_allocation strategy. Note that the open operation does not destroy values, and that a partially recycled flight_schedule can be restored by a subsequent open operation.

The pragma update(fs, fs1) indicates that the Spec input variable fs should be implemented as an Ada parameter with the mode in out, and merged with the output variable fs1. This means the Ada formal parameter fs will represent the Spec input variable fs at the start of the open operation and the Spec output variable fs1 at the end of the open operation. This packaging decision reflects the earlier decision about direct allocation, which implies that the open operation ends the lifetime of the input variable fs.

When built-in Spec types appear in the interfaces of a module, we have to consider how to map them into the types of the implementation language. We record such a decision using the pragma representation(string, text), which says the argument to the open operation should be represented using the abstract data type text, which is a reusable Ada component defined in Appendix F. The type text provides variable-length character strings, and is needed because the string types predefined in Ada provide only fixed-length strings. The unconstrained string types of Ada can be used for subprogram parameters containing strings of fixed but unknown lengths, but it is not possible to declare variables of unconstrained types without specifying a fixed length. We choose variable-length strings for object names to avoid complicating the design.

We have chosen to generate the sequence of flight descriptions produced by find_flights incrementally rather than returning an entire sequence, because this eliminates an intermediate data structure, simplifying the implementation at the lower levels. This decision is reflected in the specification of the find_flights message by using GENERATE rather than REPLY.

The type reservation_set must be refined before we can check feasibility. A specification for the type reservation_set is given in Fig. 4.3. Many of the design decisions here are similar to those we made in the flight_schedule type. We have decided to implement the concepts holds and bookings from the airline reservation system because they are needed to decide which case of the response applies. Concepts used in preconditions of a composite module are usually implemented at the next lower level for this reason. We rename the concepts because we want to use the original names for the messages. We cannot overload the names because the signatures of the concepts and the corresponding messages are the same. This renaming is

FIGURE 4.3
Specification for Reservation_Set

```
TYPE reservation_set
  INHERIT final_travel_agent_view
    -- Reservation properties from environment model.
  IMPORT single_reservation FROM final_travel_agent_interface
  IMPORT holds_concept bookings_concept
    FROM airline_reservation_system_design1

  MODEL(s: set{reservation}, name: string)
  INVARIANT ALL(rs: reservation_set
                    :: single_reservation(rs.s))
    -- PRAGMA persistent(reservation_set)
    -- PRAGMA direct_allocation(reservation_set)
```

```
MESSAGE open(name: string, rs: reservation_set)
  -- PRAGMA update(rs, rs1)
  -- PRAGMA representation(string, text)
  WHEN SOME(rs1: reservation_set :: rs1.name = name)
    REPLY (rs1: reservation_set) WHERE rs1.name = name
  OTHERWISE REPLY (rs1: reservation_set)
    TRANSITION new(rs1), rs1.s = { }, rs1.name = name

MESSAGE add(i: flight_id, d: date, p: passenger, a: agent,
            rs: reservation_set )
  CHOOSE(r: reservation SUCH THAT
         id(r) = i & date(r) = d & passenger(r) = p &
         agent(r) = a )
  TRANSITION rs.s = *rs.s U {r}

MESSAGE remove(i: flight_id, d: date, p: passenger,
               rs: reservation_set )
  CHOOSE(r: reservation SUCH THAT
         r IN *rs.s & passenger(r) = p & id(r) = i &
         date(r) = d )
  TRANSITION rs.s = *rs.s - {r}

MESSAGE remove(i: flight_id, rs: reservation_set)
  TRANSITION ALL(r: reservation ::
                 r IN rs <=> r IN *rs & id(r) ~= i )

MESSAGE remove(d: date, rs: reservation_set)
  TRANSITION ALL(r: reservation ::
                 r IN rs <=> r IN *rs & date(r) >= d )

MESSAGE holds(p: passenger, i: flight_id, d: date,
              rs: reservation_set )
  REPLY(b: boolean)
  WHERE b <=> holds_concept(p, i, d, rs.s)

MESSAGE bookings(i: flight_id, d: date, rs: reservation_set)
  REPLY(n: nat)
  WHERE n = bookings_concept(i, d, rs)

MESSAGE notify(a: agent_id, i: flight_id, d: date,
               rs: reservation_set )
  GENERATE (s: sequence{reservation})
    WHERE ALL(r: reservation :: r IN s <=>
              r IN rs & agent(r) = a & id(r) = i &
              date(r) >= d )
END
```

```
MACHINE airline_reservation_system_design1
  INHERIT airline_reservation_system_design
    RENAME holds AS holds_concept
    RENAME bookings AS bookings_concept
END
```

FIGURE 4.4
Renamed Concepts from the Functional Specification

shown in Fig. 4.4. The `reservation_set` operations needed to implement each of the airline reservation system operations are summarized in Table 4.2. We have used numbers corresponding to order of appearance in the specification to identify different versions of the overloaded operator `remove`. Inspection of this table shows all the specified messages are needed in the implementation of the airline reservation system.

We now consider the implementation of the operations of the airline reservation system. Examining the two operation correspondence tables, the designer concludes the operations are also sufficient, based on previous programming experience and the ability to sketch an implementation mentally. The designer decides each of the operations of the airline reservation system has a small and simple implementation in terms of the operations of the two data types, provided that flight attribute concepts such as `capacity` are implemented. At this time the designer classifies each of the operations as `small` for the purposes of effort estimation (see Section 4.6.1). We note that the implementation of the operations of the airline reservation system in terms of the proposed abstract data types is free of loops or recursions, so that this level of the design is unlikely to introduce any performance problems.

No additional types or functions are needed at this level, so the decompo-

TABLE 4.2
INTENDED USE OF THE RESERVATION SET OPERATIONS

A_r_s_d	Reservation_set
INITIALLY	Open
Find_flights	
Reserve	Add, holds, bookings
Cancel	Remove#1, holds
Notify	Notify
Add_flight	
Drop_flight	Remove#2
New_fare	
Retire	Remove#3

sition of the top-level module of the airline reservation system is complete. We follow the principle of working on the most difficult and uncertain part of the design first, to reduce the risks of not being able to meet the deadline for the project. We proceed with the decomposition of the components at the next level, because we judge these modules to be relatively complex.

Flight Schedule. Defining a data representation for the `flight_schedule` involves a careful choice of data structures. Since the frequent operations are `find_flights`, `member`, and `capacity`, the dominant access paths are by `[origin, destination]` and by `flight_id`. The infrequent operations do not introduce new access paths. Consulting a book on data structures such as [1] for efficient file organizations, we see the `find_flights` operation can be performed efficiently using a `B_tree` with the `origin` and `destination` as keys, and `flight_descriptions` as elements. The `member` and `capacity` operations can be performed efficiently by a `hashed_file` with key `flight_id`. There is no need to replicate the flight descriptions in the hashed file, which can contain only the `flight_id` and the `capacity` components of a `flight`. At this point, we can see there is no need for an independent implementation of the `flight` type, which has been defined as a concept. To summarize our decisions so far, a `flight_schedule` is represented by a `B_tree` and a `hashed_file`.

The abstract types `B_tree` and `hashed_file` are reusable Ada components (Appendix F). Both of these types are generic, and represent the most efficient, well known secondary storage structures for a wide class of implementations. `B_trees` are efficient for retrieving individual items as well as for sequential scans of ordered intervals on the key space. `Hashed_files` can be slightly more efficient than `B_trees` for retrieving individual items, but they do not support efficient subrange scans. The specification of `B_tree` is shown in Fig. 4.5. `B_trees` are restricted implementations of maps that require the keys to be drawn from a totally ordered data type. The `key` and `value` types are the domain and range of the map. The function parameter `le` is the total ordering relation on the key type. The `degree` of a `B_tree` is a bound on the number of descendents of an internal node of the tree structure, which affects the performance but not the results of the operations.

To adapt the generic `B_tree` type to our needs we have to determine the values of the generic parameters. We leave the choice of the `degree` parameter to the module design stage, since it does not affect the software architecture. The `flight_schedule B_tree` has keys containing the `origin`, `destination`, and `flight_id` (the `flight_id` is included to make sure each `flight` corresponds to a unique `key`). The `value` associated with a `key` contains the rest of the components of a `flight_description`: the arrival and departure times and the price. The keys are sorted with respect to the lexicographic ordering relation `lex_order{o:: airport, d:: airport,`

FIGURE 4.5
Specification of B_Tree

```
TYPE B_tree{key value: type, le: function{key, key, boolean},
            degree: nat
            SUCH THAT Total_ordering(le), degree > 2 }
    -- The degree parameter affects only the performance.
  IMPORT Total_ordering FROM total_order{key}
  IMPORT sorted FROM sequence{value}
  IMPORT One_to_one FROM function{Bt, string}

  MODEL(m: map{key, value}, n: string, open: boolean)
  INVARIANT One_to_one(name)   -- B_trees have unique names.
    -- PRAGMA direct_allocation(Bt)

  MESSAGE open(name: string, bt: Bt)
    -- PRAGMA update(bt, bt1)
    -- PRAGMA representation(string, text)
    WHEN SOME(bt1: Bt :: bt1.n = name)
      REPLY(bt1: Bt) WHERE bt1.n = name
      TRANSITION bt1.open
    OTHERWISE REPLY(bt1: Bt)
      TRANSITION new(bt1), bt1.n = name, domain(bt1.m) = { },
        bt1.open

  MESSAGE close(bt: Bt) TRANSITION ~bt.open
      -- Guarantees the B_tree will exist after termination
      -- of the main program.

  MESSAGE delete(bt: Bt) TRANSITION ~(bt IN Bt)
      -- Deletes the external file containing the B_tree.

  MESSAGE name(bt: Bt) REPLY(s: string) WHERE s = bt.n
      -- The name of the external file containing the B_tree.

  MESSAGE add(k: key, x: value, bt: Bt)
    TRANSITION bt.m = bind(i, f, *bt.m)   -- bt.m[k] = x.
      -- Replaces the previous value if there was one.

  MESSAGE remove(k: key, bt: Bt)
    TRANSITION bt.m = remove(i, *bt.m)   -- ~(k IN bt.m).

  MESSAGE fetch(k: key, bt: Bt)
    WHEN k IN bt.m
      REPLY(x: value) WHERE x = bt.m[k]
    OTHERWISE REPLY EXCEPTION domain_error
```

```
MESSAGE member(k: key, bt: Bt) REPLY(b: boolean)
   WHERE b <=> k IN bt.m

MESSAGE scan_between(k1 k2: key, bt: Bt)
   GENERATE(s: sequence(pair))
   WHERE ALL(x: pair :: x IN s <=>
             x.k IN bt.m & x.v = bt.m[k] & k1 <= x.k <= k2 ),
      sorted(le)(apply(get(k), s))
      -- s contains all of the pairs in the map with keys
      -- in the range [k1 .. k2]
      -- and the generated sequence is sorted on the keys.

MESSAGE scan_from(k: key, bt: Bt) GENERATE(s: sequence(pair))
   WHERE ALL(x: pair :: x IN s <=>
             x.k IN bt.m & x.v = bt.m[k] & k <= x.k ),
      sorted(le)(apply(get(k), s))
      -- s contains all of the pairs in the map with keys >= k
      -- and the generated sequence is sorted on the keys.

MESSAGE scan_to(k: key, bt: Bt) GENERATE(s: sequence(pair))
   WHERE ALL(x: pair :: x IN s <=>
             x.k IN bt.m & x.v = bt.m[k] & x.k <= k ),
      sorted(le)(apply(get(k), s))
      -- s contains all of the pairs in the map with keys <= k
      -- and the generated sequence is sorted on the keys.

MESSAGE scan(bt: Bt) GENERATE(s: sequence(pair))
   WHERE ALL(x: pair :: x IN s <=> x.k IN bt.m & x.v = bt.m[k]),
      sorted(le)(apply(get(k), s))
      -- s contains all of the pairs in the map
      -- and the generated sequence is sorted on the keys.

CONCEPT pair: type WHERE pair = tuple(k:: key, v:: value)
CONCEPT Bt: type WHERE Bt = B_tree(key, value, le, kf)
END
```

i:: flight_id). This function is another reusable Ada component (Appendix F) whose specification is given in Fig. 4.6. The standard ordering on character strings is a special case of the lexicographic ordering on tuples or sequences. The lexicographic ordering is determined by the leftmost component of the tuples that differ. Because the most significant fields are listed first, this specification implies that the keys of the flight_schedule

```
FUNCTION lex_order($s: type SUCH THAT
                    ALL(t: type :: t IN s =>
                        Subtype(t, total_order(t)) ))
  INHERIT field_names

  MESSAGE(x y: tuple($s))
    WHEN s = [ ] REPLY(b: boolean) WHERE b = true
    OTHERWISE REPLY(b: boolean)
      WHERE x[1] < y[1] |
        x[1] = y[1] &
          lex_order($s[2 .. length(s)])(rest(x), rest(y))

  CONCEPT rest(t1: tuple($s) SUCH THAT s ~= [ ])
    VALUE(t2: tuple($s1))
    WHERE t2 = remove(identifiers(s)[1], t1),
        SOME(tt: type :: s = [tt, $s1])
      -- Delete the first component of the tuple t1.
END
```

FIGURE 4.6
Specification of the Lexicographic Ordering

B_tree are sorted first by origin, then by destination, and then by flight_id. Since we have made the origin and destination the most significant keys in the ordering, maintaining the flight_schedule in this order keeps all of the flights with the same origin and destination in a contiguous block, which can be efficiently generated using the scan_between operation.

The lexicographic ordering is a total ordering relation whenever the orderings on the components are total orderings. In our application the components of a flight_display_key are totally ordered by the standard string ordering, so the lexicographic ordering meets the total ordering requirement of the generic B_tree module.

The B_tree operations needed to implement each of the flight_schedule operations are summarized in Table 4.3. The member and capacity operations of the flight_schedule are implemented using only the hashed_file component of the representation. Reviewing the table, we see some of the operations of the standard B_tree type such as fetch and delete are not used in our implementation. Because the type is already available, it does not save us any implementation effort to delete these operations, although it might save a small amount of program space. Since memory space is not at a premium in our example, and some compilers perform this optimization anyway, we make no changes to the standard components.

TABLE 4.3
INTENDED USE OF THE B_TREE OPERATIONS
FOR THE FLIGHT SCHEDULE

Flight_schedule	B_tree
Open	Open
Add	Add
Remove	Remove
Member	
Capacity	
Find_flights	Range

The order in which the flights are displayed by the find_flights command was not specified in the functional specification. We have decided to generate the flights with flight_ids in alphabetical order, since this ordering is provided naturally by the data structure. We are operating under tight budget constraints, and supporting a different ordering costs more because an explicit ordering procedure would be needed for an alternative ordering. We make a note of this refinement for eventual customer review, following the principle that refinements affecting the external behavior of the system should be approved before we spend much implementation effort on them. We record the refinement as shown in Fig. 4.7.

A specification for the hashed_file data type is shown in Fig. 4.8. Hashed_files are another restricted implementation of maps that requires a hashing function on keys, but does not require the key type to have an ordering. Hashed_files support the same operations as B_trees except for the subrange generators.

We have to determine the values of the generic parameters for our application. We leave the choice of the block size and the number of buckets to the

```
TYPE flight_schedule1
  INHERIT flight_schedule

  MESSAGE find_flights(fs: flight_schedule, o d: airport)
    GENERATE(s: sequence(flight_description))
    WHERE ALL(i j: nat SUCH THAT
            i IN domain(s) & j IN domain(s) ::
            s[i].id <= s[j].id )
END
```

FIGURE 4.7
Refinement of the Flight Schedule

FIGURE 4.8
Specification for Hashed_File

```
TYPE hashed_file(key value: type, hash: function(key, nat),
                 pairs block_size: nat SUCH THAT
                    Subtype(key, equality(key)), pairs > 0,
                    block_size > 0 )
    -- The last two parameters affect only the performance.
    -- Pairs is the expected number of [key, value]
    -- pairs in the hashed file.
    -- Blocksize is the number of elements per file block.
  IMPORT One_to_one FROM function(Hf, string)
  IMPORT Subtype FROM type

  MODEL(m: map(key, value), n: string, open: boolean)
  INVARIANT One_to_one(name) -- Hashed_files have unique names.
    -- PRAGMA direct_allocation(Hf)

  MESSAGE open(name: string, fs: Hf)
    -- PRAGMA update(ht, ht1)
    -- PRAGMA representation(string, text)
    WHEN SOME(ht1: Hf :: ht1.n = name)
      REPLY(ht1: Hf) WHERE ht1.n = name
      TRANSITION ht1.open
    OTHERWISE REPLY(ht1: Hf)
      TRANSITION new(ht1), ht1.n = name, domain(ht1.m) = { },
        ht1.open

  MESSAGE close(ht: Hf) TRANSITION ~ht.open
      -- Guarantees the hashed file will exist after
      -- termination of the main program.

  MESSAGE delete(ht: Hf) TRANSITION ~(ht IN Hf)
      -- Deletes the external file containing the B_tree.

  MESSAGE name(ht: Hf) REPLY(s: string) WHERE s = ht.n
      -- The name of the external file containing
      -- the hashed_file.

  MESSAGE add(k: key, x: value, ht: Hf)
    TRANSITION hf.m = bind(i, f, *hf.m)   -- hf.m[k] = x.
      -- Replaces the previous value if there was one.

  MESSAGE remove(k: key, ht: Hf)
    TRANSITION hf.m = remove(i, *hf.m)   -- ~(k IN hf.m).

  MESSAGE fetch(k: key, ht: Hf)
    WHEN k IN ht.m REPLY(x: value) WHERE x = ht.m[k]
    OTHERWISE REPLY EXCEPTION domain_error
```

```
MESSAGE member(k: key, ht: Hf)
  REPLY(b: boolean) WHERE b <=> k IN ht.m

MESSAGE scan(hf: Hf) GENERATE(s: sequence{pair})
  WHERE ALL(x: pair :: x IN s <=> x.k IN hf.m & x.v
                                          = hf.m[k])
     -- s contains all of the pairs in the map.

CONCEPT pair: type WHERE pair = tuple{k:: key, v:: value}
CONCEPT Hf: type
  WHERE Hf = hashed_file{key, value, hash, pairs,
                          block_size}
END
```

module design stage, since these parameters affect only the performance and do not impact the software architecture. The keys for the hashed_file are flight_ids and the values contain the capacity, the origin, and destination of a flight. The origin and destination are needed because the remove operation for flight_schedules identifies flights by just the flight_id; the key for the B_tree contains an origin and destination in addition to a flight_id.

Since flight_id is a restricted kind of character string, we can use the string hashing function specified in Fig. 4.9, which is another reusable Ada component (Appendix F). This function depends on all of the characters in the string, and gives different values for permutations of the same string. The base for the polynomial was chosen to be 127 because it is relatively prime to the modulus, which is a power of 2, and is close to the size of the character set, so that hash values of short strings do not overlap significantly in the code space, leading to fewer collisions. This hashing function can be used for hashed files with different numbers of buckets because the hash value is reduced modulo the number of buckets by the generic hashed file module.

The hashed file operations used in the implementation of each operation of the flight_schedule type are shown in Table 4.4. Reviewing the tables describing the implementation of the flight_schedule in terms of the B_tree and hashed_file types, we find the implementation appears to be feasible. Because an implementation using the operations specified does not need recursions or loops at this level, the only potentially slow operations are those from the underlying B_tree and hashed_file types. These data structures are among the best known for the kinds of accesses required in the application, so the architecture is a good choice for meeting the performance constraints. If we find the system is too slow after we build and run some benchmark measurements, we may have to partition for concurrency and use a multiple processor hardware configuration. Our architecture can be readily adapted to meet such a contingency, as shown in Chapter 6.

```
FUNCTION string_hash(t: type SUCH THAT
                        Subtype(t, integer), 2 ^ 7 IN t )
    -- t has an integer representation at least 8 bits long.
  IMPORT Subtype FROM type
  IMPORT Deterministic FROM function(string, t)

  MESSAGE(s: string) REPLY(n: nat)
    WHERE Deterministic(string_hash(t)), 0 <= n < modulus,
      n = SUM(i: nat SUCH THAT i IN domain(s) ::
              ordinal(s[i]) * base ^ i )
          MOD modulus
      -- Evaluates a polynomial defined by the string
      -- at the value "base".

  CONCEPT size: nat
    WHERE size = MINIMUM(i: integer SUCH THAT
                          ALL(x: t :: x < 2 ^ i) ::
                          i )
    -- Smallest number of bits needed to represent
    -- all elements of t.
  CONCEPT modulus: nat
    WHERE modulus = 2 ^ (size - 8), modulus >= 1
  CONCEPT base: nat WHERE base = 127
END
```

FIGURE 4.9
Specification of String Hash

Because we have existing implementations for the standard components B_tree, lex_order, hashed_file, and string_hash, there is no need to decompose at finer levels of detail. Similar components should be available in any mature development environment. Implementations for these components are given in Appendix F.

TABLE 4.4
INTENDED USE OF THE HASHED_FILE OPERATIONS
FOR THE FLIGHT SCHEDULE

Flight_schedule	Hashed_file
Open	Open
Add	Add, member, remove
Remove	Remove, fetch
Member	Member
Capacity	Fetch
Find_flights	

We classify the data representation of the flight_schedule as medium size and all of the messages as small. This classification is used for estimating the effort required to complete the project in Section 4.6.1.

Reservation Set. Examining the operations of reservation_set, we see that the frequent operations are add, remove#1, remove#3, holds, and bookings. The frequent access paths are therefore based on [flight_id, date, passenger], [flight_id, date], and date. The other access paths are based on flight_id and [flight_id, agent, range of dates].

Because the direct access files provided by the predefined Ada package DIRECT_IO do not allow the individual items in a file to be removed, our need to support the retire temporal of the airline reservation system via the third remove message for reservation_sets suggests we keep a separate B_tree for each reservation date. This allows the retire operation to free some disk space via the delete operation provided by Ada files, which physically removes the underlying external file. The remove operation of a B_tree returns an item in the file to a free storage pool within the file so that the space can eventually be reused. Because it does not physically remove the item from the file, the disk space needed for a given B_tree can increase but never decrease. This is a case where the properties of the implementation language affect the architectural design. Although the proposed software architecture is valid for different implementation environments, transporting the design to another language or system may change its performance characteristics.

This decision takes care of the access path based only on the date, which is needed only for the retire temporal via remove#3. The access path based on [flight_id, date] is needed for bookings. Because this operation needs only the number of reservations in the set with a given flight_id and date, we decide to maintain a redundant record of this count rather than counting the individual reservations each time we need to know the number of bookings. This suggests introducing a hashed_file for each date with flight_id as the key and the number of reservations as the value.

The access paths based on flight_id and [flight_id, agent, range of dates] can be handled by generating all of the reservations with a given flight_id and date. The need to generate ranges of elements suggests using a B_tree representation for the set of reservations, with one B_tree for each date. The key is the pair [flight_id, passenger] with the ordering lex_order{i:: flight_id, p:: passenger}. The flight_id has to be the most significant component in the ordering because we need to generate all of the reservations with a given flight_id. Since the notify operation is infrequent, we can implement it by generating all of the reservations for the given flight_id for each date in the sequence, and filter out the ones with the wrong agent.

To summarize our decisions about the representation of a `reservation_set`, there is a `B_tree` and a `hashed_file` for each `date` that has a `reservation`, where the `dates` are encoded in the file names. The `key` type for each `B_tree` is `tuple{i:: flight_id, p:: passenger}`, and the `value` type is `agent`. The `key` type for each `hashed_file` is `flight_id`, and the `value` type is `nat` (representing the number of `reservations` on the `flight` for the given `date`). The information in the `hashed_file` is redundant, and is maintained to increase the efficiency of the `bookings` operation.

The correspondence between the `reservation_set` operations and the `B_tree` operations is shown in Table 4.5 and the correspondence between the `reservation_set` operations and the `hashed_file` operations is shown in Table 4.6.

We need to maintain the set of `dates` for which reservation files exist, and to generate its elements. Because we need to generate ranges of elements, and because we want the data to survive machine crashes, we use a `B_tree` to represent the `date`-set. The `key` is a `date`, and the ordering is `"<="@date`. The values associated with `dates` are the file names for the `reservation` `B_tree` and the `bookings hashed file`, but these values are calculated from the `dates`, so there is no need to store them explicitly. Consequently, the `value` type for the `B_tree` is `null`.

The design presented here is chosen for simplicity. There is room for some improvement in efficiency, but we do not expect it to be necessary. If the date-set operations prove to be a bottleneck, we can introduce a redundant main-memory data structure to eliminate most secondary storage accesses for date-set operations. In the event we have to partition for concurrency, we may eventually have to encapsulate the date-set structure in a task to protect its operations from concurrent execution. We consider these as possible future enhancements, and note they could be added without a major impact on the proposed architecture.

The B_tree operations on the date set used in the implementation of each

TABLE 4.5
INTENDED USE OF THE B_TREE OPERATIONS
FOR THE RESERVATION SET

Reservation_set	B_tree
Open	Open
Add	Add
Remove#1	Remove
Remove#2	Range, remove
Remove#3	Delete
Holds	Member
Bookings	
Notify	Range

TABLE 4.6
INTENDED USE OF THE HASHED_FILE OPERATIONS
FOR THE RESERVATION SET

Reservation_set	Hashed_file
Open	Open
Add	Add
Remove#1	Remove
Remove#2	Range, remove
Remove#3	Delete
Holds	
Bookings	Fetch
Notify	

`reservation_set` operation are shown in Table 4.7.

We also need to generate file names from `dates`. We decide to extend the abstract data type `date` with an operation for that purpose, as shown in Fig. 4.10. We have kept only the digits of a `date` for compactness, and we have used fixed-length fields to avoid potential ambiguities of representation. We intend the `string_code` of a `date` to be concatenated with short prefix strings to generate file names for each `date`. We have introduced a new module for the `date` to keep the distinction clear between the properties of the type visible to the users and the extensions we have introduced for implementation purposes. We also expect the implementation of the type `date` to have a unique storage representation for each `date`, and we record this fact using the Spec pragma `unique_representation`. This information is needed for immutable types to determine whether they must be implemented as Ada private types or as limited private types.

We judge all of the reservation set operations to be easy to implement with the exception of `remove#2` and `notify`. To reduce the uncertainty for the feasibility of implementing these operations, we develop the rough sketches for the algorithms of these operations, shown in Figs. 4.11 and 4.12. These

TABLE 4.7
INTENDED USE OF THE DATE B_TREE OPERATIONS
FOR THE RESERVATION SET

Reservation_set	B_tree (dates)
Open	Open
Add	Add
Remove#1	
Remove#2	Scan
Remove#3	Remove
Holds	
Bookings	
Notify	Scan_from

```
TYPE date_design
  INHERIT date
  IMPORT nat FROM format
  -- PRAGMA unique_representation(date)

  MESSAGE string_code(d1: date) REPLY(s: string)
    WHERE SOME(m d y: string ::
                s = m || d || y & nat(m) = d1.month &
                nat(d) = d1.day & nat(y) = d1.year &
                length(m) = length(d) = length(y) = 2 )
END
```

FIGURE 4.10
Extension of the Type Date

```
procedure remove(i: flight_id, rs: reservation_set)
  first_key := MINIMUM(k: key SUCH THAT k.id = i :: k)
  last_key := MAXIMUM(k: key SUCH THAT k.id = i :: k)
  for d: date in scan(date_set) loop
    for r: reservation in range(first_key, last_key, rs) loop
      remove(r.p, r.i, d, rs)
    end loop
  end loop
end
```

FIGURE 4.11
Algorithm Sketch for Remove#2

```
procedure notify(a: agent_id, i: flight_id, d: date,
                 rs: reservation_set )
  first_key := MINIMUM(k: key SUCH THAT k.id = i :: k)
  last_key := MAXIMUM(k: key SUCH THAT k.id = i :: k)
  for d1: date in scan_from(d, date_set) loop
    for r: reservation in range(first_key, last_key, rs)
                         such that r.a = a
    loop
      generate(r)
    end loop
  end loop
end
```

FIGURE 4.12
Algorithm Sketch for Notify

algorithm sketches let us determine that these operations can be reasonably implemented with the primitives provided with a medium amount of effort. As a result, we classify the data representation of the `reservation_set` as medium size, the messages `remove#2` and `notify` as medium, and the rest of the messages as small. This classification is used for estimating the effort required to complete the project in Section 4.6.1.

The algorithm sketches are imperfect, but we make no effort to refine them or to verify their correctness at the architectural design stage because they are sufficient for our current purpose, which is to check feasibility, and to record the intentions of the designer about the use of the primitives provided. The sketches will be perfected in the module design stage.

At this point we must decide on the implementation of the type concepts `flight_description` and `reservation`, and two instances of the predefined Spec type `sequence`. There are no significant operations for flight descriptions or reservations, so there is no need to introduce abstract data types for these concepts. Because these types appear in the interfaces of the airline reservation system, they have to be implemented. There is no need to add any extra components, so we represent `flight_description` and `reserva-` `tion` as Ada record types with components corresponding to the attributes defined so far.

The sequence types in the airline reservation system are used to deliver sets of flight descriptions or reservations to be displayed to the travel agent. The sequences will be transmitted from the airline reservation system to the travel agent modules, which are separate tasks. The travel agent modules will transmit the displays over telephone lines, which have a relatively low speed. We consider and reject the option of generating the sequences one element at a time and producing the display incrementally because we do not want to wait for a slow display during an Ada rendezvous. Because task entries are subject to mutual exclusion, access to the airline reservation system by other travel agents would be blocked while we were transmitting the display over the tele-phone line. Because we are proposing a centralized design with a single airline reservation system task, this central task is a potential performance bottleneck, and we do not want to allow this task to be blocked while waiting for slow input/output operations. Consequently, we choose to provide a data structure for sequences, rather than generating them incrementally across the boundaries of the airline reservation system module.

We do not want to do explicit storage management and we would like to avoid the speed penalty of introducing an intermediate file, so we choose an array representation for bounded sequences rather than a linked list representa-tion or a file representation for unbounded sequences. Consequently, we have to determine bounds for the two kinds of bounded sequences in the airline reservation system. There are less than 100 airlines—most airlines do not serve very many locations, and the number for flights connecting the same origin and destination is small for a given airline—therefore 100 should be a safe upper bound for the sequence of flights produced by the find_flights command. The number of reservations on a given flight could be as large as 300 per day, there are 300 travel agents, and we expect the average lifetime of a reservation to be about 100 days; on the average, the notify command should return about 100 reservations. However, the worst case could be much worse than this, so we pick a bound of 1000 to give us a reasonable safety factor without unduly straining the memory capacity of most computers. These decisions are recorded in Fig. 4.13. A specification for the reusable component unbounded_sequence is shown in Fig. 4.14, and a specification for the reusable component bounded_sequence is shown in Fig. 4.15. As you can see, the interfaces of both types are the same except for the preconditions associated with the overflow exception. Ada implementations of both unbounded and bounded sequences are given in Appendix F. Unbounded sequences are implemented using linked lists; bounded sequences are implemented using constrained arrays.

There are no more new modules at the next level of detail, so the architectural design of the airline reservation system module is complete at this point.

Travel Agent.   This section addresses the design of the travel agent module. First we consider whether we have to partition this module for concurrency. The processing performed by each instance of the travel agent is minimal and should not cause any performance problems, so that partitioning is not likely to be needed. However, the travel agent is a generic module with multiple distinct instances. The travel agents will be using telephone connections, and according to requirement C2.5, the system must be able to support 300 travel agents. Because travel agents spend extended periods of time connected to the airline reservation system, we must provide a separate telephone connection for each

---

```
MACHINE airline_reservation_system_design2
 INHERIT airline_reservation_system_design1
  -- PRAGMA representation(sequence{flight_description},
  --                       bounded_sequence{flight_description,
  --                                  100 })
  -- PRAGMA representation(sequence{reservation},
  --                       bounded_sequence{reservation,
  --                                  1000} )
  -- PRAGMA representation(flight_description, record)
  -- PRAGMA representation(reservation, record)
END
```

FIGURE 4.13
Implementations of Type Concepts

```
TYPE unbounded_sequence(t: type)
  MODEL(s: sequence(t)) INVARIANT true

  MESSAGE create
    WHEN sufficient_memory(0)
      REPLY(s: unbounded_sequence(t)) WHERE s.s = [ ]
    OTHERWISE REPLY EXCEPTION overflow

  MESSAGE add(x: t, s: unbounded_sequence(t))
      -- PRAGMA update(s, s1)
    WHEN sufficient_memory(length(s) + 1)
      REPLY(s1: unbounded_sequence(t)) WHERE s1.s = s.s || [x]
    OTHERWISE REPLY EXCEPTION overflow

  MESSAGE append(s1 s2: unbounded_sequence(t))
    WHEN sufficient_memory(length(s1) + length(s2))
      REPLY(s3: unbounded_sequence(t))
      WHERE s3.s = s1.s || s2.s
    OTHERWISE REPLY EXCEPTION overflow

  MESSAGE fetch(s: unbounded_sequence(t), n: nat)
    WHEN 1 <= n <= length(s.s) REPLY(x: t) WHERE x = s.s[n]
    OTHERWISE REPLY EXCEPTION bounds_error

  MESSAGE length(s: unbounded_sequence(t))
    REPLY(n: nat) WHERE n = length(s.s)

  MESSAGE scan(s: unbounded_sequence(t))
    GENERATE(s1: sequence(t)) WHERE s1 = s.s

  CONCEPT sufficient_memory(n: nat) VALUE(b: boolean)
    -- True if there is enough memory available
    -- to create a new sequence of size n.
END
```

FIGURE 4.14
Specification of Unbounded Sequences

travel agent to meet the response time specified in the requirement C2.2. From
the point of view of an Ada program, a telephone connection looks like a pair
of text files: one for the input stream from the travel agent's keyboard, and one
for the output stream to the travel agent's display screen. The fact that these
files will be realized by modems and telephone lines does not affect the structure of the software. Ada files do not support checking whether a character is

```
TYPE bounded_sequence(t: type, bound: nat)
  MODEL(s: sequence(t))
  INVARIANT ALL(s: bounded_sequence(t, bound) ::
                  length(s.s) <= bound )

  MESSAGE create
    REPLY(s: bounded_sequence(t, bound)) WHERE s.s = [ ]

  MESSAGE add(x: t, s: bounded_sequence(t, bound))
      -- PRAGMA update(s, s1)
    WHEN length(s.s) < bound
      REPLY(s1: bounded_sequence(t, bound))
        WHERE s1.s = s.s || [x]
    OTHERWISE REPLY EXCEPTION overflow

  MESSAGE append(s1 s2: bounded_sequence(t, bound))
    WHEN length(s1.s) + length(s2.s) <= bound
      REPLY(s3: bounded_sequence(t, bound))
        WHERE s3.s = s1.s || s2.s
    OTHERWISE REPLY EXCEPTION overflow

  MESSAGE fetch(s: bounded_sequence(t, bound), n: nat)
    WHEN 1 <= n <= length(s.s) REPLY(x: t) WHERE x = s.s[n]
    OTHERWISE REPLY EXCEPTION bounds_error

  MESSAGE length(s: bounded_sequence(t, bound))
    REPLY(n: nat) WHERE n = length(s.s)

  MESSAGE scan(s: bounded_sequence(t, bound))
    GENERATE(s1: sequence(t)) WHERE s1 = s.s
END
```

FIGURE 4.15
Specification of Bounded Sequences

available without waiting until a character arrives, so a design with an independent task for each telephone line is desirable to avoid delaying the response of the whole system while waiting for input from a particular travel agent. We decide to have a separate instance of the travel agent module for each telephone line, where the instances of the travel agent execute as concurrent tasks. We record this decision as shown in Fig. 4.16. We have included the files to be used to communicate with the travel agent's keyboard and display screen as part of the state of the machine. As in the previous section, we define a new module for the enhancements at the top level of the architectural design to

```
MACHINE travel_agent_design(modem_id: nat)
   -- PRAGMA task(travel_agent_design)
  INHERIT final_travel_agent(modem_id)

  STATE(input output: text_file)
  INVARIANT name(input) = input_name(modem_id),
    name(output) = output_name(modem_id),
    mode(input) = #in_file, mode(output) = #out_file
  INITIALLY is_open(input), is_open(output)

  -- PRAGMA representation(string, text)
  -- PRAGMA representation(text_file, text_io.file_type)
  -- PRAGMA external_input(interpret_command)
  -- PRAGMA returned_value(flights)
  -- PRAGMA returned_value(reservations)
  -- PRAGMA returned_value(done)

  CONCEPT text_file: type

  CONCEPT input_name(id: nat) VALUE(s: string)
    -- The file name for the input stream is generated
    -- from the modem_id.

  CONCEPT output_name(id: nat) VALUE(s: string)
    -- The file name for the input stream is generated
    -- from the modem_id.
END
```

FIGURE 4.16
Top Level of the Travel Agent Module

keep a clear boundary between the functional specification and the architectural design. We decide to use variable length strings to represent file names and to use the predefined Ada text file types to represent the communication lines, as indicated by the representation pragmas.

The state of the travel agent machine consists of a pair of text files, which are provided in Ada by the predefined package TEXT_IO. Because this type is already available nothing has to be done to refine the data structure at lower levels. The invariant describes the conventions for file names and the direction of information flow for each file. The initialization description indicates the files must be opened when the system comes up. We decide that there should be a uniform convention for generating file names from modem ids, but we defer the details of these mappings until the module design stage, since this information does not affect the software architecture.

We record the implicit decisions that the interpret_command message will come from the travel agent outside the system, and that the flights, reservations, and done messages will be responses from the airline reservation system rather than independent requests. This is done using the pragmas external_input and returned_value.

Next we consider the implementation of each message. The interpret_command message is easy to implement in terms of the editing and travel agent command format concepts edit, is_find_flights, is_reserve, is_cancel, and is_notify. These concepts define command formats to be parsed and translated. The need for a translation step suggests that we seek a translator generator tool. Tools exist for automatically generating parsing and translating programs based on attribute grammars. Since a translator generator tool interfacing to Ada is not available in our installation, we implement Ada functions for each of these concepts manually. A specification for edit is shown in Fig. 4.17. We have decided to implement the edit concept exactly as it stands. The command format concepts are extended from predicates to functions returning both a boolean indicating whether the predicate is satisfiable, and a set of data objects satisfying the predicate in case such a set exists. If the predicate is not satisfiable, the data objects returned are not specified, and hence may take arbitrary or ill-formed values. Such an interface is chosen because Ada does not support variable numbers of output parameters. We have also removed the command name from the string, because it must be extracted first to determine which of the parsing functions to call. Specifications for these functions are given in Fig. 4.18.

The transformations from concepts to specifications for the functions to be implemented are relatively mechanical and should be supported by high-level editing commands in the specification tool of an automated software development environment.

The sequence of flights and the sequence of reservations in the normal responses are easy to generate one element at a time using scan@ bounded_sequence. Functions for displaying individual flights and reservations are needed for representing the bodies of these loops. These functions are specified in Fig. 4.19. Some inputs of these functions must be

---

```
FUNCTION edit_command
  INHERIT basic_edit  -- Defines the concept edit.

  MESSAGE(s1: string) REPLY(s2: string) WHERE s2 = edit(s1)
    -- PRAGMA representation(string. text)
END
```

FIGURE 4.17
Specification for Edit_Command

```
FUNCTION parse_find_flights
  INHERIT travel_agent_command_formats
  INHERIT airline_reservation_system_type_formats
  MESSAGE(s: string) -- PRAGMA representation(string, text)
    WHEN SOME(o d: airport :: is_find_flights("f " || s, o, d))
      REPLY(b: boolean, o d: airport)
        WHERE b = true, is_find_flights(s, o, d)
    OTHERWISE REPLY(b: boolean, o d: airport) WHERE b = false
END

FUNCTION parse_reserve
  INHERIT travel_agent_command_formats
  INHERIT airline_reservation_system_type_formats
  MESSAGE(s: string) -- PRAGMA representation(string, text)
    WHEN SOME(i: flight_id, d: date, p: passenger ::
              is_reserve("r " || s, a, i, d, p) )
      REPLY(b: boolean, a: agent_id, i: flight_id, d: date,
            p: passenger )
        WHERE b = true, is_reserve(s, a, i, d, p)
    OTHERWISE REPLY(b: boolean, a: agent_id, i: flight_id,
                    d: date, p: passenger )
      WHERE b = false
END

FUNCTION parse_cancel
  INHERIT travel_agent_command_formats
  INHERIT airline_reservation_system_type_formats
  MESSAGE(s: string) -- PRAGMA representation(string, text)
    WHEN SOME(i: flight_id, d: date, p: passenger ::
              is_cancel("c " || s, i, d, p) )
      REPLY(b: boolean, i: flight_id, d: date, p: passenger)
        WHERE b = true, is_cancel(s, i, d, p)
    OTHERWISE REPLY(b: boolean, i: flight_id, d: date,
                    p: passenger )
      WHERE b = false
END

FUNCTION parse_notify
  INHERIT travel_agent_command_formats
  INHERIT airline_reservation_system_type_formats
  MESSAGE(s: string) -- PRAGMA representation(string, text)
    WHEN SOME(a: agent_id, i: flight_id, d: date ::
              is_notify("n " || s, a, i, d) )
      REPLY(b: boolean, i: flight_id, d: date, a: agent_id)
        WHERE b = true, is_notify(s, a, i, d)
    OTHERWISE REPLY(b: boolean, i: flight_id, d: date,
                    a: agent_id )
      WHERE b = false
END
```

FIGURE 4.18
Specifications for Command Parsing Functions

```
FUNCTION display_flight
  INHERIT travel_agent_output_formats
  IMPORT flight_description FROM final_travel_agent_interface
  IMPORT fill FROM format

  MESSAGE(fd: flight_description, f: text_file)
    -- PRAGMA nonlocal_variable(f)
    -- PRAGMA representation(text_file, text_io.file_type)
    SEND put_line(f: text_file, s: string)
      TO text_io
      WHERE s = fill(flight_row(fd), [8, 8, 8, 10])
END

FUNCTION display_reservation
  INHERIT travel_agent_output_formats
  IMPORT reservation FROM airline_reservation_system_design
  IMPORT fill FROM format

  MESSAGE(r: reservation, f: text_file)
    -- PRAGMA nonlocal_variable(f)
    -- PRAGMA representation(text_file, text_io.file_type)
    SEND put_line(f: text_file, s: string)
      TO text_io
      WHERE s = fill(reservation_row(r), [8, 20])
END
```

FIGURE 4.19
Specifications for Display Functions

implemented as nonlocal variables due to constraints imposed by the method of implementing generators in Ada (see Section 4.4.2 and Chapter 5). These constraints are recorded using the nonlocal_variable pragma. The type text_file is implemented as the file type provided by the predefined Ada package TEXT_IO. This decision is recorded using the representation pragma.

This completes the normal responses. The exceptional responses are all very simple, and can readily be implemented directly in Ada as exception handlers, so no more new modules need be introduced at this level.

At the next level of decomposition, we find the edit operation can be implemented easily directly in Ada. The parsing functions can be implemented easily if we have a function returning the next item in a string delimited by spaces, and predicates for recognizing items of the types airport, flight_id, date, passenger, and agent_id. These functions are specified in Figs. 4.20 and 4.21. We find each of these functions can be

```
FUNCTION next_item
  IMPORT no_spaces FROM character_properties

  MESSAGE(s: string) -- PRAGMA representation(string, text)
     REPLY(next rest: string) -- PRAGMA update(s, rest)
        WHERE SOME(b1 b2: string SUCH THAT
                      spaces(b1) & spaces(b2) ::
                      s = b1 || next || b2 || rest
                                         & no_spaces(next) &
                      (b2 = "" => rest = "") ),
           next = "" => spaces(s)
        -- Extract the next nonblank string.
        -- Next is nonempty unless s has nothing but spaces.
        -- The delimiter b2 contains at least one space
        -- unless "next" goes to the end of s.
END
```

FIGURE 4.20
Specification for Next_Item

implemented easily directly in Ada. The last module differs from the previous
ones because date is an abstract data type rather than a restricted kind of character string, so that a type conversion is necessary in case the pattern matches.
We judge all of these modules to be easily implementable directly in Ada.

The modules display_flight and display_reservation would
be very easy to implement if we had an implementation of the fill concept
from the standard format definitions. Such a module is specified in Fig. 4.22.
Consulting our component library, we find an implementation of this module
already available.

We classify the data representation, all of the messages, and all of the auxiliary functions identified for the travel agent module as small and easily implementable. This classification will be used for estimating the effort required to
complete the project in Section 4.6.1.

Airline Manager.   The operations of the airline manager are relatively infrequent, and do not have any performance constraints, so that we do not need to
introduce any partitioning for concurrency. As in the case of the travel agent
module, we make the airline manager module an independent task to avoid
blocking the rest of the system while waiting for input from the airline
manager. We allocate a separate a telephone line for the use of the airline
managers, which is accessed as a pair of text files as in the travel agent interface. We decide to follow the same naming conventions for the files as in the
travel agent, and to allocate modem id 0 to the airline manager, since the

```
FUNCTION is_airport   -- PRAGMA representation(string, text)
  INHERIT airline_reservation_type_formats
  MESSAGE(s: string) REPLY(b: boolean) WHERE b
                                  <=> s IN airport
END


FUNCTION is_flight_id   -- PRAGMA representation(string, text)
  INHERIT airline_reservation_type_formats
  MESSAGE(s: string) REPLY(b: boolean) WHERE b
                                  <=> s IN flight_id
END


FUNCTION is_passenger   -- PRAGMA representation(string, text)
  INHERIT airline_reservation_type_formats
  MESSAGE(s: string) REPLY(b: boolean) WHERE b
                                  <=> s IN passenger
END


FUNCTION is_agent_id   -- PRAGMA representation(string, text)
  INHERIT airline_reservation_type_formats
  MESSAGE(s: string) REPLY(b: boolean) WHERE b
                                  <=> s IN agent_id
END


FUNCTION is_date   -- PRAGMA representation(string, text)
  INHERIT airline_reservation_type_formats
  MESSAGE(s: string)
    WHEN SOME(d: date :: d = date(s))
     REPLY(b: boolean, d: date) WHERE b <=> true, d = date(s)
    OTHERWISE REPLY(b: boolean, d: date) WHERE b <=> false
END
```

FIGURE 4.21
Specifications of Type Recognition Functions

```
FUNCTION fill_line
  IMPORT fill row FROM format
  MESSAGE(r: row, w: sequence(nat))
    REPLY(s: string) WHERE s = fill(r, w)
END
```

FIGURE 4.22
Specification for Fill_Line

modem ids 1–300 correspond to the travel agents. We also decide to use the same representations for text files and strings as in the travel agent module. These decisions are recorded in Fig. 4.23.

We record the implicit decisions that the `interpret_command` message will come from the airline manager outside the system, and that the `done` message will be a response from the airline reservation system rather than an independent request. This is done using the pragmas `external_input` and `returned_value`.

The `interpret_command` message can be implemented easily if the functions shown in Fig. 4.24 are available. None of the other messages are complicated enough to need any lower-level modules. The parsing functions can easily be implemented in terms of the functions specified in the previous section, together with those shown in Fig. 4.25.

We classify the data representation, all of the messages, and all of the auxiliary functions identified for the airline manager module as small and easily implementable. This classification will be used for estimating the effort required to complete the project in Section 4.6.1.

Date. We judge the type `date` to be easily implementable directly in Ada. The data representation and all of the operations are classified as small. This

```
MACHINE airline_manager_design
    -- PRAGMA task(airline_manager_design)
  INHERIT final_airline_manager
  IMPORT text_file input_name output_name
    FROM travel_agent_design

  STATE(input output: text_file)
  INVARIANT name(input) = input_name(0),
    name(output) = output_name(0),
    mode(input) = #in_file, mode(output) = #out_file
  INITIALLY is_open(input), is_open(output)

  -- PRAGMA representation(string, text)
  -- PRAGMA representation(text_file, text_io.file_type)
  -- PRAGMA external_input(interpret_command)
  -- PRAGMA returned_value(flights)
  -- PRAGMA returned_value(reservations)
  -- PRAGMA returned_value(done)
END
```

FIGURE 4.23
Top-Level Design for the Airline Manager

```
FUNCTION parse_add_flight
  INHERIT airline_manager_command_formats
  INHERIT airline_reservation_system_type_formats
  MESSAGE(s: string) -- PRAGMA representation(string, text)
    WHEN SOME(i: flight_id, p: money, o d: airport,
              dep arr: time, c: nat ::
              is_add_flight("add_flight " || s, i, p, o, d,
                            dep, arr, c ))
      REPLY(b: boolean, i: flight_id, p: money, o d: airport,
            dep arr: time, c: nat )
        WHERE b = true, is_add_flight(s, i, p, o, d, dep, arr, c)
      OTHERWISE REPLY(b: boolean, i: flight_id, p: money,
                      o d: airport, dep arr: time, c: nat )
        WHERE b = false
END

FUNCTION parse_drop_flight
  INHERIT airline_manager_command_formats
  INHERIT airline_reservation_system_type_formats
  MESSAGE(s: string) -- PRAGMA representation(string, text)
    WHEN SOME(i: flight_id ::
              is_drop_flight("drop_flight " || s, i) )
      REPLY(b: boolean, i: flight_id)
        WHERE b = true, is_drop_flight(s, i)
      OTHERWISE REPLY(b: boolean, i: flight_id) WHERE b = false
END

FUNCTION parse_new_fare
  INHERIT airline_manager_command_formats
  INHERIT airline_reservation_system_type_formats
  MESSAGE(s: string) -- PRAGMA representation(string, text)
    WHEN SOME(i: flight_id ::
              is_new_fare("new_fare " || s, i, p) )
      REPLY(b: boolean, i: flight_id, p: money)
        WHERE b = true, is_new_fare(s, i, p)
      OTHERWISE REPLY(b: boolean, i: flight_id, p: money)
        WHERE b = false
END
```

FIGURE 4.24
Specifications of Command Parsing Functions

completes the abstract architectural design. The abstract architectural design is
independent of implementation language, provided that implementations of the
reusable components and predefined types mentioned in the pragmas are available.

```
FUNCTION is_money  -- PRAGMA representation(string, text)
  INHERIT airline_reservation_type_formats
  MESSAGE(s: string) REPLY(b: boolean) WHERE b <=> s IN money
END

FUNCTION is_time   -- PRAGMA representation(string, text)
  INHERIT airline_reservation_type_formats
  MESSAGE(s: string) REPLY(b: boolean) WHERE b <=> s IN time
END
```

FIGURE 4.25
Specifications for Type Recognition Functions

Design Review. The design review is based on the formal specifications, which are summarized using module dependency diagrams. A module dependency diagram for the airline reservation system is shown in Fig. 4.26. Module dependency diagrams represent the "implemented in terms of" relationship, as described in Section 4.2. Modules are represented in the diagram using the symbols introduced in Section 3.2.3 (see Fig. 3.15). Reusable components are marked with an asterisk (*). The diagrams are useful for getting an overview of the system structure given by the architectural design. The diagrams are also useful for planning and system evolution activities, because they tell us which modules must be implemented or simulated to test a given module, and which modules are affected by a change in a given module. Module dependency diagrams for the travel agent and the airline manager subsystems are shown in Figs. 4.27 and 4.28.

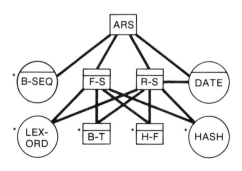

FIGURE 4.26
Module Dependency Diagram for the Airline Reservation System

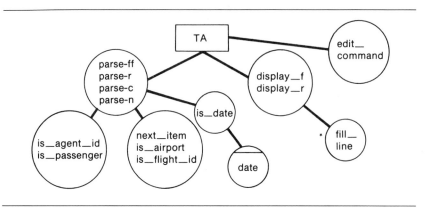

FIGURE 4.27
Module Dependency Diagram for the Travel Agent

Before we can start implementation, we have to fix the implementation language and determine the correspondence between the specified module interfaces and the constructs of the chosen programming language. The implementation language for our case study is Ada.

4.4.2 Concrete Interface Design

Concrete interface design is the process of mapping black-box specifications into concrete interface specifications for a particular implementation

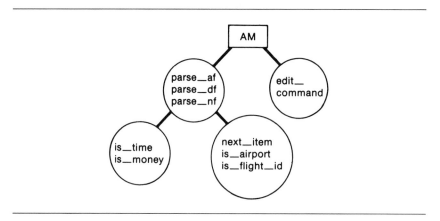

FIGURE 4.28
Module Dependency Diagram for the Airline Manager

language. The semantics of the interface are determined by the black-box specification given by the abstract functional specification. The syntax of an invocation for each operation is given by the concrete interfaces determined during concrete interface design.

The architectural design is much more difficult than the concrete interface design, and at the current state of the art requires the skill of an experienced designer. Concrete interface design is much more routine, and can be largely automated, especially if decisions about the properties of the interfaces such as task boundaries, storage allocation strategies, update parameters, and concrete type bindings have been recorded in the architectural design using pragmas. Next, we give an example of a concrete interface design for the airline reservation case study, to introduce the issues addressed at this stage; after that, we describe general rules for constructing concrete interfaces in Ada and explain some of the finer points of Spec pragmas. The creative part of concrete interface design is formulating the correspondence rules for a particular implementation language.

Concrete Interfaces for the Airline Reservation Example. This section derives Ada interface specifications from the Spec specifications for the airline reservation example. The Ada declaration for the concrete interface of the airline reservation system module is shown in Fig. 4.29. The packages mentioned in the initial `with` statements define the types appearing in the entries of the `airline_reservation_system` task. The package `concrete_types_pkg` contains declarations of all the type concepts implemented as concrete Ada types, as opposed to abstract data types such as `date` and `bounded_sequence`, which have a separate package for each type. There is no `use` statement for `bounded_sequence_pkg` because this is a generic package template rather than an individual package.

In Ada, instances of generic modules must be declared before they can be used, as illustrated by `flight_sequence_package` and `reservation_sequence_pkg`. The purpose of the subtypes `flight_sequence` and `reservation_sequence` is to provide short names for the instances of the sequence type of the generic bounded sequence package. A uniform guideline for generating such names is to concatenate the generic parameters with the name of the generic module.

The exceptions declared are those that appear in a `REPLY EXCEPTION` clause in the Spec description of the module. The embedded task, with one task entry per message or temporal, is generated because of the Spec pragma `task(airline_reservation_system)`.

The Ada specification part of the concrete types package is shown in Fig. 4.30. This package is used in the specification part of each Ada module that has the concrete types in the interfaces of its operations, and is used in the bodies of all Ada modules that refer to the concrete types in the implementation but not in the interfaces.

```
  with bounded_sequence_pkg;
  with date_pkg; use date_pkg;
  with concrete_types_pkg; use concrete_types_pkg;
package airline_reservation_system_pkg is
  -- Generic instantiations for interface types.
  package flight_sequence_pkg is
    new bounded_sequence_pkg(flight_description);
  package reservation_sequence_pkg is
    new bounded_sequence_pkg(reservation);
  use flight_sequence_pkg; use reservation_sequence_pkg;
  subtype flight_sequence is flight_sequence_pkg.sequence;
  subtype reservation_sequence is
    reservation_sequence_pkg.sequence;

  -- Exceptions.
  flight_exists: exception;
  reservation_exists: exception;
  no_such_flight: exception;
  no_reservation: exception;
  no_seat: exception;

  task airline_reservation_system is
    -- Travel agent interface.
    entry find_flights(origin, destination: in airport;
                    fs: out flight_sequence );
    entry reserve(a: in agent_id; i: in flight_id; d: in date;
                p: in passenger );
    entry cancel(i: in flight_id; d: in date; p: in passenger);
    entry notify(a: in agent_id; i: in flight_id; d: in date;
                rs: out reservation_sequence );

    -- Airline manager interface.
    entry add_flight(i: in flight_id; price: in money;
                    origin, destination: in airport;
                    departure, arrival: in flight_time;
                    capacity: in natural );
    entry drop_flight(i: in flight_id);
    entry new_fare(i: in flight_id; price: in money);

    -- Temporals.
    entry retire;
  end airline_reservation_system;
end airline_reservation_system_pkg;
```

FIGURE 4.29
Concrete Interface for the Airline Reservation System

```
with date_pkg; use date_pkg;   -- Defines date.
with text_pkg; use text_pkg;  -- Defines text_pkg_instance.
package concrete_types_pkg is   -- Concrete type definitions.
  use text_pkg_instance;   -- Defines the type text.

  subtype agent_id is text(3); -- Fixed length.
  subtype airport is text(3); -- Fixed length.
  subtype flight_id is text; -- Variable length.
  subtype money is text; -- Variable length.
  subtype flight_time is text; -- Variable length.
  subtype passenger is text; -- Variable length.

  type flight_description is
    record
      id: flight_id; dep, arr: flight_time; price: money;
    end record;

  type reservation is
    record
      id: flight_id; d: date; p: passenger; a: agent_id;
    end record;
end concrete_types_pkg;
```

FIGURE 4.30
Definitions of Concrete Ada Types

The type text is defined in the reusable generic package generic_text_pkg, which provides bounded variable-length character strings. The Ada implementation of the type text has a discriminant representing the length of the string. Constrained subtypes of text, such as agent_id and airport, have a specified constant value for the discriminant, and hence represent fixed length strings. Unconstrained subtypes such as flight_id allow different instances of the subtype to have different values for the discriminant and hence represent variable length strings. Because the discriminant has a default value, it is legal to declare Ada variables of the unconstrained type text. Such variables can hold strings of different lengths at different times, and the compiler must allocate enough storage to hold the largest value of the type. An implementation of this package is already available, and is shown in Appendix F. The generic parameter for text_pkg specifies the bound on the length of the string. The package text_pkg declares a particular instance of this generic package, which will be shared by all of the modules using the type text. The definition of text_pkg is shown in Fig. 4.31. The bound on the length of the text is based on the fact that all of the strings used by the airline reservation system have to fit on a single line of a

```
  with generic_text_pkg;
package text_pkg is
  package text_pkg_instance is
    new generic_text_pkg(max_text_length => 80);
end text_pkg;
```

FIGURE 4.31
Definition of Text_Pkg

standard display. The instance of the generic package can be used inside the
Ada code units that need to refer to the type text. This structure is used to
avoid making multiple instances of the generic package, since many Ada compilers do not automatically perform this optimization. The concrete type
definitions are derived from the specifications of the corresponding Spec type
concepts.

The types agent_id, ... , passenger are declared to be subtypes rather
than as distinct Ada types to simplify the implementation. If we made them
distinct derived types, the type checking performed by the Ada compiler would
assure us that a string representing an agent_id was never used as an airport,
but then we would have to include explicit type conversions from the type
text to the derived types in the operations for parsing commands. We choose
simplicity over security in this case because of the tight budget.

The concrete interface for the travel agent module is shown in Fig. 4.32.
The travel agent task is enclosed in a generic package so that one instance for
each telephone line can be created. This is done because there is no such thing
as a generic task in Ada, so that the task must be embedded in a generic package to provide generic instantiation with parameters. This task has no entries
because it only calls entries in other tasks, and does not accept entry calls from
other tasks. The travel agent requests services from the airline reservation system without providing any back to the system. This is determined from the
Spec pragmas external_input and returned_value in the architectural design of the module.

```
generic
  modem_id: natural;
package travel_agent_pkg is
  task travel_agent;
end travel_agent_pkg;
```

FIGURE 4.32
Concrete Interface for the Travel Agent

```
package airline_manager_pkg is
  task airline_manager;
end airline_manager_pkg;
```

FIGURE 4.33
Concrete Interface for the Airline Manager

The concrete interface for the airline manager module is shown in Fig. 4.33. There is only one instance of the airline manager package, so there are no generic parameters. The task is enclosed in a package to make it an Ada compilation unit.

The interfaces for the auxiliary operations needed only by the travel agent module are shown in Fig. 4.34. These declarations are included in the package

```
with text_pkg; use text_pkg;  -- Defines text_pkg_instance.
with date_pkg; use date_pkg;   -- Defines date.
with concrete_types_pkg; use concrete_types_pkg;
   -- Defines airport, flight_id, passenger, agent_id,
   -- flight_description, reservation.
with parse_pkg; use parse_pkg;
   -- Defines is_airport, is_flight_id, is_passenger,
   -- is_agent_id, edit_command, next_item.
package body travel_agent_pkg is
   use text_pkg_instance;   -- Defines the type text.

   -- Local subprogram declarations.
   procedure interpret_command(cmd: in text);
   procedure parse_find_flights(s: in text; o, d: out airport;
                                result: out boolean );
   procedure parse_reserve(s: in text; a: out agent_id;
                           i: out flight_id; d: out date;
                           p: out passenger;
                           result: out boolean );
   procedure parse_cancel(s: in text; i: out flight_id;
                          d: out date; p: out passenger;
                          result: out boolean );
   procedure parse_notify(s: in text; a: out agent_id;
                          i: out flight_id; d: out date;
                          result: out boolean );
end travel_agent_pkg;
```

FIGURE 4.34
Interfaces for Travel Agent Auxiliary Operations

body rather than the specification part to limit their visibility. This simplifies the visible interface because there are fewer things for the programmers concerned with other parts of the system to consider. We generate the interface declarations for these operations from the black-box specifications to reduce the opportunities for making interface errors in the implementation phase. Similar considerations apply to the declarations for the auxiliary operations needed only by the airline manager module, which are shown in Fig. 4.35. The interfaces for the auxiliary operations used by both the travel agent module and the airline manager module are given in Fig. 4.36. These operations are declared outside the package bodies of the travel agent and the airline manager modules because many of them are shared by both modules. Although all of these operations are not used by both modules, any of the operations can be used in plausible future extensions of both modules. These operations are all declared in the same module because they are all concerned with data formats and we did not want to complicate the system by introducing too many modules. We did not include these operations in concrete_types_pkg because they are unlikely to be needed in other parts of the system.

```
with text_pkg; use text_pkg; -- Defines text_pkg_instance.
with date_pkg; use date_pkg;  -- Defines date.
with concrete_types_pkg; use concrete_types_pkg;
  -- Defines airport, flight_id, money, flight_time.
with parse_pkg; use parse_pkg;
  -- Defines is_airport, is_flight_id, is_money, is_time,
  -- edit_command, next_item.
package body airline_manager_pkg is
  use text_pkg_instance;  -- Defines the type text.

  -- Local subprogram declarations.
  procedure interpret_command(cmd: string; args: in text;
                              f: in file_type );
  procedure parse_add_flight(s: in text; i: out flight_id;
                             p: out money; o, d: out airport;
                             dep, arr: out flight_time;
                             c: out natural;
                             result: out boolean );
  procedure parse_drop_flight(s: in text; i: out flight_id;
                              result: out boolean );
  procedure parse_new_fare(s: in text; i: out flight_id;
                           p: out money; result: out boolean );
end airline_manager_pkg;
```

FIGURE 4.35
Interfaces for Airline Manager Auxiliary Operations

```
   with text_pkg; use text_pkg;  -- Defines text_pkg_instance.
   with date_pkg; use date_pkg;  -- Defines date.
package parse_pkg is
   use text_pkg_instance;   -- Defines the type text.

   function edit_command(s: text) return text;
   procedure next_item(s: in out text; next: out text);
   function is_airport(s: text) return boolean;
   function is_flight_id(s: text) return boolean;
   function is_passenger(s: text) return boolean;
   function is_agent_id(s: text) return boolean;
   procedure is_date(s: in text ; d: out date; ok: out boolean);
   function is_money(s: text) return boolean;
   function is_time(s: text) return boolean;
end parse_pkg;
```

FIGURE 4.36
Interfaces for Shared Auxiliary Operations

The function `edit_command` and the procedure `next_item` are the only operations declared above that are not concerned with data formats particular to the airline reservation system. We would expect to find such general-purpose operations in our library of reusable components. We had to construct them here because our library did not contain these operations. We make a note to incorporate `edit_command` and `next_item` into our component library after they have been implemented and tested.

The concrete interface for the abstract data type `date` is shown in Fig. 4.37. The declaration for the type `date` in the private part is filled in during module design. This Ada module will not be accepted by the Ada compiler until the private part is completed.

The concrete interface for the flight schedule is shown in Fig. 4.38. Because the flight schedule is a mutable type and no pointers are used in its representation—as indicated by the Spec pragma `direct_allocation`—we must make it a limited private type in Ada. The generator `find_flights` is a generic procedure, with a procedure representing the body of the loop to be driven by the generator as a generic parameter. This illustrates our usual convention for implementing generators in Ada.

The concrete interface for the reservation set is shown in Fig. 4.39. This interface is similar to the one for the flight schedule. This completes the concrete interfaces for all of the new modules in the proposed system, and all of the types that appear in their interfaces. The interfaces for the existing modules that do not appear in the interfaces of the new modules are not shown here, since they are part of the reusable component library in Appendix F.

```
 with text_pkg; use text_pkg;  -- Defines text_pkg_instance.
package date_pkg is
  use text_pkg_instance;  -- Defines the type text.

  type date is private;

  function create(d, m, y: natural) return date;
  function "<" (d1, d2: date) return boolean;
  function "<=" (d1, d2: date) return boolean;
  function string_code(d: date) return text;

  illegal_date: exception;  -- Raised by create.
private
  type date is ?;
end date_pkg;
```

FIGURE 4.37
Concrete Interface for Date

Concrete Interface Generation Rules for Ada.   This section develops a
set of general rules for generating concrete interface specifications in Ada
corresponding to an abstract architectural design expressed in Spec. In Ada, a
concrete interface specification consists of the declaration parts of each subprogram, package, task, or generic unit. These parts of the program can be derived
from the black-box specification in a systematic way.

   This section describes our conventions for the correspondence between
Spec modules and Ada constructs. In cases where there is more than one way
to represent a Spec interface in Ada we define a default convention, and provide alternatives that can be selected by including Spec pragmas as comments
in the specification. For each Spec construct we define the default correspondence first, and then the alternatives indicated by pragmas.

   Messages normally correspond to subprograms. The subprogram implementing a message has an Ada exception corresponding to each exception
listed in a REPLY EXCEPTION clause of the message. The Ada interface is
not affected by SEND clauses. There are several cases in the default correspondence for the parameters of the subprogram, depending on the form of the message.

1. A message with a REPLY containing exactly one data component and
   without any TRANSITION clauses corresponds to an Ada function with
   an in parameter for each component of the MESSAGE and a return
   corresponding to the single data component of the REPLY.

2. A message with a GENERATE corresponds to a generic procedure with a
   single generic procedure parameter. The generic parameter represents the

```
with text_pkg; use text_pkg; -- Defines text_pkg_instance.
with concrete_types_pkg; use concrete_types_pkg;
  -- Defines flight_id, money, airport, flight_time,
  -- flight_description.
package flight_schedule_pkg is
  use text_pkg_instance;   -- Defines the type text.

  type flight_schedule is limited private;

  procedure open(name: in text; fs: in out flight_schedule);
  procedure add(i: in flight_id; price: in money;
                origin, destination: in airport;
                departure, arrival: in flight_time;
                capacity: in natural;
                fs: in out flight_schedule );
  procedure remove(i: in flight_id; fs: in out flight_schedule);
  procedure member(i: in flight_id; fs: in out flight_schedule;
                  result: out boolean );
  procedure capacity(i: in flight_id; fs: in out flight_schedule;
                  result: out natural );

  generic
    with procedure produce(fd: in flight_description);
  procedure find_flights(fs: in out flight_schedule;
                         origin, destination: airport );

  no_such_flight: exception;   -- Raised by capacity.
private
  type flight_schedule is ?;
end flight_schedule_pkg;
```

FIGURE 4.38
Concrete Interface for Flight Schedule

body of the loop to be driven by the generator, and takes one in parameter corresponding to the elements of each sequence to be generated. The state variables of the loop correspond to nonlocal variables of the actual procedure bound to the generic parameter. The implementation of Spec generators in Ada is discussed in detail in Section 5.7.5.

3. A message that does not match the previous two cases corresponds to an Ada procedure with an in parameter for each component of the MESSAGE and an out parameter for each component of the REPLY, if there is one.

A MESSAGE or REPLY with a variable number of actual parameters matching a sequence-valued formal parameter of the form $x: t corresponds to a single

```
   with concrete_types_pkg; use concrete_types_pkg;
   with text_pkg; use text_pkg; -- Defines text_pkg_instance.
   with date_pkg; use date_pkg;
package reservation_set_pkg is
   use text_pkg_instance;  -- Defines the type text.

   type reservation_set is limited private;

   procedure open(name: in text; rs: in out reservation_set);
   procedure add (a: in agent_id; i: in flight_id; d: in date;
                   p: in passenger; rs: in out reservation_set );
   procedure remove(i: in flight_id; d: in date; p: in passenger;
                     rs: in out reservation_set );
   procedure remove(i: in flight_id; rs: in out reservation_set);
   procedure remove(d: in date; rs: in out reservation_set);
   procedure holds(p: in passenger; i: in flight_id; d: in date;
                    rs: in out reservation_set; has: out boolean );
   procedure bookings(i: in flight_id; d: in date;
                       rs: in out reservation_set;
                       number_of_bookings: out natural );

   generic
     with procedure produce(r: in reservation);
   procedure notify(a: in agent_id; i: in flight_id; d: in date;
                     rs: in out reservation_set );
private
   type reservation_set is ?;
end reservation_set_pkg;
```

FIGURE 4.39
Concrete Interface for Reservation Set

Ada parameter of type array(integer range <>) of t, and the corresponding sequence of actual parameters is passed as an array aggregate. This convention can be combined with any of the variations for representing messages in Ada.

The basic conventions for representing messages can be modified by several Spec pragmas. The pragma update(x, y) indicates that the component x of a MESSAGE and a component y of a REPLY both correspond to the same in out parameter of the Ada subprogram, with the formal parameter name x.

The pragma nonlocal_variable(x) indicates that a component x of a MESSAGE or REPLY is to be implemented as a nonlocal variable reference rather than as an Ada parameter or return value.

There is also an alternative representation for generators. The pragma passive(g) indicates that the generator g should correspond to the three Ada subprograms init_g, next_g, and end_of_g rather than to a single procedure with a generic procedure parameter. The procedure init_g resets the sequence to the beginning, and has one in parameter for each data component of the MESSAGE associated with g. The procedure next_g has one out parameter corresponding to an element of the sequence to be generated. The parameterless function end_of_g has a return value of type boolean, which is true if the generated sequence has no more elements.

The two styles of representing generators have different advantages and disadvantages. The active style (the default) has the advantage of being able to represent recursive generators, as illustrated in the implementation of B_tree in Appendix F, but it is limited to only one generator per loop. The passive style allows several generators to be used in parallel to drive different state variables of the same loop, but it is limited to nonrecursive implementations. If multiple instances of a passive generator can be active at the same time, it is necessary to introduce an additional abstract data type to represent the state of each instance of the generator.

There are also correspondence rules for the different kinds of modules in Spec. A Spec FUNCTION with a single message corresponds to the Ada subprogram for that message. Any exceptions associated with the FUNCTION are declared in a separate package that is included (Ada with and use) wherever the function is called. A Spec FUNCTION with more than one message corresponds to an Ada package declaring the subprograms and exceptions corresponding to each message of the FUNCTION.

A Spec MACHINE corresponds to a package containing the subprograms and exceptions for the messages of the MACHINE. The state components do not appear in the interface.

A Spec TYPE t corresponds to an Ada package t_pkg containing declarations for the Ada type t and the subprograms and exceptions for the messages of the Spec TYPE. The type is declared to be an Ada private type in the public part, and as the representation data type in the private part. The representation data type cannot be determined from the black-box specification, so that the private declarations have to be filled in after the module design is complete.

The pragma task(m) indicates that the function, machine, or type m should be implemented as a package containing a task, and the messages should be task entries rather than subprograms. This pragma should be used for modules whose operations can be called by several concurrent tasks. The task pragma implies all data components of each MESSAGE should be implemented as in parameters of a task entry, and all data components of a REPLY should be implemented as out parameters of the task entry, except as modified by an update pragma.

The package representing a machine or type with TEMPORAL events should contain a task with an Ada task entry for each message and a parameter-less entry for each temporal. The package should also contain a driver task for each temporal, which calls the entry in the main task at the proper time. In this case, the messages must be represented as task entries to ensure mutual exclusion between the operations corresponding to the messages and those corresponding to the temporals, because the temporals are invoked based on the time by the embedded driver tasks, and those times may fall in the middle of the execution of another operation.

The default representation of a mutable Spec type is an Ada `private` type that denotes an Ada access type (pointer) inside the module. Assignments are safe for such types, and the default equality and inequality operations provided by Ada are semantically accurate.

An immutable Spec type can be represented as an Ada `private` type only if it has a unique representation, because in other cases the predefined Ada = operation gives incorrect results. The unique representation property can be specified by the designer using the Spec pragma `unique_ representation(t)`. Immutable types without unique representations must be implemented as `limited private` Ada types, because Ada allows explicit definitions of = for `limited private` types but not for `private` types. It is easy to explicitly define assignment operators for `limited private` types, but such operators must have the form of a procedure such as `assign(x, y)` since Ada does not allow the infix assignment symbol `:=` to be overloaded.

Aliasing refers to situations where several different variables are bound to the same instance of a type. Aliasing is unsafe for both mutable types and immutable types with mutable representations that are not unique, unless the representations of the instances do not directly contain any components subject to change. In the unsafe cases a state changing operation applied to one variable can make the representations contained in the other variables internally inconsistent. In such cases, assignments to variables must be controlled to prevent aliasing, or prohibited altogether. A mutable type can have a fixed representation only if the representation contains pointers, and all modifications act on indirectly referenced pieces of storage. Because Ada pointers can only designate dynamically allocated blocks of storage, assignments are unsafe for any mutable type without pointers (indicated by the Spec pragma `direct_allocation`).

The pragma `direct_allocation(t)` indicates that instances of a type `t` should be directly contained in declared program variables, so that dynamic storage allocation is not used. This means the representation of `t` should not contain pointers to dynamically allocated blocks of storage. If the specification of the type `t` contains any TRANSITION clauses, the Spec pragma `direct_allocation(t)` implies `t` should be declared as a `limited private` type in Ada. This pragma also implies any input object of type `t` mentioned in a TRANSITION clause corresponds to a parameter with mode in out, and that any result of type t corresponds to a parameter with mode out or in out. The messages of such a type cannot be represented as Ada functions.

Generic modules and messages correspond to generic program units in Ada, where each individual Spec parameter corresponds to an Ada generic parameter. Ada does not allow types or functions to be passed as ordinary parameters, therefore any message with data components of type FUNCTION or TYPE must be implemented as a generic subprogram with generic function, procedure, or type parameters. Because Ada does not allow variable numbers of generic parameters, and types and functions cannot be components of Ada arrays, Spec modules with variable numbers of type or function parameters such as the predefined type tuple{$s: type} have to be implemented by a set of overloaded Ada modules, one for each legal number of generic parameters. This requires an implementation constraint restricting the maximum number of parameters that may be supplied. An example of this is the generic lexicographic ordering defined in Appendix F.

Concepts defining concrete types that appear in the interfaces of the messages are implemented by Ada concrete type declarations. An example of such a concept is the type flight_id in the airline reservation example, which is implemented in the Ada package concrete_types_pkg, shown in Fig. 4.30. Such type concepts correspond to Ada type definitions. The default correspondence between the standard Spec types and the types of Ada is given in Table 4.8. Exceptions to these rules can be given in pragmas of the form representation(Spec_type, Ada_type).

TABLE 4.8
DEFAULT IMPLEMENTATIONS OF PREDEFINED SPEC TYPES

Spec	Ada
any	(handled by overloading)
boolean	boolean
char	character
string	string
enumeration	Ada enumeration type
null	empty Ada record
tuple	Ada record
union	Ada variant record
sequence	(abstract data type)
set	(abstract data type)
multiset	(abstract data type)
map	(abstract data type)
relation	(abstract data type)
nat	natural
integer	integer
rational	(abstract data type)
real	float
complex	(abstract data type)

4.5 Quality Assurance

Quality assurance at the architectural design level depends mostly on design reviews. Some automated consistency checking is possible, of the same general type as that performed in the functional specification stage. Execution of test cases or formal proofs of correctness must usually wait until the implementation of the modules involved is complete, or until stubs for the lower-level modules have been built. Testing by simulating lower-level modules based on their black-box specifications is possible in some situations, but at the current time such techniques are still the subject of active research.

A fair amount of the quality assurance activities done at architectural design time are preparatory steps for tests to be run once the implementations of the modules become available and do not directly address the quality of the architectural design. These activities are the development of test cases and test planning.

4.5.1 Choosing Test Cases

Test cases for testing a module can be chosen using black-box and glass-box strategies. Black-box testing is done based on the black-box specification, and glass-box testing is done based on the glass-box specification or implementation. Generating test cases for a module using the black-box strategy can begin as soon as the black-box specification for a module is complete, which occurs during functional specification for external interfaces and occurs during architectural design for internal interfaces. Generating test cases for a module using the glass-box strategy depends on the internal structure of a module, and cannot begin until the design of the module has been completed.

The conventional heuristics for black-box testing are to test every message and every case of each message, and to test the extreme values for each case if the input data domain has an ordering. It is also generally accepted that a reliable testing strategy must include some randomly chosen data values to guard against systematic bias on the part of the person or program choosing the test cases. Although there are some theoretical results available for idealized testing situations, the optimal input distribution for random testing in practical situations is still a matter of research, especially for nonnumerical data domains. A practical engineering approach is to try several different distributions to stress different aspects of the system, and to do as much testing as time allows, because errors detected after delivery are more expensive to correct than those detected earlier.

If some functions of the system have more stringent reliability requirements than others, the testing effort should spend a larger fraction of the available resources on the critical parts. The critical parts of a system are those in which potential failures can endanger people or cause expensive losses. In the absence of explicit requirements for testing critical functions, a useful rough guideline is to make the testing effort spent on each part of the system proportional to the cost of an undetected error in that part.

4.5.2 Test Planning

Test planning is determining the order in which the parts of the system are implemented and tested. This aspect of planning is specific to software systems, and requires technical judgement because the amount of work needed to test the system depends on the order in which the modules are implemented. Some general guidelines are that input and output functions and data types should be implemented first, because they usually make it easier to test the other parts of the system.

It is often useful to follow a strategy of incremental implementation that starts with the input and output interfaces, and adds and integrates modules one at a time. This has the advantage of always having a working system that does something that can be demonstrated, even though the functionality of the current state of the system may have a tenuous connection to that of the proposed system at first. Such a capability may be important for soothing the nerves of a concerned customer if schedule problems start to surface. This approach is also efficient for locating and repairing design faults. Each time a module is added, all previous test cases can be run again, helping to detect any interference between the new module and the previously working parts of the system. This generally saves time because the causes of newly detected faults can be more easily localized and hence are cheaper to diagnose and correct.

4.6 Management Aspects

With the beginning of the architectural design, the development project enters a stage in which there is a diverse set of concurrent activities that must be planned and coordinated. These include production of manuals, development of test cases, and the design, implementation, and testing of individual modules and subsystems. This is also the point at which the total effort required to complete the project becomes clear, and adjustments to staffing, schedules, or deliverables are best made.

4.6.1 Estimation

The earliest point in the development cycle when reasonably accurate effort estimation becomes possible is when a detailed module dependency diagram is available. At this point all of the tasks that have to be performed in the remainder of the development activity can be identified. The tasks that have to be performed for each module, and estimates of typical values for the relative amounts of effort needed for each are shown in Table 4.9. The quality assurance category includes review meetings, testing, and other quality assurance activities. The effort distribution depends on the design style and the degree of automation prevalent in each development environment, and should be adjusted to match individual development organizations based on records of actual time spent per module in past projects.

We have found the following method for estimating remaining effort from an architectural design to be practical. First, classify each component as small, medium, or large by guessing the amount of effort needed for implementation and getting a clean compilation. We use the classification scheme given in Table 4.10 for estimating effort. In this context, small means less than two person-hours, medium means at least two but less than four person-hours, and large means at least four but less than eight person-hours. Each function module is estimated as a single unit; the data structure and each operation of an abstract type or machine is estimated separately. There should not be any components that are expected to take more than eight person-hours, and if some components are classified in this category, then they should be decomposed further until subcomponents of the required size are reached. The limit of eight person-hours is based on our experience in classroom projects, where we found that the instances where individual estimates were off by more than a factor of two were almost always estimated to take more than eight person-hours, and were estimated incorrectly because the problem had not been understood, and because several necessary subtasks had been left out of the estimate.

An estimate of the work remaining can be obtained by adding up the individual estimates. The sum should include estimates only for those tasks that have not yet been completed for each module. Estimates for the tasks other than implementation associated with each module are derived by proportional

TABLE 4.9
APPROXIMATE EFFORT DISTRIBUTION PER MODULE

Task	Effort
Black-box specification	20%
Decomposition and module design	25%
Implementation	15%
Quality assurance	40%

TABLE 4.10
GUIDELINES FOR ESTIMATING IMPLEMENTATION EFFORT

Size	Effort for Implementation (hours)
Small	0 .. 2
Medium	2 .. 4
Large	4 .. 8

scaling using effort distribution statistics from past projects, or by using the percentages in Table 4.9. The accuracy of any estimate depends critically on the assumption that no major subsystems have been left out of the decomposition. An estimate is reliable only if the module dependency has been carefully reviewed and can be considered stable.

This method is a suitable basis for a software tool running on the project database, because it is conceptually simple. The method can require a considerable effort if performed manually, since the current status of each task must be determined. Automating the method requires keeping a record of the size classification and the status of each task in the database. The status of each task must be updated from pending to completed when the people responsible for the task complete their work. This is a relatively nondisrupting means for reporting progress, because it insulates the people doing the work from frequent interruptions to prepare status reports, and lets the management get an up to date assessment of the status of the project at any any time by running the estimation program against the project database.

To derive the accuracy of the estimates and the probability that the project can be completed by a given time, we examine the mathematical basis of this method more closely. We treat the time required for each task as a random variable, and assume the times required to complete different tasks are independent. This assumption neglects the effects of factors that can affect the project as a whole, such as power outages, delays in delivering equipment needed for testing, labor disputes, and so on. Such factors introduce correlations between the tasks and increase the expected error or the resulting estimate, although it is not easy to calculate the size of the effect. Under most normal operating conditions, such disruptive external events are rare and can be ignored, but planners should be aware of the kinds of conditions that can invalidate the accuracy estimates resulting from our analysis.

The assumption that the individual estimates are independent lets us use the following facts from probability theory:

1. The mean of the sum of a set of independent random variables is the sum of their means

2. The variance of the sum of a set of independent random variables is the sum of their variances

3. The distribution of the sum of independent random variables approaches a normal distribution as the number of random variables gets large.

If we can estimate the mean and variance of the estimates for the individual tasks, these facts let us determine the mean and variance for the entire collection of tasks left to complete the project. These individual estimates are based on guesswork. We introduce three plausible characterizations of this guesswork, to show the sensitivity of the estimates to the attitudes of the estimators. Conclusions supported by all three versions of the analysis should be considered reliable; others should be considered open to interpretation.

1. Optimistic version. Treat each estimate as a uniformly distributed random variable with bounds corresponding to the definitions of the categories. The characteristics of a uniformly distributed random variable with bounds a and b are shown in Fig. 4.40. The resulting individual means and variances for the individual tasks and the associated estimates for the project effort and expected estimation error are shown in Table 4.11. The variables s, m, and l represent the number of unfinished tasks classified as small, medium, and large, respectively. This characterization is optimistic because it assumes that the guesses correctly classify every task, and that tasks are completed in the first half of the estimation interval as often as they are completed in the second half. The optimistic estimate should be regarded as an unreachable ideal, and the actual performance of the project should not under any circumstances be expected to be any better than the optimistic estimate. If there is any appreciable probability with respect to the optimistic estimate that the project may not be complete by the deadline, the manager should consider immediate and drastic action to adjust the schedule or the scope of the project. Hiring new people should be considered only if there is enough time left in the schedule to allow for a productive working period after the expected training delay.

2. Pessimistic estimate. A pessimistic estimate corresponds to the worst case that can be expected to occur. A plausible interpretation for this is that on the average, the actual time required to complete a task is the upper bound

---

Probability density function: $f(x) = $ if $a \leq x \leq b$ then $1/(b - a)$ else 0

Mean: $\mu = (a + b)/2$

Variance: $\sigma^2 = (b - a)^2/12$

FIGURE 4.40
Characteristics of a Uniform Distribution on (a, b)

TABLE 4.11
OPTIMISTIC INTERPRETATION OF TASK ESTIMATES

	Small	Medium	Large
a	0	2	4
b	2	4	8
μ	1	3	6
σ^2	1/3	1/3	4/3

Project effort: $s + 3m + 6l$

Expected error: $\mathrm{sqrt}(s/3 + m/3 + 4l/3)$

of the estimated interval, and that the expected error in an individual estimate is also equal to the upper bound. Thus our pessimistic interpretation
expects actual completion times to vary from zero to twice the estimated
upper bound. The formulae for this characterization are shown in Table
4.12. In our experience, it is reasonable to expect that the average programmer can estimate tasks no larger than eight person-hours to at least
this accuracy.

3. Historical estimate. The means and variances of the individual estimates
are derived from statistics about the actual completion times of the same
development group for tasks that were estimated to fall in each of the
categories. This method is the most accurate because it is calibrated to
account for the biases of the estimators and the capabilities of the people
actually working on the project. Because the set of people working on any
project tend to change, it is worthwhile to keep a continuous record of
these statistics, and to use the results from the most recent time period with
a length of half the average stay of a project member. The formula for this
characterization are shown in Table 4.13. The variables μ_s, μ_m, and μ_l
represent the means of the recorded actual completion times for tasks with
the corresponding classifications, and the variables σ^2_s, σ^2_m, and σ^2_l
represent the variances of the recorded actual completion times.

TABLE 4.12
PESSIMISTIC INTERPRETATION OF TASK ESTIMATES

	Small	Medium	Large
μ	2	4	8
σ^2	4	16	64

Project effort: $2s + 4m + 8l$

Expected error: $\mathrm{sqrt}(4s + 16m + 64l)$

TABLE 4.13
HISTORICAL INTERPRETATION OF TASK ESTIMATES

	Small	Medium	Large
μ	μ_s	μ_m	μ_l
σ^2	σ^2_s	σ^2_m	σ^2_l

Project effort: $s\,\mu_s + m\,\mu_m + l\,\mu_l$

Expected error: $\mathrm{sqrt}(s\,\sigma^2_s + m\,\sigma^2_m + l\,\sigma^2_l)$

The distribution for the total project effort is a normal curve whose mean is the expected project effort μ, and whose standard deviation is the expected error σ, as illustrated in Fig. 4.41. The curve shows the meaning of the expected completion time and the expected error. There is a 50 percent chance that the project will be complete by the expected completion time, and its is reasonable to expect that the actual completion time will differ from the expected completion time by about the expected error. It is virtually certain that the project will be completed by the expected completion time plus four times the expected error, provided that the assumptions on which the analysis is based are satisfied. The three different sets of assumptions just given correspond to three different curves, which correspond informally to the best case, worst case, and expected case for a project described by the given esti-

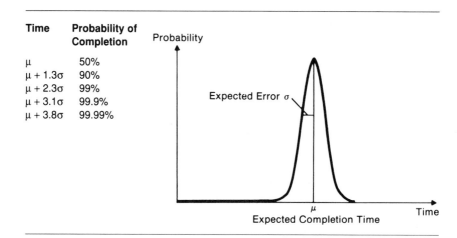

Time	Probability of Completion
μ	50%
$\mu + 1.3\sigma$	90%
$\mu + 2.3\sigma$	99%
$\mu + 3.1\sigma$	99.9%
$\mu + 3.8\sigma$	99.99%

FIGURE 4.41
Distribution of Project Completion Times

mates. In all three cases, the relative error in the estimate is roughly inversely proportional to the square root of the number of individual estimates. Thus with 100 tasks it is typical to have an expected error of about 10%, and with 10,000 tasks it is typical to have an expected error of about 1%.

It is easy to write a program that calculates the probability that a project will be completed by a given time, given the expected completion time μ, the expected error σ, and the number of person-hours available between now and the deadline d. The probability of completion by the deadline is given by

$$P = F((d - \mu)/\sigma)$$

where $F(x)$ is the cumulative normal distribution defined by

$$F(x) = 1/\sqrt{2\pi} \int_{-\infty}^{x} e^{-t^2/2} \, dt.$$

Although this integral is not solvable in closed form, numerical methods for calculating its value are included in most mathematical subroutine libraries. Tables giving values of $F(x)$ can be found in [7] as well as in most statistics textbooks.

The preceding estimates cover only the development and testing of the code. Most systems also include some manuals in the set of deliverables. The effort required for writing a users manual can be estimated using the functional specification, by counting the number of messages, types, exceptions, and output formats, and estimating the complexity of each one. The effort for producing any other deliverables of the project must also be included in the estimate of the total effort remaining.

We illustrate the application of the estimation method described above in terms of the airline reservation system case study. The results of task classification for our example are shown in Table 4.14. The total comes to 51 small tasks, 4 medium ones, and no large ones. This gives us $s = 51$, $m = 4$, and $l = 0$. At this point the specifications for the modules are complete, and none of the other work has been done. Because all of the modules are in the same stage of completion, we can determine the total effort remaining by multiplying the estimate of the implementation by the factor (80/15), which is deter-

TABLE 4.14
CLASSIFICATION OF MODULE SIZES

Module	Data	Operations	Auxiliary
ars	S	9S	
fs	M	6S	
rs	M	6S 2M	
ta	S	3S	13S
am	S	S	5S
date	S	4S	

mined from Table 4.9. According to the optimistic estimate,

$$\mu = (80/15)(s + 3m + 6l) = 5.33(51+3*4) = 336 \text{ person-hours}$$

$$\sigma = (80/15)\sqrt{s/3 + m/3 + 4l/3} = 5.33\sqrt{51/3 + 4/3} = 23 \text{ person-hours}$$

relative error: 7%

and according to the pessimistic estimate,

$$\mu = (80/15)(2s + 4m + 8l) = 5.33(2*51+4*4) = 629 \text{ person-hours}$$

$$\sigma = (80/15)\sqrt{4s + 16m + 64l} = 5.33\sqrt{4*51 + 64*4} = 114 \text{ person-hours}$$

relative error: 18%

The difference between the optimistic and pessimistic is much larger than the error tolerances predicted by the models, reflecting the differences in the under-lying assumptions in the two cases, which have a much bigger effect than the expected errors predicted by a particular set of assumptions. This illustrates the garbage-in, garbage-out principle: the estimates are only as good as the under-lying assumptions. The assumptions defining the estimation model must match reality for the conclusions derived from the model to apply to the actual perfor-mance of the development organization. For this reason, we recommend using historical estimates, since this approach bases the underlying assumptions on statistics about past performance of the organization relative to the same kind of guesswork. To calculate a historical estimate, you have to use the formulae in Table 4.13 and the statistics about the past performance of your development organization. In the absence of such statistics, the pessimistic estimate given by the formulae in Table 4.12 is suggested as a rough approximation to reality. We also note that the estimation method we have described counts only the time spent doing productive work and does not include scheduling delays due to precedence relations between tasks. If the result of one task is needed as an input to a second task, then the people responsible for the second task may be forced to wait for the first task to be completed.

To estimate the effort required to produce the user manuals, we examine the functional specification, and find seven messages visible to the user, seven data types, and six exceptions, with two outputs in tabular form. We are deal-ing with a very simple system from the users' point of view. We use a similar classification scheme for estimating effort for writing manuals, described in Table 4.15. We estimate the messages and output formats as medium, and the exceptions and types as small. Using a pessimistic estimation style, this gives the following results.

$$\mu = (100/40)(s + 2m + 4l) = 2.5(13+2*9) = 78 \text{ person-hours}$$

$$\sigma = (100/40)\sqrt{s + 4m + 16l} = 2.5\sqrt{13 + 4*9} = 18 \text{ person-hours}$$

relative error: 23%

TABLE 4.15
GUIDELINES FOR ESTIMATING MANUAL PRODUCTION EFFORT

Task	Relative Effort
Writing	40%
Summaries and indexes	20%
Review and revision	40%

Size	Effort for Writing (hours)
Small	0 .. 1
Medium	1 .. 2
Large	2 .. 4

We use the pessimistic estimates for our example to illustrate the calculation of the probability of finishing the project on time. According to the requirements, the resources available are three people for ten weeks, or $3 * 40 * 10 = 1200$ person-hours for the entire project. At this point we have already spent 380 person-hours on the requirements, functional specification, and architectural design, leaving 820 hours still available. We can combine the two estimates by adding the means and the variances, to get

$$\mu = 629 + 78 = 707 \text{ person-hours}$$

$$\sigma = \sqrt{114^2 + 18^2} = 115 \text{ person-hours}$$

$$P = F((d - \mu)/\sigma) = F((820 - 707)/115) = F(0.98) = 84\%$$

for the entire project. Note there is some chance of missing our schedule even with a fairly substantial effort reserve, although the odds are on our side. Because the pessimistic estimate gives us a good chance to finish the project on time, we consider the project to be on track. We have a reserve of 113 person-hours available beyond the expected time required to finish, and this is about the size of the expected error in the estimate. This reserve is sufficient, but by no means excessive. The current status of the project justifies the simplifications and Spartan design choices we made during requirements analysis, functional specification, and architectural design. These choices were guided by our informal judgement that the available resources were skimpy for solving the problem at hand, based on past experience with developing software.

The software engineering literature describes many methods for estimating project effort. Experimental studies show the strongest correlations between measured levels of development effort and estimates of the number of lines of code and closely related measures, out of many different measures proposed [5]. This result is hard to apply in practice, because effort estimates are needed early in the process, when the number of lines of code to be produced is still unknown. Because the best available methods are all based on guessing something, we recommend the direct approach of guessing the effort for each subtask, rather than guessing related quantities such as lines of code. Using statistics about past performance of the particular organization involved to calibrate the guesswork appears to be the best engineering approach for estimating software project costs at the current state of the art.

4.6.2 Planning

Effort estimation is subject to occasional large errors; therefore project managers should prepare several contingency plans, and keep close track of the correspondence between actual progress and the plans, so that the need to switch to a less ambitious contingency plan can be identified as early as possible.

Contingency plans should be based on the functional specification. The impact of deleting each of the functions of the system should be analyzed, and the amount of effort that would be saved by leaving out each of the functions should be estimated by adding up the individual estimates for the modules involved. The contingencies identified should allow the delivered system to be used to do some useful work, even if some of the operations needed by the users can be accomplished only partially or less conveniently than would be possible if the full system were implemented.

Our airline reservation system example does not provide many possibilities for leaving out functions, because the initial design was kept minimal due to anticipated schedule problems. The system can still be used to do some useful work if the `drop_flight` and `new_fare` operations of the airline manager interface are deleted, but these functions cannot be delayed for long. The `new_fare` operation will probably be needed before the `drop_flight` operation, so the first contingency plan would leave out `drop_flight` and the second contingency plan, which the manager hopes never to need, would leave out both `drop_flight` and `new_fare`.

The `new_fare` and `drop_flight` operations are not needed for testing the rest of the system, so we decide to schedule them late in the project, to leave our options open in case the project gets in trouble. We note that deleting these operations removes only four small implementation units (the operations and the auxiliary functions for parsing them), leading to a potential savings of roughly 40 person-hours or about 6% of the remaining work. This is a relatively small margin, emphasizing the need for the manager to keep close watch on the project.

Other possibilities for reducing the amount of work in the project are limited implementations of some operations, which work only on restricted subsets of the input space or do not meet the performance constraints under all conditions. This second kind of contingency should be avoided if possible, because limited implementations are often difficult to extend to full implementations without discarding the initial version and starting over, which is wasteful. An example of a limited implementation contingency for the airline reservation system might be a version of the system that does not meet some of the performance requirements.

To minimize risk it is important to implement the difficult parts of the system early, especially if there are any doubts about the feasibility of the approach. If such parts are built, tested, and evaluated early, there should be enough time in the schedule for a redesign if one turns out to be needed. Priority should also be given to fully elaborating the design of the parts of the system that are the least understood, so that schedule and manpower problems can be identified as early as possible.

The project manager should keep close track of the actual progress of the project, and be prepared to invoke contingency responses or to negotiate schedule and budget extensions if the probability of completing on time gets less than 50%, which occurs when the estimate of the remaining effort exceeds the amount of effort still available. When the probability of finishing the project on time gets appreciably less than 1.0, the implementation team should be informed that the schedule is tight, and that fine tuning of the implementation should be delayed until after a minimally operational system has been achieved.

We suggest using the extra time, if there still is some at the end of the project, to review and revise the manuals, to do some extra testing, make performance measurements, and introduce some optimizations. We would like to have a satisfied customer, and clarity of the documentation and consistency of the actual behavior of the system with the documentation usually have the strongest effect on user satisfaction, followed by execution speed.

4.6.3 Organization and Task Assignments

Choosing the best organization for a development team is difficult because it depends strongly on the nature and structure of the product to be built. The following guidelines are useful.

1. The structure of the organization should be based on the structure of the module dependency diagram and the nature of the tasks to be performed.

2. The module dependency diagram should be partitioned into disjoint subgraphs such that each development group is responsible for one subgraph, and the number of arcs between subgraphs owned by different groups is minimized.

3. The number of people working on operations of the same machine or type should be minimized.

4. The number of people working on the modules in a cycle of the module dependency diagram should be minimized.

5. The people responsible for testing a subsystem should be different from those responsible for implementing the subsystem.

6. The number of people reporting to each manager should be no more than seven.

The general guidelines about team organization presented in previous chapters apply also at the design and implementation stages.

Organizations concerned about the quality of their products have found problems with assembly-line type organizations and overspecialization of job functions. One of these problems is lack of any one person with responsibility for the product as a whole. This can cause unanticipated problems to go unsolved, because they may not clearly belong to the official job responsibilities of any one person in the organization. Another problem is boredom due to excessive repetition of a narrowly defined task. Giving individuals responsibility for clearly visible aspects of particular products is usually helpful for this kind of morale problem.

An alternative to an organization focused on job functions is a matrix style organization, where teams are organized by individual products, and fill different job functions in different parts of the project. In such organizations there is a single manager responsible for the project, who may have many different people reporting to him at different stages of the development. This management structure is flexible, since it can accommodate both people permanently assigned to the project and those who enter and leave the project as the phases requiring their special talents come and go. There may be other managers responsible for coordinating the activities of a given phase between many different projects who interact with the project leaders.

In addition to avoiding boredom and maintaining morale, tracing the successes and failures of each aspect of the product back to the people originally responsible for them, ensuring that the people responsible for the successes are the ones who benefit, and those responsible for the failures are the ones who bear the costs, appears to be necessary for producing high-quality products. Such policies must be supported by the highest levels of management for long-term success in producing high-quality systems.

4.7 Related Research

The classic paper on decomposing software systems is [6], and a more recent version of the approach is described in [4]. More information about managing software projects can be found in [2, 3]. Special issues in system design for minimizing risk due to system failures are discussed in [8].

Exercises

1. Develop an architectural design for a spelling correction program.
2. Develop an architectural design for a program that displays satellites orbiting the earth on a graphics terminal.

3. Develop an architectural design for a program that plays tic-tac-toe.

4. Because `hashed_files` take a long time to initialize, they have a disadvantage relative to `B_trees` in applications that create new files frequently. Modify the architectural design of the airline reservation system to replace the `hashed_file` in the representation of the `reservation_set` type with a `B_tree`. Show all changes needed to complete the modified architectural design.

Projects

1. Develop an architectural design for any of the systems specified in the projects at the end of Chapter 3.

2. Collect statistics about the past performance of your organization, and use them to determine the constants in the formulae for historical effort estimation shown in Table 4.13.

References

1. A. Aho, J. Hopcroft, and J. Ullman, *Data Structures and Algorithms*, Addison-Wesley, Reading, MA, 1985.

2. T. Gilb and S. Finzi, *Principles of Software Engineering Management*, Addison-Wesley, Reading, MA, 1988.

3. R. Gunther, *Management Methodology for Software Product Engineering*, John Wiley & Sons, New York, 1978.

4. D. Lamb, *Software Engineering: Planning for Change*, Prentice Hall, Englewood Cliffs, NJ, 1988.

5. R. Lind and K. Vairavan, "An Experimental Investigation of Software Metrics and their Relationship to Software Development Effort," *IEEE Transactions on Software Engineering 15*, 5 (May, 1989), 649–653.

6. D. Parnas, "On the Criteria to be Used in Decomposing a System into Modules," *Communications of the ACM 15*, 12 (Dec. 1972), 1053–1058.

7. S. Selby, ed., *Standard Mathematical Tables*, Chemical Rubber Co., Cleveland, OH, 1970.

8. J. Toigo, *Disaster Recovery Planning*, Yourdon Press, Englewood Cliffs, NJ, 1989.

5

Implementation

An implementation is a description of the internal structure of each module specified in the architectural design. The implementation defines the algorithms and data structures that realize each module in terms of the lower-level modules appearing in its parts list, if any. A completed implementation consists of an executable program for each module together with justifications for the main design decisions.

Architectural design is concerned mainly with identifying and defining the interfaces of the modules in the proposed system. The architectural design defines a black-box view of each module, which has both abstract and concrete aspects. Implementation is concerned mainly with identifying and defining the internal mechanisms for each module. The implementation defines a glass-box view of each module, which also has both abstract and concrete aspects.

We use Spec for abstract descriptions and Ada for concrete descriptions of implementations as well as software architectures. Because the abstract and concrete levels of an implementation are closely intertwined we combine the two notations, expressing an implementation as an Ada program unit with Spec annotations embedded in Ada comments.

5.1 Goals

The goals of implementation are to provide, justify, and verify a realization for each module, satisfying its black-box specification and meeting the performance constraints. The justifications are needed for understanding, analyzing, and modifying the system. Recording justifications is important because it can be very difficult or impossible to reconstruct them from the bare code [18]. Verification is needed because programming is an error-prone process that must be carried out nearly perfectly to get a system with acceptable reliability.

The goals in constructing a realization are to make the program as clear and simple as possible while conforming to the functional specification and meeting the performance constraints. Each part of the program should be necessary for realizing the black-box specification, and each conceptual entity in the specification should correspond to a localized and clearly identifiable region of the code to the extent allowed by the programming language. This correspondence is important for tracing the impact of requirements changes, and automated tools for maintaining and analyzing the correspondence are desirable. In the absence of tools, a neat and systematic organization of the code that directly reflects the structure of the specification can ease the process of manually maintaining the correspondence. People find code easier to understand if constructs with a similar meaning have a similar appearance. Consequently any symmetries or regularities inherent in the problem should be preserved in the specifications and in the code.

Justifications are needed for communication between designers, for determining the constraints that must be respected by future modifications to the system, and for verifying various aspects of the correctness of the code. The justifications should contain both informal explanations of why particular implementation strategies were preferred, and more detailed formal annotations. The informal annotations should provide summary information to help a designer understand the general structure and intended operating characteristics of the implementation. This information is important for helping new people learn about the design. The formal annotations are needed for more precise descriptions of critical design decisions. Annotations are used both for communication and for supporting automated tools. There may be several different kinds of formal annotations, each of which supports a different kind of verification tool.

The goals for quality assurance are locating and diagnosing faults in an initial implementation and demonstrating the absence of faults in a mature implementation. The need for quality assurance is a consequence of an imperfect software development process. In current practice, most software systems are constructed manually. Because people make errors, locating and diagnosing errors is necessary to arrive at a viable implementation using conventional technology.

The first goal for quality assurance is much easier to meet than is the second. An incorrect output on a single test case shows the presence of a fault, and the computation producing the incorrect value has a finite history that can be analyzed to locate the cause of the problem. A system without faults must produce correct outputs for all possible inputs. The set of input values for a program can be unbounded in principle, and is usually much too large in practice for exhaustive testing to be practical. In principle, the absence of faults can be established by mathematical proof techniques, but it is very difficult to do so for large systems. Consequently most software systems are not certified to be free of faults, and are used even though they do contain faults.

The goal of certifying correctness is usually impractical to meet; therefore it is often replaced by the weaker goal of checking the reliability of the implementation. Correctness is an absolute concept, and reliability is a statistical concept. A system is *correct* if it always produces results conforming to its specification. A system is *reliable* if the frequency with which it produces outputs violating its specification is low. The frequency of failures depends on the probability distribution of the actual input values, which is difficult to determine accurately. Given a fixed probability distribution, the number of test cases needed to establish confidence in a system relative to a black-box specification increases in proportion to $m * \log(m)$ [14], where m is the required mean interval between failures, so that checking stringent reliability requirements by testing can be expensive. The concept of reliability is also very sensitive to the probability distribution for the inputs. If a program contains some faults, as most large systems do, then it is possible to find an input distribution that makes the system fail every time it is invoked ($m = 1$). If the same program works correctly on some subset of its input space, as most delivered systems do, it is also possible to find input distributions where the system works correctly every time (m = infinity). This means that reliability measured by the mean interval between failures is meaningful only for systems with predictable input distributions, and that the behavior of a system under unexpected operating conditions can be wildly unpredictable even if it has been certified as reliable via a thorough program of black-box testing.

The amount of effort needed to locate and remove errors in a software system can get large, so there has been a great deal of interest in techniques that guarantee correctness of the code by construction. In such an approach, the goal is to prevent errors from entering into the design via formalized methods supported by software tools. Such techniques are still at an early stage of development, and are being addressed by many currently active research and development efforts, some of which are described in Chapter 8. At the current time it is not feasible to provide a universal guarantee of correctness by construction, but it is feasible to guarantee the absence of some classes of errors via software tools based on this approach. Some classes of errors that currently can be prevented with feasible software tools include syntax errors, type consistency errors, and use of uninitialized variables. This reduces the scope of the verification and debugging activities needed, and allows the construction of more reliable software with less effort. Some basic concepts needed to support correctness by construction, and some examples are contained in this chapter.

5.2 Basic Concepts

The following kinds of activities are part of constructing an implementation:

1. Designing data structures
2. Designing algorithms
3. Designing test instrumentation
4. Deriving detailed code
5. Locating and diagnosing errors
6. Certifying correctness of a finished product.

The algorithms and data structures are constrained by the choices made during architectural design, but many details remain to be worked out during implementation. The details should be worked out systematically, one aspect at a time, working from the highest level aspects to the finer details. This process has been called "top down design" or "stepwise refinement." The justification for considering just one aspect at a time is that the designer is more likely to make a good decision if there are fewer details affecting the decision. The justification for starting with the highest level considerations is that decisions at more detailed levels are dependent on the choices at the more abstract levels.

Details of data structures visible at a given level should be worked out before the details of algorithms at that level because the algorithms depend on the data structures. Note that similar dependency criteria lead to the opposite order during specification: The conceptual data model of a type module is worked out *after* the operations have been identified, because the model depends on the operations that must be supported. The abstract data types to be used as components of the representation of a given type or machine have been identified in the architectural design, along with the general classes of data structures and algorithms to be used. Details of the representation at the programming language level must be worked out during implementation. This includes identifying all of the components, defining how they are packaged in terms of the primitives provided by the programming language, determining the concrete data invariants, and determining the correspondence between the concrete representation and the conceptual representation appearing in the black-box specification. The packaging details are expressed as Ada declarations, and the invariants and correspondences are expressed as Spec annotations.

Determining the concrete data invariants accurately is very important because all of the operations depend on this information. All restrictions or conventions applying to the data structure should be part of the concrete data invariant. The operations can safely assume only those properties of the data structure included in the concrete data invariant, and each operation must ensure that all of the properties in the data invariant hold for any newly created or modified objects of a type or for the next state of a machine. The implementation does not work correctly unless all of the operations are based on the same conventions about the data structure. Because the conventions associated with a data structure can be quite complex, this information must be recorded, reviewed, and adjusted until consistency can be established. Recording the conventions in the concrete invariant is also important for communication purposes because different operations may be implemented by different people or by the same person at well separated points in time.

The design of algorithms for realizing the messages of each black box is also constrained by the results of architectural design, but many details remain to be determined. The architectural design should provide a list of lower level operations to be used in realizing each message, and the concrete interface design should provide declarations for the interface of the operation at the programming language level. Partial sketches of algorithms for the larger modules may be available from feasibility checks done during architectural design. The initial design of the algorithm should define carefully any local data structures to be used and work out the principles of operation for any loops or recursions in the program, because these are the most difficult aspects of the implementation. Loop invariants and bounding functions should be determined at this point.

Loop invariants document the conditions that must hold before and after every execution of the loop body. Loop invariants are an important aid in design, because it is much easier to analyze properties that do not change than to analyze those that do. Designing loops based on invariants requires a static rather than an operational thinking style that may be strange to some readers. Examples of designs using loop invariants can be found later in this chapter, and in [8, 10]. If loop invariants are available, it becomes possible to automate most of the work involved in mathematically proving the correctness of the implementation, provided the conditions to be checked are not too difficult for the theorem prover to establish without further advice from the designer. Loop invariants can also form the basis for more informal checking in design review meetings, and if implemented, they can be checked mechanically during testing.

Bounding functions are useful for demonstrating that a loop or recursion terminates for all inputs. This should be done for all recursions and loops in the implementation that are supposed to terminate. A bounding function is an upper bound on the number of iterations of a loop before it terminates, or on the depth of any remaining recursive calls.

The detailed code leading to a specified result can sometimes be derived systematically using weakest preconditions. The *weakest precondition* of a program segment s with respect to a predicate p is the least restrictive predicate $wp(s, p)$, such that the program segment s terminates in a state in which the postcondition p is true for any initial state in which $wp(s, p)$ is true. Rules for deriving weakest preconditions for a subset of the statements in Ada, and their application to systematically constructing loop-free programs satisfying given specifications are described later in this chapter.

5.3 Procedures and Guidelines

The main steps in implementation are: determining the order in which to implement the system, designing individual modules, designing test instrumentation, and testing. Guidelines for these steps are given next.

5.3.1 Determining Implementation Order

The preferred order of implementation is determined by the needs for contingency planning and testing. Contingency plans involve possible delivery of a partially implemented system lacking some of the less critical functions. The parts of the system that may have to be omitted if a contingency plan is adopted must be implemented last to preserve flexibility in making schedule adjustments.

Testing considerations indicate that input and output facilities and data types should be implemented first, because these components usually are helpful for testing the rest of the system. It is usually useful to implement everything needed to support a small subset of the externally available functions to permit early testing and possible partial demonstrations of parts of the user interface. This sometimes involves implementing a proper subset of the operations for some state machines or data types, delaying the implementations of other operations until a skeleton version of the system is working. This approach ensures that the overall system structure is sound, and allows the delivery of a working system that does some useful functions at any point near the end of the project, minimizing the risk of a total project failure.

5.3.2 Designing Modules

The recommended steps for designing a module are explained here.

1. Find and read the relevant parts of the functional specification and architectural design, including any implementation sketches developed during architectural design. Also, get a copy of the Ada specification part developed in the concrete interface design.

2. Review the Ada specification part and fill in any missing details. For machines or types, work out the concrete data representation and add the

corresponding declarations to the private part of the package specification. Determine the concrete data invariants and include them as annotations on the associated concrete type declarations. Also, give definitions for constants or parameters whose values were left unspecified in the concrete interface design.

3. Write the code for each subprogram in the module. Record any restrictions on the legal input values to the subprogram as you develop the code, using precondition annotations. Also, develop invariants and bounding functions together with the implementation of each loop, and record them as annotations. An initial version of the invariant should be developed before the code for the loop, because the initial conditions and the details of the loop body can partially be derived from the invariants. As you discover additional assumptions needed by your code, record them in the precondition, concrete data invariants, loop invariants, or annotations for the affected declarations.

4. After the code for the module has stabilized, review the entire module with respect to the black-box specifications, concrete invariants, and bounding functions. This step is important especially for types and machines, because adjustments to the concrete data invariants discovered in implementing one operation can affect the implementations of the other operations. The implementation is not done until all of the operations have a consistent view of the invariants, and all of the invariants remain true after each operation.

5. Compile the module and run any other static analysis tools available to you. Fix any errors detected by the tools and review the effects of each fix on the preconditions, invariants, and bounding functions. Repeat until no more errors are reported, and until all remaining warning messages have been carefully checked and diagnosed as harmless.

At this point the module is ready for testing.

5.3.3 Designing Test Instrumentation

After the black-box specification of a module is complete, the design of test instrumentation interfaces can begin. Test instrumentation is needed for abstract machines and data types because the internal data structures are not directly accessible from outside the module. Extra operations for observing the internal data structures of an implementation or for driving machines or mutable types into known states are known as *test instrumentation*. The amount of test instrumentation needed for a module depends on the amount and complexity of its internal data.

For modules with relatively small and simple data structures, operations for creating objects with given internal data structures and for displaying the contents of the internal data structures may suffice for glass-box testing. Modules containing large databases are difficult to test without programs for generating test data and for calculating summary views of the internal state, because manual generation and analysis of large data structures is ineffective. In such cases it may be necessary to write programs for generating random data elements, and for evaluating the preconditions, postconditions, concepts, and concrete invariants of the implementation so that the results of a test can be classified as confirming or refuting correctness automatically rather than by manual inspection of the output data. Test instrumentation is the process of adding operations for observing and controlling the internal states of implementation modules. Such operations are needed for testing purposes, and are especially important for modules with protected internal data structures, such as abstract machines and data types. Some examples of test instrumentation can be found in the implementations of the B_tree and hashed_file modules given in Appendix F.

5.4 Case Study: Airline Reservation System

The new modules identified in the architectural design of the airline reservation system are listed in Fig. 5.1. The architectural design depends on the reusable software components shown in Fig. 5.2. Ada implementations of these reusable components are given in Appendix F.

The first decision we have to make is implementation order. Recall we decided to delay implementation of the drop_flight and new_fare operations for scheduling flexibility in the event of unforeseen problems (see Section 4.6.2). We decide to implement parts of the travel_agent, airline_manager, and airline_reservation_system modules first to make it easier to test the system via the I/O facilities they provide. Priority goes to the reserve, notify, find_flights, and add_flight commands, because they let us build and observe the state of the system. Next come the flight_schedule, reservation_set, and date modules, because these data types enable the travel agent interface to be tested. The other parts of the airline reservation system come later, because their delivery could be delayed if absolutely necessary. The work of implementing the modules is done in parallel by assigning it to different team members, paying attention to the priorities imposed by the decisions above.

We present the implementation in terms of an initial skeleton containing the minimal operations to arrive at a system that can be tested through the user interface, followed by the data types, test instrumentation and the completed version of the system.

airline_reservation_system	is_passenger
flight_schedule	is_date
reservation_set	display_flight
travel_agent	display_reservation
parse_find_flights	edit_command
parse_reserve	airline_manager
parse_cancel	parse_add_flight
parse_notify	parse_drop_flight
next_item	parse_new_fare
is_airport	is_time
is_flight_id	is_money
is_agent_id	date

FIGURE 5.1
Modules to be Implemented

5.4.1 Initial Skeleton

The initial skeleton consists of the parts of the system needed for the reserve, notify, find_flights, and add_flight commands.

Main Program.   Ada requires the main program to be a procedure; the top levels of our design are tasks embedded in packages. It is easy to remedy this mismatch by adding an extra procedure to act as the main program, as shown in Fig. 5.3. The main program does nothing but declare the instances of the generic package travel_agent_pkg and include the separately compiled airline_manager_pkg. We show only two of the 300 instances of the travel_agent_pkg that should be declared in the finished system to save some space, and also to show the initial configuration we use for testing. We include two instances of the travel agent rather than just one to give any

B_tree
lex_order
hashed_file
string_hash
text
bounded_sequence
fill_line

FIGURE 5.2
Reusable Software Components Used in the Design

```
  with travel_agent_pkg;
  with airline_manager_pkg;
procedure main is
  package ta1 is new travel_agent_pkg(modem_id => 1);
  package ta2 is new travel_agent_pkg(modem_id => 2);
  -- Other instance declarations for each modem_id IN 3 .. 300.
begin
  null;
  -- All of the work is done by tasks
  -- in the packages declared above.
end main;
```

FIGURE 5.3
Implementation of Main Program

potential interference problems between multiple instantiations of the same task an opportunity to show up.

Travel Agent.   Examining the architectural design in Section 4.4.1, we find all parts of the travel agent module are needed in the initial skeleton except for parse_cancel. We have to choose concrete file names to represent the input stream and output stream of the travel agent module. These streams will be connected to modems during the actual operation of the system, and will be connected to two text files during testing. We generate concrete file names for these files systematically, based on the modem id of each instance of the generic package, and update the specification of the module to reflect this decision as shown in Fig. 5.4. The implementation skeleton for the travel agent module is shown in Fig. 5.5. Most of the information needed to produce the implementation is already available in the functional specification of the travel agent and in the module specifications associated with the architectural design. The interfaces for the local subprograms used in the implementation have been determined during architectural design, and the corresponding Ada interface specifications have been generated in the concrete interface specification stage. We leave these explicit subprogram specifications in the beginning of the package body because this removes restrictions on the order in which the subprogram bodies must be written, allowing them to be arranged in an order convenient for reading the code in a top-down fashion. This can help new people familiarize themselves with the code during later parts of the implementation and evolution activities.

Given the black-box specifications and the decomposition, writing down the details of the code is relatively straightforward. We notice the travel agent task is essentially a command interpreter, with a structure common to most

```
MACHINE travel_agent_design1(modem_id: nat)
  INHERIT travel_agent_design(modem_id)
  IMPORT nat FROM format

  CONCEPT input_name(id: nat) VALUE(s: string)
      -- The file name for the input stream
      -- is generated from the modem_id.
    WHERE SOME(ns: string ::
               s = ("ta" || ns || "_in") & nat(ns) = id )

  CONCEPT output_name(id: nat) VALUE(s: string)
      -- The file name for the output stream
      -- is generated from the modem_id.
    WHERE SOME(ns: string ::
               s = ("ta" || ns || "_out") & nat(ns) = id )
END
```

FIGURE 5.4
Elaboration of the File Name Concepts

FIGURE 5.5
Implementation Skeleton for Travel Agent

```
  with text_io; use text_io;
  with text_pkg; use text_pkg; -- Defines text_pkg_instance.
  with date_pkg; use date_pkg;  -- Defines date.
  with concrete_types_pkg; use concrete_types_pkg;
    -- Defines airport, flight_id, passenger, agent_id,
    -- flight_description, reservation.
  with parse_pkg; use parse_pkg;
    -- Defines is_airport, is_flight_id, is_passenger,
    -- is_agent_id, edit_command, next_item.
  with format_pkg; use format_pkg; -- Defines fill_line.
  with airline_reservation_system_pkg;
  use airline_reservation_system_pkg;
    -- Defines task airline_reservation_system and
    -- types flight_sequence, reservation_sequence.
package body travel_agent_pkg is
  use text_pkg_instance;  -- Defines the type text.
  use flight_sequence_pkg;
    -- Defines the flight_sequence operations.
  use reservation_sequence_pkg;
    -- Defines the reservation_sequence operations.
  -- Local subprogram declarations.
  procedure interpret_command(cmd: character; args: in text;
                              f: in file_type );
```

FIGURE 5.5 (continued)

```
procedure parse_find_flights(s: in text; o, d: out airport;
                                result: out boolean );
procedure parse_reserve(s: in text; a: out agent_id;
                          i: out flight_id; d: out date;
                          p: out passenger;
                          result: out boolean );
procedure parse_cancel(s: in text; i: out flight_id;
                          d: out date; p: out passenger;
                          result: out boolean );
procedure parse_notify(s: in text; a: out agent_id;
                          i: out flight_id; d: out date;
                          result: out boolean );


-- Constant declarations.
modem_number: constant string := natural'image(modem_id);
input_name: constant string :=
  "ta" & modem_number(2 .. modem_number'last) & "_in";
output_name: constant string :=
  "ta" & modem_number(2 .. modem_number'last) & "_out";


task body travel_agent_type is
  input, output: file_type;
  last: natural;
  buffer, command: text;
begin
  open(input, in_file, input_name);
  open(output, out_file, output_name);
  loop  -- Forever.
    get_line(input, buffer);
    buffer := edit_command(buffer);
    next_item(buffer, command);
    if length(command) = 1
    then interpret_command(char(command, 1), buffer, output);
    else -- Illegal command code.
       interpret_command(' ', buffer, output);
    end if;
  end loop;
exception
  when end_error => put_line(output, "input terminated");
  when constraint_error =>
    put_line(output,
             "Unexpected constraint_error in travel_agent" );
  when numeric_error =>
    put_line(output,
             "Unexpected numeric_error in travel_agent" );
  when program_error =>
```

```
      put_line(output,
              "Unexpected program_error in travel_agent" );
  when storage_error =>
      put_line(output,
              "Unexpected storage_error in travel_agent" );
  when tasking_error =>
      put_line(output,
              "Unexpected tasking_error in travel_agent" );
  when others =>
      put_line(output, "Unexpected exception in travel_agent");
end travel_agent_type;

procedure interpret_command(cmd: character; args: in text;
                            f: in file_type ) is
  o, d: airport;
  i: flight_id;
  da: date;
  p: passenger;
  a: agent_id;
  fs: flight_sequence;
  rs: reservation_sequence;
  ok: boolean;

  procedure display_reservation(res: in reservation) is
    -- Nonlocal_variable(f: in file_type).
  begin   -- Body of display_reservation.
    put_line(f, fill_line((string_code(res.d), res.p),
                      (8, 20) ));
  end display_reservation;
  procedure display_reservations is
    new reservation_sequence_pkg.scan(display_reservation);

  procedure display_flight(fd: in flight_description) is
    -- Nonlocal_variable(f: in file_type).
  begin   -- Body of display_flight.
    put_line(f, fill_line((fd.id, fd.dep, fd.arr, fd.price),
                      (6, 8, 8, 10) ));
  end display_flight;
  procedure display_flights is
    new flight_sequence_pkg.scan(display_flight);

begin   -- Body of interpret_command.
  case cmd is
    when 'f' =>
      parse_find_flights(args, o, d, ok);
      if ok then
        airline_reservation_system.find_flights(o, d, fs);
        if length(fs) > 0 then display_flights(fs);
```

FIGURE 5.5 (continued)

```
              else put_line(f, "no flights found"); end if;
          else put_line(f, "command not recognized"); end if;
      when 'r' =>
          parse_reserve(args, a, i, da, p, ok);
          if ok then
              airline_reservation_system.reserve(a, i, da, p);
              put_line(f, "done");
          else put_line(f, "command not recognized"); end if;
      when 'c' =>
          null;  -- Not implemented yet.
      when 'n' =>
          parse_notify(args, a, i, da, ok);
          if ok then
              airline_reservation_system.notify(a, i, da, rs);
              if length(rs) > 0 then display_reservations(rs);
              else put_line(f, "no reservations found"); end if;
          else put_line(f, "command not recognized"); end if;
      when others => put_line(f, "command not recognized");
    end case;
  exception
    when no_seat => put_line(f, "No seat available");
    when reservation_exists =>
        put_line(f, "The passenger already has a reservation");
    when no_reservation =>
        put_line(f, "The passenger does not hold a reservation");
    when no_such_flight => put_line(f, "Unknown flight id");
    when constraint_error =>
        put_line(f,
"Unexpected constraint_error in travel_agent.interpret_command"
            );
    when numeric_error =>
        put_line(f,
"Unexpected numeric_error in travel_agent.interpret_command"
            );
    when program_error =>
        put_line(f,
"Unexpected program_error in travel_agent.interpret_command"
            );
    when storage_error =>
        put_line(f,
"Unexpected storage_error in travel_agent.interpret_command"
            );
    when tasking_error =>
        put_line(f,
"Unexpected tasking_error in travel_agent.interpret_command"
            );
```

```
        when others =>
          put_line(f,
"Unexpected exception in travel_agent.interpret_command"
                );
   end interpret_command;


   procedure parse_find_flights(s: in text; o, d: out airport;
                                result: out boolean ) is
      line: text := s;
      item: text;
   begin
      next_item(line, item);
      if is_airport(item) then o := item;
         else result := false; return; end if;
      next_item(line, item);
      if is_airport(item) then d := item;
         else result := false; return; end if;
      next_item(line, item);  -- Discard any trailing spaces.
      result := length(item) = 0;
   end parse_find_flights;


   procedure parse_reserve(s: in text; a: out agent_id;
                           i: out flight_id; d: out date;
                           p: out passenger;
                           result: out boolean ) is
        line: text := s;
        item: text;
        ok: boolean;
   begin
      next_item(line, item);
      if is_agent_id(item) then a := item;
         else result := false; return; end if;
      next_item(line, item);
      if is_flight_id(item) then i := item;
         else result := false; return; end if;
      next_item(line, item);
      is_date(item, d, ok);
      if not ok then result := false; return; end if;
      trim(line);  -- Get rid of leading and trailing blanks.
      if is_passenger(line) then p := line; result := true;
         else result := false; end if;
   end parse_reserve;


   procedure parse_cancel(s: in text; i: out flight_id;
                          d: out date; p: out passenger;
                          result: out boolean ) is
```

FIGURE 5.5 (continued)

```
begin
  null;   -- Not implemented yet.
end parse_cancel;

procedure parse_notify(s: in text; a: out agent_id;
                       i: out flight_id; d: out date;
                       result: out boolean ) is
    line: text := s;
    item: text;
    ok: boolean;
begin
  next_item(line, item);
  if is_agent_id(item) then a := item;
     else result := false; return; end if;
  next_item(line, item);
  if is_flight_id(item) then i := item;
     else result := false; return; end if;
  next_item(line, item);
  is_date(item, d, ok);
  if not ok then result := false; return; end if;
  next_item(line, item);   -- Discard any trailing spaces.
  result := length(item) = 0;
end parse_notify;
end travel_agent_pkg;
```

iterative interpreters. This structure consists of a read-parse-execute loop, and a case statement for choosing which command to execute.

The implementation of generators in Ada is illustrated by the use of the generator `scan` from the type `bounded_sequence` for implementing the `find_flights` and `notify` commands in the procedure `interpret_com-mand`. Generators are implemented in Ada as procedures with a generic procedure parameter that is invoked with each individual element of the sequence to be generated. In this case, instantiations of the `scan` generator are used to turn procedures for displaying a single item (`display_flight` and `display_reservation`) into procedures for displaying sequences of items (`display_flights` and `display_reservations`). In general, a generator is a mechanism for transforming operators on individuals into the corresponding operators on sequences.

This way of looking at loops may be unfamiliar at first, but it is worthwhile to learn because it simplifies many applications by avoiding explicit descriptions of underlying data representations and control flow. The preceding example illustrates the use of generators to support the information hiding principle. We are creating loops over the components of a `bounded_sequence` without any reference to the details of the representation of a `bounded_sequence`. The program using the `scan` generator would look exactly the same whether sequences are implemented as arrays, files, linked lists, or balanced trees. This allows reimplementing data structures that turn out to be performance bottlenecks with little impact on the programs using the data structure. In large systems, tight coupling between applications programs and details of the data structure often makes such modifications prohibitively expensive. This makes information hiding important for achieving efficiency in large or rapidly evolving systems.

Information hiding can also help to achieve implementations that are easy to understand and extend. Generators are needed to allow iterative processing of the components of an abstract structure without exposing the details of the underlying data representation and control flow. These details can get quite involved for generators over more sophisticated data structures, such as `B_tree.scan_between` (Appendix F). A preprocessor for making such generator calls more readable is described in Section 5.7.6 and in Appendix G.

The remainder of the implementation of the travel agent module consists of a set of procedures for parsing user commands. The parsing procedures have a simple uniform structure: the text of each argument is extracted in order, using the `next_item` procedure, and is tested to determine if it represents an object of the expected type. The boolean output variable `result` becomes true if and only if a well formed set of arguments can be found. This uniformity makes it easy to generate code for many related procedures quickly, once the design for the first one has been carefully worked out and reviewed. The procedure `is_date`, used for parsing dates in the procedures `parse_reserve` and `parse_notify`, differs from the procedures for parsing items of the other input data types because this function must construct and return an instance of the abstract type `date`. Such a conversion is not needed for the other input types because they are represented as text strings.

Our decision to implement only the parts of the system needed in initial skeleton is reflected in the delayed implementation for `parse_cancel` and in the corresponding case of `interpret_command`. The comment in the body of this function is provided to make it easier to find all of the places that need to be completed later.

Recall that we have factored out some of the lower level parsing functions into a separate package because we expect these functions to be used in the airline manager module as well. We implement the parts of this package needed in the initial skeleton as shown in Fig. 5.6. Since the module can be used for testing even if `edit_command` is temporarily implemented as the identity transformation, we choose this simplification in the first version. This is done to allow testing of the user interface and top levels of the system early

FIGURE 5.6
Implementation Skeleton for Low-Level Parsing Functions

```
   with format_pkg; use format_pkg;
      -- Defines letter_string, digit_string.
   with text_io; use text_io;
package body parse_pkg is

   function edit_command(s: text) return text is
   begin
      null;   -- Not implemented yet.
      return s;
   end edit_command;

   procedure next_item(s: in out text; next: out text) is
      front, back: natural;
   begin
      front := 1;
      while front <= length(s) loop
         -- Invariant: spaces(s[1 .. front - 1]) & front IN s'range.
         -- Bound: length(s) - front.
         if char(s, front) = ' ' then
            front := front + 1; else exit; end if;
      end loop;
      if front > length(s)   -- Nothing but spaces in s.
        then next := min_text;
              s := min_text;
              return;
      end if;
      back := front;
      while back < length(s) loop
         -- Invariant:
         --    no_spaces(s[front .. back]) & (back + 1) IN s'range.
         -- Bound: length(s) - back.
         exit when char(s, back + 1) = ' ';
         back := back + 1;
      end loop;
      next := slice(s, front, back);
      s := slice(s, back + 1, length(s));
   end next_item;

   procedure trim(s: in out text) is
      ts: text := s;
   begin
      loop   -- Invariant:
         --     s = b || ts & spaces(b), bound: length(ts).
         exit when length(ts) = 0;
         exit when char(ts, 1) /= ' ';
         delete(ts, 1, 1);
      end loop;
```

```
  loop  -- Invariant:
        --    s = b1 || ts || b2 & spaces(b1) & spaces(b2).
        -- Bound: length(ts).
    exit when length(ts) = 0;
    exit when char(ts, length(ts)) /= ' ';
    delete(ts, length(ts), length(ts));
  end loop;
  s := ts;
end trim;

function is_airport(s: text) return boolean is
begin
  return (length(s) = 3) and then letter_string(s);
end is_airport;

function is_flight_id(s: text) return boolean is
begin
  return 2 <= length(s)
    and then (length(s) <= 6
    and then (letter_string(slice(s, 1, 2))
    and then digit_string(slice(s, 3, length(s))) ));
end is_flight_id;

function is_passenger(s: text) return boolean is
begin
  if length(s) = 0 then return false; end if;
  if not letter(char(s, 1)) then return false; end if;
  if not letter(char(s, length(s))) then return false; end if;
  for i in 1 .. length(s) loop
    if not (letter(char(s, i)) or char(s, i) = ' ')
       then return false; end if;
  end loop;
  return true;
end is_passenger;

function is_agent_id(s: text) return boolean is
begin
  return is_airport(s);
    -- Agent id's have the same format as airports.
end is_agent_id;

procedure is_date(s: in text; d: out date; ok: out boolean) is
  day, month, year, position: natural;
  found: boolean;
  item: text := s;
  slash: constant text := text_string("/");
```

FIGURE 5.6 (continued)

```
  begin
    find(item, slash, found, position);
    if not found then ok := false; return; end if;
    month :=
      natural'value(ada_string(slice(item, 1, position - 1)));
    delete(item, 1, position);
      -- Remove the prefix up to the "/".
    find(item, slash, found, position);
    if not found then ok := false; return; end if;
    day :=
      natural'value(ada_string(slice(item, 1, position - 1)));
    year := natural'value(ada_string(slice(item,
                                            position + 1,
                                            length(item) )));
    d := create(day, month, year);
    ok := true; return;
  exception
    when others => ok := false;
  end is_date;

  function is_money(s: text) return boolean is
  begin
    return length(s) >= 4
      and then char(s, 1) = '$'
      and then digit_string(slice(s, 2, length(s) - 3))
        -- Dollars.                      .
      and then char(s, length(s) - 2) = '.'
      and then digit_string(slice(s, length(s) - 1, length(s)));
        -- Cents.
  end is_money;


  function is_time(s: text) return boolean is
    colon: constant text := text_string(":");
    n, position: natural;
    found: boolean;
  begin
    find(s, colon, found, position);
    if not found then return false; end if;
    n := natural'value(ada_string(slice(s, 1, position - 1)));
      -- Hours.
    if n > 23 then return false; end if;
    n := natural'value(ada_string(slice(s,
                                        position + 1,
                                        length(s) )));
      -- Minutes.
    return (n <= 59);
  exception
    when others => return false;
  end is_time;
end parse_pkg;
```

in the project, so that potential problems can be discovered while there is still time to do something about them.

We include loop invariants and bounding functions in the loops in the `next_item` procedure to document the code. These loops have difficult logic, because there are multiple interacting conditions: either finding a delimiter character, or running off the end of the string. Explicitly formulating the invariants helps us to decide on a clear implementation strategy, and recording this strategy helps others who may later have to extend or modify the code. In particular, the invariants document our decision to keep the index expressions `front` and `back + 1` within the range of the string `s` for all possible states within the loop bodies, thus preventing Ada `constraint_error` exceptions caused by out-of-bounds references to arrays.

In working out the details of implementing functions such as `is_flight_id`, we discover a need for implementations of the concepts `letters` and `digits` from the predefined specification module `format`. This was not anticipated in the architectural design, but it does little harm since both specifications and implementations of these reusable components are already available.

We have noticed that the formats for the `airport` and `agent_id` types are exactly the same, so that the same code can be used to implement both `is_airport` and `is_agent_id`. We put a call to `is_airport` inside of `is_agent_id` rather than replacing all calls of `is_agent_id` by calls to `is_airport` because the two subprograms correspond to two different parts of the user interface, with different meanings. These parts have the same syntax by coincidence, and there is no guarantee they will remain the same in future versions. Evolution is easier if we maintain the correspondence between the structure of the implementation and the conceptual structure of the user interface.

In the function `is_date` we have taken advantage of the range constraints provided by Ada subtypes to achieve range checking on input without much explicit code on our part. The response to range constraint violations is provided by a simple catch-all exception handler, which returns false in case anything unexpected happens, signifying that a legal date could not be constructed. The range checking is done by the operation of the abstract data type `date` for creating an object of type `date` from a triple of natural numbers representing the month, day, and year. We have kept parsing details outside the definition of the abstract data type `date` on the grounds that the I/O formats for values of type `date` are more likely to change than the semantics and operations on those values.

This completes the initial skeleton implementation of the travel agent.

Airline Manager. The initial skeleton of the implementation must contain the `add_flight` operation of the airline manager to generate a nonempty flight schedule for testing the system. An initial implementation of the airline manager is shown in Fig. 5.7. This implementation is very similar to the one for the travel agent. We have kept the structure as regular as possible, and used similar coding structures as much as possible to make it easier to understand the implementation later. Such uniformity can be achieved even if there are several people implementing the functions at the same time by discussing coding conventions in advance and by examining each other's results as the work progresses.

Discrepancies in structure should be discussed, and either removed or justified. In our example there is a discrepancy between the structure of the interpret_command procedure in the travel agent and the airline manager tasks: one uses a case statement, and the other uses an if-then-else structure. This difference can be traced to a difference in the functional specifications requested by two different groups of users: the travel agents prefer single keystroke commands, but the airline managers like complete English words. Because the case statement is a conceptually simpler structure than an unrestricted if-then-else, it is the preferred choice. However, case statements can be used only for small discrete ranges and the airline manager interface does not satisfy this constraint. The difference in command formats is directly supported by user requests, so that it cannot be changed to suit the design. To achieve a uniform interface, we would either have to change the travel agent interface to an if-then-else structure, or introduce an Ada enumeration type for airline manager commands. We decide that an Ada enumeration type would probably give a better program structure, but we do not feel the cost of the change is justified at this point. We add this to our agenda for perfective system evolution, and delay action until the outcome of the project is more certain.

FIGURE 5.7
Implementation Skeleton for Airline Manager

```
with text_io; use text_io;
with text_pkg; use text_pkg;  -- Defines text_pkg_instance.
with date_pkg; use date_pkg;   -- Defines date.
with concrete_types_pkg; use concrete_types_pkg;
   -- Defines airport, flight_id, money, flight_time.
with parse_pkg; use parse_pkg;
   -- Defines is_airport, is_flight_id, is_money, is_time,
   -- edit_command, next_item.
with airline_reservation_system_pkg;
use airline_reservation_system_pkg;
   -- Defines task airline_reservation_system.
package body airline_manager_pkg is
   use text_pkg_instance;  -- Defines the type text.
```

```
-- Local subprogram declarations.
procedure interpret_command(cmd: string; args: in text;
                            f: in file_type );
procedure parse_add_flight(s: in text; i: out flight_id;
                           p: out money; o, d: out airport;
                           dep, arr: out flight_time;
                           c: out natural;
                           result: out boolean );
procedure parse_drop_flight(s: in text; i: out flight_id;
                            result: out boolean );
procedure parse_new_fare(s: in text; i: out flight_id;
                         p: out money; result: out boolean );


-- Constant declarations.
input_name: constant string := "am0_in";
output_name: constant string := "am0_out";


task body airline_manager_type is
  input, output: file_type;
  last: natural;
  buffer, command: text;
begin
  open(input, in_file, input_name);
  open(output, out_file, output_name);
  loop  -- Forever.
    get_line(input, buffer);
    buffer := edit_command(buffer);
    next_item(buffer, command);
    interpret_command(ada_string(command), buffer, output);
  end loop;
exception
  when end_error => put_line(output, "input terminated");
  when constraint_error =>
    put_line(output,
             "Unexpected constraint_error in airline_manager"
             );
  when numeric_error =>
    put_line(output,
             "Unexpected numeric_error in airline_manager" );
  when program_error =>
    put_line(output,
             "Unexpected program_error in airline_manager" );
  when storage_error =>
    put_line(output,
             "Unexpected storage_error in airline_manager" );
```

FIGURE 5.7 (continued)

```
    when tasking_error =>
      put_line(output,
                "Unexpected tasking_error in airline_manager" );
    when others =>
      put_line(output,
                "Unexpected exception in airline_manager" );
  end airline_manager_type;

  procedure interpret_command(cmd: string; args: in text;
                              f: in file_type ) is
    i: flight_id;
    p: money;
    o, d: airport;
    dep, arr: flight_time;
    c: natural;
    ok: boolean;
  begin
    if cmd = "add_flight" then
      parse_add_flight(args, i, p, o, d, dep, arr, c, ok);
      if ok then
        airline_reservation_system.add_flight(i, p, o, d,
                                                dep, arr, c );
        put_line(f, "Done.");
      else put_line(f, "command not recognized"); end if;
    elsif cmd = "drop_flight" then
      null;   -- Not implemented yet.
    elsif cmd = "new_fare" then
      null;   -- Not implemented yet.
    else put_line(f, "command not recognized"); end if;
  exception
    when flight_exists =>
      put_line(f, "The flight is already scheduled.");
      put_line(f,
"To change it, use drop_flight and then add_flight."
              );
    when no_such_flight =>
      put_line(f,
"No such flight was scheduled, check the flight id."
              );
    when constraint_error =>
      put_line(f,
"Unexpected constraint_error in airline_manager"
              );
    when numeric_error =>
      put_line(f, "Unexpected numeric_error in airline_manager");
```

```
  when program_error =>
    put_line(f, "Unexpected program_error in airline_manager");
  when storage_error =>
    put_line(f, "Unexpected storage_error in airline_manager");
  when tasking_error =>
    put_line(f, "Unexpected tasking_error in airline_manager");
  when others =>
    put_line(f, "Unexpected exception in airline_manager");
end interpret_command;


package nat_io is new integer_io(natural); use nat_io;
procedure parse_add_flight(s: in text; i: out flight_id;
                           p: out money; o, d: out airport;
                           dep, arr: out flight_time;
                           c: out natural;
                           result: out boolean ) is

  line: text := s;
  item: text;
  last: positive;
begin
  next_item(line, item);
  if is_flight_id(item) then i := item;
     else result := false; return; end if;
  next_item(line, item);
  if is_money(item) then p := item;
     else result := false; return; end if;
  next_item(line, item);
  if is_airport(item) then o := item;
     else result := false; return; end if;
  next_item(line, item);
  if is_airport(item) then d := item;
     else result := false; return; end if;
  next_item(line, item);
  if is_time(item) then dep := item;
     else result := false; return; end if;
  next_item(line, item);
  if is_time(item) then arr := item;
     else result := false; return; end if;
  get(ada_string(line), c, last);
  line := slice(line, last + 1, length(line));
  next_item(line, item);
  result := length(item) = 0;   -- Ok if no more items.
exception
  when others => result := false;
end parse_add_flight;
```

FIGURE 5.7 (continued)

```
  procedure parse_drop_flight(s: in text; i: out flight_id;
                              result: out boolean ) is
  begin
    null;   -- Not implemented yet.
  end parse_drop_flight;

  procedure parse_new_fare(s: in text; i: out flight_id;
                           p: out money; result: out boolean ) is
  begin
    null;   -- Not implemented yet.
  end parse_new_fare;
end airline_manager_pkg;
```

Airline Reservation System.   The implementation of the parts of the airline reservation system needed in the initial skeleton is shown in Fig. 5.8. The
core of the airline reservation system is a task with an entry for each user command and an internal temporal event that removes stale reservations. In accordance with the Spec pragmas in the architectural design, the `airline_`
`reservation_system` module is implemented as a task rather than a package. This is necessary to prevent concurrent requests by different travel agents
from interfering with each other. The current design processes user commands
one at a time, reflecting the decision that the initial implementation runs on a
single processor. If performance considerations require a multiprocessor version of the system in the future, this central task will have to be partitioned into
a set of independent subtasks, as discussed in Section 4.4.1 and as described in
detail in Section 6.4.1. Because the task entries correspond directly to the user
commands, it is easy to determine which of them must be implemented in the
initial skeleton. We provide null bodies for the delayed parts of the implementation, marked with comments, to make it easier to find the missing parts.
     We have to choose internal names for the flight schedule and the reserva-
tion set as part of the internal representation for the airline reservation system.
These names form part of the file names for the external file representations of
these abstract data structures. Lower levels of the implementation add suffixes
to the names to distinguish between different files serving as components of the
same abstract structure. In particular, the files implementing the components of
the reservation set have date codes in their names. Because these names are
needed for internal bookkeeping only, and some operating systems impose limits on the length of a file name, we keep them short. These names appear in the
`open` statements in the initialization section of the airline reservation system
task. The purpose of the `text_string` operations is to convert Ada string
literals, which are fixed length strings, into values of the abstract type `text`,
which are variable length strings.

FIGURE 5.8
Skeleton Implementation of Airline Reservation System

```
  with text_pkg; use text_pkg; -- Defines text_pkg_instance.
  with flight_schedule_pkg; use flight_schedule_pkg;
  with reservation_set_pkg; use reservation_set_pkg;
package body airline_reservation_system_pkg is
  use text_pkg_instance;   -- Defines the type text.

  -- Local subprogram declarations.
  procedure make_reservations(r: in out reservation_set;
                                i: in flight_id; d: date;
                                a: in agent_id;
                                rs: out reservation_sequence );
  procedure make_flights(s: in out flight_schedule;
                           o, d: airport;
                           fs: out flight_sequence );
  task retire_demon;

  task body airline_reservation_system_type is
    -- State variables.
    schedule: flight_schedule;
    reservations: reservation_set;

    -- Temporary variables.
    has, exists: boolean;
    b, c: natural;

begin
  -- Initialize.
  open(text_string("s"), schedule);
  open(text_string("r"), reservations);

  -- Start operation.
  loop  -- Forever.
    begin  -- Exception handler frame.
      select

        -- Travel agent interface.
          accept find_flights(origin, destination: in airport;
                                fs: out flight_sequence ) do
            make_flights(schedule, origin, destination, fs);
          end find_flights;
      or
          accept reserve(a: in agent_id; i: in flight_id;
                           d: in date; p: in passenger ) do
            holds(p, i, d, reservations, has);
            if has then raise reservation_exists; end if;
            begin
              bookings(i, d, reservations, b);
              capacity(i, schedule, c);
              if b = c then raise no_seat; end if;
              add(a, i, d, p, reservations);
```

307

FIGURE 5.8 (continued)

```
            exception
              when flight_schedule_pkg.no_such_flight =>
                    raise airline_reservation_system_pkg.
                          no_such_flight;
            end;
          end reserve;
    or
          accept cancel(i: in flight_id; d: in date;
                        p: in passenger ) do
            null;   -- Not implemented yet.
          end cancel;
    or
          accept notify(a: in agent_id; i: in flight_id;
                        d: in date;
                        rs: out reservation_sequence ) do
            member(i, schedule, exists);
            if not exists then
               raise airline_reservation_system_pkg.
                     no_such_flight;
            end if;
            make_reservations(reservations, i, d, a, rs);
          end notify;
    or

        -- Airline manager interface.
        accept add_flight(i: in flight_id; price: in money;
                          origin, destination: in airport;
                          departure, arrival: in flight_time;
                          capacity: in natural ) do
          member(i, schedule, exists);
          if exists then raise flight_exists; end if;
          add(i, price, origin, destination, departure,
              arrival, capacity, schedule );
        end add_flight;
    or
        accept drop_flight(i: in flight_id) do
          null;   -- Not implemented yet.
        end drop_flight;
    or
        accept new_fare(i: in flight_id; price: in money) do
          null;   -- Not implemented yet.
        end new_fare;
    or

        -- Temporals.
        accept retire do
          null;   -- Not implemented yet.
        end retire;
      end select;
    exception
```

```
              when others => null;
                 -- Exceptions are handled in the modules
                 -- invoking the task entries.
            end;  -- Exception handler frame.
         end loop;
      end airline_reservation_system_type;

      procedure make_flights(s: in out flight_schedule;
                             o, d: airport;
                             fs: out flight_sequence ) is
            -- Post: scan(fs) = generate_flights(s, o, d).
         fsl: flight_sequence;
      procedure produce_flight(fd: in flight_description) is
      begin -- Invariant: scan(fsl) = *generate_flights(s, o, d).
         add(fd, fsl);
      end produce_flight;
      procedure generate_flights is
         new find_flights(produce_flight);
   begin
      fsl := create;
      generate_flights(s, o, d);
      fs := fsl;
   end make_flights;

      procedure make_reservations(r: in out reservation_set;
                                  i: in flight_id; d: date;
                                  a: in agent_id;
                                  rs: out reservation_sequence ) is
            -- Post: scan(rs) = generate_reservations(s, o, d).
         rsl: reservation_sequence;
      procedure produce_reservation(res: in reservation) is
      begin -- Invariant:
            --     scan(rsl) = *generate_reservations(s, o, d).
         add(res, rsl);
      end produce_reservation;
      procedure generate_reservations is
         new notify(produce_reservation);
   begin
      rsl := create;
      generate_reservations(a, i, d, r);
      rs := rsl;
   end make_reservations;

   -- Driver for the temporal event "retire".
   task body retire_demon is
   begin
      null;  -- Not implemented yet.
   end retire_demon;
end airline_reservation_system_pkg;
```

The airline reservation system task initializes the state of the abstract machine and then goes into an unbounded loop for accepting commands from the travel agents and the airline manager. This reflects the fact that the airline reservation system is a passive server task. The whole system will terminate only if all of the input streams from the users reach an end of file, which is not intended to happen during actual production use of the system, when the input streams come from user keyboards. Such end of file conditions will arise during testing, however, when test input data will come from files. The user commands are processed one at a time by the airline reservation system, in an order determined by the Ada `select` statement, which makes a nondeterministic choice between the alternative `accept` statements it contains on each iteration of the loop. The definition of Ada guarantees the `select` statement provides *fair* service, which means a waiting request can be passed over at most a finite number of times.

The main loop contains an exception handler frame that catches all exceptions and goes on to the next iteration of the loop. This is needed because exceptions that occur during an Ada rendezvous (i.e., inside an `accept` statement) are raised in both the task containing the `accept` statement and in the task containing the call to the corresponding entry. In our design, it is the responsibility of the task calling each entry to respond to the exception conditions, so the airline reservation system task can safely ignore them.

The procedure `make_flights` uses a generator to create a bounded sequence data structure containing the flights to be displayed in response to a `find_flights` command from the travel agent. The procedure `produce_flights` is nested inside the procedure `make_flights` because it needs access to the variable `fs1`. This is a state variable for the loop provided by the generator, which should be local to the `make_flights` procedure.

The algorithm in the implementation can be expressed more clearly in terms of a generalized `for` loop as shown in Fig. 5.9. Here the sequence produced by the generator is used to define the range of the loop control variable `fd`. The loop shown in Fig. 5.9 is not legal in Ada, but it can be transformed into an Ada implementation of the type shown in the `make_flights` procedure via the translation rules given in Section 5.7.5. An Ada preprocessor for performing this transformation, such as the one given in Appendix G, is a

```
fs := create;
for fd in find_flights(s, o, d) loop
   if length(fs) < bound(fs) then add(fd, fs) end if;
end loop;
```

FIGURE 5.9
Algorithm for Make_flights

useful part of a tool set for supporting software development with generators.

The invariant for the state variable in the implementation of `make_flights` says the sequence in `fs1` is a prefix of the entire sequence produced by `generate_flights`, containing the elements up to but not including the most recently generated value `fd`. Generator names such as `scan` denote the sequences produced by the generator when used in assertion such as a loop invariant. When such names appear outside the body of the procedure receiving the values from the generator, they denote the entire sequence produced by the generator, just as in assertions within black-box specifications. When such a generator name appears within the body of the procedure receiving the values produced by the generator, the sequence denoted by the generator depends on the current state, and includes the elements produced by the most recent invocation of the generator, up to and including the value currently contained in the input parameter of the body procedure. If the generator name is preceded by an `*`, the value of the generator is the one in the previous state, including all of the values generated up to but not including the value currently contained in the input parameter of the body procedure. To check that the procedure `produce_flight` preserves the invariant we have to show the invariant without the `*`s on `generate_flights` holds just before the procedure returns, assuming the invariant holds at the beginning and using the relation `generate_flights(s, o, d) = *generate_flights(s, o, d) ||` `[fd]`. This follows easily from the specification of `add@bounded_` `sequence`. Invariants are discussed in Section 5.7.2.

5.4.2 Data Types

All of the abstract data types must at least be partially implemented to allow the initial skeleton of the system to be tested. The initial implementations of the data types are presented in this section.

Flight Schedule.   At this point we have to work out the details of the data representation sketched out during the architectural design (see Section 4.4.1). The concrete data representation for the flight schedule is contained in the private declarations of the package specification shown in Fig. 5.10. According to the architectural design, the representation for a flight schedule consists of a `B_tree` and a `hashed_file`. At this point we work out the detailed Ada definition of this representation. We create the appropriate instances of the generic packages defining the types `B_tree` and `hashed_file`. We define the types of the `key` and `value` of the `B_tree`, and declare the ordering function associated with the keys according to the strategy sketched during the architectural design. The declaration of the ordering function is included in the private part of the package specification because it is needed to define the instance of the generic `B_tree` package although it is not needed outside the implementation of the `flight_schedule` type. At this point we also

FIGURE 5.10
Data Representation for Flight Schedule

```
  with text_pkg; use text_pkg; -- Defines text_pkg_instance.
  with concrete_types_pkg; use concrete_types_pkg;
    -- Defines flight_id, money, airport, flight_time,
    -- flight_description.
  with B_tree_pkg;  -- Needed in private declarations.
  with hashed_file_pkg;  -- Needed in private declarations.
  with text_hash_pkg;  -- Needed in private declarations.
package flight_schedule_pkg is
  use text_pkg_instance;  -- Defines the type text.

  type flight_schedule is limited private;

  procedure open(name: in text; fs: in out flight_schedule);
  procedure add(i: in flight_id; price: in money;
                origin, destination: in airport;
                departure, arrival: in flight_time;
                capacity: in natural;
                fs: in out flight_schedule );
  procedure remove(i: in flight_id; fs: in out flight_schedule);
  procedure member(i: in flight_id; fs: in out flight_schedule;
                   result: out boolean );
  procedure capacity(i: in flight_id; fs: in out flight_schedule;
                     result: out natural );

  generic
    with procedure produce(fd: in flight_description);
  procedure find_flights(fs: in out flight_schedule;
                         origin, destination: airport );

  no_such_flight: exception;  -- Raised by capacity.
private
  type bt_key is
    record
      o, d: airport; i: flight_id;
    end record;

  type bt_value is
    record
      d, a: flight_time; p: money;
    end record;

  function bt_le(x, y: bt_key) return boolean;
  package schedule_bt_pkg is
    new B_tree_pkg(key => bt_key,
                   value => bt_value,
                   "<=" => bt_le );
    -- Use the default degree for the B_tree.
  use schedule_bt_pkg;  -- Defines B_tree.
```

```
type hf_value is
  record
    c: natural; o, d: airport;
  end record;

package hf_hash_pkg is new text_hash_pkg(natural);
package capacity_hf_pkg is
  new hashed_file_pkg(key => flight_id,
                      value => hf_value,
                      hash => hf_hash_pkg.text_hash,
                      pairs => 100_000 );
  -- Use the default block size for the hashed file.
use capacity_hf_pkg;   -- Defines hashed_file.

type flight_schedule is
  record
    schedule: B_tree; capacity: hashed_file;
  end record;   -- Invariants:
-- ALL(fs: flight_schedule :: name(fs.schedule) = name(fs) || "s"
--       & name(fs.capacity) = name(fs) || "c" ),
-- ALL(fs1 fs2: flight_schedule ::
--     name(fs1) = name(fs2) => fs1 = fs2 ),
-- ALL(k1 k2: bt_key SUCH THAT k1 IN schedule & k2 IN schedule ::
--     k1.i = k2.i => k1 = k2 ),
-- ALL(k: bt_key SUCH THAT k IN schedule :: k.i IN capacity),
-- ALL(i: flight_id SUCH THAT i IN capacity ::
--     SOME(k: bt_key SUCH THAT k IN schedule
--          :: k.i = i & k.o = capacity[i].o &
--             k.d = capacity[i].d )).

-- CONCEPT name(fs: flight_schedule)
--   -- The name with which fs was last opened.
--   VALUE(s: string).
end flight_schedule_pkg;
```

choose the values of the generic parameters related to the performance characteristics of the types. We use the default `block_size` for the `B_tree`
because the default has been chosen to give good performance for a wide range
of file sizes and typical ratios between CPU speed and disk speed, and we have
no reason to believe that hardware with unusual characteristics is used in this
application. Similarly, we declare the `key` type and the `hash` function for the
`hashed_file`. We use the default `block_size` for the `hashed_file`, and
take the expected number of `pairs` from the size estimate for the
`flight_schedule` developed in Section 4.4.1.

The most important decisions made during the detailed design of the data structures are recorded in the concrete data invariants, which are contained in the annotations immediately following the declaration of the type `flight_schedule` in the private part of the package. The concrete data invariants record the relationships we expect to hold between the components of the `flight_schedule`. The first invariant says the names of the two components share a common prefix, which is the name of the flight schedule object. This convention is a way of generating unique names for the components. The second invariant says flight schedules have unique names. This invariant is written in terms of the implementation concept `name` that is defined in an annotation at the end of the package specification. The third invariant says no two keys in the schedule `B_tree` have the same flight id. This invariant records the intentional redundancy of the keys for the schedule `B_tree`. This redundancy was introduced in the architectural design to allow subranges of the keys to be generated in the order required by the `find_flights` operation. The fourth invariant says every flight in the schedule has an entry in the capacity file. The fifth invariant says every flight with an entry in the capacity file is in the schedule, and the origin and destination of the flight in the key of the schedule entry agrees with the corresponding information in the value of the entry in the capacity file. The last two invariants record dependencies between the two parts of the representation of a flight schedule that have to be maintained by the algorithms for adding and removing entries in the flight schedule. We have taken care to thoroughly analyze and record these dependencies at the beginning of the implementation effort for the type so that the invariants can serve as a guide for producing code for the operations. This is important for ensuring that all of the algorithms are based on the same set of assumptions about the data structure.

An implementation of the flight schedule operations in the initial skeleton is shown in Fig. 5.11. The implementations of these operations are easy refinements of the approach sketched in the architectural design. In this case we find that the initial estimates of the implementation effort for each operation as small were accurate.

When reviewing the implementation against the concrete data invariants, we notice that the third invariant depends on the precondition of the `add` operation, which says that `add` should only be called with flight ids that are not already in the flight schedule. The `add` operation is called from only one place, in the `airline_reservation_system` task, and that call respects the precondition, so that the invariant is maintained correctly. However, this dependency of the invariant on the context of the calls of the `add` operation throughout the rest of the system is dangerous because it might be invalidated by a future evolutionary change. In a robust design, all of the invariants should be guaranteed to remain true for all possible invocations of the operations, including those with meaningless or unexpected parameter values. This locality consideration gets more important for larger systems. If we were not on such a tight budget, we would change the design and implementation to remove

FIGURE 5.11
Implementation Skeleton for Flight Schedule Operations

```
  with lex3;
package body flight_schedule_pkg is

  procedure open(name: in text; fs: in out flight_schedule) is
  begin
    open(name & text_string("s"), fs.schedule);
    open(name & text_string("c"), fs.capacity);
  end open;

  procedure add(i: in flight_id; price: in money;
                origin, destination: in airport;
                departure, arrival: in flight_time;
                capacity: in natural;
                fs: in out flight_schedule ) is
    -- Pre: ~member(i, fs).
  begin
    add((o => origin, d => destination, i => i),
        (a => arrival, d => departure, p => price),
        fs.schedule);
    add(i,
        (c => capacity, o => origin, d => destination),
        fs.capacity );
  end add;

  procedure remove(i: in flight_id;
                   fs: in out flight_schedule ) is
  begin
    null;  -- Not implemented yet.
  end remove;

  procedure member(i: in flight_id; fs: in out flight_schedule;
                   result: out boolean ) is
  begin
   member(i, fs.capacity, result);
  end member;

  procedure capacity(i: in flight_id; fs: in out flight_schedule;
                     result: out natural ) is
    v: hf_value;
  begin
    fetch(i, fs.capacity, v);
    result := v.c;
  exception
    when capacity_hf_pkg.domain_error => raise no_such_flight;
  end capacity;
```

FIGURE 5.11 (continued)

```
--   generic
--      with procedure produce(fd: in flight_description);
procedure find_flights(fs: in out flight_schedule;
                             origin, destination: airport ) is
   procedure produce_flight_description(k: bt_key;
                                        v: bt_value ) is
   begin
      produce((id => k.i, dep => v.d, arr => v.a, price => v.p));
   end produce_flight_description;
      -- Produce_flight_description must be declared
      -- inside find_flights to be in the scope
      -- of the generic procedure parameter "produce".
   procedure flight_range is
      new schedule_bt_pkg.
         scan_between(produce_flight_description);
begin   -- Body of find_flights.
   flight_range((o => origin, d => destination, i => min_text),
               (o => origin, d => destination, i => max_text),
               fs.schedule);
end find_flights;

function lex is new lex3(airport, airport, flight_id);
function bt_le(x, y: bt_key) return boolean is
begin
   return lex(x.o, x.d, x.i, y.o, y.d, y.i);
end bt_le;
end flight_schedule_pkg;
```

the dependency on the precondition by adding an explicit check in the add operation, with a corresponding exception condition. Because we are on a tight budget, we add this change to our agenda for perfective system evolution.

The first two and the last two invariants are respected by the code without help from preconditions. Because there are no explicit loops, and the implicit loops do not have state variables, we have no bounding functions or loop invariants. The generator find_flights always terminates because the generator range from the type B_tree terminates for all inputs. There are no invariants in the implementation of the find_flights generator because the produce_flight procedure does not contain any state variables.

We have introduced the local function bt_le for defining an instance of the lexicographic ordering on the key type bt_key because the generic mechanism in Ada is not strong enough to define a lexicographic ordering on general record types, and such an ordering is not predefined in Ada. We would like to use a generic type parameter to specify the types of the arguments to the lexicographic ordering operation <=. However, Ada does not support generic type parameters for record types, and we cannot use a generic private type because private types have no operations other than = and /=. These operations are not sufficient because the arguments of the <= operation are records whose components must be accessed to determine the result of the operation. The generic lexicographic ordering functions in Appendix F are therefore defined to work on the individual components of the records rather than on entire record objects. There has to be a separate definition of the lexicographic ordering for each record length because Ada does not allow variable numbers of generic type parameters. The purpose of the bt_le function is to bridge the mismatch between interfaces by extracting the components of a bt_key record and passing them to the appropriate instance of the generic lexicographic ordering functions.

If the generic parameter mechanism of Ada were stronger, we could have used an instance of a generic lexicographic ordering package in the definition of the B_tree type for the flight_schedule, just as we used an instance of string_hash_pkg in the definition of the hashed_file type. This would eliminate the need for introducing the bt_le function.

Reservation Set. The concrete data representation for reservation sets appears in the private part of the package specification shown in Fig. 5.12. In this case, we are using two different instances of the generic type B_tree in the data representation; one for the dates and the other for the bookings. This introduces two different definitions for the type B_tree. We define the subtypes dates_bt and reservations_bt to avoid long qualified names such as reservations_bt_pkg.B_tree. The subtype bookings_hf is included for symmetry. We define an empty record type to serve as the value part of the dates B_tree. No values are needed since we are using the B_tree to represent a set rather than a mapping.

We estimate the number of pairs in the hashed file bookings by assuming that every flight will have some bookings—this is clearly the worst case. We use the size estimate for the flight schedule from Section 4.4.1. As before, we use the default degree for the B_trees.

The representation of a reservation_set includes many data components that are not explicitly stored in the record, but that can be accessed via computed names. We include comments in the record declaration to describe the form of these implicit components, and use concrete data invariants to describe their structure more precisely.

The first three invariants describe the relationship between the base name and the names of the components of the representation in secondary storage. The base name must be explicitly stored for the reservation set because it is needed for computing the names of the implicit components of the representation containing the reservations and the bookings for each date. An encoding of the date is included in the names of the components containing the reserva-

FIGURE 5.12
Data Representation for Reservation Set

```
   with concrete_types_pkg; use concrete_types_pkg;
   with text_pkg; use text_pkg; -- Defines text_pkg_instance.
   with date_pkg; use date_pkg;
   with B_tree_pkg; with hashed_file_pkg;
     -- Needed in private declarations.
   with text_hash_pkg;
package reservation_set_pkg is
   use text_pkg_instance;   -- Defines the type text.

   type reservation_set is limited private;

   procedure open(name: in text; rs: in out reservation_set);
   procedure add (a: in agent_id; i: in flight_id; d: in date;
                  p: in passenger; rs: in out reservation_set );
   procedure remove(i: in flight_id; d: in date; p: in passenger;
                    rs: in out reservation_set );
   procedure remove(i: in flight_id; rs: in out reservation_set);
   procedure remove(d: in date; rs: in out reservation_set);
   procedure holds(p: in passenger; i: in flight_id; d: in date;
                   rs: in out reservation_set; has: out boolean );
   procedure bookings(i: in flight_id; d: in date;
                      rs: in out reservation_set;
                      number_of_bookings: out natural );

   generic
     with procedure produce(r: in reservation);
   procedure notify(a: in agent_id; i: in flight_id; d: in date;
                    rs: in out reservation_set );
private
   type res_key is
     record
       i: flight_id; p: passenger;
     end record;

   function res_le(x, y: res_key) return boolean;
   package reservations_bt_pkg is
     new B_tree_pkg(key => res_key,
                    value => agent_id,
                    "<=" => res_le );
     -- Use the default degree for the B_tree.
   use reservations_bt_pkg;
   subtype reservations_bt is reservations_bt_pkg.B_tree;
     -- Define a short name for the reservations B_tree type.
```

```
package hash_pkg is new text_hash_pkg(result => natural);
use hash_pkg;  -- Defines text_hash.
package bookings_hf_pkg is
  new hashed_file_pkg(key => flight_id,
                      value => natural,
                      hash => text_hash,
                      pairs => 100_000 );
  -- Use the default block size for the hashed file.
use bookings_hf_pkg;  -- Defines hashed_file.
subtype bookings_hf is bookings_hf_pkg.hashed_file;
  -- Define a short name for the bookings hashed_file type.

type null_type is record null; end record;
  -- An empty record type.
package dates_bt_pkg is
  new B_tree_pkg(key => date,
                 value => null_type,
                 "<=" => date_pkg."<=",
                 degree => 4 );
use dates_bt_pkg;
subtype dates_bt is dates_bt_pkg.B_tree;
  -- Define a short name for the reservations B_tree type.

type reservation_set is
  record
    base_name: text; dates: dates_bt;
    -- Implicit computed component:
    -- reservations(d: date): reservations_bt;
    -- Implicit computed component:
    -- bookings(d: date): bookings_hf;
    -- Reservations(d) and bookings(d) are
    -- sets of mappings indexed by dates.
  end record;  -- Invariants:
-- name(dates) = base_name || "d",
-- name(reservations(d)) = base_name || "r" || string_code(d),
-- name(bookings(d)) = base_name || "b" || string_code(d),
-- ALL(rs1 rs2: reservation_set ::
--     rs1.base_name = rs2.base_name => rs1 = rs2 ),
-- ALL(d: date ::
--     d IN dates => reservations(d) IN reservations_bt &
--                   bookings(d) IN bookings_hf ),
-- ALL(d: date ::a
--     reservations(d) IN reservations_bt => d IN dates ),
-- ALL(d: date :: bookings(d) IN bookings_hf => d IN dates).
end reservation_set_pkg;
```

tions and booking for that date. The fourth invariant says that reservation sets have unique base names. This property becomes important if the system is partitioned into multiple tasks, each of which maintains its own reservation set. The fifth through seventh invariants establish the correspondence between the dates in the `dates B_tree` and the legal range of computed names: there is a `reservations B_tree` and a `bookings hashed_file` for a given date if and only if the date is in the `dates B_tree`. This property allows efficient scanning of all dates with some reservations.

The conventions expressed by the above invariants are fairly complicated, and an accurate statement of them is essential for achieving a correct implementation of the operations, and for understanding the justifications for the actions they perform. If the invariants are clearly stated and completed before the implementation starts, then it is possible to avoid rewriting the operations many times. This makes it worthwhile to spend some concentrated effort on developing a coherent set of invariants describing the intended properties of the data structure before implementing the operations. It is usually difficult to anticipate all of the invariants needed in the implementation before the code is written, and new invariants are usually discovered and recorded as the implementation progresses. When a new invariant is added, there is a corresponding obligation to review the implementations of the other operations and to adjust them as needed to guarantee the truth of the invariant in all cases. The implementation is not correct unless the invariants contain all of the assumptions about the data structure used in the implementation of any of the operations, and all of the operations preserve the truth of every invariant. These checks can be time consuming, so that automated aid for reviewing the consistency of the algorithms with the proposed set of invariants would be useful. However, most existing tools for performing that function are not entirely automatic and require some human guidance. Thus in the near term, efficiency in the process of designing data structures depends on people with sufficient skill and insight to discover most of the invariants in advance. The problem cannot be solved by leaving the data invariants implicit instead of explicitly designing, specifying, and reviewing them, because the effort for achieving consistency is amplified, appearing in a longer testing and debugging cycle.

An implementation of the `reservation_set` operations is shown in Fig. 5.13. The implementation of the notify operator is a bit complicated because it involves the nested use of two generators, `range` and `scan_from`, from two different instances of the generic `B_tree` type. The definitions of the auxiliary procedures must be nested inside of each other because of the need for nonlocal variable references. The implementation is easiest to read starting from the bottom of the text, following the top-down flow of control. Because all references to nonlocal variables are read-only, the generators do not have any state variables, and there is no need for any loop invariants. Termination of the notify operation is guaranteed by the termination of the `range`

FIGURE 5.13
Implementation Skeleton for Reservation Set Operations

```
  with lex2;
package body reservation_set_pkg is

  -- Local subprogram declarations.
  procedure bookings(i: flight_id; bf: in out bookings_hf;
                     n: out natural );
  -- End local subprogram declarations.

  procedure open(name: in text; rs: in out reservation_set) is
  begin
    rs.base_name := name;
    open(name & text_string("d"), rs.dates);
  end open;

  procedure add(a: in agent_id; i: in flight_id; d: in date;
                p: in passenger; rs: in out reservation_set ) is
      -- Pre: ~holds(p, i, d, rs).
    reservations_file: reservations_bt;
    bookings_file: bookings_hf;
    n: natural;
    null_value: null_type;
      -- Uninitialized because the value does not matter.
  begin
    open(rs.base_name & text_string("r") & string_code(d),
         reservations_file );
    open(rs.base_name & text_string("b") & string_code(d),
         bookings_file );
    add((i => i, p => p), a, reservations_file);
    bookings(i, bookings_file, n);
    add(i, n + 1, bookings_file);
    add(d, null_value, rs.dates);
  end add;

  procedure remove(i: in flight_id; d: in date; p: in passenger;
                   rs: in out reservation_set ) is
  begin
    null; -- not implemented yet
  end remove;

  procedure remove(i: in flight_id;
                   rs: in out reservation_set ) is
  begin
    null; -- not implemented yet
  end remove;
```

FIGURE 5.13 (continued)

```
procedure remove(d: in date; rs: in out reservation_set) is
begin
  null; -- not implemented yet
end remove;

procedure holds(p: in passenger; i: in flight_id; d: in date;
                rs: in out reservation_set;
                has: out boolean ) is
  reservations_file: reservations_bt;
  date_exists: boolean;
begin
  member(d, rs.dates, date_exists);
  if not date_exists then has := false; return; end if;
  open(rs.base_name & text_string("r") & string_code(d),
       reservations_file );
  member((i => i, p => p), reservations_file, has);
end holds;

procedure bookings(i: in flight_id; d: in date;
                   rs: in out reservation_set;
                   number_of_bookings: out natural ) is
  bookings_file: bookings_hf;
  date_exists: boolean;
begin
  member(d, rs.dates, date_exists);
  if not date_exists then
     number_of_bookings := 0; return; end if;
  open(rs.base_name & text_string("b") & string_code(d),
       bookings_file );
  bookings(i, bookings_file, number_of_bookings);
end bookings;

procedure bookings(i: flight_id; bf: in out bookings_hf;
                   n: out natural ) is
begin
  fetch(i, bf, n);
exception
  when bookings_hf_pkg.domain_error => n := 0;
end bookings;

-- generic
--    with procedure produce(r: in reservation)
procedure notify(a: in agent_id; i: in flight_id; d: in date;
                 rs: in out reservation_set ) is
  first_key: constant res_key := (i => i, p => min_text);
  last_key: constant res_key := (i => i, p => max_text);
```

```
   procedure produce_date(d1: in date; e1: in null_type) is
      reservations_file: reservations_bt;
      procedure produce_reservation(rk: res_key; ra: agent_id) is
      begin  -- Produce_reservation.
        if ra = a then
           produce((id => rk.i, d => d1, p => rk.p, a => ra));
        end if;
      end produce_reservation;
      procedure generate_reservations is
        new reservations_bt_pkg.
           scan_between(produce_reservation);
   begin  -- Produce_date.
      open(rs.base_name & text_string("r") & string_code(d1),
           reservations_file );
      generate_reservations(first_key,
                            last_key,
                            reservations_file );

   end produce_date;
   procedure generate_dates is
      new dates_bt_pkg.scan_from(produce_date);
begin  -- Notify.
   generate_dates(d, rs.dates);
end notify;


function lex is new lex2(flight_id, passenger);
function res_le(x, y: res_key) return boolean is
begin
   return lex(x.i, x.p, y.i, y.p);
end res_le;
end reservation_set_pkg;
```

and scan generators for all possible input values. Equivalent generalized for
loops are shown in Section 4.4.1, and the mapping from generalized for loops
to implementations of generators using generic procedures with procedure
parameters is discussed in Section 5.7.5 and Appendix G.

The second and third variants of the remove operator introduce temporary local storage in the form of bounded sequences to avoid changing the
underlying files while they are being used to drive the foreach loops. Avoiding changes to the driving data structure within the body of a generator-driven
loop is recommended in general, because it makes the range of a generator
independent of the behavior of the loop body. This makes the loop more
predictable and easier to analyze. Our guideline for using generators is a generalization of the prohibition on assignments to the loop parameter in the body

of an Ada `for` loop. Generators are often designed relative to the assumption that the body of the `foreach` loop will not modify the data structure controlling the loop. In particular, the generators provided by the `B_tree` and `hashed_file` types in our library of reusable Ada components depend on this assumption, and may not work correctly if it is violated. The bounds on the bounded sequences are derived from the assumptions that there will never be more than ten years of advance reservations for a given flight, and that there will never be an airplane that carries more than 1000 passengers. These assumptions are presented to the customer for review and validation.

The use of the predefined lexicographic ordering operator is similar to the one in the `flight_schedule` shown in the previous section. The main difference is that the `reservation_set` has keys with two components, but the `flight_schedule` has keys with three components. This difference accounts for the use of two different versions of the generic `lex` operator, `lex2` and `lex3`.

An initial review of the invariants does not reveal any problems at this point. We notice the `add` operation does not guarantee that a single passenger cannot hold more than one reservation on the same flight and day. This restriction is the `single_reservation` invariant in the functional specification of the `travel_agent` interface. We find the restriction is enforced at a higher level, in the `airline_reservation_system` task. Because this corresponds to the place in the functional specification where the constraint is described, we consider this to be a virtue rather than a fault. We also note the restriction corresponds to a customer policy, and hence may be subject to change at a later date. Such a change is easier at a higher level, where fewer details are visible. The difference between this case and the one in the previous section is that a violation of the restriction would not damage the data structure at this level. In the previous case, violation of the invariant can corrupt the data structure in ways that can interfere with the correct operation of the system, causing problems that can be very difficult to trace back to their source. We leave it as an exercise for you to determine the effects of adding two different flights with the same flight id and different capacities to the same flight schedule.

Date. The concrete data representation for the abstract data type `date` is shown in Fig. 5.14. This type is relatively simple, and the only concrete data invariants are the range constraints specified in the subtype declarations. We prefer to specify the invariants directly in Ada because the compiler helps to enforce them. In the previous examples the invariants were expressed using Spec annotations because the declarations available in Ada are not strong enough to represent them. A tighter design might have an invariant expressing the variations in the lengths of the different months. Because we are on a tight budget we add this enhancement to our agenda for perfective system evolution and do not include it in the initial version of the system.

```
  with text_pkg; use text_pkg;  -- Defines text_pkg_instance.
package date_pkg is
  use text_pkg_instance;   -- Defines the type text.

  type date is private;

  function create(d, m, y: natural) return date;
  function "<" (d1, d2: date) return boolean;
  function "<=" (d1, d2: date) return boolean;
  function string_code(d: date) return text;

  illegal_date: exception;   -- Raised by create.
private
  subtype day_number is natural range 1 .. 31;
  subtype month_number is natural range 1 .. 12;
  subtype year_number is natural range 0 .. 99;

  type date is
    record
      day: day_number; month: month_number; year: year_number;
    end record;
end date_pkg;
```

FIGURE 5.14
Data Representation for Date

An implementation skeleton for the operations of the type `date` is shown in Fig. 5.15. In the `create` operation, the `constraint_error` exception signifies violations of the range constraints declared in the subtypes `day_number`, `month_number`, and `year_number`. These constraints are checked automatically in Ada, unless they are explicitly disabled. Following the principles of defensive programming, we leave range checks enabled and explicitly handle the exception, even though we believe the exception could never occur in our current design. This approach is recommended to aid in detecting faults. The initial implementation of any system is likely to contain some faults, and more may be introduced in future versions by imperfect evolution, especially for large systems.

We use the `put` operation for integers from the predefined package `text_io` rather than the predefined `image` attribute of the integer types because the length of the string resulting from `put` can be controlled. We replace any leading spaces produced by `put` by leading zeros, as specified in Section 4.4.1. This is necessary because string codes are used in constructing names for external files, and because spaces are not allowed in a file name in most operating systems, although letters and digits are. Leading spaces can

```
    with text_io; use text_io;
package body date_pkg is

    function create(d, m, y: natural) return date is
        result: date;
    begin
        result.day := d;
        result.month := m;
        result.year := y;
        return result;
    exception
        when constraint_error => raise illegal_date;
    end create;

    function "<" (d1, d2: date) return boolean is
    begin
        return (d1.year /= d2.year and
                  (((d2.year - d1.year) mod 100) < 50) )
            or else (d1.year = d2.year and d1.month < d2.month)
            or else (d1.year = d2.year and d1.month = d2.month and
                      d1.day < d2.day );
    end "<";

    function "<=" (d1, d2: date) return boolean is
    begin
        return d1 < d2 or d1 = d2;
    end "<=";

    package nat_io is new integer_io(natural); use nat_io;
    function string_code(d: date) return text is
        result: string(1 .. 6);
    begin
        put(result(1 .. 2), d.month);
        put(result(3 .. 4), d.day);
        put(result(5 .. 6), d.year);
        for i in 1 .. 6 loop
            if result(i) = ' ' then result(i) := '0'; end if;
        end loop;
        return text_string(result);
    end string_code;
end date_pkg;
```

FIGURE 5.15
Implementation Skeleton for Date Operations

occur for day, month, or year numbers less than ten. This completes the implementation of the initial skeleton of the system.

5.4.3 Test Instrumentation

This section discusses some general guidelines for test instrumentation, and then considers the kind of instrumentation needed for testing the airline reservation system.

General Guidelines.   The initial testing efforts can often be based on the input and output facilities already provided by the system. In our example, the operations find_flights and notify provide a means for examining the effects of the other user commands on the state of the system, and can form the basis for initial testing to determine if the system runs at all and provides the expected outputs for typical data values. Such testing is valuable for demonstrating the soundness of the overall system structure and for detecting integration problems at an early stage. A set of test cases based on the user interfaces can and should be derived from the functional specification prior to detailed design and implementation. These test cases should be ready at this point, and should be run as soon as a working skeleton version of the system comes up. Some manual black-box testing is useful in the initial stages, because even a small number of test cases can detect a wide variety of program faults. Running a few test cases on new code can provide valuable information.

Once the faults detected by the initial tests have been corrected, a more thorough and detailed testing effort is desirable. The problem we face at this point is to determine what additional operations or facilities are needed for supporting testing of the system. These additional facilities are called *test instrumentation*. There are two kinds of test instrumentation, one for supporting black-box testing, and the other for supporting glass-box testing.

Black-box testing can be performed without instrumentation, but only in a manual and labor-intensive fashion. A thorough job requires some automation. The most useful kinds of facilities are test oracles and random data generators. A test oracle is a program that determines if a given output is correct for a given input or sequence of inputs to the system. Test oracles are implementations of the predicates in the black-box specification of a module. Predicates without quantifiers, or with quantifiers whose variables have been restricted to finite ranges are easy to implement, and such implementations can, in principle, be generated by automated tools using current technology, if efficiency is not a large consideration. Transforming general predicates into this restricted form is much harder. Although the problem does not have a solution in the general case, the cases the occur in practice usually can be handled by a skilled person. Automating such transformations is an active research area. Test oracles are useful whether or not the input data is generated automatically, and they are necessary if a large number of test cases are to be run.

Random data generators are used for generating test data without human intervention. Predefined data generators can be provided for the data types in the library, and new generators are needed for new data types. Because all of the values of an abstract data type can be generated using the primitive operations of the type, data generators can be automatically constructed from the concrete interface specification of the type. The distribution of the resulting data values can be difficult to analyze, because it depends on the semantics of the primitive operations. Generators produced by simple mechanical means are not likely to have uniform distributions. Automatically constructed generators for new data types should be considered in practical situations, because the ability to automatically run and evaluate a large set of test cases can be valuable despite some uncertainty about the distribution of the generated values. Data generators with more predictable properties can be hand crafted given some time and effort. Such expense is most clearly justified for the reusable components in a type library.

Test instrumentation is needed to support glass-box testing in a system designed with abstractions that hide data structures, such as abstract machines and data types. Some common purposes for glass-box test instrumentation include the following.

1. Creating given states or internal data representations. Such operations are needed in cases where the sequence of operations leading to a given state or data representation is lengthy or difficult to predict.

2. Displaying or reading internal data. Because the internal data structures of abstract machines or types are protected from direct access, some additional operations may be needed for examining these structures during testing.

3. Monitoring concrete data invariants. Corruption of data invariants is a very common kind of fault in a type or machine. Extra code for monitoring invariants before and after each operation can be added for testing purposes.

4. Monitoring preconditions. Extra code for checking preconditions can be valuable for detecting incorrect calls on operations with restricted implementations.

5. Monitoring postconditions. Extra code for postconditions can be valuable for localizing faults, especially for intermediate data values or internal states, where incorrect values can indirectly cause failures at widely separated places or times.

6. Artificially triggering temporal events. Often, it is useful to be able to trigger temporal events on demand during testing, or to trigger them at much higher rates than would occur in the normal operating environment.

7. Monitoring times of events. It is useful to be able to record the actual times of events to test timing constraints.

Example. Much of the complexity of the system resides in the predefined components, notably the types B_tree and hashed_file. The implementations of these predefined components given in Appendix F include some testing instrumentation; notably operations for printing out the structure of the internal storage representation.

In a serious development environment, the predefined components have been used and tested many times previously and can be presumed reliable, so that the testing effort can focus on testing the new code. The new code in our design is relatively simple, with few explicit loops and recursions, so that we do not expect to need a great deal of instrumentation.

The parsing and display functions in the user interfaces can be tested without any instrumentation.

The airline reservation system module is also relatively easy to test, with the exception of the temporal event. We propose a temporary interface to allow the retire entry to be activated on demand, so that the functional behavior of the response can be tested independently from its timing properties. Because the relevant parts of the state can be observed using the notify command, this is sufficient for testing the functional behavior of retire. Some temporary extra code that prints out the current time can be added to retire_reservations to test the timing aspect.

The abstract data type flight_schedule has some complicated invariants. The first one can be observed directly, by using the facilities of the operating system for observing the file names in the testing directory. The second invariant is easiest to check by analysis of the code, since the open operation is the only one that affects the name of the flight schedule, and the invariant is expressed using an unbounded quantifier. This can be done informally during a design review meeting, or via a mathematical proof supported by automated tools. In this case we would choose the first alternative because the budget is tight and there are no critical reliability requirements. This check also has lower priority because there is only one instance of the flight schedule in the initial design. The last three invariants are expressed using bounded quantifiers, and hence can be implemented directly. Because we are on a tight budget and we do not have an automated tool available for generating the code to monitor these invariants, we propose to run this check only if we run into some failures that are difficult to diagnose, or if we have some time left after the other test cases run without detecting any failures. The primitive operations appear to provide adequate facilities for creating flight schedules and observing their states, so we do not propose any other instrumentation for this type.

The invariants of the reservation_set type can mostly be checked by using the operating system facilities for observing the file names in a directory, provided that we have some means for printing out the dates in the date set. We propose to add such an operation for testing purposes. The fourth invariant, which says that the base names of a reservation set must be unique, is difficult to test directly, and is best verified by analysis of the code, since it impacts only

the open operation. The operations of the type appear to be sufficient to generate states and to examine the important characteristics of a state.

The type date is easy to test without any instrumentation.

5.4.4 Testing the Initial Skeleton

We do some early testing of the initial skeleton to ensure that the overall structure of the system is sound. To do this we need some test cases to minimally
exercise the system. To get started, we need an initial flight schedule to run
tests against. Such a flight schedule can be created by the airline manager commands shown in Fig. 5.16. We would like to test the cases where there are no
flights from an origin to a destination, where there is exactly one flight, and
where there is more than one flight. This initial flight schedule is the smallest
one that will provide all of these situations. We make the capacity of the last
flight small to make it easier to demonstrate the situation where there are no
more seats available. A set of travel agent commands for checking whether the
flight schedule has been constructed as expected, and for creating some reservations and checking whether they have been created as expected is shown in
Fig. 5.17. We check instances of all three cases identified for the flight
schedule, then make some reservations, where the second one should be out of
seats, the next two should result in two bookings on the same flight, and the last
one should fail because the flight is not scheduled. We use the notify command to see if the final state of the reservation set agrees with our expectations.
The last four commands explore whether the notify command handles ranges
of dates properly, and whether it deals with empty reservation sets and
unscheduled flights. This is by no means a complete test set, but it should
suffice to minimally exercise the part of the system that has been implemented,
and to make any severe problems surface.

This is a system with concurrent inputs from multiple sources. Such
inputs can occur in an unpredictable order during a system test. We want to
make sure the flight schedule is created before the travel agents execute any
commands, so we plan two separate testing runs; first with a file containing the
given airline manager commands and an empty file of travel agent commands,
and then with an empty file of airline manager commands and a file containing

---

```
add_flight aa101 $245.00 SFO LAX 9:45 12:05 220
add_flight aa102 $225.00 SFO LAX 6:45 9:05 300
add_flight aa103 $325.00 LAX SFO 16:45 19:05 1
```

FIGURE 5.16
Test Input: Airline Manager Commands

f SFO LAX
f LAX SFO
f SFO LGA
r rvb aa103 1/17/89 Seymour Cray
r gpb aa103 1/17/89 Alonzo Church
r rvb aa101 1/17/89 Alan Turing
r rvb aa101 1/17/89 Ada Augusta Lovelace
r rvb aa104 1/17/89 Euclid
n rvb aa101 1/17/89
n rvb aa103 1/17/89
n gpb aa103 1/17/89
n rvb aa101 1/16/89
n rvb aa101 1/18/89
n rvb aa102 1/17/89
n rvb aa104 1/17/89

FIGURE 5.17
Test Input: Travel Agent Commands

the given travel agent commands. We added handlers for all of the predefined exceptions in Ada to make it easier to diagnose possible problems.

After compiling and testing the initial skeleton, several faults and inconsistencies are usually discovered and removed. The most important of these are integration problems due to inappropriate interfaces. Because such problems may require some redesign, it is important to find them before too much effort has been invested on a fruitless path. It is also more efficient to debug a skeleton system because errors are easier to locate in a smaller structure.

Although lack of space does not allow us to show faulty versions of the example, some of the problems discovered at this stage are described here. Even though Ada has a semantic constraint prohibiting parameters of functions to have mode `out`, the grammar includes such interfaces. The initial design had several interfaces violating this constraint. These faults were discovered only when the programs were first compiled. The compiler also located several errors where variables were misspelled or where the wrong variables were used, and some cases where symbols were undefined because multiple conflicting declarations were visible. Some of these problems were due to conflicts between names used in the initial version of the functional specifications and Ada reserved words or predefined symbols from the package `standard`.

Some problems due to compiler and system limitations were also discovered in the initial testing. Ada `STORAGE_ERROR` exceptions were traced to the problem that the default stack size for tasks was too small for this application. Our design takes the very conservative approach of avoiding pointers and dynamic storage allocation to improve portability, since Ada

```
generic
  modem_id: natural;
package travel_agent_pkg is
  task type travel_agent_type;

  for travel_agent_type'storage_size use 100_000;
  -- Our compiler's default stack size for tasks is too small
  -- for this application.  We have to use a task type
  -- to specify a larger limit in an Ada representation clause.

  travel_agent: travel_agent_type;
end travel_agent_pkg;
```

FIGURE 5.18
Explicit Stack Allocation for the Travel Agent Tasks

implementations are not required to provide garbage collection. All temporary
storage is therefore kept on the stack in our design, including the fairly large
buffers for the B_trees. To solve this problem, we had to change the tasks to
task types, and explicitly specify the number of bytes to be allocated for the
stack associated with each task type, as shown in Figs. 5.18 through 5.20.
Lines that have been added to or modified from the previous version are
marked with a vertical bar in the left margin. These changes were designed to
preserve the names of the tasks, to avoid any impact on the calling programs.
We also found that we had to explicitly extend the stack size limit of the underlying UNIX operating system ("limit stacksize 1024") to make this work.

Some logical faults were also discovered at this stage. In particular, our
initial architectural design had failed to provide a function for removing extra

```
package airline_manager_pkg is
  task type airline_manager_type;

  for airline_manager_type'storage_size use 100_000;
  -- Our compiler's default stack size for tasks is too small
  -- for this application.  We have to use a task type
  -- to specify a larger limit in an Ada representation clause.

  airline_manager: airline_manager_type;
end airline_manager_pkg;
```

FIGURE 5.19
Explicit Stack Allocation for the Airline Manager Task

FIGURE 5.20
Explicit Stack Allocation for the Airline Reservation System Task

```
with bounded_sequence_pkg;
with date_pkg; use date_pkg;
with concrete_types_pkg; use concrete_types_pkg;
package airline_reservation_system_pkg is
  -- Generic instantiations for interface types.
  package flight_sequence_pkg is
    new bounded_sequence_pkg(flight_description);
  package reservation_sequence_pkg is
    new bounded_sequence_pkg(reservation);
  use flight_sequence_pkg; use reservation_sequence_pkg;
  subtype flight_sequence is flight_sequence_pkg.sequence;
  subtype reservation_sequence is
    reservation_sequence_pkg.sequence;

  -- Exceptions.
  flight_exists: exception;
  reservation_exists: exception;
  no_such_flight: exception;
  no_reservation: exception;
  no_seat: exception;

  task type airline_reservation_system_type is
    -- Travel agent interface.
    entry find_flights(origin, destination: in airport;
                       fs: out flight_sequence );
    entry reserve(a: in agent_id; i: in flight_id;
                  d: in date; p: in passenger );
    entry cancel(i: in flight_id; d: in date; p: in passenger);
    entry notify(a: in agent_id; i: in flight_id; d: in date;
                 rs: out reservation_sequence );

    -- Airline manager interface.
    entry add_flight(i: in flight_id; price: in money;
                     origin, destination: in airport;
                     departure, arrival: in flight_time;
                     capacity: in natural );
    entry drop_flight(i: in flight_id);
    entry new_fare(i: in flight_id; price: in money);

    -- Temporals.
    entry retire;
  end airline_reservation_system_type;

  for airline_reservation_system_type'storage_size use 800_000;
```

FIGURE 5.20 (continued)

```
   -- Our compiler's default stack size for tasks is
   -- too small for this application.  We have to use a task type
   -- to specify a larger limit in an Ada representation clause.


   airline_reservation_system: airline_reservation_system_type;
end airline_reservation_system_pkg;
```

leading and trailing spaces from a passenger name. This required us to add a function to the architectural design, as specified in Fig. 5.21. The interface of the parse package was changed as shown in Fig. 5.22.

The code given in the previous sections corresponds to the state of the implementation after these problems were resolved.

5.4.5 Completed System

This section shows the results of filling in the missing pieces of the initial implementation.

Travel Agent.   The completed travel agent module is shown in Fig. 5.23. The only missing part of the travel agent package was `parse_cancel`. This operation is easy to implement because it is very similar to `parse_reserve`.

In the initial implementation, we did not provide any facility to edit user commands. This facility is now implemented in accordance with the functional specification, as shown in Fig. 5.24.

```
FUNCTION trim
  IMPORT space no_spaces FROM character_properties

  MESSAGE(s: string) -- PRAGMA representation(string, text)
    REPLY(ts: string) -- PRAGMA update(s, rest)
      WHERE SOME(b1 b2: string SUCH THAT spaces(b1) & spaces(b2)
                :: s = b1 || ts || b2),
        length(ts) > 0 => ts[1] ~= space ~= ts[length(ts)]
    -- Removes leading and trailing spaces.
END
```

FIGURE 5.21
Specification for the Trim Function

```
   with text_pkg; use text_pkg; -- Defines text_pkg_instance.
   with date_pkg; use date_pkg;  -- Defines date.
package parse_pkg is
   use text_pkg_instance;  -- Defines the type text.

   function edit_command(s: text) return text;
   procedure next_item(s: in out text; next: out text);
 | procedure trim(s: in out text);
   function is_airport(s: text) return boolean;
   function is_flight_id(s: text) return boolean;
   function is_passenger(s: text) return boolean;
   function is_agent_id(s: text) return boolean;
   procedure is_date(s: in text; d: out date; ok: out boolean);
   function is_money(s: text) return boolean;
   function is_time(s: text) return boolean;
end parse_pkg;
```

FIGURE 5.22
Extended Specification Part of the Parse Package

FIGURE 5.23
Completed Travel Agent

```
   with text_io; use text_io;
   with text_pkg; use text_pkg; -- Defines text_pkg_instance.
   with date_pkg; use date_pkg;  -- Defines date.
   with concrete_types_pkg; use concrete_types_pkg;
      -- Defines airport, flight_id, passenger, agent_id,
      -- flight_description, reservation.
   with parse_pkg; use parse_pkg;
      -- Defines is_airport, is_flight_id, is_passenger,
      -- is_agent_id, edit_command, next_item.
   with format_pkg; use format_pkg; -- Defines fill_line.
   with airline_reservation_system_pkg;
   use airline_reservation_system_pkg;
      -- Defines task airline_reservation_system and
      -- types flight_sequence, reservation_sequence.
package body travel_agent_pkg is
   use text_pkg_instance;  -- Defines the type text.
   use flight_sequence_pkg;
      -- Defines the flight_sequence operations.
   use reservation_sequence_pkg;
      -- Defines the reservation_sequence operations.
```

FIGURE 5.23 (continued)

```
-- Local subprogram declarations.
procedure interpret_command(cmd: character; args: in text;
                            f: in file_type );
procedure parse_find_flights(s: in text; o, d: out airport;
                             result: out boolean );
procedure parse_reserve(s: in text; a: out agent_id;
                        i: out flight_id; d: out date;
                        p: out passenger;
                        result: out boolean );
procedure parse_cancel(s: in text; i: out flight_id;
                       d: out date; p: out passenger;
                       result: out boolean );
procedure parse_notify(s: in text; a: out agent_id;
                       i: out flight_id; d: out date;
                       result: out boolean );

-- Constant declarations.
modem_number: constant string := natural'image(modem_id);
input_name: constant string :=
  "ta" & modem_number(2 .. modem_number'last) & "_in";
output_name: constant string :=
  "ta" & modem_number(2 .. modem_number'last) & "_out";

task body travel_agent_type is
  input, output: file_type;
  last: natural;
  buffer, command: text;
begin
  open(input, in_file, input_name);
  open(output, out_file, output_name);
  loop  -- Forever.
    get_line(input, buffer);
    buffer := edit_command(buffer);
    next_item(buffer, command);
    if length(command) = 1
    then interpret_command(char(command, 1), buffer, output);
    else -- Illegal command code.
       interpret_command(' ', buffer, output);
    end if;
  end loop;
exception
  when end_error => put_line(output, "input terminated");
  when constraint_error =>
    put_line(output,
             "Unexpected constraint_error in travel_agent" );
```

```ada
  when numeric_error =>
    put_line(output,
             "Unexpected numeric_error in travel_agent" );
  when program_error =>
    put_line(output,
             "Unexpected program_error in travel_agent" );
  when storage_error =>
    put_line(output,
             "Unexpected storage_error in travel_agent" );
  when tasking_error =>
    put_line(output,
             "Unexpected tasking_error in travel_agent" );
  when others =>
    put_line(output, "Unexpected exception in travel_agent");
end travel_agent_type;


procedure interpret_command(cmd: character; args: in text;
                            f: in file_type ) is

  o, d: airport;
  i: flight_id;
  da: date;
  p: passenger;
  a: agent_id;
  fs: flight_sequence;
  rs: reservation_sequence;
  ok: boolean;


  procedure display_reservation(res: in reservation) is
     -- Nonlocal_variable(f: in file_type).
  begin  -- Body of display_reservation.
    put_line(f, fill_line((string_code(res.d), res.p),
                          (8, 20) ));

  end display_reservation;
  procedure display_reservations is
    new reservation_sequence_pkg.scan(display_reservation);


  procedure display_flight(fd: in flight_description) is
     -- Nonlocal_variable(f: in file_type).
  begin  -- Body of display_flight.
    put_line(f, fill_line((fd.id, fd.dep, fd.arr, fd.price),
                          (6, 8, 8, 10) ));

  end display_flight;
  procedure display_flights is
    new flight_sequence_pkg.scan(display_flight);
```

FIGURE 5.23 (continued)

```
begin  -- Body of interpret_command.
  case cmd is
    when 'f' =>
      parse_find_flights(args, o, d, ok);
      if ok then
        airline_reservation_system.find_flights(o, d, fs);
        if length(fs) > 0 then display_flights(fs);
        else put_line(f, "no flights found"); end if;
      else put_line(f, "command not recognized"); end if;
    when 'r' =>
      parse_reserve(args, a, i, da, p, ok);
      if ok then
        airline_reservation_system.reserve(a, i, da, p);
        put_line(f, "done");
      else put_line(f, "command not recognized"); end if;
    when 'c' =>
      parse_cancel(args, i, da, p, ok);
      if ok then airline_reservation_system.cancel(i, da, p);
        put_line(f, "done");
      else put_line(f, "command not recognized"); end if;
    when 'n' =>
      parse_notify(args, a, i, da, ok);
      if ok then
        airline_reservation_system.notify(a, i, da, rs);
        if length(rs) > 0 then display_reservations(rs);
        else put_line(f, "no reservations found"); end if;
      else put_line(f, "command not recognized"); end if;
    when others => put_line(f, "command not recognized");
  end case;
exception
  when no_seat => put_line(f, "No seat available");
  when reservation_exists =>
    put_line(f, "The passenger already has a reservation");
  when no_reservation =>
    put_line(f, "The passenger does not hold a reservation");
  when no_such_flight => put_line(f, "Unknown flight id");
  when constraint_error =>
    put_line(f,
"Unexpected constraint_error in travel_agent.interpret_command"
          );
  when numeric_error =>
    put_line(f,
"Unexpected numeric_error in travel_agent.interpret_command"
          );
  when program_error =>
```

```
      put_line(f,
"Unexpected program_error in travel_agent.interpret_command"
              );
   when storage_error =>
      put_line(f,
"Unexpected storage_error in travel_agent.interpret_command"
              );
   when tasking_error =>
      put_line(f,
"Unexpected tasking_error in travel_agent.interpret_command"
              );
   when others =>
      put_line(f,
"Unexpected exception in travel_agent.interpret_command"
              );
  end interpret_command;

  procedure parse_find_flights(s: in text; o, d: out airport;
                               result: out boolean ) is
    line: text := s;
    item: text;
  begin
    next_item(line, item);
    if is_airport(item) then o := item;
       else result := false; return; end if;
    next_item(line, item);
    if is_airport(item) then d := item;
       else result := false; return; end if;
    next_item(line, item);  -- Discard any trailing spaces.
    result := length(item) = 0;
  end parse_find_flights;

  procedure parse_reserve(s: in text; a: out agent_id;
                          i: out flight_id; d: out date;
                          p: out passenger;
                          result: out boolean ) is
     line: text := s;
     item: text;
     ok: boolean;
  begin
    next_item(line, item);
    if is_agent_id(item) then a := item;
       else result := false; return; end if;
    next_item(line, item);
    if is_flight_id(item) then i := item;
       else result := false; return; end if;
    next_item(line, item);
```

FIGURE 5.23 (continued)

```
   is_date(item, d, ok);
   if not ok then result := false; return; end if;
   trim(line);   -- Get rid of leading and trailing blanks.
   if is_passenger(line) then p := line; result := true;
      else result := false; end if;
  end parse_reserve;

  procedure parse_cancel(s: in text; i: out flight_id;
                           d: out date; p: out passenger;
                           result: out boolean ) is
      line: text := s;
      item: text;
      ok: boolean;
  begin
    next_item(line, item);
    if is_flight_id(item) then
       i := item; else result := false; return; end if;
    next_item(line, item);
    is_date(item, d, ok);
    if not ok then result := false; return; end if;
    trim(line);   -- Get rid of leading and trailing blanks.
    if is_passenger(line) then
       p := line; result := true; else result := false; end if;
  end parse_cancel;

  procedure parse_notify(s: in text; a: out agent_id;
                           i: out flight_id; d: out date;
                           result: out boolean ) is
      line: text := s;
      item: text;
      ok: boolean;
  begin
    next_item(line, item);
    if is_agent_id(item) then a := item;
       else result := false; return; end if;
    next_item(line, item);
    if is_flight_id(item) then i := item;
       else result := false; return; end if;
    next_item(line, item);
    is_date(item, d, ok);
    if not ok then result := false; return; end if;
    next_item(line, item);   -- Discard any trailing spaces.
    result := length(item) = 0;
  end parse_notify;
end travel_agent_pkg;
```

FIGURE 5.24
Completed Parse Package

```
  with format_pkg; use format_pkg;
    -- Defines letter_string, digit_string.
  with text_io; use text_io;
package body parse_pkg is


  function edit_command(s: text) return text is
    command: text := min_text;
    erase: constant character := ascii.del;
    cancel: constant character := ascii.esc;
    len: natural;
  begin
    for i in 1 .. length(s) loop
      -- Invariant: command = edit(s[1 .. i - 1]).
      case char(s, i) is
        when erase => len := length(command);
          if len > 0 then delete(command, len, len); end if;
        when cancel => delete(command, 1, length(command));
        when others => append(command, char(s, i));
      end case;
    end loop;
    return command;
  end edit_command;


  procedure next_item(s: in out text; next: out text) is
    front, back: natural;
  begin
    front := 1;
    while front <= length(s) loop
      -- Invariant: spaces(s[1 .. front - 1]) & front IN s'range.
      -- Bound: length(s) - front.
      if char(s, front) = ' ' then
        front := front + 1; else exit; end if;
    end loop;
    if front > length(s)   -- Nothing but spaces in s.
      then next := min_text;
           s := min_text;
           return;
    end if;
    back := front;
    while back < length(s) loop
      -- Invariant:
      --    no_spaces(s[front .. back]) & (back + 1) IN s'range.
```

FIGURE 5.24 (continued)

```
        -- Bound: length(s) - back.
        exit when char(s, back + 1) = ' ';
        back := back + 1;
      end loop;
    next := slice(s, front, back);
    s := slice(s, back + 1, length(s));
  end next_item;

  procedure trim(s: in out text) is
    ts: text := s;
  begin
    loop  -- Invariant:
          --    s = b || ts & spaces(b), bound: length(ts).
      exit when length(ts) = 0;
      exit when char(ts, 1) /= ' ';
      delete(ts, 1, 1);
    end loop;
    loop  -- Invariant:
          --    s = b1 || ts || b2 & spaces(b1) & spaces(b2).
          -- Bound: length(ts).
      exit when length(ts) = 0;
      exit when char(ts, length(ts)) /= ' ';
      delete(ts, length(ts), length(ts));
    end loop;
    s := ts;
  end trim;

  function is_airport(s: text) return boolean is
  begin
    return (length(s) = 3) and then letter_string(s);
  end is_airport;

  function is_flight_id(s: text) return boolean is
  begin
    return 2 <= length(s)
      and then (length(s) <= 6
      and then (letter_string(slice(s, 1, 2))
      and then digit_string(slice(s, 3, length(s))) ));
  end is_flight_id;

  function is_passenger(s: text) return boolean is
  begin
    if length(s) = 0 then return false; end if;
    if not letter(char(s, 1)) then return false; end if;
    if not letter(char(s, length(s))) then return false; end if;
    for i in 1 .. length(s) loop
```

```
      if not (letter(char(s, i)) or char(s, i) = ' ')
         then return false; end if;
   end loop;
   return true;
end is_passenger;


function is_agent_id(s: text) return boolean is
begin
   return is_airport(s);
     -- Agent id's have the same format as airports.
end is_agent_id;


procedure is_date(s: in text; d: out date; ok: outboolean) is
   day, month, year, position: natural;
   found: boolean;
   item: text := s;
   slash: constant text := text_string("/");
begin
   find(item, slash, found, position);
   if not found then ok := false; return; end if;
   month :=
     natural'value(ada_string(slice(item, 1, position - 1)));
   delete(item, 1, position);
     -- Remove the prefix up to the "/".
   find(item, slash, found, position);
   if not found then ok := false; return; end if;
   day :=
     natural'value(ada_string(slice(item, 1, position - 1)));
   year := natural'value(ada_string(slice(item,
                                    position + 1,
                                    length(item) )));
   d := create(day, month, year);
   ok := true; return;
exception
   when others => ok := false;
end is_date;


function is_money(s: text) return boolean is
begin
   return length(s) >= 4
     and then char(s, 1) = '$'
     and then digit_string(slice(s, 2, length(s) - 3))
       -- Dollars.
     and then char(s, length(s) - 2) = '.'
     and then digit_string(slice(s, length(s) - 1, length(s)));
       -- Cents.
end is_money;
```

FIGURE 5.24 (continued)

```
function is_time(s: text) return boolean is
  colon: constant text := text_string(":");
  n, position: natural;
  found: boolean;
begin
  find(s, colon, found, position);
  if not found then return false; end if;
  n := natural'value(ada_string(slice(s, 1, position - 1)));
    -- Hours.
  if n > 23 then return false; end if;
  n := natural'value(ada_string(slice(s,
                                   position + 1,
                                   length(s) )));
    -- Minutes.
  return (n <= 59);
exception
  when others => return false;
end is_time;
end parse_pkg;
```

Airline Manager.   The completed airline manager module is shown in Fig.
5.25. The missing parts in the skeleton version of this module are
parse_drop_flight, parse_new_fare, and the cases in the procedure
interpret_command that invoke these procedures. The implementations
are similar to other parts of the initial version.

Airline Reservation System.   The completed airline reservation module is
shown in Fig. 5.26. The new parts of the system are the entries for cancel,
drop_flight, new_fare, and retire. The task retire_demon has been
completed and the auxiliary procedure retire_reservations has been
added.

The retire_demon task illustrates a common structure for implementing temporal events in Ada. There is a driver task for each temporal event,
which activates the event at the specified times. The times are calculated using
the predefined Ada package calendar. These times are determined based on
the original starting time to avoid any dependence on the length of time it takes
to calculate the responses to the temporal event. The Ada delay statement is
used to enable the temporal events at the calculated times. This design does not
guarantee that the events occur at exactly the specified times, because the
delay statement gives only a lower bound on the actual delay. Since the Ada
scheduler is required to be fair, we can be assured that the temporal events are
executed soon after the scheduled times if the load on the machine is not exces-

FIGURE 5.25
Completed Airline Manager

```
with text_io; use text_io;
with text_pkg; use text_pkg; -- Defines text_pkg_instance.
with date_pkg; use date_pkg;  -- Defines date.
with concrete_types_pkg; use concrete_types_pkg;
  -- Defines airport, flight_id, money, flight_time.
with parse_pkg; use parse_pkg;
  -- Defines is_airport, is_flight_id, is_money, is_time,
  -- edit_command, next_item.
with airline_reservation_system_pkg;
use airline_reservation_system_pkg;
  -- Defines task airline_reservation_system.
package body airline_manager_pkg is
  use text_pkg_instance;  -- Defines the type text.

  -- Local subprogram declarations.
  procedure interpret_command(cmd: string; args: in text;
                              f: in file_type );
  procedure parse_add_flight(s: in text; i: out flight_id;
                             p: out money; o, d: out airport;
                             dep, arr: out flight_time;
                             c: out natural;
                             result: out boolean );
  procedure parse_drop_flight(s: in text; i: out flight_id;
                              result: out boolean );
  procedure parse_new_fare(s: in text; i: out flight_id;
                           p: out money; result: out boolean );

  -- Constant declarations.
  input_name: constant string := "am0_in";
  output_name: constant string := "am0_out";

  task body airline_manager_type is
    input, output: file_type;
    last: natural;
    buffer, command: text;
  begin
    open(input, in_file, input_name);
    open(output, out_file, output_name);
    loop  -- Forever.
      get_line(input, buffer);
      buffer := edit_command(buffer);
      next_item(buffer, command);
      interpret_command(ada_string(command), buffer, output);
    end loop;
```

FIGURE 5.25 (continued)

```
exception
  when end_error => put_line(output, "input terminated");
  when constraint_error =>
    put_line(output,
             "Unexpected constraint_error in airline_manager"
             );
  when numeric_error =>
    put_line(output,
             "Unexpected numeric_error in airline_manager" );
  when program_error =>
    put_line(output,
             "Unexpected program_error in airline_manager" );
  when storage_error =>
    put_line(output,
             "Unexpected storage_error in airline_manager" );
  when tasking_error =>
    put_line(output,
             "Unexpected tasking_error in airline_manager" );
  when others =>
    put_line(output,
             "Unexpected exception in airline_manager" );
end airline_manager_type;

procedure interpret_command(cmd: string; args: in text;
                            f: in file_type ) is
  i: flight_id;
  p: money;
  o, d: airport;
  dep, arr: flight_time;
  c: natural;
  ok: boolean;
begin
  if cmd = "add_flight" then
    parse_add_flight(args, i, p, o, d, dep, arr, c, ok);
    if ok then
      airline_reservation_system.add_flight(i, p, o, d,
                                             dep, arr, c );
      put_line(f, "Done.");
    else put_line(f, "command not recognized"); end if;
  elsif cmd = "drop_flight" then
    parse_drop_flight(args, i, ok);
    if ok then airline_reservation_system.drop_flight(i);
      put_line(f, "Done.");
    else put_line(f, "command not recognized"); end if;
```

```
      elsif cmd = "new_fare" then
         parse_new_fare(args, i, p, ok);
         if ok then airline_reservation_system.new_fare(i, p);
            put_line(f, "Done.");
         else put_line(f, "command not recognized"); end if;
      elsif cmd = "retire" then
         airline_reservation_system.retire;
      else put_line(f, "command not recognized"); end if;
  exception
    when flight_exists =>
      put_line(f, "The flight is already scheduled.");
      put_line(f,
"To change it, use drop_flight and then add_flight."
              );
    when no_such_flight =>
      put_line(f,
"No such flight was scheduled, check the flight id."
              );
    when constraint_error =>
      put_line(f,
"Unexpected constraint_error in airline_manager"
              );
    when numeric_error =>
      put_line(f, "Unexpected numeric_error in airline_manager");
    when program_error =>
      put_line(f, "Unexpected program_error in airline_manager");
    when storage_error =>
      put_line(f, "Unexpected storage_error in airline_manager");
    when tasking_error =>
      put_line(f, "Unexpected tasking_error in airline_manager");
    when others =>
      put_line(f, "Unexpected exception in airline_manager");
  end interpret_command;


  package nat_io is new integer_io(natural); use nat_io;
  procedure parse_add_flight(s: in text; i: out flight_id;
                             p: out money; o, d: out airport;
                             dep, arr: out flight_time;
                             c: out natural;
                             result: out boolean ) is

    line: text := s;
    item: text;
    last: positive;
```

FIGURE 5.25 (continued)

```
begin
  next_item(line, item);
  if is_flight_id(item) then i := item;
     else result := false; return; end if;
  next_item(line, item);
  if is_money(item) then p := item;
     else result := false; return; end if;
  next_item(line, item);
  if is_airport(item) then o := item;
     else result := false; return; end if;
  next_item(line, item);
  if is_airport(item) then d := item;
     else result := false; return; end if;
  next_item(line, item);
  if is_time(item) then dep := item;
     else result := false; return; end if;
  next_item(line, item);
  if is_time(item) then arr := item;
     else result := false; return; end if;
  get(ada_string(line), c, last);
  line := slice(line, last + 1, length(line));
  next_item(line, item);
  result := length(item) = 0;   -- Ok if no more items.
exception
  when others => result := false;
end parse_add_flight;


procedure parse_drop_flight(s: in text; i: out flight_id;
                            result: out boolean ) is
  line: text := s;
  item: text;
begin
  next_item(line, item);
  if is_flight_id(item) then
     i := item; else result := false; return; end if;
  next_item(line, item);  -- Discard any trailing spaces.
  result := length(item) = 0;
end parse_drop_flight;


procedure parse_new_fare(s: in text; i: out flight_id;
                         p: out money; result: out boolean ) is
  line: text := s;
  item: text;
```

```
  begin
    next_item(line, item);
    if is_flight_id(item) then i := item;
       else result := false; return; end if;
    next_item(line, item);
    if is_money(item) then p := item;
       else result := false; return; end if;
    next_item(line, item);   -- Discard any trailing spaces.
    result := length(item) = 0;
  end parse_new_fare;
end airline_manager_pkg;
```

FIGURE 5.26
Completed Airline Reservation System

```
  with text_pkg; use text_pkg;  -- Defines text_pkg_instance.
  with flight_schedule_pkg; use flight_schedule_pkg;
  with reservation_set_pkg; use reservation_set_pkg;
  with date_pkg; use date_pkg;
  with calendar; use calendar;
package body airline_reservation_system_pkg is
  use text_pkg_instance;   -- Defines the type text.

  -- Local subprogram declarations.
  procedure make_reservations(r: in out reservation_set;
                              i: in flight_id; d: date;
                              a: in agent_id;
                              rs: out reservation_sequence );
  procedure make_flights(s: in out flight_schedule;
                         o, d: airport;
                         fs: out flight_sequence );
  procedure retire_reservations(rs: in out reservation_set);
  task retire_demon;

  task body airline_reservation_system_type is
    -- State variables.
    schedule: flight_schedule;
    reservations: reservation_set;

    -- Temporary variables.
    has, exists: boolean;
    b, c: natural;
```

FIGURE 5.26 (continued)

```
begin

  -- Initialize.
  open(text_string("s"), schedule);
  open(text_string("r"), reservations);

  -- Start operation.
  loop  -- Forever.
    begin  -- Exception handler frame.
      select

      -- Travel agent interface.
        accept find_flights(origin, destination: in airport;
                            fs: out flight_sequence ) do
          make_flights(schedule, origin, destination, fs);
        end find_flights;
      or
        accept reserve(a: in agent_id; i: in flight_id;
                       d: in date; p: in passenger ) do
          holds(p, i, d, reservations, has);
          if has then raise reservation_exists; end if;
          begin
            bookings(i, d, reservations, b);
            capacity(i, schedule, c);
            if b = c then raise no_seat; end if;
            add(a, i, d, p, reservations);
          exception
            when flight_schedule_pkg.no_such_flight =>
                 raise airline_reservation_system_pkg.
                       no_such_flight;
          end;
        end reserve;
      or
        accept cancel(i: in flight_id; d: in date;
                      p: in passenger ) do
          member(i, schedule, exists);
          if not exists then
            raise airline_reservation_system_pkg.
                no_such_flight;
          end if;
          holds(p, i, d, reservations, has);
          if has then remove(i, d, p, reservations);
            else raise no_reservation;
          end if;
        end cancel;
```

```
or
   accept notify(a: in agent_id; i: in flight_id;
                 d: in date;
                 rs: out reservation_sequence ) do
      member(i, schedule, exists);
      if not exists then
         raise airline_reservation_system_pkg.
               no_such_flight;
      end if;
      make_reservations(reservations, i, d, a, rs);
   end notify;
or

   -- Airline manager interface.
   accept add_flight(i: in flight_id; price: in money;
                     origin, destination: in airport;
                     departure, arrival: in flight_time;
                     capacity: in natural ) do
      member(i, schedule, exists);
      if exists then raise flight_exists; end if;
      add(i, price, origin, destination, departure,
          arrival, capacity, schedule );
   end add_flight;
or
   accept drop_flight(i: in flight_id) do
      member(i, schedule, exists);
      if exists then remove(i, schedule);
      else raise airline_reservation_system_pkg.
                 no_such_flight;
      end if;
   end drop_flight;
or
   accept new_fare(i: in flight_id; price: in money) do
      begin
         new_fare(i, price, schedule);
      exception
         when flight_schedule_pkg.no_such_flight =>
            raise airline_reservation_system_pkg.
                  no_such_flight;
      end;
   end new_fare;
or

   -- Temporals.
   accept retire do
      retire_reservations(reservations);
   end retire;
end select;
```

FIGURE 5.26 (continued)

```
    exception
      when others => null;
         -- Exceptions are handled in the modules
         -- invoking the task entries.
      end;  -- Exception handler frame.
   end loop;
end airline_reservation_system_type;


procedure make_flights(s: in out flight_schedule;
                       o, d: airport;
                       fs: out flight_sequence ) is
   -- Post: scan(fs) = generate_flights(s, o, d).
   fs1: flight_sequence;
  procedure produce_flight(fd: in flight_description) is
  begin -- Invariant: scan(fs1) = *generate_flights(s, o, d).
    add(fd, fs1);
  end produce_flight;
  procedure generate_flights is
    new find_flights(produce_flight);
begin
  fs1 := create;
  generate_flights(s, o, d);
  fs := fs1;
end make_flights;


procedure make_reservations(r: in out reservation_set;
                            i: in flight_id; d: date;
                            a: in agent_id;
                            rs: out reservation_sequence ) is
   -- Post: scan(rs) = generate_reservations(s, o, d).
   rs1: reservation_sequence;
  procedure produce_reservation(res: in reservation) is
  begin -- Invariant:
       --    scan(rs1) = *generate_reservations(s, o, d).
    add(res, rs1);
  end produce_reservation;
  procedure generate_reservations is
    new notify(produce_reservation);
begin
  rs1 := create;
  generate_reservations(a, i, d, r);
  rs := rs1;
end make_reservations;
```

```
procedure retire_reservations(rs: in out reservation_set) is
  now: time := clock;
  d: date := create(natural(day(now)),
                    natural(month(now)),
                    natural(year(now)) mod 100 );
begin
  remove(d, rs);
end retire_reservations;

-- Driver for the temporal event "retire".
task body retire_demon is
  hour: constant duration:= 3600.0;
  period: constant duration := 24 * hour;
  phase: constant duration := 4 * hour;
  start_up_time: constant time := clock;
  d: integer := day(start_up_time);
  m: integer := month(start_up_time);
  y: integer := year(start_up_time);
  next_retire_time: time := time_of(y, m, d, phase) + period;
begin  -- 4am the next morning.
  loop  -- Forever.
    delay next_retire_time - clock;
    airline_reservation_system.retire;
      -- Trigger the temporal event "retire".
    next_retire_time := next_retire_time + period;
  end loop;
end retire_demon;
end airline_reservation_system_pkg;
```

sive. This is permissible in this case because the timing constraints are not crit-ical, and a review of the design indicates that a longer delay does not lead to incorrect operation of the system.

In systems with hard real-time constraints, more care is needed. One way to achieve a guarantee of execution at exactly the specified time is to have a single driver task for all time-critical events, with an explicitly assigned priority that is strictly greater than the priority of any other task in the system, all of which must also have explicitly assigned priorities. Such an approach requires using dedicated hardware and checking that under all possible conditions each time critical event can be completed before the next one must start. Techniques for doing this are beyond the scope of this book, but some relevant research results are mentioned in Chapter 8.

When implementing the operation new_fare we find that the initial architectural design contains a feasibility error, because this operation was sup-posed to be implemented using the member and add operations of the flight_schedule. If we are to use add to replace the old version of the flight with a new one, we need to supply the other attributes of the flight, such as the origin, destination, and capacity, but there is currently no way to obtain that information. We decide to correct the problem by adding a new_fare operation to the flight_schedule data type. The revised specification for the flight_schedule is shown in Fig. 5.27.

Flight Schedule. The concrete interface of the flight_schedule type was extended by adding a new_fare operation to correct a problem discovered when completing the implementation of the airline_ reservation_system module. The new concrete interface is shown in Fig. 5.28. The only change is the addition of the new_fare operation.

The completed implementation of the type is shown in Fig. 5.29. The new parts of this module are remove and new_fare. The information needed for new_fare that was unavailable at the level of the airline reservation system is easy to obtain at this level, because all of the information stored in the capacity component of the flight schedule is visible.

Reservation Set. The completed implementation of the type is shown in Fig. 5.30. The new parts of the implementation are the three remove operations.

Date. The type date was fully implemented in the initial skeleton. This completes the implementation of the airline reservation system.

```
TYPE flight_schedule2
  INHERIT flight_schedule1

  MESSAGE new_fare(i: flight_id, p: money, fs: flight_schedule)
    WHEN i IN domain(fs.m)
      CHOOSE(f: flight SUCH THAT id(f) = i & price(f) = price &
             origin(f) = origin(fs.m[i]) &
             destination(f) = destination(fs.m[i]) &
             departure(f) = departure(fs.m[i]) &
             arrival(f) = arrival(fs.m[i]) &
             capacity(f) = capacity(fs.m[i]) )
      TRANSITION fs.m = bind(i, f, *fs.m)  -- Change fare.
    OTHERWISE REPLY EXCEPTION no_such_flight
END
```

FIGURE 5.27
Revised Specification for Flight Schedule

FIGURE 5.28
Revised Concrete Interface for Flight Schedule

```
  with text_pkg; use text_pkg; -- Defines text_pkg_instance.
  with concrete_types_pkg; use concrete_types_pkg;
    -- Defines flight_id, money, airport, flight_time,
    -- flight_description.
  with B_tree_pkg;  -- Needed in private declarations.
  with hashed_file_pkg;  --  Needed in private declarations.
  with text_hash_pkg;  --  Needed in private declarations.
package flight_schedule_pkg is
 use text_pkg_instance;  -- Defines the type text.


  type flight_schedule is limited private;

  procedure open(name: in text; fs: in out flight_schedule);
  procedure add(i: in flight_id; price: in money;
                origin, destination: in airport;
                departure, arrival: in flight_time;
                capacity: in natural;
                fs: in out flight_schedule );
  procedure remove(i: in flight_id; fs: in out flight_schedule);
  procedure member(i: in flight_id; fs: in out flight_schedule;
                   result: out boolean );
  procedure capacity(i: in flight_id; fs: in out flight_schedule;
                     result: out natural );
  procedure new_fare(i: in flight_id; p: in money;
                     fs: in out flight_schedule );

  generic
    with procedure produce(fd: in flight_description);
  procedure find_flights(fs: in out flight_schedule;
                         origin, destination: airport );

  no_such_flight: exception;  -- Raised by capacity.
private
  type bt_key is
    record
      o, d: airport; i: flight_id;
    end record;

  type bt_value is
    record
      d, a: flight_time; p: money;
    end record;
```

FIGURE 5.28 (continued)

```
    function bt_le(x, y: bt_key) return boolean;
    package schedule_bt_pkg is
      new B_tree_pkg(key => bt_key,
                     value => bt_value,
                     "<=" => bt_le );
      -- Use the default degree for the B_tree.
    use schedule_bt_pkg;   -- Defines B_tree.

    type hf_value is
      record
        c: natural; o, d: airport;
      end record;

    package hf_hash_pkg is new text_hash_pkg(natural);
    package capacity_hf_pkg is
      new hashed_file_pkg(key => flight_id,
                          value => hf_value,
                          hash => hf_hash_pkg.text_hash,
                          pairs => 100_000 );
      -- Use the default block size for the hashed file.
    use capacity_hf_pkg;   -- Defines hashed_file.

    type flight_schedule is
      record
        schedule: B_tree; capacity: hashed_file;
      end record;   -- Invariants:
-- ALL(fs: flight_schedule :: name(fs.schedule) = name(fs) || "s"
    --      & name(fs.capacity) = name(fs) || "c" ),
-- ALL(fs1 fs2: flight_schedule ::
    --     name(fs1) = name(fs2) => fs1 = fs2 ),
-- ALL(k1 k2: bt_key SUCH THAT k1 IN schedule & k2 IN schedule ::
    --     k1.i = k2.i => k1 = k2 ),
-- ALL(k: bt_key SUCH THAT k IN schedule :: k.i IN capacity),
-- ALL(i: flight_id SUCH THAT i IN capacity ::
    --     SOME(k: bt_key SUCH THAT k IN schedule
    --          :: k.i = i & k.o = capacity[i].o &
    --             k.d = capacity[i].d )).

-- CONCEPT name(fs: flight_schedule)
    --   -- The name with which fs was last opened.
    --   VALUE(s: string).
end flight_schedule_pkg;
```

FIGURE 5.29
Completed Flight Schedule

```
  with lex3;
package body flight_schedule_pkg is

  procedure open(name: in text; fs: in out flight_schedule) is
  begin
    open(name & text_string("s"), fs.schedule);
    open(name & text_string("c"), fs.capacity);
  end open;

  procedure add(i: in flight_id; price: in money;
                origin, destination: in airport;
                departure, arrival: in flight_time;
                capacity: in natural;
                fs: in out flight_schedule ) is
    -- Pre: ~member(i, fs).
  begin
    add((o => origin, d => destination, i => i),
        (a => arrival, d => departure, p => price),
        fs.schedule);
    add(i,
        (c => capacity, o => origin, d => destination),
        fs.capacity );
  end add;

  procedure remove(i: in flight_id;
                   fs: in out flight_schedule ) is
    v: hf_value;
  begin
    fetch(i, fs.capacity, v);
    remove((o => v.o, d => v.d, i => i), fs.schedule);
    remove(i, fs.capacity);
  exception
    when capacity_hf_pkg.domain_error =>  null;
  end remove;

  procedure member(i: in flight_id; fs: in out flight_schedule;
                   result: out boolean ) is
  begin
   member(i, fs.capacity, result);
  end member;

  procedure capacity(i: in flight_id; fs: in out flight_schedule;
                     result: out natural ) is
    v: hf_value;
```

FIGURE 5.29 (continued)

```
  begin
    fetch(i, fs.capacity, v);
    result := v.c;
  exception
    when capacity_hf_pkg.domain_error => raise no_such_flight;
  end capacity;


  procedure new_fare(i: in flight_id; p: in money;
                        fs: in out flight_schedule ) is
    hv: hf_value;
    bv: bt_value;
  begin
    fetch(i, fs.capacity, hv);
    fetch((o => hv.o, d => hv.d, i => i), fs.schedule, bv);
    add((o => hv.o, d => hv.d, i => i),
        (a => bv.a, d => bv.d, p => p),
        fs.schedule);
  exception
    when capacity_hf_pkg.domain_error => raise no_such_flight;
  end new_fare;


  --   generic
  --     with procedure produce(fd: in flight_description);
  procedure find_flights(fs: in out flight_schedule;
                        origin, destination: airport ) is
    procedure produce_flight_description(k: bt_key;
                                        v: bt_value ) is
    begin
      produce((id => k.i, dep => v.d, arr => v.a, price => v.p));
    end produce_flight_description;
      -- Produce_flight_description must be declared
      -- inside find_flights to be in the scope
      -- of the generic procedure parameter "produce".
    procedure flight_range is
      new schedule_bt_pkg.
          scan_between(produce_flight_description);
  begin   -- Body of find_flights.
    flight_range((o => origin, d => destination, i => min_text),
                (o => origin, d => destination, i => max_text),
                fs.schedule);
  end find_flights;


  function lex is new lex3(airport, airport, flight_id);
  function bt_le(x, y: bt_key) return boolean is
  begin
    return lex(x.o, x.d, x.i, y.o, y.d, y.i);
  end bt_le;
end flight_schedule_pkg;
```

FIGURE 5.30
Completed Reservation Set

```
  with lex2;
| with bounded_sequence_pkg;
package body reservation_set_pkg is
  -- Generic instantiations.
  package date_sequence_pkg is
    new bounded_sequence_pkg(date, 3000);
  use date_sequence_pkg;
  package res_key_sequence_pkg is
    new bounded_sequence_pkg(res_key, 1000);
  use res_key_sequence_pkg;


  -- Local subprogram declarations.
  procedure bookings(i: flight_id; bf: in out bookings_hf;
                     n: out natural );
  -- End local subprogram declarations.


  procedure open(name: in text; rs: in out reservation_set) is
  begin
    rs.base_name := name;
    open(name & text_string("d"), rs.dates);
  end open;


  procedure add(a: in agent_id; i: in flight_id; d: in date;
               p: in passenger; rs: in out reservation_set ) is
      -- Pre: ~holds(p, i, d, rs).
    reservations_file: reservations_bt;
    bookings_file: bookings_hf;
    n: natural;
    null_value: null_type;
        -- Uninitialized because the value does not matter.
  begin
    open(rs.base_name & text_string("r") & string_code(d),
         reservations_file );
    open(rs.base_name & text_string("b") & string_code(d),
         bookings_file );
    add((i => i, p => p), a, reservations_file);
    bookings(i, bookings_file, n);
    add(i, n + 1, bookings_file);
    add(d, null_value, rs.dates);
  end add;


  procedure remove(i: in flight_id; d: in date; p: in passenger;
                  rs: in out reservation_set ) is
```

FIGURE 5.30 (continued)

```
    reservations_file: reservations_bt;
    bookings_file: bookings_hf;
    has, date_exists: boolean;
    n: natural;
  begin
    member(d, rs.dates, date_exists);
    if not date_exists then return; end if;
    open(rs.base_name & text_string("r") & string_code(d),
        reservations_file );
    member((i => i, p => p), reservations_file, has);
    if has then
        remove((i => i, p => p), reservations_file);
        open(rs.base_name & text_string("b") & string_code(d),
            bookings_file );
        bookings(i, bookings_file, n);
        add(i, n - 1, bookings_file);
    end if;
  end remove;

  procedure remove(i: in flight_id;
                   rs: in out reservation_set ) is
    first_key: constant res_key := (i => i, p => min_text);
    last_key: constant res_key := (i => i, p => max_text);
    res_key_sequence: res_key_sequence_pkg.sequence;
    procedure produce_date(d1: in date; e1: in null_type) is
      reservations_file: reservations_bt;
      procedure produce_reservation(rk: res_key; ra: agent_id) is
      begin   -- Produce_reservation.
        add(rk, res_key_sequence);
      end produce_reservation;
      procedure generate_reservations is
        new reservations_bt_pkg.
          scan_between(produce_reservation);
      procedure remove_reservation(rk: in res_key) is
      begin
        remove(rk.i, d1, rk.p, rs);
      end remove_reservation;
      procedure remove_stale_reservations is new
        res_key_sequence_pkg.scan(remove_reservation);
    begin   -- Produce_date.
      open(rs.base_name & text_string("r") & string_code(d1),
          reservations_file );
      res_key_sequence := create;
      generate_reservations(first_key,
                            last_key,
                            reservations_file );
      remove_stale_reservations(res_key_sequence);
```

```
    end produce_date;
  procedure generate_dates is
    new dates_bt_pkg.scan(produce_date);
begin  -- Remove.
  generate_dates(rs.dates);
end remove;


procedure remove(d: in date; rs: in out reservation_set) is
  date_sequence: date_sequence_pkg.sequence;
  procedure produce_date(d1: in date; e1: in null_type) is
  begin
    if d1 < d then add(d1, date_sequence); end if;
  end produce_date;
  procedure generate_dates is
    new dates_bt_pkg.scan_to(produce_date);
  procedure remove_date(d1: in date) is
    reservations_file: reservations_bt;
    bookings_file: bookings_hf;
  begin
    open(rs.base_name & text_string("r") & string_code(d1),
        reservations_file );
    delete(reservations_file);
    open(rs.base_name & text_string("b") & string_code(d1),
        bookings_file );
    delete(bookings_file);
    remove(d1, rs.dates);
  end remove_date;
  procedure remove_stale_dates is
    new date_sequence_pkg.scan(remove_date);
begin  -- Remove.
  date_sequence := create;
  generate_dates(d, rs.dates);
  remove_stale_dates(date_sequence);
end remove;


procedure holds(p: in passenger; i: in flight_id; d: in date;
                rs: in out reservation_set;
                has: out boolean ) is
  reservations_file: reservations_bt;
  date_exists: boolean;
begin
  member(d, rs.dates, date_exists);
  if not date_exists then has := false; return; end if;
  open(rs.base_name & text_string("r") & string_code(d),
      reservations_file );
  member((i => i, p => p), reservations_file, has);
end holds;
```

FIGURE 5.30 (continued)

```
procedure bookings(i: in flight_id; d: in date;
                    rs: in out reservation_set;
                    number_of_bookings: out natural ) is
  bookings_file: bookings_hf;
  date_exists: boolean;
begin
  member(d, rs.dates, date_exists);
  if not date_exists then
     number_of_bookings := 0; return; end if;
  open(rs.base_name & text_string("b") & string_code(d),
       bookings_file );
  bookings(i, bookings_file, number_of_bookings);
end bookings;

procedure bookings(i: flight_id; bf: in out bookings_hf;
                    n: out natural ) is
begin
  fetch(i, bf, n);
exception
  when bookings_hf_pkg.domain_error => n := 0;
end bookings;

-- generic
--   with procedure produce(r: in reservation)
procedure notify(a: in agent_id; i: in flight_id; d: in date;
                 rs: in out reservation_set ) is
  first_key: constant res_key := (i => i, p => min_text);
  last_key: constant res_key := (i => i, p => max_text);
  procedure produce_date(d1: in date; e1: in null_type) is
    reservations_file: reservations_bt;
    procedure produce_reservation(rk: res_key; ra: agent_id) is
    begin  -- Produce_reservation.
      if ra = a then
        produce((id => rk.i, d => d1, p => rk.p, a => ra));
      end if;
    end produce_reservation;
    procedure generate_reservations is
      new reservations_bt_pkg.
        scan_between(produce_reservation);
  begin  -- Produce_date.
    open(rs.base_name & text_string("r") & string_code(d1),
         reservations_file );
    generate_reservations(first_key,
                          last_key,
                          reservations_file );
  end produce_date;
```

```
   procedure generate_dates is
      new dates_bt_pkg.scan_from(produce_date);
  begin  -- Notify.
     generate_dates(d, rs.dates);
  end notify;

  function lex is new lex2(flight_id, passenger);
  function res_le(x, y: res_key) return boolean is
  begin
     return lex(x.i, x.p, y.i, y.p);
  end res_le;
end reservation_set_pkg;
```

5.4.6 Summary of Deferred Enhancements

The following improvements to the design were identified and left to future versions because of budget limitations.

1. The command interpreters of the travel agent and airline manager should be reworked to use the code with the same structure (a case statement), and enumeration types should be introduced to represent the user commands in each interface.

2. The flight_schedule.add operation should be redesigned to replace the precondition with an explicit check and an exception condition, to remove the dependence of the third invariant on the conditions under which the add operation can be called.

3. The invariant of the type date should be refined to reflect differences in the number of days in different months, and the create operation should be modified accordingly.

5.5 Quality Assurance

Common quality assurance activities during the implementation stage are design reviews, testing, and static analysis. Design reviews are manual techniques for performing static checks or simulating the execution of particular test cases. Testing and static analysis are done using a computer. All of these methods are effective for locating faults in implementations. They are commonly used together because the strengths of these methods are complementary. Design reviews can perform some checks that are too difficult to automate, testing can detect faults due to unknown characteristics of the operating environment, and automated static analysis can carry out checks that are too much work to do manually.

A *fault* is a bug or design error in a program. A *failure* is an instance of incorrect program behavior. The occurrence of a failure indicates the existence of a fault, which must then be located, diagnosed, and corrected. *Locating* a fault means finding the region of incorrect program text. *Diagnosing* a fault means determining the incorrect design decisions that caused the fault. *Correcting* a fault means changing the requirements, specifications, designs, and programs as needed to eliminate all failures caused by the fault, without introducing new faults.

It is very difficult to certify that a software system is entirely free from faults. Design reviews cannot effectively certify a system to be free of faults because the probability of human error in carrying out the certification is too high. Restricted certifications by computerized techniques are possible. Checking whether a program meets a specification is algorithmically undecidable in the general case, so we have to be content with automated tools that work for many practical cases, but may run forever or terminate without producing a definite conclusion for some programs.

Testing can demonstrate the absence of faults only for finite data domains small enough for exhaustive testing, or for limited applications allowing inferences of perfect operation on infinite domains from the successful execution of carefully chosen finite subsets of the domain [2]. There are some results giving small finite test sets that detect any fault in specified classes of faults [14]. These techniques are very useful for the situations in which they apply, even though the successful execution of such a test set guarantees only the absence of the specified class of faults, and does not guarantee absolute correctness of the program. In most practical situations, testing can demonstrate the presence of faults but not their absence, so that testing should be considered primarily as a diagnostic rather than a certification technique.

Static analysis can also certify the absence of restricted classes of faults, relative to the correctness of the programs doing the certification. Commonly available static analysis tools can certify the absence of faults such as type consistency errors and references to uninitialized variables. Static analysis involving mathematical proofs can certify the absence of wider classes of faults, such as deadlocks, abnormal termination, infinite loops, or incorrect output values. Tools for performing these more advanced kinds of static analysis are mostly research prototypes, and are not widespread.

Mathematical proofs of correctness are a special kind of static analysis that can establish correctness of an implementation for all possible inputs, with respect to a formal description of the intended meaning of the programming language and the data types used in the program. Even if a proof is constructed and checked by a computer, there is still no absolute guarantee of correctness, because the proof is relative to a set of uncertain assumptions about the operating environment, which includes the compiler and operating system in addition to the characteristics of external systems not implemented in software. Proofs of correctness also depend on assumptions about the behavior of the underlying hardware that could be incorrect. At the current time, we know of no production-quality compilers or operating systems whose correctness with respect to a formal specification has been certified, and we have encountered faults in many compilers and operating systems that are in common use. Proofs of correctness are usually done with respect to specifications for the data types that do not reflect implementation limits on the number of bits in the representation, or the precision of real number representations. Although proofs incorporating implementation limits are possible, they are often much longer and more difficult than the corresponding proofs with respect to idealized data types. Even if the proofs are carried out with respect to realistic data type specifications, the compilers and operating systems are mechanically certified, and the programs for performing the certifications have been used to certify themselves, faults in the certification programs making them unable to detect their own faults are still possible. Absolute certainty about program correctness is not attainable even under very favorable conditions. Despite these possibilities for undetected faults, mathematical proofs of correctness can lead to much lower failure rates than those achieved by most current software development efforts.

Experience with mathematical proofs of correctness indicates that such certifications require about a factor of ten more effort than conventional software development methods [9]. Most of the extra effort in the project just mentioned was spent on getting a correct version of the software, and only a relatively small portion was spent on mathematical proofs for the certification. Correctness was achieved by constructing prototypes and implementing multiple versions of each module. This experience suggests that constructing correct software is much more difficult than commonly recognized, and that synthesizing a correct program can be harder than certifying its correctness.

5.5.1 Choosing Test Cases

Test cases can be chosen based on either the specification or the implementation. The two criteria are most effective at finding different kinds of faults, so that it is advisable to follow both strategies.

Black-box testing is based on the specification. The specification of a response to an event often has several cases. A minimal test set should execute each case in the specification at least once. For thoroughness, test cases near the boundaries between cases should be chosen, as well as some randomly generated values for each case. The concept of "nearness" makes sense for any data type with either a discrete ordering or a distance measure. Points near the boundaries of a predicate defining a case in a specification are often fault revealing, because they can discover differences between the boundaries in the specification and the corresponding boundaries in the code, especially for distinctions that are present in the specifications but not in the code. More precise characterizations of the effectiveness of such test sets depend on the properties of the data types involved. Specification-based black-box testing can benefit from automated tools for keeping track of the number of cases expected for each case identified in the specification, and for evaluating the postconditions to determine if each test result is consistent with the specification. Such tools may require that any unbounded quantifiers in the specifications first be transformed into bounded quantifiers, or may use sampling to check universally quantified conditions at a finite number of values for the bound variables.

Glass-box testing is based on the structure of the implementation. Common informally applied strategies are to make sure that each statement in the code is executed at least once, or that each branch in the code has been executed at least once. The benefits of these strategies are that they can be applied using commonly available tools for measuring test coverage with respect to these criteria. The corresponding disadvantages are that many faults can remain undetected by such a test set, and that it is difficult to characterize the set of faults that are guaranteed to be detected by such a test set.

Some more thorough and systematic approaches are described in [14]. One class of results describes small finite test sets that distinguish an expression from any other member of a closely related set of expressions. For example, if the expression is in the form of the ratio of two polynomials, then a single test case where the values of all the variables and the value of the entire expression are nonzero is sufficient to detect all errors where a single coefficient of the polynomial has the wrong value. Other results are available for linear arithmetic expressions, and for boolean expressions composed of arithmetic expressions. Randomly chosen test data are also shown to be fault revealing with high probability for several classes of expressions. Most of the results in this category apply to numerical data types, but there are some results available for arrays and list structures.

It would be desirable to test all of the control paths through a program, but the number of control paths in a program containing a `while` loop is infinite, and even if the number of iterations for all loops is restricted to a small finite number, the number of control paths is often still much too large for testing all paths in practice. A useful criterion for judging the control-flow coverage of a test set that exercises the program more thoroughly than statement or branch testing is data flow testing. This technique uses data reference pairs to measure the coverage of a test set. A data reference pair for a variable consists of a statement that assigns a value to the variable and a statement that reads the value of the variable produced by that assignment. There can be no other assignments to the variable between the two statements in a data reference pair. The simplest associated test coverage criterion is to execute at least one instance of each possible data reference pair. A stronger related criterion is to test all possible data contexts for each statement, where a data context for a statement consists of a data reference pair for each variable referenced in the statement. This amounts to testing all possible combinations of sources for the data referenced by the statement. Both of these techniques require the support of automated tools that are less widely available than those for statement or branch testing. These tools involve a program for recording which data reference pairs or data contexts have been exercised, and for detecting infeasible paths. Infeasible paths contain conflicting conditions at different decision points in the path. Because it is not possible to find any test cases to exercise an infeasible path, any kind of path coverage criterion requires identification of the infeasible paths. A large fraction of the infeasible paths can be detected by automated tools using symbolic evaluation techniques coupled with some simple rules for detecting contradictory predicates.

Another useful testing technique is trace fault analysis. In trace fault analysis, constraints on the expected order of the operations in a program are described by a state transition graph, and the program is analyzed to determine if it can generate any illegal sequences of operator calls. An example of the kind of constraint that can be specified is that each input file must first be opened, read zero or more times, and then closed. Such restrictions are described in Spec via atomic transactions (see Section 3.9.7). Details of the techniques mentioned above and the tools for supporting them can be found in [14].

5.5.2 Performance

Performance is another aspect of software quality that must be checked in practice. A common way to approach this problem is to specify a set of test cases, known as *benchmarks*, and to measure the actual execution time of the implementation on these cases. Sometimes the benchmarks are given as part of the requirements, along with bounds on the corresponding execution times.

If an implementation fails to meet its performance requirements, the execution of the system is measured to determine which parts of the code are being executed most often. This is usually done via an execution profile that determines either the number of times each statement in the program was executed, or the amount of time spent in each subprogram. Many modern compilers have an option for collecting this information. Most systems spend about 90% of the time executing about 10% of the code. The execution profile is used to locate the sections of the code where the system spends most of its time, which are known as performance bottlenecks. The modules containing the performance bottlenecks are then redesigned using more efficient data structures and algorithms. This process is much easier for systems designed using abstractions and the information hiding principle, because this reduces the size of the code region that must be redesigned when a data representation is changed.

Some theoretical work related to performance is complexity analysis of algorithms and queuing theory. Complexity analysis determines a formula for the worst case running time of an algorithm. Many published algorithms have known formulae for time complexity, but these are usually expressed up to an unknown proportionality constant that depends on the particular implementation to be used. The derivation of a complexity formula can be difficult, since a tight bounding function for each loop and recursion is needed. However, if the code is annotated with such bounding functions, automated tools for calculating accurate worst case running times for the entire system are feasible, and would be very useful for developing systems with hard real-time constraints. Currently such tools are not widespread. Some research results indicating the current state of the art in this area can be found in [12].

Queuing theory can be used to determine expected waiting times when a system is subjected to random loads with given probability distributions. This kind of analysis can be useful for predicting the performance of parallel programs on time sharing systems, and has been applied mostly to analyzing performance of operating systems and telephone networks. For large applications, the equations resulting from the theory can be difficult to solve, so that serious applications require the support of automated tools. A survey of the current state of the art in this area can be found in [21]. Queuing theory is useful for estimating average case behavior. Such information is useful when designing systems with performance goals of a statistical nature.

5.6 Management Aspects: Measuring Progress

The goals of the project manager include delivering a product on time and within budget. Frequent monitoring of progress is needed to achieve these goals because the effort needed to construct and debug a system is hard to predict. Nonintrusive status reporting via a set of tools operating on the project database is an effective means of achieving this. A minimal system should provide a means of marking which aspects of each component have been completed, and a tool for locating and summing the estimated effort for each task that has not yet been completed.

It is also useful to calculate the accuracy of the estimate and the probability of completing the project on time, as suggested in Chapter 4. The probability of meeting the schedule depends on the total effort available and the amount expended to date, both of which should also be maintained in the database. This probability can be used as the basis for determining when to shift to a contingency plan involving the delivery of a subset of the system. The point at which such contingency plans are to be adopted should be worked out in advance, based on the relative costs of missing the schedule and delivering an incomplete product. These costs often depend on the details of the contract agreement governing the project.

5.7 Background

This section contains some of the theoretical background material needed for systematic construction of programs.

5.7.1 Weakest Preconditions

Assertions in predicate logic form the link between specifications and programs. Assertions are used in Spec to describe the relation between input messages and output messages, or the relation between the initial and final states of a transition. Assertions can also be used to describe the states of an Ada program. The effect of a program fragment can be described by a pair of assertions, the precondition and the postcondition. The precondition describes the state just before executing the program fragment and the postcondition describes the state just after executing the fragment.

Weakest preconditions are special kinds of assertions useful for analyzing and constructing programs. Let P be a program fragment and G be an assertion expressing a goal for P. The *weakest precondition* wp(P, G) of P with respect to G is an assertion that is true for exactly those initial states in which execution of P is guaranteed to reach the point immediately after P in a finite number of steps, and to produce a final state in which G is true. The weakest precondition characterizes the set of all initial states in which execution of the program P achieves the goal condition G. For example, wp(P, $x = y + y$) is true for all initial states for which the program P produces a final state where $x = y + y$ is true. At one extreme, the goal condition `true` is satisfied in all possible final states, so that wp(P, `true`) represents the set of initial states for which P terminates normally. Thus wp(P, `true`) = `true` means that P terminates normally in all possible initial states. At the other extreme, the goal condition `false` cannot be satisfied in any state, so that wp(P, `false`) = `false` for any program P.

Weakest preconditions are the best available software correctness measure. If we take G to be the goal expressed by a specification for an operation, then wp(P, G) describes the set of inputs or initial conditions for which the program P correctly realizes the goal G. If wp(P, G) = true, then the program is correct for all possible inputs. If this is not the case, then the set of inputs or initial conditions for which the program will fail is described by ˜wp(P, G). This is a complete characterization of the set of test cases for which the program P will fail, provided that the compiler and the lower-level modules work correctly. Thus automatic procedures for calculating weakest preconditions are valuable aids for the error location aspect of debugging.

Weakest preconditions are useful for discovering the implicit assumptions in an algorithm for achieving a goal described by a given postcondition. Knowledge of such assumptions can often be used to transform a program that works in some cases into a related program that works for all possible cases. Weakest preconditions can also be used for deriving missing parts of a program and for proving that an algorithm meets a given specification. Weakest preconditions are useful for supporting computer-aided design tools because they can be mechanically derived from the program text.

The rules for deriving weakest preconditions for loop-free programs are relatively simple. The rules for deriving weakest preconditions for a small subset of Ada follow. Weakest preconditions for a wider range of programming language constructs are described in [10].

```
wp(null;, G) = G
wp(v := E;, G) = defined(E) & G[v ← E]if v not bound in G
wp(p1; p2;, G) = wp(p1, wp(p2, G))
wp(if E then p1; else p2; end if;, G) =
    defined(E) & (E => wp(p1, G)) & (˜E => wp(p2, G))
```

The first rule says the null statement achieves a given goal if and only if the goal is true in the initial state. This is accurate because executing the null statement has no effect on the program state, and because execution of the null statement is always guaranteed to terminate.

The assignment statement rule says an assignment achieves a given goal if the expression on the right hand side is defined in the initial state and the goal with the expression E substituted for the variable v is true in the initial state. The notation $G[v \leftarrow E]$ denotes textual substitution, where all free occurrences of the variable v are replaced by the expression (E), where the parentheses are used to ensure that operator precedence rules do not change the structure of the expression. For example, $(x * z)[x \leftarrow x + z] = ((x + z) * z)$, rather than $(x + z * z)$ which means $(x + (z * z))$. The rule applies only if none of the variables in E are bound by quantifiers in G, so the bound variables of G may have to be renamed before the rule can be applied. Some examples of the rule for assignment statements follow.

```
wp(x := 5;, x = 5) = defined(5) & (5 = 5) = true
wp(x := 4;, x = 5) = defined(4) & (4 = 5) = false
wp(x := y;, x = 5) = defined(y) & (y = 5) = (y = 5)
wp(x := y / z;, x = 5) = defined(y / z) & (y / z = 5)
                      = (z ~= 0 & y / z = 5)
wp(x := y;, SOME(y: integer :: 2 * x = y + 1))
   = SOME(z : integer :: 2 * y = z + 1)
```

The first assignment statement always achieves its goal, the second assignment statement never achieves its goal, and the third achieves its goal only in states where $y = 5$. The fourth example illustrates the treatment of expressions that are not always defined, since the expression y / z can produce a numeric_error exception if $z = 0$. Constants and variables are defined in all states, although the values of uninitialized variables are unpredictable. The conditions under which an operator is defined are determined from the specification of the operator. The last example illustrates renaming of a bound variable in the postcondition because of a name collision. Because the program variable y appears on the right-hand side of the assignment statement, the bound variable y in the postcondition is renamed to z, which is an arbitrarily chosen variable name that does not appear in any of the original expressions. If we had neglected renaming the bound variable, then after the substitution, the y replacing the x would refer to the arbitrary value determined by the SOME quantifier, rather than to the value of the program variable y as intended. Complications such as this do not arise if all variables bound to quantifiers in assertions are different from any of the variables appearing in the program.

The rule for sequences of statements says the subgoal for the first statement is the weakest precondition of the second statement with respect to the main goal. This describes the conditions under which the execution of the first statement p1 followed by execution of the second statement p2 achieves the main goal G. Weakest preconditions are used to analyze sequential programs starting from the end and working back towards the beginning. Working backward using weakest preconditions may appear strange at first, but it is usually preferred to working forward using strongest postconditions because knowledge of the ultimate goal can be used to keep the state descriptions smaller and simpler. This rule is illustrated by the following example.

```
wp(t:= x; x:= y; y:= t;, x = c1 & y = c2) =
wp(t:= x; x:= y;, wp(y:= t;, x = c1 & y = c2)) =
wp(t:= x; x:= y;, x = c1 & t = c2) =
wp(t:= x;, wp(x:= y;, x = c1 & t = c2)) =
wp(t:= x;, y = c1 & t = c2)) =
y = c1 & x = c2
```

This calculation shows that the given sequence of three assignment statements has the effect of interchanging the values of the variables x and y in all possible states, and demonstrates via mechanically applicable rules what most programmers know based on intuition.

The rule for conditionals says that the evaluation of the expression governing the decision must terminate normally, and that the arm of the conditional chosen for execution must lead to the specified goal. The following example assumes the program variables x and y are of type integer.

```
wp(if x > 0 then y := x; else y := -x; end if;, y > 0) =
defined(x > 0) & (x > 0 => wp(y := x;, y > 0))
             & (~(x > 0) => wp(y := -x;, y > 0)) =
true & (x > 0 => x > 0) & (~(x > 0) => -x > 0) =
true & true & ~ ~(x > 0) | (x < -0) =
x > 0 | x < 0 =
x ~= 0
```

This calculation shows that the given program fragment meets its goal only in states where $x \mathrel{\sim}= 0$, which may indicate the programmer has made a mistake. The calculation of the weakest precondition depends on a small number of rules that are easy to apply and can be readily automated. Simplification of expressions can also be automated, but it is more difficult than calculating weakest preconditions because the number of rules is larger. Simplification of the resulting expression depends on properties of the underlying data types. We have used some of the simplification rules from propositional logic and the following properties of integers in the previous simplification.

```
ALL(i j: integer :: defined(i > j))
ALL(i j: integer :: i < j <=> - i > - j)
ALL(i j: integer :: i < j | i = j | i > j)
```

Simplifying integer expressions is more difficult than simplifying expressions involving many other common data types, because some of the laws about integers are not in the form of transformation rules that are always applied in the same direction and that strictly reduce the size of the expression. Oriented size-reducing rules are easier to automate than laws of other forms because the series of transformations applicable to any expression is guaranteed to terminate after a finite number of steps. This difficulty reflects the undecidability of the first order theory of the integers. In practice we must be content with automatic procedures for simplifying integer expressions that always terminate, but may fail to simplify some expressions to the shortest possible form.

5.7.2 Invariants

Invariants are an important conceptual tool for the design of loops and data structures. An *invariant* is an assertion that is always true when control reaches a given point. For a loop, that point is usually before and after each execution of the loop body, although there may also be invariants associated with the point just before an `exit`, `return`, or `raise` statement inside a loop body. Invariants can also be associated with data structures implementing an abstract data type or abstract state machine. For data structures, the point where the invariants must be true is before and after each primitive operation of the associate abstract machine or type. In this section, we examine the use of loop invariants in the design of programs. Data invariants were used in the design of interfaces in Chapters 3 and 4. Data invariants used in program design can be found in the implementations of the types `flight_schedule` and `reservation_set` shown earlier in this chapter, and in the implementations of the types B_tree and `hashed_file` shown in Appendix F. The airline reservation example and the reusable components of Appendix F also contain examples of loop invariants.

Invariants describe constraints or conventions that relate the values of different program variables or different components of a data structure. Invariants are important for understanding programs because properties that do not change are easier to analyze than than those that do change. Invariants are important for constructing programs because many aspects of the code can be derived from a precise statement of the intended invariant. Invariants are also needed for mathematical proofs of correctness.

Loop invariants provide the basis for a systematic approach to loop design that helps the designer get the details of a loop right on the first attempt. We illustrate this approach in terms of an example.

Suppose we have to realize the concrete interface shown in Fig. 5.31. The architectural design for this module includes the advice "use binary search." Our task is to adapt this well known search strategy of repeatedly bisecting an interval to the current problem. We decide to introduce the variables `low`, `mid`, and `high`, representing the endpoints and the midpoint of the interval to be searched. We use an invariant to develop and record a precise definition of the meaning of these variables.

A binary search program compares the key at the midpoint to k. In case the two are equal, we know the key is in the table, and can return the value

---

```
type table is array(natural range <>) of key;
  -- Invariant: ALL(t: table :: sorted(t)).

function member(k: key; t: table) return boolean;
  -- Post: member(k, t) <=> SOME(n: natural :: t(n) = k).
```

FIGURE 5.31
Concrete Interface to be Implemented

true immediately. Therefore the purpose of the variables low and high should be to record which parts of the table are known *not* to contain the key we are seeking, so that the program can determine when the key is not in the table. The results of the comparison tell us that the midpoint is strictly greater or strictly less than k in the cases where the search does not terminate immediately. Because we would like to have a simple decision in the heart of the loop, we want the midpoint to qualify as the new value of one of the end-points of the interval. This leads to the program fragment shown in Fig. 5.32. This fragment contains invariants expressing an interpretation for the endpoints of the interval that is consistent with our desires for using the midpoint. The invariants state that there is a region of the array containing values known to be strictly greater than k, and another region containing values known to be strictly less than k. In the case where the key stored at the midpoint is different from k, the midpoint can serve as a boundary for one of these regions. The boundaries of these regions are defined by the variables high and low, and these boundary points are *included* in the respective regions. The precise interpretation of the boundary points must be clearly in mind to develop a correct algorithm. The designer could have chosen not to include the boundary points in the interval, but that would lead to a different program.

In Ada, the predefined attributes t'first and t'last give the lower and upper bound for the index range of the array t. These bounds on the index range define the other endpoints of the two regions, to allow all of the values in the array to be covered. We have chosen a symmetrical interpretation of the variables to make the code more uniform. The invariant does not mention the variable mid since it is not used to transmit any information from one iteration of the loop to the next.

We have used the invariants to define precisely the intended meaning of the state variables for the loop. The decisions about the details of the intended interpretation of the variables and data structures are among the most difficult and most important parts of the design of a program, making it worthwhile to concentrate on this aspect before introducing details of dynamic behavior. We

---

```
while ? loop
   -- Invariant: ALL(n: natural :: high <= n <= t'last => k < t(n)).
   -- Invariant: ALL(n: natural :: t'first <= n <= low => k > t(n)).
end loop
```

FIGURE 5.32
Loop Fragment

have worked out the static properties of the data structures in more detail than is common in informal approaches to programming. The extra effort at the beginning is justified because it takes the guesswork out of the later decisions and helps prevent common "off by one" errors.

We illustrate this by using the invariants to determine the rest of the code. The purpose of the initialization is to make the invariants true before the loop executes for the first time. No information about the array is known at that time, so the regions known not to contain the key should be empty. This corresponds to the following conditions.

```
high = t'last + 1
low = t'first - 1
```

The loop can terminate with the conclusion that the key is not in the array in case both of the regions known not to contain the key cover the entire array. This corresponds to the following condition.

```
high <= low + 1
```

The code resulting from these considerations is shown in Fig. 5.33. The comparisons together with the knowledge that the array t is sorted in increasing order establish the truth of the invariants over growing subranges of the array.

```
function member(k: key; t: table) return boolean is
   low, mid, high: natural;
begin
   high := t'last + 1;
   low := t'first - 1;
   while high > low + 1 loop
      -- Invariant: ALL(n: natural :: high <= n <= t'last => k < t(n)).
      -- Invariant: ALL(n: natural :: t'first <= n <= low => k > t(n)).
      mid := (high + low) / 2;
      if k = t(mid) then return true;
         elsif k < t(mid) then high := mid;
         else low := mid;
      end if;
   end loop;
   return false;
end member;
```

FIGURE 5.33
Completed Program

The program is designed to adjust the variables `high` and `low` accordingly. Although the binary search algorithm is simple conceptually, the details can be surprisingly difficult to get correct using informal approaches, sometimes leading to lengthy debug and test cycles. The invariants serve as a general working plan that helps the programmer fit all of the details into a consistent structure in the initial synthesis.

Next we check whether any partial operations have been invoked with values outside their domains of definition. The second argument to the only division is the constant 2, so there can be no `numeric_error` exceptions due to dividing by zero, as calculated next.

```
defined((high + low)/ 2) = (2 ˜= 0) = true
```

Showing that there can be no `constraint_error` exceptions due to the array references involves a bit more reasoning.

```
defined(t(mid)) = t'first <= mid <= t'last
```

Because we do not have any assertions about the variable `mid`, we use a weakest precondition to find the corresponding states at the beginning of the loop body.

```
wp(mid := (high + low) / 2;, t'first <= mid <= t'last) =
    t'first <= (high + low)/ 2 <= t'last
```

The first two invariants are not sufficient to establish this condition because they do not constrain the values of `high` and `low`. The required condition cannot be an invariant as it stands because it is false in an initial state where the array `t` has an empty range, and this state is perfectly legal. We consider the expected behavior of the variables `high` and `low`, and propose the following invariants.

```
-- Invariant: t'first - 1 <= high <= t'last + 1.
-- Invariant: t'first - 1 <= low <= t'last + 1.
```

These invariants are suggested by the initialization, and by our intuitive expectation that the midpoint of an interval should be between its endpoints. Noting `high` and `low` are natural numbers and that the following statement is always true,

```
(high > low + 1) => (low < (high + low) / 2 < high)
```

we can see that the loop test together with the proposed invariants is sufficient to show that the array references are always within bounds, and that the assignments to `high` and `low` maintain the truth of the new invariants.

Invariants do not provide any magic. Familiarity with the principles behind a standard algorithm applicable to a given problem makes programming easier. Insight is still necessary to invent a new algorithm. However, the use of invariants can help the programmer get the details right when turning an insight into a program, and discover and enforce symmetries that can make complicated algorithms more uniform and hence easier to understand. Starting with a set of invariants that capture the essential ideas behind an algorithm is a recommended design practice. Invariants governing more peripheral properties, such as clean termination, are often discovered and added at later stages. Automated tools for deriving weakest preconditions and for checking inferences are helpful for applying invariants to check the correctness of an implementation. A set of automated tools for turning the approach outlined here into a method that guarantees correctness by construction is not available at the current time. A more detailed discussion of the approach can be found in [10].

5.7.3 Well Founded Sets

Because all responses of a software system should be produced in a finite amount of time, checking for proper termination of a program is important. Well founded sets are used in software engineering for showing that the loops and recursions in a program terminate for all states and input values.

A set is *well founded* if it has a partial ordering without any infinite strictly decreasing sequences. For example, the set of natural numbers with the standard ordering is well founded because the set of positive whole numbers strictly less than any given number is finite. The set of integers with the standard ordering is not well founded because the negative integers can be arranged in an infinite strictly decreasing sequence $[-1, -2, -3, ...]$. The lexicographic ordering defined in Fig. 4.6 is well founded whenever the orderings on the components are well founded also. The lexicographic ordering has this property only for tuples of bounded length, as illustrated by the strictly decreasing sequence ["b", "ab", "aab", ...] over unbounded text strings.

The method for showing termination of a program involves showing that the series of steps in the execution of a program is a strictly decreasing sequence over a well founded set. If this can be done we know the program must terminate because all such sequences are finite. To show that a loop terminates, you must find a function with the following properties:

1. The domain of the function is the set of program states. Such functions are defined in terms of the program variables appearing in the loop.

2. The range of the function must be a well founded set. The most common choice is the set of natural numbers with the standard ordering.

3. For any initial state in which the loop body can be executed, the value of the function after executing the loop body once must be strictly less than the value of the function in the initial state. "Strictly less" refers to the ordering of the well founded set.

A function with these properties is called a *bounding function* (sometimes called a *progress function*). For bounding functions ranging over the natural numbers we can interpret the value of the bounding function as an upper bound on the number of iterations left before the loop terminates, since the value of the bounding function must be reduced by at least one on each iteration of the loop.

A simple example of an Ada `for` loop is:

```
for v in a .. b loop
   -- some loop body
end loop;
```

A bounding function for this loop is `length([v .. b0])`, where `b0` represents the value of the variable `b` just before the execution of the loop. This function depends on the program variable `v` and yields a natural number. The value of this function is strictly decreased on each iteration because the loop assigns the values of the range [a .. b] to the variable `v` in increasing order, and the rules of the language prohibit direct or indirect assignments to `v` in the loop body. This example shows that all Ada `for` loops of the given form are guaranteed to terminate.

An example of a `while` loop implementing a binary search can be found in the previous section. The expression `high - low` is a bounding function for this loop, since assignments must either strictly decrease `high` or strictly increase `low` on all paths through the loop body that lead to another execution of the loop body. We record this information using the following annotation.

```
-- Bound: high - low.
```

The only other path through the code leads to immediate termination of the loop via the `return` statement; therefore the loop must terminate for all possible states.

To show that a recursive subprogram terminates, you must find a function with the following properties:

1. The domain of the function is the set of input values for the recursive subprogram. This set is the cross product of the data types associated with the formal parameters with modes `in` or `in out`.

2. The range of the function must be a well founded set.

3. For each recursive call in the subprogram body, the value of the function applied to the actual parameters of the call must be strictly less than the value of the function applied to the formal parameters of the subprogram.

Such a function is also known as a bounding function. For a set of mutually recursive subprograms, all indirectly recursive calls in the bodies of the subprograms must also satisfy condition (3). The same bounding function must be used for all calls to a given subprogram. Different subprograms can have different bounding functions, even if they are mutually recursive. A simple example is shown next.

```
function fibonacci(n: in natural) return natural is
begin
  if n <= 1 then return n;
     else return fibonacci(n - 1) + fibonacci(n - 2);
  end if
end fibonacci;
```

In this case, the value of the bounding function can be taken to be the only parameter of the fibonacci subprogram. There are two recursive calls, both of which satisfy condition (3) since $n - 1 < n$ and $n - 2 < n$.

Recursion works because each recursive call corresponds to the solution of a smaller version of the original problem. The purpose of the bounding function is to document the intended meaning of smaller. Recursive subprograms over some data types may have bounding functions involving derived properties of the arguments. For example, many recursive subprograms operating on trees reduce the depth of some particular tree-valued argument to the subprogram. In such a case, the bounding function would be the depth of the tree in the given argument position. The bounding function does not have to depend on the values of all of the arguments of the recursive subprogram. For example, a recursive subprogram may be designed so that the second argument is always reduced by a recursive call, while the first argument remains the same and the third increases. A bounding function for such a subprogram is just the second argument. Such a design is sometimes described informally as a recursion "on the second argument."

Although the halting problem is known to be undecidable, this has little practical importance since most of the algorithms in software products can easily be shown to terminate using the methods just shown. Cases where it is hard or impossible to show termination usually correspond to situations where termination is not intended or is not part of the requirements. For example, an operating system is not intended to terminate, and an interpreter for a programming language is not expected to terminate for all possible inputs, since some of the inputs may represent programs with infinite loops.

5.7.4 Recurrences and Optimization

A *recurrence relation* is a set of equations giving a recursive definition for a function. A powerful class of optimizations for loops, known as "taking a relation out of the loop" or "reduction in strength," is based on finding recurrence relations for expressions used in the loop. These optimizations introduce a new state variable representing the value of an expression used in the loop, replacing the evaluation of the expression with a reference to the new state variable,

```
FUNCTION binomial_coefficients
  MESSAGE(n: nat) GENERATE(s: sequence{nat})
    WHERE ALL(i: nat SUCH THAT i <= n :: s[i + 1] = C(n, i))

  CONCEPT C(n i: nat) VALUE(bc: nat)
    WHERE bc = factorial(n)/(factorial(i) * factorial(n - i))

  CONCEPT factorial(x: nat) VALUE(y: nat)
    WHERE y = PRODUCT(n: nat SUCH THAT 1 <= n <= x :: n)
END
```

FIGURE 5.34
Specification for Binomial Coefficient Generator

and adding an incrementally maintained invariant relation for the new state variable.

We illustrate the technique using the example of generating binomial coefficients. Binomial coefficients are used in binomial expansions, and occur widely in probability and combinatorics for counting the number of subsets of size i for a set of size n. A specification for the problem is shown in Fig. 5.34.

The direct approach to implementing this generator is to make the concept C(n, i) into a subprogram that is implemented directly using the definitions in the specification. Such an implementation is shown in Fig. 5.35. Because a direct implementation of C(n, i) runs in O(n) steps, this implementation of the generator runs in O(n ^ 2) steps.

We propose taking the relation out of the loop by introducing a state vari-

```
generic
  with procedure produce(bc: in natural);
procedure binomial_coefficients(n: in natural);

procedure binomial_coefficients(n: in natural) is
begin
  for i in 0 .. n loop
    produce(C(n, i));
  end loop;
end binomial_coefficients;
```

FIGURE 5.35
Initial Implementation for Binomial Coefficient Generator

able with the invariant relation c = C(n, i). We have to invent a recurrence relation for C(n, i) to make this work.

In general, recurrence relations are discovered by pattern matching, guessing a plausible form, and checking whether it works. Since the dominant operation in the definition of C(n, i) is multiplication, we guess there may be a multiplicative recurrence, and check our guess by simplifying the ratio

$$\frac{C(n, i+1)}{C(n, i)} = \frac{n!}{i!(n-i)!} \frac{(i+1)!(n-(i+1))!}{n!} = \frac{(i+1)i!(n-i-1)!}{i!(n-i)(n-i-1)!} = \frac{i+1}{n-i}.$$

Because the result is a simple expression independent of C(n, i), we have succeeded in discovering the useful recurrence

$$C(n, i+1) = \frac{i+1}{n-i} C(n, i).$$

We also need to find the basis case for the recurrence, which is

$$C(n, 0) = \frac{n!}{0!n!} = 1.$$

This leads to the optimized implementation shown in Fig. 5.36. This version requires only O(n) operations, speeding up the algorithm by a factor of n. This can be a significant speedup, especially if the generator is used in a frequently executed part of the system.

As discussed in Section 5.5.2, in large systems it is undesirable to complicate the bulk of the code for marginal efficiency gains. The suggested approach is to produce a simple implementation, monitor the execution of the system to determine the most frequently executed modules and the most frequently executed parts of each module, and then to optimize those parts of the code using the technique just illustrated. The most frequently executed parts of any

---

```
procedure binomial_coefficients(n: in natural) is
   c: natural := 1; i: natural := 0;
begin
   loop
      produce(c);
      exit when i = n;
      c := c * (i + 1) / (n - i); i := i + 1;
   end loop;
end binomial_coefficients;
```

FIGURE 5.36
Optimized Implementation for Binomial Coefficient Generator

system are generally the bodies of the most deeply nested loops, so that loop optimizations generally have the largest effect.

Other optimizations involve the primitive operations of abstract data types. If the most frequently executed operations involve an abstract data type, the first thing to try is to look in a reference book on algorithms and data structures to find a published efficient implementation for the type. Other sources are [19] and computer science journals such as *Communications of the ACM, ACM Transactions on Programming Languages and Systems, Journal of the ACM, IEEE Transactions on Software Engineering, SIAM Journal of Computing, Acta Informatica, Science of Computer Programming*, and *Information Processing Letters*. If you cannot find a good published algorithm for your problem, you can try to find an optimization analogous to reduction in strength for loops, except that new components of the data structure with new data invariants are added instead of loop variables with new loop invariants. The principle is the same: Avoid recomputing some expression by storing some quantity that can be maintained incrementally via fast operations. Dynamic programming is a special case of this strategy.

Reduction in strength optimizations can be performed by the compiler for the built-in types and operations of the programming language, and many compilers do this. The first FORTRAN compiler did this kind of optimization automatically for array index calculations. At the current state of the art, reduction in strength optimizations for user-defined operations and data types depend on the skill of the implementor rather than the compiler, because they require application-dependent knowledge the compiler does not have. Often the largest potential efficiency gains come from just such optimizations applied to frequently used high-level types and operations, because these optimizations can decrease the asymptotic complexity of computations with long running times. An example of this kind of optimizing transformation applied to a graph problem can be found in [1].

5.7.5 Induction and Recursion

Well founded sets support the following induction rule, which forms the basis for analyzing recursive subprograms.

```
ALL(x: T SUCH THAT x < y :: p(x)) => p(y)
```
_____
```
ALL(x: T :: p(x))
```

This rule holds for any data type T that has a well founded ordering <. The rule lets us conclude that an arbitrary property p(x) is true for all values x in the data type T if we can prove the property p(y) for a previously unused variable y by using any number of assumptions of the form p(x), provided we can show x < y for each assumption. This rule is known as *structural induction* (sometimes also known as *strong induction* or *transfinite induction*).

This rule is the mathematical justification for the usual approach to designing recursive subprograms, where the body of the subprogram is developed using the assumption that all recursive calls satisfy the specification of the subprogram. If all recursive calls have arguments that are strictly less than the arguments of the original call with respect to any well founded ordering <, then this rule can be used to show that a property of a recursive function holds for all possible input values. Any conclusion established by this rule carries the implicit guarantee that the function is well defined, because termination for all inputs is implied by the conditions related to the well founded ordering.

A simple example illustrates the rule. Suppose we have a binary tree data type with a constant nil, a constructor operation make, and functions left and right giving the left and right subtrees of a given tree, as specified here:

```
ALL(x y: binary_tree :: left(make(x, y)) = x)
ALL(x y: binary_tree :: right(make(x, y)) = y)
```

A well founded ordering on this type is determined by the properties

```
ALL(x: binary_tree :: nil <= x)
ALL(x y: binary_tree :: x < make(x, y) & y < make(x, y))
```

because every tree can be generated by a finite number of make operations. Suppose we define the functions shown in Fig. 5.37.

We can use the structural induction rule to show that these functions have the property size(reflect(x)) = size(x) as follows. We consider the cases x = nil and x ~= nil separately. If x = nil then reflect(x) = x, and size(reflect(x)) = size(x) directly. Now assume x ~= nil.

```
function size(x: binary_tree) return natural is
begin
  if x = nil then return 1; else return size(left(x)) + size(right(x)); end if;
end size;

function reflect(x: binary_tree) return binary_tree is
begin
  if x = nil then return x; else return make(reflect(right(x)), reflect(left(x))); end if;
end reflect;
```

FIGURE 5.37
Functions on Binary Trees

Then `reflect(x)` = `make(reflect(right(x)), reflect(left(x)))` and `size(reflect(x))` = `size(reflect(right(x)))` + `size(reflect(left(x)))` from the definitions of `reflect` and `size`. Since `right(x)` < x and `left(x)` < x, we can assume that `size(reflect(right(x)))` = `size(right(x))` and `size(reflect(left(x)))` = `size(left(x))`. These assumptions give us `size(reflect(x))` = `size(left(x))` + `size(right(x))` = `size(x)` from the definition of `size`. The structural induction rule justifies the assumptions we made in the above case analysis, and we can conclude that `size(reflect(x))` = `size(x)` for every binary tree x.

The conclusion in our example has the form of a simplification rule, which states that a program is equivalent to a smaller and simpler program. Properties of this form can be useful for program optimization, because they can eliminate the need for some calculations in the implementation. If such transformations are used, it is important to check that they are correct, because the program resulting from a sequence of transformations may be difficult to relate to the original problem. Structural induction can also be used to prove that a recursive subprogram meets its specification.

The above proof demonstrates the pattern of reasoning used to analyze or design recursive subprograms. The example shows that reasoning based on well founded orderings can be used to check properties of programs other than termination. Such reasoning may be required to check that a recursively defined subprogram has some expected properties that are not immediately obvious from its definition. The same patterns of reasoning can be applied informally in the design and review of recursive algorithms. Reasoning based on structural induction has also been successfully automated, as described in [3].

5.7.6 Implementing Abstractions in Ada

Ada provides good support for implementing modules specified as functions, machines, or types. Functions correspond to Ada subprograms, machines correspond to packages with subprogram and exception declarations in the public part, and abstract data types correspond to packages with a private type declaration in the public part in addition to subprogram, exception, and constant declarations. If operations are used by concurrent processes, then subprograms are replaced by task entries for protection against interference between concurrent activations. All of these patterns have been illustrated in the airline reservation system example earlier in this chapter.

Implementing generators in Ada is less convenient. We have used a generic procedure with a procedure parameter to represent generators. The generic procedure parameter represents the body of the loop that is to be executed once for each element of the generated sequence. This is a powerful technique,

```
generator g(y1: t1; ... ; ym: tm) generate T1, ... , Tn is
  -- Declarations of g.
begin
  -- Statements for calculating e1, ... , en.
  generate(e1, ... , en);
  -- More statements, possibly containing "generate".
end g;
```

FIGURE 5.38
Template for Defining Generators in Ada

which can support the implementation of recursive generators (illustrated in the B_tree type shown in Appendix F). The efficiency of this technique can be improved by using the predefined Ada pragma inline for the generic procedure parameter. This expands the definition of the loop body in-line, eliminating the procedure call overhead for invoking the loop body on each iteration of the loop.

The biggest drawback for this technique is that the resulting code is hard to read, especially for nested loops. Because the loop body procedure must be in the same scope as the state variables of the loop, its definition must be nested inside the subprogram containing the loop. Nested loops lead to deeper levels of nested subprogram definitions, as illustrated by the notify operation of the reservation_set type. This problem can be cured by a preprocessor that applies the transformation explained next.

We can extend the Ada loop syntax to accommodate generators as follows. A template for defining generators is shown in Fig. 5.38. Such a template is expanded into the Ada definition shown in Fig. 5.39.

```
generic
  with procedure generate(x1: T1; ... ; xn: Tn);
procedure g(y1: t1; ... ; ym: tm) is
  -- Declarations of g.
begin
  -- Statements for calculating e1, ... , en.
  generate(e1, ... , en);
  -- More statements, possibly containing "generate".
end g;
```

FIGURE 5.39
Expansion of Generator Definition Template

```
for x1, ... , xn in g(e1, ... , em)
loop
   -- Sequence of statements in the loop body.
end loop;
```

FIGURE 5.40
Template for Generator Invocation

A template for invoking generators is shown in Fig. 5.40. The values of the index variables x1, ... , xn are supplied by the generator. The expressions e1, ... , em are the actual parameters to the generator g. This syntax is the same as an ordinary Ada for loop, except that more than one index variable is allowed and the sequence of values for the index variables is specified using a generator instead of a range expression. The Ada for loop

```
for i in a .. b loop ... end loop;
```

is equivalent to the generator-driven loop

```
for i in scan_up(a, b) loop ... end loop;
```

if the generator scan_up meets the specification shown in Fig. 5.41.

The expansion of a generator invocation into Ada involves the declaration of an auxiliary local procedure representing the body of the loop. The preprocessor should transform a generator invocation with the form shown in Fig. 5.40 into the Ada block statement shown in Fig. 5.42.

A tool for automatically applying the transformation just described allows the source code for the operations remove#2 and notify for the reservation_set type of the airline reservation example to look very close to the algorithm sketches shown in Figs. 4.18 and 4.19, rather than the less readable forms shown in Fig. 5.30. An implementation of such a tool in terms of the UNIX m4 macro processor is given in Appendix G.

```
FUNCTION scan_up
   MESSAGE(x y: integer) GENERATE(s: sequence{integer})
      WHERE s = interval@sequence{integer}(a, b)
END
```

FIGURE 5.41
Generator used in Standard Ada FOR Loop

```
declare
  procedure loop_body(x1: T1; ... ; xn: Tn) is
  begin
    -- Sequence of statements in the loop body.
  end loop_body;
  procedure execute_loop is new g(loop_body);
begin
  execute_loop(el, ... , em); -- Translation of loop.
end;
```

FIGURE 5.42
Expanded Generator Invocation

5.8 Related Research

The current state of reliability models for software that support statistical estimates of failure rates is described in [15, 17]. Criteria for when to stop testing are discussed in [16]. A well known approach to determining the adequacy of test cases based on the criterion of detecting all elementary program mutations is described in [5, 13]. Another approach to assessing adequacy of test data is [22, 23]. The use of symbolic evaluation for software validation is described in [7]. Some research on using specifications for testing implementations of abstract data types is reported in [11]. Work on testing and verification of protocols can be found in [4, 20]. A discussion of testing real-time systems can be found in [6].

Exercises

1. Calculate and simplify the weakest precondition wp(P, G) for the following programs and goals:

   a. P = "x := x + 1";"
   G = "y = x^2 + 2 * x + 1"

   b. P = "i := i + 1; s := s + a[i];"
   G = "s = SUM(k: nat SUCH THAT k <= i :: a[i])"

   c. P = "if a mod 2 = 0 then a := a / 2; b := b * 2; else p := p + b; a := a - 1; end if;"
   G = "p + a * b = x * y"

2. Find a bounding function for the following loop:

```
if b > a then t := a; a := b; b := t; end if;
while b > 0 loop
   t := a mod b; a := b; b := t;
end loop;
```

3. Find a bounding function for the following recursive program:

```
function f(x: binary_tree) return binary_tree is
begin
   if x = nil then return x;
      else return make(make(f(left(x)), f(right(x))),
                       make(f(right(x)), f(left(x))))
end f;
```

The binary_tree data type is specified in Section 5.7.4.

4. Develop an Ada while loop to achieve the postcondition z = factorial(x) & x = *x based on the invariant factorial(x) = z * factorial(a). Include the initialization for the loop and give a bounding function. The concept factorial is the usual one:

```
CONCEPT factorial(x: nat) VALUE(y: nat)
   WHERE y = PRODUCT(n: nat SUCH THAT 1 <= n <= x :: n)
```

Projects

1. Implement any of the architectural designs from the projects in Chapter 4.
2. Design and implement a program that calculates weakest preconditions for all loop-free Ada programs.

References

1. F. Bauer, B. Moller, H. Partsch, and P. Pepper, "Formal Program Construction by Transformations—Computer-Aided, Intuition-Guided Programming," *IEEE Transactions on Software Engineering 15*, 2 (Feb. 1989), 165–180.

2. J. Bicevskis, J. Borozovs, U. Straujums, A. Zarins, and E. Miller, Jr., "SMOTL—A System to Construct Samples for Data Processing Program Debugging," *IEEE Transactions on Software Engineering SE–5*, 1 (Jan. 1979), 60–66.

3. R. S. Boyer and J. S. Moore, *A Computational Logic*, Academic Press, 1979.

4. E. Brinksma, *A Tutorial on LOTOS, Protocol Specification, Testing, and Verification*, Elsevier Science Publishers B. V., 1986.

5. T. A. Budd, R. A. DeMillo, R. J. Lipton, and F. G. Sayward, "Theoretical and Empirical Studies on Using Program Mutation to Test the Functional Correctness of Programs," *Proceedings of the ACM Symposium on Principles of Programming Languages*, 1980, 220–233.

6. M. Chandrasekharan, B. Dasarathy, and Z. Kishimoto, "Requirements-Based Testing of Real-Time Systems: Modeling for Testability," *IEEE Computer 18*, 4 (Apr. 1985), 71–80.

7. L. Clarke and D. Richardson, "Symbolic Evaluation—An Aid to Testing and Verification," in *Software Validation*, North-Holland, 1984, 141–166.

8. E. W. Dijkstra, *A Discipline of Programming*, Prentice Hall, Englewood Cliffs, NJ, 1976.

9. D. Good, "Mechanical Proofs about Computer Programs," Technical Report #41, Institute for Computing Science, University of Texas at Austin, March 1981.

10. D. Gries, *The Science of Programming*, Springer Verlag, 1981.

11. I. Hayes, "Specification Directed Module Testing," *IEEE Transactions on Software Engineering SE–12*, 1 (Jan. 1986), 124–133.

12. T. Hickey and J. Cohen, "Automating Program Analysis," *Journal of the ACM 35*, 1 (Jan. 1988), 185–220.

13. W. E. Howden, "Weak Mutation Testing and Completeness of Test Sets," *IEEE Transactions on Software Engineering SE–8*, 4 (July 1982), 371–379.

14. W. Howden, *Functional Program Testing and Analysis*, McGraw-Hill, New York, 1987.

15. J. Musa, A. Iannino, and K. Okumoto, *Software Reliability: Measurement, Prediction, Application*, McGraw-Hill, New York, 1987.

16. J. Musa and A. Ackerman, "Quantifying Software Validation: When to Stop Testing?," *IEEE Software 6*, 3 (May 1989), 19–27.

17. J. Musa, "Tools for Measuring Software Reliability," *IEEE Spectrum 26*, 2 (Feb. 1989), 39–42.

18. D. L. Parnas and P. C. Clements, "A Rational Design Process: How and Why to Fake It," *IEEE Transactions on Software Engineering SE–12*, 2 (Feb. 1986), 251–257.

19. R. Renka, ed., *Collected Algorithms from ACM*, IMSL, Houston, TX.

20. D. Sidhu and T. Leung, "Formal Methods for Protocol Testing: A Detailed Study," *IEEE Transactions on Software Engineering 15*, 4 (Apr. 1989), 413–426.

21. H. Tagaki, "Queuing Analysis of Polling Models," *ACM Computing Surveys 20*, 1 (Mar. 1988), 5–28.

22. E. J. Weyuker, "Assessing Test Data Adequacy Through Program Inference," *Transactions on Programming Languages and Systems 5*, 4 (Oct. 1983), 641–655.

23. S. Zweben and J. Gourlay, "On the Adequacy of Weyuker's Test Data Adequacy Axioms," *IEEE Transactions on Software Engineering 15*, 4 (Apr. 1989), 496–500.

6

Evolution

The process of changing a software system is called *evolution* or *maintenance*. We prefer the term evolution because software does not wear out. In ordinary English usage, maintenance refers to effort spent on keeping a system functioning according to its original design and implementation. Software evolution deliberately introduces changes rather than reversing or preventing unwanted deviations from the original implementation. We take the term evolution to include changes in response to new requirements, performance improvements, repairs for design faults, changes to accommodate new operating environments, and changes to accommodate new versions of the tools used to generate the system (such as compilers).

When a large software system does not meet the needs of its users, it is usually cheaper to change the existing system rather than to develop a completely new system. Evolution accounts for more than half of the total cost of most large software systems, which typically have long lifetimes and are continually being changed. Software systems are changed for the following reasons.

1. **Requirements for additional functionality, improved performance, or new configurations.** Such requirements can be part of a phased delivery plan, or they can be the result of changing external circumstances, such as new external systems, new competitive pressures, or new hardware. This category of changes cannot be avoided.

2. **Modifications to existing requirements.** Such modifications are often sparked by user experience with the previous version of the system, which produces a better understanding of the problem and pinpoints inadequacies

in the original requirements. The incidence of changes in this category can be reduced by improved validation procedures for requirements.

3. **Errors in the existing design or implementation.** Such changes are sparked by problem reports from the users, and correspond to cases where the actual behavior of the system differs from the behavior described in the user manuals. The incidence of changes in this category can be reduced by better verification procedures for design and implementation.

4. **Excessive complexity in the design and implementation.** Changes to simplify the internal structure of the system and to bring it into correspondence with the structure of the externally visible interface are motivated by the desire to reduce the cost of future changes, and are sparked by the people responsible for evolving the system. Such changes should not affect the externally visible functional behavior of the system if they are made correctly, although they can affect its performance. The incidence of changes in this category can be reduced by better predictions of which design decisions are likely to change, and system decompositions that encapsulate such decisions in single modules.

The first two categories of changes involve reconsideration of all stages of the software development cycle, from requirements analysis to implementation; the last two kinds of changes involve only the stages from architectural design to implementation.

6.1 Goals

The main goal of software evolution is to make the software system more valuable to its users. The goals of the organization responsible for evolving a software system (the evolver) are to design, implement, and document each change correctly; to verify the correctness of the change; to keep the cost of the change low; and to control the cost of future changes.

The goals in determining which changes to make are similar to those of the initial requirements analysis. The customer and the evolver must consider tradeoffs between the cost of making a change and the added value it will bring to the customer to reach an agreement on what is to be done. The evolver's understanding of the problem domain and the goals of the customer must often be refined in this process, guided by problem reports or change requests from the users. Factors affecting what should be changed include the priorities of the customer, the cost of the change, the time it will take to deliver the new version to the users, and the amount of retraining needed for the users to adapt to the new version of the system.

A change must be made correctly and documented accurately to be useful to the customers and users. Changes are more error prone than the initial development, and require especially careful attention to quality assurance activities at all stages. Incorrect changes are often caused by interactions that are not apparent to the evolver, so that it is necessary to test the entire new version of the system and not just the part that was changed. Thorough testing of the entire system is especially critical if accurate specification and design documents are not available, because lack of accurate specification and design information increases the chances that the evolver may neglect some parts of the system affected by a change.

A goal shared by the evolver and the developer is to make the system as simple as possible. Programs should work correctly and should appear to work correctly to someone reading them for the first time. This implies that the structure of a program should correspond to its function: each part should have a single, clearly identified purpose. The designer should keep related parts together and separate unrelated parts of the code to achieve a coherent structure that helps programmers find the parts of the system affecting a given aspect of its observable behavior, and makes each aspect of the implementation easier to understand.

The goals of reducing the cost of the current change and reducing the cost of future changes conflict with each other. The cost of a single change is minimized if the evolver changes the smallest possible part of the source code and does nothing else. Such a change invalidates the requirements and design documents and can have disastrous effects on the cost of future changes. Without current requirements and design documents, changes must be based on the bare code. In such cases, the evolver must create partial reconstructions of the requirements and design information using the code and inspired guesswork, increasing the work required as well as the probability of introducing errors by inadvertently violating some undocumented restrictions vital for correct operation of the system. Such "quick and dirty" changes also complicate the behavior of the modules in the the system, and may introduce mismatches between their form and function, making the system more difficult to understand and modify. Eventually this leads to a point where the implementation of the system can no longer be understood and must be completely replaced. This conflict between goals and its economic consequences should be clearly understood by contractors and project managers. Short-sighted policies can successfully meet the next tight deadline at the expense of introducing the seeds of accelerated "software rot," which can multiply future costs.

Another goal of the evolver is to manage and keep track of the released versions of the system. Some customers may not buy every release of the system, so that it is necessary to keep track of trouble reports and corresponding repairs in evolving multiversion systems. To provide a stable and predictable system to the users, the evolver should release new versions of the system at fixed intervals that are not too frequent. The timing of new releases should be predictable to let users make meaningful plans. An exception to this guideline is early distribution of bug fixes, which may be required to solve pressing needs of customers. Such unplanned distributions should be infrequent if stringent quality control procedures are followed.

6.2 Basic Concepts

Most tasks in software evolution are similar to those in the initial development process. The main difference between evolution and the initial development of a software system is that a nonempty previous version of the system is available during evolution. It is often less work to change an existing system than to redevelop the entire system because a large part of the previous version can usually be reused in the new version. However, making changes is generally more difficult than developing new software. The extra difficulty stems from the tasks of learning how the previous version works, and from finding the parts that must be changed.

The previous version of the system ideally should include current versions of all the documents associated with the initial development, including requirements, functional specifications, module specifications, code, test cases, and manuals. The requirements, specifications, and design documents can be used to help the evolver learn about the previous version and to identify parts that are impacted by a proposed change, provided that these documents have been kept up to date. These documents are especially useful if the relationships between corresponding components of these documents are maintained in mechanically processable form. The components of each document serve as justifications for the more detailed decisions in the corresponding components of the next document. A component can be used as is if its justification remains unchanged, and must be reevaluated and possibly adjusted if its justification has been changed. The specification and design documents also record dependencies between components in the same document. A change in a component can require changes in the other components related to it via dependencies. Keeping track of the dependencies can help identify the parts of the system that may be affected by a proposed change. All parts of the documentation must be kept up to date to support this approach.

The problem of determining the impact of a change is much more severe if only the implementation is available, without current versions of the requirements, specifications, or design documents. Unfortunately, many existing systems do not have a complete set of these documents, and the available documents other than the code are often obsolete, especially for older sys-

tems. In such cases, the higher level information must be partially recon-
structed to determine the impact of a change, and to design the new version. In
practice this is usually done informally, and may not be explicitly recorded.
The process of reconstructing high-level descriptions from code is very difficult
and error prone, and there is no known method for checking when it has been
completely carried out. It can be extremely difficult to correctly modify undocumented systems in practice. If no documentation other than uncommented
code is available, the customer may be faced with the choice of either using the
system as it is, or replacing it with a newly developed system. A system with
no modifications is better than a broken system that is continuously being
changed in an attempt to correct poorly understood malfunctions. A frozen system is stable, so that users may learn what its bugs are and how to work around
them. Continuous modification of a poorly understood system is likely to produce unpredictable new bugs as fast as the old ones get fixed, making it impossible for the users to rely on any aspect of the system.

It is dangerous to change a system whose design cannot be understood
because any change is likely to inadvertently introduce faults due to unknown
interactions between different parts of the system. Modern design practice
emphasizes modular design to minimize such problems, but many of the older
systems in use today were built without regard for such considerations. In the
worst case, which sometimes arises for very old systems, even the source code
may have been lost, so that the only form of the system available may be an
executable core image. Analyzing machine code without any comments, symbolic names, or design documentation is extremely difficult, and may be more
expensive than developing a completely new system.

If an undocumented system must be changed and cannot be completely
redeveloped, then it may be necessary to incrementally reconstruct the documentation and to restructure the worst parts of the system to make them tractable. This process is sometimes called *reverse engineering*. In such cases
careful record keeping, strict version control procedures, and extensive testing
activities are essential to avoid breaking the system. Some useful common
sense guidelines for this process are:

1. Keep track of changes to the system, and incrementally redesign the parts
    of the system with the largest numbers of problem reports.

2. Keep the effort spent on restructuring proportional to the effort spent on
    making enhancements and repairs.

6.2.1 Tracing

The developer should record the links between different levels of the system, as
expressed in the requirements, specifications, designs, and implementations.
Traditionally, comments have been used to informally bridge the gap between

levels of abstraction and to supply higher-level justifications for lower-level details. Formalizing these relationships enables software tools to help locate the regions of a system impacted by a proposed change.

6.2.2 Preventative Evolution

Some requirements changes require restructuring of the system. The structure of the system must be kept consistent with its function. Interfaces must be adapted to correspond to simple and coherent abstractions. Gradual redesign is needed to keep the system understandable and to keep the cost of future changes from increasing. Consequences of not doing this are increasing reliability problems and gradual loss of control over the system.

In cases where the system structure has been degraded by uncontrolled changes, it is necessary to change the structure of the system to make it correspond to the current behavior, and to reconstruct accurate requirements, specification, and design documents. Sometimes the only way to understand a poorly structured system is to simplify and incrementally restructure it by applying transformations that do not change the meaning of the program, but do simplify its structure. Some of these transformations, such as pretty printing, affect only the appearance of the code on the listing. Other transformations, such as factoring the code and transforming it to eliminate *goto* statements, can change the execution of the program.

Another activity that is part of restructuring is reconstructing specifications that have been lost or have become obsolete. This process is known as reverse engineering. At the current state of the art, most of the available tools for doing reverse engineering involve deriving surface level properties of the actual code. Examples of tools in this category are cross-reference generators, flowchart generators, and module dependency diagram generators. Some more powerful theoretical techniques include tools for calculating weakest preconditions and reconstructing loop invariants. Weakest preconditions and loop invariants are explained in Section 5.7.

6.2.3 Evolvability Requirements

A common goal in design is to produce a structure that is easy to modify. One way to make this goal more specific is to say that any change that can be easily described by a user should be easy to make in the design. Such a goal can be made measurable by requiring the mean time for the evolution programmers to locate and identify a set of artificially inserted bugs to be less than a specified time interval for a specified fraction of the cases. Such statistical measures based on actual experiments in program modification appear to be the best available at the current time. This is not very satisfactory, because it does not provide any specific guidelines for how to design a system that is easy to modify or how to improve a design if it is discovered to be the source of frequent change requests. The general principle of information hiding appears to be the best known conceptual tool for improving ease of modification, but more research is needed to provide a solid formal basis and objective measures for this intuitive idea.

6.2.4 Achieving Fast Repairs

All realistic systems are subject to failures. A repair is a change to a system aimed at correcting an observed failure. Some systems have stringent availability requirements, expressed as bounds on the mean time to repair. The time to repair is the time interval between the occurrence of an observed software failure and the time a repair correcting the fault is installed in the working system.

A strategy for achieving a low mean time to repair is to develop a stock of spare parts for the software components in a system. This involves implementing each module in several different ways. The cost of multiple implementation is not as high as may appear at first, because the availability of several versions can make testing easier, by looking for circumstances where the behaviors of the different versions disagree.

6.3 Procedures and Guidelines

The tasks involved in changing a software system are the following:

1. Understand the problem with the current version of the system.
2. Define the requirements for the change and the intended new behavior.
3. Locate the parts of the system documents affected by the change.
4. Design and implement the new version of the system.
5. Check all changes and test the new version of the system.

   A suggested procedure for making a change to a software system is:

1. Start with the old requirements document, and identify the parts that are added, deleted, and changed.
2. Trace the correspondence links to the next level.
3. Make the indicated changes, and if you have not reached the detailed code, repeat the previous step.

4. Test the results.

5. If errors are detected, fix them and repeat the process from the step that caused the error.

At each stage in the process, you should find and review the justifications for the design decisions impacted by the proposed change.

6.4 Case Study: Airline Reservation System

We illustrate the procedures and guidelines of the previous section in terms of the airline reservation example developed in previous chapters. The changes we will consider address the following two problem reports:

1. The frequency of transactions has increased dramatically, and a single processor can no longer handle the work load with acceptable performance.

2. The current design of the system provides no way for the airline manager to review the current status of the flight schedule in support of decisions about possible future schedule changes.

We consider the steps involved in making each of these changes, assuming that you are familiar with the initial version of the case study, as developed in Chapters 2 through 5.

6.4.1 Partitioning for Concurrency

This section considers the modifications required to solve the first of the two problem reports just introduced.

Analysis. The first problem corresponds to a modified performance constraint. The modified part of the goal hierarchy is shown in Fig. 6.1. The new

---

C2: **The responses of the airline reservation system must be fast enough not to irritate the customers of the travel agents.**

    C2.4: **The system must be able to handle 50,000 reservations per day.**

FIGURE 6.1
Modified Requirement

requirement reflects an expected transaction rate five times larger than the maximum required for the initial version of the system. The customer has already found that the current single-processor implementation cannot keep up with the work load. We examine the current design and determine that a speedup of a factor of five cannot be achieved by choosing faster algorithms and data structures on the existing hardware configuration: Some small improvements are possible, but the general classes of algorithms and data structures are already the best known for the class of problems.

We conclude that the new performance requirement is impossible to meet without introducing some concurrency. The slowest operations involve accesses to secondary storage, so that the new configuration will need to have multiple disks operating concurrently, which should be driven by independent processors if we want our solution to scale up. Because the existing system cannot meet the needs of daily operations in an expanded business, the customer agrees to bear the cost of additional hardware, and authorizes the adaptation of the software to a multiprocessor system, since this enables easy future expansion.

In what follows, we assume that a multiprocessor implementation of Ada is available that is capable of executing concurrent Ada tasks on different processors.

Impact of the Proposed Change.   The proposed change does not affect the functional specification at all, since the performance constraints are soft, and do not appear in the postconditions of the commands as hard real-time constraints would. A *hard real-time constraint* is a deadline for producing each response to a particular command that must be met under all possible operating conditions for the behavior of the system to be considered correct. The performance requirements in our case study are aggregate throughput constraints that do not impose hard bounds on response times for individual commands.

To determine the impact of the change on the architectural design, we must settle on an implementation strategy. The performance bottleneck in the system is the central airline reservation task. We decide to partition this task into a set of tasks that can run independently. This can be done by partitioning the state of the airline reservation system into disjoint subspaces, and assigning responsibility for managing each subspace to a separate task. This strategy is appropriate in this case because concurrency is introduced to achieve increased speed, rather than increased reliability or availability, which would require replication rather than disjoint partitioning.

We decide to partition the state of the airline reservation system based on disjoint sets of flight ids whose boundaries are determined by a hashing function. Flight ids are strings, so we can use a standard reusable component to do the hashing.

The proposed change does not change the set of commands available to the users, so that the input and output functions remain the same. The command interpreters will have to change slightly, to use the hashing function to choose which task should serve each particular command. The airline reservation system task is already defined as a task type, so that its implementation will not have to change. The change will be in the airline reservation package, which now will declare an array of tasks rather than a single task.

This change is relatively inexpensive to implement, because it does not require the addition of any new modules other than existing reusable components, and because it affects only a small number of modules in the system. It is expected to require a moderate amount of effort since some new logical structure has to be introduced.

Design and Implementation.   The main effect on the architectural design is to make the airline reservation system into a generic module rather than an individual one. This change is shown in in Fig. 6.2. The only change is to add a generic parameter representing an instance id that will act as a hash index. This definition says that the `airline_reservation_system` is a generic module, but does not say how many instances are actually used.

We also have to decide how many components to put into the partition. Because the performance requirement has increased by a factor of five, and the original design was adequate for a single processor with a small safety margin, we partition the system into five independent tasks. This decision is recorded in Fig. 6.3. The instance declaration defines which instances of a generic module are used in the design of the system. This completes the modifications to the abstract architectural design.

The concrete architectural design must also be modified to route requests to the proper component of the partition. The required modifications are shown in Figs. 6.4 and 6.5. Working out the specification exposes an incompletely thought out aspect of the original implementation strategy: Not all of the operations operate on a single `flight_id`, as was implicitly assumed initially. The `find_flights` operation involves a search throughout the `flight_schedule`, and can potentially involve `flights` in all of the proposed partitions. Because

---

```
|MACHINE airline_reservation_system_design_2_1{i: nat}
  INHERIT airline_reservation_system_design2
END
```

FIGURE 6.2
Updated Airline Reservation System Design

```
INSTANCE airline_reservation_instances(i: nat) EXPORT partitions
  WHERE airline_reservation_instances(i) =
    airline_reservation_system_design_2_1(i)
  FOREACH(i: nat SUCH THAT 0 <= i < partitions)
    -- Declares 5 instances of the
    -- airline reservation system machine.

  CONCEPT partitions: nat WHERE partitions = 5
END
```

FIGURE 6.3
Instance Declarations for the Partition

this is a frequent operation and we are concerned about performance, we would like to avoid scanning all of the partitions. Scanning all of the partitions could introduce significant delays due to the need to synchronize with all of the airline_reservation_system tasks.

We decide instead to partition only the reservation_set part of the state, and to replicate the entire flight_schedule in each of the airline_reservation_system tasks. Because the flight_schedule is much smaller than the reservation_set, and is updated rarely, this is a reasonable choice. This choice allows each invocation of the find_flights operation to access only one of the airline_reservation_system tasks, and allows requests from different travel_agents to be handled by different airline_reservation_system tasks, which can be running on different processors.

We would prefer not to lock out other operations in the middle of an update to the multiple instances of the flight_schedule, since that could cause some lengthy delays. We consider whether temporary discrepancies between the copies of the flight schedule during the add_flight and drop_flight operations could cause any problems. None of the other operations involve more than one instance of the flight_schedule, so that no data inconsistencies can be observed if another operation runs while some but not all copies of the flight_schedule have been updated. Because flights will be dropped only after passengers have been notified well in advance, and the exact time at which the addition of a new flight takes effect does not affect the travel_agents very much, there does not appear to be any reason to insist that adding and dropping flights have an atomic effect on all of the copies of the flight_schedule. To prevent interference between concurrent instances of the add_flight and drop_flight operations, we define the atomic transaction command, which makes the airline_manager wait

```
MACHINE travel_agent_2_1(id: nat)
  INHERIT final_travel_agent(id) HIDE interpret_command
| IMPORT partitions FROM airline_reservation_instances(0)

  MESSAGE interpret_command(command: string)
     -- Command from travel agent's keyboard.
    WHEN is_find_flights(edit(command), origin, destination)
|     CHOOSE(index: nat SUCH THAT index = id MOD partitions)
      SEND find_flights(origin destination: airport)
|       TO airline_reservation_system_2_1(index)
    WHEN is_reserve(edit(command), a, i, d, p)
|     CHOOSE(index: nat SUCH THAT index = hash(i) MOD partitions)
      SEND reserve(a: agent_id, i: flight_id, d: date,
                   p: passenger )
|       TO airline_reservation_system_2_1(index)
    WHEN is_cancel(edit(command), i, d, p)
|     CHOOSE(index: nat SUCH THAT index = hash(i) MOD partitions)
      SEND cancel(i: flight_id, d: date, p: passenger)
|       TO airline_reservation_system_2_1(index)
    WHEN is_notify(edit(command), a, i, d)
|     CHOOSE(index: nat SUCH THAT index = hash(i) MOD partitions)
      SEND notify(a: agent_id, i: flight_id, d: date)
|       TO airline_reservation_system_2_1(index)
    OTHERWISE REPLY(s: string) WHERE s = "command not recognized"

| CONCEPT hash(i: flight_id) VALUE(n: nat)
END
```

FIGURE 6.4
Modified Travel Agent Module Specification

until all copies of the flight_schedule have completed the most recent change before starting the next change. Atomic transactions in Spec constrain the order in which modules accept messages, as discussed in Section 3.9.7. There is only a single airline manager interface, and the add_flight and drop_flight messages give acknowledgements, so this is easy to implement in Ada using the rendezvous mechanism.

We change the airline reservation system module to declare an array of tasks rather than a single task, as shown in Fig. 6.6. This change is straightforward. The implementations of the airline_reservation_system tasks are changed to include an initialization section for recording the partition_id for each instance of the task type, and a body is added to the

```
MACHINE airline_manager_2_1
  INHERIT final_airline_manager HIDE interpret_command
  IMPORT partitions FROM airline_reservation_instances{0}

  STATE(replies_pending: nat)
  INVARIANT replies_pending <= partitions
  INITIALLY replies_pending = 0

  MESSAGE interpret_command(command: string)
      -- Command from airline manager's keyboard.
    WHEN is_add_flight(edit(command), i, price, origin,
                        destination, departure, arrival,
                        capacity )
      SEND add_flight(i: flight_id, price: money,
                      origin destination: airport,
                      departure arrival: time, capacity: nat )
        TO airline_reservation_system_design_2_1{index}
      FOREACH(index: nat SUCH THAT
              index = hash(i) MOD partitions )
      TRANSITION replies_pending = partitions
    WHEN is_drop_flight(edit(command), i)
      SEND drop_flight(i: flight_id)
        TO airline_reservation_system_design_2_1{index}
      FOREACH(index: nat SUCH THAT
              index = hash(i) MOD partitions )
      TRANSITION replies_pending = partitions
    WHEN is_new_fare(edit(command), i, price)
      SEND new_fare(i: flight_id, price: money)
        TO airline_reservation_system_design_2_1{index}
      FOREACH(index: nat SUCH THAT
              index = hash(i) MOD partitions )
      TRANSITION replies_pending = partitions
    OTHERWISE REPLY(s: string) WHERE s = "command not recognized"

  MESSAGE done
    WHEN replies_pending = 1
      SEND(s: string) TO display WHERE s = "Done."
      TRANSITION replies_pending = 0
    OTHERWISE TRANSITION replies_pending = *replies_pending - 1

  TRANSACTION command =
    IF WHEN replies_pending = 0 -> interpret_command |
       WHEN replies_pending > 0 -> done FI
  -- The atomic transaction prevents the next interpret_command
  -- message from being accepted until all of the
  -- replies_pending have been received.
END
```

FIGURE 6.5
Modified Airline Manager Module Specification

403

FIGURE 6.6
Updated Airline Reservation System Package Specification

```
with bounded_sequence_pkg;
with date_pkg; use date_pkg;
with concrete_types_pkg; use concrete_types_pkg;
package airline_reservation_system_pkg is
  -- Generic instantiations for interface types.
  package flight_sequence_pkg is
    new bounded_sequence_pkg(flight_description);
  package reservation_sequence_pkg is
    new bounded_sequence_pkg(reservation);
  use flight_sequence_pkg; use reservation_sequence_pkg;
  subtype flight_sequence is flight_sequence_pkg.sequence;
  subtype reservation_sequence is
    reservation_sequence_pkg.sequence;

  -- Exceptions.
  flight_exists: exception;
  reservation_exists: exception;
  no_such_flight: exception;
  no_reservation: exception;
  no_seat: exception;

  task type airline_reservation_system_type is
    -- Travel agent interface.
    entry find_flights(origin, destination: in airport;
                       fs: out flight_sequence );
    entry reserve(a: in agent_id; i: in flight_id;
                  d: in date; p: in passenger );
    entry cancel(i: in flight_id; d: in date; p: in passenger);
    entry notify(a: in agent_id; i: in flight_id; d: in date;
                 rs: out reservation_sequence );

    -- Airline manager interface.
    entry add_flight(i: in flight_id; price: in money;
                     origin, destination: in airport;
                     departure, arrival: in flight_time;
                     capacity: in natural );
    entry drop_flight(i: in flight_id);
    entry new_fare(i: in flight_id; price: in money);

    -- Temporals.
    entry retire;

    -- Internal initialization interface.
    entry init(index: in natural);
  end airline_reservation_system_type;
```

```
for airline_reservation_system_type'storage_size use 800_000;
-- Our compiler's default stack size for tasks is
-- too small for this application.  We have to use a task type
-- to specify a larger limit in an Ada representation clause.

partitions: constant natural := 5;
airline_reservation_system: array(0 .. partitions - 1) of
                            airline_reservation_system_type;
end airline_reservation_system_pkg;
```

airline_reservation_system_pkg module to invoke the initialization
entries for all of the tasks in the array. The partition_id is incorporated
into the names of the files representing the states of the individual tasks, to
ensure that the files managed by different tasks are disjoint. This prevents
interference between the concurrent tasks managing the different partitions.
The implementation of the retire task must also be changed to update all of
the airline_reservation_system tasks. These changes are shown in
Fig. 6.7.

The interpret_command procedures of the travel_agent_pkg
and airline_manager_pkg modules must be changed to call the appropriate instance of the airline_reservation_system_type task type, as
shown in Figs. 6.8 and 6.9. The find_flights command interacts with only a
single copy of the flight_schedule, which is chosen based on the

FIGURE 6.7
Updated Airline Reservation System Package Body

```
  with text_pkg; use text_pkg; -- Defines text_pkg_instance.
  with flight_schedule_pkg; use flight_schedule_pkg;
  with reservation_set_pkg; use reservation_set_pkg;
  with date_pkg; use date_pkg;
  with calendar; use calendar;
package body airline_reservation_system_pkg is
  use text_pkg_instance;  -- Defines the type text.

  -- Local subprogram declarations.
  procedure make_reservations(r: in out reservation_set;
                              i: in flight_id; d: date;
                              a: in agent_id;
                              rs: out reservation_sequence );
  procedure make_flights(s: in out flight_schedule;
                         o, d: airport;
                         fs: out flight_sequence );
```

FIGURE 6.7 (continued)

```
procedure retire_reservations(rs: in out reservation_set);
task retire_demon;

task body airline_reservation_system_type is
  -- State variables.
  schedule: flight_schedule;
  reservations: reservation_set;
  partition_id: text;

  -- Temporary variables.
  has, exists: boolean;
  b, c: natural;

begin

  -- Initialize.
  accept init(index: in natural) do
    declare
      s: constant string := natural'image(index);
    begin
      partition_id := text_string(s(2 .. s'last));
    end;
  end init;
  open(text_string("s") & partition_id, schedule);
  open(text_string("r") & partition_id, reservations);

  -- Start operation.
  loop  -- Forever.
    begin  -- Exception handler frame.
      select

      -- Travel agent interface.
        accept find_flights(origin, destination: in airport;
                            fs: out flight_sequence ) do
          make_flights(schedule, origin, destination, fs);
        end find_flights;
      or
        accept reserve(a: in agent_id; i: in flight_id;
                       d: in date; p: in passenger ) do
          holds(p, i, d, reservations, has);
          if has then raise reservation_exists; end if;
          begin
            bookings(i, d, reservations, b);
            capacity(i, schedule, c);
            if b = c then raise no_seat; end if;
            add(a, i, d, p, reservations);
```

```
      exception
        when flight_schedule_pkg.no_such_flight =>
            raise airline_reservation_system_pkg.
                    no_such_flight;
      end;
   end reserve;
or
   accept cancel(i: in flight_id; d: in date;
                   p: in passenger ) do
     member(i, schedule, exists);
     if not exists then
        raise airline_reservation_system_pkg.
                no_such_flight; end if;
     holds(p, i, d, reservations, has);
     if has then remove(i, d, p, reservations);
        else raise no_reservation;
     end if;
   end cancel;
or
   accept notify(a: in agent_id; i: in flight_id;
                   d: in date;
                   rs: out reservation_sequence ) do
     member(i, schedule, exists);
     if not exists then
        raise airline_reservation_system_pkg.
                no_such_flight; end if;
     make_reservations(reservations, i, d, a, rs);
   end notify;
or

  -- Airline manager interface.
   accept add_flight(i: in flight_id; price: in money;
                     origin, destination: in airport;
                     departure, arrival: in flight_time;
                     capacity: in natural ) do
     member(i, schedule, exists);
     if exists then raise flight_exists; end if;
     add(i, price, origin, destination, departure,
        arrival, capacity, schedule );
   end add_flight;
or
   accept drop_flight(i: in flight_id) do
     member(i, schedule, exists);
     if exists then remove(i, schedule);
     else raise airline_reservation_system_pkg.
                no_such_flight;
     end if;
   end drop_flight;
```

FIGURE 6.7 (continued)

```
        or
          accept new_fare(i: in flight_id; price: in money) do
            begin
              new_fare(i, price, schedule);
            exception
              when flight_schedule_pkg.no_such_flight =>
                raise airline_reservation_system_pkg.
                          no_such_flight;
            end;
          end new_fare;
        or

          -- Temporals.
          accept retire do
            retire_reservations(reservations);
          end retire;
        end select;
      exception
        when others => null;
          -- Exceptions are handled in the modules
          -- invoking the task entries.
      end;  -- Exception handler frame.
    end loop;
  end airline_reservation_system_type;

  procedure make_flights(s: in out flight_schedule;
                         o, d: airport;
                         fs: out flight_sequence ) is
    -- Post: scan(fs) = generate_flights(s, o, d).
    fs1: flight_sequence;
  procedure produce_flight(fd: in flight_description) is
  begin -- Invariant: scan(fs1) = *generate_flights(s, o, d).
    add(fd, fs1);
  end produce_flight;
  procedure generate_flights is
    new find_flights(produce_flight);
  begin
    fs1 := create;
    generate_flights(s, o, d);
    fs := fs1;
  end make_flights;

  procedure make_reservations(r: in out reservation_set;
                              i: in flight_id; d: date;
                              a: in agent_id;
                              rs: out reservation_sequence ) is
```

```
      -- Post: scan(rs) = generate_reservations(s, o, d).
      rs1: reservation_sequence;
   procedure produce_reservation(res: in reservation) is
   begin
      -- Invariant: scan(rs1) = *generate_reservations(s, o, d).
      add(res, rs1);
   end produce_reservation;
   procedure generate_reservations is
      new notify(produce_reservation);
 begin
   rs1 := create;
   generate_reservations(a, i, d, r);
   rs := rs1;
 end make_reservations;


procedure retire_reservations(rs: in out reservation_set) is
   now: time := clock;
   d: date := create(natural(day(now)),
                     natural(month(now)),
                     natural(year(now)) mod 100 );
 begin
   remove(d, rs);
 end retire_reservations;


-- Driver for the temporal event "retire".
task body retire_demon is
   hour: constant duration:= 3600.0;
   period: constant duration := 24 * hour;
   phase: constant duration := 4 * hour;
   start_up_time: constant time := clock;
   d: integer := day(start_up_time);
   m: integer := month(start_up_time);
   y: integer := year(start_up_time);
   next_retire_time: time := time_of(y, m, d, phase) + period;
 begin  -- 4am the next morning.
   loop  -- Forever.
     delay next_retire_time - clock;
        -- Trigger the temporal event "retire" in each task.
     for i in airline_reservation_system'range loop
       airline_reservation_system(i).retire;
     end loop;
      next_retire_time := next_retire_time + period;
   end loop;
 end retire_demon;
begin -- Body of package, initialize task array.
  for k in airline_reservation_system'range loop
      airline_reservation_system(k).init(k);
  end loop;
end airline_reservation_system_pkg;
```

FIGURE 6.8
Change to Travel Agent Package

```
   with text_io; use text_io;
   with text_pkg; use text_pkg;  -- Defines text_pkg_instance.
   with date_pkg; use date_pkg;  -- Defines date.
   with concrete_types_pkg; use concrete_types_pkg;
     -- Defines airport, flight_id, passenger, agent_id,
     -- flight_description, reservation.
   with parse_pkg; use parse_pkg;
     -- Defines is_airport, is_flight_id, is_passenger,
     -- is_agent_id, edit_command, next_item.
   with format_pkg; use format_pkg; -- Defines fill_line.
   with airline_reservation_system_pkg;
   use airline_reservation_system_pkg;
     -- Defines task airline_reservation_system and
     -- types flight_sequence, reservation_sequence.
|  with text_hash_pkg;  -- Defines text_hash.
package body travel_agent_pkg is
   use text_pkg_instance;  -- Defines the type text.
   use flight_sequence_pkg;
     -- Defines the flight_sequence operations.
   use reservation_sequence_pkg;
     -- Defines the reservation_sequence operations.
   package hash_pkg is new text_hash_pkg(natural); use hash_pkg;


   -- Local subprogram declarations.
   procedure interpret_command(cmd: character; args: in text;
                               f: in file_type );
   procedure parse_find_flights(s: in text; o, d: out airport;
                               result: out boolean );
   procedure parse_reserve(s: in text; a: out agent_id;
                            i: out flight_id; d: out date;
                            p: out passenger;
                            result: out boolean );
   procedure parse_cancel(s: in text; i: out flight_id;
                           d: out date; p: out passenger;
                           result: out boolean );
   procedure parse_notify(s: in text; a: out agent_id;
                           i: out flight_id; d: out date;
                           result: out boolean );


   -- Constant declarations.
   modem_number: constant string := natural'image(modem_id);
   input_name: constant string :=
     "ta" & modem_number(2 .. modem_number'last) & "_in";
   output_name: constant string :=
     "ta" & modem_number(2 .. modem_number'last) & "_out";
```

```
task body travel_agent_type is
  input, output: file_type;
  last: natural;
  buffer, command: text;
begin
  open(input, in_file, input_name);
  open(output, out_file, output_name);
  loop  -- Forever.
    get_line(input, buffer);
    buffer := edit_command(buffer);
    next_item(buffer, command);
    if length(command) = 1
    then interpret_command(char(command, 1), buffer, output);
    else -- Illegal command code.
       interpret_command(' ', buffer, output);
    end if;
  end loop;
exception
  when end_error => put_line(output, "input terminated");
  when constraint_error =>
    put_line(output,
             "Unexpected constraint_error in travel_agent" );
  when numeric_error =>
    put_line(output,
             "Unexpected numeric_error in travel_agent" );
  when program_error =>
    put_line(output,
             "Unexpected program_error in travel_agent" );
  when storage_error =>
    put_line(output,
             "Unexpected storage_error in travel_agent" );
  when tasking_error =>
    put_line(output,
             "Unexpected tasking_error in travel_agent" );
  when others =>
    put_line(output, "Unexpected exception in travel_agent");
end travel_agent_type;

procedure interpret_command(cmd: character; args: in text;
                            f: in file_type ) is
  o, d: airport;
  i: flight_id;
  da: date;
  p: passenger;
  a: agent_id;
  fs: flight_sequence;
  rs: reservation_sequence;
  ok: boolean;
  k: natural;
```

FIGURE 6.8 (continued)

```
procedure display_reservation(res: in reservation) is
  -- Nonlocal_variable(f: in file_type).
begin  -- Body of display_reservation.
  put_line(f, fill_line((string_code(res.d), res.p),
                        (8, 20) ));
end display_reservation;
procedure display_reservations is
  new reservation_sequence_pkg.scan(display_reservation);

procedure display_flight(fd: in flight_description) is
  -- Nonlocal_variable(f: in file_type).
begin  -- Body of display_flight.
  put_line(f, fill_line((fd.id, fd.dep, fd.arr, fd.price),
                        (6, 8, 8, 10) ));
end display_flight;
procedure display_flights is
  new flight_sequence_pkg.scan(display_flight);
begin  -- Body of interpret_command.
  case cmd is
    when 'f' =>
      parse_find_flights(args, o, d, ok);
      if ok then k := modem_id mod partitions;
        airline_reservation_system(k).find_flights(o, d, fs);
        if length(fs) > 0 then display_flights(fs);
        else put_line(f, "no flights found"); end if;
      else put_line(f, "command not recognized"); end if;
    when 'r' =>
      parse_reserve(args, a, i, da, p, ok);
      if ok then k := text_hash(i) mod partitions;
        airline_reservation_system(k).reserve(a, i, da, p);
        put_line(f, "done");
      else put_line(f, "command not recognized"); end if;
    when 'c' =>
      parse_cancel(args, i, da, p, ok);
      if ok then k := text_hash(i) mod partitions;
        airline_reservation_system(k).cancel(i, da, p);
        put_line(f, "done");
      else put_line(f, "command not recognized"); end if;
    when 'n' =>
      parse_notify(args, a, i, da, ok);
      if ok then k := text_hash(i) mod partitions;
        airline_reservation_system(k).notify(a, i, da, rs);
        if length(rs) > 0 then display_reservations(rs);
        else put_line(f, "no reservations found"); end if;
      else put_line(f, "command not recognized"); end if;
    when others => put_line(f, "command not recognized");
  end case;
```

```
  exception
    when no_seat => put_line(f, "No seat available");
    when reservation_exists =>
      put_line(f, "The passenger already has a reservation");
    when no_reservation =>
      put_line(f, "The passenger does not hold a reservation");
    when no_such_flight => put_line(f, "Unknown flight id");
    when constraint_error =>
      put_line(f,
"Unexpected constraint_error in travel_agent.interpret_command"
             );
    when numeric_error =>
      put_line(f,
"Unexpected numeric_error in travel_agent.interpret_command"
             );
    when program_error =>
      put_line(f,
"Unexpected program_error in travel_agent.interpret_command"
             );
    when storage_error =>
      put_line(f,
"Unexpected storage_error in travel_agent.interpret_command"
             );
    when tasking_error =>
      put_line(f,
"Unexpected tasking_error in travel_agent.interpret_command"
             );
    when others =>
      put_line(f,
"Unexpected exception in travel_agent.interpret_command"
             );
  end interpret_command;


  procedure parse_find_flights(s: in text; o, d: out airport;
                               result: out boolean ) is

    line: text := s;
    item: text;
  begin
    next_item(line, item);
    if is_airport(item) then o := item;
      else result := false; return; end if;
    next_item(line, item);
    if is_airport(item) then d := item;
      else result := false; return; end if;
    next_item(line, item);  -- Discard any trailing spaces.
    result := length(item) = 0;
  end parse_find_flights;
```

FIGURE 6.8 (continued)

```
procedure parse_reserve(s: in text; a: out agent_id;
                            i: out flight_id; d: out date;
                            p: out passenger;
                            result: out boolean ) is
      line: text := s;
      item: text;
      ok: boolean;
  begin
    next_item(line, item);
    if is_agent_id(item) then a := item;
       else result := false; return; end if;
    next_item(line, item);
    if is_flight_id(item) then i := item;
       else result := false; return; end if;
    next_item(line, item);
    is_date(item, d, ok);
    if not ok then result := false; return; end if;
    trim(line);  -- Get rid of leading and trailing blanks.
    if is_passenger(line) then p := line; result := true;
       else result := false; end if;
  end parse_reserve;

procedure parse_cancel(s: in text; i: out flight_id;
                           d: out date; p: out passenger;
                           result: out boolean ) is
      line: text := s;
      item: text;
      ok: boolean;
  begin
    next_item(line, item);
    if is_flight_id(item) then
       i := item; else result := false; return; end if;
    next_item(line, item);
    is_date(item, d, ok);
    if not ok then result := false; return; end if;
    trim(line);  -- Get rid of leading and trailing blanks.
    if is_passenger(line) then
       p := line; result := true; else result := false; end if;
  end parse_cancel;

procedure parse_notify(s: in text; a: out agent_id;
                           i: out flight_id; d: out date;
                           result: out boolean ) is
      line: text := s;
      item: text;
      ok: boolean;
```

```
   begin
     next_item(line, item);
     if is_agent_id(item) then a := item;
        else result := false; return; end if;
     next_item(line, item);
     if is_flight_id(item) then i := item;
        else result := false; return; end if;
     next_item(line, item);
     is_date(item, d, ok);
     if not ok then result := false; return; end if;
     next_item(line, item);  -- Discard any trailing spaces.
     result := length(item) = 0;
   end parse_notify;
end travel_agent_pkg;
```

FIGURE 6.9
Change to Airline Manager Package

```
  with text_io; use text_io;
  with text_pkg; use text_pkg; -- Defines text_pkg_instance.
  with date_pkg; use date_pkg;  -- Defines date.
  with concrete_types_pkg; use concrete_types_pkg;
     -- Defines airport, flight_id, money, flight_time.
  with parse_pkg; use parse_pkg;
     -- Defines is_airport, is_flight_id, is_money, is_time,
     -- edit_command, next_item.
  with airline_reservation_system_pkg;
  use airline_reservation_system_pkg;
|    -- Defines task array airline_reservation_system.
package body airline_manager_pkg is
  use text_pkg_instance;  -- Defines the type text.

  -- Local subprogram declarations.
  procedure interpret_command(cmd: string; args: in text;
                              f: in file_type );
  procedure parse_add_flight(s: in text; i: out flight_id;
                             p: out money; o, d: out airport;
                             dep, arr: out flight_time;
                             c: out natural;
                             result: out boolean );
  procedure parse_drop_flight(s: in text; i: out flight_id;
                              result: out boolean );
```

FIGURE 6.9 (continued)

```ada
procedure parse_new_fare(s: in text; i: out flight_id;
                          p: out money; result: out boolean );


-- Constant declarations.
input_name: constant string := "am0_in";
output_name: constant string := "am0_out";


task body airline_manager_type is
  input, output: file_type;
  last: natural;
  buffer, command: text;
begin
  open(input, in_file, input_name);
  open(output, out_file, output_name);
  loop  -- Forever.
    get_line(input, buffer);
    buffer := edit_command(buffer);
    next_item(buffer, command);
    interpret_command(ada_string(command), buffer, output);
  end loop;
exception
  when end_error => put_line(output, "input terminated");
  when constraint_error =>
    put_line(output,
             "Unexpected constraint_error in airline_manager"
             );
  when numeric_error =>
    put_line(output,
             "Unexpected numeric_error in airline_manager" );
  when program_error =>
    put_line(output,
             "Unexpected program_error in airline_manager" );
  when storage_error =>
    put_line(output,
             "Unexpected storage_error in airline_manager" );
  when tasking_error =>
    put_line(output,
             "Unexpected tasking_error in airline_manager" );
  when others =>
    put_line(output,
             "Unexpected exception in airline_manager" );
end airline_manager_type;


procedure interpret_command(cmd: string; args: in text;
                             f: in file_type ) is
```

```
   i: flight_id;
   p: money;
   o, d: airport;
   dep, arr: flight_time;
   c: natural;
   ok: boolean;
begin
  if cmd = "add_flight" then
     parse_add_flight(args, i, p, o, d, dep, arr, c, ok);
     if ok then
        for k in airline_reservation_system'range loop
           airline_reservation_system(k).
              add_flight(i, p, o, d, dep, arr, c);
        end loop;
        put_line(f, "Done.");
     else put_line(f, "command not recognized"); end if;
  elsif cmd = "drop_flight" then
     parse_drop_flight(args, i, ok);
     if ok then
        for k in airline_reservation_system'range loop
           airline_reservation_system(k).drop_flight(i);
        end loop;
        put_line(f, "Done.");
     else put_line(f, "command not recognized"); end if;
  elsif cmd = "new_fare" then
     parse_new_fare(args, i, p, ok);
     if ok then
        for k in airline_reservation_system'range loop
           airline_reservation_system(k).new_fare(i, p);
        end loop;
        put_line(f, "Done.");
     else put_line(f, "command not recognized"); end if;
  elsif cmd = "retire" then
     for k in airline_reservation_system'range loop
        airline_reservation_system(k).retire;
     end loop;
  else put_line(f, "command not recognized"); end if;
exception
  when flight_exists =>
    put_line(f, "The flight is already scheduled.");
    put_line(f,
"To change it, use drop_flight and then add_flight."
           );
  when no_such_flight =>
    put_line(f,
"No such flight was scheduled, check the flight id."
           );
```

FIGURE 6.9 (continued)

```
  when constraint_error =>
    put_line(f,
"Unexpected constraint_error in airline_manager"
            );
  when numeric_error =>
    put_line(f, "Unexpected numeric_error in airline_manager");
  when program_error =>
    put_line(f, "Unexpected program_error in airline_manager");
  when storage_error =>
    put_line(f, "Unexpected storage_error in airline_manager");
  when tasking_error =>
    put_line(f, "Unexpected tasking_error in airline_manager");
  when others =>
    put_line(f, "Unexpected exception in airline_manager");
end interpret_command;

package nat_io is new integer_io(natural); use nat_io;
procedure parse_add_flight(s: in text; i: out flight_id;
                           p: out money; o, d: out airport;
                           dep, arr: out flight_time;
                           c: out natural;
                           result: out boolean ) is
  line: text := s;
  item: text;
  last: positive;
begin
  next_item(line, item);
  if is_flight_id(item) then i := item;
    else result := false; return; end if;
  next_item(line, item);
  if is_money(item) then p := item;
    else result := false; return; end if;
  next_item(line, item);
  if is_airport(item) then o := item;
    else result := false; return; end if;
  next_item(line, item);
  if is_airport(item) then d := item;
    else result := false; return; end if;
  next_item(line, item);
  if is_time(item) then dep := item;
    else result := false; return; end if;
  next_item(line, item);
  if is_time(item) then arr := item;
    else result := false; return; end if;
  get(ada_string(line), c, last);
```

```
      line := slice(line, last + 1, length(line));
      next_item(line, item);
      result := length(item) = 0;   -- Ok if no more items.
   exception
      when others => result := false;
   end parse_add_flight;

   procedure parse_drop_flight(s: in text; i: out flight_id;
                                 result: out boolean ) is
      line: text := s;
      item: text;
   begin
      next_item(line, item);
      if is_flight_id(item) then
          i := item; else result := false; return; end if;
      next_item(line, item);   -- Discard any trailing spaces.
      result := length(item) = 0;
   end parse_drop_flight;

   procedure parse_new_fare(s: in text; i: out flight_id;
                              p: out money; result: out boolean ) is
        line: text := s;
        item: text;
   begin
      next_item(line, item);
      if is_flight_id(item) then i := item;
         else result := false; return; end if;
      next_item(line, item);
      if is_money(item) then p := item;
         else result := false; return; end if;
      next_item(line, item);   -- Discard any trailing spaces.
      result := length(item) = 0;
   end parse_new_fare;
end airline_manager_pkg;
```

modem_id to spread the work load. The other travel_agent operations use a hashing function on the flight_id to choose which task to invoke, thus making the tasks act as disjoint buckets as far as reservations are concerned. The hashing function is a reusable component that was also used for the hashed_file data type in Chapter 5. The airline_manager operations now are repeated for all of the instances of the flight_schedule, and are slowed down by a factor of five. This results in a net gain only because the `travel_agent` transactions are much more frequent than the `airline_manager` transactions.

6.4.2 Feedback for Airline Managers

This section considers the modifications required to solve the second of the two problem reports introduced at the beginning of Section 6.4.

Analysis. The second problem corresponds to a missing requirement. We formulate this requirement and add it into the goal hierarchy as shown in Fig. 6.10. The original goal hierarchy is useful for relating new requirements to existing parts of the system. Examining the goal hierarchy for the initial version of the airline reservation system, we note that G1.1.1 and G1.1.2 already require a capability to display information about flights to help the travel agent find all of the flights meeting a passenger's needs.

We enquire whether the ability to display arrival and departure times, the price, and the flight id for all flights from a given origin to a given destination is sufficient to meet the new requirement, or if it is necessary to provide information about which cities are served by the airline. The customer replies that airline managers are familiar with the regions served by their airlines, and that the proposed facility is sufficient.

Impact of the Proposed Change. Based on the results of the analysis, we conclude that existing facilities for meeting requirements G1.1.1 and G1.1.2 are sufficient for meeting the new requirement G2.4. Consulting the links between the functional specification and the goals, we propose to include the existing `find_flights` command from the `travel_agent` interface in the `airline_manager` interface.

Next we identify the work needed to carry out the change. Because one of the commands will be shared by both interfaces, we propose to reorganize the functional specification to include a third view, which is shared by both inter-

---

G2: The system must provide a means for the airline manager to manage flights.

  G2.4: The system must allow the airline manager to examine the current flight schedule.

FIGURE 6.10
New Requirement

faces, and contains only the new operation. This change involves moving things around rather than inventing new facilities, and requires minimal effort, especially if the development environment provides tool support for this kind of transformation. There is no other effect on the abstract functional specification. The concrete functional specification of the `airline_manager` must be modified to include a concrete format for the new command, but the concrete functional specification for the `travel_agent` is not affected.

The architectural design for the central part of the system is affected only by adding new dependencies among existing modules. The design of the `airline_manager_pkg` module can use an existing function for parsing the new command, but a new case in the `interpret_command` procedure is needed for invoking the entry of the `airline_reservation_system` task corresponding to the new command. Because the functional specification for the `find_flights` command does not have any exception conditions, the error messages in the `airline_manager_pkg` module are not affected. The `travel_agent_pkg` module and the `date` module are not affected by the proposed change. We expect the cost of the proposed change to be low because the proposed changes are routine additions to the code that can be patterned after similar existing routines. The cost estimate is based on the facts that a small number of modules are affected and that no incompatible changes are proposed for the existing code. In general, incompatible changes are more difficult to design and debug than are pure extensions to the behavior of the existing system.

Design and Implementation.   The new functional specification is shown in Fig. 6.11. We have moved the `find_flights` command to a common interface module, which is now inherited by both the `travel_agent` interface and the `airline_manager` interface. The original definition of `find_flights` in the `travel_agent_pkg` module is hidden because the requirements tracing comments are different, and we want only the new comment, rather than copies of both comments.

The new concrete functional specification for the `airline_manager_pkg` module is shown in Fig. 6.12. We have added a new case to the `interpret_command` message, and added a new format definition for the airline manager's version of the `find_flights` command. We use the justification for the earlier change to the airline manager's concrete interface (see the end of Section 3.4.2) to determine that the airline manager's version of the new command should be spelled out in full. This illustrates that the record of previous design decisions can be helpful during evolution, provided that the structure of the record is adequately organized and indexed to allow the relevant parts to be located easily. Note that the two interfaces use two different concrete command formats to refer to the same abstract command.

```
MACHINE common_airline_reservation_interface_3_1
  INHERIT airline_reservation_state_model

  STATE(reservations: set(reservation),
        schedule: map(flight_id, flight) )
  INVARIANT existing_flights(reservations),
            no_overbooking(reservations),
            single_reservation(reservations)
  INITIALLY reservations = { }, domain(schedule) = { }
    -- Initially the reservation set and the schedule
    -- are both empty.

  MESSAGE find_flights(origin destination: airport)
    -- G1.1.1, G1.1.2, G2.4
  REPLY flights(s: sequence(flight_description))
    WHERE ALL(f: flight :: description(f) IN s <=>
              f IN range(schedule) & origin(f) = origin &
              destination(f) = destination )
    -- Flights from the origin to the destination.
END

MACHINE travel_agent_interface_3_1
  INHERIT travel_agent_interface_2_1 HIDE find_flights
  INHERIT common_airline_reservation_interface_3_1
END

MACHINE airline_manager_interface_3_1
  INHERIT airline_manager_interface_2_1
  INHERIT common_airline_reservation_interface_3_1
END
```

FIGURE 6.11
Updated Functional Specification

The changes to the functional specification thus indicate what changes are needed in the architectural design: only the airline_manager_pkg module needs to be changed, and a new module for parsing the new command needs to be added. The specification for this module is shown in Fig. 6.13. This is the same as the specification for the corresponding command parsing function for the travel_agent, except that the is_find_flights concept is applied to a different command name.

The implementation of the change is now straightforward. The code for the new version of the interpret_command procedure of the airline_ manager_pkg module is shown in Fig. 6.14. We have taken the response

```
MACHINE airline_manager_3_1
  INHERIT airline_manager_2_1 HIDE interpret_command
  INHERIT airline_manager_command_formats_3_1

  MESSAGE interpret_command(command: string)
     -- Command from airline manager's keyboard.
    WHEN is_find_flights(edit(command), origin, destination)
      SEND find_flights(origin destination: airport)
        TO airline_reservation_system_design_2_1{0}
    WHEN is_add_flight(edit(command), i, price, origin,
                       destination, departure, arrival,
                       capacity )
      SEND add_flight(i: flight_id, price: money,
                      origin destination: airport,
                      departure arrival: time, capacity: nat)
        TO airline_reservation_system_design_2_1{index}
      FOREACH(index: nat SUCH THAT
              index = hash(i) MOD partitions )
      TRANSITION replies_pending = partitions
    WHEN is_drop_flight(edit(command), i)
      SEND drop_flight(i: flight_id)
        TO airline_reservation_system_design_2_1{index}
      FOREACH(index: nat SUCH THAT
              index = hash(i) MOD partitions )
      TRANSITION replies_pending = partitions
    WHEN is_new_fare(edit(command), i, price)
      SEND new_fare(i: flight_id, price: money)
        TO airline_reservation_system_design_2_1{index}
      FOREACH(index: nat SUCH THAT
              index = hash(i) MOD partitions )
      TRANSITION replies_pending = partitions
    OTHERWISE REPLY(s: string) WHERE s = "command not recognized"
END

DEFINITION airline_manager_command_formats_3_1
  INHERIT final_airline_manager_command_formats

  CONCEPT is_find_flights(command: string,
                          origin destination: airport )
    VALUE(b: boolean)
    WHERE b <=> is_list(command, "find_flights",
                        origin, destination )
END
```

FIGURE 6.12
Updated Airline Manager Interface

```
FUNCTION parse_find_flights
  INHERIT airline_manager_command_formats_2_1
  INHERIT airline_reservation_system_type_formats
  MESSAGE(s: string) -- PRAGMA representation(string, text).
    WHEN SOME(o d: airport ::
             is_find_flights("find_flights " || s, o, d) )
      REPLY(b: boolean, o d: airport)
        WHERE b = true, is_find_flights(s, o, d)
    OTHERWISE REPLY(b: boolean, o d: airport) WHERE b = false
END
```

FIGURE 6.13
Specification for New Module

FIGURE 6.14
New Version of the Airline Manager Package

```
  with text_io; use text_io;
  with text_pkg; use text_pkg; -- Defines text_pkg_instance.
  with date_pkg; use date_pkg;  -- Defines date.
  with concrete_types_pkg; use concrete_types_pkg;
    -- Defines airport, flight_id, money, flight_time.
  with parse_pkg; use parse_pkg;
    -- Defines is_airport, is_flight_id, is_money, is_time,
    -- edit_command, next_item.
| with format_pkg; use format_pkg; -- Defines fill_line.
  with airline_reservation_system_pkg;
  use airline_reservation_system_pkg;
    -- Defines task array airline_reservation_system.
package body airline_manager_pkg is
  use text_pkg_instance;  -- Defines the type text.
  use flight_sequence_pkg;
    -- Defines the flight_sequence operations.

  -- Local subprogram declarations.
  procedure interpret_command(cmd: string; args: in text;
                              f: in file_type );
| procedure parse_find_flights(s: in text; o, d: out airport;
                              result: out boolean );
  procedure parse_add_flight(s: in text; i: out flight_id;
                              p: out money; o, d: out airport;
                              dep, arr: out flight_time;
                              c: out natural;
                              result: out boolean );
```

```
procedure parse_drop_flight(s: in text; i: out flight_id;
                            result: out boolean );
procedure parse_new_fare(s: in text; i: out flight_id;
                            p: out money; result: out boolean );


-- Constant declarations.
input_name: constant string := "am0_in";
output_name: constant string := "am0_out";

task body airline_manager_type is
  input, output: file_type;
  last: natural;
  buffer, command: text;
begin
  open(input, in_file, input_name);
  open(output, out_file, output_name);
  loop   -- Forever.
    get_line(input, buffer);
    buffer := edit_command(buffer);
    next_item(buffer, command);
    interpret_command(ada_string(command), buffer, output);
  end loop;
exception
  when end_error => put_line(output, "input terminated");
  when constraint_error =>
    put_line(output,
              "Unexpected constraint_error in airline_manager"
            );
  when numeric_error =>
    put_line(output,
              "Unexpected numeric_error in airline_manager" );
  when program_error =>
    put_line(output,
              "Unexpected program_error in airline_manager" );
  when storage_error =>
    put_line(output,
              "Unexpected storage_error in airline_manager" );
  when tasking_error =>
    put_line(output,
              "Unexpected tasking_error in airline_manager" );
  when others =>
    put_line(output,
              "Unexpected exception in airline_manager" );
end airline_manager_type;

procedure interpret_command(cmd: string; args: in text;
                            f: in file_type ) is
```

FIGURE 6.14 (continued)

```
i: flight_id;
p: money;
o, d: airport;
dep, arr: flight_time;
c: natural;
ok: boolean;
fs: flight_sequence;

procedure display_flight(fd: in flight_description) is
  -- Nonlocal_variable(f: in file_type).
begin  -- Body of display_flight.
  put_line(f, fill_line((fd.id, fd.dep, fd.arr, fd.price),
                        (6, 8, 8, 10) ));
end display_flight;
procedure display_flights is
  new flight_sequence_pkg.scan(display_flight);

begin
  if cmd = "find_flights" then
      parse_find_flights(args, o, d, ok);
      if ok then
         airline_reservation_system(0).find_flights(o, d, fs);
         if length(fs) > 0 then display_flights(fs);
         else put_line(f, "no flights found"); end if;
    else put_line(f, "command not recognized"); end if;
  elsif cmd = "add_flight" then
     parse_add_flight(args, i, p, o, d, dep, arr, c, ok);
     if ok then
        for k in airline_reservation_system'range loop
           airline_reservation_system(k).
             add_flight(i, p, o, d, dep, arr, c);
        end loop;
        put_line(f, "Done.");
     else put_line(f, "command not recognized"); end if;
  elsif cmd = "drop_flight" then
     parse_drop_flight(args, i, ok);
     if ok then
        for k in airline_reservation_system'range loop
           airline_reservation_system(k).drop_flight(i);
        end loop;
        put_line(f, '"Done.");
     else put_line(f, "command not recognized"); end if;
  elsif cmd = "new_fare" then
     parse_new_fare(args, i, p, ok);
     if ok then
```

```
         for k in airline_reservation_system'range loop
             airline_reservation_system(k).new_fare(i, p);
         end loop;
         put_line(f, "Done.");
      else put_line(f, "command not recognized"); end if;
   elsif cmd = "retire" then
      for k in airline_reservation_system'range loop
         airline_reservation_system(k).retire;
      end loop;
   else put_line(f, "command not recognized"); end if;
 exception
   when flight_exists =>
     put_line(f, "The flight is already scheduled.");
     put_line(f,
"To change it, use drop_flight and then add_flight."
             );
   when no_such_flight =>
     put_line(f,
"No such flight was scheduled, check the flight id."
             );
   when constraint_error =>
     put_line(f,
"Unexpected constraint_error in airline_manager"
             );
   when numeric_error =>
     put_line(f, "Unexpected numeric_error in airline_manager");
   when program_error =>
     put_line(f, "Unexpected program_error in airline_manager");
   when storage_error =>
     put_line(f, "Unexpected storage_error in airline_manager");
   when tasking_error =>
     put_line(f, "Unexpected tasking_error in airline_manager");
   when others =>
     put_line(f, "Unexpected exception in airline_manager");
 end interpret_command;

 procedure parse_find_flights(s: in text; o, d: out airport;
                              result: out boolean ) is
   line: text := s;
   item: text;
 begin
   next_item(line, item);
   if is_airport(item) then
      o := item; else result := false; return; end if;
   next_item(line, item);
   if is_airport(item) then
```

FIGURE 6.14 (continued)

```
      d := item; else result := false; return; end if;
   next_item(line, item);  -- Discard any trailing spaces.
   result := length(item) = 0;
end parse_find_flights;

package nat_io is new integer_io(natural); use nat_io;
procedure parse_add_flight(s: in text; i: out flight_id;
                           p: out money; o, d: out airport;
                           dep, arr: out flight_time;
                           c: out natural;
                           result: out boolean ) is
   line: text := s;
   item: text;
   last: positive;
begin
   next_item(line, item);
   if is_flight_id(item) then i := item;
      else result := false; return; end if;
   next_item(line, item);
   if is_money(item) then p := item;
      else result := false; return; end if;
   next_item(line, item);
   if is_airport(item) then o := item;
      else result := false; return; end if;
   next_item(line, item);
   if is_airport(item) then d := item;
      else result := false; return; end if;
   next_item(line, item);
   if is_time(item) then dep := item;
      else result := false; return; end if;
   next_item(line, item);
   if is_time(item) then arr := item;
      else result := false; return; end if;
   get(ada_string(line), c, last);
   line := slice(line, last + 1, length(line));
   next_item(line, item);
   result := length(item) = 0;  -- Ok if no more items.
exception
   when others => result := false;
end parse_add_flight;

procedure parse_drop_flight(s: in text; i: out flight_id;
                            result: out boolean ) is
   line: text := s;
   item: text;
```

```
begin
   next_item(line, item);
   if is_flight_id(item) then
       i := item; else result := false; return; end if;
   next_item(line, item);  -- Discard any trailing spaces.
   result := length(item) = 0;
end parse_drop_flight;

procedure parse_new_fare(s: in text; i: out flight_id;
                         p: out money; result: out boolean ) is
       line: text := s;
       item: text;
begin
   next_item(line, item);
   if is_flight_id(item) then i := item;
       else result := false; return; end if;
   next_item(line, item);
   if is_money(item) then p := item;
       else result := false; return; end if;
   next_item(line, item);  -- Discard any trailing spaces.
   result := length(item) = 0;
  end parse_new_fare;
end airline_manager_pkg;
```

---

in the new case and the definition of the display_flights procedure from the implementation of the travel_agent_pkg module. The choice of which task should serve the find_flights command had to be modified because the airline_manager_pkg module does not have a modem_id parameter. We determined the corresponding value, and substituted the constant 0 for the parameter k. The interface to display_flights indicates that the type flight_sequence is now needed by both the airline_manager_pkg module and the travel_agent_pkg module. The name of the package where this type is defined is already visible in the airline_manager_pkg module; all we have to do is to add a use flight_sequence_pkg statement.

The implementation of the parse_find_flights procedure does not require any new code. Because the parsing function works only on the arguments to the command, which are exactly the same for both the travel_agent and the airline_manager command formats, we can copy the corresponding function from the travel_agent_pkg module without any changes. We decide to copy the code rather than to factor it out into a shared package because this lets us change fewer modules, and because the command formats for the two modules are logically distinct concepts, which happen to coincide at the moment by accident.

6.5 Quality Assurance

Quality assurance is an essential part of software evolution because the evolvers may not completely understand the system they are changing, especially if it is complex and poorly documented. There are two types of quality assurance activities; one aimed at keeping the system conceptually manageable, and the other aimed at discovering faults introduced by a change.

6.5.1 Evolution Reviews

There should be separate review processes for acceptance of a system by its users and acceptance of a system by the organization responsible for the evolution of the system. The purpose of the review by the evolvers is to make sure that everything needed for evolution has been provided—most notably, complete and accurate documentation—and that the design of the system is free from features likely to be detrimental to future changes. The main things to look for are modular designs without the potential for implicit interactions between widely separated parts of the system, and proper application of the information hiding principle to localize design decisions likely to change to single modules. Many potential problems in evolution can be avoided if the evolver has the right to refuse responsibility for a system until it has been cleaned up and properly documented. The developer should be responsible for making repairs and changes to the system until the point at which the system passes its evolution review.

6.5.2 Testing

Changes to a system are often checked by running test cases. The purpose of testing during evolution is to detect faults introduced by a change to the software. Running the same set of test cases on each new version of a system is a popular strategy because of its low cost and its low requirements for supporting software tools. However, this choice is not statistically sound, because it can systematically miss large classes of errors. It may be useful to run a standard set of test cases each time if this can be done at low cost, but this set should be augmented with some newly chosen test cases to achieve a high degree of fault detection.

Common sense suggests including sufficient new test cases chosen to thoroughly exercise the changed aspects of the system. It is also important to include some randomly chosen test cases that are different each time. The purpose of these new test cases is to detect faults in parts of the system that were not supposed to be affected by the change, because the change may have broken some other part of the system via some unintended interaction, such as violation of an undocumented assumption about the behavior of the system. Randomly chosen test cases are appropriate because you are trying to detect unknown and unpredictable interactions. Random test data generation avoids systematic biases caused by the tester's potentially mistaken understanding of the system. There are also many types of programs for which randomly chosen test cases are fault revealing with high probability[4].

6.6 Management Aspects

Some current difficulties in software evolution stem from management problems. For example, maintenance programmers in this country have traditionally been given low pay and low status in the organization, and have few rewards. Such positions typically get filled by people with little experience and ability. However, it is often more difficult to change a program without breaking it than to develop the initial design and implementation. It is not surprising that changes to systems made in such circumstances do not always produce the desired results.

The widespread policies of associating low status and little reward with software evolution or maintenance activities are in conflict with the high proportion of software costs associated with these activities, and appear to be linked to a widespread misconception among high level managers that software is *produced* by a manufacturing process rather than being *developed* by a research and engineering effort. The activities comprising software development are more similar to research and engineering than to manufacturing, since unpredictable discovery and design processes are involved rather than predictable and repetitive steps aimed at replication of a fixed design. Management policies treating software development projects more like research and development efforts than manufacturing efforts should help improve the effectiveness of the software evolution process.

Another common problem is that current procurement policies in many organizations do not request requirements, specifications, and designs to be delivered along with the source code, and current system maintenance policies do not require the documents to be kept up to date as the system evolves. Accurate high-level descriptions and design justification information are needed to safely and efficiently modify a system; it is not surprising that software systems get progressively harder to change and often become less reliable as they are changed.

Other common problems with software evolution from the management point of view are cost and unpredictability of changes. Many of the available guidelines for responding to these problems are common-sense principles such as the following.

1. Maintain a log of changes made and costs associated with each change. This historical information forms the basis for planning and estimation.

2. Keep track of evolution costs per module, and redesign the modules with the highest evolution costs.

3. Plan to redesign the worst parts of the system incrementally, keeping effort spent on redesign roughly proportional to effort spent on handling problem reports.

4. Have separate review meetings for validation and maintainability. Meetings of the first type authorize release of the system to the customer. Meetings of the second type authorize release of the system to the organization responsible for evolving the system.

5. Schedule change cycles at regular intervals. This encourages users to be more careful in their choice of change requests, and helps organize work schedules more efficiently.

Many systems are too big to allow changes to be made one at a time by a single person. Having groups of people working on different changes concurrently introduces a coordination problem, because the changes being developed can interact and interfere with each other. This coordination problem is difficult because changes can interfere even if the modified parts of the documents do not overlap. This makes it difficult to tell when it is safe to combine the work of two teams with responsibilities for different changes. Software tools for combining changes and detecting interference are needed. Some work has been done in this direction [2, 3], but more theoretical and practical work is needed before reliable tools for combining enhancements to a software system will become available. In the short term, it is desirable to hold periodic meetings between groups responsible for making concurrent changes to a system, to review each other's work, and to detect areas of potential interference. In the absence of reliable automated tools for detecting conflicts between proposed modifications, it is essential to assign the responsibility to evaluate proposed changes and the authority to determine which ones are incorporated into the software product at which times to a clearly identified person or group in charge of the configuration of the system.

6.7 Related Research

An approach to changing systems by reconstructing abstractions, particularly in the context of porting a system from one operating environment to another, is discussed in [1]. Some recent work on automatically reconstructing design information from bare code is [7]. Database and tool support for automated evolution is discussed in [5]. A discussion of some of the management problems associated with software maintenance can be found in [6].

Exercises

1. Change the design of the travel agent and airline manager modules of the airline reservation system to represent commands as Ada enumeration types, and rewrite the command interpreters in both modules to have the same structure, as discussed at the end of Section 5.4.1. Also, update the parsing functions as necessary to complete the change.

2. Change the design of the flight schedule and the airline reservation system task to remove the dependence on the precondition for calling the add operation, as discussed in Section 5.4.2.

Projects

1. Extend the airline reservation system to handle flights with multiple stops, and add capabilities for finding flights with the lowest cost and the lowest transit time. For an advanced project, include options to consider constraints on departure and arrival times, and to consider itineraries that involve changing flights when seeking the least-cost route. To be realized with practical delay times, searches for least cost routes must be pruned, and some information may have to be precomputed.

2. Redesign the types B_tree and hashed_file so that the open operation will detect and repair any violations of the invariants caused by a previous machine crash in the middle of any of the operations that modify the data structures.

References

1. G. Arango, I. Baxter, P. Freeman, and C. Pidgeon, "TMM: Software Maintenance by Transformation," *IEEE Software 3*, 3 (May 1986), 27–39.

2. V. Berzins, "On Merging Software Extensions," *Acta Informatica 23*, 6 (Nov. 1986), 607–619.

3. S. Horowitz, J. Prins, and T. Reps, "Integrating Non-Interfering Versions of Programs," Technical Report 690, Computer Sciences Department, University of Wisconsin, Madison, Mar. 1987.

4. W. Howden, *Functional Program Testing and Analysis*, McGraw-Hill, New York, 1987.

5. G. Kaiser and D. Perry, "Workspaces and Experimental Databases: Automated Support for Software Maintenance and Evolution," *Proceedings of the IEEE Conference on Software Maintenance*, 1987, 108–114.

6. G. Parikh, *Techniques of Program and System Maintenance*, Winthrop, Cambridge, MA, 1982.

7. L. Wills, "Automated Program Recognition," Technical Report 904, MS Thesis, MIT Artificial Intelligence Laboratory, Feb. 1987.

7

Support Environment

Formal methods are most effective when supported by a computer-aided software engineering (CASE) environment. Such a CASE environment should contain an integrated set of software tools that support the entire development process, from requirements analysis to evolution.

The support environment is a complex software system that should be developed according to the principles of software engineering. The problem domain for this system is software development. This problem domain is still poorly understood, and is an active research area. Consequently the detailed requirements for a CASE environment are uncertain, and are likely to change as we learn more about what can be automated and how the software development process can be improved. However, the high-level goals for such a system are relatively clear, as discussed in Chapter 1 and explored in more detail in Chapters 2 through 6.

7.1 Goals

The primary goal of the support environment is to automate the most error-prone and labor-intensive tasks in the software development process. People have a limited capability to understand systems with many details. Computer-aided design tools can extend the power of the software systems that can be developed by insulating designers from many of the conceptually simpler details. Error checking and debugging are two areas where significant gains can be made by insulating the programmer from massive amounts of uninteresting detail. Tools for performing these functions at a syntactic level are widespread, and tools operating at the semantic level are becoming feasible. Tools for providing decision-support functions to the designer are also valuable and feasible to develop at the current state of the art. Some functions in this category include: answering questions about the structure, development history, and intended functionality of a software system; and assessing the effects of proposed changes. Tools that go significantly beyond the syntactic level require automated reasoning capabilities. These facilities must be reasonably efficient, and may have to be limited with respect to the difficulty of the conclusions they can draw to achieve practical levels of efficiency.

Practical software systems often have complicated designs that are intolerant of design errors, in the sense that almost any variation from a perfect design leads to a system that does not meet the requirements. Such accuracy is practically impossible to achieve by manual methods, especially for very large systems. Thus helping designers and implementors to achieve the accuracy required to meet software requirements is an important goal, which justifies the investment of effort in developing and using CASE environments.

Another goal of CASE environments is to speed up the software development process. Speed of development is a limiting factor because customers cannot afford to wait for many years after they work out the requirements for a new system before starting to use it. CASE environments seek to automate parts of software development, especially routine aspects that are simple conceptually, but that involve many details. Collectively, these details can be a formidable problem, even though they are simple individually, because even conceptually trivial errors can lead to software failures. For applications governed by formalized policies, people make individual decisions much more slowly and introduce many more errors than properly constructed software tools. Finding and correcting the errors is a major part of the effort in developing large systems. A substantial part of the contribution of a CASE environment to improved productivity lies in preventing or automatically locating many classes of errors. There is generally some overhead for the designers to learn how to use the tools and to enter their designs into the system in a format the tools can use. Thus the productivity gains are greatest for large systems, and for small applications the overheads can mask the gains. CASE environments increase the size of the systems that can be built in the available time but do not necessarily decrease development times for all systems.

CASE also enables construction of higher-quality software. By automating the more routine tasks in software development, CASE environments enable software engineers to concentrate on the creative part of their work, thus allowing them to produce better conceptual models and designs. The result should be software systems that are easier to use, although this is hard to measure objectively. CASE tools also enable more thorough error checking, which leads to more reliable software.

7.2 Basic Concepts

Problems have to be formalized for successful automation. Formal languages and notations are a key factor in enabling the use of CASE tools, because software tools need precisely defined problem representations to operate effectively. The tools in a CASE environment need formal representations for the results of all stages of software development. In this book, we have focused on the specification language Spec and the programming language Ada since we needed particular notations to represent our examples, and since both of these languages have been designed for supporting development of large systems. CASE environments can be based on any formal languages. However, it is much easier to create and integrate the tools if there is only a single representation for each type of software object, so that it is desirable to choose only one notation for each aspect of software development.

The general guidelines for designing a CASE environment are similar to those for any large software system addressing a novel application and expected to change significantly as it evolves. A complete CASE environment is a very complex system with many different functions, and the individual functions involve sophisticated processing. The requirements are to some extent open, in the sense that it is impossible to identify all of the functions that the final version of the system should perform before starting to build the system. This occurs because the process the system is trying to support has not been formalized, and is not completely understood. As software development is economically important and intellectually challenging, we expect research efforts in software engineering to lead to conceptual advances and requirements for new and different types of tools. A software development environment should therefore be designed to be easy to extend. Some suggestions for how to produce a CASE environment are:

1. Plan on a phased development, where the most basic tools are developed first, and the system is extended as new tools become available. Include interfaces in the basic tools for expected future capabilities, even if those capabilities will not be implemented for some time.

2. Use an open architecture that provides standard interfaces and mechanisms for adding new tools and new aspects to the data as compatible extensions. These standards can be represented as general interface constraints that can be inherited and specialized by future extensions to the system. Such constraints can be described using virtual modules in Spec.

3. Classes of tools should be generated automatically based on a tool-definition language to the extent this is feasible. This allows tools to be generic and flexible, and makes it easier to adapt the system to respond to issues that will not be discovered until initial versions of the system have been developed and used on real software projects. The tool generators should be part of the environment to support expansion. The outputs of the tool generators should be represented in the same implementation language used for the hand-crafted parts of the system. The implementation language should be standardized and have widely available compilers to simplify porting the system to new computing environments.

4. Each command should have a single clearly defined function. Conceptual complexity is an important limitation on technology transfer: The system will not get used unless it is quick and easy for a typical user to attain a skill level sufficient to get some useful work done with an efficiency comparable to the previous approach to software development. This makes it imperative to organize the user interface into simple coherent units, to make the commands correspond to the actions performed by the engineer at a natural level of description, and to choose command names that are meaningful to most users without explanations, especially for the most common operations.

5. There should be a single powerful command for each function perceived by the user. Thus commands should be generalized, and simplified by removing restrictions on their use. Duplicated or overlapping functions should be avoided, and the same commands should be used to perform a given function throughout the system. This requires thorough analysis and standardization.

6. Tools should be integrated to work together. This means that information produced by any tool should be accessible to any other tool. This requires standardized abstract data types that can be used throughout the system. If special data representations are needed in several different contexts for performance reasons, these should be provided as alternative implementations of the standard abstract data types. The system or its implementation language should provide generic data transformation facilities for converting between alternative representations of any abstract data type, to support the suggested design style.

7. Unplanned extensions to the data model should be realized by compatible subtypes of the abstract data types in the previous versions of the system. The instances of such subtypes can be used by previously designed tools, but can also provide new and unanticipated capabilities required by new tools.

These considerations make it attractive to choose an implementation language that provides full support for abstract subtypes and multiple representations of abstract types. If a language without explicit support for these considerations will be used, such as Ada, then higher-level design representations and automated tools for providing these capabilities are needed.

7.3 Currently Feasible Tools

Some important categories of tools include configuration control, decision support, error checking, synthesis, and project management. These application areas, and the currently feasible types of tools for each area are discussed next.

7.3.1 Configuration Control Tools

Configuration control is the process of coordinating the activities of a set of software engineers working on a software system consisting of many related parts. This is a critical function in practical software development efforts because many difficulties can be traced to coordination problems in development teams and consistency problems in software families consisting of many different but closely related systems. Most software engineers are competent at writing and debugging individual programs. However, confusion and major delays can result when the consistency of the project data is destroyed by interference between locally correct changes made by different engineers, or by occasional individual errors. We emphasize configuration control because it is an unavoidable limiting factor in developing large software systems that can be effectively addressed by automated tools.

Configuration control acts on the state of the software development project, which consists of many related software objects such as requirements, specifications, code, test cases, user manuals, project plans, and work schedules. In this chapter we use the term *object* to denote instances of abstract data types in long term storage, and we will be concerned mainly with data types representing such software objects. For most practical software development projects, the project data consists of many instances of these types of data objects. Software objects are not usually created directly in their final form, but rather are developed gradually, in a series of refinements and modifications. The goal of configuration control is to provide a consistent view of these objects at all times, and to control access by the members of the development team to maximize useful work. This is done by making a distinction between private copies of the project data and the official copy visible to the development team as a whole, which is sometimes known as the *baseline*. Decisions do not take effect and do not become visible to the rest of the project until they are incorporated into the current baseline. Private copies of project data can be changed freely without affecting anyone else, but those in the baseline are controlled to ensure that everyone can get well formed and up-to-date copies of the project information.

Configuration control can be achieved by a combination of policies and procedures. Project management must set up the proper policies, as discussed in Section 7.5. The procedures involved can be both automatic and manual. The traditional approach is to assign the responsibility for controlling the configuration of the project data to a senior programmer or designer, known as the *configuration manager*, who must approve and sign off on all changes. This can work well for small projects, but is critically dependent on a single person unless all of the policies and constraints to be checked are recorded. Dependency on such a single critical person is undesirable because it can cause major difficulties if the configuration manager becomes incapacitated or leaves the project. Completely manual approval procedures can also introduce significant delays, especially in larger projects where the configuration manager can have difficulty in keeping up with a large volume of changes. Manual procedures also have relatively high error rates.

For larger projects, automated procedures for at least the routine configuration management tasks are desirable. In such a context, the configuration manager sets up tool usage policies, and personally approves only those special cases where changes are necessary, such as those that violate the usual policies or are incorrectly rejected by the automated tools. A mechanism for bypassing the tools is often needed in practice because it is much less expensive to design the tools for the most common cases than it is to handle every conceivable situation automatically. It is often more cost effective to provide flexibility by relying on the judgement of an experienced designer than to try to provide it in the software tool. The configuration manager should allow the tools to be bypassed only in cases where there are clear and compelling justifications for doing so. For example, it is desirable to bypass the automated mechanism in cases where there is a bug in a tool for checking a correctness constraint, and where the programmer can demonstrate that a proposed change is correct even though the tool says otherwise. When this happens, the configuration manager should submit a request to fix the tool, and should decide the fate of the proposed change personally to avoid delaying the entire project until the tool is repaired.

Two different aspects of configuration control can be identified: concurrency control and correctness. The goal of concurrency control is to ensure that concurrent updates do not interfere with each other, and that the effects of an update do not get lost. This condition is often interpreted as *serializability*, which means that the effect of a concurrent set of updates is acceptable if and only if it is the same as applying the same set of updates one at a time in some order. This is a common definition of the goal of concurrency control in databases that also makes sense in the context of configuration control. Identifying weaker constraints that allow more concurrency while still providing practical levels of noninterference is a current research area. The concurrency control problem is compounded by long software development transactions that can take days or weeks, and by the need to avoid aborting ongoing transactions.

The goal of correctness constraints is to ensure that a version of an object is not released to the rest of the development team unless the object is correct in some respects. There are different degrees of correctness constraints. It is not currently practical to insist on absolute correctness before a version of an object is made public. Some correctness constraints that can be checked in practice are that all baseline versions of objects produced by software tools are derived from the current versions of the corresponding source objects, and that constraints that can be checked by completely automatic software tools are satisfied by all baseline versions. An automatic configuration management system can also provide an interface for recording the status and results of manual quality control procedures such as design review meetings.

Concurrency Control.   Tools for automatically enforcing concurrency control constraints are feasible at the current state of the art, although some of the widely available tools address only part of the problem. The concurrency control facilities of most configuration management tools are based on the following concepts.

1. A configuration associates a set of *versions* with each object. Each version is a copy of the object at some particular time.

2. Existing versions cannot be modified. The state of an object under configuration control can change only via the creation of new versions. This allows individual versions to be read in parallel without conflict, and provides stable working conditions for the engineers working on a project.

3. Each version has a permanent unique identifier. This is necessary for recording dependency relationships between versions and providing the capability to recreate past states.

4. Each object has a designated *current version*, which identifies the version of the object belonging to the baseline at the current time. This is necessary to automatically provide the most recent information on demand. In some systems there may be a current version of an object for each alternative if an object has multiple alternatives. Alternatives are discussed later.

5. Any version of an object can be read by project members at any time, possibly relative to access privileges associated with the role of each project member. Access to past versions is necessary to allow all previous states of the project to be recreated as needed. Old versions therefore are never discarded, although they might be migrated to archival storage media such as magnetic tape if required by storage constraints.

6. The creation of new versions is controlled by the configuration management system as needed to avoid conflicts.

A configuration control tool can be viewed as the interface to a database containing all of the versions for the objects under configuration control. There are two basic kinds of access to the database: read-only and update. A read-only access provides a private copy of a version that can be manipulated but not put back into the database after it has been modified. For example, read-only versions of specification modules are useful for testing a new version of a code module, together with read-only versions of other code modules used by the new version. The advantage of a read-only access is that any existing version can be retrieved at any time.

Concurrency control is achieved via restrictions on the operations for updating the configuration database. There are usually two operations involved in an update, *read-for-updating*, which retrieves a writable copy of the current versions of a set of objects, and *add*, which adds a set of finished new versions to the configuration database. A read-for-updating access differs from a read-only access by *locking* the retrieved objects. Because only one person or software process can hold a lock on any given object at any given time, these locks prevent other updates to the objects while they are held. The locks are released by the corresponding add operation after the new versions are added to the database. This ensures that the effects of an update are not lost, since the next update to the object will be based on the new version rather than a previous one. To prevent deadlocks, all of the objects involved in an update should be locked as a unit by the same read-for-updating operation. A read-for-updating operation that cannot lock the required objects immediately must be delayed until all of the objects are available. Objects can be locked by long transactions, therefore a read-for-updating operation that must be delayed should print a message indicating the cause of the delay and return control to the engineer immediately after requests for the required locks have been queued. When the locks are obtained, the engineer can be notified by the system, perhaps by electronic mail.

In actual projects there are often tight deadlines, and strong incentives to work in parallel on simultaneous updates to the same object. This requires special care and extra work, but it can sometimes get the job done in less calendar time than waiting until all of the required locks are available. Success requires continuous communication between the engineers making concurrent changes to the same objects. To support this mode of operation, whenever an update transaction is delayed because some of the objects it needs are already locked, the configuration control system should report which engineer has locked those objects.

Parallel development of interacting changes is asymmetric: one engineer holds the required locks, and is working on the current version of the object. The other engineer cannot get the required locks, and wants to create a change based on the version of the object that will be produced by the first engineer at some future time. Because the desired version is not yet available, the second engineer works on a read-only copy of the current version augmented with informal information about the nature of the ongoing changes and with copies of the current experimental version of the object. The second engineer may have to rework the change several times as the experimental version being developed by the first engineer changes, and will have to review and possibly revise the design when the final versions of the other objects are frozen and become part of the baseline.

A different way to approach parallel development of changes to shared objects is for the second engineer to create a new alternative for the object, representing an independent line of development. Creating a new alternative does not require any locks, and does not influence the current baseline. When both engineers finish their work, the version produced by the first engineer must be combined with the version produced by the second engineer to produce a new version for the official baseline, which incorporates the work of both engineers. The additional work associated with this final process can be automated to some extent.

Alternative Versions. In the simplest possible world, the versions of an object are linearly ordered according to their development history, as illustrated in Fig. 7.1. In this case, each version is intended to supercede the previous versions due to improvements or repairs. In such a structure, the current version is always at the end of the chain, such as version V4 in the example. Such a simple view of the world rarely corresponds to actual software development practice.

Software systems often exist in multiple variations, which are different members of a software family that are intended to coexist, rather than supercede each other. We refer to such variations as *alternative versions*. Some possible motivations for introducing alternative versions into a software design are:

1. Different hardware interfaces. For example, a standard graphics package might have alternative versions corresponding to several different types of display terminals with different capabilities and command sets.

2. Different software interfaces. For example, a software package might have alternative versions for different host operating systems.

3. Different customer options. A system may come with optional features, and different customers may buy different subsets of the system. In

FIGURE 7.1
A Linearly Ordered Version Set

phased delivery situations, not every customer will buy every major release, so that different releases of the system will have to coexist, thus acting as alternative versions.

4. Different optimization criteria. On small machines it may be necessary to optimize storage; on larger machines it may be desirable to use more storage to gain execution speed.

5. Different design decisions. Exploratory designs for unfamiliar application areas may develop several different algorithms or data structures for the same module to compare accuracy or performance. Fault-tolerant systems are sometimes designed to calculate critical values using several different methods, comparing and combining the results to get correct answers even in the presence of a limited number of failures.

Each alternative has its own path in the development history, and its own current version, which is the most recent version on the path. The alternative versions of an object are often strongly related, and may share part of the development history. A structure typical of multiple system releases is illustrated in Fig. 7.2. The example illustrates a structure that might arise if the development of a major new release of a system is started before all of the required repairs and improvements for the previous version have been completed. In this case, the two alternatives share part of the development history. The history of Alternative 1 consists of the version sequence [V1.1, V1.2, V1.3], and the history of Alternative 2 consists of the version sequence [V1.1, V1.2, V2.1, V2.2]. We have used a simple two-part numbering scheme to provide unique identifiers for the versions—the first number identifies the alternative and the second number identifies which revision of the alternative a given version represents.

The history structure associated with the version set can, in principle, be any partial ordering relation, and need not be restricted to a tree. For example, in a case where we are implementing the same display behavior for several completely different hardware devices, the development histories of the different alternatives can be completely disjoint, as illustrated in Fig. 7.3. A more interesting case, corresponding to a later stage in the parallel development of the two major releases discussed previously, is illustrated in Fig. 7.4.

FIGURE 7.2
A Version Set with Two Alternatives

V1.1 ⟶ V1.2 ⟶ V1.3 ⟶ V1.4

V2.1 ⟶ V2.2

V3.1 ⟶ V3.2 ⟶ V3.3 ⟶ V3.4 ⟶ V3.5

FIGURE 7.3
Independent Alternatives

In this example, V1.4 represents a completed version of Alternative 1, in which all known bugs have been fixed. The early versions of Alternative 2 were based on version V1.2, since this was the current version of the module at the time the development of the next major release started. Now that the bugs in Alternative 1 have been fixed, it is desired to incorporate the corresponding changes in Alternative 2. This produces version V2.3, which is derived directly from two different versions, V1.4 and V2.2, and is intended to combine the semantic features of both those versions. The resulting version V2.3 is intended to be the same as if the changes leading to versions V2.1 and V2.2 were done based on version V1.4 instead of V1.2.

Some automatic aid for the process of combining two alternatives is available. However, most of the widely available tools such as sccs and rcs on UNIX operate at the syntactic level, without any regard for the semantics of the objects they are processing. These general-purpose tools treat objects as text strings and view changes in terms of editing operations on text files rather than in terms of operations on semantic structures. Mechanisms sensitive to the semantics of the source language are required to produce results that can be trusted without human inspection and review. Automating the process of combining alternatives completely and reliably for formal specification and programming languages is a current research area.

Progress on combining alternatives and automatically reorganizing development histories depends on better formal interpretations of the relationships between versions. The traditional interpretation of the partial ordering

FIGURE 7.4
Reconverging Alternatives

between the versions of an object has been a historical "derived from" relationship, which records a trace of the steps that were actually taken to produce the current version. Such steps can involve arbitrary changes, without any distinctions between compatible extensions, incompatible changes, or retractions that undo previous extensions. The historical development relationship between versions has a very weak connection to the semantics of the objects and the design process that produced them. Parnas has convincingly stated the case for a design documentation style that documents systems as if they had been developed by a rational and orderly process, even though the actual development may have followed a tortuous path containing many false starts, incorrect decisions, and repairs [11]. A rational design process is one in which there are good reasons for each decision. Although the actual process of developing software may not have a rational structure because of incomplete information and human error, documenting a system as if it had been developed by such an ideal process helps to organize, evaluate, and review the design. The purpose of the documentation is to explain the current version of the system, not to record all imperfections of the actual development. This implies that the historical information should be summarized and reorganized to make it more useful. The alternative designs that were considered and rejected should be recorded along with the reasons why they were rejected, and linked to the corresponding decisions for the current system, to guide maintainers who may have to reconsider those decisions later when responding to requirements changes.

Because much of the documentation currently produced is not very useful, documentation is often viewed as a waste of time. This is due largely to poor organization and poor choice of what to document—often fine details are described, and the fundamental decisions are ignored, since they are assumed to be "obvious." Properly organized documents, which can provide answers to questions and serve as the basis for testing and modifying a system, can be useful long after they were originally developed. For example, the A7–E requirements are still used to maintain the system many years after they were developed [7, 11].

An approach to version control consistent with this viewpoint interprets the ordering on versions as the *specialization* relation (also known as *refinement*). A specialization of an object is another object that has all of the properties of the first, and may have additional properties. Thus a specialization is a compatible extension, which respects all of the features of the original object, and adds further features and constraints. Specialization is a semantic concept, which corresponds to historical development in an idealized process of design by stepwise refinement without any backtracking. The specialization relation is mathematically a partial ordering, which is transitive, reflexive, and antisymmetric. Specialization can be defined precisely for any formal language.

For example, in ordinary two-valued logic, specialization corresponds to the *implies* relation =>: A is a specialization of B if and only if A => B. The inverse of the approximation ordering used in denotational semantics of programming languages is a different example of a specialization relation. Subtypes in Ada are also specializations of the corresponding base types. However, subclasses in Smalltalk are not always specializations of the inherited parent classes. A subclass that just adds new methods and new instance variables is a specialization of the parent class. A subclass that introduces an incompatible change by overriding an inherited method is not a specialization.

We use specializations and generalizations to describe the development of the functional specification and architectural design for the case study on the airline reservation system in Chapters 3 and 4. The Spec inheritance relation is used to record the refinement structures in the case study. This relation corresponds exactly to specialization on specifications in the absence of the HIDE and RENAME constructs. A Spec INHERIT with a HIDE is an abbreviation for the composition of two relationships, a generalization followed by a specialization. The *generalization* relationship is the inverse of specialization: A is a generalization of B if and only if B is a specialization of A. Generalization corresponds to a HIDE, which removes a specified name together with all of the associated properties and constraints. Thus an incompatible change can be decomposed into the combination of a generalization that removes the properties and constraints associated with an inappropriate decision, and a specialization that adds the constraints associated with an alternative decision. Renaming is a notational convenience, and can be treated as an abbreviation for a transformation on the source text that does not affect its semantics.

Using the specialization relation rather than a historical derivation relation to organize versions can make alternative decisions explicit, and can simplify tracing the derivation of the current version by moving the decisions that are no longer in effect into alternative branches of the design space. Thus all of the decisions on the path to the current version are in effect in the current version, and other alternatives are described on different branches of the version graph. A simple example is shown in Fig. 7.5. The figure shows the two different views for a change that affects the type of a parameter. The historical view

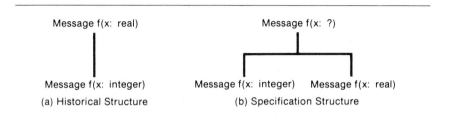

Message f(x: real)

Message f(x: integer)

(a) Historical Structure

Message f(x: ?)

Message f(x: integer)   Message f(x: real)

(b) Specification Structure

FIGURE 7.5
Historical Structure vs. Specialization Structure

organizes the versions according to the "stream of consciousness" of the designer, which shows a single incompatible change. The specialization structure introduces a new version representing the most specific common generalization of the previous version and the new version, and shows the two versions of the design as alternative specializations of the most specific common generalization. This makes the structure of the version set correspond to the structure of the design space being explored, which contains a choice between two incompatible design decisions.

The most specific common generalization represents the aspects of the design that are common to both of the incompatible alternatives. In the example, the type of x in the most specific common generalization is represented by the undefined value ? of the Spec language, which can be read as "to be determined." Most specific common generalizations can be constructed mechanically if we accept a conservative approximation that assumes that two objects have the same semantics if and only if they have equal representations. This should be acceptable in practice because the same constructs should be coded in the same way in related alternatives. This restriction aids evolution of software families, because it makes constructs with the same meaning have the same appearance in all related versions. Tools for maintaining the design history based on its specialization structure should help prevent divergence between the code of equivalent parts of alternative versions, which is a common problem that increases the cost and complexity of evolving software families.

In general, a historical view interleaves different logical threads of the development representing alternative designs in the somewhat arbitrary order in which the changes were entered into the database. The specialization structure separates the alternative choices more clearly, and shows an induced node in which the decision that introduces a distinction between two alternatives has not yet been made. This distinction provides a criterion for classifying and separating subsequent decisions in the historical development. In terms of the example shown in Fig. 7.5, any decisions that depend on the interpretation of x as a real value appear only on the left branch of the derivation; those that depend on the interpretation of x as an integer appear only in the right branch of the specialization structure. This helps designers preparing to change the system to focus on the chain of decisions that leads to the current version, and to identify alternatives that have been explored previously. Computer support for such a process requires recording the refinement structure of a development at a more detailed level than showing just the public releases traditionally captured by most configuration management systems. An effective tool should also support transformations on the derivation history that clarify the logical structure of the design by introducing alternatives and factoring out common decisions. In particular, decisions that do not depend on the distinction between two alternatives should be moved into the most specific common generalization even if they were made after the decision that distinguished between the two alternatives in the original historical development.

An issue in effectively managing the derivation history is the existence of many different but equivalent derivations of an object that differ in the order in which decisions were made. Often decisions are independent and can be made in either order without affecting the final outcome, leading to multiple distinct representations for equivalent derivation histories. In such a case, the order in which the decisions were made does not have any semantic significance, and should be considered a historical accident. It can be useful to automatically transform derivations by reordering the decisions when this can be done without changing the meaning of the derived object. Software tools for determining when two refinements can be reordered without changing their meaning, and for deriving representations of the reordered refinements is useful for supporting evolution. It is easier to understand a derivation history with alternatives if corresponding decisions occur on all of the paths in the same order. In particular, more than two alternatives for the same decision may have been made at widely separated points in time, especially for difficult or uncertain aspects of the design. The structure of the design space is greatly clarified if the derivations are transformed so that all of the alternative refinements are applied to the same version, and if common decisions have been factored out so that they appear in the part of the derivation before the alternatives diverge. Because these decisions may have been made in unrelated orders by different designers in the actual historical development, some transformations to reorder the decisions may be necessary to maintain an understandable record of the development. Any real project cannot afford errors in such simplifications of the development history, so the transformations involved must be applied by trusted software tools.

A common problem in evolution is the need to reverse a particular decision, while preserving many other independent decisions that were made later. The facility to automatically reorder the decisions in a derivation tree allows the decisions that should be preserved to be automatically moved before the decision that has to be changed, thus simplifying the work of software maintenance by increasing the number of versions that can be shared by two alternatives, thus reducing the number of versions that need to be recorded. The theory and tools for such transformations are current research areas.

Correctness and Consistency Constraints. In addition to concurrency control and recording the derivations of the objects comprising the project state, a major concern of configuration control is correctness. Much effort of the other team members can be wasted by incorporating a faulty version into the baseline, because this can create mysterious bugs that can be hard to trace. For this reason, the configuration control system should guarantee that the aspects of correctness that can be checked mechanically are checked before a new version becomes part of the official baseline. The constraints that are practical to check depend on the software tools available, and on the amount of time required to run them. The types of correctness checks that can be performed are discussed in detail in Section 7.3.3.

Because some checks can take a long time, especially for larger systems, there is often a distinction made between releasing a new version and marking it as certified. This a pragmatic issue related to project deadlines, and whether other team members can afford to wait for all of the certifications to be complete before starting the next step based on the new version of a released object. Starting the next task based on faulty objects leads to repeated work, which uses up some of the time gained by starting earlier. It is desirable to wait until all of the checks have been passed if this can be done without requiring engineers to remain idle. The project manager must choose the best policy based on the particular circumstances of the project, such as the average error rate, the average amount of time for correcting an error, and actual distributions of running times for the error-checking tools. It is also worthwhile to note that the amount of time it takes to run even a slow software tool is usually less than the time it takes to schedule a design review meeting for performing a design certification using manual techniques.

A common policy is to separate the checks into two categories, the quick ones and the slow ones. The quick checks are performed automatically when a new version is added into the database, and the new version is not released to the public unless the checks succeed. In case the checks fail, the proposed new version is returned to its author for corrective action. The checks in the slow category are also performed automatically, but the system does not wait for the results before releasing the new version. The slow checks can be done in the background at a low priority level, or queued for an overnight run when the system is lightly loaded. Each version must have an attribute for each slow check that records its current status: in progress, passed, or failed. Similar attributes also can be used to record the status of slow manual procedures, such as design reviews or acceptance tests performed by the customer. The error diagnostics resulting from a failed slow check should be sent to the author of the object, and the system should issue a warning to engineers using a version if the version is used while a slow check is incomplete, or if a slow check later determines that the version contains a fault.

For example, a practical policy might require a clean compile and successful run of a brief set of standard test cases for a code module as a quick check, and might run an extensive set of test cases as a slow check, perhaps based on randomly generated test cases and a test result evaluation program that is derived automatically from the specification of the module.

It is not feasible at the current state of the art to absolutely guarantee that every version in the baseline is correct; therefore the configuration management tools should record which versions of the source objects and tools were used to create each version of each object in the baseline. This enables a designer to determine what has changed in case a bug appears in a module test that did not show up in the same tests run the day before, and the current version of the module being tested is still the same.

For effectively localizing new faults based on derivation histories, the configuration management system should record at least the following attributes for each new version of an object:

1. A record of the purpose of the refinement represented by the version

2. Who created it

3. When it was created

4. Any dependencies between the version of the object and particular versions of tools or other objects. These dependencies should include any options or inputs required by the tools to recreate the new version.

The tools for performing the analysis should be able to display the differences between the versions of source objects or tools used in the construction of two versions of an object generated at two different times, which can require recursively tracing dependency threads to an arbitrary depth. The attributes just listed should be selectively displayed for the versions that differ. The informal comments recording the purpose of each refinement are particularly important since they can often enable identification of probable faults without examining the code. Faults due to incomplete propagation of the consequences of a change, such as a new restriction on a data structure or a new interpretation for an argument to a procedure, are particularly amenable to detection by this kind of analysis of the differences in the derivations of two versions of an object.

Consistency constraints are dependencies between corresponding versions of different objects. The simplest kind of consistency constraint to enforce automatically is the functional dependency between a source object and another object that is mechanically derived from the source object by a software tool. The most familiar example of this is the relation between the source code and the object code of a program, which are expected to be related by the function computed by a compiler. Similar constraints are associated with many other types of software tools. Maintaining this kind of consistency relationship is simple conceptually, but it is very important in practice because much time can be wasted in trying to track down a bug due to using an obsolete version of the object code. Debugging can be very difficult if the observed behavior does not correspond to the intended versions of the specifications and source code.

The dependency attributes used for supporting the analysis of derivation histories can also be used for mechanically maintaining consistency between the current versions of the source objects and the other objects that are mechanically derived from them. A simple example of this kind of facility is provided by the UNIX make tool. This tool records the dependencies between files representing versions of objects in a database called the makefile, together with the commands needed to generate the mechanically derived files. The tool approximates functional dependencies using the creation times associated with the files. Make assumes that a derived file is up to date if and only if it has been created after all of the files it depends on. The tool creates a current version of a specified file by tracing the dependency chains leading to the demanded file in depth-first order, and recomputing the files on these chains that are not up to date. This simple algorithm works most of the time. The algorithm can fail if the creation times of the sources do not increase monotonically, which can happen when restoring old versions from tape. The algorithm can also fail if the creation times of the derived files do not remain fixed, which can happen when objects are copied. A more reliable algorithm can be based on the unique ids associated with each version, provided that they are machine readable and protected from tampering or human error.

Consistency constraints generally stem from multiple representations of a design decision. In cases where the representations are related by mechanical translation steps, the consistency constraints can be treated as functional dependencies and can be maintained by the kind of tool just described. Some dependencies do not have a clear direction associated with them: Two objects may be related by a consistency constraint, but there may be no way to determine whether the first object is derived from the second or vice versa. Such bidirectional constraints can be addressed by constraint networks.

A *constraint network* is a kind of system for maintaining a set of constraints relating a set of objects. Such a system allows attribute values to be entered only if all of the constraints are satisfied. Constraints in such a system are active, in the sense that they have rules for adding derived values whenever enough attribute values have been defined to allow the value of a missing attribute to be determined via a constraint. For example, a constraint such as $x = y * z$ can be used to calculate the value of any one of the variables x, y, and z if the values of the other two are known. Thus constraint networks can provide automatically computed attributes without a fixed commitment about which values must be derived from which other values. Instead, the constraints can be applied in either direction, depending on the circumstances.

Constraint networks can also detect inconsistencies when two different constraints require an attribute of an object to take on two different values. When an inconsistency arises in a constraint network, the system can trace the derivation chains backwards to determine which pieces of information that originated from outside the constraint network led to the conflict, thus helping to localize the error and helping the designer determine which attribute values should be removed to resolve the inconsistency. When a piece of information is removed, all of the other pieces of information derived from it are removed also, unless they can be rederived using the remaining constraints. This kind of processing has been most highly developed for numerical constraints because the theory of solving equations has been most extensively studied for number systems. Similar facilities for other types of data are also possible. An important potential application of this technology is to determine which parts of a software system should be removed when a requirement is dropped. Some research has explored this idea [4], but more work is needed to fully realize its benefits.

Versions of Composite Objects. A *composite object* is composed of other objects, known as its *components*. Large systems are built using hierarchical decompositions; therefore facilities for managing versions of composite objects are important for engineering applications in general, and for software development in particular. We discuss briefly some of the issues involved in managing the versions of composite software objects.

A version of an object is intended to be a fixed snapshot of the object. This concept must be refined for composite software objects to determine the interpretation of references to other objects, such as the components of a composite object. There are two plausible alternatives: a reference to another object can either specify a particular version of that object, or it can denote the current version of the object. Under the first alternative, a version of a composite includes the definitions of all the component objects used in the definition of the composite; under the second alternative, a version of a composite includes the names of the components but not their definitions.

The first alternative is appropriate for a version control system for software development, because the properties of a software object are usually influenced by the properties of the other modules it uses. This interpretation of object references in versions guarantees that the properties of a version are completely fixed, which is desirable to provide a stable working environment. Adoption of the first alternative prevents situations where a version of a program module successfully passes all tests on one day, and mysteriously fails the same tests the next day. Such situations can arise under the second alternative in cases where the source code of the program module is unchanged, but where one of the components it uses has changed. This example illustrates why a version of a composite module should fix the definitions of the component objects in addition to the definition of the composite object itself.

Building a configuration management system based on this interpretation requires attention to the representation of versions and the automated processing needed for effectively managing composite objects. An object reference in a version of a composite object must identify not only an object, but also an alternative and a version for that object. To avoid burdening the designer with many routine details, the operation for adding a new version of a composite object to the baseline should use the current alternative and version of each component object as a default, and provide a convenient way to override the defaults when necessary. It is also important to use a representation that can efficiently use storage by sharing parts of object definitions between versions. This is necessary to avoid storing multiple complete copies of composites that differ only in the versions of the subcomponents, since a complete copy of a large system can require substantial amounts of secondary storage.

The second alternative appears plausible because it is often desirable to use a version of a composite object with the most recent versions of its components. For example, this occurs when testing a program module. However, the second interpretation is not an appropriate basis for a version control system for the reasons just outlined. A better way to support access to the most up-to-date version of a composite object is to provide an automation configuration control operation that delivers such a version, constructing one if necessary. Such an operation creates a new version of a composite object whenever the current version of the object refers to an obsolete version of at least one of its subcomponents, where up-to-date versions of all subcomponents are produced by recursively applying the same mechanism. Such an operation illustrates the need for the efficient shared storage representation mentioned previously, because large numbers of new versions for composite objects can be automatically created by a single user operation. In an advanced system, this capability should be integrated with the facility for managing computed objects and attributes, since the processing involved is essentially the same. Computed objects and attributes can be considered to be abstract subcomponents of the source objects that can be either computed on demand or stored, depending on whether the system is trying to optimize performance in time or space.

A configuration control system should also provide the designer with a single operation for retrieving an old version of a composite object. The results of such an operation should include the corresponding versions of all other objects referenced either directly or indirectly by the composite object. Such a facility is missing in many current systems, which commonly treat all modules as self-contained units and provide no support for maintaining the relationships between the versions of a composite object and the versions of its components. This becomes a serious problem for engineers working on large projects, because manipulating versions of large composites without the appropriate support from the configuration control system can involve large amounts of manual effort, and offers ample opportunities for introducing errors.

Relationships Between Objects.   A configuration control system should help maintain relationships between objects with multiple versions. For example, a software module has a specification and an implementation, and it is desirable to keep a record of which versions of the implementation correspond to each version of the specification. This process is easier in systems that maintain the distinction between refinements and alternatives, and treat refinements as specializations, as defined earlier in this section (Alternative Versions).

The specialization structure is useful because many common relationships are *monotonic* with respect to specialization. For example, if a program p

satisfies a specification s, then every specialization of p satisfies s and p satisfies every generalization of s. This provides an inheritance structure that allows the system to make inferences about relationships. This can be used to reduce the amount of information the designer has to explicitly specify, as well as the amount of information that has to be explicitly stored by the system. To make this kind of inference reliable, the specialization structure must be maintained by trusted programs.

To summarize, configuration control is essential for successful software development by a team. In the near future, it is reasonable to expect that configuration control will be provided by a mixture of automated tools and manual procedures. Because coordination problems get more severe as the size of the project increases, success in building very large reliable systems depends on increasing the power and sophistication of automated tools for supporting configuration control.

7.3.2 Decision Support and Synthesis Tools

Another limiting aspect of software development is conceptual complexity. Decision-support tools can help to control conceptual complexity by helping designers understand and manipulate project data. This class of tools provides display, editing, analysis, and synthesis capabilities. The most advanced tools provide all of these aspects in a single integrated framework. A promising approach to constructing such a framework is based on a class of syntax-directed editors that are coupled with a general attribute-grammar processing capability.

Syntax-Directed Editors. A syntax-directed editor is designed for a specific formal language, and has built-in knowledge of at least the syntax and the preferred display format for that language. Syntax-directed editors can be developed for languages representing requirements, specifications, programs, bug reports, or any other kind of data object involved in software development. Such editors can guide the construction and manipulation of well formed state-ments in the language, and can provide visual feedback about the logical struc-ture of those statements.

Syntax-directed editors are attractive as a framework for providing decision-support capabilities because they can be extended with the capabilities to calculate, display, synthesize, and transform attributes of the language related to its semantics as well as its syntax. Some of the benefits that can be provided by such an editor follow.

Helping people learn how to write a formal language. A syntax-directed editor can display the expected category of statement that can appear in a given place in a document, and can provide menus showing the legal choices for that place. The menu choices insert entire templates for different types of legal statements. The templates already have balanced sets of keywords and provide empty places for subexpressions. The subexpressions can be filled in later using the same mechanism, in a process of template expansion rather than linear text entry. This can be valuable for people using unfamiliar notations. The benefits are not limited to novice users since the rarely used features of a language can be unfamiliar even to expert users. Many syntax-directed editors also let users enter subexpressions as ordinary text, which is then parsed and converted into templates by the editor. This facility is most useful for rapid entry of frequently used types of subexpressions that do not contain keywords and whose structures are familiar to the designer, such as arithmetic and assignment statements.

Providing formatted displays. A syntax-directed editor usually contains a definition of a standardized display format for the source language, which can include indenting conventions similar to those created by a pretty printer, and can show the minimum number of parentheses necessary to disambiguate expressions relative to operator-precedence rules. This can keep the display in a neat and standardized format irrespective of the way in which the designer entered the code. There have been questions raised as to whether display formats should be standardized. Different people may have different preferences about how they like to see the code, but on team projects display standards are useful to aid review processes and to help many different people examine the same documents. This consideration suggests that there should be a standard display format, and that the tools should support the standard format, but it does not rule out the possibility that the tools can also support alternative formats. Syntax-directed editors represent documents as trees rather than as text internally. Display formats are computed from the internal representation, and can be flexible. Existing syntax-directed editors can support several different display formats for the same document, and can thus let each team member see any document using their own preferred layout, if this is considered desirable.

Providing summary views that hide the details of selected parts of a complicated statement. By selectively hiding some of the lower-level details, the editor can provide an overview of the basic structure of a complex specification or program. For example, the syntax of a language can be organized using *comment blocks*, which are templates that contain a comment and a list of statements. Such a template is a single structural unit, which unambiguously defines the scope of the comment. Comment blocks have two alternative display formats, a complete display and a short form that shows only the comment part, as illustrated in Fig. 7.6. Because comment blocks can be nested, this provides a useful facility for constructing and reviewing a design by stepwise refinement. Each comment block is used to record and explain a refinement. The editor can provide a facility similar to the outline processors that have been developed for personal computers: Different paths of the stepwise refinement can be selectively expanded for review, and uninteresting paths can be collapsed into the

(a) Short Form   (b) Expanded Display

```
if a(i) > a(i + 1) then                 if a(i) > a(i + 1) then
   -- swap a(i), a(i + 1)                   -- swap a(i), a(i + 1)
end if;                                      t := a(i);
                                             a(i) := a(i + 1);
                                             a(i + 1) := t;
                                         end if;
```

FIGURE 7.6
Comment Blocks

short form to avoid cluttering the display with details that are not relevant to the designer's current purpose. This can make it much easier for a designer to grasp the structure of a complex document.

Providing meaningful facilities for searching and manipulation. Because the editor is aware of the structure of the source language, it can support searches and global replacements throughout a region defined by a language construct, such as a procedure or package body. Anyone who has tried to use an ordinary text editor to rename a program variable is familiar with the frustrations of having the same text string replaced even in contexts where it denotes something other than a variable name, such as parts of string literals or procedure names. The syntax-directed editor is aware of the syntactic category of each construct, so it can support a much more accurate pattern matching capability. The editor can also be aware of the scoping and overloading rules for the identifiers in a particular language; it can support language-specific operations such as "rename this procedure name throughout its scope" or "change the order of the parameters to this procedure." Such commands should affect both the definition of the procedure and all of the places where it is called, but do not affect occurrences of the procedure name that do not denote the procedure, such as string literals, local variables or distinct overloaded variants.

Providing values of computed attributes for analysis purposes. Computed attributes can capture many semantic properties of software objects, and can integrate the editor with many types of static analysis, which can be carried out as the design is entered. For example, attributes can be used to maintain cross-reference information, which can be used to guide the operations of the editor. Such a facility can be used to support commands that display or edit all of the places in a system where a particular procedure is called, a particular variable is referenced, a particular exception is raised or handled, and many other sets of locations defined by the structure of a formal language. Other uses of computed attributes are type checking, providing an execution facility that integrates the editor with a debugger or program animation facility, data flow analysis, requirements tracing, and many other kinds of processing. For example, computed attributes can link error messages that might be produced by stand-alone tools in loosely coupled environments directly to the source text visible from the editor, perhaps by adding special kinds of comments in the appropriate places. The editor can inform the designer that there are outstanding errors, and can provide commands for finding and displaying the error locations. For example, data flow analysis can flag attempts to read uninitialized variables or assignments of values to variables that are never read, thus helping the designer locate missing parts of the code. Providing immediate feedback about errors can save time by helping the designer to avoid developing further refinements based on flawed aspects of a design. For aspects of a design that are difficult to check automatically, computed attributes can be used to generate input data for other tools operating in the background, such as theorem proving programs. Examples of applications where this structure may be useful include checking that every procedure call satisfies declared preconditions, and that every instantiation of a generic module satisfies declared restrictions on the values of the generic parameters. The resulting lists of conditions to be checked can be filtered by resolving common special cases using fast procedures with limited capabilities, and the remaining more difficult cases can be checked manually or submitted to a general-purpose theorem-proving program with bounds on the amount of time it will spend searching for a proof.

Providing automated design completion facilities. The computed attributes supported by a syntax-directed editor can be used to fill in automatically aspects of the design that are implied by details that have been explicitly entered by the designer. For example, types of variables can often be inferred from the context of their use, allowing the editor to produce the corresponding type declarations automatically. Similarly, procedure interface declarations can be created automatically when the procedures are first used. Such a facility can also generate declarations for exception conditions, and default exception handlers for all possible exceptions that can be raised directly or indirectly in each procedure. For example, default handlers can be generated that raise the exception again explicitly at each level to remind the designer of all the possible exceptional cases. This relationship can be maintained incrementally. When a procedure is changed, perhaps by replacing a default exception handler by one that explicitly responds to the exception, the new version or the procedure can be automatically reanalyzed to determine if the set of exceptions it can raise has changed, and the places where the procedure is called can be automatically adjusted to add or remove exception handlers as needed. Such facilities can be valuable for producing robust Ada software, because exceptions can propagate from remote places in the source code, and manual techniques for determining whether all possible exceptions have been handled in a large system can be extremely tedious. Filling in details automatically can prevent errors and can let the designer concentrate on the creative parts of a design. Examples of automatic design completion at the specification level include deriving declarations and import/export relationships for messages and concepts.

Attribute Grammars. Several different systems exist for generating syntax-directed editors automatically from annotated forms of the grammar for the source language [10, 12]. Such systems allow generic designs for syntax-directed editors to be reused for many different languages, and mitigate the cost of developing many language-specific tools. Most of these systems are based on some form of attribute grammar. Attribute grammars can also be used to generate many kinds of translators and analyzers for formal notations. Such translators can realize preprocessors implementing language extensions, pretty printers, diagram generators, routines for converting data from one database format to another, and many other CASE tools. Automatically generated translators can also perform input functions in applications programs.

An *attribute grammar* is an ordinary context-free grammar augmented with a set of equations for each production. These equations define the values of a set of attributes for the symbols in the production. The attributes and equations can be specified by the tool designer to calculate many kinds of properties of the language defined by the grammar.

A simple example of an attribute grammar is shown in Fig. 7.7. This example shows a fragment of a simple expression language, defined by an abstract syntax that leaves out the keywords. The cases of each production are identified by uppercase labels to make the grammar easier to read, and to provide unique representations for derivation trees. The instances of each grammar symbol are numbered to identify them uniquely in the attribute equations. The equations define the type attribute for each kind of expression in the example. This attribute represents the expected data type for each expression. The values of this attribute are determined by the context in which the expression appears, as illustrated by the first equation. If the fragment shown in the example is embedded in a functional language, then the expected type of the expression forming the body of a function definition will be determined by the

---

```
exp0      : IF exp1 exp2 exp3
            { type(exp1) = boolean, type(exp2) = type(exp0),
                                type(exp3) = type(exp0) }
          | VARIABLE id1
            { type(id1) ˙= type(exp0) }
          ;
```

FIGURE 7.7
Simple Attribute Grammar

declaration of the type returned by the function. A type checker can be constructed by extending this attribute grammar with other attributes representing the actual type of each expression, and representing the type bindings induced by variable and function declarations. These attributes can be used to check whether the actual type of each expression is compatible with the expected type for the expression. Attribute equations can be used to pass information up and down the syntax tree in any pattern, and can be used to check context sensitive constraints with reasonable efficiency. Traditionally, circular definitions are not allowed, although in some systems they are interpreted as fixpoint equations that are solved by iteratively recomputing the attribute values until the values stabilize. Such circular definitions can be useful for calculating closure properties, but they must be designed with care to avoid infinite iterations. An example of a closure property useful in software development applications is the transitive module dependency relation. This relation has a potentially circular definition for software systems with recursive procedures.

The processor for an attribute grammar can produce relatively efficient code for calculating the attributes, although current methods sometimes require substantial storage space for the resulting attribute values. Both monolithic and incremental algorithms for computing attributes have been developed. Improving the space efficiency of attribute grammar processors is a current research area.

Diagram Tools. Diagram tools provide another form of decision support. The simplest kinds of diagram tools generate graphical representations for design objects defined by formal languages. Such graphical representations can be useful for providing summary views. Diagrams can help a designer or customer gain a global understanding of the structure of a system, and are often used to support review meetings. The more advanced forms of diagram tools allow both the graphical forms and the text forms of design objects to be edited, and can automatically create or modify both forms of the information to maintain consistency between the graphical view and the text view of the object.

The advanced forms of the tools can be difficult to implement because each of these two views often contains information that is not present in the other view. For example, the graphical view contains information about the layout of the diagram that is not usually contained in the text view, and the text view often contains semantic information that is not captured by the structures shown in the graphical views, such as detailed algorithms or assertions. Thus facilities for editing the graphical view must define how all possible transformations on the graphics affect the text views, and the facilities for editing the text views must similarly define how all possible transformations on the text affect the graphical view. Such transformations must provide computed default values for the missing information, to allow completion of the other view in case new components are added to an object. Because the computed default values can be replaced by subsequent editing operations in the other view, providing automated support for maintaining consistency and providing useful derivation information are substantial problems.

Browsers and Component Finders. Another kind of decision support tool helps locate relevant reusable components. The simplest type of tool in this category is a browser. A browser provides a window into a database that can be used to examine its contents. Browsers are useful for exploring libraries of reusable components. Browsers were originally applied to programs, and can also be used for software objects of any other type: requirements, specifications, bug reports, and so on. A browser is similar to an editor, except that it provides additional facilities for navigating through the structures provided by the database.

A common mechanism for visualizing tree-structured collections is to provide a set of menus that show the alternative choices at each point in the path from the root of the tree to the current point in the collection. The benefit provided by a browser is critically dependent on the organization of the database. To succeed, the tree structure must be based on a disjoint categorization, with independent choices for each level. The designer must be able to easily and unambiguously decide at each level which category contains the item of interest. Such categorizations are relatively difficult to construct and maintain for large and evolving collections.

Other tools for retrieving reusable components provide automatic object-retrieval facilities. The simplest ones are based on linear searches for text patterns, such as the grep facility of UNIX. Keyword searching restricted to particular attributes of the objects represents the next level of sophistication. Such searches typically are based on patterns consisting of boolean combinations of keywords or on frequency vectors for keywords. This is sometimes coupled with a facility for recognizing synonyms, which is often implemented using normalization. The basic idea is to choose a unique representative member for each equivalence class of synonyms, and to standardize each keyword in all queries and all entries in the database by replacing each keyword with the unique representative of its equivalence class of synonyms.

Retrieving programs based on their formal specifications is a more powerful approach because the search can be based on the semantics of the desired object. In addition to being more selective than a keyword search, such an approach can incorporate transformations on and combinations of stored objects to synthesize an object satisfying a query. Such searches typically involve logical inferences, and can be time consuming. This technique can be coupled with some of the faster and less specific methods such as keyword searching to reduce the size of the search space. Such systems are the subject of current research.

Performance Evaluation Tools. Execution profilers and timing analyzers are commonly used to improve the performance of a software system.

An execution profiler gives the number of times each statement in a program is executed, or the amount of time spent in each subroutine. This can be valuable for locating the parts of the system that should be redesigned to use more efficient data structures and algorithms. Execution profilers are useful for improving the performance of large systems by locating the modules where the system spends most of its time. Once the frequently executed parts of the code have been located, they can be reimplemented to use more efficient algorithms and data structures.

A timing analyzer determines the time it takes to execute each path through a straight-line program, and locates the longest path, or the set of paths that exceed a specified time bound. Timing analyzers are used in the design of real-time systems to determine the critical paths through the code that must be redesigned if a tight worst-case timing constraint is not being met. Such tools give results for a specific target architecture. Timing tools that apply to many different target machines can be effectively created via tool generators that take descriptions of instruction sets and their timing properties as input and generate timing analyzer tools tailored to the described machine. Timing analysis is significantly more difficult for machines with virtual memory and interrupts, languages with dynamic garbage collection, and algorithms with loops or recursions. Such features are tightly constrained or avoided in many current real-time systems to enable guarantees of meeting real-time deadlines in the worst case.

Other performance evaluation tools include packages for constructing and solving queuing theory models. These tools are commonly used to estimate average waiting times and system throughput for systems with multiple concurrent users, such as operating systems or telephone switching networks. The tools for solving queuing theory models provide symbolic solutions that cover all possible load conditions and can be analyzed to determine the impact of varying load and resource parameters and optimal operating ranges. However, symbolic solutions are feasible only for restricted sets of assumptions about the distributions of arrival times and service times, such as independent exponential distributions. Solutions for historical or mathematically intractable distributions are generally done via simulations. Although simulations can treat unrestricted distributions, each simulation gives results only for a specific load distribution, rather than a family of related distributions, and the accuracy of the results is influenced by statistical sampling errors that decrease slowly as the number of samples increases. Accurate estimation of properties influenced by rare events can require very large sample sets to get sufficiently many instances of the rare events during the simulation run. Exploring the effects of varying load parameters via simulations can be very expensive, especially for systems with many independent parameters, because the entire simulation must be executed once for each assignment of values to the parameters.

Design Completion Tools.   Other software synthesis tools provide design completion facilities. The simplest tools in this category are discussed earlier in this section (Syntax-Directed Editors). More sophisticated tools of this type use formal specifications to automatically synthesize code. There are several different known approaches to this problem, which can be separated into proto-typing tools and production-quality tools. Prototyping tools generate correct but possibly inefficient code for the purposes of evaluating requirements and functional specifications. Tools in this category must require a minimum of design effort to be useful. Production-quality synthesis tools attempt to con-struct efficient implementations for the delivered version of the system. Tools in this category must produce reliable and efficient code to be useful.

Some prototyping tools are based on executable subsets of a specification language. Some such subsets are axioms in conditional equational form, which can be translated into recursive programs, and Horn clause logic, which can be executed using resolution-based inference techniques. These approaches are valuable when they work, but often they require the specifications to be transformed considerably to provide a feasible level of execution efficiency.

Another approach is based on module interconnection facilities and a set of reusable software components. This approach can provide much better efficiency for large systems than the executable specification approach, because the reusable software components can embody the most efficient known algo-rithms. The disadvantage of the approach is that it takes more effort on the part of the designer, who must develop a decomposition, and must often adjust the behavior of available components to tailor them to the current problem. The additional effort is not entirely a disadvantage since much of the decomposition information developed in such a prototype can evolve into the architectural design for the delivered version of the system. This approach can be realized with the help of a translator program that maps a simplified notation into detailed code for adjusting and interconnecting the components. Such transla-tors can be created using attribute grammars.

Special-purpose application generators represent a variation of this approach that increases efficiency at the expense of generality. By fixing the problem domain, it is possible to develop a generic class of solution algorithms and embed them into a translator for a special-purpose language designed specifically for the application domain. This allows a simple specification of the problem to be mapped automatically into a fairly efficient implementation. This type of system sometimes is called an *application generator* or a *fourth-generation language*. Tools in this category are very useful, provided that the customer's problem fits into the domain of a particular tool. The main advan-tage of such systems is the flexibility they provide, which makes it easy to adapt the system to the changing needs of the customer, provided that the changes do not change the problem so radically that it no longer can be expressed in the language supported by the application generator. The best known uses of application generators include business data processing, where interactively specified forms are used to interact with a database.

Tools for synthesizing production quality code for unrestricted applica-tions can be based on weakest preconditions and transformations. Tools in this category are the goals of current research, and are not yet widespread. However, we shall briefly examine the principles on which they are based.

Synthesis methods based on weakest preconditions are used on a small scale, to automatically derive sequences of assignment statements that satisfy given postconditions. The advantage of such tools is that they guarantee the correctness of the synthesized code with respect to the given specification in the cases where the tools succeed. This problem is difficult in general, but can be solved in many cases for straight-line code. These special cases are sufficient to support the automatic generation of initialization code for many loops with given loop invariants, for example. The loop body can often also be synthesized if a bounding function and a fragment of the loop body decreasing the bounding function is given in addition to the loop invariant. The techniques are based on deriving weakest preconditions for programs consisting of sequences of assignment statements containing unknown expressions to be assigned to the variables mentioned on the postconditions. This process often results in a set of equations or inequalities. The process succeeds if the resulting set of relations can be solved to determine the unknown parts of the assignment statements.

Transformation techniques are used to improve the efficiency of a program, where in the extreme case, a black-box specification can be viewed as a program involving enumerations and infinite operations to determine the output. The core of a transformation system is a knowledge base containing a set of meaning-preserving transformations that can be used to improve the efficiency of a program. Such systems can succeed in improving the efficiency of a program only if the knowledge base contains transformations that apply to the given problem specification. This approach also guarantees the correctness of the resulting programs if it succeeds, provided that all of the transformations in the knowledge base are valid.

Meaning-preserving transformations often have associated preconditions that must be met in order for the transformation to be applicable. The tools for applying the transformations require a reasoning capability for determining whether particular transformations are applicable. A system that relies on a human engineer for choosing which transformations to apply is described in [1]. This system is capable of checking whether the transformations are applicable, and of carrying out the specified transformations. A different system that attempts to find applicable transformations automatically and to use performance estimates to guide the search is described in [6]. This system is capable of making choices of data representations for a common set of predefined data types to produce efficient algorithms for particular problems.

7.3.3 Error-Checking Tools

Another limiting factor in software development is accuracy. A reliable software system must be free of errors, but the mean distance between errors in text produced by people is much smaller than the descriptions of most large software systems. Some tools can guarantee the absence of some types of errors because of special restrictions on how the tools construct the documents. For example, a syntax-directed editor can guarantee the absence of syntax errors because of the way it constructs well formed expressions in a formal language. However, such guarantees are not yet practical for all aspects of software development. This makes tools for detecting and locating the kinds of errors that cannot be prevented by special construction techniques important for the development of large software systems. For example, each formal language used in software development should have either a syntax-directed editor or a syntax-checking tool.

A basic kind of check is type consistency. Type-consistency checking applies at the requirements and specifications levels as well as at the programming language level. Although the checking is conceptually simple, it is valuable because many logical errors manifest themselves as type mismatches. It is possible to use type constraints to automatically generate type declarations, and to integrate type inference mechanisms into a syntax-directed editor, which can prevent type inconsistencies by construction. If such a tool is not available, then the next best thing is a type checker that produces error messages pinpointing any inconsistencies. The consistency constraints that should be checked by such a tool for the Spec language are described in Section 3.9.4.

Another relatively simple kind of check is requirements coverage. It is desirable for every requirement to be met by some nonempty set of user commands in the functional specification, and for each user command to correspond to a nonempty set of requirements. This kind of checking can be provided by keeping the relationship describing which commands support which requirements in a database, and providing queries that locate all of the requirements and commands that do not participate in the relationship.

Tools for deadlock detection are useful for evaluating specifications containing atomic transactions. Such a tool can trace the paths in all of the stimulus-response diagrams and all of the atomic transactions in the specification to determine if there are situations where an atomic transaction can fail to terminate because it is waiting for the arrival of messages that have not been sent. For example, a graph containing all of the stimulus-response paths for the file transfer protocol specified in Figs. 3.65 and 3.66 is shown in Fig. 7.8. This graph is derived from the specifications. Each node in the graph represents a set of events, where all of the events in each node correspond to the same case in the response to a message. The edges in the graph show which events cause which other events. This graph is used to check the atomic transactions defined at the sender module. The atomic transaction constrains only those events that occur at the sender module and are mentioned in the transaction. The constrained events are shown in **boldface** type in the example. The graph is generated from the initial events in the atomic transaction. In the example, there is only one initial event, `send@sender`. A necessary condition for absence of deadlocks is that every finite path in the graph must be extendible into a complete path through the atomic transaction. For example,

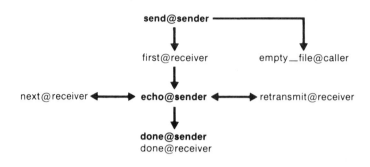

FIGURE 7.8
Stimulus-Response Graph for the File Transfer Protocol

the path [send@sender,echo@sender,done@sender] is a complete path through the atomic transaction shown in Fig. 3.67. The analysis discovers a potential deadlock because the path [send@sender, empty_file@caller] cannot be extended into a complete path through the atomic transaction. The problem can be fixed by adding the response

    SEND done TO sender

to the send@sender message in the case where the file is empty. Another way to fix the problem is to eliminate the done message at the sender and to replace the atomic transaction with the following.

    TRANSACTION transfer = IF WHEN data = [ ] -> send FI

This fulfills the purpose of the original atomic transaction, which is used to delay the next file transfer until the previous one has been completed.

The condition checked previously is necessary but not sufficient to establish the absence of deadlocks. To give a complete guarantee, it is necessary to check that the postconditions associated with sending a message imply the preconditions associated with receiving the message along each path through the atomic transaction, to make sure that the completions for the paths represent feasible computations. This requires the capability to check implications in the underlying logic.

The absence of starvation can be checked by showing that there are no feasible infinite paths through the atomic transaction. This can be done using the technique of bounding functions discussed in Section 5.7.3. It is sufficient to consider just the cycles in the stimulus-response graph. For example, the cycle [echo$sender, next@receiver] can be repeated at most a finite number of times because it decreases the bounding function length(data) at the sender module. However, the cycle [echo@sender, retransmit @receiver] can be repeated infinitely often, so that the protocol has the

potential of introducing starvation if the transmission of a block is always corrupted. If the transmission channel is noisy we cannot prevent this possibility if
we must guarantee delivery of the file. One way to avoid the possibility of starvation is to modify the protocol to put a bound on the number of times a
retransmission may be attempted for a given block or for a given file, and to
abort any transmission that cannot be successfully completed within the bound.
This extension is left to you.

Other kinds of checks at the specification level include instance consistency, input coverage, satisfiability, and congruence consistency. These
constraints are also discussed in Section 3.9.4. Tools for checking these constraints generally require proving theorems in the underlying logic, which is an
undecidable problem in general, and which can be time consuming in many
cases where solutions are possible. For example, instance consistency requires
checking the validity of logical implications, input coverage requires checking
whether a given expression is well defined under a given set of conditions, and
satisfiability requires proving theorems of the form $\texttt{ALL(x: t1 :: pre}$
$\texttt{(x) => SOME(y: t2 :: post(x, y)))}$. This does not mean that we
must give up on trying to build tools, but it does suggest that we should design
tools that have limited goals, and can produce results corresponding to three
cases: constraint ok, error detected, or could not decide. The cases where the
tool could not decide can be output from each tool. This output can be examined manually or fed to other more powerful tools. Practical systems for
automating semantic checks in this category should have a series of tools,
where the faster ones are run first and handle many of the common simple
cases, and the more powerful ones are run only on the questions that could not
be decided by the fast special-case methods. This structure is suggested
because many of the theorems involved in checking the consistency of a
software design are in fact very easy to prove, and many of them can be handled by simple facilities that can recognize a relatively small set of special
cases. For example, most of the cases for checking whether an expression is
well defined can be handled by a simple set of rules for the operations of the
predefined data types, which can be derived from the associated specifications.

Error checking at the programming language level can be classified into
static and dynamic approaches. Static approaches involve analysis of the code
that is independent of the actual inputs to the program; dynamic approaches
involve execution of the code on particular sets of input data.

Most compilers perform syntax and type consistency checking. Another
kind of static checking is data flow analysis, which is carried out by some
optimizing compilers. Data flow analysis can detect cases where variables are
read before they are initialized or variables are assigned values that are never
read. This kind of checking can be generalized to include constraints on the
order in which the operations of particular data types are applied to the
instances of the type. For example, files must be opened before they can be
read, and must be closed before the program terminates.

A more powerful category of static checks involves mathematical proof techniques. The types of properties that are of interest include proving that a program will meet its specification for all possible inputs, and that a program will terminate without raising any exceptions. The concepts on which such tools are based are discussed in Section 5.7. Methods for automating these checks depend on algebraic simplification using term rewrite techniques, induction principles, and other automatable theorem proving techniques. Tools in this category exist but have not been used widely.

The second category of tools at the programming language level are concerned with dynamic checking or testing, which is done while executing programs on particular sets of input data. Dynamic checking tools usually determine statistical properties of programs such as estimates of failure rates. Although such tools usually cannot guarantee that a system operates correctly under all possible situations, testing can be very effective at locating faults, especially those that impact the most common operations performed by a system. Testing is most effective if it is supported by a set of software tools for the following purposes.

Preparing test data. To support manual choices of test data, it is desirable to have a concise test-case definition language providing a syntax for compactly describing instances of all data types, including complex structured types and user-defined types. The test-case definition language should support definitions of sequences of data instances as well as individual instances, so that test sets with given properties can be generated without excessive effort. The processor for the data definition language should generate a driver procedure that invokes the program to be tested with the proper input data, and records the results. To support testing of state machines, the test-case definition language should also support defining the state of the machine in which the test is to be executed and generating code that puts the machine into the specified state before the specified inputs are supplied. To support random testing, it is desirable to have tools for generating random samples from all of the data types that can be expressed in the test-case definition language.

Analyzing test results. The most basic facility computes the differences between a test result file and a previous version of the test result file. More sophisticated facilities automatically generate test oracle programs from the specifications for the module to be tested. A test oracle program determines whether the results of executing a particular program on a particular test case conform to the specification or not. Test oracles are needed to support random testing on a large scale. In the absence of a test oracle generator, a test oracle can be coded manually, or the results of two different implementations for the same program can be compared. An automatically generated test oracle is preferable if the necessary tools can be provided, because there is a smaller chance that faults in the test oracle will prevent the detection of faults in the program to be tested. Testing of large programs is most effective if the code can be instrumented to check specifications of intermediate points in the program in addition to checking the final outputs against their specifications. In particular, it is desirable to check preconditions for internal procedures before each call, loop invariants before and after each execution of the loop body, and data invariants before and after the execution of each operation on a state machine or abstract data type. However, some of these checks can be computationally expensive.

Evaluating test case adequacy. The simplest and most common tool in this category is an execution profiler, which can be used to determine if each statement in the program has been executed at least once. More advanced tools check whether each branch of every possible control path has been tested, or whether each statement has been tested using each possible source of the input data, as determined by a data flow analysis. Other kinds of tools estimate the probability that the program contains an error based on the results of a given set of test cases, to help determine when to stop testing.

7.3.4 Project Management Tools

Support for project management includes tools for estimation, scheduling, and checking on the current status of the project. These functions involve a common set of attributes and are natural to combine into a single tool. The basic idea is to identify the tasks associated with each type of object, and to provide attributes in the project database for recording the following information for each task:

1. The person responsible for carrying out the task
2. The estimated time required to accomplish the task
3. The amount of time that has been spent on the task so far
4. The current status of the task, complete or not.

The principles discussed in Section 4.6.1 can be used to calculate the expected completion date for the project and the probability that the project will be completed by a given deadline. The amount of time actually spent on each part of the system can be used to determine the constants to use in deriving values of the constants needed for the historical interpretation of task effort estimates listed in Fig. 4.41. If the project database is preserved through the system evolution phase, these numbers can also be used to determine the parts of the system that have required the most maintenance effort. This information is useful for identifying parts of the system that should be redesigned to ease evolution problems.

Task assignments can be recorded in the database using the attributes listed previously, and the results of scheduling can be recorded using an additional attribute that lists the immediate predecessors of each task. A task can be started as soon as all of the immediate predecessor tasks are completed. The order in which the tasks must be completed is subject to some uniform constraints; for example, a module must be specified before it is implemented. These are augmented with additional decisions about the order in which parts of the system should be implemented. The considerations affecting these additional decisions involve ease of testing, contingency planning, and reducing project risk by working on the most uncertain things first. These considerations are discussed in Chapter 5. Once the constraints on the order in which the tasks can be done are entered into the database, a planning tool can determine the earliest time each task can start, and the latest time the task should be started to avoid delaying the project. The tasks for which the earliest starting time is the same as the latest starting time are said to be on the *critical path*, since they cannot be delayed at all without delaying the entire project. It is useful to iden-tify the critical tasks to ensure that they get the highest priority.

A task schedule can be analyzed to determine a rough distribution of man-power requirements as a function of time, and the schedule can be adjusted to smooth out the manpower distribution or to adjust the constraints and the schedule to match given availability patterns for workers if the times at which people will enter or leave the project are known in advance. The problem of constructing an optimal schedule for many manpower distributions is at least NP hard, which implies that exact solutions for large problems are not likely to be practical. However, this does not mean that we should not seek to construct approximate automated procedures, since the manager is not likely to be able to construct optimal schedules for large projects using manual techniques either. Knowledge of the difficulty of the optimal scheduling problem should lead us instead to seek approximate heuristics that provide good solutions most of the time. One such heuristic is to schedule the tasks so that of those that can be started, the one with the least slack is chosen first, where the slack is the differ-ence between the latest starting time and the earliest starting time. This is the simplest of the plausible heuristics that lead to fast, greedy scheduling methods. A greedy scheduling method always chooses the best task next, with respect to some readily computable ordering. The least slack criterion is not necessarily the best heuristic, but it is easy to implement and gives reasonable results. Better heuristics are the subject of current research.

Tools for reporting the current status of the project are relatively straight-forward. A typical status report might list the tasks that are behind schedule, the tasks that are ahead of schedule, and give the net number of person-hours that the actual status of the project is ahead or behind the projected status. The estimated completion time and the probability of completion by the deadline are also useful indicators of the current status and are easy to compute based on the methods discussed in Section 4.6.1.

Tools for supporting contingency planning are also useful. Such tools should help identify and estimate the cost of the tasks that could be avoided if a given function or user capability were not implemented. The output of such a tool should be both the set of component tasks affected by the contingency plan, and an assessment of the amount of time that would be saved by adopting such a plan. The tool should also support assessment of the amount of time that would be saved by not implementing groups of user capabilities, since the com-ponents supporting several different user capabilities can overlap, and the savings associated with deleting a group of user capabilities is not a simple combination of the savings associated with the individual capabilities.

7.4 Engineering Databases

Engineering databases provide the framework for constructing automated software development environments. Such databases provide the means for communications between different tools and different users, thus integrating tools, supporting global consistency checking, and providing the means for nondisruptive status reports for a development project.

An effective software development environment is more than the sum of its parts: the individual tools in the environment should be able to work together to solve problems, so that the users are not impeded by the boundaries between the tools. This property is known as tool integration. The easiest and most efficient way to achieve tool integration *in a fixed system* is to design the tools with common interfaces so that they can share data freely and provide uniform interfaces to the users. However, the global consistency constraints inherent in this approach introduce dependencies between the tools that hinder evolution. Tool integration is difficult to achieve in practice because a practical environment must be easy to modify and extend. Evolution is particularly important in this context because the requirements for automated software development environments are uncertain, development costs are high, and new technologies are likely to enable greatly improved environments in the future.

Evolution is easiest if the tools are loosely coupled in an open architecture that provides mechanisms for adding new tools easily. The easiest and fastest way to expand an environment is to incorporate a tool developed by someone else with a new idea. Such *foreign tools* are developed independently of the environment, and are unlikely to respect its conventions and interfaces. Thus foreign tools usually use data structures and input/output formats incompatible with those of the integrated environment. This can make it difficult to share data with the other tools, and it can complicate user interfaces by introducing redundant commands and multiple formats for the same sorts of data.

One way to provide tool integration in the presence of foreign tools is to provide facilities for translating between the different data formats used by the system. The gain in flexibility and new functionality often justifies the loss of some efficiency due to extra translation steps. However, introducing a large number of translations can complicate the design of the environment, and maintaining multiple copies of the same data can introduce consistency problems. These problems can be addressed by using an engineering database to manage the data rather than creating many independent and uncontrolled translation tools.

An *engineering database* is a specialized database mangement system designed for managing engineering data. Such a database can serve as a framework for integrating tools by providing a shared repository for all project data. An engineering database should provide the following facilities to support computer-aided software development environments:

1. Reliable persistent storage

2. Name spaces

3. Data translation to and from tool formats

4. Concurrency control

5. Version control

6. Managing computed objects and attributes.

The most fundamental service provided by a database is reliable persistent storage. This means the objects in the database continue to exist after the processes that created them have terminated. It is a controversial question whether an engineering database should allow objects to be destroyed, but it is clear that operations for destroying objects must be tightly controlled if they are provided, to ensure that the results of development work are not lost. Because it can be very hard to tell when an object is no longer useful, engineering databases should allow selected sets of objects to be designated as permanent. Conceptually, the lifetime of permanent objects is unbounded, although permanent objects may be migrated to archival storage and permanent objects that can be mechanically recreated may be removed from physical storage, at the discretion of the database management system or the database administrator. Engineering time is much more expensive than magnetic tape; therefore it is a reasonable policy to make all of the manually created objects in the state of a software project permanent, perhaps relative to some consistency and correctness conditions.

Objects in an engineering database should have unique identifiers that act as abstract addresses, in the sense that the database should be able to efficiently retrieve an object based on its identifier. This retrieval mechanism supports tools that follow dependency chains from given objects, which is a common situation in computer-aided design. Object identifiers differ from pointers since they are bound to objects rather than physical locations, so that object identifiers do not change when objects are moved to different machines or storage media. Support for object relocation is important to provide permanent objects at a reasonable cost and to reduce remote communication and balance processor loads in distributed environments.

Managing the storage associated with an engineering database differs from managing storage in most programming languages because permanent objects should never become inaccessible. This implies that an engineering database should provide a mechanism for enumerating all the instances of a type to support queries for locating objects whose names are not known, that there is no need for garbage collection of objects in the database, and that access rights should be associated with objects rather than with names. The mechanism for enumerating all instances of a type is likely to be slow and may be used relatively rarely, but it can retrieve objects that are not even indirectly accessible via *external names*. An external name is a symbol that can be manipulated directly by the users of the system, such as a character string or an icon.

An engineering database should support the concept of a name space to aid management of external names. A *name space* binds external names to internal identifiers for the objects in the database. Name spaces are generalizations of directories in a file system, which bind external names to files. A facility for binding external names to internal object identifiers is needed to help users manipulate objects, because internal object identifiers can not be meaningfully displayed to users, and hence are difficult to remember. Internal object identifiers should be mechanically generated by the database system to ensure that they are unique throughout the entire database. Name spaces, users, and tools should all be object types that can be stored in the database so that the standard mechanisms for managing relationships can be used to maintain associations between users, tools, design objects, and name spaces. A name space should provide operations for retrieving the object bound to an external name, checking whether an external name has a binding, enumerating all of the bindings in a name space, adding and removing bindings, and importing bindings from other name spaces. Some of the concepts of Ada are useful in this context: a name space should contain a public and a private part, where the bindings in the public part can be imported by other name spaces, and those in the private part cannot. It can be useful to import the entire set of public bindings from another name space, to import a selected subset, or to rename specified bindings from another name space.

A database should support data translation via a uniform view mechanism, which can provide different views of the data in the database to different tools. Each view of the database can define a different representation for the data, and possibly different sets of primitive operations. The database has a main view that is defined by the *database schema*, which may be a static document, or a set of objects contained in the database itself and maintained using the standard version control mechanism it provides. The schema defines the set of abstract data types whose instances are contained in the database, including the primitive operations available on those types. It is important for an engineering database to support objects corresponding to the instances of all abstract data types, because a computer-aided software engineering environment must deal with a large and extensible set of data types. The types that are likely to arise include operator trees for a variety of formal languages, graph structures, diagrams, text, name spaces, object spaces, and the entire range of data types used in tool interfaces.

Each view of the database defines a different set of abstract data types, which are linked to the types in the main view by mappings specified in the definition of the view. The types in a view can correspond to a subset of the types in the main view, the set of instances of a type in a view can correspond to a subset of the instances of the corresponding type in the database schema, and the properties and operations of the types in a view can be more restricted than those of the corresponding types in the database schema. A view can provide read-only access or update access to types in the database schema. In the first case, mappings are required only from the database schema to the view, and in the second case, mappings are required in both directions. The database schema and the view mechanism should be integrated with the specifications of the types in the database and the associated subtype structure.

Tools designed as part of the environment operate directly on implementations of the abstract types defined in views of the database. The views for such tools have the choice of either materializing the objects in the view, or translating the operations of the view types into operations on the corresponding types of the database schema, whichever is more efficient. Views supporting foreign tools must specify concrete data representations for each abstract data type in the view, in addition to just the interface of the abstract type, to maintain consistency with the data representations expected by the foreign tools. The purpose of a view supporting a foreign tool is to enable use of the tool without modifying it; therefore such a view must materialize the data in the format expected by the tool.

Concurrency control and version control are two configuration control functions that should be provided by the database. The issues associated with these functions are discussed in Section 7.3.1.

Automatic management of computed objects and attributes is important for maintaining the consistency of the database. A computer-aided software engineering environment provides many tools for constructing derived objects and attributes, such as executable files, concrete interface specifications, cross-reference information, and certifications. An engineering database should provide facilities for automatically and reliably managing this information. Some useful facilities are:

1. Protected derivations

2. Derivation policies

3. Space management policies.

The requirements for an engineering database differ substantially from those for a business database. For example, most business systems are concerned only with the current state of the operational data for an organization; in engineering applications, information about the development history and alternative choices must also be recorded. Also, the transactions in a business database are short, do not depend on human interactions, and can be rolled back if necessary to preserve consistency. In contrast, engineering transactions are long, interactive, cannot be rolled back, and cannot block read access to the database. Another difference is the variety of data in the database. Business data often contains many instances of just a few types of data, and can be covered to a large degree with just relationships over numbers and character strings with predictable sizes. In contrast, engineering data contains just a few instances of a wide variety of abstract data types, and these instances have a complex and varied structure, with diverse storage sizes.

Most of the available database management systems are designed for business applications, and are not well suited for engineering applications such as software development environments. When traditional database management systems are used to support engineering applications, mismatches between the application and the original requirements for the database management system often lead to cumbersome interfaces and poor performance. This is why specialized database management systems are needed for effectively implementing project databases.

Engineering database systems are a recent development, and mature systems are not widely available yet. Engineering databases are a current focus for software research because such databases are expected to enable and enhance the feasible levels of automated tool support for software development. This situation should change as a result of many currently active research and development efforts focused on engineering database systems. The object-oriented databases being developed now are better suited to engineering applications than the traditional database systems based on the relational, network, and hierarchical data models common in business applications.

7.5 Management Aspects

A computer-aided software development environment is essential for developing reliable large-scale software systems. However, a high level of automation cannot be achieved without suitable policies addressing several significant problems. Some of the issues are: how to acquire a useful set of tools, how to adapt development practices to take advantage of the tools, and how to take advantage of new developments.

Many of the best software tools are carefully guarded commercial secrets, because they are viewed as providing an edge over the competition. This leads to a situation where most companies develop their own tools, in a massive and wasteful duplication of effort. Progress is also slowed because parallel tool development efforts cannot learn from each other's mistakes. This problem can be addressed by cooperation between companies, as shown by MCC in the United States and the Esprit program in Europe. The situation in the United States is affected by government policies and laws that limit cooperation between the government and private industry. Effective cooperation between competitors is difficult to achieve without government support.

Careful planning and systematic investment policies are needed because the cost of the tools can be substantial. Many software development organizations in the United States treat tool development costs as part of project costs, rather than as a separate line item in the long-term investment plan. This type of policy handicaps the software industry in the United States relative to countries that follow different policies, particularly Japan. Treating tools as part of project costs is detrimental because it encourages cutting corners to reduce overhead costs associated with tool development. The result is special-purpose tools that must be thrown away at the end of the project because they do not generalize well to other applications, are not reliable, and are not documented well enough to be fixable. Thus tool development becomes a true overhead cost, because nothing of value is left over at the end of the project. With better incentive structures and planning, the same expenditures can be used to gradually build up and improve a reliable and integrated set of software development tools that improve productivity in all future projects.

Similar policy issues apply to building up libraries of reusable components. It requires additional effort and investment to generalize, document, and certify existing components to make them reusable, thus reducing future synthesis and debugging efforts, and enhancing future productivity.

Strong management support for using automated tools and strict configuration management policies are needed to reap the potential benefits of automation. Introducing tools presents classical technology transfer problems, because of the need for retraining, and new approaches to get the maximum benefits from automated tools. The following analogy expresses the frustrations of a toolsmith in a computer-aided design shop for digital hardware, and applies equally well to software development tools. Suppose a suborganization complains about traffic problems when going to work each morning, and you deliver a helicopter to them. They try to taxi it down the freeway, and complain bitterly that it is much more cumbersome than a car, and makes it even harder to get to work in the morning. The difficulty is that to realize the potential benefit of using the helicopter, the members of the suborganization must abandon their accustomed approach to fighting traffic and learn to fly. Similarly, software tools often enable better solutions to a problem that involve totally different approaches, but the powerful new tools may not be very good at supporting the old way of doing business. It can be difficult to convince people to use tools that may initially degrade performance while the people learn how to use them. Effective automation requires strong management support for training, and incentives for learning how to get the most out of new systems. The process is easier if tools can be designed to allow a gradual transition from accustomed practices to new approaches without degrading performance too much during the transition. This requires a long term view that can see past the next deadline to a future in which the tools enable the successful delivery of products that would have been impossible to create using old techniques.

Strict configuration-management policies require even stronger management support, because they often permanently degrade individual performance to improve the productivity of the group as a whole. Although adhering to strict configuration-management policies enforced by software tools can make the individual tasks of the development team take longer, these policies can prevent many hours searching for problems due to incompatibilities between versions. Nothing can be more frustrating than spending a week trying to debug a system only to discover that the object code does not correspond to the current version of the source, or to find that a correctly repaired bug has reappeared because someone accidentally overwrote the corrected version of a module and lost the changes that fixed the bug. It may be possible for an individual to meet a tight deadline by circumventing configuration control procedures, but this often causes many other members of the project to miss their deadlines. Management should establish and enforce firm configuration control policies and make sure that everyone understands why they are necessary and how they benefit the team as a whole. The purpose of these policies is to prevent lost work and destructive unpredictable changes to critical parts of a system in the middle of someone's enhancement or error location efforts.

7.6 Related Research

Many papers related to advanced tools for software development can be found in [3]. A formalization of refinements and a discussion of algorithms for combining refinements to programs can be found in [2, 8]. An approach for creating specialized specification languages for particular problem domains with associated application generators is described in [5]. Details of versions and alternatives are discussed in [9].

Exercises

1. Make a list of all the software development tools available in your organization, and determine which of the capabilities described in this chapter are available to you.

Projects

The following projects are fairly substantial, and correspond roughly to student theses at the master's level.

1. Design and construct a tool for generating a test driver for a program with a given concrete interface specification. The test driver should execute the program with a specified number of randomly chosen input data sets from the appropriate abstract data types.

2. Design and construct a tool for evaluating the results of a test case. The inputs to the tool are the specifications of a program, the actual inputs defining a test case, and the actual outputs of the tested program. The result is a boolean indicating whether the results of the test case conform to the specification.

3. Design and construct a tool for determining the worst-case execution time of a straight-line program (without loops or recursions). The input to the tool is a source program, the corresponding compiled object program, and a table giving the worst-case execution times for each instruction on a given machine.

References

1. F. Bauer, B. Moller, H. Partsch, and P. Pepper, "Formal Program Construction by Transformations—Computer-Aided, Intuition-Guided Programming," *IEEE Transactions on Software Engineering 15*, 2 (Feb. 1989), 165–180.

2. V. Berzins, "On Merging Software Extensions," *Acta Informatica 23*, 6 (Nov. 1986), 607–619.

3. R. Conradi, T. Didriksen, and D. Wanvik, eds., *Advanced Programming Environments*, Springer-Verlag, 1986.

4. A. Czurchry and D. Hines, "KBRA: A New Paradigm for Requirements Engineering," *IEEE Expert 3*, 4 (Winter 1988), 21–35.

5. P. Freeman, "A Conceptual Analysis of the Draco Approach to Constructing Software Systems," *IEEE Transactions on Software Engineering SE–13*, 7 (July 1987), 830–844.

6. A. Goldberg, "Technical Issues for Performance Estimation," *Proceedings of the Second Annual RADC Knowledge-Based Assistant Conference*, RADC(COES), Griffiss AFB, NY, 1987.

7. K. Henninger, J. Kallander, D. Parnas, and J. Shore, "Software Requirements for the A7-E Aircraft," NRL Report 3876, Nov. 1978.

8. S. Horowitz, J. Prins, and T. Reps, "Integrating Non-Interfering Versions of Programs," Technical Report 690, Computer Sciences Department, University of Wisconsin, Madison, Mar. 1987.

9. M. Ketabchi and V. Berzins, "The Theory and Practice of Representing and Managing the Refinements, Alternatives, and Versions of Composite Objects," Technical Report 85–40, Computer Science Department, University of Minnesota, 1985.

10. D. Notkin, "The GANDALF Project," *The Journal of Systems and Software 5*, 2 (May 1985), 91–105.

11. D. L. Parnas and P. C. Clements, "A Rational Design Process: How and Why to Fake It," *IEEE Transactions on Software Engineering SE–12*, 2 (Feb. 1986), 251–257.

12. T. Reps and T. Teitelbaum, *The Synthesizer Generator: A System for Constructing Language-Based Editors*, Springer-Verlag, New York, 1988.

8

Research Directions

This chapter provides a brief survey of current research directions in software engineering. We focus on areas contributing to increased automation and productivity.

8.1 Prototyping

As discussed in Chapter 2, it is very difficult to develop firm requirements for novel software systems. This is a matter for concern because errors in requirements have a large effect on software costs. Requirements errors cannot be prevented just by talking to users, especially for aspects of applications that have not been automated before. Introducing a computer system may change the way customers deal with their problems so radically that they often cannot predict or understand all of the implications of switching to an automated system. This makes requirements analysis a discovery process for the customer that may substantially change the customer's perceptions of the application. Many people cannot visualize what an unfamiliar system will be like unless they see it demonstrated and can try to use it to solve typical problems from their application area. In such cases the customers do not know exactly what the proposed system should do, but they can usually recognize what they want or don't want when they see it in action, especially if expert guidance on how to use the system to solve their problems is provided during the demonstration.

If the first time the customer sees the system run is when the system is completed and delivered, it is very likely that the customer will not find the delivered system acceptable, and that extensive modification and rebuilding will be required.

Prototypes provide inexpensive demonstrations of the essential aspects of proposed new system behavior. Prototypes are constructed prior to the production version to:

1. Gain information that guides analysis and design, and

2. Support generation of the production version.

This approach is based on the assumption that many iterative changes to proposed system behavior are necessary to formulate an acceptable version of the requirements. This assumption is likely to be valid whenever the proposed software system will introduce substantial changes in the way the customers do their business. In such circumstances, it is attractive to make many of the initial changes based on demonstrations of cheap mockups of the system before starting the detailed and time-consuming engineering work needed to construct efficient and reliable software systems. This approach seeks to reduce software evolution costs by making the foreseeable changes to the requirements before investing substantial resources in building a production quality system, as illustrated in Fig. 8.1. Such an approach can eliminate most of the change requests due to an inappropriate initial set of requirements, concentrating software evolution effort on responses to environmental changes affecting the problems the system must solve.

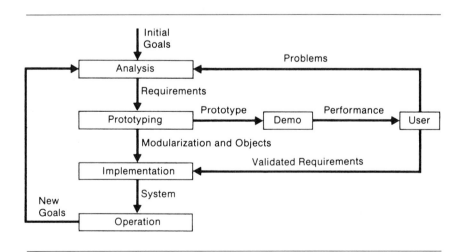

FIGURE 8.1
The Prototyping Process

The prototype can be useful in the maintenance of the production version of the system in two different capacities. The first is exploratory evaluation of alternative changes. The prototype is a simpler and more flexible description of the system than the production version. A prototype should capture the logical structure of a system more clearly than a production version because it is expressed in a higher level language and presents a simple view of the system before optimization transformations add incidental details and introduce dependencies between logically unrelated parts of the system. The tools in the prototyping system should also provide analysis capabilities that help the designer assess the impact and effects of a proposed change more easily than when working with the production version of the system.

The second use of the prototype in the evolution of the production version depends on having a mature tool set that helps the designer transform the prototype into the production version. Ideally this should be a cooperative effort by the designer and the tools. The tools should keep a record of the decisions that were made by the designer to transform each version of the prototype into the corresponding production version. This record should be used in creating the next release of the production version from the updated prototype. An iterative process of prototype modification is triggered by each major change request. After the new release of the prototype has stabilized, the tools should be able to use the record of the designer's previous set of decisions to guide the creation of the new release of the production version of the system. The tools should determine which decisions are affected by the change, and automatically apply the decisions that are not affected. The designer must reconsider only the parts of the transformation process that affect the changed parts of the system. Computer-aided rederivation avoids the need to identify and undo optimizations that are not applicable to the new release of the production system, and helps prevent introducing details into the production version that are no longer supported by the changed requirements.

To be useful, prototypes must be constructed quickly and economically. Manual approaches to prototyping require too much time and effort, although some limited gains can be obtained by using high-level programming languages designed to be expressive and flexible rather than efficient. Some programming languages that have been used in this way include LISP, APL, AWK, SETL, PROLOG, and EqL. A more promising way to realize rapid prototyping in practice is to combine a special prototyping language with a computer-aided prototyping system. A prototyping language must make it easy to construct, modify, and analyze a prototype, possibly at the expense of efficiency, completeness, capacity, or robustness, and must form a sound basis for an integrated set of supporting tools forming the computer-aided prototyping system. The purposes of a computer-aided prototyping system are to:

1. Aid the designer in constructing and evaluating a prototype,

2. Provide an execution, debugging, and monitoring capability, and

3. Support transformation of a prototype into the corresponding production version of the system.

Most of the commercially available prototyping systems have narrow ranges of application, typically geared towards business data processing. Such packages typically provide convenient interfaces to databases via graphical query languages and graphical report definition facilities, and generate code automatically. These packages can significantly speed up the development process and may produce software that can be used in a production environment, although they may not provide the best efficiency. Currently available packages do not include comprehensive treatments of error handling, crash recovery, concurrency control, and data integrity, although there is no inherent reason why such systems could not be extended to provide good service in these areas. The biggest problem with these approaches is limited applicability: they are effective for prototyping systems in a particular type of application, but are not much use for other types of applications, such as word processing, real-time systems, scientific computing, systems programming, distributed systems, or expert systems.

Another type of application-specific prototyping system is aimed at the development and processing of special-purpose languages. Most of the systems in this category are based on attribute-grammar technology. The most basic use of attribute grammars is to define translations from one formal language into another. Systems for automatically generating parsers and translators from attribute-grammar specifications of the required transformation can significantly speed up this kind of work. Attribute grammars can also be used to generate other classes of tools for formal languages, such as syntax-directed editors, interpreters, diagram generators, flow analysis tools, pretty printers, types checkers, and so on. This technology is described in Chapter 7. Other kinds of application-specific code-generation systems are discussed in [9].

A more comprehensive approach to computer-aided prototyping is based on a general-purpose prototyping language. The Defense Advanced Projects Research Agency (DARPA) is currently seeking to develop a comprehensive rapid prototyping language and the associated computer-aided prototyping system, indicating growing research interest in this area. The DARPA common prototyping language and system is supposed to apply to real-time systems, concurrent systems, distributed systems, and expert systems when it becomes available. The goals of the common prototyping language include support for verification and transformation to a production quality implementation in addition to a capability for rapid formulation and execution.

It is difficult to design a prototyping language because the goals of expressiveness and executability are in conflict. A prototyping language should be expressive to allow concise and natural descriptions of complex system behaviors. Such descriptions should be formulated at a level natural for human thought and communication, to allow the prototype designers to work as quickly as possible. Such high-level descriptions leave out many of the details necessary for efficient execution. For example, the second-order logic and the generalized set of quantifiers used in this book can enable simple descriptions of complex processes that are difficult to compute. Such descriptions are simple precisely because they do not provide the details of an effective algorithm for producing the desired result. This capability is useful in many practical situations, but it also provides the power to describe infinite processes and functions that are not computable. It is therefore not realistic to expect an expressive language to be completely executable, although such a language may have a large executable subset.

A working definition of executable is the following. A language is *executable* if there is a correct compiler for the language, and the compiler terminates for all possible specifications, where a specification is any well formed sentence in the language. A compiler is considered to be correct if it produces a program that successfully produces a result satisfying the specification in all cases where there exists such a result. If we consider a source program to be a kind of specification for the desired output, then all programming languages are designed to be executable with respect to this definition. Practical compilers are designed to terminate for all source programs, and are expected to produce results that correspond to the semantics of the source program. We do not doubt that correct compilers for programming languages exist in the mathematical sense, even though most real compilers contain faults. Source programs representing infinite loops are accepted by our definition of correctness because they correspond to specifications that cannot be satisfied.

Languages powerful enough to define functions that are not computable are not executable under our working definition. Such languages can have executable subsets, and some of the executable subsets may be easy to recognize. However, none of the executable subsets of such a language can include the entire language. These considerations suggest that execution facilities for practical prototyping languages should not be expected to cover the entire language and should be allowed to ask the designer for more information if they cannot realize a given prototype description.

The goals of verification and transformation to efficient implementations indicate that a prototyping language should have a specification component capable of describing the intended semantics of the prototypes. This allows intended properties of the prototype and its design structure to be recorded and checked. Thus modules of a prototype should have a specification part and an implementation part. The specification part is used for formulation, documenting the design, retrieval of reusable software, verification, and possibly execution. The implementation part contains the additional information that must be supplied by the designer in case the execution capabilities of the prototyping system fail to realize the specification part automatically.

There are two approaches for making a prototyping language executable, one based on meta-programming, and the other based on executable specifications. The meta-programming approach provides facilities for adapting and interconnecting available software components. The processor for a meta-programming language generates the skeleton of an implementation, with empty places for the available components. These components can be drawn from a library, simulated, or manually programmed as needed.

The executable specification approach uses the specifications of a module for direct execution, and can succeed only if the specification is executable or can be transformed into a semantically equivalent form that is executable. The advantage of this approach is that it does not require the designer to give any information in addition to the specification. The disadvantage of the approach is that it can be extremely inefficient in some cases. The only known technique for realizing arbitrary computable specifications is enumeration: generating a potentially infinite sequence that exhausts all possible values of the specified result type, and checking each one to see if it happens to meet the specification.

The execution mechanism of logic programming languages such as PRO-LOG is a symbolic version of enumeration. Such an approach is more efficient than enumeration by brute force because each logical step considers a potentially unbounded class of individuals rather than a single individual. However, the number of such classes can still be unbounded, and the number of steps required to arrive at an answer can still be very large if the logic program contains only the abstract essence of a specification, without extra information to help narrow down the search. In practical situations, this approach is suitable only for realizing relatively simple computations. To use this method in the prototyping of large systems, it is necessary to augment the pure specifications with annotations for speeding up execution.

The two approaches can effectively be used together in the context of large prototypes. The meta-programming approach allows the use of efficient algorithms for parts of the system whose functions match available reusable components. The executable specification approach allows the simulation of special-purpose modules that are not in the software base, and that are executed rarely enough that slow realizations are acceptable. In cases where modules realized by executable specifications turn out to be frequently executed, performance can sometimes be improved to a sufficient degree for prototyping purposes by adding annotations that give hints about faster ways to realize the function, or by efficiency improving transformations. The details of carrying out these steps in practice have not been worked out in complete detail, and require further research and development before they will be available in a commercially available product suitable for production use.

An example of an existing general-purpose prototyping language is PSDL (Prototype System Description Language) [11]. PSDL is geared towards the development of real-time systems and large-scale Ada programs. PSDL is based on the meta-programming approach to execution, and gains its expressive power via a natural computational model, a simple decomposition mechanism, automated code generation and scheduling, and an interface to a computerized repository of reusable software components known as the *software base*.

Modules in PSDL have a specification part and an implementation part. The specification part serves as the basis for automated retrieval of available components from the software base. PSDL specifications are executable without additional information from the designer whenever this retrieval is successful. In other cases, the designer must supply an implementation part. The implementation part usually consists of a decomposition into more primitive components using an augmented data flow model, although in cases where the component is so simple that decomposition is not useful, the designer also has the option of directly coding the component in a programming language. The approach can be used together with any underlying programming language. The initial version of the computer-aided prototyping system (CAPS) for PSDL is designed to use Ada for this purpose. Ongoing work is exploring facilities for direct simulation of specifications as another alternative for realizing a module that cannot be retrieved from the software base.

The decomposition of a module is described in PSDL using a combination of graphics and text. The elements of a decomposition are operators communicating by data streams. An example of a PSDL decomposition is shown in Fig. 8.2. Operators are either functions or state machines, and data streams carry instances of abstract data types. The interconnection pattern of the streams and operators is given by a data flow diagram, which also gives maximum execution times for the operators with hard real-time constraints. The precedence constraints on the order in which the operators can be fired are derived from the data flow diagram. The diagram is augmented with a set of nonprocedural control constraints that determine the conditions under which each

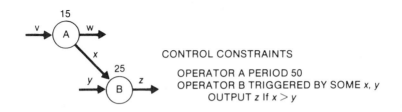

FIGURE 8.2
A PSDL Decomposition Description

operator must fire. PSDL data flow diagrams differ from the data flow diagrams used in many informal approaches to software design because they have definite execution semantics.

Operators can be triggered either by the arrival of new data, or by periodic temporal events, as determined by the associated control constraints. The circumstances under which each operator fires are part of the interconnection rather than part of the specification of the behaviors of the individual operators. This allows small adjustments to the behavior of each operator to be made as part of the interconnection. In particular, the control constraints support conditional execution, conditional output, exception handling, and timers. A PSDL timer is like a software stopwatch, which can be used to control the activity of an operator. Data streams can be of two different types, sampled or dataflow, according to the triggering conditions associated with the operators that consume the stream. The most recent data value in a sampled stream is continuously available, and can be read zero or more times before it is updated. A data flow stream is a discrete sequence of values, each of which is written exactly once and read exactly once, in first-in, first-out order.

The control constraints are realized by a translator, which provides a framework for the reusable components and realizes the data streams. The hard real-time constraints associated with the operators in the critical subsystems of the prototype are realized by the schedulers in the CAPS. The static scheduler guarantees that hard real-time constraints are met under worst-case conditions if it succeeds in constructing a schedule. The dynamic scheduler uses the CPU time not needed by the operators with hard real-time constraints to run the operators without timing constraints. The other facilities provided by CAPS include aids for constructing PSDL descriptions, such as graphical editors and syntax-directed editors, software base management facilities, and debugging facilities.

A different strategy for prototyping is the transformation approach, which seeks to incrementally transform a logical specification into relatively efficient code. An example of this approach is the Refine system, which is a commercial product based on recent research on software transformations. This system represents fragments of reusable components as transformation rules. These rules are intended to be meaning-preserving and efficiency improving, including some transformations that map potentially unbounded quantifiers into finitely executable processes in some special cases. Specifications that do not match any of the available efficiency improving transformations are realized by enumeration techniques. This approach differs from direct execution of specifications because it tries to improve the efficiency of the formulation provided by the designer. This approach can successfully handle common predefined types such as sets and mappings. Current techniques do not address automatic generation of transformations for user-defined types, which is an area for future research.

8.2 Reusing Software

The goal of software reuse is to construct systems by selecting existing components rather than creating new versions for each application. This is done by maintaining a software base containing many instances of each kind of software component. This approach can be applied to all types of software-related objects, including concepts for formulating requirements, component specifications, code, theorems about programs, proofs, results of analyses, test cases, manual descriptions, diagrams, and so on. Usually several types of software components are related to each other. Such a set of related parts should be retrieved as a unit. The benefits of software reuse depend on the difference between the effort required to assemble existing components and that required to construct new ones. The concept of software reuse is simple and appealing, but it is difficult to realize in practice. Some of the research areas relevant to overcoming the difficulties are the following.

Finding appropriate reusable components. The classical approaches to finding software components have been either to rely on a person who is familiar with all of the components in a given software library, or to rely on a catalog and a classification scheme. However, these approaches are not adequate for large software bases, which contain too many components for a single person to remember. Manual searches through large collections can be so time consuming that the benefits of reuse are lost. Current classification schemes are generally unable to determine a unique place in which a component meeting a given need can be found, so that designers may have to examine many components. Better techniques are needed for describing and indexing components and automating retrieval of relevant components from large collections.

Assessing the usefulness of an existing component. Early software libraries contained little more than the code and brief English descriptions. Examining and evaluating code can be very time consuming, so that reusable components should be stored together with specifications and evaluations. This information should enable an automated evaluation process to find which of the many available components provide solutions to the designer's problem with the least amount of additional designer effort. A current research problem is to find representations for designer queries and component descriptions that enable accurate computed rankings for the set of available and potentially relevant components. Some of the relevant properties for code modules include specifications of their functions, time and space requirements, and degree of reliability (proof of correctness or degree of test coverage).

Adapting components to particular needs. At the current state of the art, a software base can contain only a small fraction of all possible software components, which is infinite in principle and enormously large in practice. This implies that usually the retrieved component will not quite match what the designer needs, and that some modifications will be necessary. The classical approach of storing individual software components in a library is therefore inadequate for achieving widespread software reuse. A software base should contain representations of large classes of related components rather than individual components, and the retrieval process should include automated construction of the element of the class most nearly matching the designer's needs. After this has been done, the component may still not quite match the designer's need, and there may be need for a further interactive process to make small variations in the behavior of the component.

Maintaining the collection of reusable components. The previous discussion implies that building and maintaining a software base is a major undertaking. There must be some agent responsible for deciding how to organize the software base and which components to include. In the near term, this agent is likely to be a person, and research goals include providing computer aid or completely automatic procedures for the functions involved in managing a large software base. Some of these functions include quality control, generalizing components to widen their range of application, transforming components to standardize their interfaces and make them compatible with other components in the software base, factoring out common functions, establishing structured sets of alternatives, refining specifications of previous components to ensure they are distinguished from newly added components, and removing components when the set of circumstances under which they are superior to other components in the software base becomes empty.

Progress on finding components depends on finding computationally tractable representations for descriptions of software components. Such descriptions are associated with the stored components, and also represent queries from designers seeking particular components. The essence of the problem is to provide fast and accurate procedures for determining the degree to which the description attached to a software component satisfies a given query description.

A promising approach to this problem is *normalization*. A normalization procedure provides a unique standard representation for classes of equivalent descriptions or description fragments. The goal of normalization is to provide a standard vocabulary for descriptions, to make them easier to compare. This approach can be applied at both the formal and informal level. Normalization can be applied to keyword-based classifications via a standard synonym table that replaces all synonyms for a keyword with the same standard symbol. Normalization can be applied to formal descriptions via rewrite techniques, which can use semantic equivalences to provide unique normal forms for some classes of formal statements. This process is related to algebraic simplification techniques.

Normalization can help to detect subsumption relationships as well as equivalences. For example, standard keywords can be arranged in a generalization hierarchy that provides the basis for assessing the strength of a partial match. Normalization contributes to this approach by removing redundancies and reducing the size of the hierarchy. If a keyword attached to a software component is a generalization of a keyword in a query, then the number of intermediate nodes in the generalization hierarchy is an inverse measure of the closeness of an inexact match. For example, a fragment of a generalization hierarchy for some keywords is shown in Fig. 8.3. With respect to the given generalization hierarchy, the keyword *accounting* appearing in a query would register partial matches for descriptions containing the keyword *financial* or the keyword *business*. The first kind of partial match is stronger than the second because the length of the path between the two keywords is 1 in the first case and 2 in the second. The keyword *inventory* would not be accepted as a partial match for *accounting* because it is not on the generalization chain going up from the query keyword. Keywords can be used to describe many different attributes of a software component, and a separate generalization hierarchy can be given for each attribute. Attributes other than application area include the function the component performs, the type of data it operates on, implementation language, operating system, peripherals required, and so on. A query can specify the relative importance of these attributes in determining the strength of a match.

Normalization can be useful in checking for inexact matches in formal descriptions as well. Checking the subsumption relation for logical specifications requires an implication checker, which can be computationally expensive in the general case. Normalization can help speed up this process in two different ways. An initial keyword search can narrow down the search space to a relatively small subset of the entire software base, and can impose a rough ordering on the candidate components based on the closeness of the keyword matches and performance attributes of the components. These can then be submitted to an implication checker in best-first order, reducing the number of implications to be checked. Normalizing the property names in a formal specification can provide a quick syntactic check for some types of implications, based on laws of the form A & B => A. This mechanism leads to fast recognition if the normalization process can convert a condition in the query to

FIGURE 8.3
A Keyword Generalization Hierarchy

the same form as one of the conjuncts in a component specification. Such fast recognition methods can be applied to larger sets of possibilities than implication checks involving deeper analysis. The general implication checks can be limited to candidates with strong keyword matches, and need to be performed only if the fast screening process fails.

Retrieval of components based on formal specifications can provide partial matches that are useful as subcomponents of a synthesized implementation in cases where there is no existing reusable component that meets the query specification completely. One instance of this is a case where the postcondition of an available component implies the postcondition of the query, but where the available component produces the desired result only in a limited set of circumstances defined by a precondition. This allows the component to be used as one of the alternatives of a guarded command or conditional decomposition. Such a partial match leaves the system with the task of finding another component to cover the remaining cases, or the designer with the task of manually creating such a component. For example, a search for a module to calculate the maximum value of a set might result in a component that works only for nonempty sets. In such a case, the designer might complete the design by supplying the minimum value of the entire data type in the cases where the set is empty, or might discover the need to introduce an exception condition into the design if the data type does not have a minimum element.

Another way to increase the possibilities of finding a match is to provide the retrieval mechanism with a limited capability to do bottom-up design by automatically composing some of the available components to produce a combination of components that can meet a specification. This can be done by associating composition templates with the components in the software base. A composition template describes how a given component can be combined with an unknown component to achieve a specification of a given form. The composition template also provides a scheme for deriving the specification of the unknown component. This concept is illustrated by the following example of a composition template for using a *sort* function as a postprocessing filter. The composition template says that any function with a specification of the form

```
MESSAGE($x: any) REPLY (s: sequence{t})
   WHERE sorted(s), ALL(x: t :: x IN s <=> P(x))
```

can be realized by a composition of the form shown in Fig. 8.4. The predicate P is a parameter of the composition template, and can match any condition in a query specification. The component F is an unknown function that must satisfy the specification shown in Fig. 8.4. The function F can be realized by another retrieval from the software base, or it can be constructed by the designer. This kind of composition rule can be derived from the specification of an available component, together with a characterization of the properties that are left invariant by the component. The invariance property for the

FUNCTION F
 MESSAGE ($x: any) REPLY (s: sequence {t})
 WHERE ALL (x: t :: x IN s <=> P(x))
END

FIGURE 8.4
Composition Template for Sort

example is

```
ALL(s: sequence{t}, x: t :: frequency(x, s)
                   = frequency(x, sort(s)))
```

and the relation between the invariance property and the description of the unknown function *F* is

```
ALL(s: sequence{t}, x: t :: x IN s
           <=> frequency(x, s) > 0).
```

Automatically assessing the usefulness of an existing component is a largely unexplored area. The reliability aspect can be quantified using existing concepts. One approach is to provide a trusted subset of the software base that contains only components that have been proven to meet the specifications. Although this can be expensive, it can be useful in reducing the cost of developing critical subsystems that must be certified to meet certain specifications, such as safety-critical applications. Other approaches include keeping statistical estimates of the reliability of a component derived from randomly chosen sets of test cases. A reasonable policy is to run some additional test cases each time a component is retrieved and used, thus gradually increasing the confidence level for the correctness of frequently used components. If faults are discovered, then the fault must be fixed, the software base must be updated, and all applications using the faulty version of the component must be repaired. This implies that version control and tracing facilities should be integrated with the software base. Automatically estimating the amount of effort needed to transform a given component into a form meeting a specification that is close but does not exactly match the query is another aspect of this problem that is largely unexplored.

The problem of adapting components can be viewed as the problem of representing families of software components [6]. Generic modules are a first step in this direction. A smart retrieval algorithm should be able to determine whether there exists an instantiation of a generic component that meets a query specification, and if so it should automatically construct one. Some research questions in this area are finding parameterization mechanisms that provide a single representation for the specification or implementation of large classes of software components. In Ada, generic implementation modules are limited to representing classes of modules that all share the same Ada source code. Existing technology extends this on an ad-hoc basis via conditional compilation facilities. A research goal in this area is to provide higher level representations for general implementation patterns, which can lead to significantly different forms of the source code at the programming language level for different instances of a single generic component. This area is related to meta-programming and translation technology. For example, an attribute grammar processor is an example of a powerful generic component representing a trans-lator, which is specified by a generic parameter representing an attribute gram-mar. The attribute grammar processor constructs the source code of each par-ticular instance based on a fixed set of rules, but the construction of an instance can involve a significant amount of computation, and the actual source code can be quite different for different instances. Other examples of software com-ponents that are logically individual units but which cannot be expressed by a single unit of source code in Ada include polymorphic operators and operators with a variable number of arguments, such as the Pascal writeln procedure. Investigations of general-purpose facilities for representing and generating the instances of a large class of algorithms for meeting a single parameterized specification are needed. A different approach to the problem is to provide general purpose transformations for generating alternative implementations of a wide class of programs. For example, any data type can have both a single-process version, such as an Ada package, and a protected version that can be shared by multiple processes, such as an Ada task. A transformation that can generate the protected version of any data type would reduce the number of instances that need to be explicitly stored in a software base. This can be viewed as a special instance of the previous problem, where all data types inherit a boolean parameter that specifies whether or not the implementation of the type should be protected. Further research should identify other attributes defining alternative versions of software modules and provide methods for automatically constructing the required alternatives on demand. Such an approach can be eventually integrated with stored sets of guidelines for which variations are best in which circumstances. Such guidelines can provide automatic default values for many of the decisions a designer must make. Such an extension would avoid the need for the designer to consider the details of many choices except in cases where the observed properties of a given system do not correspond to user needs.

Very little is known about systematic methods for maintaining components in a software base. Compatibility makes a large difference in the usefulness of a set of reusable components. Attention to compatibility appears to be one of the reasons for the success of the UNIX system and other toolkits providing sets of building blocks for given applications. Another important property is orthogonality, because a space of functions is much easier to search if it is not cluttered with many small variations of the same concept. Relevant research questions are how to define and maintain sets of compatible interfaces in a general setting, and how to detect and eliminate overlaps. Some possible mechanisms are generalization and inheritance. When several components are recognized to be different instances of the same theme, they should be replaced by a single generic component representing a larger class of components that includes the previous components. Inheritance mechanisms can be used to factor out common fragments of software functions, and can provide the ability to combine these fragments in different combinations on demand. Progress in these areas may eventually invalidate the idea that a useful software base must be very large: sufficiently powerful representations for classes of components may enable software bases with a relatively small number of elements at the conceptual level to cover a very large number of concrete variations for a given application area.

8.3 Constraints and Truth Maintenance

One of the most time-consuming aspects of software development is propagating the consequences of a design decision and detecting inconsistencies. Some early work in this area has investigated the idea of truth maintenance systems, which seek to represent consistency constraints as active networks that automatically derive properties of a system as enough constraints are added to uniquely determine different attributes [3, 16]. Such systems also record the derivation of each attribute of a system, and contain rules for determining which alternative takes precedence in cases of conflict. For example, some attributes can have default values that have a lower priority than values specified by a designer, and can be automatically replaced by better or more accurate information. If two conflicting pieces of information have the same priority, then derivation chains can be traced back to determine which of the facts directly entered by the designer are in conflict. If a designer retracts a fact, then the system can use the derivation records to remove the derived attribute values that were based on that fact, and can rederive alternative attribute values based on the remaining information. An application of this technology to requirements analysis is described in [5].

Constraint network technology is best developed for constraints involving numbers. The existing technology is well suited for project management aspects such as maintaining current estimates of completion times, project status information, and project plans. More work is needed on ways to combine independent pieces of knowledge to partially constrain the value of an attribute, constraint maintenance based on symbolic rather than concrete values, and constraint propagation rules for data types other than the numeric ones, including user-defined abstract data types. This technology should eventually be integrated with automatic design completion techniques such as type inference.

8.4 Automated Reasoning Capabilities

Progress on automating tasks currently performed by programmers and software engineers depends on advances in automated reasoning capabilities. Some of the important subproblems are checking the validity of implications, checking whether two conditions are mutually exclusive, checking whether a set of conditions covers all possibilities, and determining satisfiability of particular specifications. Although theoretically, these problems are equivalent, it may be useful to distinguish them in practice because doing so may enable the use of faster special-case algorithms. Although the general cases of these problems are undecidable, it is not necessary for a useful engineering tool to do a perfect job. The tool must not produce incorrect answers, but it can on occasion terminate without producing any conclusion. In general, different types of checking require different degrees of proficiency, and hence different kinds of resource-bounded algorithms are desirable.

Implication checking is used in the context of checking preconditions, both for uses of software components and for checking the validity of software transformations. For implication checking, it is desired that the program be able to recognize the validity of the class of implications that can be easily recognized by a person, to provide the capability of mechanically filtering out the trivial cases, and focusing the designer's attention on just the difficult ones. Thus it is important to find limited inference techniques that can handle the surface level inferences easy for humans while avoiding the possibility of long or unbounded computations.

Determining satisfiability may require deeper reasoning. Satisfiability checks are needed to show feasibility of given specifications, and are potentially useful for synthesizing algorithms, since a method for constructing an output can often be derived from a proof that at least one value for the required output exists for all possible input conditions. Constructive logic is of potential interest in this regard. Other uses of satisfiability checking include detection of unreachable code segments or execution paths in construction of test cases.

Logical reasoning contains many solvable subproblems with known decision procedures. Some of these include propositional logic, propositional temporal logic, and Presburger arithmetic. More research is needed to identify other subsets of the general automated reasoning problem that have practical significance in software applications and have comprehensive decision procedures or fast partial decision procedures. For example, experience has shown that many of the theorems arising in program verification can be established by algebraic simplification techniques based on term rewrite technology.

Some of the known techniques for automated reasoning include resolution, tableaux techniques, techniques based on mathematical induction [4], and equation-solving techniques based on the Knuth-Bendix algorithm [8, 14]. Future research should address the problems of determining which techniques are best for which kinds of problems, and of determining extensions of these techniques for subsets of second-order temporal logic. Better techniques for allowing the designer to guide the tools by supplying conjectures and advice are needed. On the development side, there is need to create reasoning systems that provide a combination of methods in a compatible framework and which interface smoothly to the rest of a software development environment. For example, the notations of the specification language and the implementations languages should be compatible with the reasoning capabilities, and the reasoning capabilities should be able to make use of general-purpose version control and engineering database facilities.

8.5 Transformations

Software transformations come in three different varieties:

1. Meaning preserving
2. Constraining
3. Relaxing.

Meaning-preserving transformations are used mostly for optimization, where effective implementation of nonconstructive specifications is a limiting case. Such transformations have been used at a low level by optimizing compilers for a long time. A mature system for applying meaning-preserving transformations to the problem of bridging the gap between specifications and code is described in [1]. This system is aimed at producing implementations that are correct by construction, in the sense that the code is guaranteed to be consistent with a given formal specification. The system aids the designer in applying transformations, and makes sure that the preconditions of each transformation are satisfied, thus ensuring that the formulation of the program is correct at all stages. The system is aimed at the development of reliable software, rather than rapid prototyping. The current version depends on the skill of the designer to choose which transformations to apply, and may require considerable effort to apply to a practical problem. Future research should address the problems of guiding the transformations at a higher level, and of automating the easier choices. Other applications for meaning-preserving transformations that should be addressed by future research include simplification and restructuring to ease evolution.

Constraining transformations represent design decisions that make consistent refinements of a previous design by imposing additional constraints. Such transformations can add restrictions to a specification to enable efficient implementations. This type of transformation has not been explored as thoroughly as the class of meaning-preserving transformations, and is a subject for future research. Constraining transformations are important for modeling the decisions made by software developers, which often involve changes to the specifications as part of the implementation process.

Relaxing transformations remove restrictions on a software component, and are inverses of constraining transformations. Such transformations are needed when a design decision is abandoned, perhaps after other valid transformations have been made. Many incompatible changes to a software system can be described as the combination of a relaxing transformation and a constraining transformation. Such transformations are also important for supporting software evolution involving incompatible changes in terms of the configuration management process. Formal models and automated support for constraining and relaxing transformations are an important area for future research.

8.6 Conclusions

Software engineering is a new field that is just beginning to form a solid scientific foundation. The informal approaches popular in the beginning are slowly being replaced by more formal approaches supported by software tools for computer-aided software development. This trend is fueled by the demand for increasingly sophisticated systems, which cannot be built effectively using manual techniques. The essential elements of computer-aided software development are the use of formal methods and notations, systematic use of abstractions, and the application of software tools to increasingly many aspects of the software development process.

Tools for computer-aided software engineering are an important factor in making this approach practical. Many useful tools already exist, and better tools are possible. Many active areas of research and development are establishing the basis for new types of powerful software tools, and reducing these new principles to practice. Continued research and systematic policies for investment in software tools are essential for making this approach a reality. Because tools are expensive and take time to develop, the most practical path to highly automated software factories is one of gradual evolution. Such automation is essential for constructing reliable software systems on a large scale.

Hardware designers have been forced into using computer-aided design methods because there is no way to fix a design error in a chip—if it does not work, you have to throw it away. We are getting to the point where we cannot afford software errors in many of our important systems. This requires us to move in the direction of computer-aided design in software development as well. Our purpose has been to integrate and present a practical set of concepts and techniques for achieving this goal. The job is by no means completed. A great deal of research, development, and technology transfer will be required before we can expect software systems to operate correctly as a matter of course, and to be responsive to changes in user needs and operating environments.

8.7 Related Research

The application of attribute grammars to the prototyping of special-purpose languages is discussed in [7]. The use of special-purpose languages and language processors for prototyping is discussed in [9]. The prototyping language PSDL and its associated computer-aided prototyping system are described in [10–13]. A discussion of Presburger arithmetic can be found in [2, 15].

Projects

1. Do a literature survey on automated reasoning techniques, characterize the types of problems for which each technique is best suited, and formulate a decision rule for which technique to apply to each type of problem.

2. Assemble a compatible and comprehensive set of reusable software components for a particular application area, and report on the structures you found most useful in organizing your software base.

References

1. F. Bauer, B. Moller, H. Partsch, and P. Pepper, "Formal Program Construction by Transformations—Computer-Aided, Intuition-Guided Programming," *IEEE Transactions on Software Engineering 15*, 2 (Feb. 1989), 165–180.

2. W. Bledsoe and L. Hines, "Variable Elimination and Chaining in a Resolution-Based Prover for Inequalities," in *5th Conference on Automated Deduction: Lecture Notes in Computer Science*, W. Bibel and R. Kowalski (editors), Springer-Verlag, New York, 1980, 70–87.

3. A. Borning, "The Programming Language Aspects of ThingLab, A Constraint-Oriented Simulation Laboratory," *ACM Transactions on Programming Languages and Systems 3*, 4 (Oct. 1981), 353–387.

4. R. Boyer and J. Moore, *A Computational Logic Handbook*, Academic Press, 1988.

5. A. Czurchry and D. Hines, "KBRA: A New Paradigm for Requirements Engineering," *IEEE Expert 3*, 4 (Winter 1988), 21–35.

6. J. A. Goguen, "Parameterized Programming," *IEEE Transactions on Software Engineering SE–10*, 5 (Sep. 1984), 528–543.

7. R. Herndon and V. Berzins, "The Realizable Benefits of a Language Prototyping Language," *IEEE Transactions on Software Engineering SE–14*, 6 (June 1988), 803–809.

8. B. Jayaraman and G. Gupta, "EqL: The Language and its Implementation," *IEEE Transactions on Software Engineering 15*, 6 (June 1989), 771–779.

9. L. Levy, "A Metaprogramming Method and Its Economic Justification," *IEEE Transactions on Software Engineering SE–12*, 2 (Feb. 1986), 272–277.

10. Luqi, "Knowledge Base Support for Rapid Prototyping," *IEEE Expert 3*, 4 (Nov. 1988), 9–18.

11. Luqi, V. Berzins, and R. Yeh, "A Prototyping Language for Real-Time Software," *IEEE Transactions on Software Engineering SE–14*, 10 (Oct. 1988), 1409–1423.

12. Luqi and V. Berzins, "Rapidly Prototyping Real-Time Systems," *IEEE Software*, Sep. 1988, 25–36.

13. Luqi, "Software Evolution via Rapid Prototyping," *IEEE Computer 22*, 5 (May 1989), 13–25.

14. P. Rety, C. Kirchner, H. Kirchner, and P. Lescanne, "Narrower: a New Algorithm for Unification and its Application to Logic Programming," in *Rewriting Techniques and Applications*, Springer-Verlag, 1985.

15. R. Shostak, "A Practical Decision Procedure for Arithmetic with Function Symbols," *Journal of the ACM 26*, 2 (Apr. 1979), 351–360.

16. G. L. Steele Jr., *The Definition and Implementation of a Computer Programming Language Based on Constraints*, Ph.D. Thesis, MIT, 1980.

A

APPENDIX
Spec Syntax Diagrams

This appendix gives syntax diagrams for the Spec language, augmented with some lexical definitions and operator precedences.

Definitions of Lexical Classes

DIGIT = [0-9]

LOWER CASE LETTER = [a-z]

UPPER CASE LETTER = [A-Z]

CHAR = [^" \] | \" | \\

ASCII = [^x] | x

COMMENT = -- [^ \n]* \n

These definitions are expressed using the extended regular expression notations explained next. [x-y] indicates a choice of any character between x and y in the ASCII collating sequence, including x and y; [^xy] indicates a choice of any ASCII character other than x and y; a vertical bar represents a choice; \n represents the newline character; and a star (*) represents zero or more repetitions of the preceding pattern.

Operator Precedences, Weakest Binding to Strongest Binding

;

,

<=>

=>

|

&
~

< > = >= <= ˜= ˜> ˜< ˜>= ˜<= == ˜==
IN ..
U ‖
+ -
* / \ MOD;
UNARY_MINUS;
^

$ [({ .
UNARY_STAR

All spec operators are left associative; for example x+y+z means (x+y)+z.

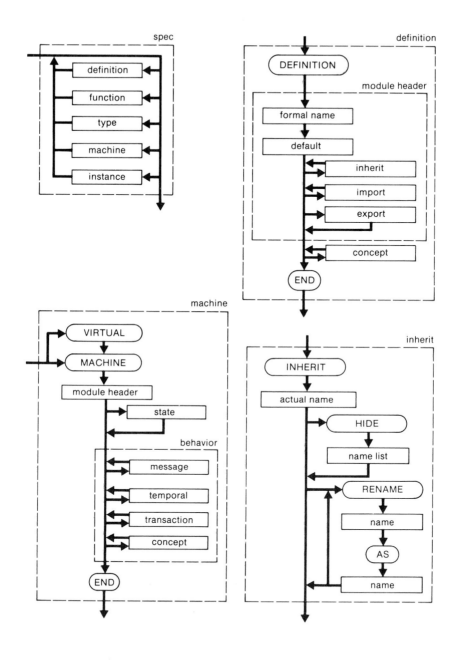

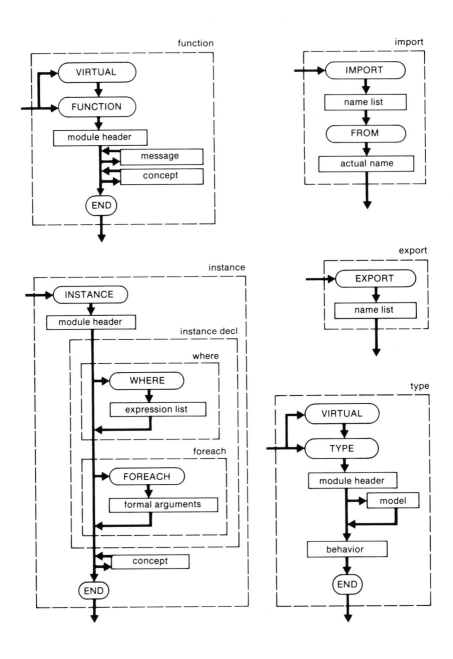

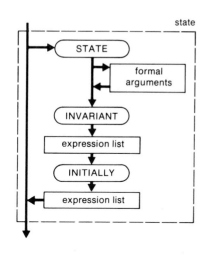

state

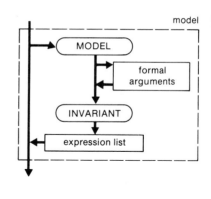

model

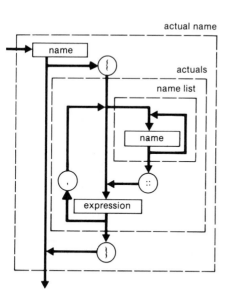

actual name

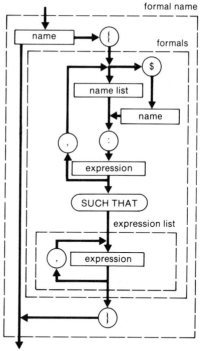

formal name

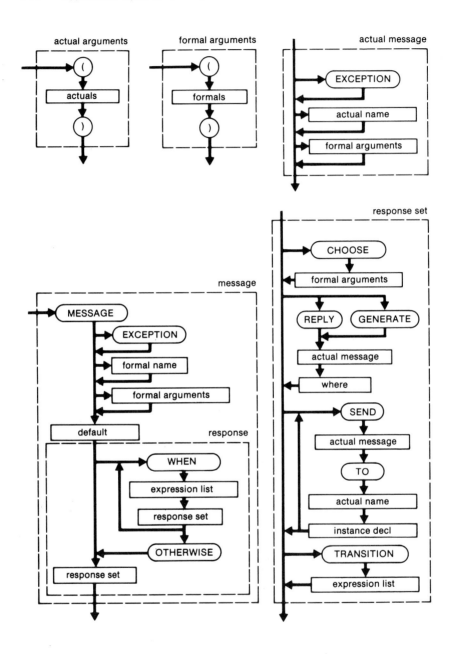

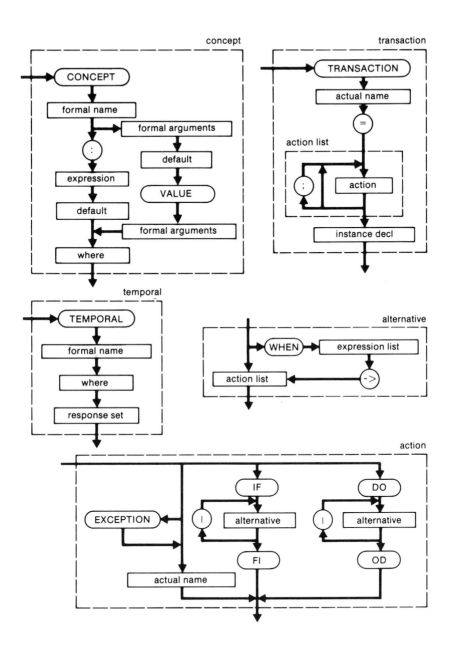

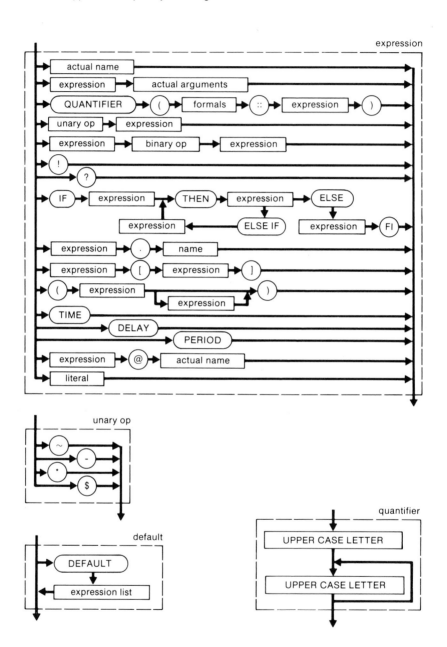

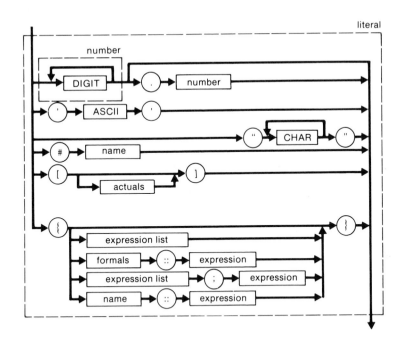

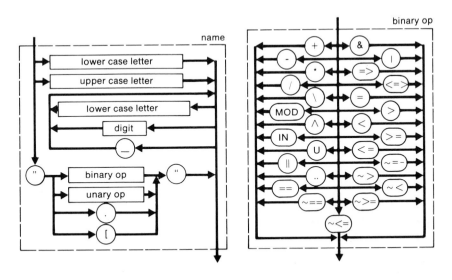

APPENDIX

Spec Operators

The following table gives the standard interpretations of the predefined infix and prefix operators in the Spec type library. User-defined types can also use these operators, but to avoid confusion we recommend using the symbols consistently with their standard interpretations.

˜x	not(x)	boolean
x & y	and(x, y)	boolean
x | y	or(x, y)	boolean
x => y	implies(x, y)	boolean
x <=> y	equivalent(x, y)	boolean
x = y	equal(x, y)	equality{t} (inherited)
x ˜= y	˜(x = y)	equality{t} (inherited)
x == y	equivalent(x, y)	equivalence{t} (inherited, for mutable types)
x ˜== y	˜(x == y)	equivalence{t} (inherited, for mutable types)
x < y	less(x, y)	partial_order{t}, total_order{t} (inherited)
x <= y	x < y | x = y	partial_order{t}, total_order{t} (inherited)
x ˜< y	˜(x < y)	partial_order{t}, (inherited)
x ˜<= y	˜(x <= y)	partial_order{t}, (inherited)
x > y	y < x	partial_order{t}, total_order{t} (inherited)
x >= y	y <= x	partial_order{t}, total_order{t} (inherited)
x ˜> y	y ˜< x	partial_order{t}, (inherited)

x ˜>= y	y ˜<= x	partial_order{t}, (inherited)
-x	minus(x)	integer, rational, real, complex
x + y	plus(x, y)	nat, integer, rational, real, complex
x - y	difference(x, y)	nat, integer, rational, real, complex
x * y	times(x, y)	nat, integer, rational, real, complex
x / y	quotient(x, y)	nat, integer, rational, real, complex
x MOD y	remainder(x, y)	nat, integer, rational, real
x \ y	remainder(x, y)	nat, integer, rational, real
x ^ y	expt(x, y)	nat, integer, rational, real, complex
x U y	union(x, y)	set{t}, multiset{t}, relation{$ts}
x ‖ y	append(x, y)	string, sequence{t}, tuple{$ts}
x IN y	member(x, y)	set{t}, multiset{t}, sequence{t}, map{t1, t2}, type
x .. y	interval(x, y)	set{t}, sequence{t}
x.y	get(x, "y")	tuple{$ts}, union{$ts}
x[y]	fetch(x, y)	sequence{t}, map{t1, t2}

C

APPENDIX
Spec Concept Library

This appendix gives the definitions of the predefined Spec concepts. The module *standard* is special because it is implicitly inherited by all other Spec modules. All of the other predefined concepts must be explicitly imported or inherited before they can be used.

```
DEFINITION standard
  INHERIT quantifiers
END
```

```
DEFINITION requirement_goals
  -- Defines a relationship linking concepts to
  -- goals for the system.
  INHERIT system
  IMPORT concept FROM requirement_model

  CONCEPT goal(c: concept, s: system) VALUE(b: boolean)
    -- True if a goal of the system s is to provide
    -- an implementation of the concept c.
END
```

```
DEFINITION system_actions
  -- Defines types of actions corresponding to
  -- common goals of proposed systems.
  IMPORT User_class FROM user
  IMPORT attribute FROM requirement_model

  CONCEPT displayed_to(c: concept, uc: User_class)
     VALUE(b: boolean)
    -- True if the concept c can be displayed
    -- to the user class uc.

  CONCEPT creates(uc: User_class, t: type) VALUE(b: boolean)
    -- True if members of the user class uc can create
    -- new instances of the type t.

  CONCEPT destroys(uc: User_class, t: type) VALUE(b: boolean)
    -- True if members of the user class uc can destroy
    -- instances of the type t.

  CONCEPT updates(uc: User_class, t: type, a: attribute)
     VALUE(b: boolean)
    -- True if members of the user class uc can update
    -- the attribute a of the type t.
END
```

```
DEFINITION user
  -- Concepts for describing users and user classses.
  INHERIT system
  INHERIT person
  IMPORT Subtype FROM type
  IMPORT Covers_domain FROM relationship

  CONCEPT user: type
     -- A user is a person that uses a software system.
     WHERE Subtype(user, person), Covers_domain(uses, 1, user)

  CONCEPT User_class: type
     -- A user class is a set of users that use the same system.
     WHERE Subtype(User_class, type),
        -- Every user class is a type.
       ALL(uc: User_class :: Subtype(uc, user)),
          -- The elements of each user class are users.
       ALL(uc: User_class ::
          SOME(s: software_system :: ALL(u: uc :: uses(u, s)))) )
```

```
            -- Every user in a user class uses
            -- the same software system.

  CONCEPT Uses(uc: User_class, s: software_system)
    VALUE(b: boolean)
    -- True if every user in the user class
    -- interacts with the software system s.
    WHERE ALL(u: user SUCH THAT u IN uc :: uses(u, s))

  CONCEPT uses(u: user, s: software_system)
    VALUE(b: boolean)
    -- True if the user u interacts with the software system s.

  CONCEPT Maintains(uc: User_class, t: type)
    VALUE(b: boolean)
    -- True if the instances of the type t can be created,
    -- modified, and destroyed only on the request
    -- of some user in the user class.
    WHERE ALL(uc: User_class, s: system, t: type ::
              Maintains(uc, t) & Controls(s, t) => Uses(uc, s) )
END
```

```
DEFINITION system
  -- Concepts for describing systems.
  IMPORT Subtype FROM type

  CONCEPT system: type

  CONCEPT software_system: type
    WHERE Subtype(software_system, system)

  CONCEPT hardware_system: type
    WHERE Subtype(hardware_system, system)

  CONCEPT proposed(s: system)
    VALUE(b: boolean)
    -- True if a goal of the current project
    -- is to construct a system of type st.

  CONCEPT complete(s: system)
    VALUE(b: boolean)
    -- True if s has been completely developed.
```

```
CONCEPT pending(s: system)
  VALUE(b: boolean)
  -- True if s must be built but is not yet completed.
  WHERE b <=> proposed(s) & ~complete(s)

CONCEPT System_class: type
  -- A system class is a set of systems with the same purpose.
  WHERE Subtype(System_class, type),
      -- Every system class is a type.
    ALL(sc: System_class :: Subtype(sc, system))
      -- The elements of each system class are systems.

CONCEPT Controls(sc: System_class, t: type)
  VALUE(b: boolean)
  -- True if the instances of the type t can be created,
  -- modified, and destroyed only via a system of type s.
  WHERE b <=> SOME(s: system :: s IN sc & Controls(s, t))

CONCEPT Controls(s: system, t: type)
  VALUE(b: boolean)
  -- True if the instances of the type t can be created,
  -- modified, and destroyed only via the system s.
END
```

```
DEFINITION hardware_concepts
  INHERIT system
  INHERIT processor_concepts
  INHERIT memory_concepts
  INHERIT time_unit

  CONCEPT implemented_on(s: system, h: hardware_system)
    VALUE(b: boolean)
    -- True if s will have to run on the hardware system h.

  CONCEPT processors(h: hardware_system)
    VALUE (ps: set{processor})
    -- The set of processors in the system h.

  CONCEPT number_of_processors(h: hardware_system) VALUE(n: nat)
    WHERE n = size(processors(h))   -- The number of cpu's in h.

  CONCEPT connected_to(ps: set{processor}, n: network)
    VALUE(b: boolean)
    -- True if all the processors in the set ps
    -- are connected to the network n.
```

```
  CONCEPT network: type

  CONCEPT speed(n: network) VALUE (r: real)  -- Bits / second.
END
```

```
DEFINITION processor_concepts
  INHERIT memory_concepts

  CONCEPT processor: type
    -- The set of computers.

  CONCEPT main_memory_size(p: processor) VALUE(n: nat)
    -- The amount of main memory attached to the processor p.

  CONCEPT secondary_memory_size(p: processor) VALUE(n: nat)
    -- The amount of secondary memory, such as disk,
    -- attached to the processor p.

  CONCEPT processor_speed(p: processor) VALUE(r: real)
    -- The speed of the processor p.

  CONCEPT mips: real
    -- Unit of processor speed,
    -- millions of instructions per second.

  CONCEPT flops: real
    -- Unit of processor speed,
    -- number of floating point operations per second.

  CONCEPT mega_flops: real WHERE mega_flops = flops * 10 ^ 6
  CONCEPT giga_flops: real WHERE giga_flops = flops * 10 ^ 9
END
```

```
DEFINITION memory_concepts

  CONCEPT bit: nat
    -- Unit of memory size.

  CONCEPT kb: nat WHERE kb = bit * 2 ^ 10  -- Kilobits.

  CONCEPT Mb: nat WHERE Mb = bit * 2 ^ 20  -- Megabits.
```

```
   CONCEPT Gb: nat WHERE Gb = bit * 2 ^ 30   -- Gigabits.

   CONCEPT byte: nat WHERE byte = bit * 8

   CONCEPT kbyte: nat WHERE kbyte = byte * 2 ^ 10   -- Kilobytes.

   CONCEPT Mbyte: nat WHERE Mbyte = byte * 2 ^ 20   -- Megabytes.

   CONCEPT Gbyte: nat WHERE Gbyte = byte * 2 ^ 30   -- Gigabytes.
END
```

```
DEFINITION business
   -- Concepts for describing business activities.
   INHERIT cause   -- Defines agent, activity, wants.
   INHERIT transfer   -- Defines supplies, gives_to.
   IMPORT Covers_domain FROM relationship
   IMPORT Subtype FROM type

   CONCEPT product: type
     -- Every product is bought and sold.
     WHERE Covers_domain(sells, 2, product),
           Covers_domain(buys, 2, product)

   CONCEPT price(p: product, v: vendor)
     VALUE(m: money)
     -- The amount of money needed to buy an instance
     -- of the product from the vendor.

   CONCEPT price(p: product)
     VALUE(m: money)
     WHERE m = MINIMUM(v: vendor SUCH THAT sells(v, p) ::
                       price(p, v) )
     -- The price of a product is the lowest price
     -- offered by any vendor.

   CONCEPT vendor: type
     -- Every vendor sells some product.
     WHERE Covers_domain(sells, 1, vendor), Subtype(vendor, agent)

   CONCEPT money: type
     WHERE Subtype(money, number)

   CONCEPT customer: type
     -- Every customer buys some product.
```

```
    WHERE Covers_domain(buys, 1, customer),
      Subtype(customer, agent),
      ALL(c: customer, p: product :: wants(c, p) => buys(c, p))
      -- Customers have the resources to satisfy their wishes.

  CONCEPT sells(v: vendor, p: product)
    VALUE(b: boolean)
    -- True if the vendor v sells the product p.
    WHERE b <=> SOME(c: customer :: sells_to(v, p, c)),
      Subtype(sells, activity),
      ALL(v: vendor, p: product SUCH THAT sells(v, p) ::
          supplies(v, p) )

  CONCEPT sells_to(v: vendor, p: product, c: customer)
    VALUE(b: boolean)
    -- True if the vendor v sells the product p
    -- to the customer c.
    WHERE Subtype(sells_to, activity),
      ALL(v: vendor, p: product, c: customer SUCH THAT
          sells_to(v, p, c) :: gives_to(v, p, c) )

  CONCEPT buys(c: customer, p: product)
    VALUE(b: boolean)
    -- True if the customer c buys the product p.
    WHERE b <=> SOME(v: vendor :: buys_from(c, p, v)),
      Subtype(buys, activity)

  CONCEPT buys_from(c: customer, p: product, v: vendor)
    VALUE(b: boolean)
    -- True if the customer c buys the product p
    -- from the vendor v.
    WHERE b <=> sells_to(v, p, c),
      Subtype(buys_from, activity),
      ALL(c: customer, p: product, v: vendor SUCH THAT
          buys_from(c, p, v) :: pays(c, v) )

  CONCEPT pays(c: customer, v: vendor)
    VALUE(b: boolean)
    -- True if the customer c pays the vendor v.
    WHERE b <=> SOME(p: product :: pays_for(c, v, p)),
      Subtype(pays, activity)

  CONCEPT pays_for(c: customer, v: vendor, p: product)
    VALUE(b: boolean)
    -- True if the customer c pays the vendor v.
    WHERE b <=> gives_to(c, price(p, v), v),
      Subtype(pays_for, activity)
END
```

```
DEFINITION transfer
  -- Concepts for describing transfers of items
  -- from one agent to another.
  INHERIT cause
  INHERIT relationship
  IMPORT Subtype FROM type

  CONCEPT supplier: type
    -- Every supplier supplies instances of some type.
    WHERE Covers_domain(supplies, 1, supplier),
      Subtype(supplier, agent) -- Suppliers are active agents.

  CONCEPT supplies(supplier: agent, x: any)
    VALUE(b: boolean)
    -- True if the supplier gives the object x to some receiver.
    WHERE b <=> SOME(receiver: agent ::
                    gives_to(supplier, x, receiver) ),
      Subtype(supplies, activity)

  CONCEPT gives_to(supplier: agent, x: any, receiver: agent)
    VALUE(b: boolean)
    -- True if the supplier gives the object x to the receiver.
    WHERE Subtype(gives_to, activity)
END
```

```
DEFINITION cause
  -- Concepts for describing cause and effect relations.
  IMPORT Covers_domain FROM relationship

  CONCEPT agent: type
    -- Every agent is the cause of some activity.
    WHERE Covers_domain(causes, 1, agent)

  CONCEPT activity: type
    -- Every activity is caused by some agent.
    WHERE Covers_domain(causes, 2, activity)

  CONCEPT causes(actor: agent, action: activity)
    VALUE(b: boolean)
    -- True if the agent causes the activity.

  CONCEPT Produces(action: activity, object: type)
    VALUE(b: boolean)
    -- True if the activity produces instances of the object.
```

```
CONCEPT Consumes(action: activity, object: type)
  VALUE(b: boolean)
  -- True if the activity consumes instances of the object.
  WHERE ALL(a: activity, o: type ::
            Consumes(a, o) => Needed_for(o, a) )

CONCEPT wants(actor: agent, object: any)
  VALUE(b: boolean)
  -- True if the agent wants the object.

CONCEPT Needed_for(object: type, action: activity)
  VALUE(b: boolean)
  -- True if an agent must have the object
  -- to cause the activity.
  WHERE ALL(actor: agent, object: any, action: activity ::
            wants(actor, action) &
            Needed_for(object, action) =>
            wants(actor, object) ),
    ALL(actor: agent, object: any, action: activity ::
        wants(actor, object) & Produces(action, object) =>
        wants(actor, action) )
    -- Agents want the means to attain their goals.
END
```

```
DEFINITION person   -- Concepts for describing people.
  INHERIT cause   -- The module "cause" defines the type "agent".
  IMPORT Subtype FROM type

  CONCEPT person: type   -- The set of human beings.
    WHERE Subtype(person, agent)   -- People are active agents.

  CONCEPT name(p: person) VALUE(s: string)
END
```

```
DEFINITION relationship
  -- Concepts for describing the connection between
  -- types and relationships.
  CONCEPT relationship{$domains: type}: type
    -- A relationship is a predicate.
    WHERE relationship = function{$domains, boolean}
```

```
CONCEPT Covers_domain(t: type, r: relationship($domains),
                      role: nat SUCH THAT
                      t = domains[role] )
  -- "role" is the index of t in the type sequence "domains".
VALUE(b: boolean)
-- True if every element of the type t participates
-- in the relationship r in the specified role position.
WHERE b <=> ALL(x: t ::
                  SOME(s: sequence(any) SUCH THAT
                       s IN domains :: r($s) & s[role] = x ))
END
```

```
DEFINITION time -- Concepts for describing time.
  CONCEPT time: type -- The absolute local time.
    WHERE Subtype(time, real)

  CONCEPT time_of_day: type
    -- The local clock time, which repeats every 24 hours.
    WHERE Subtype(time_of_day, real)

  CONCEPT date: type -- Identifies a particular day.

  CONCEPT time(tod: time_of_day, d: date) VALUE(t: time)
    -- The time of day and the date determine
    -- the absolute local time.

  CONCEPT time_of_day(t: time) VALUE(tod: time_of_day)
    -- The clock time at a given absolute time.

  CONCEPT date(t: time) VALUE(d: date)
    -- The date at a given absolute time.

  CONCEPT second(t: time) VALUE(r: real)
    WHERE 0.0 <= r < 60.0
  CONCEPT second(t: time_of_day) VALUE(r: real)
    WHERE 0.0 <= r < 60.0,
      ALL(t: time :: second(t) = second(time_of_day(t)))

  CONCEPT minute(t: time) VALUE(n: nat) WHERE 0 <= r < 60
  CONCEPT minute(t: time_of_day) VALUE(n: nat)
    WHERE 0 <= r < 60,
      ALL(t: time :: minute(t) = minute(time_of_day(t)))
```

```
CONCEPT hour(t: time) VALUE(n: nat) WHERE 0 <= r < 24
CONCEPT hour(t: time_of_day) VALUE(n: nat)
  WHERE 0 <= r < 24,
    ALL(t: time :: hour(t) = hour(time_of_day(t)))

CONCEPT day(t: time) VALUE(n: nat) WHERE 0 <= r < 366
CONCEPT day(d: date) VALUE(n: nat)
  WHERE 0 <= r < 366, ALL(t: time :: day(t) = day(date(t)))

CONCEPT weekday(t: time) VALUE(w: weekday)
CONCEPT weekday(d: date) VALUE(w: weekday)
  WHERE ALL(t: time :: weekday(t) = weekday(date(t)))
CONCEPT weekday: type
  WHERE weekday =
    enumeration{monday, tuesday, wednesday, thursday, friday,
                saturday, sunday }

CONCEPT year(t: time) VALUE(i: integer)
CONCEPT year(d: date) VALUE(i: integer)
  WHERE ALL(t: time :: year(t) = year(date(t)))
END
```

```
DEFINITION time_unit -- Concepts for describing time intervals.
  CONCEPT duration: type -- The length of a time interval.
    WHERE Subtype(duration, real)

  CONCEPT second: duration
    -- A time interval one second long.

  CONCEPT millisec: duration
    WHERE millisec = second * 10 ^ -3

  CONCEPT microsec: duration
    WHERE microsec = second * 10 ^ -6

  CONCEPT nanosec: duration
    WHERE nanosec = second * 10 ^ -9

  CONCEPT picosec: duration
    WHERE picosec = second * 10 ^ -12

  CONCEPT minutes: duration
    WHERE minutes = second * 60
```

```
    CONCEPT hours: duration
      WHERE hours = minutes * 60

    CONCEPT days: duration
      WHERE days = hours * 24

    CONCEPT weeks: duration
      WHERE weeks = days * 7
END
```

```
DEFINITION period
   -- Concepts for describing periodic activities.
   INHERIT time
   IMPORT activity FROM cause

   CONCEPT periodic(action: activity)
     VALUE(b: boolean)
     -- True if the activity occurs at regular time intervals.

   CONCEPT period(action: activity)
     VALUE(t: time)
     -- The time interval between consecutive instances
     -- of the activity.

   CONCEPT phase(action: activity)
     VALUE(t: time)
     -- The absolute time at which the first instance
     -- of the activity starts.
END
```

```
DEFINITION location
   -- Concepts for describing locations.
   CONCEPT location: type

   CONCEPT at(x: any, l: location) VALUE(b: boolean)
     -- The current location of the object x.

   CONCEPT distance(l1 l2: location) VALUE(d: distance)
     -- The distance between two locations.
```

```
  CONCEPT distance: type
    WHERE Subtype(distance, number)
END
```

```
DEFINITION requirement_model
  -- Defines types representing the basic building blocks
  -- for environment models.

  CONCEPT concept: type
    -- The most general category of building blocks
    -- for environment models.
  WHERE ALL(c: concept :: c IN type | c IN individual |
            c IN attribute | c IN relationship )
    -- Every concept is a type, individual, attribute,
    -- or relationship.  See the Spec type library
    -- for a definition of the type "type".

  CONCEPT individual: type
    -- The union of all types whose instances are
    -- individual objects rather than types.
  WHERE ALL(x: any :: x IN individual <=> ~(x IN type))
    -- Any object that is not a type is an individual.

  CONCEPT attribute: type
    -- The union of all types whose instances are
    -- attribute functions.
  WHERE ALL(x: any :: x IN attribute <=>
            SOME(d: sequence{type}, r: type ::
                x IN function{$d, r} & r ~= boolean ))
    -- Attributes are functions with non-boolean values.
    -- See the Spec type library for a definition
    -- of the type "function".

  CONCEPT relationship: type
    -- The union of all types whose instances are
    -- relationship predicates.
  WHERE ALL(x: any :: x IN relationship <=>
            SOME(d: sequence{type} ::
                x IN function{$d, boolean} ))
    -- Relationships are functions with boolean values.
END
```

```
DEFINITION format
  INHERIT character_properties

  CONCEPT is_list(line: string, $items: string)
    VALUE(b: boolean)
      -- The line consists of zero or more items
      -- separated by spaces.
    WHERE length(items) = 0 => (b <=> spaces(line)),
      ALL(i: string, r: sequence(string) SUCH THAT
          items = [i, $r] :: b <=>
          SOME(s1 s2 back: string SUCH THAT
              spaces(s1) & spaces(s2) ::
              line = s1 || i || s2 || back & is_list(back, r) &
              (s2 = "" => back = "") ))

  CONCEPT table(rows: sequence(row), widths: sequence(nat))
    VALUE(lines: sequence(string))
    WHERE length(lines) = length(rows),
      ALL(n: nat SUCH THAT n IN domain(rows) ::
          lines[i] = fill(rows[i], widths) )

  CONCEPT row: type
    WHERE row = sequence(string)

  CONCEPT fill(r: row, widths: sequence(nat)
              SUCH THAT length(row) = length(widths) )
              -- Each item in the row must fit in a field
              -- of the corresponding width.
    VALUE(s: string)
      -- Pad each item in the row to fit
      -- in the corresponding field width.
    WHERE fill([ ], [ ]) = [newline],
      ALL(col: string, r1: row, n: nat, w1: sequence(nat)
          SUCH THAT length(col) < n ::
          fill([col, $r1], [n, $w1]) =
            [$pad(col, n), $fill(r1, w1)] )

  CONCEPT pad(col: string, width: nat)
    VALUE(s: string)
    -- Pad with spaces from the left to the given width.
    -- Exceeds specified width if the string does not fit.
    WHERE IF length(col) < width THEN
            SOME(b: string ::
                s = b || col & length(s) = n & spaces(b) )
          ELSE s = " " || col FI
```

```
CONCEPT nat(s: string SUCH THAT digits(s))
   VALUE(n: nat)
     -- The number represented by a string of digits, base ten.
   WHERE ALL(s: string, n: nat SUCH THAT s = "0123456789"
             :: nat([s[n]]) = n - 1 ),
     ALL(s: string, c: char SUCH THAT digits(s) & digit(c)
         :: nat([$s, c]) = 10 * nat(s) + nat([c]) )
END
```

```
DEFINITION character_properties
  IMPORT digit letter FROM char

  CONCEPT digits(s: string) VALUE(b: boolean)
    WHERE ALL(c: char SUCH THAT c IN s :: digit(c))

  CONCEPT letters(s: string) VALUE(b: boolean)
    WHERE ALL(c: char SUCH THAT c IN s :: letter(c))

  CONCEPT spaces(s: string) VALUE(b: boolean)
    WHERE ALL(c: char SUCH THAT c IN s :: c = space)

  CONCEPT no_spaces(s: string) VALUE(b: boolean)
    WHERE b <=> ALL(c: char SUCH THAT c IN s :: c ~= space)

  CONCEPT space: char WHERE space = create@char(32)
    -- Ascii space character.

  CONCEPT tab: char WHERE tab = create@char(9)
    -- Ascii tab character.

  CONCEPT newline: char WHERE newline = create@char(10)
    -- Ascii linefeed character.
END
```

```
DEFINITION basic_edit
  CONCEPT edit(s: string)
    VALUE(es: string)
    WHERE ~(erase IN s | cancel IN s) => es = s,
     ALL(s1 s2: string, c: char ::
         edit([$s1, c, erase, $s2]) = edit([$s1, $s2]) ),
       ALL(s1 s2: string :: edit([$s1, cancel, $s2]) = edit(s2))
```

```
  CONCEPT erase: char
    WHERE erase = create@char(127)   -- Ascii delete.

  CONCEPT cancel: char
    WHERE cancel = create@char(27)   -- Ascii escape.
END
```

```
DEFINITION field_names
  IMPORT Subtype FROM type
  IMPORT letter FROM char
  EXPORT identifiers identifier

  CONCEPT identifiers(s1: sequence{any})
    VALUE(s2: sequence{identifier})
      -- s2 is the sequence of formal parameter or argument names
      -- associated with the sequence of actual parameter or
      -- argument values s1.  This concept is meaningful
      -- only when applied to parameter lists.

  CONCEPT identifier: type
    WHERE Subtype(identifier, string),
      ALL(i: identifier :: length(i) > 0 & letter(i[1])),
      ALL(i: identifier, c: char ::
          c IN i => letter(c) | digit(c) | c = '_' )
    -- Identifiers are special strings representing Spec names.
    -- Identifiers are written without quotes when used as
    -- {actual parameters}.  Identifiers are written with quotes
    -- when used as (actual arguments).
END
```

```
DEFINITION mutable{t: type}
  CONCEPT new(x: t) VALUE(b: boolean)
    WHERE b <=> x IN t & ~(x IN *t),
        -- An object is new if it belongs to the type
        -- in the current state and it did not belong
        -- to the type in the previous state.
      ALL(a c: t :: new(a) & c IN *t => id(a) ~= id(c))
        -- A new object is distinct from any object existing
        -- in the previous state.
```

```
  CONCEPT id(x: t) VALUE(n: nat)
    WHERE ALL(y z: t :: id(y) = id(z) => y = z),
      ALL(y: t :: *y IN *t => id(y) = id(*y))
      -- Every object has a permanent unique identifier.
END
```

```
DEFINITION quantifiers{t: type}
  IMPORT Identity Commutative Associative FROM number{t}
  IMPORT Bottom Top FROM partial_order{t}

  CONCEPT All(s: set{boolean}) VALUE(b: boolean)
    WHERE b <=> s = {true} | s = { }

  CONCEPT Some(s: set{boolean}) VALUE(b: boolean)
    WHERE b <=> true IN s

  CONCEPT reduction_quantifier(f: function{t, t, t}, i: t
                               SUCH THAT Identity(i, f),
                               Commutative(f), Associative(f) )
    VALUE(g: function{unbounded_set{t}, t})
      -- Quantifier defined by repeated applications of f.
      -- Defined for infinite sets only if
      -- all subset decompositions give the same result.
    WHERE g({ }) = i, ALL(x: t :: g({x}) = x),
      ALL(s1 s2: unbounded_set{t} SUCH THAT
          intersection(s1, s2) = { } ::
          g(s1 U s2) = f(g(s1), g(s2)) )

  CONCEPT Sum(s: set{t}) VALUE(y: t)
    WHERE Sum = reduction_quantifier("+"@t, zero@t)

  CONCEPT Product(s: set{t}) VALUE(y: t)
    WHERE Product = reduction_quantifier("*"@t, one@t)

  CONCEPT Number(s: set{any}) VALUE(n: nat)
    WHERE Number({ }) = 0, Number({!}) = 1,
      ALL(x: any :: Number({x}) = 1),
      ALL(s1 s2: set{any} SUCH THAT intersection(s1, s2) = { }
          :: Number(s1 U s2) = Number(s1) + Number(s2))

  CONCEPT Average(s: set{any}) VALUE(n: nat)
    WHERE n = Sum(s)/Number(s)
```

```
CONCEPT lub{le: function{t, t, t} SUCH THAT
            Partial_ordering(le) }
            (s: unbounded_set{t}) VALUE(b: t)
    -- b is the least upper bound of s in the ordering "le".
  WHERE ALL(x: t :: x IN s => le(x, b)),
    ALL(y: t SUCH THAT ALL(x: t :: x IN s => le(x, y)) ::
        le(b, y) )

CONCEPT Maximum(s: set{t}) VALUE(y: t)
  WHERE Maximum = lub{"<="}

CONCEPT Minimum(s: set{t}) VALUE(y: t)
  WHERE Minimum = lub{">="}

CONCEPT Union(s: set{t}) VALUE(y: t)
  WHERE Union = lub{subset}

CONCEPT Intersection(s: set{t}) VALUE(y: t)
  WHERE Intersection = lub{contains}
END
```

APPENDIX
Spec Type Library

This appendix gives the definitions of the predefined data types in the Spec language.

```
TYPE any  -- The union of all other types.
  IMPORT Subtype FROM type

  MODEL
  INVARIANT ALL(t: type :: Subtype(t, any))
END
```

```
VIRTUAL TYPE equality {t: type}
  IMPORT Deterministic FROM function{any, any}
  EXPORT Reflexive Symmetric Transitive Identity_relation Eternal

  MESSAGE equal(x y: t)  -- Weak equality, can be computed.
    REPLY(b: boolean)
    WHERE Reflexive(equal), Symmetric(equal), Transitive(equal),
      Identity_relation(equal),
        -- Equals can be substituted for equals.
      Eternal(equal)
        -- If two objects are equal,
        -- they are equal in all states.
```

```
MESSAGE not_equal(x y: t)
  REPLY(b: boolean) WHERE b <=> ~equal(x, y)

CONCEPT "="(x y: t) VALUE(b: boolean)
    -- Strong logical equality, not computable.
  WHERE Strongly_reflexive("="),
      -- (! = !) = true but equal(!, !) = !.
    ALL(x y: t :: (x = y) <=> equal(x, y))
      -- "=" is the same as "equal" for all well defined
      -- data values.

CONCEPT "~="(x y: t) VALUE(b: boolean)
  -- Strong logical inequality, not computable.
  WHERE b <=> ~(x = y)

CONCEPT Reflexive(f: function{t, t, boolean}) VALUE(b: boolean)
  WHERE b <=> ALL(x: t :: f(x, x))
    -- x ranges over well defined values of type t.

CONCEPT Strongly_reflexive(f: function{t, t, boolean})
  VALUE(b: boolean)
  WHERE b <=> Reflexive(f) & f(!, !)
    -- Reflexive also for the undefined element "!".

CONCEPT Symmetric(f: function{t, t, boolean}) VALUE(b: boolean)
  WHERE b <=> ALL(x y: t :: f(x, y) => f(y, x))

CONCEPT Transitive(f: function{t, t, boolean})
  VALUE(b: boolean)
  WHERE b <=> ALL(x y z: t :: f(x, y) & f(y, z) => f(x, z))

CONCEPT Identity_relation(f: function{t, t, boolean})
  VALUE(b: boolean)
  WHERE b <=>
    ALL(a b: t, ts1 ts2: sequence{type}, s1: ts1, s2: ts2,
        range: type, g: function{$ts1, t, $ts2, range}
        SUCH THAT Deterministic(g) ::
        f(a, b) => g($s1, a, $s2) = g($s1, b, $s2) )
          -- If f(x, y) there is no way
          -- to distinguish x from y.
          -- This means x and y are identical,
          -- so you can substitute x for y.

CONCEPT Eternal(f: function{t, t, boolean}) VALUE(b: boolean)
  WHERE b <=> ALL(a b: t :: f(a, b) => always(f(a, b)))
    -- This means the relation f cannot be affected by
    -- state changes.
END
```

```
TYPE boolean
  INHERIT equality{boolean}
  IMPORT Partial_ordering FROM partial_order{boolean}
    -- Generated by {true, false}.

  MESSAGE true REPLY(b: boolean)

  MESSAGE false REPLY(b: boolean)
    WHERE true ~= false

  MESSAGE "~"(b1: boolean) REPLY(b2: boolean)
    WHERE ~true = false, ~false = true, ~! = !

  MESSAGE and(b1 b2: boolean) REPLY(b3: boolean)
    WHERE ALL(b: boolean :: and(b, true) = b = and(true, b)),
      ALL(b: boolean :: and(b, false) = false = and(false, b)),
      ALL(b: boolean :: and(b, !) = ! = and(!, b))

  MESSAGE or(b1 b2: boolean) REPLY(b3: boolean)
    WHERE ALL(b: boolean :: or(b, true) = true = or(true, b)),
      ALL(b: boolean :: or(b, false) = b = or(false, b)),
      ALL(b: boolean :: or(b, !) = ! = or(!, b))

  MESSAGE implies(b1 b2: boolean) REPLY(b3: boolean)
    WHERE b3 = or(~b1, b2), Partial_ordering(implies),
      ALL(b: boolean :: implies(b, !) = ! = implies(!, b))

  MESSAGE "<=>"(b1 b2: boolean) REPLY(b3: boolean)
    WHERE b3 = ((b1 => b2) & (b2 => b1)),
      ALL(b: boolean :: (b <=> !) = ! = (! <=> b))

  CONCEPT "&"(b1 b2: boolean) VALUE(b3: boolean)
    -- "and" extended to undefined values, not strict.
    WHERE ALL(b: boolean :: (b & true) = b = (true & b)),
      ALL(b: boolean :: (b & false) = false = (false & b)),
      (! & true) = ! = (true & !),
      (! & false) = false = (false & !),
      (! & !) = !

  CONCEPT "|"(b1 b2: boolean) VALUE(b3: boolean)
    -- "or" extended to undefined values, not strict.
    WHERE ALL(b: boolean :: (b | true) = true = (true | b)),
      ALL(b: boolean :: (b | false) = b = (false | b)),
      (! | true) = true = (true | !),
      (! | false) = ! = (false | !),
      (! | !) = !
```

```
  CONCEPT "=>"(b1 b2: boolean) VALUE(b3: boolean)
    -- "implies" extended to undefined values, not strict.
    WHERE b3 = (~b1 | b2), Partial_ordering("=>")
END
```

```
VIRTUAL TYPE total_order {t: type}
  INHERIT partial_order{t} HIDE "~<" "~>" "~<=" "~>="
    -- These operations are redundant for a total order,
    -- use >=, <=, >, and < instead.
  EXPORT Exhaustive Total_ordering

  MESSAGE "<="(x y: t) REPLY(b: boolean)
    WHERE Exhaustive("<=")

  MESSAGE max(x y: t) REPLY(z: t)
    WHERE z = IF x >= y THEN x ELSE y FI

  MESSAGE min(x y: t) REPLY(z: t)
    WHERE z = IF x <= y THEN x ELSE y FI

  CONCEPT Exhaustive(f: function{t, t, boolean})
    VALUE(b: boolean)
      WHERE b <=> ALL(x y: t :: f(x, y) | f(y, x))

  CONCEPT Total_ordering(f: function{t, t, boolean})
    VALUE(b: boolean)
      WHERE b <=> Partial_ordering(f) & Exhaustive(f)
END
```

```
TYPE char
  INHERIT equality{char}
  INHERIT total_order{char}

  MODEL(code: nat)  -- ASCII codes.
  INVARIANT ALL(c: char :: 0 <= c.code <= 127)

  MESSAGE create(n: nat)  -- literal 'a' = create(97) and so on.
    WHEN 0 <= n <= 127 REPLY(c: char) WHERE c.code = n
    OTHERWISE REPLY EXCEPTION illegal_code
```

```
  MESSAGE ordinal(c: char) REPLY(n: nat)
    WHERE n = c.code

  MESSAGE equal(c1 c2: char) REPLY(b: boolean)
    WHERE b <=> (c1.code = c2.code)

  MESSAGE "<"(c1 c2: char) REPLY(b: boolean)
    WHERE b <=> (c1.code < c2.code)

  CONCEPT letter(c: char) VALUE(b: boolean)
    WHERE b <=> (c IN ['a' .. 'z'] | c IN ['A' .. 'Z'])

  CONCEPT digit(c: char) VALUE(b: boolean)
    WHERE b <=> c IN ['0' .. '9']
END
```

```
TYPE enumeration{$s: identifier}
  -- Example: traffic_signal = enumeration{red, yellow, green}.
  INHERIT equality{enumeration{$s}}
  INHERIT total_order{enumeration{$s}}
  IMPORT identifier FROM field_names  -- See Appendix C.

  MODEL(code: nat)
    -- Position numbers in the generic parameter list.
  INVARIANT ALL(c: enumeration{$s} :: 1 <= c.code <= length(s))

  MESSAGE create(n: nat)
      -- Literal #s[k] = create(k), e.g. #yellow = create(2).
    WHEN 1 <= n <= length(s)
      REPLY(c: enumeration{$s}) WHERE c.code = n
    OTHERWISE REPLY EXCEPTION illegal_code

  MESSAGE ordinal(e: enumeration{$s}) REPLY(n: nat)
    WHERE n = c.code

  MESSAGE equal(e1 e2: enumeration{$s}) REPLY(b: boolean)
    WHERE b <=> (e1.code = e2.code)

  MESSAGE "<"(e1 e2: enumeration{$s}) REPLY(b: boolean)
    WHERE b <=> (e1.code < e2.code)
END
```

```
TYPE null
  INHERIT equality{null}
  -- Generated by {nil}.

  MESSAGE nil REPLY(n: null)

  MESSAGE equal(n1 n2: null) REPLY(b: boolean)
    WHERE b = true
END
```

```
TYPE tuple{$s: type SUCH THAT distinct(identifiers(s))}
  -- Two tuple types are the same if and only if they have
  -- the same actual parameters WITH THE SAME FIELD NAMES.
  -- Identifiers(s) is the sequence of identifiers used as
  -- field names in the actual parameter list.

  INHERIT equality{tuple{$s}}
  INHERIT partial_order{tuple{$s}}
    RENAME ">=" AS contains
    RENAME ">" AS properly_contains
  IMPORT identifiers identifier FROM field_names
  IMPORT distinct remove FROM sequence{identifier}

  MODEL(c: sequence{any})
  INVARIANT ALL(t: tuple{$s} :: t.c IN s)

  MESSAGE create($a: any)
    -- Literal [i1:: v1, ... , in:: vn] =
    -- create(i1:: v1, ... , in:: vn).
    WHEN a IN s & identifiers(a) = identifiers(s)
      REPLY(t: tuple{$s}) WHERE t.c = a
    OTHERWISE REPLY EXCEPTION type_error

  MESSAGE "."{id: identifier SUCH THAT id IN identifiers(s)}
          (t: tuple{$s})
    -- "."{b}(a) is written a.b, component selection.
    CHOOSE(k: nat, ct: type SUCH THAT
          identifiers(s)[k] = id & ct = s[k] )
    REPLY(x: ct) WHERE x = t.c[k]

  MESSAGE get(t: tuple{$s}, id: identifier)
    WHEN id IN identifiers(s)
      CHOOSE(n: nat, ct: type SUCH THAT ct = s[n])
      REPLY(x: ct) WHERE x = t.c[n]
```

```
      OTHERWISE REPLY EXCEPTION tuple_selection_error
      -- Get(t, "x") = t.x,
      -- this form allows the id to be calculated.

   MESSAGE "["(t: tuple{$s}, n: nat)
     -- "["(t, n) is written t[n].
     WHEN 1 <= n <= length(s)
       CHOOSE(ct: type SUCH THAT ct = s[n])
       REPLY(x: ct) WHERE x = t.c[n]
     OTHERWISE REPLY EXCEPTION tuple_selection_error.

   MESSAGE remove(id: identifier, t1: tuple{$s})
     WHEN id IN identifiers(s)
       CHOOSE(n: nat, ss: sequence{type}
              SUCH THAT id = identifiers(s)[n]
              & ss = s[1 .. n - 1] || s[n + 1 .. length(s)])
       REPLY(t2: tuple{$ss}) WHERE contains(t1, t2)
     OTHERWISE REPLY EXCEPTION tuple_selection_error

   MESSAGE "||"(t1: tuple{$s}, t2: tuple{$ss})  -- Concatenation.
     WHEN distinct(s || ss)
       REPLY(t3: tuple{$s, $ss}) WHERE t3.c = t1.c || t2.c
     OTHERWISE REPLY EXCEPTION type_error
     -- Tuple || is defined in terms of sequence ||.

   MESSAGE equal(t1 t2: tuple{$s})
     REPLY(b: boolean) WHERE b <=> t1.c = t2.c

   MESSAGE contains(t1: tuple{$s}, t2: tuple{$ss})
     REPLY(b: boolean)
       -- True if and only if t1 contains all of the components
       -- of t2.
     WHERE b <=> ALL(i: identifier SUCH THAT i IN identifiers(ss)
                     :: get(t1, i) = get(t2, i) )
END
```

```
TYPE union{$s: type SUCH THAT distinct(identifiers(s))}
   -- A union type is a tagged disjoint union of a set of types.
   -- Two union types are the same if and only if they have
   -- the same actual parameters WITH THE SAME FIELD NAMES.
   -- Identifiers(s) is the sequence of identifiers used as
   -- field names in the actual parameter list.

   INHERIT equality{union{$s}}
   IMPORT identifiers identifier FROM field_names
   IMPORT distinct FROM sequence{identifier}
```

```
  MODEL(tag: identifier, value: any)
  INVARIANT ALL(u: union{$s} :: u.tag IN identifiers(s)),
    ALL(u: union{$s} :: u.value IN type_of(u.tag))

  MESSAGE create{id: identifier SUCH THAT id IN identifiers(s)}
             (x: any)
    -- Literal {t :: v} = create{t}(v).
    WHEN x IN type_of(id)
      REPLY(u: union{$s}) WHERE u.tag = id & u.value = x
    OTHERWISE REPLY EXCEPTION type_error

  MESSAGE is{id: identifier SUCH THAT id IN identifiers(s)}
            (u: oneof{$s})
    REPLY(b: boolean) WHERE b <=> u.tag = id
    -- Check if you have a given variant.

  MESSAGE "."{id: identifier SUCH THAT id IN identifiers(s)}
             (u: oneof{$s})
    -- "."{b}(a) is written a.b, projection.
    WHEN u.tag = id
      CHOOSE(rt: type SUCH THAT rt = type_of(id))
      REPLY(x: rt) WHERE x = u.value
    OTHERWISE REPLY EXCEPTION type_error
    -- Extract the value assuming a given variant,
    -- succeeds only if the tag matches the assumed variant.

  MESSAGE equal(u1 u2: union{$s})
    REPLY(b: boolean)
    WHERE b <=> u1.tag = u2.tag & u1.value = u2.value

  CONCEPT type_of(id: identifier SUCH THAT id IN identifiers(s))
    VALUE(t: type)
    -- The type corresponding to the id
    -- in the formal parameter list s.
      WHERE SOME(n: nat :: t = s[n] & id = identifiers(s)[n])
END
```

```
TYPE sequence{t: type}
  INHERIT equality{sequence{t}}
  INHERIT total_order{sequence{t}}
  IMPORT Subtype FROM type
  EXPORT prefix suffix sorted distinct permutation frequency
    -- Generated by {empty, add}.

  MESSAGE empty
    -- Literal [ ] = empty.
    REPLY(s: sequence{t})
```

```
MESSAGE add(x: t, s1: sequence{t})
  -- Literal [x] = add(x, empty).
  -- Literal [x, $s] = add(x, s).
  REPLY(s2: sequence{t})

MESSAGE remove(x: t, s1: sequence{t})
  -- Remove all instances of x from s.
  REPLY(s2: sequence{t})
  WHERE ALL(x: t :: remove(x, empty) = empty),
    ALL(x: t, s: sequence{t} ::
        remove(x, add(x, s)) = remove(x, s) ),
    ALL(x y: t, s: sequence{t} SUCH THAT x ~= y
        :: remove(x, add(y, s)) = add(y, remove(x, s)) )

MESSAGE "||"(s1 s2: sequence{t})  -- Concatenation.
  -- Literal [$s1, $s2] = s1 || s2.
  REPLY(s2: sequence{t})
  WHERE ALL(s: sequence{t} :: empty || s = s),
    ALL(x: t, s1 s2: sequence{t} ::
        add(x, s1) || s2 = add(x, s1 || s2) )

MESSAGE "["(s: sequence{t}, n: nat)
  -- Indexing, "["(a, b) is written a[b].
  WHEN 1 <= n <= length(s)
    REPLY(x: t)
    WHERE ALL(x: t, s: sequence{t} :: add(x, s)[1] = x),
      ALL(n: nat, x: t, s: sequence{t} SUCH THAT n > 1
        :: add(x, s)[n] = s[n - 1] )
  OTHERWISE REPLY EXCEPTION bounds_error

MESSAGE "["(s1: sequence{t}, s2: sequence{nat})
  -- Indirect indexing.
  -- Subrange is a special case:
  -- s[1 .. 3] is the same as s[[1, 2, 3]].
  WHEN ALL(n: nat SUCH THAT n IN s2 :: n IN domain(s1))
    REPLY(s3: sequence{t})
    WHERE length(s3) = length(s2),
      ALL(n: nat SUCH THAT n IN domain(s2) ::
          s3[n] = s1[s2[n]] )
  OTHERWISE REPLY EXCEPTION bounds_error

MESSAGE length(s: sequence{t})
  REPLY(n: nat)
  WHERE length(empty) = 0,
    ALL(x: t, s: sequence{t} ::
        length(add(x, s)) = length(s) + 1 )

MESSAGE domain(s: sequence{t})
  REPLY(d: set{nat})
  WHERE d = {1 .. length(s)}
```

```
MESSAGE "IN"(x: t, s: sequence{t})
  -- "IN"(x, s) is written x IN s.
  REPLY(b: boolean)
  WHERE b <=> SOME(n: nat SUCH THAT n IN domain(s) :: s[n] = x)

MESSAGE "IN"(s1 s2: sequence{t})
  REPLY(b: boolean)
  WHERE b <=> SOME(x y: sequence{t} :: x || s1 || y = s2)

MESSAGE equal(s1 s2: sequence{t})
  REPLY(b: boolean)
  WHERE b <=> ALL(n: nat :: s1[n] = s2[n])

MESSAGE "<"(s1 s2: sequence{t})
  -- Lexicographic ordering (dictionary ordering on strings).
  WHEN Has_operation{t, t, boolean}(t, "<") &
       Partial_ordering("<"@t)
    REPLY(b: boolean)
    WHERE ALL(s: sequence{t}, x: t :: [ ] < [x, $s]),
      ALL(s1 s2: sequence{t}, x1 x2: t
          :: [x1, $s1] < [x2, $s2] <=>
             x1 < x2 | x1 = x2 & s1 < s2 )
  OTHERWISE REPLY EXCEPTION operation_not_applicable

MESSAGE subsequence(s1 s2: sequence{t})
  REPLY(b: boolean)
  -- True if the elements of s1 are embedded in s2,
  -- in the same order.
  WHERE ALL(s: sequence{t} :: subsequence([ ], s)),
    ALL(s1 s2: sequence{t}, x: t :: subsequence([x, $s1], s2)
          <=> SOME(s3 s4: sequence{t}
                   :: s2 = [$s3, x, $s4] &
                      subsequence(s1, s4) )),
    Partial_ordering(subsequence)

MESSAGE ".."(x1 x2: t)  -- ".."(x1, x2)" is written [x1 .. x2].
  WHEN Subtype(t, total_order)
    REPLY(s: sequence{t})
    WHERE sorted{"<"@t}(s),
         ALL(x: t :: x IN s <=> x1 <= x <= x2)
  OTHERWISE REPLY EXCEPTION operation_not_applicable

MESSAGE apply{rt: type}(f: function{t, rt}, s1: sequence{t})
  REPLY(s2: sequence{rt})
  WHERE length(s2) = length(s1),
    ALL(n: nat SUCH THAT n IN domain(s1) :: s2[n] = f(s1[n]))

MESSAGE reduce{f: function{t, t, t}, identity: t SUCH THAT
               ALL(y: t :: f(y, identity) = y) }
          (s: sequence{t})
```

```
      REPLY(x: t)
      WHERE IF s = { } THEN x = identity
            ELSE x = f(s[1], reduce{f}(s[2 .. length(s)]))) FI

  MESSAGE reduce1{f: function{t, t, t}} (s: sequence{t})
      WHEN length(s) > 1 REPLY(x: t)
        WHERE x = f(s[1], reduce1{f}(s[2 .. length(s)]))
      WHEN length(s) = 1 REPLY(x: t) WHERE x = s[1]
      OTHERWISE REPLY EXCEPTION empty_reduction_undefined

CONCEPT prefix(s1 s2: sequence{t})
  VALUE(b: boolean)
  -- True if s1 is a prefix of s2.
  WHERE b <=> SOME(s: sequence{t} :: s1 || s = s2)

CONCEPT suffix(s1 s2: sequence{t})
  VALUE(b: boolean)
  -- True if s1 is a suffix of s2.
  WHERE b <=> SOME(s: sequence{t} :: s || s1 = s2)

CONCEPT sorted{le: function{t, t, boolean} SUCH THAT
                Total_ordering(le) }
          (s: sequence{t})
  VALUE(b: boolean)
  -- True if s is sorted in nondecreasing order
  -- with respect to le.
  WHERE b <=> ALL(n1 n2: nat SUCH THAT
                  1 <= n1 < n2 <= length(s) ::
                  le(s[n1], s[n2]) )

CONCEPT distinct(s: sequence{t})
  VALUE(b: boolean)
  -- True if there are no repeated elements in s.
  WHERE b <=> ALL(n1 n2: nat SUCH THAT
                  1 <= n1 < n2 <= length(s) ::
                  s[n1] ~= s[n2] )

CONCEPT permutation(s1 s2: sequence{t})
  VALUE(b: boolean)
  -- True if s1 is a permutation of s2.
  WHERE b <=> ALL(x: t :: frequency(x, s1) = frequency(x, s2))

CONCEPT frequency(x: t, s: sequence{t})
  VALUE(n: nat)
  -- The number of times x appears as an element of s.
  WHERE n = NUMBER(k: nat SUCH THAT s[k] = x :: k)
END
```

```
VIRTUAL TYPE partial_order{t: type}
  INHERIT equality{t}
  IMPORT Reflexive Transitive FROM equality{t}
  EXPORT Acyclic Antisymmetric Partial_ordering

  MESSAGE "<"(x y: t) REPLY(b: boolean)
    WHERE b <=> (x <= y & x ~= y), Acyclic("<"), Transitive("<")

  MESSAGE "~<"(x y: t) REPLY(b: boolean)
    WHERE b <=> ~(x < y)

  MESSAGE ">"(x y: t) REPLY(b: boolean)
    WHERE b <=> y < x

  MESSAGE "~>"(x y: t) REPLY(b: boolean)
    WHERE b <=> ~(x > y)

  MESSAGE "<="(x y: t) REPLY(b: boolean)
    WHERE Partial_ordering("<=")

  MESSAGE "~<="(x y: t) REPLY(b: boolean)
    WHERE b <=> ~(x <= y)

  MESSAGE ">="(x y: t) REPLY(b: boolean)
    WHERE b <=> y <= x

  MESSAGE "~>="(x y: t) REPLY(b: boolean)
    WHERE b <=> ~(x >= y)

  CONCEPT Acyclic(f: function{t, t, boolean})
    VALUE(b: boolean)
    WHERE b <=> ALL(x: t :: ~f(x, x))

  CONCEPT Antisymmetric(f: function{t, t, boolean})
    VALUE(b: boolean)
    WHERE b <=> ALL(x y: t :: f(x, y) & f(y, x) => x = y)

  CONCEPT Partial_ordering(f: function{t, t, boolean})
    VALUE(b: boolean)
    WHERE b <=> Reflexive(f) & Antisymmetric(f) & Transitive(f)
END
```

```
TYPE set{t: type SUCH THAT Subtype(t, equality{t})}
    -- The element type t must have an equality operation
    -- with the standard interpretation.
  INHERIT equality{set{t}}
```

```
INHERIT partial_order{set{t}}
  RENAME "<=" AS subset
  RENAME "<" AS proper_subset
IMPORT Commutative Associative FROM number{t}
IMPORT Subtype FROM type
  -- Generated by {empty, add} and partitioned by {"IN"}.

MESSAGE empty
  -- Literal { } = empty.
  REPLY(s: set{t})
  WHERE ALL(x: t :: ~(x IN empty))

MESSAGE add(x: t, s1: set{t})
  -- Literal {x} = add(x, empty).
  -- Literal {x, $s} = add(x, s).
  REPLY(s2: set{t})
  WHERE ALL(x y: t, s: set{t} ::
            x IN add(y, s) <=> (x = y | x IN s) )

MESSAGE remove(x: t, s1: set{t})
  REPLY(s2: set{t})
  WHERE ALL(x y: t, s: set{t} ::
            x IN remove(y, s) <=> (x ~= y & x IN s) )

MESSAGE "IN"(x: t, s: set{t})   -- "IN"(x, s) is written x IN s.
  REPLY(b: boolean)
  -- True if x is an element of the set s.

MESSAGE "U"(s1 s2: set{t})   -- Literal {$s1, $s2} = s1 U s2.
  REPLY(s3: set{t})
  WHERE ALL(x: t :: x IN s3 <=> (x IN s1 | x IN s2))

MESSAGE "-"(s1 s2: set{t}) REPLY(s3: set{t})
  WHERE ALL(x: t :: x IN s3 <=> (x IN s1 & ~(x IN s2)))

MESSAGE intersection(s1 s2: set{t}) REPLY(s3: set{t})
  WHERE ALL(x: t :: x IN s3 <=> (x IN s1 & x IN s2))

MESSAGE "*"{t1: type}(s1: set{t}, s2: set{t1})
  -- Cartesian product.
  REPLY(s3: set{tuple{c1:: t, c2:: t1}})
  WHERE ALL(x: t, y: t1 ::
            [c1:: x, c2:: y] IN s3 <=> (x IN s1 & y IN s2) )

MESSAGE size(s: set{t}) REPLY(n: nat)   -- Cardinality.
  WHERE n = NUMBER(x: t SUCH THAT x IN s :: x)

MESSAGE equal(s1 s2: set{t}) REPLY(b: boolean)
  WHERE b <=> ALL(x: t :: x IN s1 <=> x IN s2)
```

```
MESSAGE subset(s1 s2: set{t}) REPLY(b: boolean)
   WHERE b <=> ALL(x: t :: x IN s1 => x IN s2)

MESSAGE ".."(x1 x2: t)   -- ".."(x1, x2) is written {x1 .. x2}.
   WHEN Subtype(t, partial_order) REPLY(s: set{t})
     WHERE ALL(x: t :: x IN s <=> x1 <= x <= x2)
   OTHERWISE REPLY EXCEPTION operation_not_applicable

MESSAGE apply{rt: type}(f: function{t, rt}, s1: set{t})
   REPLY(s2: set{rt})
   WHERE ALL(y: rt :: y IN s2 <=>
             SOME(x: t :: x IN s1 & y = f(x)) )

MESSAGE reduce{f: function{t, t, t}, identity: t
               SUCH THAT Commutative(f), Associative(f),
                 ALL(y: t :: f(y, identity) = y) } .
           (s: set{t})
     REPLY(x: t)
     WHERE IF s = { } THEN x = identity
           ELSE ALL(y: t :: y IN s =>
                     x = f(y, reduce{f}(s - {y})) ) FI

MESSAGE reduce1{f: function{t, t, t} SUCH THAT
               Commutative(f), Associative(f) }
           (s: set{t})
     WHEN size(s) > 1 REPLY(x: t)
       WHERE ALL(y: t :: y IN s =>
                 x = f(y, reduce1{f}(s - {y})) )
     WHEN size(s) = 1
       REPLY(x: t) WHERE x IN s
     OTHERWISE REPLY EXCEPTION empty_reduction_undefined
END
```

```
TYPE unbounded_set{t: type}
  INHERIT set{t}

  MESSAGE construct(p: function{t, boolean})
    REPLY(s: unbounded_set{t})
      WHERE ALL(x: t :: x IN s <=> p(x))
      -- S = {x: t SUCH THAT p(x) :: x}, may not be finite.
END
```

```
TYPE multiset{t: type}
  INHERIT equality{multiset{t}}
  IMPORT frequency FROM sequence{t}

  MODEL(n: map{t, nat})
  INVARIANT ALL(m: multiset{t} :: default(m.n) = 0)

  MESSAGE empty REPLY(m: multiset{t})
    WHERE ALL(x: t :: m.n[x] = 0)

  MESSAGE add(x: t, m1: multiset{t}) REPLY(m2: multiset{t})
    WHERE m2.n[x] = m1.n[x] + 1,
      ALL(y: t SUCH THAT y ~= x :: m2.n[y] = m1.n[y])

  MESSAGE remove(x: t, m1: multiset{t})
    WHEN x IN m1 REPLY(m2: multiset{t})
      WHERE m2.n[x] = m1.n[x] - 1,
        ALL(y: t SUCH THAT y ~= x :: m2.n[y] = m1.n[y])
    OTHERWISE REPLY(m1: multiset{t})

  MESSAGE "U"(m1 m2: multiset{t}) REPLY(m3: multiset{t})
    WHERE ALL(x: t :: m3.n[x] = m1.n[x] + m1.n[x])

  MESSAGE "IN"(x: t, m: multiset{t}) REPLY(b: boolean)
    WHERE b <=> m.n[x] > 0

  MESSAGE frequency(x: t, m: multiset{t}) REPLY(n: nat)
    WHERE n = m.n[x]

  MESSAGE size(m: multiset{t}) REPLY(n: nat)
    WHERE n = SUM(x: t :: m.n[x])
    -- The number of occurrences for all items in the multiset.

  MESSAGE domain(m: multiset{t}) REPLY(s: set{t})
    WHERE s = domain(m.n)
    -- The set of elements that appear in the multiset
    -- at least once.

  MESSAGE scan(m: multiset{t})
    GENERATE(s: sequence{t})
    WHERE ALL(x: t :: frequency(x, m) = frequency(x, s))
    -- The order of the elements is not specified.
    -- Note the overloading of frequency:
    -- sequence concept & multiset message.
END
```

```
TYPE map {key result: type SUCH THAT Subtype(key, equality{t})}
    -- The domain of the map must have an equality operation
    -- with the standard interpretation.

INHERIT partial_order{map{key, result}}
IMPORT Subtype FROM type

MODEL(default: result, pairs: set{pair})
INVARIANT ALL(m: map{key, result} :: single_valued(m.pairs)),
  ALL(m: map{key, result}, p: pair SUCH THAT
      p IN m.pairs :: p.y ~= default )

  MESSAGE create(v: result)
    REPLY(m: map{key, result})
      WHERE m.default = v, m.pairs = { }
      -- m[x] = v for all x.

  MESSAGE bind(x: key, y: result, m: map{key, result})
    REPLY(mm: map{key, result})
      WHERE mm[x] = y, mm.default = m.default
        ALL(z: key SUCH THAT z ~= x :: mm[z] = m[z])

  MESSAGE remove(x: key, m: map{key, result})
    REPLY(mm: map{key, result})
      WHERE mm[x] = m.default, mm.default = m.default
        ALL(z: key SUCH THAT z ~= x :: mm[z] = m[z])

  MESSAGE remove(s: set{key}, m: map{key, result})
    REPLY(mm: map{key, result})
      WHERE ALL(x: key :: IF x IN s THEN mm[x] = m.default
                           ELSE mm[x] = m[x] FI ), mm.default = m.default

  MESSAGE "["(m: map{key, result}, x: key)
    -- "["(m, x) is written m[x].
    REPLY(y: result)
      WHERE IF x IN m
            THEN SOME(p: pair :: p IN m.pairs &
                                   p.x = x & p.y = y )
            ELSE y = m.default FI

  MESSAGE "IN"(x: key, m: map{key, result}) REPLY(b: boolean)
    WHERE b <=> x IN domain(m)
    -- b <=> m[x] ~= m.default.

  MESSAGE equal(m1 m2: map{key, result})
    REPLY(b: boolean)
      WHERE b <=> ALL(x: key :: m1[x] = m2[x])
```

```
MESSAGE "<="(m1 m2: map{key, result})
  REPLY(b: boolean)
    WHERE b <=> subset(m1.pairs, m2.pairs) &
                m1.default = m2.default
      -- b <=> ALL(x: key :: m1[x] = m2[x] |
      --                      m1[x] = default(m2) ).

MESSAGE domain(m: map{key, result})
  REPLY(s: set{key})
    WHERE s = SET(p: pair SUCH THAT p IN m.pairs :: p.x)
      -- s = {x | x in m}.

MESSAGE range(m: map{key, result})
  REPLY(s: set{result})
    WHERE ALL(y: result :: y IN s <=>
              SOME(x: key :: m[x] = y) )
      -- s = {y | y = m[x] for some x},
      -- includes the default value.

MESSAGE default(m: map{key, result})
  REPLY(y: result)
    WHERE y = m.default
      -- The default value of the map.

CONCEPT pair: type
  WHERE pair = tuple{x :: key, y :: result}

CONCEPT single_valued(s: set{pair})
  VALUE(b: boolean)
  WHERE b <=> ALL(p1 p2: pair SUCH THAT p1 IN s & p2 IN s
                  :: p1.x = p2.x => p1.y = p2.y )
    -- The map associates at most one y value with each x value.
END
```

```
TYPE relation{$s: type SUCH THAT distinct(identifiers(s))}
  -- Two relation types are the same if and only if they have
  -- the same actual parameters WITH THE SAME FIELD NAMES.
  -- Identifiers(s) is the sequence of identifiers used as
  -- field names in the actual parameter list.

  INHERIT equality{relation{$s}}
  INHERIT partial_order{relation{$s}}
    RENAME "<=" AS subset
    RENAME "<" AS proper_subset
```

```
IMPORT distinct remove FROM sequence{identifier}
IMPORT identifiers identifier FROM field_names
IMPORT type_of FROM union{$s}

MODEL(s: set{tuple{$s}})
INVARIANT true

MESSAGE create
  -- Literal { } = create.
  REPLY(r: relation{$s}) WHERE r.s = { }

MESSAGE add(t: tuple{$s}, r1: relation{$s})
  -- Literal {t} = add(t, empty).
  -- Literal {t, $r} = add(t, r).
  REPLY(r2: relation{$s})
  WHERE r2.s = r1.s U {t}

MESSAGE "IN"(x: tuple{$s}, r: relation{$s}) REPLY(b: boolean)
  WHERE b <=> x IN r.s

MESSAGE domain{id: identifier SUCH THAT id IN identifiers(s)}
              (r: relation{$s})
  CHOOSE(ct: type SUCH THAT ct = type_of(id))
  REPLY(d: set{ct})
  WHERE ALL(x: ct :: x IN d <=>
            SOME(t: tuple{$s} :: t IN r & get(t, id) = x) )
  -- The set of values that appear in a given column
  -- of the relation.
  -- Example: relation{a:: char, b:: nat}
  -- domain{a}({[a:: 'x', b:: 1],
  --            [a:: 'y', b:: 2],
  --            [a:: 'x', b:: 3] }) = {'x', 'y'}.

MESSAGE select{id: identifier SUCH THAT
               id IN identifiers(s) & ct = type_of(id) }
              (r1: relation{$s}, x: ct)
  REPLY(r2: relation{$ss})
  WHERE ss = remove(id, s),
    ALL(t2: tuple{$ss} :: t2 IN r2.s <=>
        SOME(t1: tuple{$s} :: t1 IN r1 & get(t1, id) = x &
                              contains(t1, t2) ))
  -- Select all of the tuples with a given value
  -- in one of the columns.
  -- Example: relation{a:: char, b:: nat}
  -- select{a}({[a:: 'x', b:: 1],
  --            [a:: 'y', b:: 2],
  --            [a:: 'x', b:: 3] }, 'x') = {[b:: 1], [b:: 3]}.
```

```
MESSAGE project{id: identifier SUCH THAT id IN identifiers(s)}
               (r1: relation{$s})
  REPLY(r2: relation{$ss})
  WHERE ss = remove(id, s),
    ALL(t2: tuple{$ss} :: t2 IN r2.s <=>
      SOME(t1: tuple{$s} :: t1 IN r1 & contains(t1, t2)) )
  -- Ignore the information in one of the columns
  -- of the relation.
  -- Example: relation{a:: char, b:: nat}
  -- project{a}({[a:: 'x', b:: 1],
  --             [a:: 'y', b:: 2],
  --             [a:: 'x', b:: 3] }) =
  -- {[b:: 1], [b:: 2], [b:: 3]}.

MESSAGE join{id: identifier SUCH THAT
             ALL(i: identifier :: i = id <=>
                 i IN identifiers(s) & i IN identifiers(ss) )}
           (r1: relation{$s}, r2: relation{$ss})
  REPLY(r3: relation{$sss})
  WHERE sss = remove(id, [$s, $ss]),
    ALL(t3: tuple{$sss} :: t3 IN r3.s <=>
      SOME(t1: tuple{$s}, t2: tuple{$ss} SUCH THAT
           t1 IN r1 & t2 IN r2 & get(t1, id) = get(t2, id) ::
           t3 = remove(id, t1) || remove(id, t2) ))
  -- Natural join from relational databases.

MESSAGE "U"(r1 r2: relation{$s})
  -- Literal {$r1, $r2} = r1 U r2.
  REPLY(r3: relation{$s})
  WHERE ALL(x: tuple{$s} :: x IN r3 <=> (x IN r1 | x IN r2))

MESSAGE "-"(r1 r2: relation{$s}) REPLY(r3: relation{$s})
  WHERE ALL(x: tuple{$s} :: x IN r3 <=> (x IN r1 & ~(x IN r2)))

MESSAGE intersection(r1 r2: relation{$s})
  REPLY(r3: relation{$s})
  WHERE ALL(x: tuple{$s} :: x IN r3 <=> (x IN r1 & x IN r2))

MESSAGE size(r: relation{$s})
  REPLY(n: nat)
  WHERE n = NUMBER(t: tuple{$s} SUCH THAT t IN s :: t)

MESSAGE equal(r1 r2: relation{$s})
  REPLY(b: boolean)
  WHERE b <=> r1.s = r2.s

MESSAGE subset(r1 r2: relation{$s}) REPLY(b: boolean)
  WHERE b <=> subset(r1.s, r2.s)
END
```

```
VIRTUAL TYPE number{t: type}
  INHERIT equality{t}
  EXPORT Commutative Associative Distributive Identity

  MESSAGE zero REPLY(n: t)
    WHERE Identity(zero, "+")

  MESSAGE one REPLY(n: t)
    WHERE Identity(one, "*")

  MESSAGE "+"(n1 n2: t) REPLY(i3: t)
    WHERE Commutative(plus), Associative(plus)

  MESSAGE "*"(n1 n2: t) REPLY(i3: t)
    WHERE ALL(n: t :: n * zero = zero),
      Commutative(times), Associative(times),
      Distributive(plus, times)

  CONCEPT Commutative(f: function{t, t, t})
    VALUE(b: boolean)
    WHERE b <=> ALL(x y: t :: f(x, y) = f(y, z))

  CONCEPT Associative(f: function{t, t, t})
    VALUE(b: boolean)
    WHERE b <=> ALL(x y z: t :: f(x, f(y, z)) = f(f(x, y), z))

  CONCEPT Distributive(f g: function{t, t, t})
    VALUE(b: boolean)
    WHERE b <=> ALL(x y z: t ::
                    g(x, f(y, z)) = f(g(x, y), g(x, z)) )

  CONCEPT Identity(i: t, f: function{t, t, t})
    VALUE(b: boolean)
    WHERE b <=> ALL(x: t :: f(x, i) = x = f(i, x))
END
```

```
TYPE nat
  INHERIT number{nat}
  INHERIT total_order{nat}
    -- Generated by {zero, succ}.

  MESSAGE zero -- Literal 0 = zero.
    REPLY(n: nat)
```

```
MESSAGE one -- Literal 1 = one.
  REPLY(n: nat) WHERE n = succ(zero)

MESSAGE succ(n1: nat)
  -- Literal 2 = succ(1), literal 3 = succ(2), ...
  REPLY(n2: nat)

MESSAGE pred(n1: nat)
  WHEN n1 > zero REPLY(n2: nat)
    WHERE ALL(n: nat :: pred(succ(n)) = n)
  OTHERWISE REPLY EXCEPTION undefined_pred

MESSAGE "+"(n1 n2: nat) REPLY(n3: nat)
  WHERE ALL(n m: nat :: n + succ(m) = succ(n + m))

MESSAGE "-"(n1 n2: nat)
  WHEN n1 >= n2 REPLY(n3: nat)
    WHERE ALL(n: nat :: n - zero = n),
      ALL(n m: nat :: n - succ(m) = pred(n) - m)
  OTHERWISE REPLY EXCEPTION undefined_difference

MESSAGE "*"(n1 n2: nat) REPLY(n3: nat)
  WHERE ALL(n m: nat :: n * succ(m) = n + (n * m))

MESSAGE "/"(n1 n2: nat)
  WHEN n2 ~= zero REPLY(q: nat)
    WHERE SOME(r: nat :: n1 = q * n2 + r & n2 > r)
  OTHERWISE REPLY EXCEPTION divide_by_zero

MESSAGE "MOD"(n1 n2: nat)
  -- n1 MOD n2 is also written n1 \ n2.
  WHEN n2 ~= zero REPLY(r: nat)
    WHERE SOME(q: nat :: n1 = q * n2 + r & n2 > r)
  OTHERWISE REPLY EXCEPTION divide_by_zero

MESSAGE "^"(n1 n2: nat)
  WHEN n1 ~= 0 | n2 ~= 0 REPLY(n3: nat)
    WHERE ALL(n: nat SUCH THAT n ~= 0 ::
              n ^ 0 = 1 & 0 ^ n = 0 ),
      ALL(n m: nat :: n ^ succ(m) = (n ^ m) * n)
  OTHERWISE REPLY EXCEPTION undefined_expt

MESSAGE equal(n1 n2: nat) REPLY(b: boolean)
  -- The properties of equal are determined by
  -- the definition of < and the inherited properties
  -- of equality and total_order.

MESSAGE "<"(n1 n2: nat) REPLY(b: boolean)
  WHERE ALL(n: nat :: n < succ(n))
```

```
MESSAGE "|"(n1 n2: nat)   -- n1 | n2 means n1 is a factor of n2.
  REPLY(b: boolean)
  WHERE b <=> SOME(n: nat :: n * n1 = n2), Partial_ordering("|")

CONCEPT prime(n: nat)
  VALUE(b: boolean)
  WHERE b <=> n > 1 & ALL(m: nat SUCH THAT m | n ::
                          m = 1 | m = n )
  -- Note overloading: first "|" is "divides",
  -- second "|" is "or".
END
```

```
TYPE integer
  INHERIT number{integer}
  INHERIT total_order{integer}
    -- Generated by {zero, succ, pred}.

  MESSAGE nat_to_integer(n: nat)
    -- Type conversion operation for mixed-mode arithmetic.
    REPLY(i: integer)
    WHERE nat_to_integer(zero) = zero,
      ALL(n: nat ::
          nat_to_integer(succ(n)) = succ(nat_to_integer(n)) )

  MESSAGE is_nat(i: integer) REPLY(b: boolean)
    WHERE SOME(n: nat :: i = nat_to_integer(n))

  MESSAGE zero -- Literal 0 = zero.
    REPLY(i: integer)

  MESSAGE one -- Literal 1 = one.
    REPLY(i: integer) WHERE i = succ(zero)

  MESSAGE succ(i1: integer)
    -- Literal 2 = succ(1), literal 3 = succ(2), ...
    REPLY(i2: integer)

  MESSAGE pred(i1: integer)
    -- Literal -1 = pred(0), literal -2 = pred(-1), ...
    REPLY(i2: integer)

  MESSAGE "-"(i1: integer) REPLY(i2: integer)
    WHERE ALL(i: integer :: -i = 0 - i)

  MESSAGE abs(i1: integer) REPLY(i2: integer)
    WHERE i2 = IF i1 >= 0 THEN i1 ELSE -i1 FI
```

```
MESSAGE "+"(i1 i2: integer) REPLY(i3: integer)
  WHERE ALL(i j: integer :: i + succ(j) = succ(i + j)),
    ALL(i j: integer :: i + pred(j) = pred(i + j))

MESSAGE "-"(i1 i2: integer) REPLY(i3: integer)
  WHERE i1 = i2 + i3

MESSAGE "*"(i1 i2: integer) REPLY(i3: integer)
  WHERE ALL(i j: integer :: i * succ(j) = (i * j) + i),
    ALL(i j: integer :: i * pred(j) = (i * j) - i)

MESSAGE "/"(i1 i2: integer)
  WHEN i2 ~= zero REPLY(q: integer)
    WHERE SOME(r: integer ::
               i1 = q * i2 + r & abs(i2) > r >= 0 )
  OTHERWISE REPLY EXCEPTION divide_by_zero

MESSAGE "MOD"(i1 i2: integer)
  -- i1 MOD i2 is also written i1 \ i2.
  WHEN i2 ~= zero REPLY(r: integer)
    WHERE SOME(q: integer ::
               i1 = q * i2 + r & abs(i2) > r >= 0 )
  OTHERWISE REPLY EXCEPTION divide_by_zero

MESSAGE "^"(i: integer, n: nat)
  WHEN i ~= 0 | n ~= 0 REPLY(j: integer)
    WHERE ALL(i: integer SUCH THAT i ~= 0 ::
               i ^ 0 = 1 & 0 ^ i = 0 ),
      ALL(i: integer, n: nat :: i ^ succ(n) = (i ^ n) * i)
  OTHERWISE REPLY EXCEPTION undefined_expt

MESSAGE equal(i1 i2: integer) REPLY(b: boolean)
  WHERE ALL(i: integer :: succ(pred(i)) = i = pred(succ(i)))

MESSAGE "<"(i1 i2: integer) REPLY(b: boolean)
  WHERE ALL(i: integer :: pred(i) < i < succ(i))
END
```

```
TYPE rational
  INHERIT number{rational}
  INHERIT total_order{rational}

  MODEL(num den: integer)
  INVARIANT ALL(r: rational :: r.den ~= zero)
```

```
MESSAGE ratio(i1 i2: integer)
  WHEN i2 ~= zero REPLY(r: rational)
    WHERE r.num = i1, r.den = i2
  OTHERWISE REPLY EXCEPTION zero_denominator

MESSAGE integer_to_rational(i: integer)
  -- Type conversion operation for mixed-mode arithmetic.
  REPLY(r: rational) WHERE r = ratio(i, 1)

MESSAGE nat_to_rational(n: nat)
  -- Type conversion operation for mixed-mode arithmetic.
  REPLY(r: rational)
    WHERE r = integer_to_rational(nat_to_integer@integer(n))

MESSAGE is_integer(r: rational) REPLY(b: boolean)
  WHERE SOME(i: integer :: r = integer_to_rational(i))

MESSAGE is_nat(r: rational) REPLY(b: boolean)
  WHERE SOME(n: nat :: r = nat_to_rational(n))

MESSAGE zero REPLY(r: rational)
  WHERE r = integer_to_rational(zero)

MESSAGE one REPLY(r: rational)
  WHERE r = integer_to_rational(1)

MESSAGE "-"(r1: rational) REPLY(r2: rational)
  WHERE r2 = zero - r1

MESSAGE abs(r1: rational) REPLY(r2: rational)
  WHERE r2 = IF r1 >= zero THEN r1 ELSE -r1 FI

MESSAGE "+"(r1 r2: rational) REPLY(r3: rational)
  WHERE r3.num = r1.num * r2.den + r2.num * r1.den,
        r3.den = r1.den * r2.den

MESSAGE "-"(r1 r2: rational) REPLY(r3: rational)
  WHERE r1 = r2 + r3

MESSAGE "*"(r1 r2: rational) REPLY(r3: rational)
  WHERE r3.num = r1.num * r2.num, r3.den = r1.den * r2.den

MESSAGE "/"(r1 r2: rational)
  WHEN r2 ~= zero REPLY(r3: rational)
    WHERE r1 = r2 * r3
  OTHERWISE REPLY EXCEPTION divide_by_zero
```

```
  MESSAGE "MOD"(r1 r2: rational)
    -- r1 MOD r2 is also written r1 \ r2.
    WHEN r2 ~= zero REPLY(r: rational)
      WHERE SOME(q: rational ::
                  r1 = q * r2 + r & abs(r2) > r >= zero &
                  is_integer(q) )
    OTHERWISE REPLY EXCEPTION divide_by_zero

  MESSAGE "^"(r1: rational, i1: integer)
    WHEN r1 = zero & i1 <= zero REPLY EXCEPTION undefined_expt
    OTHERWISE REPLY(r2: rational)
      WHERE ALL(r: rational :: r ^ one = r),
        ALL(r: rational, i: integer ::
            r ^ succ(i) = (r ^ i) * r ),
          ALL(r: rational, i: integer SUCH THAT r ~= zero ::
            r ^ pred(i) = (r ^ i) / r )

  MESSAGE equal(r1 r2: rational) REPLY(b: boolean)
    WHERE b <=> (r1.num * r2.den = r2.num * r1.den)

  MESSAGE "<"(r1 r2: rational) REPLY(b: boolean)
    WHERE b <=> IF r1.den * r2.den > zero
                THEN r1.num * r2.den < r2.num * r1.den
                ELSE r1.num * r2.den > r2.num * r1.den FI
END
```

```
TYPE real
  INHERIT number{real}
  INHERIT total_order{real}

  MESSAGE rational_to_real(r1: rational)
    -- Type conversion operation for mixed-mode arithmetic.
    REPLY(r2: real)
    WHERE rational_to_real(zero) = zero,
      rational_to_real(one) = one,
      ALL(x y: rational ::
          rational_to_real(x - y) =
          rational_to_real(x) - rational_to_real(y) ),
        ALL(x y: rational SUCH THAT y ~= zero ::
          rational_to_real(x / y) =
          rational_to_real(x) / rational_to_real(y) )

  MESSAGE integer_to_real(i: integer)
    -- Type conversion operation for mixed-mode arithmetic.
    REPLY(r: real)
    WHERE r = rational_to_real(integer_to_rational@rational(i))
```

```
MESSAGE nat_to_real(n: nat)
  -- Type conversion operation for mixed-mode arithmetic.
  REPLY(r: real)
  WHERE r = rational_to_real(nat_to_rational@rational(n))

MESSAGE is_rational(r: real)
  REPLY(b: boolean)
  WHERE SOME(i: integer :: r = rational_to_real(i))

MESSAGE is_integer(r: real)
  REPLY(b: boolean)
  WHERE SOME(i: integer :: r = integer_to_real(i))

MESSAGE is_nat(r: real)
  REPLY(b: boolean)
  WHERE SOME(n: nat :: r = nat_to_real(n))

MESSAGE zero -- Literal 0.0 = zero.
  REPLY(i: real)

MESSAGE one -- Literal 1.0 = one.
  REPLY(i: real)

MESSAGE "-"(r1: real) REPLY(r2: real)
  WHERE r2 = zero - r1

MESSAGE abs(r1: real) REPLY(r2: real)
  WHERE r2 = IF r1 >= zero THEN r1 ELSE -r1 FI

MESSAGE "+"(r1 r2: real) REPLY(r3: real)

MESSAGE "-"(r1 r2: real) REPLY(r3: real)
  WHERE r1 = r2 + r3

MESSAGE "*"(r1 r2: real) REPLY(r3: real)

MESSAGE "/"(r1 r2: real)
  WHEN r2 ~= zero REPLY(r3: real)
    WHERE r1 = r2 * r3
  OTHERWISE REPLY EXCEPTION divide_by_zero

MESSAGE "MOD"(r1 r2: real)
  -- r1 MOD r2 is also written r1 \ r2.
  WHEN r2 ~= zero REPLY(r: real)
    WHERE SOME(q: real :: r1 = q * r2 + r &
                          abs(r2) > r >= zero &
                          is_integer(q) )
  OTHERWISE REPLY EXCEPTION divide_by_zero
```

```
    MESSAGE "^"(r1 r2: real)
      WHEN (r1 = zero & r2 <= zero) | (r1 < zero & ~is_integer(r2))
        REPLY EXCEPTION undefined_expt
      OTHERWISE REPLY(r3: real)
        WHERE ALL(r: real :: r ^ 1.0 = r),
          ALL(r: real SUCH THAT r > zero :: zero ^ r = zero),
          ALL(r x y: real SUCH THAT
                r > zero | r < zero & is_integer(x) &
                is_integer(y) ::
                r ^ (x + y) = (r ^ x) * (r ^ y) )

  MESSAGE equal(r1 r2: real) REPLY(b: boolean)

  MESSAGE "<"(r1 r2: real) REPLY(b: boolean)
    WHERE ALL(x y: rational ::
                rational_to_real(x) < rational_to_real(y) <=>
                x < y ),
      ALL(x y z: real :: x + y < x + z <=> y < z),
      ALL(x y z: real SUCH THAT x > zero ::
          x * y < x * z <=> y < z ),
      ALL(x y z: real SUCH THAT x < zero ::
          x * y < x * z <=> y > z )
END
```

```
TYPE complex
  INHERIT number{complex}

  MODEL(re im: real) INVARIANT true

  MESSAGE real_to_complex(r: real)
    -- Type conversion operation for mixed-mode arithmetic.
    REPLY(c: complex)
    WHERE c.re = r, c.im = zero

  MESSAGE rational_to_complex(r: rational)
    -- Type conversion operation for mixed-mode arithmetic.
    REPLY(c: complex)
    WHERE c = real_to_complex(rational_to_real@real(r))

  MESSAGE integer_to_complex(i: integer)
    -- Type conversion operation for mixed-mode arithmetic.
    REPLY(c: complex)
    WHERE c = real_to_complex(integer_to_real@real(i))
```

```
MESSAGE nat_to_complex(n: nat)
  -- Type conversion operation for mixed-mode arithmetic.
  REPLY(c: complex)
  WHERE c = real_to_complex(nat_to_real@real(n))

MESSAGE is_real(c: complex) REPLY(b: boolean)
  WHERE b <=> c.im = zero

MESSAGE is_imaginary(c: complex) REPLY(b: boolean)
  WHERE b <=> c.re = zero

MESSAGE is_rational(c: complex)
  REPLY(b: boolean)
  WHERE SOME(r: rational :: c = rational_to_complex(r))

MESSAGE is_integer(c: complex)
  REPLY(b: boolean)
  WHERE SOME(i: integer :: c = integer_to_complex(i))

MESSAGE is_nat(c: complex)
  REPLY(b: boolean)
  WHERE SOME(n: nat :: c = nat_to_complex(n))

MESSAGE zero REPLY(c: complex)
  WHERE c = real_to_complex(zero)

MESSAGE one REPLY(c: complex)
  WHERE c = real_to_complex(1.0)

MESSAGE i REPLY(c: complex)
  WHERE i * i = - one

MESSAGE conjugate(c1: complex) REPLY(c2: complex)
  WHERE c2.re = c1.re, c2.im = -c1.im

MESSAGE magnitude(c1: complex) REPLY(r: real)
  WHERE r = (c.re ^ 2 + c.im ^ 2) ^ 0.5, r >= 0.0

MESSAGE "-"(c1: complex) REPLY(c2: complex)
  WHERE c2 = zero - c1

MESSAGE "+"(c1 c2: complex) REPLY(c3: complex)
  WHERE c3.re = c1.re + c2.re, c3.im = c1.im + c2.im

MESSAGE "-"(c1 c2: complex) REPLY(c3: complex)
  WHERE c1 = c2 + c3

MESSAGE "*"(c1 c2: complex) REPLY(c3: complex)
  WHERE c3.re = c1.re * c2.re - c1.im * c2.im,
    c3.im = c1.re * c2.im + c1.im * c2.re
```

```
  MESSAGE "/"(c1 c2: complex)
    WHEN c2 ~= zero REPLY(c3: complex)
      WHERE c1 = c2 * c3
    OTHERWISE REPLY EXCEPTION divide_by_zero

  MESSAGE "^"(c1 c2: complex)
    WHEN (c1 = zero & c2.re <= zero)
      REPLY EXCEPTION undefined_expt
    OTHERWISE REPLY(c3: complex)
      WHERE ALL(c: complex :: c ^ one = c),
        ALL(c: complex SUCH THAT c.re > zero :: zero ^ c = zero),
        ALL(c x y: complex SUCH THAT c ~= zero
            :: c ^ (x + y) = (c ^ x) * (c ^ y) )

  MESSAGE equal(c1 c2: complex)
    REPLY(b: boolean)
      WHERE b <=> c1.re = c2.re & c1.im = c2.im
END
```

```
TYPE type
  INHERIT equality{type} RENAME equal AS Equal
  IMPORT Partial_ordering FROM partial_order{type}
  EXPORT Has_operation Subtype Immutable Mutable
    Immutable_instances Static Indestructible Irreplaceable

  MESSAGE "IN"(x: any, t: type) REPLY(b: boolean)
    WHERE ALL(t: type, x: t :: x IN t), ALL(t: type :: ~(! IN t))
    -- True if x is a proper element of the data type t.
    -- The undefined element "!" can appear in expressions
    -- of any type, but it is not a proper element of any type.

  MESSAGE "IN"(s1: sequence{any}, s2: sequence{type})
    REPLY(b: boolean)
      -- True if corresponding elements match.
      -- Example: [1.5, true] IN [real, boolean].
    WHERE b <=> length(s1) = length(s2) &
              ALL(n: nat SUCH THAT n IN domain(s1) ::
                  s1[n] IN s2[n] )

  MESSAGE Equal(t1 t2: type) REPLY(b: boolean)
    WHERE b <=> ALL(x: any :: x IN t1 <=> x IN t2) &
          ALL(ts: sequence{type}, f: function{$ts}
              :: Has_operation{$ts}(t1, f) <=>
                 Has_operation{$ts}(t2, f) )
    -- Two types are equal if and only if they have
    -- the same elements and the same operations.
```

```
CONCEPT Has_operation(ts: type_sequence)
                     (t: type, f: function($ts))
  VALUE(b: boolean)
  -- True if the type t accepts the message f.

CONCEPT Subtype(t1 t2: type) VALUE(b: boolean)
  WHERE ALL(t1 t2: type SUCH THAT
             Subtype(t1, t2) :: ALL(x: t1 :: x IN t2)),
    Partial_ordering(Subtype)
  -- True if t1 satisfies the specification of t2.

CONCEPT Immutable(t: type) VALUE(b: boolean)
  -- True if the properties of the type cannot change.
  WHERE b <=> always(t = *t | *t = !),
      -- Always is a modal operator, which means that the
      -- enclosed predicate is true in all possible states.
      -- In the initial state *t = !.
    ALL(t: type :: Immutable(t) <=>
        Static(t) & Immutable_instances(t) )
      -- A type is immutable if the set of instances
      -- cannot change and the state of each
      -- individual instance cannot change.

CONCEPT Mutable(t: type) VALUE(b: boolean)
  WHERE b <=> ~Immutable(t)

CONCEPT Immutable_instances(t: type) VALUE(b: boolean)
  -- True if the states of the instances
  -- of the type cannot change.
  WHERE b <=> always(ALL(x: t :: x = *x | *x = !))

CONCEPT Static(t: type) VALUE(b: boolean)
  -- True if the set of instances of the type cannot change.
  WHERE b <=> always(ALL(x: Completion(t) ::
                         x IN t <=> *x IN *t | *t = !) ),
    ALL(t: type :: Static(t) <=>
        Indestructible(t) & Irreplaceable(t) )

CONCEPT Indestructible(t: type) VALUE(b: boolean)
    -- True if instances of the type t can never be destroyed.
  WHERE b <=> always(ALL(x: Completion(t) ::
                         (*x IN *t => x IN t) | *t = !) )

CONCEPT Irreplaceable(t: type) VALUE(b: boolean)
    -- True if new instances of the type t
    -- can never be created.
  WHERE b <=> always(ALL(x: t ::
                         (x IN t => *x IN *t) | *t = !) )
```

```
CONCEPT Completion(t1: type): type
    -- The set of all present and future
    -- instances of the type t.

  WHERE ALL(x: any :: x IN Completion(t) <=> sometime(x IN t))
        -- Sometime is a modal operator, which means that the
        -- enclosed predicate is true now or
        -- in some future state.
END
```

```
TYPE function{$d: type, r: type}
  INHERIT equality{function{$d, r}}
  EXPORT Domain Range Total One_to_one Onto Strict Deterministic

  CONCEPT Domain(f: function{$d, r}) VALUE(s: sequence{type})
    -- The sequence of argument types for the function f.
    -- Example: MESSAGE(x: t1, y: t2) has domain [t1, t2].
    WHERE s = d

  CONCEPT Range(f: function{$d, r}) VALUE(t: type)
    -- The type of the value returned by the function
    -- in the normal case.
    WHERE t = r

  CONCEPT Total(f: function{$d, r}) VALUE(b: boolean)
    -- True if f is well defined for all values in its domain.
    WHERE ALL(s: sequence{any} SUCH THAT s IN d :: f($s) IN r )
    -- Improper values such as ! do not belong to any data type.

  CONCEPT One_to_one(f: function{$d, r}) VALUE(b: boolean)
    -- True if f has a unique value
    -- for every element of the domain h.
    WHERE ALL(s1 s2: sequence{any} SUCH THAT s1 IN d & s2 IN d
             :: f($s1) = f($s2) => s1 = s2 )

  CONCEPT Onto(f: function{$d, r}) VALUE(b: boolean)
    -- True if the range of f covers the entire type r.
    WHERE ALL(y: r :: SOME(s: sequence{any} SUCH THAT
                           s IN d :: f($s) = y ))

  CONCEPT Strict(f: function{$d, r}) VALUE(b: boolean)
    -- True if the value of f is undefined
    -- whenever at least one input is undefined.
    WHERE ALL(s1 s2: sequence{any}, x: any SUCH THAT
             s1 || [x] || s2 IN d :: f($s1, !, $s2) = ! )

  CONCEPT Deterministic(f: function{$d, r}) VALUE(b: boolean)
    -- True if f is single-valued.
```

```
      WHERE ALL(s: sequence{any}, x y: r SUCH THAT
                s IN d :: x = f($s) & y = f($s) => x = y )
END
```

```
VIRTUAL TYPE equivalence {t: type}
  INHERIT equality{t}
  INHERIT Mutable{t}
  IMPORT Immutable FROM type
  IMPORT Reflexive Symmetric Transitive FROM equal{t}
  IMPORT Deterministic FROM function{any, any}

  MESSAGE equivalent(x y: t)
    REPLY(b: boolean)
    WHERE Reflexive(equivalence), Symmetric(equivalence),
      Transitive(equivalence),
      ALL(a b: t :: a == b => same_state{t}(a, b))
  -- State equivalence: two distinct copies of the same object
  -- are equivalent but not equal.

  MESSAGE not_equivalent(x y: t)
    REPLY(b: boolean)
    WHERE b <=> ~equivalent(x, y)

  MESSAGE copy(x: t)
    REPLY(y: t) WHERE y == x, y ~= x
    TRANSITION new(y)

  CONCEPT same_state{t1:type}(x y: t1)
    VALUE(b: boolean)
    WHERE Immutable(t1) =>
          ALL(c d: t1 :: same_state{t1}(c, d) => c = d),
        -- For Immutable types equality and equivalence
        -- are the same.
      ALL(c d: t1, ts1 ts2: sequence{type}, s1: ts1, s2: ts2,
          range: type, f: function{$ts1, t1, $ts2, range}
          SUCH THAT f ~= equal@t1 & Deterministic(f) ::
          same_state{t1}(c, d) =>
            same_state{range}(f($s1, c, $s2), f($s1, d, $s2)) )
  -- Two equivalent objects can only be distinguished
  -- by the equal operation or applying a state changing
  -- operation to one of the objects.  This is a restriction
  -- on the functional operations of well formed mutable types.

  CONCEPT "=="(x y:t) VALUE(b: boolean)

  CONCEPT "~=="(x y:t) VALUE(b: boolean)
    WHERE b <=> ~(x == y)
END
```

APPENDIX
Spec Pragmas

This appendix gives brief explanations of the Spec pragmas. Pragmas in Spec provide advice about how to realize specified components.

PRAGMA task(module_name)

Implement the given module as an Ada task.

PRAGMA update(input_message_component, output_message_component)

Implement both message components as an Ada in out parameter called input_message_component.

PRAGMA nonlocal_variable(message_component)

Implement the message component as a reference to a nonlocal variable called message_component.

PRAGMA representation(Spec_type, Ada_type)

Implement the Spec type as the Ada type.

PRAGMA persistent(type_name)

Implement the type using secondary storage. Implies instances of the type survive from one run of the program to the next in the absence of system failures.

PRAGMA unique_representation(type_name)

Implement the type using Ada private. Should be applied to immutable types. Requires the implementor to pick a unique representation for each instance of the abstract type.

PRAGMA direct_allocation(type_name)

Restrict the storage representation so that all main memory storage for each instance of the type is associated with some program variable. This restriction rules out access types, dynamic storage allocation, and garbage collection in main memory. See Section 4.4.2 for a discussion of the relation to Ada limited private. The pragma does not constrain use of secondary storage.

PRAGMA stable(type_name)

The instances of the type and all state changes due to completed operations are guaranteed to survive system crashes. This implies an implementation using redundant secondary storage.

PRAGMA external_input(message_name)

The message will come from outside the system, and must be implemented by input operations, rather than as a subprogram or entry that will be called from within the software system.

PRAGMA returned_value(message_name)

The message will be implemented as the return value or output variables of another subprogram or task entry, and does not correspond to a separate item in the Ada interface.

PRAGMA passive(generator_name)

The generator is implemented using three distinct operations, init_ generator_name, next_generator_name, and end_of_ generator_name, in an interface similar to that provided by sequential files.

APPENDIX
Reusable Ada Components

This appendix gives the implementations of the reusable Ada components used in this book.

```
with B_tree_degree_pkg; use B_tree_degree_pkg;
    -- Defines degree_type.
  with text_pkg; use text_pkg; -- Defines text_pkg_instance.
  with max;
    -- The binary maximum function on the natural numbers.
  with direct_io; -- For random access to the disk.
generic
  type key is private;
  type value is private;
    -- A B_tree is a mapping from keys to values.
  with function "<="(k1, k2: key) return boolean is <>;
    -- "<=" must be a total ordering on the keys.
  degree: degree_type := 128;  -- Degree >= 3.
    -- The degree is the maximum number of children for an
    -- internal node.  The default degree is chosen to give
    -- good performance for most typical ratios of CPU speed
    -- to disk speed.
package B_tree_pkg is
  use text_pkg_instance;  -- Defines the type text.
```

```
type B_tree is limited private;
  -- Limited because direct access files
  -- are limited types in Ada.

procedure open(bt_name: in text; bt: in out B_tree);
procedure close(bt: in out B_tree);
procedure delete(bt: in out B_tree);
function name(bt: B_tree) return text;
procedure add(k: in key; x: in value; bt: in out B_tree);
procedure remove(k: in key; bt: in out B_tree);
procedure fetch(k: in key; bt: in out B_tree;
                result: out value );
procedure member(k: in key; bt: in out B_tree;
                  result: out boolean );

generic
  with procedure produce(k: in key; v: in value);
procedure scan_between(k1, k2: in key; bt: in out B_tree);

generic
  with procedure produce(k: in key; v: in value);
procedure scan_from(k1: in key; bt: in out B_tree);

generic
  with procedure produce(k: in key; v: in value);
procedure scan_to(k1: in key; bt: in out B_tree);

generic
  with procedure produce(k: in key; v: in value);
procedure scan(bt: in out B_tree);

-- Testing interface.
procedure free_list_length(bt: in out B_tree;
                            result: out natural );

generic
  with procedure print_key(k: in key);
procedure print_keys(bt: in out B_tree);

-- Exceptions.
domain_error: exception;  -- Raised by fetch.
quit: exception;
-- Raised by produce.
-- Handled by scan_between, scan_from, scan_to, scan.

private

subtype file_index is natural;
-- Represents a node index in a B_tree file.
```

```
-- Corresponds to direct_io.count, but must be defined as a
-- distinct type to avoid a circular type definition.
-- 1 <= i <= size(bt.file) if i is the file_index of a node
-- in bt.
empty: constant file_index := 0;
  -- Terminator for the free list.

max_keys: constant natural := degree - 1;
-- The maximum number of keys in a subtree node.
max_pairs: constant natural :=
  max(1, (max_keys * key'size + degree * file_index'size) /
       (key'size + value'size) );
-- The maximum number of pairs in a leaf node,
-- must be at least one.
-- Max_pairs is chosen to make a leaf node and
-- a subtree node about the same size.

subtype subtree_size_range is natural range 1 .. degree;
subtype subtree_keys_range is natural range 1 .. max_keys;
subtype subtree_children_range is natural range 0 .. max_keys;
subtype leaf_size_range is natural range 0 .. max_pairs;
subtype leaf_pairs_range is natural range 1 .. max_pairs;

type subtree_keys_array is array(subtree_keys_range) of key;
type subtree_children_array is
  array(subtree_children_range) of file_index;
type leaf_keys_array is array(leaf_pairs_range) of key;
type leaf_values_array is array(leaf_pairs_range) of value;

type node_type is (subtree, leaf, free);
type node(tag: node_type := leaf) is
  record
    case tag is
      when subtree =>
        subtree_size: subtree_size_range;
        subtree_keys: subtree_keys_array;
        children: subtree_children_array;
      when leaf =>
        leaf_size: leaf_size_range := 0;
        leaf_keys: leaf_keys_array;
        values: leaf_values_array;
      when free =>
        next: file_index := empty;
    end case;
  end record;
-- n.subtree_keys(i) is bound in n.children(i)
-- for any subtree node n, 1 <= i < n.subtree_size.
-- subtree_keys and leaf_keys are sorted in strictly
```

```
-- increasing order.
-- k IN n.children(i) => key(n, i) <= k < key(n, i + 1)
-- for any subtree node n.
-- size(n) <= max_size(n) for all nodes n.
-- n.subtree_size >= min_size(n) for any non-root subtree node n.
-- n.leaf_size >= min_size(n) for any non-root leaf node n.
-- subtree_size >= 2 for any root subtree node,
-- except during a remove operation.
-- subtree_keys(1 .. subtree_size - 1) and
-- children(0 .. subtree_size - 1) contain data.
-- leaf_keys(1 .. leaf_size) and
-- values(1 .. leaf_size) contain data.
-- c1, c2 IN children(0 .. subtree_size - 1) => c1.tag = c2.tag.
-- All leaves are at the same depth.
-- tag ~= free for the root and all children c of a subtree node.
-- tag = free for every node in the free list.
-- Justification for free list:
-- the size of an Ada direct file cannot decrease.

  package node_io is new direct_io(node);
  use node_io;   -- Defines file_type and file operations.

  type B_tree is
    record
      name: text;
      file: file_type;
    end record;
-- The root node has file_index 1 and tag IN {leaf, subtree}.
-- The header node for the free list has
-- file_index 2 and tag = free.

-- Implementation concepts:

-- CONCEPT min_key: any
--    WHERE ALL(k: key :: min_key < k)
--    -- An extra key value less than any normal key.

-- CONCEPT max_key: any
--    WHERE ALL(k: key :: max_key < k)
--    -- An extra key value greater than any normal key.

-- CONCEPT key(n: subtree_node, i: nat)
--    VALUE(k: key U {min_key, max_key})
--       -- Extend the explicitly stored keys with
--       -- min_key and max_key.
--    WHERE key(n, 0) = min_key, key(n, n.subtree_size) = max_key,
--       ALL(i: nat SUCH THAT 0 < i < n.subtree_size ::
--          key(n, i) = n.subtree_keys(i) )
```

```
-- CONCEPT key(n: leaf_node, i: nat)
--   VALUE(k: key U {min_key, max_key})
--      -- Extend the explicitly stored keys with
--      -- min_key and max_key.
--   WHERE key(n, 0) = min_key,
--      key(n, n.leaf_size + 1) = max_key,
--      ALL(i: nat SUCH THAT 0 < i <= n.leaf_size ::
--          key(n, i) = n.leaf_keys(i) )

end B_tree_pkg;
```

```
package B_tree_degree_pkg is
   subtype degree_type is integer range 3 .. integer'last;
   -- Range of values for the degree of a B_tree.
   -- For node balancing, every nonroot node must have a sibling.
   -- Thus minimum node size >= 2 and
   -- degree = maximum node size >= 3.
end B_tree_degree_pkg;
```

```
function max(n1, n2: natural) return natural is
begin
   if n1 >= n2 then return n1; else return n2; end if;
end max;
```

```
  with text_io;
package body B_tree_pkg is

   root_position: constant file_index := 1;
     -- File_index of the root node.
   free_list_position: constant file_index := 2;
     -- File_index of the free list header node.

   subtype subtree_node is node(subtree);
   subtype leaf_node is node(leaf);
   subtype free_node is node(free);
   subtype extended_subtree_range is
     natural range 0 .. max_keys + 1;
```

```
subtype extended_leaf_range is
  natural range 0 .. max_pairs + 1;
subtype fp is positive_count;
  -- Used for coverting file_index-es to file pointers
  -- for read and write.

invariant_broken: exception;
  -- Raised only if the data invariant is damaged by a bug,
  -- should never occur in a correct implementation.

-- Local subprogram declarations.
procedure add_new_root(f: in file_type; sibling_key: in key;
                       sibling_position: in file_index );
procedure add_to_node(k: in key; x: in value; i: in file_index;
                      f: in file_type;
                      has_new_sibling: out boolean;
                      sibling_key: out key;
                      sibling_position: out file_index );
function find_subtree_index(k: key; n: subtree_node)
  return subtree_children_range;
procedure find_leaf_index(k: in key; n: in leaf_node;
                          i: out extended_leaf_range;
                          found: out boolean );
procedure add_child(k: in key; child_position: in file_index;
                    n: in out subtree_node;
                    f: in file_type;
                    has_new_sibling: out boolean;
                    sibling_key: out key;
                    sibling_position: out file_index );
procedure add_to_subtree(k: in key;
                         child_position: in file_index;
                         n: in out subtree_node );
procedure add_to_leaf(k: in key; x: in value;
                      i: in leaf_pairs_range;
                      n: in out leaf_node );
procedure split_subtree(k: in key;
                        child_position: in file_index;
                        n: in out subtree_node;
                        new_subtree: in out subtree_node;
                        new_subtree_key: out key );
procedure split_leaf(k: in key; x: in value;
                     key_position: in extended_leaf_range;
                     n: in out leaf_node;
                     new_leaf: in out leaf_node;
                     new_leaf_key: out key );
procedure update_root(root: in out node; f: in file_type);
```

```
procedure remove_from_node(k: in key; n: in out node;
                           f: in file_type;
                           node_changed,
                             node_key_changed: out boolean;
                           node_key: out key);
procedure update_node_key(parent: in out node;
                          child_key: in key;
                          child_index: in
                            subtree_children_range;
                          parent_changed,
                            parent_key_changed: out boolean;
                          parent_key: out key);
procedure adjust_child(parent, child: in out node;
                       child_index: in subtree_children_range;
                       f: in file_type );
procedure adjust_children(parent: in out subtree_node;
                          c1, c2: in out node;
                          i: in subtree_keys_range;
                          f: in file_type );
procedure remove_child(parent: in out subtree_node;
                       child_position: in subtree_keys_range);
procedure combine(n1: in out node; n2: in node;
                  n2_key: in key );
procedure balance(n1, n2: in out node; n2_key: in out key);
procedure remove_from_leaf(k: in key; n: in out leaf_node;
                           node_changed,
                             node_key_changed: out boolean;
                           node_key: out key );
function find_leaf(k: key; bt: B_tree) return leaf_node;
function size(n: node) return natural;
function min_size(n: node) return natural;
function max_size(n: node) return natural;
procedure allocate_file_position(f: in file_type;
                                 i: out file_index );
procedure recycle_file_position(f: in file_type;
                                i: in file_index );
function "<"(k1, k2: key) return boolean;
-- End of local subprogram declarations.

-- pragma inline(add_new_root,
--               add_child,
--               split_subtree,
--               split_leaf,
--               update_root,
--               update_node_key,
--               adjust_child,
```

```
--              remove_child,
--              combine,
--              balance,
--              remove_from_leaf );

procedure open(bt_name: in text; bt: in out B_tree) is
  root_node: leaf_node;
  free: free_node;
begin
  bt.name := bt_name;
  open(bt.file, inout_file, ada_string(bt_name));
exception
  when name_error =>
    -- The file does not exist yet, make a new one.
    create(bt.file, inout_file, ada_string(bt_name));
    -- Make a root node for an empty B_tree.
    write(bt.file, root_node, fp(root_position));
    -- Make a free list for the file.
    -- Note the initial file size is implementation dependent.
    if size(bt.file) = 1 then
        write(bt.file, free, fp(free_list_position));
        -- In this case the free list is empty.
    else for i in reverse 2 .. size(bt.file) loop
            write(bt.file, free, fp(i));
            free.next := file_index(i);
        end loop;
        -- Collect all initial nodes with file_index >= 2
        -- in the free list.
    end if;
    close(bt);  -- Make sure initialization takes effect.
    open(bt_name, bt);
        -- Open the B_tree again, should work normally this time.
  when status_error =>
    -- The file is already open.
    if name(bt.file) /= ada_string(bt_name) then close(bt);
        open(bt.file, inout_file, ada_string(bt_name));
    end if;
end open;

procedure close(bt: in out B_tree) is
begin
  close(bt.file);
exception when status_error => null;
  -- Do nothing if the file is already closed.
end close;
```

```ada
procedure delete(bt: in out B_tree) is
begin
  if not is_open(bt.file) then
     open(bt.file, inout_file, ada_string(bt.name));
  end if;
  delete(bt.file);
end delete;

function name(bt: B_tree) return text is
begin
  return bt.name;
end name;

procedure add(k: in key; x: in value; bt: in out B_tree) is
  root_has_sibling: boolean;
  sibling_key: key;
  sibling_position: file_index;
begin
  if not is_open(bt.file) then
     open(bt.file, inout_file, ada_string(bt.name));
  end if;
  add_to_node(k, x, root_position, bt.file, root_has_sibling,
              sibling_key, sibling_position );
  if root_has_sibling then
     add_new_root(bt.file, sibling_key, sibling_position);
  end if;
  close(bt);
end add;

procedure add_new_root(f: in file_type; sibling_key: in key;
                       sibling_position: in file_index) is
  r: subtree_node;
  n: node;
  new_position_for_old_root: file_index;
begin
     -- Move the old root to a new position.
   read(f, n, fp(root_position));
   allocate_file_position(f, new_position_for_old_root);
   write(f, n, fp(new_position_for_old_root));
     -- Create a new root with two children.
   r.subtree_size := 2;
   r.children(0) := new_position_for_old_root;
   r.subtree_keys(1) := sibling_key;
   r.children(1) := sibling_position;
     -- The new sibling for the old root.
   write(f, r, fp(root_position));
end add_new_root;
```

```
procedure add_to_node(k: in key; x: in value;
                      i: in file_index; f: in file_type;
                      has_new_sibling: out boolean;
                      sibling_key: out key;
                      sibling_position: out file_index ) is
-- Pre: is_open(f).
-- Post: k is bound to x in the subtree rooted at file index i.
-- Post: has_new_sibling <=>
--       there is a new sibling for the node at position i.
-- Post: has_new_sibling =>
--       the file_index of the new sibling is sibling_position.
-- Post: has_new_sibling =>
--       the first key of the new sibling is sibling_key.
-- Post: all changes below the node at position i
--       are reflected in the file f.
  n: node;
  has_new_child: boolean;  -- True if n has a new child.
  child_key: key;  -- First key of new child of n.
  child_position: file_index;  -- File_index of new child of n.
  key_position: extended_leaf_range;
  found: boolean;
  sibling: leaf_node;
  sp: file_index;
begin
  read(f, n, fp(i));
  case n.tag is
    when subtree =>
      add_to_node(k, x, n.children(find_subtree_index(k, n)),
                  f, has_new_child, child_key,
                  child_position );
      if has_new_child then
        add_child(child_key, child_position, n, f,
                  has_new_sibling, sibling_key,
                  sibling_position );
        write(f, n, fp(i));
      end if;
    when leaf =>
      find_leaf_index(k, n, key_position, found);
      if found then has_new_sibling := false;
        n.values(key_position) := x;  -- Replace old binding.
      elsif size(n) < max_size(n) then
        has_new_sibling := false;
        add_to_leaf(k, x, key_position, n);
      else has_new_sibling := true;
        split_leaf(k, x, key_position, n,
                   sibling, sibling_key );
        allocate_file_position(f, sp);
```

```
            write(f, sibling, fp(sp));
            sibling_position := sp;
         end if;
         write(f, n, fp(i));
      when free => raise invariant_broken;
         -- Should never get here.
   end case;
end add_to_node;


function find_subtree_index(k: key; n: subtree_node)
   return subtree_children_range is
      -- Post: key(n, find_subtree_index(k, n)) <= k.
      -- Post: k < key(n, find_subtree_index(k, n) + 1).
   low: extended_subtree_range := 0;
   high: extended_subtree_range := n.subtree_size;
      -- n.subtree_size >= 2.
   mid: subtree_keys_range;
begin
   loop  -- Invariant: key(n, low) <= k < key(n, high).
         -- Invariant: 0 <= low < high <= n.subtree_size.
         -- Bound: high - low.
      if high = low + 1 then return low; end if;
      mid := (low + high) / 2;
         -- low < mid < high since low + 1 < high.
      if n.subtree_keys(mid) <= k then
         low := mid; else high := mid; end if;
   end loop;
end find_subtree_index;


procedure find_leaf_index(k: in key; n: in leaf_node;
                          i: out extended_leaf_range;
                          found: out boolean ) is
      -- Post: if found then n.leaf_keys(i) = k
      --          else key(n, i - 1) < k < key(n, i) &
      --                1 <= i <= n.leaf_size + 1.
   low: extended_leaf_range := 0;
   high: extended_leaf_range := n.leaf_size + 1;
   mid: leaf_pairs_range;
begin
   loop  -- Invariant: key(n, low) < k < key(n, high).
         -- Invariant: 0 <= low < high <= n.leaf_size + 1.
         -- Bound: high - low.
      if high = low + 1 then
         i := high; found := false; return; end if;
      mid := leaf_pairs_range((low + high) / 2);
      if n.leaf_keys(mid) = k then
         i := mid; found := true; return;
```

```
      elsif n.leaf_keys(mid) <= k then low := mid;
      else high := mid; end if;
    end loop;
  end find_leaf_index;

  procedure add_child(k: in key; child_position: in file_index;
                      n: in out subtree_node; f: in file_type;
                      has_new_sibling: out boolean;
                      sibling_key: out key;
                      sibling_position: out file_index ) is
    -- Add a new child to a subtree node,
    -- and split the node if it is too big.
    -- Pre: is_open(f).
    -- Post: k bound to child_position.
    -- Post: has_new_sibling <=> node n has a new sibling.
    -- Post: has_new_sibling =>
    --          first_key(new sibling) = sibling_key.
    -- Post: has_new_sibling =>
    --          new sibling is stored in f
    --          at file_index sibling_position.
    sibling: subtree_node;
    sp: file_index;
  begin
    if size(n) < max_size(n) then has_new_sibling := false;
       add_to_subtree(k, child_position, n);
    else has_new_sibling := true;
       split_subtree(k, child_position, n, sibling, sibling_key);
       allocate_file_position(f, sp);
       write(f, sibling, fp(sp));
       sibling_position := sp;
    end if;
  end add_child;

  procedure add_to_subtree(k: in key;
                           child_position: in file_index;
                           n: in out subtree_node ) is
    -- Pre: size(n) < max_size(n).
    -- Post: k bound to child_position in n.
    i: subtree_children_range;
  begin
    i := find_subtree_index(k, n) + 1;
      -- Node index of child containing k.
    n.subtree_keys(i + 1 .. n.subtree_size) :=
      n.subtree_keys(i .. n.subtree_size - 1);
    n.children(i + 1 .. n.subtree_size) :=
      n.children(i .. n.subtree_size - 1);
    n.subtree_keys(i) := k;
```

```
    n.children(i) := child_position;
    n.subtree_size := n.subtree_size + 1;
end add_to_subtree;

procedure add_to_leaf(k: in key; x: in value;
                      i: in leaf_pairs_range;
                      n: in out leaf_node ) is
  -- Pre: size(n) < max_size(n).
  -- Post: k bound to x in n.
begin
    n.leaf_keys(i + 1 .. n.leaf_size + 1) :=
      n.leaf_keys(i .. n.leaf_size);
    n.values(i + 1 .. n.leaf_size + 1) :=
      n.values(i .. n.leaf_size);
    n.leaf_keys(i) := k;
    n.values(i) := x;
    n.leaf_size := n.leaf_size + 1;
end add_to_leaf;

procedure split_subtree(k: in key;
                        child_position: in file_index;
                        n: in out subtree_node;
                        new_subtree: in out subtree_node;
                        new_subtree_key: out key ) is
  -- Pre: size(n) = max_size(n) &
  --        ~(k IN keys(n)) & k > first_key(n).
  -- Post: n.subtree_keys U new_subtree.subtree_keys =
  --        *n.subtree_keys U {k}.
  -- Post: n.subtree_keys < new_subtree.subtree_keys.
  -- Post: n.subtree_size = min_size(n).
  -- Post: new_subtree.subtree_size >= min_size(new_subtree).
  -- Post: new_subtree_key is the smallest key in new_subtree.
  subtree_index: subtree_children_range;
    -- Index of new child.
  minsize: natural := min_size(n);
  maxsize: natural := max_size(n);
begin
  subtree_index := find_subtree_index(k, n);
    -- New key at subtree_index + 1.
  if subtree_index + 1 < minsize then  -- k goes in n.
    new_subtree_key := n.subtree_keys(minsize - 1);
    n.subtree_size := minsize - 1;
    new_subtree.subtree_size := maxsize - minsize + 1;
      -- size(n) + size(new_subtree) = maxsize.
    new_subtree.subtree_keys(1 .. maxsize - minsize) :=
      n.subtree_keys(minsize .. maxsize - 1);
```

```
        new_subtree.children(0 .. maxsize - minsize) :=
          n.children(minsize - 1 .. maxsize - 1);
        add_to_subtree(k, child_position, n);
          -- size(n) = minsize.
      elsif subtree_index + 1 = minsize then
          -- The new entry is the first child of new_subtree.
        new_subtree_key := k;
        n.subtree_size := minsize;
        new_subtree.subtree_size := maxsize + 1 - minsize;
          -- size(n) + size(new_subtree) = maxsize + 1.
        new_subtree.subtree_keys(1 .. maxsize - minsize) :=
          n.subtree_keys(minsize .. maxsize - 1);
        new_subtree.children(1 .. maxsize - minsize) :=
          n.children(minsize .. maxsize - 1);
        new_subtree.children(0) := child_position;
      else  -- The new entry is a later child of new_subtree.
        new_subtree_key :=  n.subtree_keys(minsize);
        n.subtree_size := minsize;
        new_subtree.subtree_size := maxsize - minsize;
          -- size(n) + size(new_subtree) = maxsize.
        new_subtree.subtree_keys(1 .. maxsize - minsize - 1) :=
          n.subtree_keys(1 + minsize .. maxsize - 1);
        new_subtree.children(0 .. maxsize - minsize - 1) :=
          n.children(minsize .. maxsize - 1);
        add_to_subtree(k, child_position, new_subtree);
      end if;
      if size(n) < min_size(n) or
        size(new_subtree) < min_size(new_subtree)
      then raise invariant_broken; end if;
    end split_subtree;

    procedure split_leaf(k: in key; x: in value;
                        key_position: in extended_leaf_range;
                        n: in out leaf_node;
                        new_leaf: in out leaf_node;
                        new_leaf_key: out key ) is
      -- Pre: size(n) = max_size(n) &
      --      key(n, key_position - 1) < k < key(n, key_position).
      -- Post: n.leaf_keys < new_leaf.leaf_keys.
      -- Post: n.leaf_size = min_size(n).
      -- Post: new_leaf.leaf_size >= min_size(new_leaf).
      -- Post: new_leaf_key is the smallest key in new_leaf.
      -- Post: n.leaf_keys U new_leaf.leaf_keys =
      --      *n.leaf_keys U {k}.
      minsize: natural := min_size(n);
      maxsize: natural := max_size(n);
```

```ada
begin
  if key_position <= minsize then   -- k goes in n.
    n.leaf_size := minsize - 1;
    new_leaf.leaf_size := maxsize - minsize + 1;
      -- size(n) + size(new_leaf) = maxsize.
    new_leaf.leaf_keys(1 .. maxsize - minsize + 1) :=
      n.leaf_keys(minsize .. maxsize);
    new_leaf.values(1 .. maxsize - minsize + 1) :=
      n.values(minsize .. maxsize);
    add_to_leaf(k, x, key_position, n);
  else  -- key_position > minsize, k goes in new_leaf.
    n.leaf_size := minsize;
    new_leaf.leaf_size := maxsize - minsize;
      -- size(n) + size(new_leaf) = maxsize.
    new_leaf.leaf_keys(1 .. maxsize - minsize) :=
      n.leaf_keys(minsize + 1 .. maxsize);
    new_leaf.values(1 .. maxsize - minsize) :=
      n.values(minsize + 1 .. maxsize);
    add_to_leaf(k, x, key_position - minsize, new_leaf);
  end if;
  new_leaf_key := new_leaf.leaf_keys(1);
  if size(n) < min_size(n) or
     size(new_leaf) < min_size(new_leaf)
  then raise invariant_broken; end if;
end split_leaf;

procedure remove(k: in key; bt: in out B_tree) is
  root_node: node;
  root_changed, root_has_new_key: boolean;
    -- root_changed => root_node has been changed.
  root_key: key;
begin
  if not is_open(bt.file) then
    open(bt.file, inout_file, ada_string(bt.name));
  end if;
  read(bt.file, root_node, fp(root_position));
  remove_from_node(k, root_node, bt.file, root_changed,
                   root_has_new_key, root_key );
  if root_changed then update_root(root_node, bt.file);
    write(bt.file, root_node, fp(root_position));
  end if;
  close(bt);
end remove;

procedure update_root(root: in out node; f: in file_type) is
  child_position: file_index;
```

```
begin
   if size(root) = 1 and root.tag = subtree then
      -- Replace root node with only child.
      child_position := root.children(0);
      read(f, root, fp(child_position));
      recycle_file_position(f, child_position);
   end if;
end update_root;


procedure remove_from_node(k: in key; n: in out node;
                           f: in file_type; .
                           node_changed,
                             node_key_changed: out boolean;
                           node_key: out key ) is
-- Pre: is_open(f).
-- Post: the key has been removed from the B_tree.
-- Post: all changes to nodes below n are in f.
-- Post: node_changed <=> the node n has been changed.
-- Post: node_key_changed <=> n has a new first key.
-- Post: node_key_changed => the first key of n is node_key.
  child: node;
  child_changed, child_key_changed: boolean;
  child_key: key;
  i: subtree_children_range;
begin
  case n.tag is
    when subtree =>
      i := find_subtree_index(k, n);
      read(f, child, fp(n.children(i)));
      remove_from_node(k, child, f, child_changed,
                       child_key_changed, child_key );
      if child_key_changed then
        update_node_key(n, child_key, i, node_changed,
                           node_key_changed, node_key );
      end if;
      if size(child) < min_size(child) then
        node_changed := true;
        adjust_child(n, child, i, f);
      elsif child_changed then
        write(f, child, fp(n.children(i)));
      end if;
    when leaf =>
      remove_from_leaf(k, n, node_changed,
                       node_key_changed, node_key );
    when free => raise invariant_broken;
      -- Should never get here.
  end case;
end remove_from_node;
```

```
procedure update_node_key(parent: in out node;
                          child_key: in key;
                          child_index:
                             in subtree_children_range;
                          parent_changed,
                             parent_key_changed: out boolean;
                          parent_key: out key ) is
  -- Pre: the new key of the child at child_index is child_key.
  -- Post: parent_changed <=> parent ~= *parent.
  -- Post: parent_key_changed <=>
  --        first_key(parent) ~= first_key(*parent).
  -- Post: parent_key_changed =>
  --        first_key(parent) = parent_key).
begin
  if child_index = 0 then
     -- The new key goes at some level above parent.
     parent_changed := false;
     parent_key_changed := true;
     parent_key := child_key;
  else parent_changed := true;
     parent_key_changed := false;
     parent.subtree_keys(child_index) := child_key;
  end if;
end update_node_key;

procedure adjust_child(parent, child: in out node;
                       child_index: in subtree_children_range;
                       f: in file_type ) is
  -- Pre: is_open(f) & size(child) < min_size(child).
  -- Post: bindings in the subtree rooted at parent
  --        are unchanged.
  -- Post: size(child) >= min_size(child).
  -- Post: size(sibling) >= min_size(sibling).
  -- Post: changes to children of the parent node are
  --        reflected in the file.
  sibling: node; -- Sibling node adjacent to child.
begin
    if size(parent) < 2 then raise invariant_broken; end if;
    if child_index > 0 then
       read(f, sibling, fp(parent.children(child_index - 1)));
       adjust_children(parent, sibling, child,
                       child_index, f );
    else read(f, sibling, fp(parent.children(1)));
       adjust_children(parent, child, sibling, 1, f);
    end if;
end adjust_child;
```

```
procedure adjust_children(parent: in out subtree_node;
                          c1, c2: in out node;
                          i: in subtree_keys_range;
                          f: in file_type ) is
  -- Pre: file_index of c1 = parent.children(i - 1).
  -- Pre: file_index of c2 = parent.children(i).
  -- Pre: c1.keys < c2.keys.
  -- Pre: parent.tag = subtree.
  -- Post: min_size(c) <= size(c) <= max_size(c)
  --       for each child c of parent.
  -- Post: the bindings in the subtree rooted at parent
  --       are unchanged.
begin
  if size(c1) + size(c2) <= max_size(c1) then
     combine(c1, c2, parent.subtree_keys(i));
     recycle_file_position(f, parent.children(i));
     remove_child(parent, i);
  else balance(c1, c2, parent.subtree_keys(i));
     write(f, c2, fp(parent.children(i)));
  end if;
  write(f, c1, fp(parent.children(i - 1)));
end adjust_children;


procedure remove_child(parent: in out subtree_node;
                       child_position:
                          in subtree_keys_range ) is
  -- Remove the child at position child_position
  -- from the parent node.
begin
  parent.subtree_keys(child_position ..
                      parent.subtree_size - 2 ) :=
    parent.subtree_keys(child_position + 1 ..
                        parent.subtree_size - 1 );
  parent.children(child_position .. parent.subtree_size - 2) :=
    parent.children(child_position + 1 ..
                    parent.subtree_size - 1 );
  parent.subtree_size := parent.subtree_size - 1;
end remove_child;


procedure combine(n1: in out node; n2: in node;
                  n2_key: in key ) is
  -- Pre: n1.tag = n2.tag &
  --      size(n1)`+ size(n2) <= max_size(n1).
  -- Pre: n1.keys < n2.keys.
  -- Post: n1.keys = *n1.keys || *n2.keys.
  s: natural;  -- New size of n1.
```

```ada
begin
  case n1.tag is
    when subtree =>
      s := n1.subtree_size + n2.subtree_size;
      n1.subtree_keys(n1.subtree_size) := n2_key;
      n1.subtree_keys(n1.subtree_size + 1 .. s - 1) :=
        n2.subtree_keys(1 .. n2.subtree_size - 1);
      n1.children(n1.subtree_size .. s - 1) :=
        n2.children(0 .. n2.subtree_size - 1);
      n1.subtree_size := s;
    when leaf =>
      s := n1.leaf_size + n2.leaf_size;
      n1.leaf_keys(n1.leaf_size + 1 .. s) :=
        n2.leaf_keys(1 .. n2.leaf_size);
      n1.values(n1.leaf_size + 1 .. s) :=
        n2.values(1 .. n2.leaf_size);
      n1.leaf_size := s;
    when free => raise invariant_broken;
      -- Should never get here.
  end case;
  if size(n1) < min_size(n1) then
    raise invariant_broken; end if;
end combine;

procedure balance(n1, n2: in out node; n2_key: in out key) is
  -- Pre: n1.tag = n2.tag.
  -- Pre: size(n1) + size(n2) > max_size(n1).
  -- Pre: n1.keys < n2.keys.
  -- Post: n1.keys || n2.keys = *n1.keys || *n2.keys.
  -- Post: size(n1) = (size(*n1) + size(*n2)) / 2.
  -- Post: n2_key = first_key(n2, f).
  s1: natural := (size(n1) + size(n2)) / 2;  -- New size of n1.
  s2: natural := size(n1) + size(n2) - s1;  -- New size of n2.
begin
  case n1.tag is
    when subtree =>
      if n1.subtree_size < s1 then
        n1.subtree_keys(n1.subtree_size) := n2_key;
        n1.subtree_keys(n1.subtree_size + 1 .. s1 - 1) :=
          n2.subtree_keys(1 .. s1 - 1 - n1.subtree_size);
        n1.children(n1.subtree_size .. s1 - 1) :=
          n2.children(0 .. s1 - 1 - n1.subtree_size);
        n2_key := n2.subtree_keys(s1 - n1.subtree_size);
        n2.subtree_keys(1 .. s2 - 1) :=
          n2.subtree_keys(s1 - n1.subtree_size + 1 ..
                          n2.subtree_size - 1 );
        n2.children(0 .. s2 - 1) :=
          n2.children(n2.subtree_size - s2 ..
                      n2.subtree_size - 1 );
```

```
        else
          n2.subtree_keys(n1.subtree_size + 1 - s1 .. s2 - 1) :=
            n2.subtree_keys(1 .. n2.subtree_size - 1);
          n2.children(n1.subtree_size - s1 .. s2 - 1) :=
            n2.children(0 .. n2.subtree_size - 1);
          n2.subtree_keys(n1.subtree_size - s1) := n2_key;
          n2.subtree_keys(1 .. n1.subtree_size - 1 - s1) :=
            n1.subtree_keys(s1 + 1 .. n1.subtree_size - 1);
          n2_key := n1.subtree_keys(s1);
          n2.children(0 .. n1.subtree_size - 1 - s1) :=
            n1.children(s1 .. n1.subtree_size - 1);
        end if;
        n1.subtree_size := s1;
        n2.subtree_size := s2;
      when leaf =>
        if n1.leaf_size < s1 then
          n1.leaf_keys(n1.leaf_size + 1 .. s1) :=
            n2.leaf_keys(1 .. s1 - n1.leaf_size);
          n1.values(n1.leaf_size + 1 .. s1) :=
            n2.values(1 .. s1 - n1.leaf_size);
          n2.leaf_keys(1 .. s2) :=
            n2.leaf_keys(n2.leaf_size -s2 + 1 .. n2.leaf_size);
          n2.values(1 .. s2) :=
            n2.values(n2.leaf_size -s2 + 1 .. n2.leaf_size);
        else
          n2.leaf_keys(s2 + 1 - n2.leaf_size .. s2) :=
            n2.leaf_keys(1 .. n2.leaf_size);
          n2.values(s2 + 1 - n2.leaf_size .. s2) :=
            n2.values(1 .. n2.leaf_size);
          n2.leaf_keys(1 .. n1.leaf_size - s1) :=
            n1.leaf_keys(s1 + 1 .. n1.leaf_size);
          n2.values(1 .. n1.leaf_size - s1) :=
            n1.values(s1 + 1 .. n1.leaf_size);
        end if;
        n1.leaf_size := s1;
        n2.leaf_size := s2;
      when free => raise invariant_broken;
        -- Should never get here.
    end case;
    if size(n1) < min_size(n1) or size(n2) < min_size(n2)
    then raise invariant_broken; end if;
  end balance;

  procedure remove_from_leaf(k: in key; n: in out leaf_node;
                             node_changed,
                               node_key_changed: out boolean;
                             node_key: out key) is
```

```
  -- Post: k not in n.
  -- Post: node_changed => n ~= *n.
  -- Post: node_key_changed => first_key(n) ~= first_key(*n).
  -- Post: n.size = 0 => node_key = !
  -- -- node_key is undefined if the B_tree becomes empty.
  i: extended_leaf_range;  -- i is the node index of k in n.
  found: boolean;
begin
  find_leaf_index(k, n, i, found);
  if not found then node_changed := false;
     node_key_changed := false;
     return;
  end if;
  n.leaf_keys(i .. n.leaf_size - 1) :=
    n.leaf_keys(i + 1 .. n.leaf_size);
  n.values(i .. n.leaf_size - 1) :=
    n.values(i + 1 .. n.leaf_size);
  n.leaf_size := n.leaf_size - 1;
  node_changed := true;
  if i = 1 then node_key_changed := true;
     node_key := n.leaf_keys(1);
  else node_key_changed := false; end if;
end remove_from_leaf;

procedure fetch(k: in key; bt: in out B_tree;
                result: out value ) is
  n: leaf_node;
  i: extended_leaf_range;
  found: boolean;
begin
  if not is_open(bt.file) then
     open(bt.file, inout_file, ada_string(bt.name));
  end if;
  n := find_leaf(k, bt);
  find_leaf_index(k, n, i, found);
  close(bt);
  if found then result := n.values(i);
     else raise domain_error; end if;
end fetch;

function find_leaf(k: key; bt: B_tree) return leaf_node is
    -- Pre: is_open(bt.file).
    -- Post: find_leaf(k, bt) is the leaf node containing k.
  i: file_index := root_position;  -- Start at the root node.
  n: node;
```

```
begin
  loop
    read(bt.file, n, fp(i));
    case n.tag is
      when leaf => return n;
      when subtree =>
        i := n.children(find_subtree_index(k, n));
      when free => raise invariant_broken;
        -- Should never get here.
    end case;
  end loop;
end find_leaf;

procedure member(k: in key; bt: in out B_tree;
                 result: out boolean ) is
  i: extended_leaf_range;
begin
  if not is_open(bt.file) then
    open(bt.file, inout_file, ada_string(bt.name));
  end if;
  find_leaf_index(k, find_leaf(k, bt), i, result);
  close(bt);
end member;

--  generic
--     with procedure produce(k: in key; v: in value);
procedure scan_between(k1, k2: in key; bt: in out B_tree) is
--  scan_between uses the local procedure scan_tree.
--  scan_tree must be declared inside scan_between
--  because it calls produce.
  procedure scan_tree(f: in file_type; i: in file_index) is
    n: node;
    a, b: natural;
    found: boolean;
  begin
    read(f, n, fp(i));
    case n.tag is
      when subtree =>
        a := find_subtree_index(k1, n);
        b := find_subtree_index(k2, n);
        for j in a .. b loop
          scan_tree(f, n.children(j));
        end loop;
      when leaf =>
        find_leaf_index(k1, n, a, found);
        find_leaf_index(k2, n, b, found);
```

```ada
        if not found then b := b - 1; end if;
        for j in a .. b loop
          produce(n.leaf_keys(j), n.values(j));
        end loop;
      when free => raise invariant_broken;
        -- Should never get here.
    end case;
  end scan_tree;
begin  -- Body of scan_between.
  if not is_open(bt.file) then
     open(bt.file, inout_file, ada_string(bt.name));
  end if;
  scan_tree(bt.file, root_position);
  close(bt);
exception
  when quit => close(bt);
    -- Stop if produce raises the "quit" exception.
end scan_between;


--  generic
--     with procedure produce(k: in key; v: in value);
procedure scan_from(k1: in key; bt: in out B_tree) is
  -- scan_from uses the local procedure scan_tree.
  -- scan_tree must be declared inside scan_from
  -- because it calls produce.
  procedure scan_tree(f: in file_type; i: in file_index) is
    n: node;
    a: natural;
    found: boolean;
  begin
    read(f, n, fp(i));
    case n.tag is
      when subtree =>
        a := find_subtree_index(k1, n);
        for j in a .. n.subtree_size - 1 loop
          scan_tree(f, n.children(j));
        end loop;
      when leaf =>
        find_leaf_index(k1, n, a, found);
        for j in a .. n.leaf_size loop
          produce(n.leaf_keys(j), n.values(j));
        end loop;
      when free => raise invariant_broken;
        -- Should never get here.
    end case;
  end scan_tree;
```

```
begin  -- Body of scan_from.
  if not is_open(bt.file) then
      open(bt.file, inout_file, ada_string(bt.name));
  end if;
  scan_tree(bt.file, root_position);
  close(bt);
exception
  when quit => close(bt);
    -- Stop if produce raises the "quit" exception.
end scan_from;


--  generic
--     with procedure produce(k: in key; v: in value);
procedure scan_to(k1: in key; bt: in out B_tree) is
-- scan_to uses the local procedure scan_tree.
-- scan_tree must be declared inside scan_to
-- because it calls produce.
  procedure scan_tree(f: in file_type; i: in file_index) is
    n: node;
    b: natural;
    found: boolean;
  begin
    read(f, n, fp(i));
    case n.tag is
      when subtree =>
        b := find_subtree_index(k1, n);
        for j in 0 .. b loop
          scan_tree(f, n.children(j));
        end loop;
      when leaf =>
        find_leaf_index(k1, n, b,found);
        if not found then b := b - 1; end if;
        for j in 1 .. b loop
          produce(n.leaf_keys(j), n.values(j));
        end loop;
      when free => raise invariant_broken;
          -- Should never get here.
    end case;
  end scan_tree;
begin  -- Body of scan_to.
  if not is_open(bt.file) then
      open(bt.file, inout_file, ada_string(bt.name));
  end if;
  scan_tree(bt.file, root_position);
  close(bt);
exception
  when quit => close(bt);
    -- Stop if produce raises the "quit" exception.
end scan_to;
```

```
--   generic
--     with procedure produce(k: in key; v: in value);
procedure scan(bt: in out B_tree) is
-- scan uses the local procedure scan_tree.
-- scan_tree must be declared inside scan
-- because it calls produce.
  procedure scan_tree(f: in file_type; i: in file_index) is
    n: node;
  begin
    read(f, n, fp(i));
    case n.tag is
      when subtree =>
        for j in 0 .. n.subtree_size - 1 loop
          scan_tree(f, n.children(j));
        end loop;
      when leaf =>
        for j in 1 .. n.leaf_size loop
          produce(n.leaf_keys(j), n.values(j));
        end loop;
      when free => raise invariant_broken;
        -- Should never get here.
    end case;
  end scan_tree;
begin  -- Body of scan.
  if not is_open(bt.file) then
    open(bt.file, inout_file, ada_string(bt.name));
  end if;
  scan_tree(bt.file, root_position);
  close(bt);
exception
  when quit => close(bt);
    -- Stop if produce raises the "quit" exception.
end scan;

function size(n: node) return natural is
begin
  case n.tag is
    when subtree => return n.subtree_size;
    when leaf => return n.leaf_size;
    when free => raise invariant_broken;
      -- Should never get here.
  end case;
end size;

function min_size(n: node) return natural is
begin
  return (max_size(n) + 1) / 2;
end min_size;
```

```
function max_size(n: node) return natural is
begin
  case n.tag is
    when subtree => return subtree_size_range'last;
    when leaf => return leaf_size_range'last;
    when free => raise invariant_broken;
      -- Should never get here.
  end case;
end max_size;

procedure allocate_file_position(f: in file_type;
                                      i: out file_index ) is
  -- Pre: is_open(f).
  -- Post: i is the file_index of a free node.
  n: free_node;
begin
  read(f, n, fp(free_list_position));
  if n.next = empty then i := file_index(size(f) + 1);
  else i := n.next;
      read(f, n, fp(n.next));
      write(f, n, fp(free_list_position));
  end if;
end allocate_file_position;

procedure recycle_file_position(f: in file_type;
                                     i: in file_index ) is
  -- Pre: is_open(f).
  -- Post: i is in the free list.
  header, new_node: free_node;
begin
  read(f, header, fp(free_list_position));
  new_node.next := header.next;
  header.next := i;
  write(f, new_node, fp(i));
  write(f, header, fp(free_list_position));
end recycle_file_position;

function "<"(k1, k2: key) return boolean is
begin
  return not(k2 <= k1);
end "<";

-- Testing functions.

procedure free_list_length(bt: in out B_tree;
                           result: out natural ) is
  -- Post: result is the number of free nodes in the free list.
```

```ada
    i: file_index := free_list_position;
       -- Start at the free list header.
    node_found: natural := 0;
       -- Number of free nodes found so far.
    n: node;
begin
  if not is_open(bt.file) then
      open(bt.file, inout_file, ada_string(bt.name));
  end if;
  loop
    read(bt.file, n, fp(i));
    case n.tag is
      when free => if n.next = empty
        then result := node_found; return;
        else node_found := node_found + 1; i := n.next;
        end if;
      when leaf => raise invariant_broken;
        -- Should never get here.
      when subtree => raise invariant_broken;
        -- Should never get here.
    end case;
  end loop;
  close(bt);
end free_list_length;

-- generic
  -- procedure print_key(k: in key);
procedure print_keys(bt: in out B_tree) is
    -- print_tree_keys must be nested inside print_keys because
    -- it calls the generic parameter "print_key".
  procedure print_tree_keys(f: in file_type; i: in file_index;
                            prefix: in string) is
    n: node;
  begin
    read(f, n, fp(i));
    case n.tag is
      when subtree =>
        text_io.put(prefix);
        for j in 1 .. n.subtree_size - 1 loop
          print_key(n.subtree_keys(j));
        end loop;
        text_io.new_line;
        for j in 0 .. n.subtree_size - 1 loop
          print_tree_keys(f, n.children(j), prefix & "   ");
        end loop;
      when leaf =>
        text_io.put(prefix);
```

```
            for j in 1 .. n.leaf_size loop
              print_key(n.leaf_keys(j));
            end loop;
            text_io.new_line;
          when free => raise invariant_broken;
            -- Should never get here.
      end case;
    end print_tree_keys;
  begin
    if not is_open(bt.file) then
       open(bt.file, inout_file, ada_string(bt.name));
    end if;
    print_tree_keys(bt.file, root_position, "");
    text_io.new_line;
    close(bt);
  end print_keys;
end B_tree_pkg;
```

```
generic
  type t1 is private;
  type t2 is private;
  with function "<"(x, y: t1) return boolean is <>;
  with function "<"(x, y: t2) return boolean is <>;
function lex2 (x1: t1; x2: t2; y1: t1; y2: t2) return boolean;
```

```
function lex2 (x1: t1; x2: t2; y1: t1; y2: t2) return boolean is
begin
  return x1 < y1
    or else (x1 = y1
      and then (x2 < y2 or else x2 = y2));
end lex2;
```

```
generic
  type t1 is private;
  type t2 is private;
  type t3 is private; ·
  with function "<"(x, y: t1) return boolean is <>;
```

```
  with function "<"(x, y: t2) return boolean is <>;
  with function "<"(x, y: t3) return boolean is <>;
function lex3 (x1: t1; x2: t2; x3: t3;
               y1: t1; y2: t2; y3: t3) return boolean;
```

```
function lex3 (x1: t1; x2: t2; x3: t3;
               y1: t1; y2: t2; y3: t3) return boolean is
begin
  return x1 < y1
    or else (x1 = y1
      and then (x2 < y2
         or else (x2 = y2
            and then (x3 < y3 or else x3 = y3))));
end lex3;
```

```
  with pairs_pkg; use pairs_pkg;   -- Defines pairs_type.
  with text_pkg; use text_pkg; -- Defines text_pkg_instance.
  with direct_io;
generic
  type key is private;
  type value is private;
  with function hash(k: in key) return natural;
  pairs: pairs_type;   -- Expected number of keys, pairs >= 0.
  block_size: positive := 128;
    -- Keys per disk block, block_size >= 1.
package hashed_file_pkg is
  use text_pkg_instance;   -- Defines the type text.

  type hashed_file is limited private;

  procedure open(hf_name: in text; hf: in out hashed_file);
  procedure close(hf: in out hashed_file);
  procedure delete(hf: in out hashed_file);
  function name(hf: in hashed_file) return text;
  procedure add(k: in key; x: in value; hf: in out hashed_file);
  procedure remove(k: in key; hf: in out hashed_file);
  procedure fetch(k: in key; hf: in out hashed_file;
                  result: out value );
  procedure member(k: in key; hf: in out hashed_file;
                   result: out boolean );
```

```
  generic
    with procedure produce(k: in key; v: in value);
  procedure scan(hf: in out hashed_file);

-- Testing interface.
  procedure free_list_length(hf: in out hashed_file;
                             result: out natural );
  procedure print_bucket_lengths(hf: in out hashed_file);

  domain_error: exception;   -- Raised by fetch.
  quit: exception;   -- Raised by produce. Handled by scan.

private

  subtype file_index is natural;
    -- The file index of a node in a hashed file.
    -- 1 <= i <= size(hf.file) if
    --    i is the file index of a node in hf.
  empty: constant file_index := 0;
    -- Terminator for all node chains.

  subtype node_size is natural range 0 .. block_size;
  subtype node_index is natural range 1 .. block_size;

  type keys_type is array(node_index) of key;
  type values_type is array(node_index) of value;

  type node is
    record
      size: node_size := 0;
      keys: keys_type;
      values: values_type;
      next, previous: file_index := empty;
    end record;
  -- Each bucket is a doubly-linked list of nodes.
  -- previous = empty for all bucket header nodes.
  -- next ~= empty => size = block_size
  --    for all nodes in the buckets.
  -- The free list is a singly-linked list of nodes.
  -- size = 0 and previous = empty
  --    for all nodes in the free list.

  package node_io is new direct_io(node);
  use node_io;   -- Defines file_type and file operations.
  type hashed_file is
```

```
    record
      name: text;
      file: file_type;
    end record;

end hashed_file_pkg;
```

```
package pairs_pkg is
  type pairs_type is range 1 .. 100_000_000;
end pairs_pkg;
```

```
  with text_io;
package body hashed_file_pkg is

  buckets: constant file_index :=
    file_index(1 + (pairs / pairs_type(block_size)));
  -- The bucket header nodes have a file index in 1 .. buckets.

  free_list_position: constant file_index := buckets + 1;
  -- The free list header node has a
  --    file index = free_list_position.
  -- The minimum number of nodes in a hashed file
  --    is free_list_position.
  -- The bucket overflow nodes have a
  --    file index > free_list_position.
  -- The nodes in the free list have a
  --    file index > free_list_position.

  subtype fp is positive_count;
    -- Used for coverting file_index-es to
    --    file pointers for read and write.

  invariant_broken: exception;
    -- Raised only if the invariant is damaged by a bug.

  -- Local subprogram declarations.
  procedure add_to_node(k: in key; x: in value; f: in file_type);
  procedure find(k: in key; f: in file_type; fi: out file_index;
                 n: out node; i: out node_index;
                 found: out boolean );
```

```
procedure find_key(k: in key; n: in node; i: out node_index;
                    found: out boolean );
procedure remove_from_node(k: in key; f: in file_type;
                           i: in file_index );
procedure find_last_node(f: in file_type; fi: in file_index;
                         last_node: out node;
                         li: out file_index );
procedure allocate_node(f: in file_type; i: out file_index);
procedure recycle_node(f: in file_type; i, pi: in file_index);
-- End of local subprogram declarations.

procedure open(hf_name: in text; hf: in out hashed_file) is
  n: node;
begin
  hf.name := hf_name;
  open(hf.file, inout_file, ada_string(hf_name));
exception
  when name_error =>
    -- The file does not exist yet, make a new one.
    create(hf.file, inout_file, ada_string(hf_name));
    -- Initialize the buckets.
    for i in 1 .. buckets
        loop write(hf.file, n, fp(i)); end loop;
    -- Initialize the free list.
    if size(hf.file) = count(buckets) then
       write(hf.file, n, fp(free_list_position));
       -- The free list is empty
       -- if the initial file size is small.
    else for i in reverse free_list_position ..
                          file_index(size(hf.file))
         loop write(hf.file, n, fp(i)); n.next := i; end loop;
         -- Collect nodes with file_index >= free_list_position
         -- in the free list.
    end if;
  when status_error =>
    -- The file is already open.
    if name(hf.file) /= ada_string(hf_name) then
       close(hf.file);
       open(hf.file, inout_file, ada_string(hf_name));
    end if;
end open;

procedure close(hf: in out hashed_file) is
begin
  close(hf.file);
exception when status_error => null;
  -- Do nothing if the file is already closed.
end close;
```

```ada
procedure delete(hf: in out hashed_file) is
begin
  if not is_open(hf.file) then
     open(hf.file, inout_file, ada_string(hf.name));
  end if;
  delete(hf.file);
end delete;

function name(hf: in hashed_file) return text is
begin
  return hf.name;
end name;

procedure add(k: in key; x: in value;
              hf: in out hashed_file ) is
begin
  if not is_open(hf.file) then
     open(hf.file, inout_file, ada_string(hf.name));
  end if;
  add_to_node(k, x, hf.file);
  close(hf);
end add;

procedure add_to_node(k: in key; x: in value;
                      f: in file_type ) is
  fi: file_index;
  n, new_node: node;
  ni: node_index;
  found: boolean;
begin
  find(k, f, fi, n, ni, found);
  if found then n.values(ni) := x;
     elsif n.size < block_size then
       n.size := n.size + 1;
       n.keys(n.size) := k;
       n.values(n.size) := x;
     else new_node.size := 1;
       new_node.keys(new_node.size) := k;
       new_node.values(new_node.size) := x;
       new_node.previous := fi;
       allocate_node(f, n.next);
          -- Puts new file index in n.next.
       write(f, new_node, fp(n.next));
  end if;
  write(f, n, fp(fi));
end add_to_node;
```

```
procedure remove(k: in key; hf: in out hashed_file) is
begin
  if not is_open(hf.file) then
      open(hf.file, inout_file, ada_string(hf.name));
  end if;
  remove_from_node(k, hf.file,
                    1 + (file_index(hash(k)) mod buckets) );
  close(hf);
end remove;

procedure remove_from_node(k: in key; f: in file_type;
                           i: in file_index ) is
    -- Pre: is_open(f).
    -- Post: ~(k IN f).
  fi, li: file_index;   -- f(fi) = n, f(li) = last_node.
  n, last_node: node;
  ni: node_index;
  found: boolean;
begin
  find(k, f, fi, n, ni, found);
  if not found then return;
  elsif n.size = 1 and n.next = empty and
        n.previous /= empty then
    recycle_node(f, fi, n.previous);
    return;
  elsif n.next = empty then
    n.keys(ni) := n.keys(n.size);
    n.values(ni) := n.values(n.size);
    n.size := n.size - 1;
    write(f, n, fp(fi));
    return;
  else find_last_node(f, n.next, last_node, li);
    n.keys(ni) := last_node.keys(last_node.size);
    n.values(ni) := last_node.values(last_node.size);
    write(f, n, fp(fi));
  end if;
  if last_node.size = 1 then
     recycle_node(f, li, last_node.previous);
  else last_node.size := last_node.size - 1;
    write(f, last_node, fp(li));
  end if;
end remove_from_node;

procedure find_last_node(f: in file_type; fi: in file_index;
                         last_node: out node;
                         li: out file_index ) is
  -- Pre: fi ~= empty.
  -- Post: f(li) = last_node & last_node.next = empty.
  -- Post: bucket(li, f) = bucket(fi, f).
```

```ada
  index: file_index := fi;
  n: node;
begin
  loop
    read(f, n, fp(index));
    if n.next = empty then
       last_node := n; li := index; return; end if;
    index := n.next;
  end loop;
end find_last_node;

procedure fetch(k: in key; hf: in out hashed_file;
                result: out value ) is
  fi: file_index;
  n: node;
  ni: node_index;
  found: boolean;
begin
  if not is_open(hf.file) then
     open(hf.file, inout_file, ada_string(hf.name));
  end if;
  find(k, hf.file, fi, n, ni, found);
  close(hf);
  if found then result := n.values(ni);
     else raise domain_error; end if;
end fetch;

procedure member(k: in key; hf: in out hashed_file;
                 result: out boolean ) is
  fi: file_index;
  n: node;
  ni: node_index;
begin
  if not is_open(hf.file) then
     open(hf.file, inout_file, ada_string(hf.name));
  end if;
  find(k, hf.file, fi, n, ni, result);
  close(hf);
end member;

procedure find(k: in key; f: in file_type; fi: out file_index;
               n: out node; i: out node_index;
               found: out boolean ) is
  -- Pre: is_open(f).
  -- Post: if found then n.keys(i) = k else k not in f.
  -- Post: f(fi) is the node where k will be stored if added.
  -- Post: n = f(fi).
```

```
  n1: node;
  ok: boolean;
  index: file_index := 1 + (file_index(hash(k)) mod buckets);
begin
  loop  -- Invariant:
        -- f(index) is a node in the bucket containing k.
    read(f, n1, fp(index));
    find_key(k, n1, i, ok);
    if ok then fi := index; n := n1; found := true; return;
    elsif n1.next = empty then
       fi := index; n := n1; found := false; return;
    else index := n1.next;
    end if;
  end loop;
end find;

procedure find_key(k: in key; n: in node; i: out node_index;
                   found: out boolean ) is
  -- Post: if found then n.keys(i) = k else ~(k IN n.keys).
begin
  for j in 1 .. n.size loop
    -- Invariant: ~(k IN n.keys(1 .. j - 1)).
    if n.keys(j) = k then
       i := j; found := true; return; end if;
  end loop;
  found := false;
end find_key;

procedure allocate_node(f: in file_type; i: out file_index) is
  -- Pre: is_open(f).
  -- Post: i is the file_index of a free node.
  n: node;
begin
  read(f, n, fp(free_list_position));
  if n.next = empty then i := file_index(size(f) + 1);
  else i := n.next;
       read(f, n, fp(n.next));
       write(f, n, fp(free_list_position));
  end if;
end allocate_node;

procedure recycle_node(f: in file_type;
                       i, pi: in file_index ) is
  -- Pre: is_open(f) & f(i).previous = pi.
  -- Post: i is in the free list.
  header, previous_node, new_node: node;
```

```
begin
  read(f, previous_node, fp(pi));
  previous_node.next := empty;
  write(f, previous_node, fp(pi));
  read(f, header, fp(free_list_position));
  new_node.next := header.next;
  header.next := i;
  write(f, new_node, fp(i));
  write(f, header, fp(free_list_position));
end recycle_node;

--   generic
--      with procedure produce(k: in key; v: in value);
procedure scan(hf: in out hashed_file) is

  -- produce_node must be declared inside scan
  -- because it calls produce.
  procedure produce_node(n: in node) is
  begin
    for ni in 1 .. n.size loop
      produce(n.keys(ni), n.values(ni));
    end loop;
  end produce_node;

  -- produce_bucket must be declared inside scan
  -- because it calls produce_node.
  procedure produce_bucket(f: in file_type;
                           fi: in file_index ) is
    n: node;
    index: file_index := fi;
  begin
    loop
      read(f, n, fp(index));
      produce_node(n);
      index := n.next;
      if index = empty then return; end if;
    end loop;
  end produce_bucket;

begin  -- Body of scan.
  if not is_open(hf.file) then
    open(hf.file, inout_file, ada_string(hf.name));
  end if;
  for fi in 1 .. buckets loop
    produce_bucket(hf.file, fi);
  end loop;
  close(hf);
exception
```

```
    when quit => close(hf);
      -- Stop if produce raises the "quit" exception.
  end scan;

-- Testing interface.

  procedure free_list_length(hf: in out hashed_file;
                             result: out natural ) is
    -- Post: result is the number of free nodes in the free list.
    i: file_index := free_list_position;
      -- Start at the free list header.
    node_found: natural := 0;
      -- Number of free nodes found so far.
    n: node;
  begin
    if not is_open(hf.file) then
       open(hf.file, inout_file, ada_string(hf.name));
    end if;
    loop
      read(hf.file, n, fp(i));
      if n.next = empty then result := node_found; return;
      else node_found := node_found + 1; i := n.next;
      end if;
    end loop;
    close(hf);
  end free_list_length;

  function bucket_length(f: in file_type;
                         fi: in file_index ) return natural is
    n: node;
    bucket_size: natural := 0;   -- Number of nodes found so far.
    index: file_index := fi;
  begin
    loop
      read(f, n, fp(index));
      bucket_size := bucket_size + n.size;
      if n.next = empty then return bucket_size; end if;
      index := n.next;
    end loop;
  end bucket_length;

  procedure print_bucket_lengths(hf: in out hashed_file) is
  begin
    if not is_open(hf.file) then
       open(hf.file, inout_file, ada_string(hf.name));
    end if;
    text_io.put_line("bucket_lengths:");
```

```
       for fi in 1 .. buckets loop
           text_io.put(natural'image(fi));
           text_io.put(" ");
           text_io.
             put_line(natural'image(bucket_length(hf.file, fi)));
       end loop;
       text_io.new_line;
       close(hf);
   end print_bucket_lengths;

-- CONCEPT bucket(i: file_index, f: file_type)
-- VALUE(bi: file_index)
-- WHERE if f(i).previous = empty then bucket(i, f) = i
--        else bucket(i, f) = bucket(f(i).previous, f) end if
end hashed_file_pkg;
```

```
   with text_pkg; use text_pkg; -- Defines text_pkg_instance.
generic
   type result is range <>;
       -- The result of the hash is an integer type.
       -- Pre: result'size >= 8.
package text_hash_pkg is
   use text_pkg_instance;   -- Defines the type text.

   bits: constant natural := result'size;
   modulus: constant result := result(2 ** (bits - 8));
   subtype hash_result is result range 0 .. modulus - 1;
   function text_hash(s: text) return hash_result;

end text_hash_pkg;
```

```
package body text_hash_pkg is
   base: constant result := 127;
       -- Base should be relatively prime to 2**n,
       -- small enough to allow a large modulus without overflow,
       -- and large enough to avoid many small strings
       -- in the same bucket.

       -- This hash function depends on all of the characters
       -- in the string and distinguishes between permutations
       -- of the same string.
```

```
function text_hash(s: text) return hash_result is
  n: result := 0;
begin
  for i in reverse 1 .. length(s) loop  -- Invariant:
    -- SOME(s1: string SUCH THAT s1 = s[i+1 .. length(s)] ::
    --         n = SUM(k: nat SUCH THAT k IN domain(s1) ::
    --                 ordinal(s[k]) * base ** k ) MOD modulus ).
    n := (base * n + result(character'pos(char(s, i))))
         mod modulus;
  end loop;
  return n;
end text_hash;
end text_hash_pkg;
```

```
  with generic_text_pkg;
package text_pkg is
  package text_pkg_instance is
    new generic_text_pkg(max_text_length => 80);
end text_pkg;
```

```
  with text_io; use text_io;
generic
  max_text_length: natural := 80;
package generic_text_pkg is

  subtype text_length_type is natural range 0 .. max_text_length;
  type text(length: text_length_type := 0) is private;

  -- Constants.
  min_text: constant text;   -- ALL(s: text :: min_text <= s).
  max_text: constant text;   -- ALL(s: text :: s <= max_text).

  -- String operations.
  function text_string(s: string) return text;
  function ada_string(t: text) return string;
  function length(t: text) return natural;
  function max_length(t: text) return natural;
  function "<"(t1, t2: text) return boolean;
  function "<="(t1, t2: text) return boolean;
  -- The functions "=" and "/=" are predefined.
  function char(t: text; i: natural) return character;
  function slice(t: text; low, high: natural) return text;
  function substring(t: text;
                     start, length: natural ) return text;
```

```ada
      function "&"(t1, t2: text) return text;
      function "&"(s: string; t: text) return text;
      function "&"(t: text; s: string) return text;
      procedure append(t: in out text; c: in character);
      procedure append(t: in out text; new_text: in text);
      procedure replace(t: in out text; replacement: in character;
                      position: in natural );
      procedure replace(t: in out text; replacement: in text;
                      position: in natural );
      procedure delete(t: in out text; low, high: in natural);
      procedure find(t, pattern: in text; found: out boolean;
                   start: out natural );

      -- Input/output.
      procedure get(t: out text;
                  length: in natural := max_text_length );
      procedure get(f: in file_type;
                  t: out text;
                  length: in natural := max_text_length );
      procedure get_line(t: out text);
      procedure get_line(f: in file_type; t: out text);
      procedure put(t: in text);
      procedure put(f: file_type; t: in text);
      procedure put_line(t: in text);
      procedure put_line(f: file_type; t: in text);
   private
      type text(length: text_length_type := 0) is
        record contents: string(1 .. length); end record;

      min_text: constant text := (0, "");
        -- The empty string is the minimum element
        -- in the standard string ordering.

      max_text: constant text :=
        (max_text_length, (others => ascii.del));
        -- ascii.del is the last character
        -- in the ascii collating sequence.
   end generic_text_pkg;
```

```ada
   package body generic_text_pkg is
      function text_string(s: string) return text is
      begin
         if s'length > max_text_length then
            raise constraint_error; end if;
         declare
           t: text(s'length);
```

```ada
  begin
    t.contents(1 .. s'length) := s;
    return t;
  end;
end text_string;

function ada_string(t: text) return string is
begin
  return t.contents(1 .. t.length);
end ada_string;

function length(t: text) return natural is
begin
  return t.length;
end length;

function max_length(t: text) return natural is
begin
  return max_text_length;
end max_length;

function "<"(t1, t2: text) return boolean is
begin
  return t1.contents(1 .. t1.length) <
         t2.contents(1 .. t2.length);
end "<";

function "<="(t1, t2: text) return boolean is
begin
  return t1.contents(1 .. t1.length) <=
         t2.contents(1 .. t2.length);
end "<=";

-- The functions "=" and "/=" are predefined.

function char(t: text; i: natural) return character is
begin
  if i not in 1 .. t.length then
     raise constraint_error; end if;
  return t.contents(i);
end char;

function slice(t: text; low, high: natural) return text is
begin
  if ((low not in 1 .. t.length) or else
      (high not in 1 .. t.length)) and then low <= high
  then raise constraint_error; end if;
  return text_string(t.contents(low .. high));
end slice;
```

```ada
function substring(t: text;
                   start, length: natural) return text is
begin
  if ((start not in 1 .. t.length) or else
      (start - 1 + length not in 1 .. t.length))
     and then length > 0
  then raise constraint_error; end if;
  return text_string(t.contents(start .. start - 1 + length));
end substring;

function "&"(t1, t2: text) return text is
begin
  return text_string(ada_string(t1) & ada_string(t2));
end "&";

function "&"(s: string; t: text) return text is
begin
  return text_string(s & ada_string(t));
end "&";

function "&"(t: text; s: string) return text is
begin
  return text_string(ada_string(t) & s);
end "&";

procedure append(t: in out text; c: in character) is
  s: string(1 .. 1) := (1 => c);
begin
  if t.length + 1 > max_text_length then
     raise constraint_error; end if;
  t := t & s;
end append;

procedure append(t: in out text; new_text: in text) is
begin
  if t.length + new_text.length > max_text_length
  then raise constraint_error; end if;
  t := t & new_text;
end append;

procedure replace(t: in out text;
                  replacement: in character;
                  position: in natural ) is
begin
  if (position < 1) or else (position > t.length) then
     raise constraint_error; end if;
  t.contents(position) := replacement;
end replace;
```

```ada
procedure replace(t: in out text;
                  replacement: in text;
                  position: in natural ) is
begin
  if replacement.length = 0 then return;
  elsif position in 1 .. (t.length - replacement.length + 1)
  then t.contents(position ..
                  position - 1 + replacement.length) :=
       replacement.contents(1 .. replacement.length);
  else raise constraint_error; end if;
end replace;

procedure delete(t: in out text; low, high: in natural) is
begin
  if low > high then return;
  elsif ((low in 1 .. t.length) and then
         (high in 1 .. t.length))
  then t := slice(t, 1, low - 1) &
            slice(t, high + 1, length(t));
  else raise constraint_error; end if;
end delete;

procedure find(t, pattern: in text;
               found: out boolean;
               start: out natural ) is
  i: natural := pattern.length;
begin
  while i <= t.length
  loop -- Invariant: pattern not in t[1 .. i - 1].
       -- Bound: t.length - i.
    if t.contents(i + 1 - pattern.length .. i) =
       pattern.contents(1 .. pattern.length)
    then found := true;
         start := i + 1 - pattern.length;
         return;
    else i := i + 1; end if;
  end loop;
  found := false;
end find;

-- Input/output.
procedure get(t: out text;
              length: in natural := max_text_length) is
  temp: text(length);
begin
  if length not in 0 .. max_text_length then
     raise constraint_error; end if;
  get(temp.contents(1 .. length));
  t := temp;
end get;
```

```ada
   procedure get(f: in file_type; t: out text;
               length: in natural := max_text_length ) is
     temp: text(length);
   begin
     if length not in 0 .. max_text_length then
        raise constraint_error; end if;
     get(f, temp.contents(1 .. length));
     t := temp;
   end get;

   procedure get_line(t: out text) is
     temp: string(1 .. max_text_length);
     length: natural;
   begin
     get_line(temp, length);
     t := text_string(temp(1 .. length));
   end get_line;

   procedure get_line(f: in file_type; t: out text) is
     temp: string(1 .. max_text_length);
     length: natural;
   begin
     get_line(f, temp, length);
     t := text_string(temp(1 .. length));
   end get_line;

   procedure put(t: in text) is
   begin
     put(ada_string(t));
   end put;

   procedure put(f: file_type; t: in text) is
   begin
     put(f, ada_string(t));
   end put;

   procedure put_line(t: in text) is
   begin
     put_line(ada_string(t));
   end put_line;

   procedure put_line(f: file_type; t: in text) is
   begin
     put_line(f, ada_string(t));
   end put_line;
end generic_text_pkg;
```

```ada
generic
  type t is private;
package sequence_pkg is
  type sequence is private;

  function create return sequence;
  procedure add(x: in t; s: in out sequence);
  function append(s1, s2: sequence) return sequence;
  function fetch(s: sequence; n: natural) return t;
  function length(s: sequence) return natural;

  generic
    with procedure produce(x: in t);
  procedure scan(s: in sequence);

  bounds_error: exception;   -- Raised by fetch.
  overflow: exception; -- Raised by create, add, append.
private
  type node;
  type sequence is access node;
end sequence_pkg;
```

```ada
package body sequence_pkg is

  type node is
    record
      first: t;
      rest: sequence;
    end record;

  function create return sequence is
  begin
    return null;
      -- In this implementation create will never overflow.
  end create;

  procedure add(x: in t; s: in out sequence) is
  begin
    s := new node'(first => x, rest => s);
  exception
    when storage_error => raise overflow;
  end add;
```

```
   function append(s1, s2: sequence) return sequence is
   begin
     if s1 = null then return s2;
     else return
        new node'(first => s1.first, rest => append(s1.rest, s2));
     end if;
   exception
     when storage_error => raise overflow;
   end append;

   function fetch(s: sequence; n: natural) return t is
   begin
     if s = null or n = 0 then raise bounds_error;
     elsif n = 1 then return s.first;
     else return fetch(s.rest, n - 1); end if;
   end fetch;

   function length(s: sequence) return natural is
   begin
     if s = null then return 0;
     else return 1 + length(s.rest); end if;
   end length;

   --   generic
   --      with procedure produce(x: in t);
   procedure scan(s: in sequence) is
     s1: sequence := s;
   begin
     while s1 /= null loop
         produce(s1.first);
         s1 := s1.rest;
     end loop;
   end scan;
end sequence_pkg;
```

```
generic
  type t is private;
  max_size: natural := 100;
package bounded_sequence_pkg is
  type sequence is private;

  function create return sequence;
  procedure add(x: in t; s: in out sequence);
  function append(s1, s2: sequence) return sequence;
  function fetch(s: sequence; n: natural) return t;
```

```
   function length(s: sequence) return natural;
   function bound(s: sequence) return natural;

   generic
      with procedure produce(x: in t);
   procedure scan(s: in sequence);

   overflow: exception;    -- Raised by add, append.
   bounds_error: exception;   -- Raised by fetch.
private
   subtype size_type is natural range 0 .. max_size;
   type elements_type is array(1 .. max_size) of t;

   type sequence is
      record
         size: size_type := 0;
         elements: elements_type;
      end record;
end bounded_sequence_pkg;
```

```
package body bounded_sequence_pkg is
   function create return sequence is
      s: sequence;   -- Size has the default value 0.
   begin
      return s;
   end create;

   procedure add(x: in t; s: in out sequence) is
   begin
      if s.size < max_size
         then s.size := s.size + 1; s.elements(s.size) := x;
         else raise overflow;
      end if;
   end add;

   function append(s1, s2: sequence) return sequence is
      s: sequence;
   begin
      if s1.size + s2.size <= max_size then
         s.size := s1.size + s2.size;
         s.elements(1 .. s1.size) := s1.elements(1 .. s1.size);
         s.elements(s1.size + 1 .. s.size) :=
            s2.elements(1 .. s2.size);
         return s;
      else raise overflow;
      end if;
   end append;
```

```ada
   function fetch(s: sequence; n: natural) return t is
   begin
     if n in 1 .. s.size then return s.elements(n);
     else raise bounds_error; end if;
   end fetch;

   function length(s: sequence) return natural is
   begin
     return s.size;
   end length;

   function bound(s: sequence) return natural is
   begin
     return max_size;
   end bound;

   --  generic
   --     with procedure produce(x: in t);
   procedure scan(s: in sequence) is
   begin
     for i in 1 .. s.size loop
         produce(s.elements(i));
     end loop;
   end scan;
end bounded_sequence_pkg;
```

```ada
   with text_pkg; use text_pkg; -- Defines text_pkg_instance.
package format_pkg is
   use text_pkg_instance;   -- Defines the type text.

   type row is array(integer range <>) of text;
   type widths is array(integer range <>) of natural;

   function fill_line(r: row; w: widths) return text;
   function blanks(n: natural) return text;
   function letter_string(s: text) return boolean;
   function letter(c: character) return boolean;
   function digit_string(s: text) return boolean;
end format_pkg;
```

```
package body format_pkg is
  function fill_line(r: row; w: widths) return text is
    padding: natural;
    result: text := min_text;   -- Initially empty.
  begin
    for i in r'range loop
      if length(r(i)) < w(i)
        then padding := w(i) - length(r(i));
        else padding := 1;
      end if;
      result := result & blanks(padding) & r(i);
    end loop;
    return result;
  end fill_line;

  function blanks(n: natural) return text is
  begin
    return text_string((1 .. n => ' '));
  end blanks;

  function letter_string(s: text) return boolean is
  begin
    for i in 1 .. length(s) loop
        if not letter(char(s, i)) then return false; end if;
    end loop;
    return true;
  end letter_string;

  function letter(c: character) return boolean is
  begin
    return c in 'a' .. 'z' or else c in 'A' .. 'Z';
  end letter;

  function digit_string(s: text) return boolean is
  begin
    for i in 1 .. length(s) loop
        if not (char(s, i) in '0' .. '9') then
           return false; end if;
    end loop;
    return true;
  end digit_string;
end format_pkg;
```

APPENDIX
Generator Preprocessor for Ada

This appendix gives an implementation of the transformations from generalized for-loop notation into the equivalent Ada representation. These transformations are discussed in Section 5.7.6. The implementation consists of a set of macro definitions for the m4 macro processor of UNIX, and was developed and tested on Sun UNIX 4.2 Release 3.5. The notation was adapted to fit the conventions of the m4 macro processor. The quotes are necessary to permit correct argument identification. The macros are designed to work for nested foreach loops and foreach loops inside of generator definitions. The output of the macro processor is intended for consumption by the Ada compiler rather than a human reader, and does not have a readable indentation pattern. Readers wishing to examine the output are advised to pass it through an Ada pretty printing program first.

The macros do not allow loop bodies to contain instances of the quoting characters "`" and "'", even though the "'" character is meaningful in Ada programs. The easiest way to fix this is to rename the m4 quoting characters within the definitions of the macros to control characters that cannot appear in a legal Ada program, such as ^A and ^B. This renaming can be accomplished via the m4 macro `changequote`. The renaming was not done here to improve readability by using only printable characters in the source code.

```
dnl -- m4 comments describing input and output formats
dnl --
dnl -- format: generator(inputs, outputs, body)
dnl --
```

```
dnl -- sample invocation:
dnl --
dnl -- generator('g(y1: t1; ... ; ym: tm)', '(x1: T1, ... , xn: Tn)',
dnl -- 'is
dnl --    -- declarations of g
dnl -- begin
dnl --    -- statements for calculating e1, ... , en
dnl --    generate(e1, ... , en);
dnl --    -- more statements, possibly containing "generate"
dnl -- end g;' )
dnl --
dnl -- expands to:
dnl --
dnl -- generic
dnl --    with procedure generate(x1: T1; ... ; xn: Tn);
dnl -- procedure g(y1: t1; ... ; ym: tm);
dnl -- procedure g(y1: t1; ... ; ym: tm) is
dnl --    -- declarations of g
dnl -- begin
dnl --    -- statements for calculating e1, ... , en
dnl --    generate(e1, ... , en);
dnl --    -- more statements, possibly containing "generate"
dnl -- end g;
dnl --
define('generator',
'generic
  with procedure generate $2;
procedure $1 ;
procedure $1 $3')
dnl --
dnl -- format: foreach(loop variables, generator name, generator arguments,
dnl --                  statements in loop body)
dnl --
dnl -- sample invocation:
dnl --
dnl -- foreach((x1: T1, ... , xn: Tn), g, (e1, ... , em),
dnl --    -- sequence of statements in the loop body
dnl -- )
dnl --
dnl -- expands to:
dnl --
dnl -- declare
dnl --    procedure loop_body(x1: T1; ... ; xn: Tn) is
dnl --    begin
dnl --       -- sequence of statements in the loop body
dnl --    end loop_body;
dnl --    procedure execute_loop is new g(loop_body);
```

```
dnl -- begin
dnl --    execute_loop(el, ... , em); -- translation of loop
dnl -- end;
dnl --
define('foreach',
'declare
  procedure loop_body $1 is
  begin
    $4
  end loop_body;
  procedure execute_loop is new $2 (loop_body);
begin
  execute_loop $3 ;
end;')
dnl -- get rid of all predefined macro names
undefine('ifdef')
undefine('changequote')
undefine('divert')
undefine('undivert')
undefine('divnum')
undefine('ifelse')
undefine('incr')
undefine('eval')
undefine('len')
undefine('index')
undefine('substr')
undefine('translit')
undefine('include')
undefine('sinclude')
undefine('syscmd')
undefine('maketemp')
undefine('errprint')
undefine('dumpdef')
undefine('unix')
undefine('shift')
undefine('dnl')
undefine('define')
undefine('undefine')
```

Index